Frommer's®

SKOKIE PUBLIC LIBRARY

3 1232 00507 8292

Sicily

JUN 2011

5th Edition

by Conchita Vecchio

WITHDRAWN

D0720265

WILEY

A John Wiley and Sons, Ltd, Publication

SKOKIE PUBLIC LIBRARY

Published by:

WILEY PUBLISHING, INC.

Copyright © 2011

John Wiley & Sons Ltd, The Atrium, Southern Gate, Chichester,

West Sussex PO19 8SQ, UK

Telephone (+44) 1243 779777

Email (for orders and customer service enquiries): cs-books@wiley.co.uk. Visit our Home Page on www.wiley.com

All Rights Reserved. No part of this publication may be reproduced, stored in a retrieval system or transmitted in any form or by any means, electronic, mechanical, photocopying, recording, scanning or otherwise, except under the terms of the Copyright, Designs and Patents Act 1988 or under the terms of a licence issued by the Copyright Licensing Agency Ltd, Saffron House, 6-10 Kirby Street, London EC1N 8TS, UK, without the permission in writing of the Publisher. Requests to the Publisher should be addressed to the Permissions Department, John Wiley & Sons Ltd, The Atrium, Southern Gate, Chichester, West Sussex PO19 8SQ, England, or emailed to permreq@wiley.co.uk, or faxed to (+44) 1243 770620.

Designations used by companies to distinguish their products are often claimed as trademarks. All brand names and product names used in this book are trade names, service marks, trademarks or registered trademarks of their respective owners. The Publisher is not associated with any product or vendor mentioned in this book.

This publication is designed to provide accurate and authoritative information in regard to the subject matter covered. It is sold on the understanding that the Publisher is not engaged in rendering professional services. If professional advice or other expert assistance is required, the services of a competent professional should be sought.

UK Publisher: Sally Smith

Project Manager: Daniel Mersey

Commissioning Editor: Fiona Quinn

Development Editor: Matthew Brown/Fiona Quinn

Project Editor: Hannah Clement

Cartography: Guy Ruggier

Photo Editor: Jill Emeny

Front cover photo: © Martin Child/ Robert Harding. Description: Baroque balcony, Palazzo Nicolaci, Noto, Sicily.

Back cover photo: © Nordic Photos / awl-images. Description: Cefalù.

Wiley also publishes its books in a variety of electronic formats. Some content that appears in print may not be available in electronic books.

For information on our other products and services or to obtain technical support, please contact our Customer Care Department within the U.S. at 877/762-2974, outside the U.S. at 317/572-3993 or fax 317/572-4002.

British Library Cataloguing in Publication Data

A catalogue record for this book is available from the British Library

ISBN 978-0-470-97396-7 (pbk)

ISBN 978-1-119-97254-9 (ebk)

ISBN 978-1-119-99447-3 (ebk)

ISBN 978-1-119-99463-3 (ebk)

Typeset by Wiley Indianapolis Composition Services

Printed and bound in the United States of America

5 4 3 2 1

CONTENTS

LIST OF MAPS

ABOUT THE AUTHOR

Conchita Vecchio is a born and raised New Yorker. As a child and as a teen she often traveled to Sicily with her family, spending her summers there. After graduating high school she moved to northern Italy, traveling extensively whenever the opportunity came. After living in the north, however, she managed to find her way down to her genetic homeland of Sicily, where she now lives. She is a frequent contributor to the *Best of Sicily* website, and was a consultant for the History Channel's *Cities of the Underworld* episode titled "Real Mafia Underground" (season 3, episode 3), on which she also appeared.

ACKNOWLEDGMENTS

The editors would like to thank Matthew Brown and Sicilian-based author, Carol King, for their help and patience in putting together the 5th edition of this book.

HOW TO CONTACT US

In researching this book, we discovered many wonderful places—hotels, restaurants, shops, and more. We're sure you'll find others. Please tell us about them, so we can share the information with your fellow travelers in upcoming editions. If you were disappointed with a recommendation, we'd love to know that, too. Please email frommers@wiley.com or write to:

Frommer's Sicily, 5th Edition
Wiley Publishing, Inc. • 111 River St. • Hoboken, NJ 07030-5774

AN ADDITIONAL NOTE

Please be advised that travel information is subject to change at any time—and this is especially true of prices. We therefore suggest that you write or call ahead for confirmation when making your travel plans. The authors, editors, and publisher cannot be held responsible for the experiences of readers while traveling. Your safety is important to us, however, so we encourage you to stay alert and be aware of your surroundings. Keep a close eye on cameras, purses, and wallets, all favorite targets of thieves and pickpockets.

FROMMER'S STAR RATINGS, ICONS & ABBREVIATIONS

Every hotel, restaurant, and attraction listing in this guide has been ranked for quality, value, service, amenities, and special features using a **star-rating system.** In country, state, and regional guides, we also rate towns and regions to help you narrow down your choices and budget your time accordingly. Hotels and restaurants are rated on a scale of zero (recommended) to three stars (exceptional). Attractions, shopping, nightlife, towns, and regions are rated according to the following scale: zero stars (recommended), one star (highly recommended), two stars (very highly recommended), and three stars (must-see).

In addition to the star-rating system, we also use **seven feature icons** that point you to the great deals, in-the-know advice, and unique experiences that separate travelers from tourists. Throughout the book, look for:

special finds—those places only insiders know about

fun facts—details that make travelers more informed and their trips more fun

best bets for kids and advice for the whole family

special moments—those experiences that memories are made of

overrated—places or experiences not worth your time or money

insider tips—great ways to save time and money

great values—where to get the best deals

The following **abbreviations** are used for credit cards:

AE   American Express   DISC   Discover   V   Visa

DC   Diners Club   MC   MasterCard

TRAVEL RESOURCES AT FROMMERS.COM

Frommer's travel resources don't end with this guide. Frommer's website, **www.frommers. com,** has travel information on more than 4,000 destinations. We update features regularly, giving you access to the most current trip-planning information and the best airfare, lodging, and car-rental bargains. You can also listen to podcasts, connect with other Frommers. com members through our active-reader forums, share your travel photos, read blogs from guidebook editors and fellow travellers, and much more.

THE BEST OF SICILY

A t 25,708 sq km (9,926 sq miles), Sicily is not only the largest island in the Mediterranean but also the largest region in Italy. This triangle-shaped land symbolized by the mythological three-legged Trinacria is home to the first known parliament in the western world (**Palermo**), the oldest continental tree (**Sant'Alfio,** near Catania), the highest and most active volcano in Europe (**Mount Etna**) and the vastest archaeological park (**Selinunte**).

Additionally, there are jewels that testify to Sicily's glorious Classical past (**Agrigento, Syracuse, Segesta, Tindari, Morgantina, Piazza Armerina**), unique styles of baroque architecture crafted in response to devastating earthquakes in the southeast (**Catania, Noto, Scicli, Ragusa, and Modica**), and, sadly, modern yet hideous postwar concrete monsters (**Palermo, Catania, Messina, Agrigento**).

The colors and natural contrasts are shaped by the elements like nowhere else on earth; African and Alpine fauna live spectacularly on the same island. At times you might think Sicily is some sort of paradise, but it takes only an SUV or a scooter roaring down a chaotic Palermo or Catania street to give you a reality check. Then, of course, there are the Sicilians themselves: The descendants of Greek, Carthaginian, Roman Vandal, Arab, Norman, and Spanish conquerors are welcoming yet suspicious, taciturn and at the same time garrulous, deeply tied to traditions yet always yearning to break away from distasteful precedents, namely the Mafia. Thousands of years of domination may have created these stark contradictions, but they have left an archaeological, cultural, and culinary legacy like no other in this world. In Goethe's words, "the key to it all is here."

THE best TRAVEL EXPERIENCES

o **Swimming with the fish in Ustica:** One of the late Jacques Cousteau's favorite places, this protected marine reserve on the island northwest of Palermo lets you get up-close and personal with the fish and allows irchaeological underwater expeditions. If you're really lucky, a school will escort your ferry ride to and from the island. See p. 143.

Mount Etna: Making your way up the highest volcano in Europe is ive you goose bumps, but lava flows aren't the only things happening can ski down the mountain with the Ionian Sea as a backdrop or trek through its lush Alpine vegetation. See p. 220.

o **Exploring the Sicilian Countryside:** Sicily isn't all sun-kissed beaches and islands. The internal countryside, with its rolling wheat hills, tortuous river bends, centuries-old farmhouses, and magnificent medieval castles, is the real key to what Sicily was like hundreds of years ago. In towns within the verdant mountains of the Madonie, you sense that time hasn't caught up with modernity—and the locals don't mind at all. See p. 194.

o **Crossing the Straits of Messina:** If you want to make a dramatic entrance to Sicily, then this is it. Do it the way it's been done for thousands of years, possibly early in the morning, with the port of Messina as your beacon to the island. Just make sure not to irritate Scylla and Charybdis. See p. 226.

o **Watching a Volcanic Eruption from the Sea:** Volcanic activity isn't limited to Etna; the Aeolian Islands are known for their fits and spurts now and then, especially on Stromboli, where the volcano huffs and puffs continuously. Get a bottle of Malvasia and enjoy the show from a boat, at dusk. See p. 247.

o **Visiting Medieval Erice:** This picturesque village perched on top of a rocky crag dominating Trapani was founded by the mythical Eryx and has withstood many an invasion, remaining almost intact throughout the centuries. The sweeping views over land and sea are incomparable, the sunsets are like no other, and, on a clear day, you can see forever—or at least to Cape Bon, in Tunisia. See p. 150.

o **Participating in a Town Festival:** This is really when you get to see cities, towns, and villages come to life and understand the idiosyncrasies of the locals. Everyone comes out of hiding to take part, dressing to the nines, and age-old traditions and rituals are respected. There's no shortage of festivals in Sicily throughout the year—every town has feasts for their patron saint. The most spectacular ones are **St. Rosalie in Palermo** (July 14; p. 125) and **St. Agatha in Catania** (Feb 5; p. 36). Non-religious festivals are the **Almond Blossom Festival** in Agrigento (first week of Feb; p. 36), the **Palio dei Normani** at Piazza Armerina (mid-Aug; p. 190), and the **International Couscous Festival** at San Vito Lo Capo (last week of Sept; p. 37).

THE best ROMANTIC GETAWAYS

o **Cefalù:** This quaint fishing village an hour east of Palermo is the second most popular seaside town after Taormina. With its medieval homes and alleyways dominated by the imposing 12th-century cathedral, as well as its charming shops and restaurants, this is where the locals come to fall in love all over again. See p 135.

- **Erice:** Considered by some to be the Taormina of the west, minus the pizzazz and glitz, Erice is a sleepy medieval town dominating land and sea. Its up-and-down cobblestone streets, relaxed atmosphere, and extraordinary views and sunsets will have many hearts fluttering. See p. 150.
- **Pantelleria:** This southwestern island, closer to Africa than to Italy, is the stage for exotic wilderness, unspoiled seas, secluded hideaways, and timeless *dammusi,* all of which set it apart from "mainland" Sicily, making it the place for a romantic respite. Why else would they have a lake named after Venus here? See p. 179.
- **Ragusa:** Baroque elegance is exuded everywhere in this southernmost province of Sicily, and the old-world charm that still lives on gives you the feeling that baronial courtships haven't gone anywhere. See p. 277.
- **Stromboli:** On the volcanic island where Ingrid Bergman and Roberto Rossellini fell madly in love, this easternmost of the Aeolians is a haven for those who want to be surrounded by rugged yet pristine landscapes away from the rest of the world—and quite possibly not come back. See p. 247.
- **Taormina:** It may have lost some of its luster in the last few years, but the magic is still there in this hilltop town: It's the place lovers from around the world flock to for romance, enticed by the astounding scenario offered by Etna, Greek ruins, charming streets and alleyways, and the Ionian Sea. It is, after all, where Richard Burton wooed Liz Taylor. See p. 197.

THE best MUSEUMS

- **Galleria di Arte Moderna Santa Anna** (Palermo; ✆ 091-8431605): At its new permanent location in the ex-convent of same name, the Modern Art Gallery showcases a fine collection of works from the 1900s onward, many of which were exhibited during various Biennales in Venice. See p. 106.
- **Galleria Regionale della Sicilia** (Palermo; ✆ 091-6230011): The recently reopened museum is home to some of the finest medieval artwork in Sicily; the stunning *Triumph of Death,* an anonymous work, will leave you gaping at the details for hours. Works by Sicily's very own Antonello Da Messina are also housed here, including his world-famous *Annunciation.* See p. 97.
- **Museo Archeologico Luigi Bernabo' Brea** (Lipari; ✆ 090-9880174): Housing what are quite possibly the earliest elements of Sicilian civilization, this museum's artifacts from prehistoric archaeology and volcanic eruptions are testament to the island's millennial history. See p. 238.
- **Museo Archeologico Regionale A. Salinas** (Palermo; ✆ 091-6116805): Partially closed for restoration until 2012, this former convent houses Sicily's greatest archaeological collection, among which is the exquisite Palermo Stone, inscribed with the chronicles of the Egyptian pharaohs until 300 B.C. See p. 96.
- **Museo Archeologico Regionale di Agrigento** (Agrigento; ✆ 0922-401565): Tucked away in the Valley of the Temples is this extraordinary collection of artifacts from the ancient Akragas and the environs. The most impressive remains are the gargantuan *telamoni,* or giants, as tall as columns that held up the temples. See p. 313.

- **Museo Archeologico Regionale Paolo Orsi** (Syracuse; ✆ **0931-464022**): Syracuse's museum showcases what was once the power and wealth of the rival of Athens. The Landolina Venus is only one of the star pieces of the collections. See p. 288.
- **Museo Regionale di Arte Mediovale e Moderna** (Syracuse; ✆ **0931-69511**): The Palazzo Bellomo displays a priceless collection of Sicilian medieval and modern works, including *The Burial of St. Lucy,* from bad-boy artist Caravaggio, who sojourned here for a while. Another extraordinary work by Antonello da Messina, a more elaborate *Annunciation,* is also here. See p. 294.
- **Riso: Museo d'Arte Contemporanea della Sicilia** (Palermo; ✆ **091-320532**): Palermo's newest museum in the restored Palazzo Belmonte-Riso showcases the works of local, national, and international contemporary artists. As befits a new museum, a cafe, a bookshop, and a Wi-Fi hotspot are all on the premises. See p. 107.

THE best CATHEDRALS & CHURCHES

- **Duomo** (Cefalù): The first Norman cathedral in western Sicily, it was built by Roger II and initially intended as his final resting place. Its imposing size dominates the landscape of the town, while the interior is embellished with the first in a series of brilliant mosaics found in this part of Sicily. See p. 136.
- **Santa Maria dell'Ammiraglio** (aka La Martorana; Palermo): One of the best expressions of Arabo-Norman architecture, this 12th-century Orthodox church was considerably altered during the baroque heyday but, miraculously, the splendid mosaics were spared. It was at this convent that the marzipan fruits known as *frutta* Martorana were created. It also houses the only known portrait of Roger II. See p. 99.
- **San Giovanni degli Eremiti** (St. John of the Hermits) (Palermo; Via dei Benedettini 18, no phone.): This is the epitome of Arabo-Norman architecture in the city. Capped by five red domes, it would seem like a mosque when seen from afar. It is set amid a splendid garden of palm and fragrant citrus trees. See p. 95.
- **Monreale Duomo** (Monreale): This is the most spectacular of all Arabo-Norman churches, and also the last. Commissioned by William II in 1174 after a dream, with its 6,400 sq m (21, 000 sq ft.) of mosaics, it is truly one of the best churches in Italy. See p. 127.
- **Oratorio del Rosario di San Domenico** (Palermo; ✆ **091-332779**): The Oratory was founded in the closing years of the 16th century by the Society of the Holy Rosary. One of the Society's most outstanding members, Giacomo Serpotta, decorated this oratory with his delightfully expressive putti (cherubs). See p. 103.
- **Oratorio del Rosario di Santa Cita** (Palermo): Giacomo Serpotta took 32 years to complete this Rococo masterpiece festooned with *puttis* and biblical scenes and inlaid with marble and mother of pearl; the most amazing piece among the sculptures is the *Battle of Lepanto.* The oratory was miraculously spared damage during the Allied bombings of 1943. See p. 100.

o **Oratorio di San Lorenzo** (Palermo; © **091-582370**): Of extraordinary elegance, the interior's stucco decoration is the masterpiece of Giacomo Serpotta. Art historians have written of these wall paintings as "a cave of white coral." See p. 103.

THE most AWE-INSPIRING RUINS

o **Mozia:** A Punic stronghold for many centuries, this tiny island in the Stagnone lagoon off the coast of Marsala is an open-air museum that gives insight to the everyday life of the intriguing Phoenician and Carthaginian civilizations that dominated this area of Sicily. The Whitakers, who made their fortunes exporting Marsala wine, owned the island for many years and financed excavations on the island; many of the artifacts are housed in the Villa Whitaker, including the 5th-century statue of the Youth of Mozia. There is also a working vineyard on the island, managed by the Tasca D'Almerita winery. See p. 175.

o **Ortygia Island** (Syracuse): Getting its name from the Greek word for "quail," Ortygia is home to the oldest Greek temple on the island (dedicated to Apollo) and the temple dedicated to Athena, incorporated within the walls of the cathedral. Ortygia is also the setting for the legend of Arethusa, and the Maniace castle dominates the sea from the tip of the island. See p. 293.

o **Parco Archeologico della Neapolis** (Syracuse): One of the most spectacular archaeological sites, it bears testament to the power of the ancient Syracuse. The Greek Theater is the largest in Sicily and still puts on classical plays like in the days of Aeschylus, while the so-called Ear of Dionysius, hewn out of the rock, is the most amazing site at the quarries of the Latomie del Paradiso. See p. 287.

o **Parco Archeologico di Selinunte** (Selinunte): At 270 hectares (667 acres) it's the largest archaeological park in Europe. The temples, many of which were painstakingly rebuilt after being reduced to heaps of rubble, are denoted with letters of the alphabet as dedications to a certain divinity (which one is still uncertain). Some of the temple floors bear traces of mosaics, thought to be the forerunners of those in Piazza Armerina. See p. 170.

o **Teatro Greco-Romano** (Taormina): The second largest ancient theater in Sicily after Syracuse, the Teatro was built in the 4th century B.C. and expanded to an amphitheater by the Romans, who also added a partial roof, now destroyed. With Etna serving as a dramatic backdrop, this theater is still in use today. See p. 202.

o **Tempio & Teatro Greco di Segesta** (Segesta): This limestone temple is one of the best preserved in the world, with its 36 columns all in excellent condition. It was left uncompleted, adding to its aura of mystery. The restored Greek Theater set on Monte Barbaro has a spectacular land and sea backdrop. See p. 148.

o **Villa Romana del Casale** (Piazza Armerina): Romans liked to live large, and this mansion is an example, complete with Roman baths and the like. But the real attraction here is the 3,500 sq m (37,700 sq ft.) of mosaics that embellish the floors. They depict hunting scenes and everyday life, and there's even one of a girl athlete with stitches on her leg. See p. 191.

o **Valle dei Templi** (Agrigento): Perched on top of the Mediterranean, the Valley of the Temples is home to the best-preserved temples in the world. The most impressive is the Temple of Concord, which is in near-intact condition. The rubble that once formed the temple of Zeus was thought to be the largest temple in the world, and the surviving four columns topped with remains of a pediment and entablature of the Temple of Castor and Pollux is one of the symbols of Sicily. See p. 310.

THE best WALKS

- **Erice:** Set high upon a rocky crag dominating western Sicily, this medieval village seems like a place that time forgot. Give yourself 4 hours to make your way around this enchanting city, visiting the recently reopened Castle of Venus, the neighboring Torre Pepoli, and the beautiful gardens of the Baglio Pepoli. As you head toward Porta Trapani, you'll encounter breathtaking views stretching out over land and sea. See p. 150.

- **The Kalsa and the Albergheria, Palermo:** Zigzagging through these two neighborhoods, the oldest quarters of the city, you'll find treasure troves of their unique past, offering remnants of all foreigners and civilizations that found a home here. Medieval and baroque *palazzi* and churches line the streets, and every corner you turn is steeped in history—and laundry hanging out the windows. Some of the streets are signposted in three languages, Italian, Hebrew, and Arabic, to highlight where their communities once stood in this multilingual, multicultural city. See p. 72.

- **Ragusa Ibla:** The old part of the city has some of the most amazing panoramas in southeastern Sicily and quaint little corners that can only be explored on foot. Start from the cathedral, and make your way east (bypassing a series of elaborate baroque buildings in need of repair) to the Giardini Iblei, at the tip of the city, for some respite.

- **Salt Marshes:** Enclosed between Trapani and Marsala is a protected area that will bring you back hundreds of years to show you how salt was harvested, using centuries-old windmills. While the whole stretch down to Marsala is rather long, you can start from Trapani and finish the 1-hour walk at Nubia, along a coastal road, and stop in to visit the Museo del Sale (Salt Museum). See p. 163.

- **Taormina:** It may sound like a cliché, but when you're at the main tourist hotspot you might as well go with the flow. In its defense, the walk that starts from the public gardens and heads west toward the cathedral offers one of the most dramatic panoramas in the world, overlooking the bay of Naxos and a smoking Etna in the distance. See p. 197.

- **Valley of the Temples:** By far the most impressive of walks, it takes under 2 hours to traverse the best-preserved ruins outside Greece in a valley laden with almond trees overlooking the Mediterranean Sea. The best times to go: Early in the morning, as the sun rises in the east; late afternoon, when the sandstone temples have a spectacular auburn hue; and at night, when the temples are floodlit. See p. 310.

THE best LUXURY HOTELS

- **Capofaro Resort** (Salina; ✆ **090-9844330;** www.capofaro.it): This stylish resort on the island of Salina gives new meaning to Mediterranean living—stylish rooms and amenities on a property surrounded by grape vines with the most spectacular views over the Aeolians. See p. 251.

○ **Grand Hotel Mazzarò Sea Palace** (Mazzarò; ℂ **0942-612111;** www.mazzaro seapalace.it): The elegant, genuinely charming hotel opens onto the most beautiful bay in Sicily and has its own private beach. Big windows in the rooms let in cascades of light and offer views of the coast. See p. 205.

○ **Grand Hotel Ortigia** (Siracusa; ℂ **0931-464600;** www.grandhotelsr.it): A very appealing mix of modernity and old-world charm. It's set directly on the waterfront in a stately four-story building that contains lots of inlaid marble and polished Belle Epoque hardwoods. See p. 298.

○ **Grand Hotel Piazza Borsa** (Palermo; ℂ **091-320075;** www.piazzaborsa.it): This brand-new hotel in the Kalsa was once the stock exchange of Palermo. The Belle Epoque decor has been preserved throughout. Some rooms overlook the beautiful Basilica of St. Francis of Assisi. See p. 77.

○ **Kempinski Hotel Giardino di Costanza** (Mazara Del Vallo; (ℂ **0923-675000;** www.kempinski.com): The only Kempinski property in Italy is in the heart of wine-and-olive country in a state-of-the-art, refurbished villa just outside the town of Mazara del Vallo. See p. 174.

○ **NH Liberty** (Messina; ℂ **090-6409436;** www.nh-hotels.it): One of the finest hotels in Sicily. Throughout, you'll find rich paneling, marble-inlaid floors, ornate plasterwork, and lavish stained-glass windows. See p. 230.

○ **Principe di Villafranca** (Palermo; ℂ **091-6118523;** www.principedivilla franca.it): The finest boutique-style hotel in Palermo. Stylish, and intimate, its Sicilian theme includes enough antiques and architectural finesse to make you think the place is a lot older. See p. 82.

○ **San Domenico Palace** (Taormina; ℂ **0942-613111**): A former convent, San Domenico has attracted elite and literati from all over the world. Not as centrally located as is its historical rival, the Timeo, San Domenico offers a sense of peace and tranquility, as well as mouth-watering views that make a stay here worth it. See p. 206.

○ **Villa del Bosco** (Catania; ℂ **095-7335100;** www.hotelvilladelbosco.it): Guests enjoy a true taste of the aristocratic life of a landowning Sicilian family during the early 19th century. The dignified boutique hotel is rich with antiques. See p. 257.

○ **Villa Iglea Grand Hotel** (Palermo; ℂ **091-6312111;** www.hilton.com): This is to Palermo what the Ritz is to Paris or Claridge's is to London. Set inside an exquisite Art Nouveau gem on the outskirts of town, it overlooks the sea and hasn't lost any of its luster. See p. 77.

THE best INEXPENSIVE HOTELS

○ **Ambasciatori** (Palermo; ℂ **091-6166881;** www.ambasciatorihotelpalermo.net): Offering five-star views at three-star prices, Ambasciatori is right in the middle of everything. A nondescript entrance on Via Roma takes you into clean, comfortable accommodations and away from the death-defying Palermo traffic. See p. 85.

- **B&B Del Centro** (Enna; ✆ 327-7460800 (mobile); www.bedandbreakfastenna. com): This hidden B&B is a true gem—an old palazzo refurbished back to its original splendor. Cozy rooms have wrought-iron beds and bathrooms come with massage showers. See p. 186.

- **Hotel Condor** (Taormina; ✆ 0942-23124; www.condorhotel.com): This hidden gem is an absolute rarity in Taormina—a family-run two-star hotel that offers comfortable rooms and wonderful views, and doesn't charge you an arm and a leg for staying at one of most expensive vacation towns in Italy. See p. 210.

- **Hotel La Ville** (Catania; ✆ 095-322709; www.hotellavillecatania): A friendly hotel with a splendid mix of old-world charm and modern furnishings in spacious rooms. For its location and quality of service, the accolades are well-deserved. See p. 260.

THE best RESTAURANTS

- **Al Fogher** (Piazza Armerina; ✆ 0935-684123): There's another reason to come here besides the mosaics. In the heartland of the island, chef Angelo Treno honors the local flavors, but he's also traveled the world in search of new ones. The combinations of the two are simply divine. See p. 193.

- **Casa Grugno** (Taormina; ✆ 0942-21208; www.casagrugno.it): Austrian-born chef Andreas Zangerl presides over this increasingly famous place. The sublime food here is reinvented Sicilian cuisine at its finest, haute cuisine that draws from a pan-European sensibility. See p. 211.

- **Da Calogera** (Mondello; ✆ 091-6841333): A stones' throw away from the shoreline, this little place is one of the area's best. The colorful, ceramic-tiled exterior of the eatery is a clam bar. Indoors, enjoy an array of fish pasta dishes or the restaurant's original dish: Boiled octopus. See p. 127.

- **Il Duomo** (Ragusa Ibla; ✆ 0932-651265): One of the finest restaurants in southern Sicily, Il Duomo has been awarded Michelin stars. Its greatest devotees maintain that it is the best restaurant in Sicily, serving a deluxe island cuisine. In many cases, chefs perpetuate age-old cooking traditions in turning out their sublime culinary offerings. See p. 283.

- **Osteria I Tre Bicchieri** (Catania; ✆ 095-7153540; www.osteriaitrebicchieri.it): The finest restaurant in Catania welcomes visitors to the three high-ceilinged, vaulted rooms outfitted in a graceful 18th-century style. The best pasta I tasted in Catania was the tagliatelle with ragout of suckling pig here. See p. 261.

- **Osteria dei Vespri** (Palermo; ✆ 091-6171631): In the stables of the princely palazzo where scenes from *The Leopard* were filmed, you'll find one of Palermo's finest restaurants. Brothers Andrea and Alberto Rizzo keep the devotees coming by taking classic Palermitan staples to the next level with variations that are innovative yet tied to tradition. See p. 88.

- **Ristorante Il Dehor** (Agrigento; ✆ 0922-511061): One of the best restaurants in all of Sicily. Damiano Ferraro, an Agrigento-born, London-educated culinary whizz has reinvented traditional Sicilian cuisine. See p. 315.

- **Zia Pina** (Palermo; no phone): You might risk passing
  altogether, as the surroundings are very off-putting. But
  outdoor kitchen is actually one of the busiest eateries in
  cooked right in front of you. See p. 91.

THE best TRADITION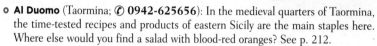
EATERIES

- **Al Duomo** (Taormina; ☎ 0942-625656): In the medieval quarters of Taormina, the time-tested recipes and products of eastern Sicily are the main staples here. Where else would you find a salad with blood-red oranges? See p. 212.
- **Don Camillo** (Syracuse; ☎ 0931-67133): One of the city's finest and most affordable dining rooms was constructed on the foundations of a 15th-century monastery. The cuisine of seafood and Sicilian recipes is among the most creative in town. It's a charmer. See p. 301.
- **Monte San Giuliano** (Erice; ☎ 0923-869595): In the medieval hilltop village of Erice, the most spectacular in Sicily, you can dine at this undiscovered garden hideaway after making your way through narrow labyrinthine streets. Most of the foodstuffs are plucked from the sea. Some of the dishes, such as a seafood couscous, are inspired by North Africa. See p. 156.
- **Nangalarruni** (Castelbuono; ☎ 0921-671428): People come from all over Italy to try Giuseppe Carollo's critically-acclaimed dishes; they are a nod to the flavors of the Parco delle Madonie, which produces almost all his ingredients, and to the simple country preparations of long ago. See p. 196.

SICILY IN DEPTH

t is the largest island in the Mediterranean, and for centuries it was the most important island in the pre-Columbian world. It's blessed with a wealth of natural beauty, agricultural abundance, rich history, and more impressive monuments than most countries have. Yet when they're asked about their island, Sicilians tend to sigh, then sarcastically chuckle that "We are an island with a special statute"—ironically alluding to the fact that nothing has really changed since the Italian government granted Sicily semi-autonomous status in 1946.

The mainland, reached in 20 minutes by ferry, seems a world away: The wealth and the bustling industries of northern Italy are a stark contrast to Sicily's seemingly lackadaisical status quo and stunted economic growth, and that's not even considering the Mafia, which has always infiltrated the island's economy; even though the crime syndicate has been decimated in the last few years, it is a leviathan always ready to spring back into action.

Sicily is a land that has always yearned for independence from something or someone throughout the centuries, and this feeling comes across tangibly in the reactions of its own people who, when asked if they're Italian, will automatically retort, "We're not Italian, we're *Sicilian*." But what actually defines "Sicilian" is intriguing: Mix Greek, Teutonic, Berber, Norman, and Iberian together, shake well, and you'll have a unique bloodline that was a melting pot centuries ago. This extraordinary mix of genes and heritages is blended in just about everything: Food, architecture, landscapes, customs, and traditions. As one expat living here puts it: "You might not ever understand Sicily if you weren't born here, yet if it didn't exist, we'd have to invent it."

SICILY TODAY

To the outsider, Sicily, the largest region in Italy and with a population of roughly 5 million, could thrive on tourism alone as its major source of income—it boasts endless beaches and monuments are scattered just

IT ALL sounds GREEK TO ME... OR ARABIC...OR SPANISH...

If you listen to a conversation in Sicilian dialect (one of more than 20 variations, depending on the area) it may seem nearly incomprehensible. However, you'll probably be able to pick up a few words that are a testament to the various dominations on the island, and still incorporated in the current vernacular. For example, if you hear someone hollering "'*va travagghia!*" (Go to work!) to a ne'er-do-well, note that the Sicilian verb for "to work" is derived from the French *travailler* and not from the Italian *lavorare*. Similar instances can also be found for Spanish (*carnezzeria* is what a butcher shop is called in Palermo, as opposed to *macelleria*). Newborns to this day are still rocked in the *naca* (from the Greek *naka,* cradle), and bread is often sold with *giuggiulena* (from the Arabic *giulgiulan,* sesame seeds). And that's not even considering the descendants of the Albanian refugees who settled in Piana degli Albanesi and who are bilingual in Italian and Albanian—they even have bilingual signs around town.

about everywhere. It is also one of the major exporters of olive oil, wine, and fish to the rest of the world which should also be a note of pride. Sicilian hospitality is according to native standards, where "the guest is sacred," and they love to pride themselves on cordiality. The love of food and slow living is renowned. Yet, despite its membership along with the rest of Italy in the European Union, Sicily still presents the complexities and idiosyncrasies left by the consequences of its history: Where it can be burgeoning miraculously in some areas, it can be woefully neglected in others. The bridge to the mainland that never was (and quite possibly never will be) is one such example—the link connecting Messina to Reggio Calabria has been in the works since time immemorial. Another such sour note is Sicily's airports— why one fully-outfitted, ready-for-use airport at Ragusa still remains closed, while local politicos argue for the necessity to build one in Agrigento, is a mystery.

When it comes to education, Sicily presents an alarmingly diachronic reality: While the level of high school drop-outs is considered one of the highest in the nation, teens who continue their studies, particularly at classical studies or science at high school, have a syllabus that in theory is one of the best in Europe—the 5 years of ancient Greek or Latin studied at Classical institutions is superior to Greece itself. Despite this, education reforms in Italy have led to a decline in the quality of studies, and Sicily has not been spared.

In stark contrast to what macho stereotyping would lead the visitor to believe, women have come a long way from the male-dominated Sicilian society portrayed in postwar films. No longer kept under lock and key to protect their honor, they are on a par with men in all fields of education and employment, including the armed forces—although grown men are still considered mama's boys. Even the traditional southern Italian family has become a thing of the past: Divorce rates are high, second marriages or couples living together is not uncommon, and offspring are never more than two, often entrusted to foreign-born nannies while the mothers work outside the home. In postwar years it was not unusual for families to have no less than eight children; nowadays the birthrate in Sicily is augmented by the immigrants who come here, naively, in search of a better life: Coming from northern Africa, eastern Europe, and even as far away as China, they are, ironically, recreating the melting pot that Sicily was a millennium ago.

In some ways, you would never think that Sicily is a world away from the mainland—it has all the latest gadgets and baubles—yet unemployment is a big problem. More often than not, the only way to find a job here is through *clientelismo*: It's not what you know, but who you know. It is estimated that some 1 million people left Sicily over a 20-year period beginning in 1951, (the current population is about 5 million), and many young people still flee today's staggering unemployment levels in search of jobs elsewhere. Paradoxically, immigrants are repopulating the island. There are those who are still willing to reinvest in their territory, such as vintners and hoteliers, but the number is still minimal. Talk about making tourism the number one source of the island's income hasn't yielded results. Maybe Sicily, and Sicilians, could use a bit of the spirit their forebears had nearly 800 years ago, when the rebellion of the Sicilian Vespers led to change.

LOOKING BACK AT SICILY
Earliest Settlers

Because Sicily is at a strategic point in the Mediterranean, on a route where east meets west, it's unsurprising that everyone wanted a piece of this fertile land. Yet to understand Sicily's complex history you have to understand the many peoples who have come and gone from the island, and their legacies that are still embedded in the architecture, the culture, and the language. Sicily has been inhabited since the megalithic times, as evidenced by graffiti and etchings in caves near Palermo and on the Egadi Islands. Before recorded Greek colonization took place, the island had its own "indigenous" people, but even they came from elsewhere: The Sikanians, the

DATELINE

734 B.C. Corinthians found Syracuse.	**827** Saracens' invasion of Sicily launched.
480 B.C. Syracusans overrun the Carthaginian beachhead at the Battle of Himera.	**1032** Roger seizes Palermo, launching the Norman dynasty.
415 B.C. Athens sails a great armada against Syracuse but is defeated.	**1190–97** Henry, a Hohenstaufen, rules Sicily after defeating the Normans.
409 B.C. Carthage attacks and destroys Selinunte and Himera.	**1231** Frederick II issues the antifeudal Constitution of Melfi.
211 B.C. Syracuse is sacked as Romans declare victory.	**1282** A rebellion—the so-called Sicilian Vespers—breaks out in Palermo, spreading across the island.
535 Belisarius annexes Sicily to the Eastern Roman Empire.	

oldest of the natives, are said to have come from the southeast Iberian peninsula sometime between 3000 B.C. and 2000 B.C., settling predominantly in southwest Sicily. Around 1000 B.C., other settlers made their home here: The Sicels (after whom the island is named), an Italic people thought to have come from the southern Italian peninsula to settle along the east coast; and the Elymians, who, according to myth, were led by Aeneas after the Trojan War to a small patch of land in western Sicily (not much greater than 65 sq km/25 sq miles). Historical evidence, however, indicates that the Elymians were likely a people from present-day central Anatolia. The fact that they would have made their way here long before the first Greek colonizers is not so far-fetched: There are traces of Mycenaean and Minoan artifacts and architecture that attest to a Greek presence on the island. These were probably people primarily interested in trade since the island was on such a bustling commercial route. It is known that these Greek merchants traded with the Ausonians, another Italic people who settled predominantly on the Aeolian Islands.

Greeks & Carthaginians

The first recorded colonization of the island began in 800 B.C., in quests for greener pastures and more elbow room. The Phoenicians (master sea-farers from present-day Syria) landed in a natural harbor in northwest Sicily; the place they dubbed Zyz (flower) would go on to become modern-day Palermo. They also established trading posts in Solunto and on the island of Motya, off the coast of Marsala. When their strength faded, the Carthaginians became the heirs of their civilization. They took control of Erice and expanded the Phoenician settlements on the island.

Meanwhile, on the east coast, settlers from Greece were sowing the seeds of what would become Magna Graecia: The Chalchidians founded Naxos (735 B.C.), the Corinthians, Syracuse (734 B.C.), and the Rhodians and Cretans, Gela (689 B.C.). The Megarans, who would go on to found Selinunte around 650 B.C., occupied a small area of land not too far from Syracuse; Akragas (Agrigento) was a subcolony of

1302	Peace treaty between the Angevins and the Aragonese gives Sicily to the Spaniards.	1816	Ferdinand abrogates the constitution, creates Kingdom of the Two Sicilies.
1513	Spanish Inquisition introduced.	1860	Garibaldi's forces chase out the Bourbons, as Sicilians vote for unification.
1693	Earthquake destroys much of eastern Sicily, including Catania.		
1713	Treaty of Utrecht assigns Sicily to House of Savoy.	1908	Earthquake in Messina takes 80,000 lives.
1734	Spanish reclaim Sicily under Bourbon king, Charles I.	1943	Allied armies under Patton and Montgomery capture Sicily from the Nazis.
1812	A liberal constitution spells the doom of the feudal system.	1946	Sicily granted semi-autonomous status.

continues

Gela founded in 581 B.C. This corner of the world became known as Magna Graecia, or Greater Greece, as it was more Hellenized than Greece itself.

The growing power of Carthage in North Africa threatened all of Sicily. By the 7th century B.C., Carthage had started an expansionist campaign, eyeing the colonies of Magna Graecia. However, as the Greek colonies grew more powerful in Sicily, they fought each other out of greed and jealousy; the cliché of Athens versus Sparta is a notable example.

The Rule of the Tyrants

In ancient times, the word "tyrant" described men who grabbed power instead of inheriting it, as in a royal lineage. Tyrants ruled over the Greek city-states of Sicily. Some were so-called enlightened tyrants, such as Dion, while the most ruthless was Agathocles. Tyrants were good at protecting what was theirs. In 480 B.C. the Carthaginians, lead by Hamilcar, mounted a massive attack on the western possessions of Greece, and sailed into Himera on the northern coast with an army of roughly 30,000 soldiers. The Carthaginian general led the siege on behalf of his old friend Terillus, who had been ousted as tyrant of Himera. This prompted the tyrant of Akragas (Agrigento)—the new the tyrant of Himera—to appeal to Syracuse for help. Syracuse sent about 25,000 men. Hamilcar, still not satisfied, wanted additional reinforcements, and asked Selinunte on the south coast for help.

The Carthaginians, according to some historians of the time, mistook the Syracuse forces for reinforcements from Selinunte. When it was too late, some 15,000 soldiers were slain and their ships torched. As a result, the winner of that battle, Gelon, the tyrant of Syracuse, became a force to contend with in the Greek world. It is said that Hamilcar threw himself to the flames with embarrassment. Seven decades would pass before Carthage would return to invade Sicily.

The defeat of the Carthaginians led to a golden age for Sicily, as scientists such as Archimedes, Theocritus, and Empedocles became famous all over the

1951 A massive emigration from the island begins, eventually totaling one million Sicilians.

1980s–1990s In spite of a campaign against it by the government, the Mafia maintains a strong influence on the island.

1992 Anti-Mafia judges Giovanni Falcone and Paolo Borsellino are killed within months of each other, sparking popular outrage.

2002 The strongest earthquake in Sicily in 20 years causes $500 million of devastation. Six weeks later, Mount Etna announces itself once again, with the most powerful eruption this century, belching smoke and fire and threatening tourist facilities near Catania.

2006 Mafia's number-one boss, Bernardo Provenzano, arrested near Corleone.

2009 Floods cause devastation to the province of Messina, leaving 24 people dead and 35 missing, and sweeping away cars and buildings.

then-known world. Plato and Aeschylus often visited from Greece (the latter visiting for good—he died in Gela); Plato even surmised that if there were ever a place to put into practice his model of Utopia, it would be in Sicily. Pindar would wax lyrical about the wonders of the island, composing odes to the tyrants. Agrigento boasted the largest (and to this day still best-preserved) temples, while Syracuse had the biggest theater. The period of growth and expansion was set back only by infighting among the city-states. The fierce rivalry between Athens and Sparta back in the motherland sparked off the same sentiments in the new Greek world.

Syracuse became the unrivaled dominant power in Sicily, and the time became ripe to challenge the supremacy of Athens itself. In 413 B.C., Athens sent the largest fleet ever assembled to subdue Syracuse. As recounted by the historian Thucydides, the Great Expedition from Athens suffered a crushing defeat, and 7,000 Athenian soldiers were taken prisoner and condemned to a slow death in the quarries. The great city of Syracuse reached its cultural and political apex, becoming the most dominant force in the Mediterranean.

The Revenge of Carthage

Trouble was brewing from afar. Hannibal Mago, grandson of Hamilcar, arrived on the southern coast of Sicily with his mercenaries in 409 B.C. He destroyed Selinunte, which had been a great city, and a former ally. Its modern-day ruins are a testament to his victory. After the wrath of Carthage, the once-mighty Selinunte faded into history forever.

Hannibal didn't stop there. He then headed north with one thing in mind— to seek his revenge against Himera. This time around Hannibal and Carthage came out on top. He won a great victory, subsequently torturing and killing all the male survivors.

Hannibal had an appetite for destruction. He came back in full force once again, in 406 B.C., destroying Agrigento, the second most powerful city in Sicily after Syracuse. Hannibal wasn't stopped by a military setback but by a plague that swept through his camp and killed him. Himilkon took over for the Carthaginians, offering his son Moloch as a sacrifice to demonstrate his seriousness. After 8 months of relentless siege, the ancient Akragas finally fell to the Carthaginians. The Carthaginians ultimately set their sights on the mighty Syracuse, but, as had happened before, a plague swept over their troops, forcing them to return home. Still, for the Carthaginians, three out of four wasn't bad.

The Romans in Sicily

The Greek heyday in Sicily was coming to an end. A new threat was rising for the city-states: Rome. Sicily was largely spared during the First Punic War (264–241 B.C.), but the people of Syracuse sided with Carthage during the Second Punic War (218–202 B.C.). For this, the newly emerged powers of Rome did not forgive Sicily, and in 211 B.C. the Romans conquered the island full force. In its defeat, Sicily became a "subcolony," the first outside of Rome, and the formerly proud, enlightened inhabitants of the island became slaves or servants who were mercilessly taxed and lived in abject poverty. Slave revolts broke out periodically but were brutally suppressed by the Romans, who used the island as a breadbasket after felling its trees to make room for wheat crops; the lumber was used to make warships. In the

3rd century A.D., when Sicilians were finally declared free citizens of the Roman Empire, it was a too little too late: The barbarians from the north were on their way to pillage Sicily.

Barbarians, Byzantines, & the Saracens

As the Roman Empire collapsed to the Visigoths in A.D. 410, Sicily came under increasing attack from the Vandals under Genseric. The barbarian invasion of the island was short-lived, but for a brief period Sicily was reunited with Italy under the Ostrogoth Theodoric. Fourteen centuries would pass before this would happen again.

In A.D. 535, the Byzantine general Belisarius occupied Sicily, setting off a second wave of Hellenization of the island. For a brief time in 663, Syracuse became the center of the eastern Byzantine Empire.

The Arabs, Berbers, and Spanish Muslims—known collectively as the Saracens—had all set their sights on Sicily, given its geographic proximity. By 700, the island of Pantelleria became theirs. By 827, the Arabs mounted a full-force invasion of Sicily. They set foot on the island at Mazara del Vallo, in the southwest. Four years later Palermo succumbed to the Saracens, and by 965 the invading African forces had moved across the island to the Straits of Messina.

The Arabs made Palermo the capital of their new emirate, decorating it with lush gardens (said to rival those of Baghdad), parks, mosques (hundreds of them), and palaces with innovative ventilation systems. Unlike the Roman occupation that deprived Sicily of any cultural enhancement, Sicily actually prospered under the Arab rulers, who made substantial breakthroughs in agriculture, introducing citrus trees, date palms, cotton, pistachios, eggplants, and other crops. The farming and irrigation methods they introduced to the island are still in use today. Even religious tolerance was practiced, and many Christians converted to Islam.

But the Saracen rule, like so many others before it, would be short-lived. Because of Arab infighting, the Byzantine general George Maniakes wanted to capitalize on the situation. Although he didn't get very far, another invasion was waiting to happen: The Normans were about to lay claim to Sicily.

The Men of the North

If you wonder why not all Sicilians are short, dark haired, and dark skinned, but also tall, blond, and blue eyed, well, it's thanks to the Normans. In 1061, an Arab emir in Messina called on the Norman Roger Hauteville, who was already leading his forces down the peninsula, for help in putting down a rebellion among fellow Saracens. Into this internecine fighting, then, the Normans came, they saw, and they conquered, although it would take them another 30 years to seize the island completely, often enlisting Arab soldiers to fight against other Arabs. The final blow to the Arabs came in 1072, 10 years after they crossed the Straits of Messina, when they captured Palermo and made it their capital.

The Hauteville dynasty ruled for less than a century but left a cultural and social legacy that was unseen and unheard of at the time. This was the true harbinger of the melting pot. Arabs, Jews, and Christians lived in harmony. The multi-ethnic atmosphere so championed by the Normans also lives on in the architecture, especially in Palermo. Sometimes they took over an already existing Arab structure—houses and buildings didn't last long because they were made of mud and clay—fortified it, and turned it into the unique "Arabo-Norman" style building, with typical Norman arches surmounted by domes, almost always red. By 1200, the Arabic language, which had been the official court language, was becoming rarer. French and Italian were becoming the lingua franca among the people, while Latin became the language of the erudite.

Count Roger, or Roger I (1031–1101), started the Sicilian branch of the Norman dynasty. He was followed by his son, Roger II (1105–54), one of the most enlightened kings of the Middle Ages. He championed the arts in Sicily (the cathedral in Cefalù and the Palatine Chapel in Palermo were built on his commission), calling in artists and craftsmen from all over the Mediterranean basin. He established the pretext for the first meeting of dignitaries that would eventually become the first known parliament in Europe. His son, William the Bad (1154–66), who had earned his moniker not for any ruthless rule but for his lascivious lifestyle, did not live up to his father's reputation.

The Reign of the Hohenstaufens

When William II (1166–89)—called William the Good, he of the cathedral of Monreale—died in 1189 at the age of 36, the throne went to Tancred, his illegitimate son. The ascension to the throne was challenged by King Henry VI, a German Hohenstaufen, or Swabian. Tancred clung to the throne until his death in 1194, surviving a sacking of Messina in 1190 by Richard the Lion-Heart on his way to join the Third Crusade.

William III succeeded Tancred, but by then the Hohenstaufen fleet had already called in at Messina, capturing William and imprisoning him in a castle, where he would eventually die. Henry (later to become the Holy Roman Emperor Henry VI) was declared king of Sicily on Christmas Day in 1194, as his wife was giving birth to their only child, Frederick, in Jesi.

Henry died of dysentery in 1197, the throne passing to Frederick I of Sicily, his son, who was only 3 years old. His mother, Constance, acted as queen regent, but she died 18 months later. When Frederick grew up, he proved to be a strong yet wise king. As a promoter of science, medicine, and law, he was called Stupor Mundi, or "Wonder of the World." When he became Holy Roman Emperor Frederick II, Palermo became the most important city in Europe, a cultural center without equal in the Western world, continuing the precedent set by his Norman grandfather, Roger II. In 1231, he issued the antifeudal Constitution of Melfi, stripping the barons of much of their power. Upon his death in 1250, Sicily entered a period of decline.

All too willing to strip the anti-papist Hohenstaufens of their power, a French pope awarded the title of king of Sicily to Charles of Anjou, the brother of Louis IX, the French king. Under Charles, in 1266 Angevin forces fought and beat the armies of the Hohenstaufen rulers, killing all the heirs. Once enthroned, Charles of Anjou launched a cruel attack against those Sicilians who were loyal to the Hohenstaufens.

The War of the Vespers

The harsh rule of the Angevins sparked an uprising, known as the Sicilian Vespers, which began on Easter Monday in 1282. After a French soldier insulted and molested a local woman in Palermo near the church of Santo Spirito, the Sicilians decided that they had had enough of this 20-year despotism. The tolling of a church bell for evening services, or vespers, set off a riot. Every French soldier in sight was slaughtered, the rebellion fanning out to cover the island. Any man who pronounced the word *"cicero"* with a guttural accent was killed on the spot.

The Sicilians were able finally to send the French packing—for a while, at least. A group of noblemen appealed to Peter of Aragon, as they were now without a king, and offered him the crown of Sicily on dynastic grounds: He was a descendant of Constance of Aragon, the wife of Frederick II. He landed in Trapani 5 months after that initial riot of the Sicilian Vespers, and within just a few days he was proclaimed king.

The actual War of the Vespers was fought between the armies of Aragon and Anjou, the latter based in Naples, over a period of two decades. Spain was tightening its grip on Sicily, paving the way for (yet another) domination. Although the Sicilians had offered the crown to Peter on the condition that Sicily be made an independent nation after his death, that didn't happen; in fact, it was another 500 years before the Spaniards would leave the island.

Rule by the Spaniards

In 1302, the Peace of Caltabelotta concluded the war between the papist Angevins and the imperial Aragonese. The Kingdom of Two Sicilies was created, the Angevins retaining the territories around Naples, with Sicily itself going to the Spaniards. The Aragonese kings ruled from Palermo directly until 1458.

Isolated and no longer the great crossroads of civilization, the great artistic and cultural movements sweeping mainland Europe in the 14th and 15th centuries, such as the Renaissance, never made it to Sicily. If anything, Sicily was going backward as the rest of the continent was going forward. The Spanish Inquisition, introduced to Sicily in the early 1500s and lasting over 150 years, put a muzzle on any questions posed by luminaries.

The 17th & 18th Centuries

As the Spanish Empire faded, Sicily likewise declined. The rule of corrupt and indifferent viceroys only enhanced this. Meanwhile in the countryside, bands of outlaws, protesting against vast estates and inhumane work conditions, started retaliating. They butchered livestock, burned crops, and slaughtered local bailiffs to protest against the outmoded feudal system. It was this climate that paved the way for the most infamous criminal organization in the world, the Mafia, "founded" in Sicily.

As if the suffocating feudal system weren't enough, in the 17th century Sicily was struck by natural disasters. Mount Etna erupted in 1669, causing massive damage to the east coast and destroying Catania. The eruption was followed in 1693 by earthquakes along the same coastline, killing about 5% of Sicily's population and completely destroying nearly everything in sight. The bubonic plague also made its way here, decimating the population. Politically, the island had become nothing more than an insignificant pawn among the powers of Europe. After the death of Charles II of Habsburg in 1700, Spain plunged into the Wars of the Spanish Succession. In 1713, Sicily was handed to the House of Savoy, according to the terms of the Treaty of Utrecht. In 1720, the uninterested Savoys traded it to the Austrians for Sardinia.

Spain rose from the ashes again in 1734, reclaiming Sicily and this time placing it under a Bourbon king, Charles I (1734–59), who was to visit Sicily only once. In time he gave up the kingdom to assume the title of King Charles III of Spain. He was succeeded by Ferdinand IV, who assumed the throne as Ferdinand IV of Naples in 1806. The island's so-called noblemen were living parasitically off the people of Sicily while they tightened their feudal grip on the island, yet new ideas unleashed by the French Revolution brought in winds of change.

The Coming of Napoleon

Although Napoleon Bonaparte never actually invaded Sicily, his new repartition of the lands of Europe had an impact on the island. When Napoleon conquered Naples in 1799, The Bourbons were forced out and the crown was passed to Napoleon's brother, Joseph. King Ferdinand sought refuge in Sicily, where he found protection with British troops. Pressured by the commander of British forces in Sicily, Lord William Bentinck, Ferdinand was forced to draw up a constitution for Sicily in 1812 similar to the one that governed Britain. The constitution put an end to feudal power in Sicily, creating a two-chamber Sicilian parliament in Palermo. The court established in Palermo was independent of the one presiding in Naples.

Once Napoleon was defeated in 1815, and British forces left the island, Ferdinand went back to Naples. He declared himself Ferdinand I, king of the Two Sicilies, in 1816, and abrogated the constitution he had been forced to draw up. Sicily rebelled against the repeal, but resistance was quelled with the aid of mercenaries from Austria. Ferdinand died in 1825, and life on the island only worsened under Ferdinand II (1830–59), who was named Re Bomba (King Bomb) after his 5-day bombardment of Messina to suppress uprisings there and in Palermo in 1848. Although the king suppressed the rebellions, the spirit of revolution was gaining more ground. By April 1860, the name Garibaldi had become the buzzword across the island.

Garibaldi & Unification

On April 4, 1860, an island-wide revolt against the Bourbon regime broke out. Capitalizing on the situation, the revolutionary leader Giuseppe Garibaldi decided the time was right to intervene. Along with his famous *mille*, 1,000 red-shirted soldiers, he arrived at Marsala on the west coast of Sicily on May 11, 1860. He set about to free the island from the Bourbons, aided by the lower classes that joined his ranks.

A Bourbon army of 15,000 soldiers was defeated at Calatafimi on May 15, and within 2 weeks the capital at Palermo was taken. By the time Garibaldi declared victory at the port of Milazzo on July 20, the Bourbons were in serious retreat. For the first time in nearly 600 years, Sicily was no longer in the chokehold of the Bourbon regime.

On October 21 of that same year, an island-wide referendum was held and, as was expected, 99% of the eligible voters (only a marginal number of the population) opted to follow Garibaldi's plan and unify with mainland Italy. Many poor and illiterate Sicilians who were not allowed to vote saw no good in this outcome, viewing the Piedmontese House of Savoy, which had traded them for Sardinia years earlier, as just a new "occupier" of the island.

Fascism & Wars

The peasants and lower classes were right: Under the House of Savoy, Sicily indeed found itself back to square one and in the same conditions it had endured over the centuries under their predecessors. The so-called aristocracy remained firmly in charge of the economy, and the peasants got nothing, not even the right to vote. In 1866, Turin crushed a rebellion in Palermo.

If that weren't enough, the Mafiosi acted as regents for the landowners, extracting exorbitant rents from the peasant farmers. Exasperated by these living conditions, some 500,000 Sicilians emigrated to Australia, North America, and South America. Many of these people came from the Messina area, which was devastated in the earthquake of 1908, leaving over 80,000 people dead. The 20th century brought even harsher realities, with the Italian conquest of Libya in 1912, followed by World War I, which devastated the economy of Sicily and took the lives of many of its young men.

The aftermath of World War I was followed, in 1922, by the emergence of Benito Mussolini, who had gained power in Rome after his infamous march on the city. The Italian dictator decided to crack down on Sicily's Mafiosi so that they knew who was boss. Mussolini sent his agent, Cesare Mori, to restore law and order to Sicily, a move that simply drove the criminals into hiding until the Allied forces came to shore in 1943.

Mori won the support of the landed gentry. To reward these large estate holders for their help, he revised all the agrarian reforms that were favorable to the land workers. By the 1930s, Mussolini, emulating the ancient Romans, designated Sicily as a breadbasket to feed his armies in his quest for empire.

In 1939 Sicily found itself caught up in a new war, World War II. Preceding the invasion with aerial bombardments, the Allies attacked most of Sicily's major cities. Catania, Messina, and Palermo were heavily bombed, and much of the damage is still visible today.

In July 1943, General Patton and the American Seventh Army landed at Licata on the southern coast, as Montgomery's British forces put ashore at a point to the east. The Sicilians offered little resistance and welcomed the Allies, but the Nazis fought back with a vengeance, hoping to delay the Allied advance until they could move their men and equipment across the Straits of Messina into Calabria.

Palermo fell to the Allied advance, followed by Messina. On September 3, as the Germans escaped to southern Italy, Sicilian authorities signed an armistice at Cassibile, becoming the first region of Italy to be freed by the Allies, long before the invasion of Normandy in 1944. Ironically, the Allies were aided by the Mafiosi, who resurfaced for the occasion, eager to rid Sicily of the Fascists who had tried to wipe them out.

49th State for the U.S.?

With the devastation of World War II behind them, Sicilians reviewed their link with the Italian mainland, with thousands deciding the union had been a disaster, as had been foretold by the lower classes. A Separatist movement gained hold, demanding complete independence for the island.

Sicilian Communists called for massive land redistribution. In an unlikely marriage, the landed gentry allied itself with the Mafia to snuff out the "dangerous left-wing uprisings" throughout the land.

In 1946, the government in Rome agreed to give Sicily limited independence. Regional autonomy called for Sicily to have its own assembly and president. The role is similar to what Scotland enjoys with England.

Many of the Separatists were even lobbying to be linked to the United States, becoming the 49th state. But with the coming of the elections of 1951, the Separatists faded into history.

For most of the latter part of the 20th century, Sicily was dominated by the Christian Democrats, a political party founded by Father Luigi Sturzo of Caltagirone. This was the party more or less of the Catholic Church, with right-of-center to conservative leanings. In an unspoken, almost hidden alliance, the Christian Democrats worked with the Mafia, as *clientilismo*—political patronage—became the rule of the land. Many a developmental fund ended up in the pocket of a Mafia don.

Even in the late 20th century and early 21st century, the Mafia has remained a strong influence on the island, in spite of a campaign against it by the governments presiding in the 1980s and 1990s. Many anti-Mafia lawmakers were gunned down, and in 1992, the Mafia-fighting magistrates Giovanni Falcone and Paolo Borsellino were killed within months of each other, sparking island-wide indignation. In 2004, the annual report of the Interior Ministry to the parliament in Rome claimed that the Mafia in Sicily was experiencing "a moment of renewal to overcome a structural crisis following the arrest of many top-ranking elements." The report also concluded that the so-called Cosa Nostra was trying to "regain credibility and competitiveness." The ministry report ominously concluded that the Cosa Nostra was pressing ahead with its traditional activities, such as gaining control of public-works contracts and practicing widespread extortion of Sicilian businesses for "protection" money.

One novel approach to dealing with the Cosa Nostra is taking place in the town of Corleone, home of the most sanguinary Mafia bosses. Corleone has been confiscating the property of some of the more notorious Mafiosi and making this blood-soaked land bloom. Agronomists are planting melons, lentils, wheat, grapes, and chickpeas on estates once owned by the Mafia, and selling the products from these lands. And how is the mob striking back at this agricultural bounty? To this point, retaliation has been relatively minor.

In 2006 the Italian government continued its relentless pursuit of Mafia leaders, arresting Italy's reputed number-one Mafia boss, Bernardo Provenzano. The don was found 60km (37 miles) south of Palermo in Corleone, even though his former lawyer was telling newspapers that the elusive Mafia leader was dead. He was found very much alive after 43 years on the run, living on a diet of ricotta and chicory; he's now incarcerated in total isolation.

SICILY'S ART & ARCHITECTURE

For decades, scholars have claimed that if you want to uncover the history of Western civilization, you need look no further than the island of Sicily. The original melting pot is a showcase of art and architecture of the Mediterranean, as each conqueror brought a different style and artistic statement to the island over 10,000 years of history. From the earliest graffiti found in caves, to the glorious Doric temples at Agrigento, to the pinnacle of the unique Late Sicilian Baroque in the southeast, each wave of civilization has left its mark. Sometimes the styles of two different occupiers have been uniquely blended, as evidenced in the combination of Arabic and Norman art and architecture.

Much of Sicily's artistic legacy has been damaged by volcanic explosions, earthquakes, and a range of man-made forces, from Hannibal's invading troops from North Africa to the Allied bombardments of 1943. Much that remains is threatened by decay.

The Mafia hasn't helped, either. The looting of the island's treasures for sale abroad to wealthy anonymous buyers has taken a vast toll on Sicily's artistic heritage, and the precious painting by Caravaggio that once adorned the Oratory of San Lorenzo in Palermo is said to have been fed to pigs (and only for spite).

Prehistoric Art

Artists have been at work in Sicily since prehistoric times, as rock paintings and graffiti discovered at the Addaura caves in Palermo and in Messina reveal. Even in the Neolithic period, the first indigenous cultures, such as those who settled Lipari, were turning out artful **ceramics** and **terra-cotta,** many of which remain to this day (see the Museo Archeologico Eoliano in Lipari, p. 238).

The most remarkable **cave paintings** were those found at Grotta del Genovese on Levanzo, one of the Egadi Islands off the western coast of Sicily. Discovered by accident in 1949, the Paleolithic wall paintings and Neolithic drawings are anywhere from 6,000 to 10,000 years old. Most of the drawings are of wild animals, such as deer and horses. Even the mighty tuna, traditionally found in these waters, show up here.

The Legacy of the Greeks

From the 8th century B.C. onward, the Greeks settled on Sicily, leaving great contributions to architecture before they were replaced by other conquerors. Much of their heritage was destroyed by pillagers, but much still remains to delight us. The Greeks left a legacy of some of the best-preserved Doric **temples** in the Western world, especially those at Agrigento in the Valley of the Temples, those in the ruined city of Selinunte, those in the archaeological gardens at Syracuse, and (best of all) the magnificent and still-standing temple at Segesta. The temples constructed in Sicily were more innovative than even those of classical Greece.

The archaeological museums of Sicily are filled with artifacts from the Greek occupation: Painted **ceramics** and **amphorae, sculptures** and **metopes,** and **bronzes** and **carved ornaments** for temple buildings.

The Coming of the Romans

Unlike the Greeks, the Romans did not leave a great artistic legacy in Sicily, except for the **Villa Romana (Roman villa)** at Casale, outside the town of Piazza Armerina (p. 191). The vast polychrome floor mosaics at this 40-room villa from the 3rd century A.D. are worth the trek across Sicily. Villas on much smaller scales, and not as well-preserved, are found in Palermo, at Durrueli near Agrigento, at Tellaro near Noto, and in Patti on the northern coast. Other traces of Roman architecture can be found in the amphitheaters of Taormina, Syracuse, and Catania, as well as in Syracuse's Christian catacombs.

Artistic Flowering under the Normans

Subsequent conquerors such as the Byzantines and the Arabs made little artistic impact on Sicily until invited back by later conquerors, the Normans. The Byzantines transformed Greek temples into Christian basilicas, while the Arabs built palaces, private residences, and religious buildings with such Asian characteristics as domes piercing the roofs. Arabo-Norman architecture represented an innovation of art and architecture.

From the 11th century on, the Normans began to transform Sicily, and much of their achievement remains today. The Normans erected huge **cathedrals,** or *duomos.* Their achievements—the cathedrals at Monreale and Cefalù, and the Palatine Chapel within the Norman Palace in Palermo—remain among the greatest sightseeing attractions on the island today.

Roger II (1131–54) founded the first major cathedral in northwest Sicily at Cefalù, using a Latin cross plan with a chevron pattern. Pointed arches and angled columns particular to Sicily, as opposed to mainland cathedrals, still characterize this landmark church. The mosaic decorations in the central apse alone would make this one of Sicily's greatest churches.

The mosaics in the cathedral at Monreale cover the entire surface of the interior and are therefore even more stunning and beautiful. It was at Monreale that Sicily reached the apex of its contribution to medieval art in Europe. The Monreale Duomo also contains the most examples of Norman sculpture on the island, more than 200 slender columns with twin capitals. Each of these capitals is graced with a singular composition. Similar capitals, though not as elaborate, can be found at the cloisters at Cefalù, with a stunning capital depicting Noah's Ark.

Palermo also has a splendid cathedral and important **churches** of the period, such as Santa Maria dell'Ammiraglio (La Martorana), San Cataldo, San Giovanni degli Eremiti (St. John of the Hermits) and San Giovanni dei Lebbrosi (St. John of the Lepers), the first Norman church in Palermo, along with the Arab-influenced palaces that served as summer retreats, like La Cuba and La Zisa.

But the Normans lavished the most attention on the seat of their power, the mammoth Palazzo dei Normanni in Palermo. This sumptuous palace became the seat of the Hauteville dynasty. Using a palace originally constructed by the Arabs in the 9th century, the Normans greatly extended it between 1132 and 1140. The crowning architectural glory of this palace is the **Cappella Palatina (Palatine Chapel),** with its Arab-inspired cupola and a stunning modern honeycomb ceiling decorated with Arab designs. With the passing of the Normans and the arrival of the Hohenstaufen rulers in the 13th century, the great flowering of Sicilian art slowly died. The Hohenstaufens were more interested in fortifications and castles than in art, as evidenced in Milazzo, Catania, and Syracuse. The dark ages of Sicilian art had descended on the island and would last for 4 centuries.

Sicily Sleeps Through the Renaissance

At the height of the Renaissance, Sicily remained under Spanish occupation. That may explain why Sicily virtually slept through the Renaissance, which began in Florence and swept across the rest of Italy. Although no great architectural heritage remains in Sicily from this era, painting and sculpture was preeminent, revealing mainly Spanish but also Flemish influences.

Sicily's greatest artist, **Antonello da Messina** (1430–79), emerged during this period, initially inspired by the Flemish school and later showing the influence of his encounters with Piero della Francesca and Giovanni Bellini in Venice. One painting more than any other exemplifies his work: *Portrait of an Unknown Man,* in the Museo Mandralisca at Cefalù. His other notable works, the greatest of Renaissance art in Sicily, are the *Polyptych of St. Gregory,* in the Museo Regionale in Messina, and his two versions of the *Annunciation.* (One, a simple portrait of the Virgin Mary, is housed at the Palazzo Abatellis in Palermo, while a more detailed version is in the Palazzo Bellomo in Syracuse.)

The **Gagini family** of sculptors and architects moved down from Lake Lugano and had an enormous impact on Sicily. The founding father of the Gagini school was Domenico Gagini (1420–92), who often worked in conjunction with his son, Antonello, born in Palermo in 1478. Their sculptures still adorn many of the churches of Palermo, and a Gagini school flourished in Sicily until the mid-1600s.

Baroque & Neoclassical Overkill

The baroque style swept Sicily, awakening the island from a long slumber since the Normans' departure centuries earlier. The baroque came into vogue as a result of a devastating earthquake in 1693 in eastern Sicily that leveled such cities as Catania, paving the way for their own unique brand of the style, the Late Sicilian Baroque, which combined the Spanish-inspired version of the baroque with Sicilian decorative and structural elements. **Rosario Gagliardi** (1700–70) designed the magnificent **Cattedrale San Giorgio** at Ragusa Ibla. The baroque city that emerged after the earthquake in Catania was created in part by **Giovanni Battista Vaccarini** (1702–69), who devoted 3 decades of his life to pulling a new Catania out of the ashes.

Noto, in southeastern Sicily, is another city that was rebuilt in the baroque style after the earthquake. The unity of the baroque style here remains unequaled anywhere else on the island.

In Palermo, the baroque style came under the influence of Spanish dons who preferred *spagnolismo,* or a love of rococo ostentation. The **Quattro Canti** crossroads of the city remains today as the most lavish example of the dons' taste for overly adorned squares and streets. Private palaces, or *palazzi,* were also richly adorned, with sculptures ranging from angels to nymphs to gargoyles. Chiesa dell'Immacolata Concezione (Church of the Immaculate Conception) at the Capo, and the convent of Santa Caterina, among others, were adorned with dizzying intarsias of marble that reek more of opulence than charity.

The master of the Palermitan oratories, **Giacomo Serpotta,** born in Palermo in 1656, specialized in adorning church oratories with molded plasterwork in ornamental frames. You can see one of his masterpieces today, Palermo's **Oratory of the Rosary,** in the church of Santa Cita. The neoclassical movement that soon followed yielded some less-elaborate but more elegant edifices (the two theatres of Palermo, the Massimo, and the Politeama, are prime examples).

Art Nouveau

Along with Paris, Vienna, and Brussels, Palermo was also one of the shining stars of Art Nouveau, the artistic and architectural movement that blossomed in the late 19th century and lasted into the 1930s. Also known as Liberty, it introduced to Sicily a first: Stained-glass windows and decor. (Gothic architecture, which utilized stained-glass windows, never made it on the island.) Palermo stood out when it came to the Art Nouveau style, thanks to the genius and innovation of such architects as Giovan Battista Basile and his son Ernesto, and artists such as Salvatore Gregorietti and Ettore Maria de Begler, who painted the dining room of the Villa Igiea hotel. Furniture design was also at the forefront thanks to the Ducrot factory. Regrettably, during what was known as the "rape of Palermo," between 1960 and 1980, many of these buildings were torn down and replaced by uglier ones. The two kiosks in front of the Massimo Theater are still great examples of Art Nouveau, and **Villa Malfitano** (p. 106) and **Villino Florio** (p. 177) deserve a visit.

Contemporary Art

Contemporary art in Sicily is synonymous with two artists: **Salvatore Fiume** (1915–97) and **Renato Guttuso** (1911–87). Fiume was an eclectic painter, sculptor, playwright, and set designer whose works are housed in some of the most prestigious museums around the world, including the Vatican Museums and the Hermitage in St. Petersburg, Russia. Painting in a style often called visceral, Guttuso became renowned for his nudes, landscapes, and still-lifes. His most famous work, *The Vuccuria,* is housed at the Steri Palace in Palermo.

THE LAY OF THE LAND

Of all the islands of the Mediterranean, Sicily is the largest, spread across 40,965km (25,454 miles), and lying halfway between Gibraltar and the Suez Canal. It is surrounded by several archipelagos, the most numerous of which are the Aeolian Islands (see Chapter 10). Other island groups include the Egadi in the west and the Pelagie, the latter centered at Lampedusa. Two other islands are Pantelleria and Ustica.

Sicily enjoys a Mediterranean climate—it's the first part of Italy to heat up in the spring and the last to get chilly in winter. It also suffers the longest, hottest summers, with July and August being veritable scorchers.

An island of rivers, many of which dry up in summer, Sicily is also volcanic, the most threatening menace being Mount Etna, on the eastern coast. Some of the islands in the various archipelagos also have volcanoes, notably Stromboli. Most are long dormant, but Vulcano is known to huff and puff now and then.

Geology

The geology of Sicily is similar to that of other Mediterranean islands, which were conditioned by the slow contraction of the vast ocean between Africa and Eurasia. In the last 50 million years, this process has pushed the predominantly limestone sea bed of the Cretaceous period toward the surface, causing the formation of mountain and hill ranges. This has also been accompanied by volcanic activity, making Sicily rich in tuff (lithified volcanic ash) and widely used for building materials. It is also characterized by the formation of precipitated sulfur, which had enormous importance to the economy of the island until the 1970s, as mines were set up to extract the much-in-demand mineral for export. (Salt deposits are also abundant, though, like sulfur, they are not part of today's Sicilian economy.) The sulfur deposits resulted from a tectonic event in the western Mediterranean, which caused the rising and the subsequent closure of the Strait of Gibraltar. The lack of water flow from the Mediterranean to the Atlantic Ocean determined the hypersalinity that derived from excessive evaporation. Once the Pliocene era began, a new tectonic event lowered the threshold and thus generated the flow once more of oceanic waters into the sea, covering the evaporated sediments with the deep-sea formations of fine clay and pelagic carbonates.

Flora & Fauna

The deforestation of Sicily has been disastrous for the island from as far back as Roman times. Once rich in forests that provided it with abundant water, Sicily had vast tracts of woodland razed over the years to turn the island into the grain belt of the Roman Empire. The brush fires set deliberately by arsonists haven't helped much, either. Massive deforestation has left Sicily with a hotter, drier climate.

The ancient Greek settlers brought with them the cultivation of the grape and the olive tree. The Arab conquerors brought date palms from Africa and encouraged the cultivation of citrus groves. From the New World came the prickly pear cactus, which has now become one of the symbols of Sicily.

Typical Mediterranean flora is still present in the maquis along the coastlines and on the islands, while cities at higher altitudes—such as Enna, Erice—and towns in the foothills of Etna have Alpine vegetation, namely oaks and chestnuts. Aleppo pines are present along the coastlines. Broom bushes set the countryside alive in spring, with miles of sunflower-yellow coloring. The spiny shrub, the so-called bastard olive, grows wild almost everywhere.

Island fauna have been horrendously affected by the gradual deforestation of Sicily. Other than sheep grazing in country fields, it is rare to see much wildlife as you travel the country roads of Sicily. Along the coast, of course, there is still plenty of birdlife, notably cormorants, herons, and seagulls. The viper is the only poisonous snake on the island, frightening tourists as it suns itself at various archaeological sites in summer. In the Madonie and Nebrodi mountains, you might run into the occasional wild boar.

The western coast dwellers of Sicily, who for centuries have depended on the mammoth schools of tuna for their livelihoods, are now facing diminishing returns. Huge Japanese trawlers in international waters are capturing more and more of these fish for shipment to the markets of Tokyo.

SICILY IN POPULAR CULTURE: BOOKS, FILM, & MUSIC

Books

SICILIAN AUTHORS Considering that Italian literature was founded at the court of Frederick II in Palermo, it comes as no surprise that Sicily has produced brilliant writers whose works have become world-renowned classics. Oddly enough, there would be a very long gap between the poems and sonnets composed by the court minstrels Ciullo d'Alcamo and Jacopo da Lentini and the next wave of writers, but Sicily made up for it.

One of the great writers of Italian fiction, **Giovanni Verga** (1840–1922) was from Catania. His works depicting the Sicily of his life and times are among the most important of the Realist movement, and his verses relay the story with a stark, frank poignancy. He published his *Little Novels of Sicily* in 1886, and his *I Malavoglia (House by the Medlar Tree)* was part of a trilogy dedicated to the *vinti,* the defeated, a common theme in his works. The *Cavalleria Rusticana,* one of the most popular operas in the world, is based on one of his stories. Like Verga, fellow Catania-area born **Luigi Capuana** (1839–1915) was also deeply influenced by French realism. **Federico De Roberto** (1861–1927) wrote the compelling *I Vicerè (The Viceroys)*, a novel about a rich and powerful Sicilian family during the time of Italian unification.

In the last century the Nobel Prize was awarded twice to two of Sicily's sons—**Luigi Pirandello** (1867–1936), from Agrigento, and Salvatore Quasimodo, from Modica. The outstanding playwright and dramatist Pirandello is considered the forerunner of the Theatre of the Absurd for his interpretations of human nature and genuine mistrust of what would seem to be the truth. His masterpiece, *Six Characters in Search of an Author,* is a poignant tragicomedy that questions the relationship between reality and fantasy. *Il Fu Mattia Pascal (The Late Mattia Pascal)* is a humorous novel with bizarre twists about escape from a stifling life. It can be emphatically said that reading Pirandello is compulsory for understanding what makes Sicily tick.

Poet **Salvatore Quasimodo** (1901–68) is considered one of the greatest Italian lyrical writers of the last century but, unlike Pirandello whose stories were deeply rooted in his home territory, his writing was not greatly influenced by his homeland; his works were more inspired by his repugnance of the war (he was an outspoken anti-Fascist). His most famous poems are *And It's Suddenly Evening* and *Day After Day*; his works gave way to the movement known as Hermeticism. His brother-in-law, **Elio Vittorini** (1908–66), from Syracuse, wrote the brilliant *Conversazioni in Sicilia (Conversations in Sicily)* in which he denounced Fascism. The first U.S. edition was prefaced by Ernest Hemingway, who had a great influence on Vittorini's writing style.

Giuseppe Tomasi di Lampedusa (1896–1957) was a descendant of nobility and a dilettante writer, yet his only novel, *Il Gattopardo (The Leopard)*—published posthumously in 1958—has been acclaimed as one of the great novels of its time. It traces the decline and fall of the House of Salina, a family of Sicilian aristocrats during the tumultuous time of Italy's Unification in 1860, which mirrored the fate of di Lampedusa's own ancestors. The words uttered by Prince Fabrizio Salina in the novel ("change everything so as to not change anything") would become an eerie omen about the state of Sicily today.

Leonardo Sciascia, (1921–89), from Racalmuto, was a keen observer of postwar Sicily in a period of political upheaval. Mafia domination and the role of Mafia in politics are themes reflected in his works. His outspoken positions on certain issues often made him unpopular, yet Gore Vidal heralded him as the vigil of the Sicily of the times. *The Wine Dark Sea,* a collection of short stories, explores "the Sicilian mind," as well as Mafia culture. The book presents a history of the island as it travels over the centuries.

Two authors who are still producing works today and who draw inspiration from their home territory are **Giuseppe Consolo,** who published the *Sorriso di un Marinaio Ignoto (Smiles from an Unknown Seaman)* and **Andrea Camilleri,** who still pens the widely-successful Inspector Montalbano series based on the character of police commissioner Salvatore Montalbano.

HISTORY   *The Kingdom In The Sun,* by John Julius Norwich, is a formidable book that explains and explores how the Normans conquered Sicily and how they were able to maintain the delicate balance among the existing inhabitants on the island while creating the most important cultural center in the Western world.

Arabs and Normans in Sicily and the South of Italy, by Adele Cilento, is a coffee-table book of 275 full-color glossy pictures. It is the best-illustrated account of the architecture, tapestries, manuscripts, paintings, and relics of the culture created in Sicily under both Arab and Norman rule. With the coming of the Normans, the artistic legacy of the Byzantine world was fused with Christian motifs.

The Kingdom of Sicily, 1100–1250: A Literary History, by Karla Mallette, is for serious readers who want an insight into medieval life on the island. The book deals with the complex nature of Sicily as a cultural crossroads between East and West, Islam and Christianity. The literary production of the island is surveyed in Arabic, Latin, Greek, and Romance dialects.

FICTION & MEMOIR   *Sicily: Where Love Is,* by Gerry Battista, captures a closely-knit family and their friends. The lives and adventures of several generations of the Salerno family, strong on family ties and cultural values, are beautifully portrayed. You are transported to Sicily when reading this book.

A House in Sicily, by Daphne Phelps with Denis Mack Smith, is a captivating memoir, recounting how Phelps inherited "the most beautiful house in Sicily." Arriving in Taormina with little money, she planned to sell the house but fell in love with Taormina, and began receiving guests, including illustrious ones such as Tennessee Williams and Bertrand Russell.

Casa Nostra: A Home in Sicily, by Caroline Seller Manzo, does for Sicily what Frances Mayes did for Tuscany in another memoir. Food, family, and culture—even culture shock—are captured in this English woman's tale of her unpredictable adventures when she set out to renovate a villa. The unique beauty and history of western Sicily are also captured in this tale.

WAR NOVELS   *The Day of Battle: The War in Sicily and Italy (1943–44),* by Rick Atkinson, is a riveting story of the U.S. Army's campaign to capture Sicily in World War II. This is a warts-and-all detailed story of the Sicilian campaign, focusing on the major personalities (and sometimes the minor players) as well as the flaws and successes of the battle.

A Bell for Adano, by John Hersey, is a Pulitzer Prize-winning World War II novel set in the fictitious Sicilian town of Adano (which was really Licata, where Allied forces landed in 1943). The story tells the tale of an Italian–American army major who wins over the trust and respect of the locals when he helps find a way to replace the 700-year-old town-hall bell that was melted down by the Fascists to make ammunition.

Films

Cinema Paradiso brought a 1989 Oscar to Giuseppe Tornatore for this romantic tale of growing up in a remote Sicilian village. A filmmaker returns to his Sicilian hometown for the first time in 3 decades and takes a look back at his life. That life included time spent helping the projectionist at the local movie house.

Giuseppe Toratore followed *Cinema Paradiso* in 1995 with *L'Uomo Delle Stelle* (*The Star Maker*), which was the story of a Roman con man who arrives in Sicily posing as a talent scout. He journeys with his camera to poor villages in 1950s Sicily, promising stardom for a fee to the gullible islanders. Tornatore would make two more films about Sicily: *Malena* in 2000, about a young boy's infatuation with a war widow who happens to be the most beautiful woman in town, coveted by men and viciously envied by their women; and *Baaria* in 2009, an epic recounting the postwar history of his hometown of Bagheria.

Stromboli (1949), shot on one of the Aeolian Islands, was a failure at the box office, although it received worldwide publicity. Later generations have appreciated it more than those who first saw it. Ingrid Bergman was the star, Roberto Rossellini the director. The couple's "illicit" affair virtually destroyed the married Bergman's career (at least temporarily), and she was even denounced in the U.S. Senate. (In my view, Rossellini and Bergman should have been denounced for this movie, not their love affair.)

Politics and crime are bedfellows in Francesco Rosi's neorealist drama *Salvatore Giuliano* (1962). The body of Giuliano, one of Italy's most "beloved" gangsters, was found on July 5, 1950, in Castelvetrano in Sicily. His body was punctured with bullet holes. Rosi paints a vivid portrait of this legendary bandit.

Il Gattopardo (The Leopard) was Luchino Visconti's 1968 film version of the celebrated Giuseppe di Lampedusa novel set in the revolutionary Sicily of the mid-1800s. A lush drama with a memorable ballroom scene, the film is a perfect evocation of a lost world. The masterpiece traces the decline and fall of the House of Salina, starring Burt Lancaster as a Sicilian prince trying to preserve his fading aristocratic way of life.

Visconti in 1948 also used Sicily as a backdrop for *La Terra Trema (The Earth Trembles)*, an adaptation of Verga's novel *Malavoglia*. This story of a fisherman failed at the box office upon its release but came to be viewed as a classic of the neorealism movement.

Playing a Sicilian aristocrat, Marcello Mastroianni starred in Pietor Germi's 1961 comedy *Divorzio all'italiana (Divorce, Italian Style)*. Facing a midlife crisis, Mastroianni wants a divorce when it was not legal in Italy. He finds his wife (played by Daniela Rocca) annoying, and he devises a scheme to make it appear that she is unfaithful and then to kill her.

In 2002 Marco Tullio Giordana's *I Cento Passi (The 100 Steps)* received wide critical acclaim. Documenting the life of anti-Mafia activist Peppino Impastato, he recounts the story of the 100 steps that separated Impastato's house from the home of the Mafioso who had him brutally killed.

Music

As the crossroads of the Mediterranean, Sicily has had a wide range of music, from *à capella* devotional songs to the vibrant jazz scene of today. Over the years the island has been a cultural melting pot of music, beginning with the Greeks, and going on to the Normans, French, Spanish, and even Arabs from the Maghreb.

As the "granary of Italy," Sicily is home to harvest songs and work songs. Sicily's flute music *(friscaletto)*, accompanied by a *schiacciapensieri* (Jew's harp), has deep roots on island, with Carmelo Salemi the best-known performer of these traditional sounds. Another notable folk singer was Rosa Balistreri, who sung of the hardships of life in a ripping, moving voice accompanied by a lone guitar, which has influenced a generation of artists. Many festivals are held in her name throughout the island, as are folk-song contests.

Catania, with its splendid Teatro Massimo Bellini, built in 1890, is the hometown of the great **Vincenzo Bellini** (1801–35), who regrettably lived a very short life. The young composer still remains "the favorite son" of Catania.

A popular musician, Franco Battiato, fused rock 'n' roll with traditional and classical influences. His masterpiece, released in 1979, was called *L'era del cinghiale bianco*. Catania is still the musical capital of the island; many contemporary Italian chart-toppers and internationally appreciated artists like Carmen Consoli and Mario Biondi are from here.

Messina's male choirs enjoy island renown, and Giancarlo Parisi is known for his traditional Sicilian music. In 1975, Luciano Maio founded the band Taberna Mylaensis, and recovered much traditional Sicilian music before it died out—folk songs, folkloric dance music, provincial ballads, romantic poetry, and instrumental songs played on traditional instruments.

Alan Lomax, an American musicologist, made many recordings of traditional island music in the 20th century, including epic storytelling, religious music, dance music, and lullabies.

Recorded in 1954, the album *Sicily* (Rounder Records) is a digitally remastered selection of mostly unreleased music from Lomax's sweeping Columbia World Library of Folk and Primitive Music project. Lomax was fortunate enough to record this music in preindustrial Italy, and he was able to capture on record every sound, from the plaintive a cappella chorus of female almond sorters to a frenzied tarantella. He even managed to capture the sounds of a *ciaramedda a paru* (twin-chanter bagpipe). Yes, the bagpipe is not just confined to Scotland, and you'll see the odd bagpipe player or two roaming the streets at Christmastime, playing the classic traditional carols.

EATING & DRINKING IN SICILY

Good food is usually a priority for travelers to Sicily, as it should be: Ingredients are always fresh, and the recipes simple and time-tested. Whether you dine in a hole-in-the-wall dive or have five-star service, the choices are plentiful.

A Melting-Pot Cuisine

Island fare is a blend of the cuisines of Sicily's many conquerors and cultures. The lush citrus groves around Catania were originally planted by the Arabs. Even those magnificently intricate pastries and rich desserts are a direct result of the Arab invasions, which brought a taste of North Africa to the shores of Catania.

In time, subsequent invaders, including Norman rulers and Spanish viceroys, left their own legacy of "aristocratic food," often as part of huge banquets prepared by enormous staffs (no respectable aristocrat would have been without a *monsù*, or house chef) and presented by servants. These extravagant excesses were in direct contrast to the diet of the fishermen, the land tillers, and other working people who set a simple table based mainly on fish and the bountiful harvest of vegetables from the Sicilian countryside. But it's the rediscovery of these simple dishes, made with ingredients offered by the land and sea, that's finding favor once more in the kitchens of the best restaurants on the island.

Sicily at the Table

Sicily is blessed with some of the finest raw culinary materials in Italy. Using this incredible array of fresh ingredients from the sea and field, the chefs of Sicily fashion a delectable display of enticing platters, many of them better and more original than those found anywhere on the mainland of Italy.

STARTERS Sicilian antipasti are meals in themselves. My favorite opening to a meal is the island specialty *caponatina* (eggplant stew). It's made with eggplant, fresh tomatoes, olives, capers, onions, and celery in a sweet-and-sour sauce of vinegar and sugar, served at room temperature for full flavor.

Another savory starter is the *antipasto caldo,* made of bite-size *arancine* (rice balls), potato croquettes, *panelle* (chickpea fritters), diced pieces of omelet, and French fries. This starter is a meal alone, and most diners can't get through the first course after one of these. An *antipasto misto* is usually sun dried tomatoes, artichokes in vinaigrette, and local cheese and cured meats. I also could begin any meal in Sicily with an *insalata di mare,* a seafood salad of boiled squid, tasty bits of octopus, fat shrimp, and chopped fresh vegetables with a dressing of olive oil flavored with lemon juice or vinegar. Marinated raw anchovies doused with olive oil and red pepper are another classic seafood starter. The *impepata di cozze,* fresh mussels steamed in wine with garlic, red pepper, and parsley, is also another premeal classic.

FIRST COURSES For your *primi,* or first course—especially if you've skipped the antipasti—you'll be treated to delicious pasta and rice dishes or even couscous, the latter deriving from Sicily's centuries-old links with North Africa. Couscous dominates around western Sicily, where the *cous cous alla trapanese* is made with fish instead of the classic meat or mutton. *Cous cous al nero di seppia,* a variation of the more-famous rice-based dish, is also a favorite round these parts.

Spaghetti alla Norma (pasta with eggplant and aged ricotta), is a classic out of Catania, while *pasta con le sarde,* a simple but savory pasta with fresh sardines, served in a tomato and wild fennel sauce with raisins, pine nuts, and capers, is a staple of Palermo. *Pesto alla siciliana* varies, but the classic ingredients are olive oil, tomatoes, crushed almonds, pine nuts, ricotta, garlic, and basil. If you can have only one pasta dish, make it *spaghetti con i ricci* (pasta with sea urchin). It's simply sautéed in garlic and olive oil and is a sheer delight to the palate that leaves you wanting more. **Note:** For seafood first courses, adding any grated cheese on top is a big no-no.

VEGETABLES & FRUITS Luscious local vegetables, used liberally in pastas and main courses, include vine-ripened tomatoes, spring-green zucchini (the yardstick-long variety), wild asparagus, tangy capers, many varieties of olives, broccoli and cauliflower the size of a child's head, thorny artichokes, fava beans, and *tinniruma* (tiny, tender leaves of the zucchini plant used in soups). Fruit is just as abundant: Flat peaches with intoxicating aromas, cantaloupes from the plains east of Agrigento, prickly pears in three different colors, the world-famous *Uva Italia,* a grape variety from Canicattì, and, of course, the citrus fruits that abound—from the blood-red oranges of eastern Sicily, which get their distinctive color from the lavaenriched soil, to the tangy varieties the size of grapefruits, to the lemons, cedars, and bergamots.

SEAFOOD Naturally, fresh fish and crustaceans are the dominant feature at most tables. The most popular fish dishes are tuna from the west and swordfish from the Straits of Messina. For most connoisseurs, fish is best served *alla griglia* (simply grilled), *arrosto* (roasted), *al cartoccio* (wrapped in tin foil), *all'acquapazza* (cooked in sea water), or simply boiled (the way octopus is always served). **Involtini di pesce spada,** grilled roulades of swordfish, are covered with breadcrumbs and sautéed in olive oil. Another swordfish classic is *pescespada alla messinese,* topped with olives, tomatoes, and capers. Sardines, another staple of Sicily, are used to create the succulent **sarde a beccafico**—fried sardine filets covered with spiced breadcrumbs and sandwiched between two bay leaves. You can wholeheartedly bet that any **fritto misto** (small fish fried together) will include shrimp, calamari, and mullet.

MEATS Traditionally, Sicilian cuisine is based largely on vegetables and the catch of the day harvested from coastal waters. But you can also fill your plate with marvelous meat specialties, including **grigliata alla palermitana,** which is a mixed variety of meats—usually sausage, beef, and pork—breaded and grilled (not fried). One of the better-known meat dishes is **falsomagro,** meaning "false lean;" it's the Sicilian answer to meatloaf. This rich, bountiful dish, a family favorite that fed hungry mouths when times were tough and the choice of ingredients limited, is composed of a large slab of beef wrapped around Sicilian sausages, prosciutto, raisins, pine nuts, cheese, a boiled egg or two, or whatever is available. The treat is tied with a string and stewed in a savory tomato sauce. This peasant's dish has now been elevated to gourmet status, as more and more local chefs are reworking this classic and serving it their way.

One Sicilian dish now served around the world is **pollo alla Marsala** (chicken in Marsala wine). A variation on this famous dish is veal Marsala, which originated among western Sicily's English families living here in the 19th century. Appearing on almost every menu is some form of **involtini,** a roulade made from grilled or roasted chicken or sliced beef, stuffed with a vegetable or meat filling. Sometimes a leafy vegetable such as radicchio is added to the filling. And no Sicilian barbeque would be complete without meat; pork, and sausage from the Nebrodi mountain range, mutton, and the classic **stigghiole** (lamb or veal intestines on a spit).

DESSERTS Sicily knows no bounds when it comes to desserts and sweets—an exhaustive list would require an entire chapter! Narrowing it down, though, I'll start with **cassata,** perhaps the crowning glory of Sicilian desserts. It's a treat for the eyes and the taste buds alike—layers of sponge cake are covered with sweetened ricotta, mixed with chocolate bits and candied fruit, and held together with a frosting of multicolored marzipan so elaborately decorated it's almost a shame to slice (but you will).

Another ricotta-based classic is the **cannolo,** a crunchy, deep-fried tube-like wafer filled with the same mix used for cassata, and sprinkled with pistachios. This is the real deal, not the makeshift varieties filled with cream. A word to the wise: The best pastry shops won't make *cassata* or *cannoli* in the summer, when ricotta is scarce around the island. Chocolate also figures prominently (and that's putting it mildly) in the lush **setteveli**—seven layers of chocolate cake doused with different types of chocolate and pralines, then frosted with a syrupy fudge. Dare to resist this one, if you can. Sicily also lays claim to having invented **gelato,** when Sicilian Francesco Procopio opened his cafe in Paris and exported the stuff abroad. Softer in consistency than regular ice cream, the flavor varieties of gelato are endless, but my absolute favorite is the one made with *pistacchio di Bronte,* pistachios from the town on the slopes of Etna.

The dietetic version of gelato is **granita,** an ice with an almost ice-cream like consistency often eaten after meals but also for breakfast, accompanied by a **brioche,** shaped like a hamburger bun (the best ones always have a "cap"). There's no shortage of flavors here either, the classics being lemon, coffee, and blackberry. Don't say you weren't warned!

The Wines of Sicily

Sicilian wines have seen a renaissance in the last 20 years, thanks to the island's world-renowned wineries that have won prestigious international awards, as well as to the love and dedication of the local vintners. The wines are made from either autochthonous or transplanted grape varieties, and there isn't an area of the island that isn't known for a typical wine. Western Sicily is synonymous with **Bianco d'Alcamo,** a crisp white, and of course the sweet, thick **Marsala** has delighted palates for centuries. **Nero d'Avola** and **Cerasuolo di Vittoria,** with their deep red hues, are products of southeastern Sicily. The **Nerello Mascalese** comes from the foothills of Etna, where the lava-enriched soil confers its distinctive ruby-red color. The **Mamertino,** yet another red, comes from the Messina area and has been around since the times of Julius Caesar. The area around **Menfi,** on the southern coast, is renowned for its whites. Even the tiny islands surrounding Sicily have left their mark in the oenological world: **Malvasia** from Salina and **Passito** from Pantelleria are both golden-to-amber colored dessert wines with distinctive aromas and flavors. Wineries throughout Sicily open their doors to visits and tastings.

WINERIES TO visit

If you want to do some wine tasting during your trek around the island, consider visiting some of these wineries that offer visits and tastings.

- **Florio/Duca di Salaparuta,** Marsala (☏ **0923-781111;** www.cantine florio.it)
- **Pellegrino,** Marsala (☏ **0923-719911;** www.carlopellegrino.it)
- **Donnafugata,** Marsala (☏ **0923-724245;** www.donnafugata.it)
- **Rallo,** Marsala (☏ **0923-721633;** www.cantinerallo.net)
- **Firriato,** Paceco (☏ **0923-882755;** www.firriato.com)
- **Serramarrocco,** Fulgatore (☏ **063-220973;** www.serramarrocco.com)
- **Calatrasi,** San Cipirello (☏ **091-856767;** www.calatrasi.it)
- **Baglio di Pianetto,** Santa Cristina Gela (☏ **091-8570002;** www.bagliopianetto.com)
- **Planeta,** Contrada Ulmo (☏ **091-6124335;** www.pianeta.it)
- **Tasca D'Almerita,** Sclafani Bagni (☏ **092-1544011;** www.tascadalmerita.it)
- **Milazzo,** Campobello di Licata (☏ **0922-878207;** www.milazzovini.com)
- **La Lumia,** Licata (☏ **0922-891709;** www.baronelalumia.it)
- **Quignones,** Licata (☏ **0922-891007;** www.quignones.it)
- **Cos,** Acate (☏ **0932-876145;** www.cosvittoria.it)
- **Murgo,** Santa Venerina, Catania (☏ **095-950520;** www.murgo.it)
- **Benanti,** Viagrande, Catania (☏ **095-7893533;** www.vinicolabenanti.it)
- **Feudo Maccari,** Noto (☏ **0931-596894;** www.feudomaccari.it)
- **Riofavara,** Ispica (☏ **0932-701530;** www.riofavara.it)

PLANNING YOUR TRIP TO SICILY

3

Many first-time visitors to Sicily wrongly believe that it doesn't take much time to see the entire island. Nothing could be farther from the truth—not only is it the largest island in the Mediterranean but it is Italy's largest region. Travel from Palermo to Syracuse, at opposite ends of the island, can take up to 4 hours by car.

Given this vastness, plan to stay at least a week, and that's just to see the highlights with lots of traveling in between. Unless you've decided to stay in one place and make daytrips, the best—if not the sanest—way to see most of the island is to fly into either Palermo or Trapani, located in western Sicily, and travel eastward, winding up your trip in Catania and flying out from there. Although the considerable network of buses and trains will take you where you want, renting a car at the airport gives you the most flexibility, as motorways are efficient and, for the most part, free of charge. That is, of course, if you're ready to take on the daredevil road rules of Sicily.

VISITOR INFORMATION

For a general overview of Sicily and to start drawing up ideas, visit the websites of the Italian Government Tourist Board: www.italiantourism. com and www.enit.it. You can also contact the tourist board offices in your country.

In the United States: 45 Rockefeller Plaza, New York, NY 10111(© **212/ 245-4822;** fax 212/586-9249); 500 N. Michigan Ave., Ste. 2240, Chicago, IL 60611 (© **312/644-0996;** fax 312/644-3019); and 12400 Wilshire Blvd., Ste. 550, Los Angeles, CA 90025 (© **310/820-0098;** fax 310/820-6357).

In Canada: 175 Bloor St. E., South Tower, Ste. 907, Toronto, ON, M4W 3R8 (© **416/925-4882;** fax 416/925-4799).

In the United Kingdom: 1 Princes St., London W1R 8AY (© **020/7408-1254;** fax 020/7399-3567).

For in-depth research on a city or area, visit the websites of the regional, provincial, or local tourist boards of the places you plan to visit. The **Regione Siciliana Assessorato al Turismo** (www.regione.sicilia.it/turismo/web_turismo) handles things on a regional level, while the various provincial tourist boards (**Ente Provinciale per il Turismo**) operate individually in each of the nine provinces. Local tourist boards (**Azienda Autonoma di Soggiorno e Turismo** or **Azienda Autonoma per l'Incremento del Turismo;** in smaller towns and villages these are also referred to as **Pro Loco**) are found in every city.

MAPS　　A map is most helpful when arriving in large cities. The tourist offices offer a map, free of charge, highlighting the main attractions. Larger street maps are usually sold at bookshops and newsagents. If you're renting a car, a map is normally included with the rental—but make sure to ask for one if it's not already in your car.

WHEN TO GO

April to early June and **late September to October** are the best times to visit, as the temperatures are not as sweltering as they are in the summer. However, April to June are the months when school buses packed with children visit the most important sites. Easter is considered high season.

The real tourist boom picks up in mid-June, when schools are closed. From **July to mid-September,** the coastal areas are crammed. Unless you plan to spend time at a seaside resort or on an island, avoid **August** if you can: The heat is unbearable and most establishments in the cities are closed.

From **late October to mid-December,** things are quieter, there are fewer tourists in the cities; sites and attractions do tend to close earlier. Things pick up again briefly during the **Christmas holidays** (Dec 20–Jan 7), when many shops and museums have extended hours. Otherwise, between **November and February,** hotels and restaurants in resort towns are closed, and the temperatures take a plunge, especially in the mountainous areas.

High season on most airline routes to Sicily usually stretches from June to the beginning of September and around holiday periods (Christmas and Easter). **Shoulder season** is from April to May and from early September to October; **low season** is from November 1 to December 19 and from mid-January to March.

Weather

Sicily enjoys a relatively mild climate; high temperatures begin in May, often lasting until sometime in October. While the summers can be very hot and dry, the spring and winter months often bring on torrential rains. Surprisingly, even Sicily has its cold waves in winter, with temperatures falling below zero, especially inland. As of late, it's not been uncommon to see minimal snowfall in Palermo.

Although humidity is not stifling, save for the big cities, there is one element that can be brutal: the wind. Being surrounded by three seas Sicily is exposed to all of them, from the scorching sirocco from the Sahara or the blustery north winds that cause trees to uproot and do serious damage.

Average Temperatures & Rainfall in Palermo & Syracuse

		JAN	FEB	MAR	APR	MAY	JUNE	JULY	AUG	SEPT	OCT	NOV	DEC
Palermo	Temp (°F)	54	55	56	60	66	72	78	79	75	69	62	56
	Temp (°C)	12	13	13	16	19	22	26	26	24	21	17	13
	Rainfall (in.)	2.80	2.60	2.30	1.70	1.00	.50	.20	.50	1.60	3.90	3.70	3.20
Syracuse	Temp (°F)	54	54	55	59	60	72	78	79	75	69	58	56
	Temp (°C)	12	12	13	15	16	22	26	26	24	21	14	13
	Rainfall (in.)	2.40	1.70	1.30	.70	.50	1.00	.10	.20	1.00	3.10	2.00	2.80

Sicily Calendar of Events

For an exhaustive list of events beyond those listed here, check http://events.frommers. com, where you'll find a searchable up-to-the-minute roster of what's happening in Sicily.

JANUARY

Epifania (Epiphany), Piana degli Albanesi. Located 29km (18 miles) from Palermo in one of the Albanian colonies founded at the end of the 15th century, the celebration of Epiphany is an ostentatious affair in the Orthodox Christian rite. A joyous procession of residents in traditional Albanian costumes parades through the streets. Call ✆ **091-8574144** or go to www.pianalbanesi. it. January 6.

Carnevale, Acireale. Carnevale is celebrated all over Sicily, but this one is one of the most famous in Italy. In a town north of Catania between Mount Etna and the sea, it's marked by a colorful parade of masked participants and giant floats. Lemons and oranges from nearby citrus fields are used in abundance to create statues and figures, creating an aromatic atmosphere. It's a weeklong party of fun and revelry. Contact the Catania tourist office at ✆ **095-7306211.** End of January/ beginning of February, according to Lenten calendar.

FEBRUARY

Almond Blossom Festival, Agrigento. Literally thousands of almond trees are in bloom around the Valley of the Temples at this festival heralding the arrival of the first fruits of spring. In Phrygian myths, the almond tree was viewed as the "father of the world." The event is marked with music, folkloric dances from around the world, parades, and puppet shows. All kinds of sweets made with almonds are sold. Contact the Agrigento tourist office at ✆ **0922-20454** or 0922-20391. First week of February.

Feast of Saint Agatha, Catania. This is the spectacular religious celebration of the martyred patron saint of the city, which takes place over three days. A procession of huge candle holders called *candelore,* representing the historical guilds of Catania, parades through the city, preceding the procession of the relics of Saint Agatha. There's also street theater and fireworks. Sweets based on centuries-old recipes from nunneries are sold. All-around mayhem prevails. Contact the Catania tourist office at ✆ **095-7306211.** February 3 to February 5.

APRIL

Holy Week Observances, island-wide. Processions and age-old ceremonies—some from pagan days, some from the Middle Ages—are staged in every city and town in Sicily. No matter where you are, you're likely to come across observances of this annual event. Trapani's procession of the *Misteri* is the island's most famous event staged during Holy Week. But the most dramatic and moving is in the inland city of Enna, about an hour west of Catania. Events are staged on such days as Holy Thursday, Good Friday, and, of course, Easter Sunday itself. Local tourist offices can supply details. Week leading up to Easter.

The Dance of the Devils, Prizzi. Unique in Italy, the dance of the devils (*Il Ballo dei Diavoli*) takes place on Easter Sunday in this town, a 2-hour drive south of Palermo, deep in the Sicilian interior. The festival represents the age-old struggle between good and evil. Figures dressed as red devils, their faces covered with grotesque masks, parade through the streets, searching for souls to devour. Death is seen dressed in yellow and carrying a crossbow. All ends well when "angels" appear later to subdue the devils. Call ☏ **095-7306255**. Easter Sunday.

MAY

Infiorata (Flower Festival), Noto. The residents of this little southeastern town prepare a magnificent carpet of flowers along Via Nicolaci, in the historic core. Themes are taken from religion and mythology. The festival features crafts shows, performances of sacred music, and tours of religious sites, followed by dances and parades of flower-bedecked antique carriages. Check with the tourist office at ☏ **0931-573779** for exact dates.

JUNE

Festa del Muzzini, Messina. *Muzzini* are ancient vases draped in silk, which was a local product of the city, and are carried in parades. This observance is actually a pagan rite to honor Demeter, the goddess of earth and fertility. It's rumored that many young women trying to have a child find themselves impregnated on the night of this celebration. Contact the Messina tourist office at ☏ **090-674236.** June 24.

JULY

Luglio Musicale, Trapani. A month-long series of outdoor events takes place at the Villa Margherita celebrating the finest in ballet, opera, and modern musicals since 1948. Contact the Trapani tourist office at ☏ **0923-545511** or visit www.lugliomusicale.it. July 23 to July 25.

The Feast of Santa Rosalia, Palermo. Holding a special place in the hearts of many residents, this is the celebration of the patron saint of the city. During the week-long festivities Palermo becomes an open-air theater. The highlight is when a 15m-high (49 ft.) float known as the *carro*, shaped like a boat and bearing a statue of the saint, is paraded along Corso Vittorio Emanuele from the Cathedral to the Foro Umberto at the sea, drawn by male devotees. Bands, dancers, circus performers, religious

choruses, fireworks, theatrical performances, and food stalls (featuring everything from delectable tiny snails to the ubiquitous *arancini* (rice balls)) characterize the event. Contact the Palermo tourist office at ☏ **091-583847.** July 10 to July 15.

Scalinata Infiorata, Caltagirone. The spectacular, arduous stairs of Caltagirone, where all of the 102 steps are decorated in local ceramics yet no two are alike, are embellished from top to bottom with flowers by day and candles by night that create an effigy of Saint James, the patron saint of the city. Contact the Caltagirone tourist board ☏ **0933 41363**; visit www.comune. caltagirone.ct.it.

AUGUST

Ferragosto (Assumption Day). This national holiday virtually shuts down the island of Sicily, marking both the religious festival of the Assumption of Mary and the proletarian *Ferie di Agosto* or August holidays. This event always includes religious processions; the real spectacle however is the night before, when bonfires are lit on all the beaches, giving way to all-night dancing and mayhem. August 15.

Palio dei Normanni, Piazza Armerina. Sicily's Norman past is observed during this historic celebration in which locals dress in medieval costumes and parade around town. Even jousting takes place among knights in period costumes, looking like refugees from the pages of *Ivanhoe*. They fight against a puppet representing the dreaded Saracens. Contact the Piazza Armerina tourist office at ☏ **0935-682911.** Mid-August.

SEPTEMBER

International Couscous Festival, San Vito Lo Capo. This annual event on the shores north of Trapani is a week-long festival of live music and a bounty of local foods. The couscous competition draws some of the best cooks in the world, including those from North Africa where the dish originated. You are guaranteed to put on weight if you participate in all of the feasting. Contact the Trapani tourist office at

WHAT TO pack

Sicily enjoys a Mediterranean climate, and days are pretty mild. That's not to say that Sicily does not get its cold spells, particularly inland, and the summers are nothing less than scorching. For summer, pack light clothing and a sweater for the evening, and a pair of good walking shoes for the ancient sites. If visiting Mount Etna, dress in layers; as the temperatures can be rather cold even in August. Winter days are rather blustery, so a good down jacket is necessary. Whatever the season bring a good pair of sunglasses, as the wind can be awfully bothersome, and take high-protection suntan lotion.

☎ **0923-545511** or visit www.couscousfest. it. Last week of September.

OCTOBER

Ottobrata Zafferanese, Zafferana Etnea. At the foothills of Mount Etna, this month-long festival celebrates the local products of the area, and each weekend revolves around different themes: Honey, pistachios, wine, chestnuts, and grapes. Samplings abound, folkloristic dances, local artisans selling their crafts, and art exhibitions enliven the event. Contact the pro loco of Zafferana Etnea ☎ **095-7082825** or visit www.ottobrata zafferanese.net. Month-long.

NOVEMBER

Tutti i Santi (All Saints' Day), island-wide. This ancient observance is celebrated all over Italy and is also a national religious holiday. In Sicily, the spirits of the dead are said to come back to visit children, leaving them toys and other goodies. On this holiday, people take the time to make sure the tombs of their late beloveds are squeaky clean and, in most towns, it is not uncommon for families to sit by the tombs all day long, creating a veritable town festival at the cemetery. Pastry shops prepare a delectable confection, the ominously named "bones of the dead", and the *frutta martorana*, the almond paste shaped to resemble fruits and vegetables. November 1 and 2.

DECEMBER

Chocolate Festival, Modica. Cocoa lovers from around the world flock to the baroque city of Modica, where the celebrated chocolate, still crafted according to recipes from the 16th century, is sold by the tons and local confectioners offer samples of their sweets made with top-secret recipes. A week of entertainment, overeating, and overall pre-holiday gaiety prevails. Contact the Modica Tourism board ☎ **0932-759634;** www.chocobarocco.it. Second week of December.

Christmas Fair, Syracuse. This is the island's most colorful Christmas market. Many islanders drive for miles to purchase gifts here, including sweets, clothing, special embroidery, ornaments, and other items. It's held in the Epipoli section of Syracuse. Contact the Syracuse tourist office at ☎ **0931-481200.** From the second Saturday in December to December 21.

ENTRY REQUIREMENTS

Passports

If you're coming from the U.S., Canada, Australia, or New Zealand, you must have a valid passport issued by your home country. Upon arrival, the border police will stamp it as proof of entry. Insist on getting one should there not be anyone on duty—it's your only proof of entry to Italy (plane tickets, even if they show departure dates, are not considered official documents).

E.U. citizens can enter with passports or valid government-issued identification.

Visas

Visas are not required for stays up to 90 days. For non-E.U. citizens expecting to stay more than 90 days, visit the Italian State Police website, www.poliziadistato.it, for detailed information; there is a section entirely in English that explains how to obtain a *Permesso di Soggiorno* (permission of stay) and what visa requirements are mandatory. For further information, contact the nearest Italian embassy or consulate in your country. For a list of consulates in the U.S., visit www.italyemb.org; in the U.K., www.amblondra.esteri.it; in Canada, www.ambottawa.esteri.it; in Australia, www.ambcanberra.esteri.it; and in New Zealand, www.ambwellington.esteri.it.

Customs

WHAT YOU CAN TAKE HOME FROM SICILY

For information on what you're allowed to bring home, contact one of the following agencies:

U.S. Citizens: **U.S. Customs & Border Protection (CBP),** 1300 Pennsylvania Ave., NW, Washington, DC 20229 (✆ **877/287-8667;** www.cbp.gov).

Canadian Citizens: Canada Border Services Agency, Ottawa, Ontario, K1A 0L8 (✆ **800/461-9999** in Canada, or 204/983-3500; www.cbsa-asfc.gc.ca).

U.K. Citizens: HM Customs & Excise, Crownhill Court, Tailyour Road, Plymouth, PL6 5BZ (✆ **0845/010-9000;** from outside the U.K., 020/8929-0152; www.hmce.gov.uk).

Australian Citizens: Australian Customs Service, Customs House, 5 Constitution Avenue, Canberra City, ACT 2601 (✆ **1300/363-263;** from outside Australia, 612/6275-6666; www.customs.gov.au).

New Zealand Citizens: New Zealand Customs, The Customhouse, 17–21 Whitmore St., Box 2218, Wellington, 6140 (✆ **04/473-6099** or 0800/428-786; www.customs.govt.nz).

GETTING THERE & GETTING AROUND

Getting to Sicily

BY PLANE

Sicily is served by three airports: **Palermo Falcone-Borsellino Airport** (✆ **091-7020111;** www.gesap.it) at Punta Raisi 31km (19 miles) west of the city, **Trapani Vincenzo Florio Airport** (✆ **0923-842502;** www.airgest.it) at Birgi 15kms (9 miles) from Trapani, and **Catania Vincenzo Bellini Airport** (✆ **095-7239111;** www.aeroporto.catania.it), the third largest airport in Italy, at Fontanarossa 7km (4½ miles) from the city center. A fourth airport has been built in Ragusa at **Comiso,** which will serve the southeast, but at the time of writing it had taken more than a year for anyone to sign the go-ahead. It remains to be seen if this will open or not.

Direct flights from the U.S. to Sicily are rare, although **Eurofly** (www.meridiana.com) operates flights from JFK to Palermo twice a week from June to

September. Tickets go like hot cakes, so book early. Italy's major carrier to and from the U.S. is **Alitalia** (© 1-800-2235730, (from Italy, © 06-2222); www.alitaliausa. com). Alitalia flies to Italy in code sharing with **Delta Airlines** (© 1-800-2211212, from IU.S. © 02-38591087 (in Italy); www.delta.com). These two airlines fly directly to either Rome Fiumicino or Milan Malpensa airports.

When **flying from Italy's** mainland, you can catch a connecting flight to Sicily, with Alitalia or **Air One** (from Italy © 199-207080; www.alitalia.com/ap_it/), Italy's second domestic carrier and Alitalia partner, **Ryanair, easyJet,** and **Wind Jet.** Other domestic airlines with service to Sicily (including Lampedusa and Pantelleria) are **Blu Express** (© 199-419777; www.blu-express.com) and **Air Italy** (© 89-55895589; www.airitaly.it).

There's no shortage of **direct flights from the U.K. and Ireland** to Sicily. **British Airways** (© 0844-4930787 from UK; from Italy © 199-712266; www. ba.com) operates a daily service from London Gatwick to Catania. **Ryanair** (© 0871-2460000 from UK; from Ireland © 0818-303030; from Italy © 899-018880; www.ryanair.com) has flights to Trapani from Dublin, London Luton, London Stansted, and Liverpool). **easyJet** (© 0871-2442366 from UK; from Italy © 848-887766; www.easyjet.com) offers flights to Palermo from June to October. An Italian carrier, **Windjet** (© 892020; www.3.volawindjet.it), has seasonal flights from London Gatwick to Palermo and Catania.

To compare airfare for all flights to Sicily and search for the best prices, visit www. itasoftware.com or www.travelsupermarket.com.

BY CAR

If you're feeling particularly adventurous and have time it's also possible to drive from London to Palermo (allow at least 3 days for the journey), a distance of 1,822km (1,132 miles). Once across the channel, factor at least 24 hours of driving to the Italian border.

Rather than driving all through Italy, from here you could pick up a ferry from Genoa (**Grandi Navi Veloci;** www.gnv.it) which sails to Palermo in 20 hours.

BY TRAIN

For many visitors, especially backpackers, this is the most convenient way to reach Sicily from the Italian mainland. Depending on where you start your journey, and which category of train, the trip can take anywhere from 12 to 15 hours (Milan or Venice) or 9 to 12 hours (Rome or Naples). All trains from the mainland arrive at the port of Villa San Giovanni or Reggio Calabria, the toe of the Italian peninsula, and from there trains roll onto enormous barges for the 1-hour crossing to Messina. Trains either stop at Messina Centrale or continue on to Palermo, Catania, or Syracuse.

For fares and information within Italy, call © 892021 or visit www.trenitalia.it, also available in English.

Rail Passes for North American & Australian Travelers

Many travelers to Europe take advantage of the **Eurailpass,** which permits unlimited first- and second-class rail passage in most countries in western Europe (although not in the U.K.). Passes are available for purchase online (www.eurail. com) and at various offices/agents around the world. In North America, railway and travel agents in major cities sell passes, but the biggest supplier is **Rail Europe** (℡ 877/272-RAIL [7245]; www.raileurope.com). In Australia you can buy them at CIT Holidays (www.web.cit.com.au).

Rail Passes for British & Other European Travelers

For European travelers, three passes are designed for unlimited travel within a designated region during a predetermined number of days.

Many different rail passes are available in the United Kingdom for travel to Sicily. Stop in at the **International Rail Centre,** Victoria Station, London SWIV 1JY (℡ 0870/5848-848 in the U.K.; www.raileurope.co.uk). Some of the most popular passes, including InterRail and Euro Youth, are offered only to travelers 25 and under; these allow unlimited second-class travel through most European countries. The **InterRail Pass** (www.interrail.net) is available to passengers of any nationality, with some restrictions—passengers must be able to prove at least 6 months of residency in a European or North African country (Morocco, Algeria, Tunisia) before buying the pass. It allows unlimited travel throughout Europe (except Albania and the republics of the former Soviet Union). See website for more details.

Passengers 25 and older can buy an **InterRail Global Pass.** The cost varies according to the pass purchased, which can be valid from 10 days to 1 month. Passengers must meet the same residency requirements that apply to the InterRail Pass (described above).

For information on buying individual rail tickets or any of the aforementioned passes, contact **National Rail Enquiries,** Victoria Station, London (℡ 020/7278-5240 or 08457/484950; www.nationalrail.co.uk). Tickets and passes are also available at any of the larger railway stations as well as select travel agencies throughout Britain and the rest of Europe.

BY BOAT & FERRY

As an island, Sicily is well linked via sea to mainland Italy. The major connection is from Villa San Giovanni in Calabria, the last mainland city approached before the ferry trip over to Messina, in eastern Sicily. Ferries (*traghetti*) depart frequently from Villa San Giovanni, making the trip of 12km (7½ miles) across the straits. If you don't have a car, you can also make the crossing by hydrofoil (*aliscafo*) from Reggio Calabria, which is faster but does not allow passengers to stand outside during the trip. If you have time to spare, take the ferry, and watch the crossing from the deck.

If you're already in Italy there are many options to choose from. **Traghetti Lines** (℡ 0565-912191; www.traghettilines.it) shows all the possible boat and ferry connections from mainland Italy, Sardinia, and Malta to Palermo, Catania, Messina, Trapani, and Pozzallo. Service to Palermo from Naples and Civitavecchia (Rome) is offered by **SNAV** (℡ 081-4285555; www.snav.it) while **Ustica Lines** (www.usticalines.it) handles service from Naples to the outer-lying islands (Ustica and the Egadi Islands). **TTT lines** (℡ 800-915365; www.tttlines.it) runs a service from Naples to Catania, while **Grimaldi Lines** (℡ 081-496444; www.grimaldi-lines.com) handles service from Civitavecchia. From further north, **Grandi Navi Veloci** (℡ 010-2094591; www.gnv.it) sails from Genoa (year-round) and Livorno (seasonal) to Palermo. Departure times are always subjected to weather and sea conditions, so always call to ask for confirmation.

BY BUS

Europe's major bus carrier, **Eurolines** (✆ 0870/514-3219 in London; www.euro lines.com), has its main office at Grosvenor Gardens, Victoria, London SW1. It runs buses to Rome in 33 hours, with stops along the way. After that, you can take an Italian bus to Sicily. Buses leave England on Wednesday and Friday, heading for Milan and Rome.

If you're in Rome and want to travel overland by bus into Sicily, you can book tickets at **Segesta,** Piazza della Repubblica (✆ 0935-565111; www.interbus.it). It has two departures daily from Rome's Piazza Tiburtina to Palermo; the trip takes 12 hours. The line also goes to Syracuse in southern Sicily in 11 hours.

Getting Around Sicily

BY PLANE

There are domestic flights from Palermo to the Pélagie Islands (Lampedusa and Linosa), and from Trapani to the island of Pantelleria. The flights last about 30 minutes.

BY TRAIN

All major Sicilian cities such as Palermo, Catania, Messina, Syracuse, Agrigento, Taormina, and Trapani have good rail links. A single ticket can be bought up to 2 months before scheduled travel. Eurail passes are honored on trains around the island, but don't waste money on a first-class pass if you intend on using it just in Sicily—few trains have first-class carriages.

Trains are operated by **Trenitalia (or Ferrovie dello Stato (FS)),** the Italian State Railways (✆ 892021 from Italy; from other countries ✆ 06-68475475; www.trenitalia.com). Train fares are generally very affordable. Children ages 4 to 11 receive a discount of 50% off the adult fare, and children 3 and younger travel free with a parent. Second-class travel usually costs about two-thirds the price of an equivalent first-class trip.

InterCity trains (designated **IC** on train schedules) are modern, air-conditioned, limited-stop trains and you have to pay an often heavy supplement; a second-class IC ticket can provide a first-class experience. In Sicily, ICs run only between Messina and Palermo and Messina and Catania.

Slower Sicilian trains—called **Diretto, Espresso,** and **Interregionale**—stop at major towns or cities. A **Regionale** train (sometimes known as the **Locale**), stops in every hamlet and takes forever, but some experienced travelers insist that it's part of the charm.

For fares, visit www.trenitalia.it; it's also important to check if your ticket also requires paying a supplement for express or InterCity trains. Prices are also determined by the route—for example, from Palermo to Catania it will be cheaper cutting inland via Caltanissetta/Enna than from Messina. A trip to Syracuse from Palermo will cost a minimum of 14.30€ to a maximum of 27.05€. If you're under the age of 26 or over 60 and plan to use the train extensively you might want to consider purchasing a **Carta Verde** or a **Carta Argento.** The Carta Verde is available to youths between 12 and 26 years of age at the price of 40€. It offers a 10% discount on all national trains (including couchettes) and up to 25% off international travel. The Carta Argento, designed for senior travelers, costs 30€ (free for travelers over 75) and offers a 15% discount on all trains and up to 25% off international travel.

BY BUS

Buses are becoming the travel means of choice in Sicily, as numerous train stations on the island are closing due to downsizing and general lack of interest by the regional government. Bus fares are generally less than train tickets and are even cheaper when a round trip ticket is bought.

For individual city and town links refer to the specific sections on cities and towns in later chapters. **AST** (☎ **848-000323;** www.aziendasicilianatrasporti.it) has the largest network on the island. **SAIS** (☎ **091-616028** in Palermo, or 095-536168 in Catania; www.saisautolinee.it), offers a service from Palermo to Messina, Enna, Catania, and Syracuse. **Cuffaro** (☎ **091-6161510;** www.cuffaro.info) links Palermo in the north with Agrigento in the south. **Interbus** (☎ **094-2625301;** www.interbus.it) has service between the cities of Catania, Messina, Taormina, and Syracuse. **Salemi** (☎ **092-3981120;** www.autoservizisalemi.it) links Palermo to western Sicily (Trapani and Marsala). For all bus links, visit www.regione.sicilia.it/turismo/trasporti. In large cities, most buses stop at the main train station.

Sundays have a reduced service, and the bus can be packed with students traveling back to the big cities. Holidays often have a reduced service or don't operate at all.

Tickets for intercity services are most often purchased right on the bus. However, in some instances, for example, from Palermo to Trapani or vice versa, you have to book a ticket in advance at one of the local bus offices. **Note**: both tickets bought on-board and booked tickets are non-refundable.

Tickets for city buses are bought before boarding at ticket booths, *tabacchi* (tobacco shops), and newsagents, and must be validated once you get on, or else you'll be fined up to 60€ if stopped by a bus controller. If the validating machine is not working, notify the driver immediately. Most city buses charge from 1€ to 1.30€ for a ticket that is valid for only 60 to 90 minutes.

In Palermo and Catania you can purchase a 24-hour bus ticket that can save you money if you plan to use the bus network extensively. See relevant city chapters for more info.

BY CAR

For U.K. and European drivers, full driving licenses are valid for Sicily. U.S. and Canadian drivers are required to have an **International Driving Permit** (IDP) to drive a rented or private car in Italy. You can apply for an IDP at any **AAA or CAA** branch. You must be at least 18 and have two 2×2-inch (4cm x 5cm) photos and a photocopy of your U.S. driver's license with your AAA application form. Remember that an International Driver's License is valid only if physically accompanied by your original driver's license and only if signed on the back. To find the AAA office nearest you, call ☎ **800/222-4357,** or go to www.aaa.com. In Canada, you can get the location of the **Canadian Automobile Association** office closest to you by calling ☎ **800/267-8713** or going to www.caa.ca.

RENTALS Many of the loveliest parts of Sicily are only reachable by car. Be prepared however to experience some of the most aggressive and daredevil maneuvers in the western world. Sicilian drivers have road rules of their own, and everyone has the right of way.

To rent a car in Sicily, a driver must have a valid driver's license, a valid passport, and must be (in most cases) more than 25 years old. Insurance is compulsory, though any reputable rental firm will arrange it in advance before you're even given the keys. It is generally cheaper to make arrangements for car rentals before you leave home. Of course, you can also rent a car once you arrive in Sicily, although the rates will be higher. The price can vary greatly depending on the vehicle, the average rental on the island costs from 80€ to 120€ per day, cheaper if rented weekly or longer.

The main rental agencies in Sicily include **Avis** (© 800/331-1212; www.avis.com) and **Hertz** (© 800/654-3131; www.hertz.com). Other firms are **Auto Europe** (© 800/223-5555; www.autoeurope.com), **Europe by Car** (© 888/223-1516 or 212/581-3040; www.europebycar.com), **Kemwel Holiday Auto** (© 800/678-0678; www.kemwel.com), and **Dollar** (© 1800-800-3665; www.dollar.com).

Internet resources can make comparison shopping cheaper. Expedia (www.expedia.com) and Travelocity (www.travelocity.com) help you compare prices and make reservations.

FUEL *Benzina* (gasoline/petrol) is expensive in Sicily. In today's uncertain economy, prices can change from week to week, even day to day. Gas stations on the autostrade are open 24 hours, but stations on regular roads are rarely open on Sunday; also, many close from noon to 3pm for lunch, and most shut down after 7pm. Almost all stations have self-service. Make sure the pump registers zero before an attendant starts refilling your tank. A popular scam in Sicily is to fill your tank before resetting the meter, so you pay not only your bill but also the charges run up by the previous motorist.

DRIVING RULES Driving is on the right; passing is on the left. In cities and towns, the speed limit is 50 kmph (31 mph). For all cars and motor vehicles on main roads and local roads, the limit is 90 kmph (56 mph). For the autostrade, the limit is 130 kmph (81 mph). Use the left lane only for passing. If a driver zooms up behind you on the autostrada with his or her lights on (or honking away), that's your sign to get out of the way. Use of seat belts is compulsory and using a cell phone while driving is illegal. Don't be surprised to see children sitting in the front seat or in the laps of their parents when driving—child seats are considered by most here to be "unnecessary."

BREAKDOWNS & ASSISTANCE The **Automobile Club Italiano (ACI)** does not offer free roadside emergency help to stranded motorists in Sicily. Members have discounts and in some cases protection packages that include free assistance. If you call the ACI emergency number (© 803116) in the event of a breakdown, you must pay a minimum of 110€, plus another 45€ to have your car towed to the nearest garage, plus tax and 1€ per kilometer. So getting stranded in Sicily has a serious cost. Not only that, but 20% is added to the bill between 10pm and 6am and on Saturday and Sunday. ACI offices are at Via delle Alpi 6, in Palermo (© 091-300468; www.aci.it), and at Via Sabotino 1, in Catania (© 095-533380).

SICILIAN ROADS The autostrade are not as extensive on Sicily as they are on the Italian mainland. The most traveled route is the A19 between Palermo and Catania, a convenient link between the island's two major cities. The other oft-traveled route is the A20 going between Palermo and Messina. The A18 links Messina and Catania on the eastern coast, whereas the A29 goes from Palermo to Mazara del Vallo to the south, with a detour to Trapani.

Sicily has nowhere near the burdensome tolls of mainland Italy, but there are some: For example, taking the autostrada from Messina to Catania costs 4.50€, while from Cefalù to Palermo the cost is .80€. Unless you're traveling from city to city, you'll use the state roads, or *Strade statali,* single-lane, and toll-free routes. To reach remote villages, you'll sometimes find yourself going along a country lane and watching out for goats. These are the bona-fide scenic routes, with roads sometimes just steps away from the shore.

BY TAXI

Taxi rates vary from town to town, but in general are very pricey. In most cities, the meter begins at 3.50€, and then charges you 2.50€ for the first 154m (505ft.), plus another .85€ per kilometer thereafter. There are supplements of 2€ from 10pm to 7am, Sundays and on holidays. Depending on the size of the taxi, four or as many as five passengers are allowed. Taxis are found at all airport arrival terminals; always ask how much the tariff to your destination is—there are normally flat fees from the airport to the city. In some cities, taxis can be called. When you reserve by phone, the taxi meter goes on when the cabbie pulls out of his station. In Sicily, taxis rarely stop if hailed on the street. Although most taxi drivers are honest and hard-working, you will occasionally encounter an unscrupulous bad apple: If the front seat is inclined forward so as to block the vision of the meter, ask the driver to pull it up.

BY BICYCLE

Most Sicilian cities have bike-rental firms; otherwise, your hotel might help you make arrangements for one. Rentals in cities start at 10€ a day or 60€ a week. Even though helmets and lights are not legally required, it is prudent to have them, especially in a city like Palermo, where bike lanes are virtually non-existent. It is forbidden to bike along the autostrade. Bikes are transported free on Sicilian ferries, but you must pay to carry them on most trains. Fast trains generally do not allow bikes, although conductors on IC trains let you put a bike in the baggage train for an extra 5€. Most regional and local trains allow bike transport. Check www.trenitalia.it for more information about bicycle transport.

MONEY & COSTS

Currency

THE VALUE OF THE EURO VS. OTHER POPULAR CURRENCIES

€	US$	Can$	UK£	Aus$	NZ$
1	$1.36	C$1.38	£0.85	A$1.38	NZ$1.76

The currency used in Italy is the **euro,** whose official abbreviation is EUR. The symbol of the euro is a stylized *E:* €.

Frommer's lists exact prices in the local currency, euros. The currency conversions were correct at the time of going to press. However, rates fluctuate, so before departing consult a currency exchange website such as **www.xe.com** to check up-to-the-minute rates. The price of meals at a *trattoria* serving home-cooked meals is much more affordable than in New York or London, (expect to pay no more than 20€ to

WHAT THINGS COST IN PALERMO	€
Taxi from the airport to city center	40.00
Bus from airport to city center	5.80
Ride on city bus	1.30
Double at Villa Igiea (very expensive)	320.00
Double at Grand Hotel Piazza Borsa (expensive)	110.00
Double at Crystal Palace (moderate)	90.00
Double at Hotel Moderno (inexpensive)	60.00
Lunch for two, without wine, at Cin Cin (expensive)	60.00
Lunch for two, without wine, at Shanghai (inexpensive)	16.00
Dinner for two, without wine, Charme (expensive)	100.00
Dinner for two, without wine, at U Strascinu (moderate)	50.00
Dinner for two, without wine, Trattoria Primavera (inexpensive)	30.00
Slice of pizza	2.00
Glass of wine	4.00
Admission to Palazzo dei Normanni	8.50
Theater ticket	20.00

30€ for a full meal for two). Bus fares in Palermo are the most expensive in Italy although, at 1.30€, U.K. visitors will find them very reasonable in comparison to prices at home.

ATMs

The easiest and best way to get cash away from home is from an ATM (automated teller machine). ATMs are found in all Sicilian cities, towns, and villages that have a bank. Be sure you know your personal identification number (PIN) before you leave home and be sure to find out your daily withdrawal limit before you depart. Also keep in mind that many banks impose a fee every time a card is used at a different bank's ATM, and that fee can be higher for international transactions (up to $5 or more) than for domestic ones. On top of this, the bank from which you withdraw cash may charge its own fee. For international withdrawal fees, ask your bank.

You can also get cash advances on your credit card at an ATM. Keep in mind that credit card companies try to protect themselves from theft by limiting the funds someone can withdraw outside their home country, so call your credit card company before you leave home. And keep in mind that you'll pay interest from the moment of your withdrawal, even if you pay your monthly bills on time. If you feel unsure about using your credit card at an ATM for cash advances, you can ask for an *anticipo contanti* (cash advance) in person at exchange bureaus or at most banks.

Important note: Make sure that the PINs on your bank cards and credit cards will work in Sicily. You'll need a **four-digit code** (six digits won't work).

Credit & Debit Cards

Credit and debit cards are a safe way to carry money. They generally offer relatively good exchange rates. You can also withdraw cash advances from your credit cards at banks or ATMs, provided you know your PIN (see above).

Keep in mind that when you use your credit card abroad, most banks apply a 2% fee above the 1% fee charged by Visa, MasterCard, or American Express for currency conversion on credit charges. But credit cards still may be the smart way to go when you factor in things like exorbitant ATM fees and higher traveler's check exchange rates (and service fees).

For tips and telephone numbers to call if your wallet is stolen or lost, see "Lost & Found" in the "Fast Facts: Sicily" section of Chapter 14.

In Sicily, the most commonly accepted credit cards are MasterCard and Visa. Of secondary importance are American Express and Diners Club.

STAYING HEALTHY

In general, Sicily is viewed as a "low-risk" destination, although problems, of course, can and do occur anywhere. You don't need to get vaccines; most foodstuffs are safe; and tap water in most cities and towns is potable. When in doubt, drink bottled water. If you are traveling around Sicily over the summer, limit your exposure to the sun, especially during the first few days, and thereafter until 11 am and then from 4 pm. Use a sunscreen with a high protection factor and apply it liberally. Remember to apply it repeatedly to children. Not only will you prevent sunburn you'll also avoid heatstroke—two things that can land you immediately at the hospital.

If You Get Sick

In case of **emergency,** dial ✆ 113 for the police, or ✆ 112 for the *Carabinieri* (military police): They can call an ambulance or help you in many ways. If your situation is life-threatening, go to the *pronto soccorso* (emergency ward) at the local hospital.

Many doctors in Sicily understand English to some degree. If you get sick, your hotel concierge will call or recommend a doctor. Another option is to go to the *guardia medica* (doctor on duty) or the *guardia medica turistica* at vacation resorts. In the chapters that follow, we list hospitals and emergency numbers under "Fast Facts" in the sections on various cities.

Under the Italian national healthcare system, you're eligible only for free *emergency* care. If you're admitted to a hospital as an in-patient, you're required to pay (unless you're a resident of the EEA). You're also required to pay for follow-up care. If you do end up paying for healthcare, some health insurance plans will cover at least part of the hospital visits and procedures. Be prepared to pay the bills up front, however. Once you've filed all the necessary paperwork back home, you'll be refunded.

Before leaving home, find out what medical services your health insurance covers. To protect yourself, consider buying medical travel insurance (see "Medical Insurance," under "Insurance," in Chapter 14).

U.K. nationals will need a **European Health Insurance Card (EHIC)** (© 0845/606-2030; www.ehic.org.uk) to receive free or reduced-cost health benefits during a visit to a European Economic Area (EEA) country (European Union countries plus Iceland, Liechtenstein, and Norway) or Switzerland. For advice, ask at your local post office or see www.dh.gov.uk/travellers. European travelers will need additional insurance for repatriation after a medical emergency.

Very few U.S. health insurance plans pay for medical evacuation back (which can cost $10,000 and up). If you're ever hospitalized more than 150 miles from home, **MedjetAssist** (© 800/527-7478; www.medjetassistance.com) will pick you up and fly you to the hospital of your choice virtually anywhere in the world in a medically equipped and staffed aircraft 24 hours day, 7 days a week. Annual memberships are $225 individual, $350 family; you can also purchase short-term memberships.

If you suffer from a chronic illness, consult your doctor before your departure. Pack **prescription medications** in your carry-on luggage, and carry them in their original containers, with pharmacy labels—otherwise they won't make it through airport security. If your medication requires the use of hypodermic needles (such as diabetes) ask your doctor for a signed statement, or take your prescription, indicating the name of the medicine and what it is used to treat. Also, it's a good idea to keep a list of the active ingredients alongside the name of each prescription drug you take—though the brand name might differ in Italy, a doctor or pharmacist will immediately recognize the active ingredient.

CRIME & SAFETY

Contrary to popular culture spawned by urban legends, you will not come face-to-face with a Mafioso during your visit. There is, however, a better chance that you might encounter pickpockets, thieves, and purse-snatchers. Although most tourists have trouble-free visits to Sicily each year, the principal tourist areas have been experiencing an increase in crime. Palermo and Catania, in particular, have reported growing incidents of muggings and attacks. Criminals frequent tourist areas and major attractions such as museums, monuments, restaurants, hotels, beach resorts, trains, train stations, airports, subways, and ATMs. Travelers should exercise caution, carry limited cash and credit cards, and leave extra cash, credit cards, passports, and personal documents in a safe location. Crimes have occurred at all times of day and night. Sexual assaults are rare but do take necessary precautions—use a taxi at night to take you back to your hotel and don't accept rides from locals who seem "nice." If you feel threatened don't be afraid to shout and cause a scene to attract attention. It works as an excellent deterrent.

Drivers should be cautious about accepting help from anyone other than a uniformed police officer, *Carabiniere, Finanziere* (finance & revenue police, who often do random roadside checks on major roadways), or Municipal police.

The loss or theft abroad of a passport should be reported immediately to the local police and the nearest embassy or consulate (p. 326).

For more information on health, safety, and what to do in case of passport loss or theft see Chapter 14—"Fast Facts: Sicily."

SPECIALIZED TRAVEL RESOURCES

LGBT Travelers

Even though it still has a long way to go, homosexuality is moving by baby steps in Sicily toward social acceptance, but macho traditions and mentality are still deeply rooted in society. While public displays of affection between homosexual couples are rare, when it does happen it's often met with a lot of staring and the occasional comment. Except in the very primitive areas violence against homosexuals is unheard of. The first gay association in Italy was founded in Palermo in 1980 (ArciGay; www.arcigay.it) to protest the suicide of a homosexual couple tormented by ferocious public opinion. The current mayor of Gela, Rosario Crocetta, is openly gay in a city known for its high Mafia density.

Taormina, however, is a world apart and most certainly gay friendly. The Aeolian Islands, Pantelleria and Lampedusa, are also vacation spots of choice. To help plan your trip, the following resources may be helpful.

The **International Gay and Lesbian Travel Association (IGLTA; ℂ 954/630-1637;** www.iglta.org) is the trade association for the gay and lesbian travel industry, and offers an online directory of gay- and lesbian-friendly travel businesses and tour operators.

Many agencies offer tours and travel itineraries specifically for gay and lesbian travelers. San Francisco-based **Now, Voyager (ℂ 800/255-6951;** www.nowvoyager.com) offers worldwide trips and cruises. And **Olivia (ℂ 800/631-6277;** www.olivia.com), a members-only site, offers lesbian cruises and resort vacations. **Gay.com Travel (ℂ 415/834-6500;** www.gay.com/travel or www.outandabout.com) is an excellent online provider of information about gay-owned, gay-oriented, and gay-friendly lodging, dining, sightseeing, nightlife, and shopping establishments in every important destination worldwide. Another good resource is **Purple Roofs** (www.purpleroofs.com) which lists gay-friendly accommodation in Sicily. The Canadian website **GayTraveler** (www.gaytraveler.ca) offers ideas and advice for gay travel all over the world.

For more gay and lesbian travel resources, visit frommers.com.

Travelers with Disabilities

Sicily was almost always off-limits to travelers with disabilities. However, new laws require establishments to have bathrooms and other areas in order to facilitate wheelchair access, and more and more B&Bs are refurbishing and keeping the needs of the differently abled in mind. Most buses are now equipped to accommodate a wheelchair, as are the newer trains, but many historical sites are still inaccessible, such as Erice or Segesta. In this book, wheelchair accessible sites will be pointed out—often you need to book a tour guide at the site beforehand to show you around.

We recommend that those with disabilities consider visiting Sicily on an organized tour specifically geared to provide assistance, which is vitally needed.

Access-Able Travel Source (ℂ 303/232-2979; www.access-able.com) offers a comprehensive database on travel agents from around the world with experience in accessible travel; destination-specific access information; and links to such resources as service animals, equipment rentals, and access guides.

Many travel agencies offer customized tours and itineraries for travelers with disabilities. Among them are **Flying Wheels Travel** (② 507/451-5005; www.flying wheelstravel.com) and **Accessible Journeys** (② 800/846-4537 or 610/521-0339; www.disabilitytravel.com).

British travelers should contact **Tourism for All** (② 0845-1249971 in the U.K. only; www.tourismforall.org.uk) to access a wide range of travel information and resources for disabled and elderly people. **Accessible Accommodation** offers accessible accommodations listings via its website, www.accessibleaccommodation. com, or call ② **0208-1441278.**

For more on organizations that offer resources to travelers with disabilities, go to frommers.com.

Family Travel

Sicilians may love children, but they don't offer a lot of child-friendly places or amenities for them. For example, a kids' menu in a restaurant is a rarity. You can, however, request a half portion (*mezza porzione*), and most waiters will oblige—though be prepared to pay full price in some uncompromising eateries. Most Sicilian hoteliers will let children 12 and younger stay for free in a room with a parent.

At attractions, inquire if a kids' discount is available; Italians call it *sconto bambino*. European Community youths 17 and under get a big break: They're admitted free to all state-run museums.

Babysitting services are available through most hotel desks or by going to the local tourist office in the town where you're staying. Many hotels have children's game rooms and playgrounds.

Recommended family travel websites include **Family Travel Forum** (www. familytravelforum.com), a comprehensive site that offers customized trip planning; **Family Travel Network** (② 703/905-9858; www.familytravelnetwork.com), an award-winning site that offers travel features, deals, and tips; **Traveling Internationally with Your Kids** (www.travelwithyourkids.com), and **Family Travel Files** (www.thefamilytravelfiles.com), which offers a directory of off-the-beaten-path tours and tour operators for families.

In the U.K. check out websites such as **www.havingalovelytime.com, www. family-travel.co.uk,** and **www.travellingwithchildren.co.uk** for reviews of family-friendly locations.

Women Travelers

Travel to Sicily for women is safe, but do take necessary precautions. You will encounter at least once along your journey a flirtatious man who wants to be "helpful" to foreign ladies. Though most of the time they mean well, use your best judgment when dealing with complete strangers. Sexual assaults are rare, and harassment is almost always limited to a wolf's whistle.

Women travelers may also want to check out the award-winning website **Journeywoman** (www.journeywoman.com), a "real life" women's travel information network where you can sign up for a free e-mail newsletter and get advice on everything from etiquette, to dress, to safety.

Senior Travel

Many establishments and hotels offer discounts for seniors. In most cities, people over the age of 60 qualify for reduced admission to theaters, museums, and other attractions, as well as discounted fares on public transportation.

Members of **AARP**, 601 E St. NW, Washington, DC 20049 (© **888/687-2277;** www.aarp.org), get discounts on hotels, airfares, and car rentals. AARP offers members a wide range of benefits, including *AARP The Magazine* and a monthly newsletter. Anyone 50 and over can join. Many reliable agencies and organizations target the 50-plus market. **Elderhostel** (© **800/454-5768;** www.elderhostel.org) arranges worldwide study programs for those aged 55 and over.

Note: being a U.S. senior in Sicily doesn't have much clout at national and regional museums—there are no reduced prices offered as there is no bilateral agreement between the E.U. and the U.S. with regards to museum admissions.

In the U.K., the largest senior citizens holiday company, **Saga Holidays** (© **0800-096-0074;** www.sagaholidays.co.uk) offers holidays to Sicily as well as other locations worldwide. It is also a good resource for insurance and other related products for the over-50s.

Frommers.com offers more information and resources on travel for seniors.

RESPONSIBLE TOURISM

With regards to responsible and **eco-** or **sustainable tourism,** Sicily is undergoing a renaissance, as landowners and locals alike are re-discovering the riches of their territory. Farming methods have been the same for centuries, and more and more farms and *agriturismi* owners are opening up their property to visitors to show them how it's done with little or no impact on the environment. Sustainable tourism also applies to the sea and coastal areas, as Sicily was one of the first zones in Europe to designate areas specifically for the protection and preservation of marine life (Ustica, Filicudi, Riserva dello Zingaro, Lampedusa). Fishing and building in these areas is forbidden and tour facilities are threadbare so as not to interfere with the surroundings.

A synonymous type of tourism is dubbed **ethical tourism.** It differs slightly in theory from eco-tourism, having a propensity toward travel with socially conscious issues in mind. Social awareness on the island was raised in the 1960s by anthropologist Danilo Dolci, who was appalled at the living and working conditions of the people in postwar Sicily, and made it his life's mission to recruit volunteers from all over the world to rectify the situation. Nowadays ethical tourism is best represented by working on farms that were once property of the Mafia, attracting volunteers from all over Italy, and the sale of pasta and other products harvested from the land goes toward the upkeep of the farm. To plan a trip to Sicily with ecological and social issues in mind start from: **Responsible Travel** (www.responsibletravel.com), an excellent resource for understanding the ideology behind ecotourism and has suggestions for Sicily; **Sustainable Travel International** (www.sustainabletravel international.org) is chock-full of resources on sustainable travel for those who want to make a difference.

For general information on eco hotels throughout the world, including some in Sicily, visit www.ecohotelsoftheworld.com. For specific destinations in Sicily, **Eco-turismo Italia** (www.ecoturismo-italia.it) gives you an insight into ecotourism on

FROMMERS.COM: THE complete TRAVEL RESOURCE

It should go without saying, but we highly recommend **frommers.com**, voted Best Travel Site by *PC Magazine*. We think you'll find our expert advice and tips; independent reviews of hotels, restaurants, attractions, and preferred shopping and nightlife venues; vacation giveaways; and online booking tool indispensable before, during, and after your travels. We publish the complete contents of over 128 travel guides in our **Destinations** section, covering nearly 3,600 places worldwide, to help you plan your trip. Each weekday, we publish original articles reporting on **Deals and News** via our free **Frommers.com Newsletter** to help you save time and money and travel smarter. We're betting you'll find our new **Events** listings (http://events.frommers.com) an invaluable resource; it's an up-to-the-minute roster of what's happening in cities everywhere—including concerts, festivals, lectures, and more. We've also added weekly **podcasts, interactive maps,** and hundreds of new images across the site. Check out our **Travel Talk** area featuring **Message Boards** where you can join in conversations with thousands of fellow Frommer's travelers and post your trip report once you return.

the island. If you are interested in volunteering on the Mafia-free territories, visit **Libera** (www.libera.it) for detailed information about the project.

SPECIAL INTEREST & ESCORTED TRIPS

Special Interest Trips

Many tourists like the idea of engaging in their hobbies while visiting another country. In Sicily, both can be done.

If cycling is your fancy, **Backroads** (© 800/462-2848 or 510/527-1555; www.backroads.com), runs a 6-day biking and walking trip up Etna and through southeast Sicily that also includes food and wine tastings. It also offers a bike tour for families that's suitable for children as young as 9 years old. **Butterfield & Robinson** (© 866/551-9090 or 416/864-1354; www.butterfield.com) also operates a 6-day bike tour of Sicily, covering both the east and west of the island. In the U.K. and Ireland, the best bike tour operator is **Iron Donkey** with tours of west Sicily (© 028-90-813200; www.irondonkey.com). Before embarking on your two-wheel journey, you should also visit www.sicilybike.com.

Sicilytravel.net also offers cycling tours as well as Food & Wine tours of the island. For more information contact © 0922-402257; www.sicilytravel.net. **The International Kitchen** (© 800-945-8606; www.theinternationalkitchen.com) offers 7-day culinary tours of Sicily that depart several times a year for groups or upon request. The tours are based in and around southeast Sicily.

For bird-watching enthusiasts, **Birding Sicily** is run by two local twitchers. For more information see www.birdingsicily.com.

Escorted General Interest Tours

Escorted tours are escorted by a group leader, and the itinerary is scripted, leaving little or no room for improvisation, although they offer a great way to socialize with travelers who share the same interests.

Consider all of the following before making a booking: This type of tour requires payment up front, and often you'll have to fork out before the trip with no say in the matter on accommodations or meals, unless you specifically request a variation (read: pay more). Make sure you have a clear, itemized list of what's included and what's not, and what are optional services you can choose to pay for along the way. Before parting with your cash, it makes sense to ask what the **cancellation policy** entails. Tours can be cancelled, for example, if the participant quorum isn't met or due to severe weather conditions (such as volcanic ash). Also, inquire about what happens if *you* have to pull out of the tour, and what the policy is, and get it in writing. Another element of escorted tours is that they are often designed to visit high-tourist-density areas in minimum time, where you are literally herded from one place to another at speed, leaving you little if any time to experience the place you're visiting or fathom where you are.

Other factors to consider when choosing an escorted tour are the expected **size** of the group, and the **demographics.** There is better interaction and cohesion in a smaller group, while large groups are a little impersonal—and there's always someone who's bound to get lost and hold up the bus. Ask specifically to whom a certain type of tour is aimed—a couple on their honeymoon, for example, might not want to be on a busload of families with rowdy children.

The following are a list of reputable tour operators that have a wide range of tours to Sicily, for every budget.

Visit Italy Tours, based in Los Angeles (© 800/255-3537 or 310/649-9080; www.visititalytours.com) offers year-round treks to Sicily. You can join one of the pre-packaged tours around the island or build your own. **Perillo Tours** (© 800/431-1515; www.perillotours.com) has been in the business of tourism to Italy since 1945 and offers tours to suit every wallet.

Globus and Cosmos Tours are another top contender in the business with **Globus** (© 800/338-7092; www.globusandcosmos.com) catering more to the budget-conscious traveler. Globus offers a cuisine-themed tour around the island while **Cosmos** (© 800/276-1241) includes Sicily as part of a tour of southern Italy.

Another choice is **Insight Vacations** (© 800/582-8380; www.insightvacations.com), which offers an 8-day tour of Sicilian highlights. For a truly cultural immersion **Collette Vacations** (© 800/340-5158; www.collettevacations.com) in conjunction with the Smithsonian Institution, offers an 11-day tour of the island aimed at better understanding the art and history of Sicily, with lectures held by local experts in the field. For a truly vast range of choices, nothing tops **Academic Tours** (© 800/875-9171 or 718/417-8782; www.academictours.com).

From the U.K., **Titan Hi-Tours** (© 0800/988-5823; www.titanhitours.co.uk) offer two tours: The 7-day Taste of Eastern Sicily and a 10-day Sicily Jewel of the Mediterranean tour, including flights from the U.K. **Travelsphere** (© 0844/567-9960; www.titanhitours.co.uk) have an 8-day Classic Sicily Tour. Also check the national newspapers for special deals and discounted tours.

Packages for the Independent Traveler

Package tours can be as basic as air travel and hotel to an all-inclusive package that may include meals, guided tours, transfers to and from airports, and so on. While on the one hand everything is planned out and (hopefully) sorted for you from beginning to end, on the other it allows minimum flexibility, which is something to think about if you are an adventure-seeker and like to decide on your sleeping accommodations as you go along. If basing your choices on price range, search engines will often show you very different packages for the same price, but analyze carefully: If one package includes a flight with lots of connections to your destination but a very good three star hotel, another may offer a direct flight but an absolute rat hole as a hotel room. Read the fine print carefully about what's included in the package. If you need specific accommodations (an extra bed in the room or a bathroom that allows wheelchair accessibility) request it, and get it in writing. The same goes for dietary restrictions: Ask if there are gluten-free options or if meals that respect religious affiliation are offered. Check what their policy is regarding cancellation fees: A dirt-cheap package almost always offers no cancellation refund while more expensive ones might allow some compensation. See Chapter 14, "Fast Facts: Sicily", regarding trip cancellation insurance.

Sometimes you may need to look no further than the airline companies themselves to book a package tour. Try **Alitalia Vacations** (© 800/914-9000; www. alitaliavacations.com). All the major online travel companies such as **Last Minute** (www.lastminute.com), **Expedia** (www.expedia.com), **Travelocity** (www.travelocity. com), and **edreams** (www.edreams.com) have packages to suit all ranges.

Vacation Together (© 800/839-9851 or 877/444-4547; www.vacationtogether. com) allows you to search for a package and compare prices between different agencies and air lines. The **United States Tour Operators Association** (© 212/599-6599; www.ustoa.org) also allows you to multi-search for a specific destination. **Liberty Travel** (© 888/271-1584; www.libertytravel.com) heavily advertises their package deals in the Sunday papers. **Perillo Tours,** a company that has long specialized in travel to Italy, also offers a wide range of packages and services (© 1-800/431-1515; www.perillotours.com).

In the U.K., one of the leading Italian specialists with holiday packages to Sicily is **Citalia** (© 0844-415-1987; www.citalia.com). To compare package prices, also check out TravelSupermarket (www.travelsupermarket.com). It is always advisable to make sure your holiday company has an ABTA bond, so that in the unfortunate event your holiday company goes bust while you're abroad, you won't be left stranded.

Travel packages are also found in print media. You may also want to check out www.bestofsicily.com for advice on package tours to Sicily.

STAYING CONNECTED
Cellphones/Mobile Phones

Italians are probably the biggest users of cellphones in Europe, and Sicily is no exception. It is not unusual for someone to own two or three. Cellphones in Italy operate on a 900/1800 GSM frequency, so make sure your phone falls into this category if you intend on using your phone here. Except for remote areas reception is good. Check the international roaming rates (the rates charged by your company when you use your phone in another country) with your company before leaving, otherwise your phone bill might cost you more than your entire trip. Most U.K. mobile handsets work in Sicily. For cheaper calls: See buying a SIM card below.

For U.S./Canadian visitors there are, however, ways to save on cellphone use. Renting a phone is an option. You can arrange rental from the U.S. and pickup upon arrival in Sicily. U.S. or Canadian citizens can rent one before leaving home from **InTouch USA** (☎ **800/872-7626** or 703/222-7161; www.intouchglobal.com) or **RoadPost** (☎ **888/290-1616** or 905/272-5665; www.roadpost.com).

Buying an unlocked cellphone and SIM card when in Italy may sound like a good and simple alternative, but in order to buy an unlocked SIM you must have valid ID and a *Codice Fiscale* (Italian VAT number). To request one go to an *Agenzia delle Entrate* (you can find all the offices listed at www.agenziaentrate.gov.it) tax office with your passport. If you intend on staying for a while it would make sense to get one, otherwise for very brief stays it's not worth going through all the bureaucratic red tape. SIM cards are available at the major carrier shops—TIM, Vodafone, Wind, and 3. The Post Office also has SIM cards, called Posta Mobile.

Internet & E-mail
WITH YOUR OWN COMPUTER
More and more hotels, cafes, and retailers are signing on as **Wi-Fi** (wireless fidelity) hotspots. Many outdoor places in large cities are also hotspots; your computer or smartphone will pick up the signal immediately. For **broadband or ADSL** access, most hotels offer such connections in rooms. Make sure to have a connection kit, phone adapters, a spare phone cord, and a spare Ethernet network cable. A smart alternative is to buy an unlocked SIM (on how to obtain one, see section on cellphones above) and an Internet Key that goes into the USB port. All the major mobile phone companies offer diverse plans based on pricing and usage. Note that international roaming charges will apply.

ONLINE traveler's TOOLBOX

Veteran travelers usually carry some essential items to make their trips easier. The following is a selection of handy online tools to bookmark and use.

- **Airplane Food** (www.airline meals.net)
- **Airplane Seating** (www.seatguru. com and www.airlinequality.com)
- **Foreign Languages for Travelers** (www.travlang.com)
- **Maps** (www.viamichelin.com)
- **Subway Navigator** (www.subway navigator.com)

- **Time and Date** (www.timeand date.com)
- **Travel Warnings** (http://travel. state.gov, www.fco.gov.uk/travel, www.voyage.gc.ca, or www.dfat. gov.au/consular/advice)
- **Universal Currency Converter** (www.xe.com/ucc)
- **Visa ATM Locator** (www.visa. com), **MasterCard ATM Locator** (www.mastercard.com)
- **Weather** (www.intellicast.com and www.weather.com)

WITHOUT YOUR OWN COMPUTER

To find the cybercafe nearest you visit www.cybercaptive.com and www.cyber cafe.com. Cybercafes are found in large Sicilian cities, especially Catania and Palermo. Aside from formal cybercafes, most **youth hostels** and **public libraries** have Internet access. Avoid **hotel business centers** unless you're willing to pay exorbitant rates.

Telephones

To call Sicily from the United States, dial the **international prefix, ℂ 011;** then Italy's **country code, 39;** and then the area code (for example, **091** for Palermo or **095** for Catania), which is now built into every number. Then dial the actual **phone number.** To call the United States and Canada from Sicily, dial ℂ **001,** then the area code, then the number. To place a **local call,** the number must always be preceded by the area code.

Public phones are becoming a thing of the past in Italy, where everyone has a cellphone, making them nearly obsolete. For those rare few that are still found, they accept coins, prepaid phone cards (*scheda* or *carta telefonica*), or both. You can buy a *carta telefonica* at any *tabacchi* (tobacco shop; most display a sign with a white T on a brown background) in increments of 5.00€ and 10.00€. To make a call, pick up the receiver and insert .50€ or your card (break off the corner first). Dial the number, at the tone, and after the call wait a few seconds for the card to eject.

To call from one area code to another, dial the area code, then dial the number. **To dial direct internationally,** dial ℂ **00** and then the country code, the area code, and the number. **Country codes** are as follows: The United States and Canada, **1;** the United Kingdom, **44;** Ireland, **353;** Australia, **61;** New Zealand, **64.** Italy offers various international prepaid phone cards (*carta telefonica internazionale*) which offer dirt-cheap rates. They cost either 5€ or 10€. A toll-free access phone number (some have instructions in English) is printed on the card; you must first scratch the space where the personal identification number (PIN) is printed in order to make the call. To make a phone call, dial the access number and then enter the PIN. An automated voice will ask you to enter the phone number you are calling and will tell you how much time you have left on your card.

For **national telephone information** in Italy, dial ℂ **1254;** for **international information** call ℂ **892412.** Both services cost 3€ per minute.

TIPS ON ACCOMMODATIONS

Surfing for Hotels

There's no shortage of sites from which to choose and book a hotel— **Travelocity, Expedia, Orbitz, Priceline,** and **Hotwire Hotels.com, Quikbook** (www. quikbook.com), and **Travelaxe** (www.travelaxe.net). To do a Sicily-specific hotel search, you can try Best of Sicily (www.bestofsicily.com). Once you've booked, it's a good idea to **get a confirmation number** and **make a printout** of your receipt.

IT'S A lovely POOL...BUT CAN YOU USE IT?

When booking a hotel, especially in summer, don't automatically assume that just because it has a pool you'll be able to lounge around poolside all day long—many hotels and *agriturismi* are popular venues for weddings, which means holding a poolside reception in the warmer months is often the norm, therefore inconveniencing hotel clients who choose the hotel purposely for the pool facilities. If in doubt, call or e-mail first, and then make your final decision.

Saving on Your Hotel Room

The **rack rate** is the maximum rate that a hotel charges for a room. Hardly anybody pays this price, however, except in high season or on holidays. To lower the cost of your room:

- **Ask about special rates or other discounts.** You may qualify for corporate, student, military, senior, frequent flier, trade union, or other discounts.
- **Dial direct.** When booking a room in a chain hotel, you'll often negotiate a better deal by calling the individual hotel rather than the chain's main number.
- **Book online.** Many hotels offer Internet-only discounts, or supply rooms to Priceline, Hotwire, or Expedia at rates much lower than the ones you can get through the hotel itself.
- **Remember the law of supply and demand.** You can save big on hotel rooms by traveling in a destination's off season or shoulder seasons, when rates typically drop, even at luxury properties.
- **Look into group or long-stay discounts.** If you come as part of a large group, you should be able to negotiate a bargain rate. Likewise, if you're planning a long stay (at least 5 days), you might qualify for a discount. As a general rule, expect 1 night free after a 7-night stay.
- **Sidestep excess surcharges and hidden costs.** Many hotels have adopted the unpleasant practice of gouging their guests with ambivalent surcharges. When you book a room, ask what is included in the room rate, and what is extra. Avoid dialing direct from hotel phones, which can have exorbitant rates. And don't be tempted by the room's minibar offerings: Most hotels charge through the nose for water, soda, and snacks. Finally, ask about local taxes and service charges, which can increase the cost of a room by 15% or more.

SUGGESTED SICILY ITINERARIES

4

S icily offers such a wealth of sights and places to see that narrowing down your choices can be difficult. In order to optimize time, your best bet is to fly into one of the airports on the west coast (Palermo or Trapani) and leave from the one on the east coast (Catania) or vice versa; this allows you to see more without having to rush back to the airport at which you arrived.

Even when you've finally settled on an itinerary, you'll still have to travel a few hours a day getting from one place to another. The following itineraries aim to help you maximize your time in Sicily. Ideally designed for car travel, with no backtracking from one end of the island to the other, they are also suitable for bus or train, should you not have or not want a car.

THE REGIONS IN BRIEF

PALERMO The capital of Sicily is also the island's largest city. It's crowded, loud, and very unkempt in most areas, and driving in the city can take 10 years off your life. But outstanding artistic and architectural gems, such as the **Norman Palace,** the **Palatine Chapel,** and the **Quattro Canti,** convey the elegance and grandeur that once reigned here and show how Sicily was a crossroads for many different cultures. The three historical markets—**Capo, Vucciria,** and **Ballarò**—give you an inside peek at everyday life in the city. Not too distant from the center of Sicily you can have sweeping views of the city from **Monte Pellegrino,** or head to the beach in **Mondello.** A short distance away lies **Monreale,** with its exquisite cathedral adorned with some of the best mosaics in the western world.

THE WEST The Arabs called the area Val di Mazara, and it is emphatically wine, salt, and olive country. The world famous Alcamo wine is produced in and around the town of **Alcamo,** and the equally famous sweet **Marsala** wine is made in and around the city of the same name. The prized olives grown in the area are used to make some of the best

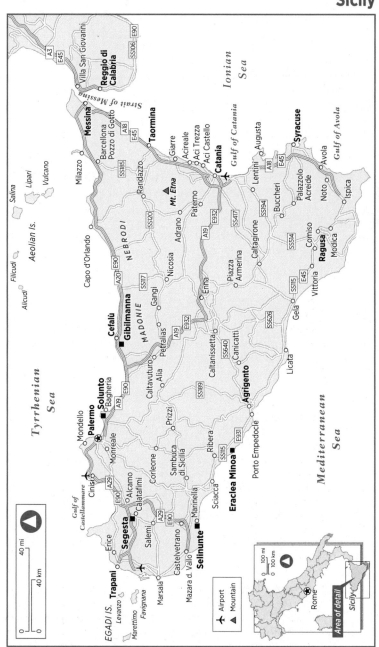

olive oils in the world, and sea salt is still harvested as it was in Carthaginian times using centuries-old windmills. The waters along the coast are crystalline and have either rocky (**Riserva Naturale dello Zingaro**) or sandy (**San Vito Lo Capo**) shores, and the town of **Mazara del Vallo** is one of the fishing capitals of Italy. And, yes, the region does have its fair share of history and monuments as well: The Doric temple and Greek Theater of **Segesta,** the ruins of **Selinunte,** and the Carthaginian stronghold of **Motya,** to name just a few.

CENTRAL SICILY   This is about as close as you'll ever get to Sicily as it once was, when back in the times of *The Leopard* in the mid-1800s (pre-Unification in 1860) the economy of the island was based on agriculture. The rolling hills with wheat fields, the endless fruit orchards, and citrus groves are still here, along with the centuries-old stone farmhouses and castles on top of isolated hills. The ones in **Mussomeli** and **Caccamo** are exceptional, while the one in **Enna,** the highest provincial capital in Italy, commands views over the entire island. **Sutera,** at the base of a lone hill, is picturesque. The **Madonie Mountains** are the highest on the island and feel more Alpine than Mediterranean.

THE SOUTHERN COAST   The southern coast, known for fishing and agriculture, is an area that has some of the most stunning landscapes on the island. As you wind your way down the coastal road you'll encounter vineyards, citrus orchards, wheat fields, and the odd sheepherder or two who sees nothing wrong with leading his flocks along state roads. As can be expected, the beaches are sandy and go on forever, with the one extraordinary exception of the **Scala dei Turchi,** a white, rippled limestone and clay cliff carved by the elements. History surely left its mark here, exemplified by the **Valley of the Temples** in **Agrigento** and in other Greek colonies such as **Eraclea Minoa** and **Gela,** though, sadly, the latter is in poor condition. Punctuating the hilltops and coastlines are castles, such as the ones in **Caltabellotta** and **Falconara,** near Butera.

THE NORTHEAST   This verdant area with lush forests carpeting the **Nebrodi** mountains and its hidden villages gives you the feeling that time has stopped, but for all the sleepiness there is one town that's always hopping: The incomparable **Taormina,** once the playground of the jet set. It's also the gateway to the island (**Messina**) and was the place where the first Greeks colonized Sicily (**Naxos**).

MOUNT ETNA   Overshadowing the eastern areas and visible from as far away as Erice and Calabria on the mainland, Europe's highest (over 3,000m/9,843 ft.) and most active volcano has determined the history, architecture, and agriculture of its environs for centuries, if not millennia: The cooled lava has been used to rebuild many of the cities after earthquakes, and the lava-rich soil produces the blood-red oranges that are unique to this part of the island. Thick vegetation surrounds the foothills, creating a microclimate of flora not seen anywhere else in Sicily. Treks up to the craters are possible, depending on weather and volcanic activity; dress warmly, even in summer.

CATANIA   The second-largest city in Sicily is more industrialized than Palermo; some say that its proximity to the mainland is the reason. There's no denying that Catania is loud and brash. Old Catania still lives on in places such as the daily **fish market.** Its architecture is certainly homogeneous: Literally forced to rebuild from the ground up after a devastating earthquake in 1693, it developed its own twist on

KNOW before YOU GO

Before visiting monuments and sites, it's always a good idea to call ahead or check their websites to confirm when they are open. Schedules can change from one day to the next, and you'll spare yourself needless expense and disappointment.

the baroque, the Late Sicilian Baroque, which defines not only Catania but all of southeastern Sicily. The **Roman Amphitheater** and **Odeon** are vestiges of Roman domination, but it's the harmonious style of the buildings post-earthquake that define the city. Worth visiting also are **Sant'Alfio**, to see the oldest tree in continental Europe, and **Bronte**, to taste the delectable pistachios.

THE SOUTHEAST This area is different from the rest of the island, and what has come to be known as "Ragusashire" is a territory of plateaus where the sheep and cows graze on its green pastures, even in summer, so it's no wonder it has become the dairy capital of Sicily. Delicacies like the sharp *caciocavallo* or smoked *ragusano* have earned government DOP status (Denomination of Protected Origin) to safeguard the quality and the heritage of the products. Chocolate in **Modica** is still made artisanally; a typical variety is chocolate with chili pepper. Wines and other delights are typical of the area; the city of **Avola** is known for its wine and almonds. In this area the mighty **Syracuse,** the rival of the Greek capital, Athens, developed and prospered, and the ruins are a testament to its former greatness; the Greek Theater was considered the most prominent cultural venue in Greater Greece. The southeast is also the capital of the Sicilian Baroque style, and the **Val di Noto** has been granted Unesco World Heritage status for its unique post-seismic architecture.

THE ISLANDS Even an island can have its own islands. Mostly of volcanic origin, they are the hotspots to visit during the summer, owing to their sparkling blue or green seas and uncontaminated beaches. They are a nature-lover's paradise, with protected marine reserves (**Ustica**) and designated beaches for the sea turtles to lay their eggs (**Lampedusa**), luring visitors like the call of a siren. The earliest traces of Sicilian history are found on the **Aeolian** and **Egadi** islands, while **Pantelleria,** with a feel more African than Italian, offers culinary delights such as capers and the sweet Passito wine.

SICILY IN 1 WEEK

Designed to let you see the highlights of the island on a very tight schedule, this itinerary touches upon the classical vestiges of Sicily, yet allows for some outdoor fun and relaxation: The splendid temples and ruins that outnumber those in Greece itself, amphitheaters and a plush villa that are a testament to Roman opulence, and three breathtaking heights from which to admire the island—Erice, Taormina, and Mount Etna are all included. The tour winds up in the capital city of Palermo, where medieval jewels stand side-by-side with baroque treasures.

Day 1: Arrival in Catania

Flights to Fontanarossa Airport or trains from Messina will bring you to Sicily's second-largest city. Once you've checked into your hotel or B&B, spend the rest of the day on a **walking tour** (p. 269), viewing the vestiges of the centuries side-by-side (Roman theaters, baroque gems, hideous new buildings), all against the backdrop of the menacing Etna. If you get there early enough, make your way to the **fish market,** close to **Piazza Duomo,** to feel the pulse of the city. (Be sure to wear slip-resistant shoes that you won't mind being soiled by the putrid waters on the ground.) The city can be dizzying, stifling, and clamorous, yet Via Etnea is one of the most elegant boulevards in Italy. No visit to Catania would be complete without a *granita* (a flavored ice with the consistency close to that of ice cream) and a *brioche* (bread similar to a hamburger bun) in one of its many mouth-watering flavors: lemon, coffee, or blackberry. Better yet, do it the way a real Catanese would: Have your *brioche* for breakfast. Wind up your day with a visit to the magnificent **Castello Ursino.**

Day 2: Mount Etna & Taormina

Once you are better acquainted with Catania, it's time to move on to its main attraction, the highest volcano in Europe, at 3,292m (10,801 ft.). There are a few access points from which to reach the top craters; the best organized one is from the **Rifugio Sapienza,** on the southern slope. Be forewarned however that things here can change in a nanosecond—if meteorological conditions are prohibitive or the volcano starts to show signs of activity, tours are immediately suspended. From the top, the scenery is like no other. Once your visit to Etna is over, it's time to head back to the hotel, change, and seek some R&R in the chicest town in Sicily, **Taormina.** It has attracted visitors for centuries, renowned for its sheer beauty and fame as a hideaway for trysting lovers. Stroll along the main street, **Corso Umberto I,** and, if time allows, visit the **Greco-Roman Theater** that has Etna as its backdrop. Have an *aperitivo* at the Wünderbar in Piazza IX Aprile, which faces the breathtaking **Bay of Naxos.** It might cost you an arm and a leg, but consider it a necessary expense.

Day 3: Syracuse & Piazza Armerina

It's time to leave Catania and head south to visit two of the most important archaeological sites in the world, the **Neapolis Park of Syracuse** and the **Villa Romana del Casale at Piazza Armerina.** Start your day by visiting the archaeological area of Syracuse and explore the still-working **Greek Theater,** the **Ear of Dionysius** (said to have been cunningly used by the tyrant himself to eavesdrop on rebels), and the **Roman Amphitheater,** where the shows were man vs. man or man vs. beast (the latter often won). After your visit, proceed to the delightful **Ortygia** Island and have lunch at one of the many eateries that surround the splendid **Piazza Duomo,** but make sure you pop in to have a look inside the cathedral beforehand—a Greek temple is part of the cathedral. After lunch, travel northwest to **Piazza Armerina** to view the **Villa Romana del Casale.** You'll get a taste of how Romans loved to live large—this

Suggested Itineraries

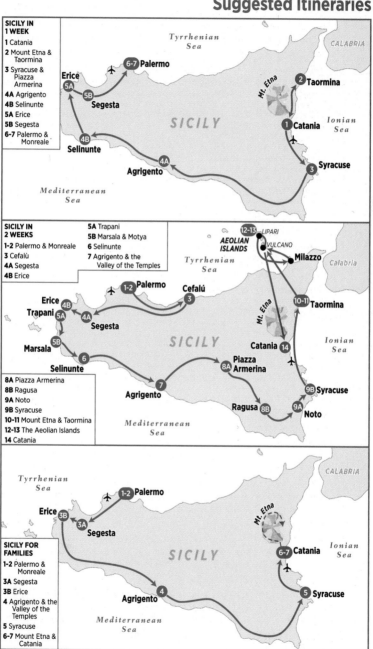

**SICILY IN
1 WEEK**
1 Catania
2 Mount Etna &
Taormina
3 Syracuse &
Piazza
Armerina
4A Agrigento
4B Selinunte
5A Erice
5B Segesta
6-7 Palermo &
Monreale

**SICILY IN
2 WEEKS**
1-2 Palermo & Monreale
3 Cefalù
4A Segesta
4B Erice
5A Trapani
5B Marsala & Motya
6 Selinunte
7 Agrigento & the
Valley of the Temples

8A Piazza Armerina
8B Ragusa
9A Noto
9B Syracuse
10-11 Mount Etna & Taormina
12-13 The Aeolian Islands
14 Catania

**SICILY FOR
FAMILIES**
1-2 Palermo &
Monreale
3A Segesta
3B Erice
4 Agrigento & the
Valley of the
Temples
5 Syracuse
6-7 Mount Etna &
Catania

hunting lodge houses magnificent floor mosaics that illustrate scenes from everyday life with astounding precision (one girl athlete is depicted with stitches on her leg). If you're lucky, you'll also see the experts in art restoration at work; they volunteer their time to preserve the precious tiled artwork.

Day 4: Agrigento & Selinunte

Prepare to spend the day exploring two of the most impressive and powerful cities of Magna Graecia. When Pindar praised **Agrigento** as "the most beautiful of the mortal cities," he was not overstating his case. The splendid **Valley of the Temples,** a Unesco World Heritage site, preserves the vestiges of what was once a main player in the Mediterranean and surpasses Greece's Athens itself for the quantity and quality of ruins. The near-intact **Temple of Concord** is the best-preserved temple in the world (check it out at night, when it's floodlit) and one of the symbols of Sicily.

After taking in the temples in Agrigento, travel west to witness more of the glories of Greater Greece. The almighty **Selinunte** is a vast archaeological park (270 hectares/667 acres) that's home to the most impressive ruins in the western world and still the subject of much study; some of the temples have been painstakingly reconstructed while many of the precious embellishments like the **Metopes** are safeguarded at the Archaeological Museum of Palermo. As the afternoon sun sets, head down to the beach below the site promontory and swim out to see the temples in front of you.

Day 5: Erice & Segesta

Day 5 of the journey brings you to the westernmost reaches of Sicily. As you make your way up to the hilltop village of **Erice,** take in the stunning views over land and sea as you head to this peaceful oasis far removed from city chaos. Be sure to re-energize at Maria Grammatico's pastry shop, and take some of her divine sweets for the road. Head back down by cable car and make your way to **Segesta** to view the miraculously well-preserved **Doric temple** and the still-working **Greek theater,** with a hillside backdrop stretching out to sea.

Days 6 & 7: Palermo & Monreale

The capital of Sicily has been a crossroads for cultures and civilizations for 8 millennia. Start at the **Norman Palace** (open only Fri–Mon) bright and early to avoid the crowds; make sure to visit the **Palatine Chapel** to see the formidable mix of eastern and western art, especially the **mosaics.** Walk along Villa Bonanno to the **Cathedral** in Corso Vittorio Emanuele, just to admire the exterior; continue along Vittorio Emanuele to the imposing **Four Corners.** Admire the Tuscan fountain in **Piazza Pretoria** and, just behind it, take in two splendid Arabo-Norman churches, **La Martorana** and **San Cataldo.** Make your way down Corso Vittorio Emanuele again; on the first left after Via Roma you'll stumble upon the raucous **Vucciria market.** Lunch like a Palermitan would: Standing up, eating food from any of the impromptu fry-up places in the neighborhood (don't ask, just eat). Spend the afternoon taking in the area of the new city, and unwind in the chic pedestrian area of Via Principe di Belmonte. See p. 109 for a suggested **walking tour** of the city.

The following day, spend the morning gaping at the impressive mosaics in **the Duomo of Monreale,** which lies 15km (12 miles) south of Palermo. Make your way next door to visit the annexed **Cloisters,** where no two-column capitals are alike. Spend your last evening in Sicily blending in with the locals: Enjoy a meal or a cocktail in Via Principe di Belmonte, the elegant pedestrian area of town. For the truly adventurous, take a walking tour of old Palermo: The floodlit monuments are spectacular.

SICILY IN 2 WEEKS

This 2-week tour includes all the classical sites that would be visited in a 1-week tour, but this itinerary takes a more in-depth look at the history of the island, exploring the unique baroque heritage in southeast Sicily, the Carthaginian strongholds of Marsala and Mozia in the west, and the Aeolian islands, where the oldest traces of Sicilian civilization are found. It's not all museum and archaeological sites though: The tour includes exploration of the endless, crystalline coastlines of Sicily, permitting a day or two of total relaxation.

Days 1 & 2: Palermo & Monreale

Follow Days 6 and 7, in the "Sicily in 1 Week" itinerary, above.

Day 3: A Side Trip to Cefalù

This splendid Norman gem, about an hour east of Palermo, is a sleepy fishing village for most of the year, but in the summer it comes alive with tourists and hubbub. Arrive in the morning to view the imposing 12th-century **cathedral** that dominates the town and is adorned on the inside with impressive mosaics, the first commissioned by the Normans in western Sicily. Visit the recently reopened **cloisters** next to the cathedral, and then make your way down to the sea for lunch. Spend the afternoon wandering the winding cobblestone streets and cool off at the **Medieval Wash Basin.** End your visit with one of the delectable sweets concocted by **Pasticceria Serio,** in Via Giglio.

Day 4: Segesta to Erice

See Day 5, in the "Sicily in 1 Week" itinerary, above, but begin in Segesta and finish in Erice.

Day 5: Trapani to Marsala & Motya

After making your way down from Erice, stop and have a brief look around the center and port area of **Trapani,** with its distinct African feel. As you head down this Carthaginian territory you'll bypass the centuries-old windmills used for harvesting salt. This is unequivocally wine country, and you'll want to visit one of the two **Marsala** producers, Florio or Pellegrino. After your visit to the wineries (if you're not too inebriated), head to the jetty to cross the lagoon to the island of **Motya,** to see Carthaginian life up close and personal.

Day 6: Selinunte

The largest archaeological park in Europe offers a glimpse of the mighty Greek commercial power before it was turned into heaps of rubble. The temples are simply called by letters of the alphabet as they are still being studied and many have been painstakingly restored. **Temple E** is in particularly good condition and is one of the best examples of Sicilian Doric. Spend the rest of the day on the beach at **Marinella,** with the temples as your backdrop.

Day 7: Agrigento & the Valley of the Temples

Head east along the scenic coastal route to make your way to the spectacular **Valley of the Temples** to view the best-preserved group of temples in the world. **The Temple of Concord,** in near-perfect condition, is the most amazing. Try to see them at night or when they are floodlit; the visual is truly stunning. After visiting the temples, head to the nearby **Archeological Museum** to witness some of the most impressive artifacts of the area, especially the *telamoni*—the giants who held up the temple of Zeus. Although the city itself offers some fine churches, don't waste too much time visiting there. Overnight in the area.

Day 8: Piazza Armerina & Ragusa

As you trek farther east, make your way inland to visit **Piazza Armerina** and the marvelous dwelling of **Villa Romana del Casale.** Discovered by pure chance, it had been underground for centuries, perhaps covered by a mudslide. Besides the trappings of Roman luxury, the main reason to come here is the 3,500 sq m (11,500 sq ft.) of splendid **mosaics** that depict scenes of everyday life. When you're finished, make your way to something very different: The elegant **Ragusa,** the southernmost provincial capital in Italy. This baroque gem overlooking the **Hyblean Mountains** is actually two cities, **Ragusa Superiore** and the more ancient **Ragusa Ibla.** After exploring the town, spend the night at one of the fine hotels on the beach, at **Marina di Ragusa.**

Day 9: Noto & Syracuse

The southeast is famed for its unique baroque architecture, and **Noto** offers many examples. It has been declared a Unesco World Heritage site for its distinctive urban planning. After wandering around what seems like a throwback to the baronial era of the 18th century, make your way farther east to even more remote times, in **Syracuse.** It was one of the most powerful colonies of Magna Graecia, and its grand **Greek Theater** and endless ruins are a testament to its former glory. Have dinner at the delightful **Ortygia Island,** the old town center, in one of the many eateries in and around the **Piazza Duomo,** but have a look inside the cathedral first. If time allows, visit **Palazzo Bellomo,** home to Caravaggio's *The Burial of St. Lucy.*

Days 10 &11: Mount Etna & Taormina

Make your way north to visit the highest active volcano in Europe for a spectacular blend of fire, ice, and moonlike scenarios. If the weather is good and the volcano inactive, start from the base at **Rifugio Sapienza** and take the cable car and jeep up to the main crater to witness a thrilling combination of fire, ice, mountains, and sea. (Bring warm clothes for the trip.) Make your way down and continue your trip to **Taormina,** the island's chicest town. Get there in time for an *aperitivo* at the Wünderbar in Piazza IX Aprile and feel as if you're living *La Dolce Vita.* Spend the next morning visiting the majestic **Greco-Roman Theater** and shopping in the lovely little boutiques—yes, they're pricey, but it's location, location, location. Spend the afternoon down at the beach at **Mazzarò** or exploring the first Greek colony in Sicily, at **Naxos.**

Days 12 & 13: The Aeolian Islands

The earliest traces of Sicilian civilization lie here on these unspoiled, verdant islands. Take an early ferry or hydrofoil from **Milazzo** and make your first stopover at **Vulcano,** if you're not put off by the stench of sulphur coming from the nearby mud baths. Hop on the next boat to **Lipari** and make your base there. Hire a scooter and head to **Cava di Pomice,** where the waters are emerald green due to the pumice washed up on the shore. Spend the next day island hopping: Either head east to the tiny yet exclusive **Panarea** and then to romantic **Stromboli,** or head west to the idyllic **Salina,** the natural reserve of **Filicudi,** or the remote **Alicudi,** where cars are prohibited.

Day 14: Catania

Your last day in Sicily should allow you enough time to visit Sicily's second-largest city. Start in the morning with a *granita* and *brioche* and head to the **fish market** to see what makes the locals tick. Visit the nearby **cathedral** and pay your respects to Vincenzo Bellini, one of Catania's most famous sons, who is buried here. Next, make your way west along Via Vittorio Emanuele II (walk, don't even think of using a car), to visit the **Roman Amphitheater and Odeon;** try not to miss the other **Roman Theater** at Piazza Stesicoro. Have a scrumptious *cannolo* and bid goodbye to Sicily. Follow my suggested tour on page 269 in Chapter 11.

SICILY FOR FAMILIES

When touring with young children, you're bound to hear the phrase "Are we there yet?" more than once. Keeping the kids happy and interested and getting them involved is no easy feat, but this tour makes for enjoyment and priceless memories for the entire family, as well as giving the kids something to brag about once they're home.

Days 1 & 2: Palermo & Monreale

Start the day at the **Norman Palace** to see how kings lived, and, if it's open, visit the **Segrete** (dungeons), where the enemies of the kings were locked up; head even farther below, to the Punic Foundations, dating back to 8 B.C. When you come back up, follow the sweeping staircases that lead you to the **Palatine Chapel** and its scintillating **mosaics.** Call ahead to book a visit to the **Astronomical Observatory** to see the site where the first asteroid was spotted. (Note: There are many steps to climb to reach the top.) After all the climbing, head for the **Parco D'Orleans,** where the bird zoo houses species from all over the world, and take a breather. After lunch knock on the door of Franco

Bertolino, in Salita Ramirez behind the cathedral. His studio is devoted to a dying craft, painting **Sicilian carts,** a tradition that's been in his family for generations. For more folklore, but this time involving puppets, go to the workshop of **Vincenzo Argento,** at 445 Corso Vittorio Emanuele; his handcrafted puppets of medieval knights come in all shapes and sizes. He even puts on a daily **puppet show.** Spend the next day at the magnificent cathedral at **Monreale,** and watch the kids gape in amazement at the scintillating **mosaics**— make sure to point out the one depicting the story of Noah. They'll be so fascinated they'll probably want to see how mosaics are made; on Via Arcivescovado there's a small workshop where you can buy a kit for the little ones to keep them busy.

Day 3: Segesta & Erice

On Day 3, set out for Segesta, where the kids will think they're on a movie set when they see the Doric Temple; they'll even be able to act out their own plays at the Greek Theater. When they've got the thespian mood out of their systems it's time for the medieval magic of Erice—climbing the cathedral bell tower will make kids feel as though they're one of the king's soldiers, and romping around the Castle of Venus will make them feel as if they're part of the royal court. Just don't tell them what actually went on here during Roman times.

Day 4: Agrigento & the Valley of the Temples

After spending time on the west coast, head south along the coastal route, where the kids might be lucky enough to see sheep grazing along the hills. Visit the **Valley of the Temples,** in **Agrigento,** where the kids will marvel at where the gods were worshipped. The *telamoni* (the giants) will get their attention; they are both within the park and at the **Archaeological Museum.** Head down to the beach area at **San Leone** for lunch, and spend the rest of the day relaxing on the beach.

Day 5: Syracuse

Hoping that the kids are still interested, head east to **Syracuse,** the mighty rival of Athens. After visiting the **Greek Theater,** they'll really look forward to visiting the **Ear of Dionysius,** where they can scream and hear their echoes to their hearts' content (and so will other children—be prepared). Have lunch at **Ortygia** and then take a stroll to the **Maniace Castle,** at the tip of the island.

Days 6 & 7: Mount Etna & Catania

This is probably what they've been waiting for with baited breath—finally coming face-to-face with the volcano—although warn the kids that if the weather conditions aren't good or the volcano is showing signs of activity, the trip will be cancelled. Start from the base at **Rifugio Sapienza** and ride the cable car, and then board the jeep that will take you to top. There's cooled lava everywhere; the kids can scoop some up to take home as souvenirs. Should you stay grounded because of inclement weather, there's always the **Toy Museum,** on Via Vittorio Emanuele, at Palazzo Bruca. Toys and children's pastimes from the 18th century onward are on display, and there's also a workshop that organizes games and activities for kids. In summertime, children and adults alike cool off at **Etnaland,** the island's most popular water theme park.

PALERMO

I t has been as fabled as it has been feared, as loved as it has been loathed, it has been described as heaven and hell on earth, and it has served as the headquarters for kings and kingpins alike. One thing is certain about Palermo: It always leaves a lasting impression on those who visit.

Although often overlooked on the grand tour of Italy, this city is a veritable open-air museum, boasting the largest historical center in Europe (240 hectares/593 acres) that includes more than 500 *palazzi* and churches. It is definitely not short on cultural richness. But it's also a city where lovely Art Nouveau villas are dwarfed by concrete behemoths and where traffic is so bad that walking will get you there faster than any moving vehicle.

For many centuries, Palermo was a crossroads of innovations and ideas. The home for numerous social, political, and cultural breakthroughs, it was where the first known parliament in Europe convened, where the roots of Italian literature took hold, where paper evolved from the fragile papyrus, and where a fellow named Jawhar as-Siquilli set out to found the city of Cairo in 969 A.D.

As the capital city of Sicily, Palermo has witnessed more political turmoil and exchanges of power than many independent nations. Little did the Phoenicians know what would become of this natural harbor when they landed here sometime around 800 B.C.

Palermo's golden age came to full fruition under Norman domination led by Count Roger of Hauteville, who captured Palermo in 1072. Under his son, King Roger, Palermo became a bastion of social, cultural, and religious tolerance. Christians, Jews, and Muslims lived in harmony.

Under Roger's grandson, the Holy Roman Emperor Frederick II, the grandeur of the city started to decline once he set up court outside Palermo, creating fertile terrain for yet another takeover, this time by the Angevins. Other dynasties were to follow, yet Palermo never regained the spirit of its golden age.

In the 1980s the unthinkable happened: Mafia dons and family members started spilling the beans about Cosa Nostra. Entire families of some informants were murdered. In 1992, the people of Palermo had finally had enough. Although these days Palermo has a staggering level of unemployment, young people are willing to invest in their city instead of moving away. In the process, they hope to restore it to its original splendor of long ago.

ORIENTATION
Arriving

BY PLANE Flights into Palermo from mainland Italy or directly from the U.K. arrive at Palermo's airport, **Punta Raisi Falcone-Borsellino,** which lies 31km (19 miles) west of Palermo. The number to call for general airport information is *©* **091-7020111;** for real-time flight times and other information log on to www.gesap.it.

Birgi Airport in Trapani (see p. 158), lying southwest, has become an alternative hub for reaching Palermo. See p. 39 for information about flying to Sicily.

From the airport, **Prestia and Comandé coach service** (www.prestiae comande.it) to the Politeama and Piazza Giulio Cesare (central train station) will cost 5.80€. The **Trinacria Express train** (www.trenitalia.it) runs to the central station from arrivals and costs 5.50€; tickets must be purchased before boarding. In fact, if there is no way to purchase a ticket—if the vending machine is out of order or the ticket office is closed—forgo using the train and take the bus instead. You'll be fined at least 52€ for not having a ticket. A **taxi** is by far the fastest way of getting into town, but also the most expensive—expect to pay at least 35€ to get to the city center if pre-booked; otherwise make sure to negotiate a price with the driver beforehand to avoid nasty surprises later on. To book a taxi call *©* **091-513311,** or visit www.autoradiotaxi.it. If you want the freedom of getting around by yourself—even if the experience can be hair-raising at times—you can **rent a car** (p. 43) at the airport with any of the well-known companies and drive into the city. If you can, arrange rental before arriving—it saves time and rates are somewhat cheaper.

BY TRAIN Palermo is well linked to and from Italy as well as to most major cities on the island. All major trains arrive at Palermo's main terminal, **Stazione Centrale,** at Piazza Giulio Cesare (*©* **892021;** www.trenitalia.it). The ticket and information office operates from 6:45am to 8:40pm, while automatic ticket-vending machines can be found near the entrance. The luggage deposit (see "Fast Facts: Palermo," p. 76) is located on the right facing the tracks.

Arriving from Catania takes at least 3½ hours; not all services from here are direct—somewhere along the way you'll have to change trains; trains cost between 15€ one way and 32€ for the InterCity. From Messina, expect a 3-hour ride costing between 12€ one way and 25€ for the InterCity. From Trapani, for 7.40€, the train takes about 2½ hours, with frequent service throughout the day. From Agrigento it's a 2-hour ride through the countryside and costs 8€. If you don't mind spending time on trains (and love the so-called scenic routes), then the ride from Syracuse is for you—you'll get there in anywhere from 4½ to 7 hours; trains cost between 15€ one way and 32€ for the InterCity.

There are also direct rail links from major Italian cities—from Rome it's at least 12 hours, with both daily and overnight service and costs between 52€ to 101€ one way. From Naples expect to travel 9 hours. For those willing to ride to Palermo all the way from Milan, allow anywhere between 15 and 20 hours.

BY BUS Buses that run from the mainland to Palermo arrive in Via Balsamo, adjacent to the Central Station, but unless you're willing to sit immobilized for endless hours—not to mention risking thrombosis—I discourage it: The ride is long, boring, and not for those prone to car sickness. **SAIS** runs two buses daily from Rome (costing 44€) and one from Naples, with connecting buses from northern cities operated by the same company. For information, call ✆ **091-6166028,** or visit www.saistrasporti.it.

Bus travel is a good option for trips around Sicily, as it reaches some places trains don't. There are convenient links to major cities by **SAIS** (see above). From Messina, it takes 3¼ hours and costs 15€ to reach Palermo; from Catania, 2½ hours with no stops along the way, and costs 14.20€. **Segesta** (✆ **091-6167919;** www. segesta.it) also has links from Trapani in about 2 hours, costing around 9€. **Cuffaro** (✆ **091-6161510;** www.cuffaro.info) runs between Palermo and Agrigento in 2½ hours. For the long haul from Syracuse, **Interbus** (✆ **091-6167919;** www.interbus. it) will get you there in 3½ hours. All these lines also have Via Balsamo as their final destination.

BY CAR   Three autostrade (superhighways) are linked to Palermo: the A19 from Catania, running inland; the coastal A20 from Messina; and the A29 from Mazara del Vallo, in the southwest. Except for certain points, they are free of charge. In addition, there are also national roadways linked to Palermo: The SS113 from Trapani (eastbound) or Messina (westbound), the SS121 from Catania and central Sicily, and the SS189 from Agrigento. If you are up to driving to Palermo from the mainland, you'll have to load your car onto a ferry and cross the Straits of Messina at either Villa San Giovanni or Reggio Calabria. Cars cost about 28€ and passengers are extra. **Trenitalia** (✆ **892021;** www.trenitalia.it) and **Caronte & Tourist** (✆ **800-627414;** www.carontetourist.it) offer service from Villa San Giovanni, while **Meridiano Lines** (✆ **0965-810414;** www.meridianolines.it) operates from Reggio Calabria.

Once the 20-minute crossing is over and the ferry is docked in Messina, it's far from over: Be prepared to drive about 3 more hours to Palermo on the A20 autostrada. Don't say you weren't warned.

BY BOAT   A viable option if you don't want to drive down the perilous, oft-roadwork-burdened Salerno–Reggio Calabria portion of the A1 highway, boat crossings to Palermo from Naples are provided by **SNAV** (✆ **081-4285555;** www.snav.it) and **Tirrenia Lines** (✆ **892123** toll-free in Italy, or 02-26302803; www.tirrenia. it), while **Grimaldi Lines** (✆ **081-496444;** www.grimaldi-lines.com) offers a service a few times a week from Salerno. The ferry trip takes 11 hours and prices start from 40€. SNAV also offers a ferry service three times a week from Civitavecchia, near Rome. **Grandi Navi Veloci** (✆ **010-2094591;** www.gnv.it) also operates ships from Civitavecchia as well as from Genoa and Livorno, with prices starting from around 36€. Scheduled times may vary due to weather conditions, so always call to confirm departure.

Visitor Information

Tourist offices and kiosks are located at strategic points near the main monuments and at the Palermo airport (✆ **091-591698**). The principal office is the **Azienda Autonoma Turismo,** Piazza Castelnuovo 34 (✆ **091-6058351;** www.aapit.it), open Monday to Friday 8:30am to 2pm and 3 to 6pm. In July and August this office is also open on Saturday 9am to 1pm. To make getting your way around less confusing, ask for a map *"Carta Monumentale,"* preferably with an index. Should you need one when offices are closed, you can purchase one at most newsagents and bookshops. For planning ahead before coming to Palermo, visit www.seepalermo.com for updates, news, and a real feel for the place.

City Layout

The capital of Sicily has an Old City that built up around the old harbor of La Cala, which expanded north toward Monte Pellegrino. The street plan of the Middle Ages is still in effect in the old parts of town, so it's easy to get lost.

Two main roads cut across medieval Palermo, the **Old City,** virtually quartering it. The first main road is **Corso Vittorio Emanuele,** which begins at La Cala, the ancient harbor, and cuts southwest to the landmark Palazzo dei Normanni and the Duomo (the Palermo cathedral). Corso Vittorio Emanuele runs east–west through this ancient maze of streets known to the Arabs of long ago. The other street splitting the town into two sections is **Via Roma,** which runs north and south.

The Old City is split into quadrants at the **Quattro Canti,** the virtual heart of Palermo. This is the point where Vittorio Emanuele crosses **Via Maqueda,** an artery beginning to the west of the rail depot, heading northwest. Running roughly parallel to Via Maqueda to its east is **Via Roma,** which heads north from Piazza Giulio Cesare. Via Roma and the much older Via Maqueda, virtually parallel streets, shoulder the burden of most of the inner city's heavy traffic.

La Kalsa, the medieval core of Palermo, lies to the southeast of the busy hub of Quattro Canti. The residential neighborhood of **Albergheria** is to the southwest of Quattro Canti. This is the center of the sprawling Ballarò market. Like La Kalsa, Albergheria was heavily bombed in World War II.

Via Cavour divides the medieval core to the south and the **New City** to the north. Despite its heavy traffic, the more modern section of Palermo is much easier to navigate. At the heart of this grid are the double squares of **Piazza Castelnuovo** and **Piazza Ruggero Séttimo.** Palermitans call this piazza maze **Piazza Politeama** (or just Politeama). At the double square, Via Ruggero Séttimo (a continuation of Via Maqueda; see above) crosses **Via Emerico Amari.**

Heading northwest from Politeama is Palermo's swankiest street, **Viale della Libertà,** home to smart stores and tiny boutiques. It is also the street of many upmarket restaurants, bars, office blocks, and galleries. Via Libertà races its way to the southern tip of **Parco della Favorita.**

Neighborhoods in Brief

Palermo retains the urban planning of medieval times; the three outdoor markets that date back hundreds of years still define the boundaries of the area, and the four historical districts, or *mandamenti,* still retain the feel of long ago—each had its own patron saint. Back then neighborhoods were rigidly confined (not unlike caste systems), but today that practice is long gone. Still, the maze-like, narrow streets that defined each neighborhood remain.

LA KALSA

In the quadrilateral of Via Lincoln, Via Roma, Corso Vittorio Emanuele, and the Foro Italico, the Arabs made this their headquarters, locating all the government headquarters here. In fact, Kalsa derives from the old Arabic "Khalisa," which means pure, elected; the second meaning seems to have more feasibility. Distinctly the most Arab in feel, this was a highly insalubrious area in which to wander up until 10 years ago. But now, thanks to investors refurbishing and restoring the old, bombed-out palazzi, it has attracted young, hip, urbane residents and is home to city hotspots such as the **Mikalsa** (p. 121) and the **Kursaal Kalhesa** (www.kursaalkalhesa.it). It still houses fine noble dwellings such as the **Palazzo Mirto** and **Palazzo Ajutamicristo** (www.palazzo-ajutamicristo.com), the latter having been a palace of Charles V. One of the finest art museums in Sicily, the **Galleria Regionale della Sicilia** in the **Palazzo Abbatellis,** is on Via Alloro, while in Piazza Marina you'll find the imposing, austere **Palazzo Steri** (www.palazzosteri.it).

LA VUCCIRIA

Enclosed within the Castellammare *emendameto* and accessible from Via Roma, Corso Vittorio Emanuele, and the Cala, this centuries-old market was once the pulse and beating heart of Palermo, with people flocking from everywhere to buy the foodstuffs displayed on spectacular stands with which to prepare the day's meals. Today only a smattering of its vibrancy lives on, but the feeling of what once was still remains, with butcher shops still called *carnizzerie,* fishmongers scaring shoppers with large heads of swordfish, precarious houses that look as though they might crumble any time, and tiny, hole-in-the-wall eateries that may seem shady and improvised, but are the best in town.

IL BALLARÒ

Another of Palermo's historical markets, this is enclosed within the Albergeria *mandamento*. Starting from the buildings behind Piazza Bologni and extending as far as Corso Tukory, it is also crammed with shoppers and visitors alike buying the food from the art-like stalls and snacking out on the occasional *pane e panelle* sandwich. It's become a multicultural area reminiscent of Palermo's golden age, where many immigrants have decided to set up their shops as well. The crowning glories of this neighborhood are the **Chiesa del Carmine** and the **Casa Professa** (p. 99).

IL CAPO

This is both a *mandamento* and a market, the largest and the most bazaar-like in ambience, enclosed within an area that includes Via Papireto, Via Volturno, Via Maqueda, and Corso Vittorio Emanuele. Filled with tiny, winding streets and alleyways that draw you like a magnet, the **Teatro Massimo** seems to dominate over it all. Two splendid churches—the very baroque **Chiesa dell'Immacolata Concezione**, in Via Porta Carini, and the medieval **Chiesa di Sant'Agostino** (p. 101) are worth stopping in as you wander around the market. The Capo was also the headquarters of the secret society of the *Beati Paoli,* the legendary sect that robbed from the rich and gave to the poor.

ALBERGHERIA

This is the oldest of the four *mandamenti;* it is also known as the *mandamento* Palazzo Reale because the Phoenicians first laid the foundations of what would become the royal place on the highest part of the city. Like the Kalsa, it is filled with tiny, dimly lit alleyways barely wide enough for a person and with decaying buildings in dire need of repair. It is also unsavory in some patches of the neighborhood, despite the fact that cafes and eateries are popping up everywhere. These were the streets roamed by the soothsayer and charlatan Cagliostro, its native son. There are, however, some very exquisite corners—the splendid **Piazza Bologni,** with is noble palaces and statue of Charles V, and the facade of the **Palazzo Sclafani,** which once housed the *Trionfo della Morte* (*Triumph of Death*) which is now at the **Galleria Regionale della Sicilia** (p. 97).

CASTELLAMMARE

Owing its name to the castle that once overlooked the sea—now open again to the public— it is an area bordered by Corso Vittorio Emanuele, Via Cavour, Via Roma, and Via Crispi. Also heavily bombed during 1943, it nonetheless houses some spectacular palazzi and churches, such as the **Oratorio del Rosario di Santa Cita** (p. 100) and the **Oratorio di San Lorenzo** (p. 103), **San Giorgio dei Genovesi,** and the Catalan Gothic **Santa Maria La Nova**. Encompassing the Vucciria as well, the Pantheon of Palermo,

San Domenico is also here. Author Giuseppe Tomasi di Lampedusa had his ancestral palazzo here, but it was bombed during World War II and is now being rebuilt.

NEW CITY

As you head north from Via Maqueda, the streets grow broader but also more nondescript. The monumental **Teatro Massimo,** at Piazza Verdi, roughly marks the division between the Old City and the New City. Where Via Maqueda cuts through the medieval district, it becomes Via Ruggero Séttimo as it heads north through the modern town. This street explodes into the massive double squares at Piazza Politeama, site of the Teatro **Politeama Garibaldi.** North of the square is Palermo's swankiest street, **Viale della Libertà,** running up toward **Giardino Inglese.** This is the area where the Art Nouveau movement triumphed in the city, as is still visible in the kiosks at Piazza Castelnuovo and in Piazza Verdi, but many of these priceless edifices were torn down by unscrupulous builders with the blessing of the then-mayors in the 1960s, to make way for the ugly cement behemoths that do not blend with the elegance of the neighborhood.

Getting Around

I highly recommend walking to see the city, but there are alternative means of getting around—after all, feet can only do so much walking!

BY BUS   The vast bus network will get you to all the main sites in Palermo and its environs, including Monte Pellegrino, Mondello, and Monreale. Municipal bus service is run by **AMAT,** Via Borrelli 16 (✆ **848-800817;** www.amat-pa.it).

A ride on a bus costs 1.30€. Tickets are sold at AMAT kiosks and at most *tabacchi* (tobacco shops) and newsagents (tickets expire after 90 minutes). Once on board, put the ticket in the validating machine, or—if that's not possible—on the top part of your ticket write the date and start time of your journey (month/day/year and time, using a 24 hr. clock). Not having a validated ticket will land you a hefty fine, and ticket checkers love nothing more than stopping unknowing tourists. If you plan on using the bus extensively during the day, a good option is to purchase a 24-hour ticket (3.50€), which expires at midnight of the day you use it. If you are not venturing beyond the city center, you can use one of the three convenient circular bus lines (Linea Rossa, Linea Gialla, Linea Verde) at a fraction of the cost of a regular bus ticket (.52€, valid all day).

A tourist bus called *City Sightseeing,* also operated by AMAT, begins and ends its circuit at the landmark Teatro Politeama (the Emerico Amari side). It stops at many major monuments, including the Duomo and the Royal Palace. From April to November 4 departures are daily at 9:30am; from November 5 to March 31, departures are at 10am. Tickets are sold on board; there are no advance reservations. The cost is 20€ per person, children 11 and under 10€. For information, call ✆ **091-589429.** Another sightseeing bus, a red double decker, is operated by **WorldWide City Sightseeing** (✆ **091-589429;** www.city-sightseeing.com) and offers a 24-hour hop-on, hop-off service on two different routes around the city. Adults ride for 20€, children 15 and under for 10€; families (2 adults, up to 3 children) ride for 50€; advanced booking is available. Departures are from Via Emerico Amari (Politeama) on the corner of Via Wagner.

BY TAXI   Getting around the inner core of Palermo by bus is very time-consuming and not easy, and driving a car around Palermo is a nightmare. In most cases, taxis are the best way to navigate the city center. Taxi stands are found at the main rail depot, at Piazza Verdi, at Piazza Indipendenza, and at Piazza Ruggero Séttimo, among other locations. The meter starts at 3.80€ and charges 2.55€ for the first 154m (505 ft.), plus .85€ per kilometer thereafter. If you can't find a taxi on the street, call Auto Radio Taxi ✆ **091-513311.**

If you can afford it, consider renting a taxi for the day to explore Palermo attractions; it will cost 70€ to 100€. Most drivers speak only a few words of English, but somehow they manage. You can request an English-speaking driver; perhaps one will be available. For further information on taxi sightseeing, call ✆ **091-512737.**

BY METRO   Palermo has a very limited metro system that operates on the same line as the national railway. At press time it is undergoing major expansion. From the central station, it is the easiest way to get to the tourist area around the Norman Palace, as many sites are concentrated there. It's also convenient if you are staying in other parts of town, such as Notarbartolo. Tickets cost 1.30 €.

BY CAR   Driving around Palermo can be done, but it is guaranteed to take years off your life. Roberto Benigni, in one of his films set in Palermo, joked about "the traffic" (vehicular and otherwise), but traffic in Palermo is no laughing matter. Each driver seems to have his own personalized road rules; mass transit can be painfully slow, and main thoroughfares can have cars backed up for miles. You may want to rent a car for side trips to places such as Monreale, however. Rentals can be arranged at airport desks or at offices within central Palermo. Try **Avis,** Punta Raisi Airport (✆ **091-591684;** www.avis.com), and Via Francesco Crispi 115 (✆ **091-586940**), or Hertz, at the airport and at Via Messina 7/E (✆ **091-331668;** www.hertz.com). There are two leading Italian car-rental firms: **Maggiore** (✆ **091-591681;** www.maggiore.com) is at the airport, with another branch at the Notarbartolo Railway Station (✆ **091-6810801**); **Sicily By Car** (✆ **091-591250;** www.autoeuropa.it) is also at the airport, as well as at Via Stabile Mariano 6A (✆ **091-581045**).

Finding a place to park your car is like finding a needle in a haystack, as free parking is scarcer and scarcer. ***Note:*** Those blue spaces you might see along the street are subject to fees, for which you'll have to buy timed scratch tickets at a *tabbacchi* or newsagent. If you choose to park your car in a garage you'll find one near the rail station, **Garage Stazione Centrale** (✆ **091-6168297**), which charges 15€ per night (closed Sun). Two other convenient garages—identified simply by the word GARAGE—are at Via Stabile 10 (✆ **091-321667**), charging 15€ per night, and at Piazza Oliva (✆ **091-325444**), charging 20€ per night. Piazzale Ungheria, an outdoor municipal car par, charges hourly and up to 30€ in a 24-hour period.

BY ORGANIZED TOUR   Your hotel or B&B can arrange tours to suit your interests. To contact and book a tour with a serious, highly recommended organization before traveling, go to **www.palermoguide.net.** For top-of-the-line personalized service visit **www.sicilyconcierge.com.**

ON FOOT   Once you arrive in Palermo, park your car, and leave it parked. Walk everywhere you can; Palermo is best discovered on foot.

[FastFACTS] PALERMO

American Express The local agency is at **Giovanni Ruggieri e Figli,** Emerico Amari 40 (© **091-587144**), open Monday to Friday 9am to 1pm and 4 to 7:30pm, Saturday 9am to 1pm. In the event of a lost or stolen card, call © **06-72900347.**

Bookstores Bestsellers and classics in English can be found at **la Feltrinelli,** Via Cavour 133 (© **091-781291; www.lafeltrinelli.it**) or at **Mondadori,** Via Ruggero Settimo 18 (www.librimondadori.it). Both are open daily from 9am to 8pm.

Consulates The **U.S. Consular Agency,** on Via Vaccarini 1 in the new part of town (© **091-305857**), is open Monday to Friday 9am to 1:30pm. The **British Consulate,** Via Cavour 117 in the city center (© **091-326412**), is open Monday to Friday 9am to 1pm. **Note:** Consulates observe both their home county's and Italy's national holidays, and will therefore be closed on those days.

Emergencies For the police, dial © **112**; the *Carabinieri* (army police corps) can be reached at © **113.** For an ambulance dial © **118**; to report a fire, © **115.** For road assistance call ACI (Italian Automobile Club) at © **803116** or toll-free © **800-116800.**

Hospital The two main hospitals are **Ospedale Civico** at Via Carmelo Lazzaro (© **091-6661111**) and the **Policlinico** at Via del Vespro 129 (© **091-6551111**). The **Children's Hospital** is at Piazza Porta Montalto (© **091-6666224**). In the new part of town the closest hospitals are **Villa Sofia**, Piazza Salerno 1 (© **091-6700350**), and **Ospedale Cervello,** at Via Trabucco (© **091-6802111**).

Internet Access Though most areas in the center have Wi-Fi coverage, the computer-less can check e-mail at the **Aboriginal Internet Café** at Via Spinuzza 51 (© **091-6622229; www.aboriginalcafe.com**), which has 20 computers and charges 1.90€ per half-hour; open Monday to Saturday 9am to midnight. For free Internet service go to **Palazzo Ziino** on Via Dante (© **091-7407618**); open Monday to Saturday from 9:30am to 6:30pm and Sunday from 9:30am to 1:30pm. **Note:** ID is required to use the Internet at public points.

Laundromat L'Oblò is located at Via Volturno 62 (© **333 8032824**), just steps away from the Capo market. Open Monday to Friday from 8:30am to 7pm and Saturday from 9am to 2pm.

Lost Property This service is handled by **Ufficio Oggetti Smarriti** at Via Macello 21 (© **091-7405082**). It's open Monday, Tuesday, and Thursday 9am to noon. To reach it, take bus no. 211 from the Stazione Centrale.

Luggage Storage You can leave luggage at the storage at the Central Station, open daily 6am to midnight. It charges from 4€ per suitcase for the first 5 hours to 11€ for 24 hours. For information, call © **091-6033440.** A photocopy of ID is required to leave luggage.

Pharmacies Pharmacies in the city center are found at Via Roma 113 (© **091-6164339**); Via Mariano Stabile 175 (© **091-334482**); and Via Emerico Amari 2 (© **091-585383**). Nonprescription, over-the-counter medicine can be found at *Parafarmacie;* these have a blue cross to distinguish them from full pharmacies, denoted by green crosses. **Note:** Pharmacies are closed on weekends; check the listings posted next to the door of each pharmacy for the closest one on weekend duty. There is a surcharge applied to items bought at night-duty pharmacies.

Post Office The main post office is at Via Roma 320 (© **091-7535193**), open Monday to Friday

8am to 6:30pm, Saturday 8am to noon. Branches can be found at the train station (no phone), observing the same opening hours as the main post office, and at the airport (℡ 091-212176), open Monday to Friday 8:30am to 3:30pm. The branch at Via Mariano Stabile 277 (℡ 091-7494811) has the friendliest staff; it's open from Monday to Friday 8:30am to 1:30pm and on Saturdays 8:30am to 12:30pm.

Shipping If you want to send back all those heavy souvenirs via parcel as fast as possible, go to **Mail Boxes Etc. Point Service** at Via XX Settembre 62/A (℡ **091-6251830**).

Transit Information Local transportation is run by **AMAT** (℡ **848-800817,** or from a cellphone ℡ **199-240800;** www.amat-pa.it).

Travel Agencies See **"American Express,"** above.

WHERE TO STAY

There are a plethora of accommodations to choose from in Sicily's capital, from no-frills B&Bs to five-star luxury hotels, and everything else in between. In keeping with the rest of European standards, many lodgings are entirely smoke-free and are equipped to cater to the needs of families and those with limited mobility. The high season, just like in the rest of Sicily, is June to September and the Christmas holidays, while the shoulder period is from Easter to May. *Note:* Check in at many hotels begins at 2:00pm.

Very Expensive

Grand Hotel Piazza Borsa ★★★   This brand-new hotel in the Kalsa was once the stock exchange of Palermo. The Belle Epoque decor has been preserved throughout, and the modern furnished, soundproofed rooms are mid-sized to spacious; some overlook the beautiful Basilica of St. Francis of Assisi. The bathrooms have either tub or shower, with Jacuzzis in the deluxe rooms. In warmer weather breakfast is served on the terrace overlooking the rooftops of the Kalsa. A rarity these days, the hotel also has a specially designated smoking lounge.

Via Cartari 18, 90133 Palermo. ℡ **091-320075.** www.piazzaborsa.it. 127 units. 145€–182€ double; 324€–700€ suite. Discounts for children 11 and under. Rates include breakfast. AE, DC, MC, V. Limited street parking. Bus: 101, 102, 107, or Linea Rossa. **Amenities:** Restaurant; bar; room service; smoke-free rooms. *In room:* A/C, TV, minibar, hair dryer, Internet.

Villa Igiea Grand Hotel ★★★   Located in the suburb of Acquasanta, 2.4km (1½ miles) north of the center, this is still arguably the best place to stay in town. Villa Igiea was once a sanatorium, but it's now a remarkable, rare example of Sicilian Art Nouveau. Managed by Hilton, it is in better shape and more comfortable than the also highly rated Grand Hotel et Des Palmes (see below), Palermo's other historic property. However, its location on the outskirts of town (where there aren't frequent bus links) may seem inconvenient to some travelers. With a 1920s feel steeped within its walls, the hotel is surrounded by terraced gardens overlooking the sea and the marina. The old architecture has been preserved, including the precious dining room frescoed by Ettore Maria de Begler. Guest rooms contain valuable furnishings such as comfortable wrought-iron beds.

Salita Belmonte 43, 90142 Palermo. ℡ **091-6312111.** Fax 091-547654. www.hotelvillaigieapalermo.com. 124 units. 150€–424€ double; 455€–600€ suite. Rates include breakfast. AE, DC, MC, V. Free parking. Bus: 139. **Amenities:** Restaurant; bar; outdoor saltwater pool; tennis court; health club; room service; smoke-free rooms. *In room:* A/C, TV, minibar, hair dryer, Internet (5€/hr).

Where to Stay & Eat in Palermo

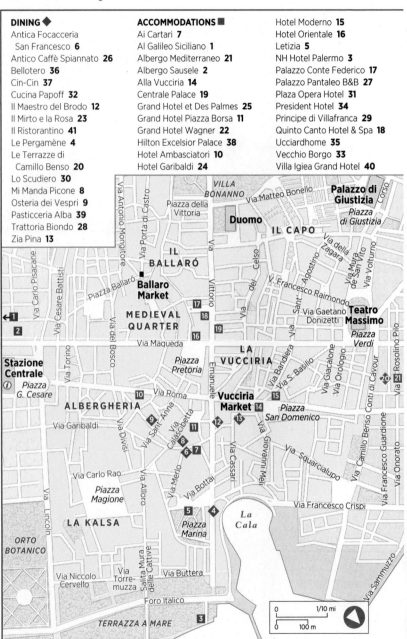

DINING ◆

Antica Focacceria
 San Francesco **6**
Antico Caffè Spiannato **26**
Bellotero **36**
Cin-Cin **37**
Cucina Papoff **32**
Il Maestro del Brodo **12**
Il Mirto e la Rosa **23**
Il Ristorantino **41**
Le Pergamène **4**
Le Terrazze di
 Camillo Benso **20**
Lo Scudiero **30**
Mi Manda Picone **8**
Osteria dei Vespri **9**
Pasticceria Alba **39**
Trattoria Biondo **28**
Zia Pina **13**

ACCOMMODATIONS ■

Ai Cartari **7**
Al Galileo Siciliano **1**
Albergo Mediterraneo **21**
Albergo Sausele **2**
Alla Vucciria **14**
Centrale Palace **19**
Grand Hotel et Des Palmes **25**
Grand Hotel Piazza Borsa **11**
Grand Hotel Wagner **22**
Hilton Excelsior Palace **38**
Hotel Ambasciatori **10**
Hotel Garibaldi **24**

Hotel Moderno **15**
Hotel Orientale **16**
Letizia **5**
NH Hotel Palermo **3**
Palazzo Conte Federico **17**
Palazzo Pantaleo B&B **27**
Plaza Opera Hotel **31**
President Hotel **34**
Principe di Villafranca **29**
Quinto Canto Hotel & Spa **18**
Ucciardhome **35**
Vecchio Borgo **33**
Villa Igiea Grand Hotel **40**

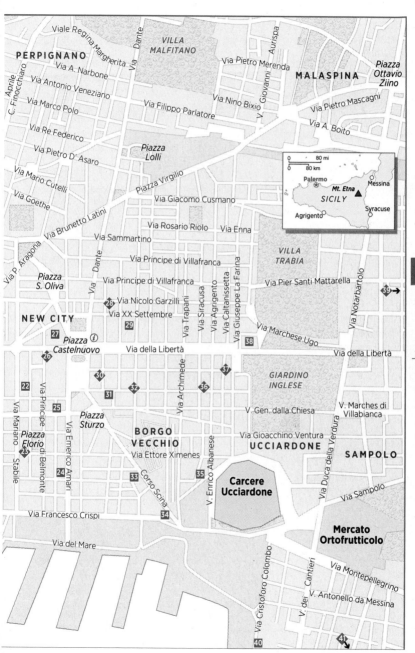

Expensive

Centrale Palace ★★ For atmosphere and comfort, I'd still give the edge to Villa Igiea (see above)—but Centrale Palace is close. At the heart of Quattro Canti, the core of the hotel is a 17th-century palazzo, although guest rooms occupy adjacent buildings that are newer. The original palazzo was converted into a hotel in 1892 during Palermo's Belle Epoque golden age. The lobby is daringly painted in vivid colors associated with the Italian Renaissance. Some period or Empire antiques are placed about to take the curse off the *moderno*. But many furnishings, especially those in the guest rooms, have more function than flair. Doubles are medium-size to spacious. The quietest rooms are on the side streets; double-glazing on the front rooms block, but does not entirely keep out, Palermo's horrific street noise. My favorite perch is the top-floor dining room, taking in views over the Palermo rooftops to Monte Pellegrino.

Corso Vittorio Emanuele 327 (at Via Maqueda), 99134 Palermo. ✆ **091-336666.** Fax 091-334881. www.centralepalacehotel.it. 104 units. 188€–271€ double; 221€–312€ junior suite; 231€–850€ suite. Rates include buffet breakfast. AE, DC, MC, V. Parking 18€. Bus: 103, 104, or 105. **Amenities:** 2 restaurants; bar; exercise room; sauna; room service; babysitting; smoke-free rooms. *In room:* A/C, TV, minibar, hair dryer, Internet (in most rooms).

Grand Hotel et Des Palmes ★ This is the most legendary hotel in Sicily, and it's still receiving guests even though its heyday has long passed. For nostalgia buffs, however, there's nothing to top it. Since the 19th century, it has sheltered some of the island's most illustrious visitors, including Richard Wagner, who finished *Parsifal* here. The hotel has seen enough murders, suicides of poets, romantic but off-the-record liaisons, and aristocratic intrigue to fill a book the size of *War and Peace*. Classy furnishings, towering pillars, and antique chandeliers still evoke the greatness of a bygone era. The charm of this antique grande dame glows on its rooftop terrace as well.

Management is working to revive the place to its former glory—while the public rooms are still glamorous, some guest rooms can be disappointingly simple. The best ones feature antiques, heavy Italian fabrics, stucco ceilings, and parquet floors.

Via Roma 398, 90139 Palermo. ✆ **091-6028111.** Fax 091-331545. www.grandhoteldespalmes.com. 183 units. 115€–251€ double; 371€–401€ suite. AE, DC, MC, V. Parking 18€. Bus: 101, 102, 103, 104, or 225. **Amenities:** Restaurant; bar; health club; spa; room service; babysitting; smoke-free rooms; Wi-Fi. *In room:* A/C, TV, minibar, hair dryer, Wi-Fi (free).

Grand Hotel Wagner On four floors set right behind the Des Palmes hotel (where Wagner really *did* stay) and within walking distance of the main shopping artery and pedestrian area, this hotel puts you right in the heart of it all without charging you Des Palmes prices. Created out of a former aristocratic palazzo, the comfortable, soundproof rooms are decorated in neoclassical style; some of the more expensive units have balconies. The well-lit, spacious bathrooms have showers only (senior suites have Jacuzzis). It's officially rated as five-star but it doesn't have the typical amenities of such, like a pool, but for everything else expect top-notch service.

Via R. Wagner 2, 90139 Palermo. ✆ **091-336572.** Fax 091 335627. www.grandhotelwagner.it. 61 units. 125€–180€ double; 208€–399€ suite. Rates include breakfast. AE, MC, V. Parking 15€. Bus: 101,102,103,104,107, or Linea Rossa. **Amenities:** Bar; health club; room service; smoke-free rooms; roof garden; Wi-Fi (free). *In room:* TV, minibar, hairdryer.

Hilton Excelsior Palace ★ Even though it was completely restored in 2005, this nostalgic favorite still exudes much of the aura of the 19th century. It was built for the National Exhibition of 1891, when it was called Hotel de la Paix. Much of the Art Nouveau decor of that elegant era remains, at least in the public rooms with their atmosphere of Palermitan Belle Epoque. The location is in a quiet neighborhood at the northern end of Via Libertà, 5 minutes away from the Politeama. Bedrooms range from midsize to large and have been completely modernized, with well-equipped bathrooms; some have been outfitted for wheelchair access. Many rooms open onto a view of the hotel garden. The formal restaurant, where the staff is elegantly uniformed, serves first-rate Sicilian and international dishes. Pets welcome.

Via Marchese Ugo 3, 90141 Palermo. © **091-7909001.** Fax 091-342139. www.palermoexcelsiorpalace hotel.com. 117 units. 216€–302€ double; 366€ junior suite. Rates include buffet breakfast. AE, DC, MC, V. Free parking. Bus: 101, 102, 106, or 806. **Amenities:** Restaurant; bar; health club; room service; baby-sitting; smoke-free rooms. *In room:* A/C, TV, minibar, Wi-Fi (free).

Hotel Garibaldi A favorite with airline crew coming in and out of town, this hotel directly across from the Politeama has an unassuming side entrance. The brightly-colored yet minimalist decor is welcoming. The rooms are relaxing, and roomy, but I don't understand why so many units have twin beds—must be a flight-attendant thing. Some corner rooms look out directly onto the Politeama, while the marble bathrooms have either tub or shower. All in all, an excellent choice in the heart of the city.

Via Emerico Amari 146, 90139 Palermo. © **091-6017111.** Fax 091-323141. www.ghshotels.it/garibaldi. 71 units. 105€ double; 190€ suite. Rates include breakfast. AE, DC, MC, V. Free parking. Bus: 101, 102, 103, 104, or 107; airport buses from Palermo and Trapani. **Amenities:** Bar; smoke-free rooms, Wi-Fi. *In room:* A/C, TV, minibar, hair dryer, Internet.

NH Hotel Palermo ★ ☺ Now part of the prestigious NH chain, this hotel has been considerably improved. Still, its major selling point is that it's the only hotel in the center with a swimming pool—and on an August day in Palermo, that's one heck big bonus. Its location overlooking the sea and the Foro Italico adds to its allure. A few steps from the Villa Giulia, and a stone's throw from the Kursaal Kalhesa, the hotel is also close to the harbor and the rail station. Rooms tend to be small, but they are comfortable, and well organized, with lots of built-ins, frequently renewed bed linens, and tiled bathrooms. All units have either balconies or terraces. To escape the traffic noise, ask for one of the more tranquil units on the upper floors, which also have better views of the sea. Pets welcome.

Via Foro Italico 22, 90133 Palermo. © **848-390398.** Fax 091-6161441. www.nh-hotels.it. 237 units. 121€–196€ double; 286€–383€ suite. Rates include breakfast. AE, DC, MC, V. Free parking. Bus: 139. **Amenities:** Restaurant; bar; outdoor pool (seasonal); room service; babysitting; smoke-free rooms. *In room:* A/C, TV, minibar, hair dryer, Internet.

Plaza Opera Hotel ★★ If you want a contemporary spin, check into this cosmopolitan hotel, one of the sleekest and most sophisticated in Palermo. It occupies a restored palace. In the heart of the city, it is convenient to theaters, restaurants, art galleries, and wine bars, and you can visit most of the celebrated monuments on foot from the hotel's front door. Although the setting is completely modern, paintings and antiques add grace notes. From the moment you walk in the door to check in, you experience Sicilian hospitality, including a welcome cocktail. Bedrooms are beautifully designed and comfortably appointed with a sleek minimalist ambience. The helpful staff will book theater tickets, make restaurant reservations, and perform any number of other tasks.

Via Nicolò Gallo 2, 90139 Palermo. ℂ **091-3819026.** Fax 091-6127343. 47 units. 250€–300€ double; 450€ suite. AE, DC, MC, V. Bus: 101, 102, 106, 107, or Linea Rossa. Parking 10€ for standard rooms, free for superior, deluxe & suites. **Amenities:** Bar; babysitting; steam room nearby. *In room:* A/C, TV, hair dryer, Wi-Fi.

Principe di Villafranca ★★★ This charming 1998 property is the finest boutique-style hotel in Palermo. Stylish, intimate, and evocative of an elegant, unfussy private home, it occupies two floors of what was originally a low-rise apartment house. Its Sicilian theme includes enough antiques and architectural finesse to make you think the place is a lot older. Grace notes include Oriental rugs, marble floors, vaulted ceilings, and a baronial fireplace. The hotel and some of its neighbors were built within what was once one of Palermo's most beautiful gardens, the Ferriato, owned long ago by the princes of Villafranca.

Guest rooms are midsize to spacious, with tile, granite, and travertine bathrooms and a welcome variety of postmodern comfort and style. The excellent restaurant, Hippopotamus, specializes in a Sicilian and Argentine cuisine. In the bar, notice the valuable Liberty-era writing desk crafted by Basile, one of the luminaries of his era.

Via G. Turrisi Colonna 4, 90141 Palermo. ℂ **091-6118523.** Fax 091-588705. www.principedivillafranca.it. 34 units. 230€ double; 280€ suite. Rates include buffet breakfast. AE, DC, MC, V. Free parking. Bus: 101 or 102. **Amenities:** Restaurant; bar; exercise room; room service; babysitting. *In room:* A/C, TV, minibar, hair dryer, Wi-Fi (free).

Quinto Canto Hotel & Spa ★★ 📠 I can't rave enough about this one. Putting you right at the Quattro Canti and giving the Centrale Palace (p. 80) a run for its money, this new hotel, converted from a stately home, has truly outdone itself when it comes to comfort in limited spaces. The luminous, spacious rooms overlooking the cupola of the church next door all have terraces and are soundproofed and well appointed with modern and period pieces. Bathrooms have either a shower stall, a tub, or both. The twin classic room is specifically designed for wheelchair accessibility. The hotel also has one of the best spas in town, which is why I give it the edge over the Centrale, right across the street. Pets welcome.

Corso Vittorio Emanuele 310, 90142 Palermo. ℂ **091-584913.** Fax 091-7574117. www.quintocantohotel. com. 21 units. 140€ double; 180€–210€ suite. Parking 15€. Rates include American buffet breakfast. AE, DC, MC, V. Bus: 104, 105, or Linea Verde. **Amenities:** Restaurant; bar; spa; room service; babysitting; smoke-free rooms. *In room:* A/C, TV, minibar, hair dryer, Wi-Fi (free).

Vecchio Borgo ★ This post-millennium hotel was created by recycling an eight-floor building constructed in 1937. Don't expect grand surroundings outside the hotel—you are, after all, in the Borgo Vecchio, one of the oldest quarters in town. The decor throughout is not cluttered but contains certain decorative flourishes. The midsize bedrooms are well furnished and beautifully maintained, each with a neatly kept and well-equipped bathroom with a hydromassage shower. Many good, unknown-to-the-multitudes *trattorie* are found in the neighborhood.

Via Quintino Sella 1–7, 90139 Palermo. ℂ **091-6111446.** Fax 091-6093318. www.hotelvecchioborgo.eu. 38 units. 180€ double; 290€ junior suite. Rates include buffet breakfast. AE, DC, MC, V. Parking (nearby) 10€. Bus: 101, 102, 107, or 806. **Amenities:** Bar; room service; smoke-free rooms. *In room:* A/C, TV, minibar, hair dryer, Wi-Fi (4€/hr).

Moderate

Palazzo Conte Federico ★★★ Still inhabited by aristocracy, the Count and Countess of Federico, this is the most elegant and refined B&B in Palermo. Actually it is an antiques-laden castle that dates from the 12th century. In the heart of the old city, near the cathedral, it was constructed on the site of Roman city walls. The tower on the south side is one of the few remaining parts of the former city wall, and has been converted into a private suite. Restored and changed over the centuries, the castle still has high painted ceilings from the 1300s, baroque ceiling frescoes, a bifora from the 1200s, and sculptures and fountains. Guest apartments are rented in the inner courtyard, complete with elegant beds, a kitchen area, a bathroom, and small living room. If you're lucky, the countess will also entertain you musically: She is a trained opera singer and classical pianist.

Via dei Biscottari 4, 90134 Palermo. ✆ **091-6511881.** www.contefederico.com. 6 units. 150€–400€ double. No credit cards. Free parking. Bus: 104, 105, or Linea Verde. **Amenities:** Dining room; cooking classes. *In room:* TV, no phone, Wi-Fi (free).

Palazzo Pantaleo B&B 👬 In an elegant courtyard hidden away from Via Ruggero Settimo, the Palazzo Pantaleo is the city's best-kept secret. The owners have meticulously restored the hotel with modern specifications, and are always ready to give their guests personal attention. The five rooms are a throwback to the Belle Epoque, with period furniture and the original tiles of the palazzo, and the bathrooms are functional and spacious with showers only. One of the units is specifically designed for limited mobility. Breakfast is served in the black-and-white tiled panoramic glass veranda, leading you right into the Palermo of the 1920s. Free, guests-only parking in the courtyard, a true rarity in the city center, is another boon.

Via Ruggiero Settimo 74H, 90141 Palermo. ✆ **091-325471.** www.palazzopantaleo.it. 5 units. 100€ double; 140€ suite. Rates include breakfast. Free parking. MC, V. Bus: 101, 102, 103, 104, 106, 107, or 108. **Amenities:** Room service; smoke-free rooms. *In room:* A/C, TV, minibar, Wi-Fi (free).

President Hotel This eight-story concrete-and-glass structure rising above the harbor remains a reliable choice in Palermo. After a much-needed renovation, the President emerged as one of the better and more moderately priced options in town. You'll pass beneath a soaring arcade before entering the informal stone-trimmed lobby. The amenities here are simple but comfortable. There's little stylish about the small rooms, but they are well kept, as are the adjoining tiled bathrooms. You needn't bother with the on-site restaurant and its clientele of tired businesspeople. All you have to do is walk out along the harbor to find a number of fine trattorie serving excellent fish.

Via Francesco Crispi 228, 90139 Palermo. ✆ **091-580733.** Fax 091-611588. www.presidenthotelpalermo sicily.com. 129 units. 195€–230€ double. Rates include buffet breakfast. AE, DC, MC, V. Parking 10€. Bus: 139. **Amenities:** Restaurant; bar; room service. *In room:* A/C, TV, minibar, hair dryer, Wi-Fi (free).

Ucciardhome ★ 👬 One of the better boutique hotels of Palermo, this is an unexpected find. Rated four stars by the government, the hotel is known for its personal service by one of the city's most helpful staff Ucciardhome has special features such as an exclusive wine bar that is both elegant and *intime*. The staff can make arrangements for you to visit a nearby gym, Turkish bath, or beauty salon. Room service will also provide special lunches and dinners. Honeymooners make up a part of the clientele. Each of the spacious bedrooms is furnished with acute attention to detail, including minimalist designer furniture, precious materials, and dark wood—prominently featured throughout the hotel. Much use is made of ivory-white marble floors, and each of the bedrooms comes with soundproofing, big windows, and terraces or balconies.

Via Enrico Albanese 34–35, 90139 Palermo. ✆ **091-348426.** Fax 091-7303738. www.hotelucciardhome.com. 16 units. 102€–150€ double; 162€–190€ junior suite; 213€–250€ suite. Rates include breakfast. AE, DC, MC, V. Bus: 101. **Amenities:** Wine bar; room service. *In room:* A/C, TV, minibar, hair dryer, Wi-Fi (free).

Inexpensive

Ai Cartari ★★   When Rosi and Salvo opened up one of the first B&Bs in the city over 10 years ago, their friends thought they were nuts; since then, many B&Bs have come and gone, but this one is still around. In what was once an old paper mill directly across from the Basilica of St Francis, the Lorias have poured their heart and soul into restoring the property—soaring wood-beamed ceilings in the living room and the country decor make it a very cozy atmosphere, where Rosi herself serves substantial breakfasts. The two suite-like rooms have independent entrances—a rarity for a B&B. One of the guest rooms has a small cooking area. The rooms are decorated with period furniture from around Sicily, and the majolicas that decorate the bathroom were part of the original building.

Via Alessandro Paternostro 62, 90133 Palermo. ✆ **091-6116372.** www.aicartari.it. 2 units 80€–120€ double, 140€–180€ quadruple. Minimum 2-night stay. Rates include breakfast. MC, V. Parking 10€. Bus: 101, 102, 107, or Linea Rossa. **Amenities:** *In room:* A/C, TV, minibar, Internet.

Albergo Mediterraneo   One of my preferred government-rated three-star hotels, this angular 1956 building sits on a narrow commercial street in a blandly modern neighborhood. The granite-sheathed lobby leads to six upper floors with wide hallways and spacious dimensions, evoking a well-designed contemporary hospital. Rooms are bigger than you might imagine, with a sense of calm but absent of a lot of unnecessary furniture. Overall, this place is businesslike and highly recommendable.

Via Rosolino Pilo 43, 90139 Palermo. ✆ **091-581133.** Fax 091-586974. www.abmedpa.com. 106 units. 118€ double. Rate includes continental breakfast. AE, DC, MC, V. Parking 13€. Bus: 101, 102, 104, or 107. **Amenities:** Restaurant; bar. *In room:* A/C, TV, minibar.

Albergo Sausele 🔱   This family-run inn stands out amid the dreary rail-station-area hotels. It boasts high ceilings, globe lamps, modern art, and new modular furnishings. The staff is hospitable, as is the resident Saint Bernard, Eva. Guest rooms with shower-only bathrooms are certainly small and modest, but they are a pleasant choice. To avoid street noise, light sleepers should request a unit overlooking the peaceful courtyard. What make this place special are the handcrafted and antique artifacts from around the world, collected by Giacomo Sausele on his travels.

Via Vincenzo Errante 12, 90127 Palermo. ✆ **091-6161308.** Fax 091-6167525. www.hotelsausele.it. 36 units. 92€ double; 123€ triple. Rates include continental breakfast. AE, DC, MC, V. Parking 10€. Bus: Any to Stazione Centrale. **Amenities:** Bar; 2 lounges. *In room:* A/C, TV, hair dryer.

Al Galileo Siciliano 🛍   A few blocks away from the train station, in what seems like an unsavory neighborhood, you'll find this clean, quiet B&B run by efficient young hosts. Popular with traveling theater companies, and one of the few openly gay-friendly places in town, the ample, well-appointed guest rooms have wooden ceilings, and each has a private bathroom with shower. All in all, if you're not too fussy about your surroundings and are traveling on a shoestring budget, give this one a go.

Via GB Odierna 40, 90127 Palermo. ℃ **091-6163031.** Fax 091-6101463. www.algalileosiciliano.it. 6 units; 40€ double; 100€ quadruple. Rates include breakfast. Limited street parking; garage parking can be arranged for a fee. Bus: Any to Stazione Centrale. **Amenities:** In room: A/C, TV, fridge, Wi-Fi (free).

Alla Vucciria 🏨 Come here to experience true Vucccuria living, and see it unfold before your eyes every morning. In one of the market side streets, you enter a building that looks as if it's been bombed out and climb three flights of steep, haphazard stairs as the neighbors peer behind the door. But once you get to the top, you're actually in a very clean, cozy and well-run B&B with three very spacious, well-lit rooms. The owner is helpful and very knowledgeable about the city, which is a bonus. Two of the three rooms have en suite bathrooms. Many visitors to Palermo who have stayed here consider this their home, and won't stay anywhere else.

Via Coltellieri, 46, 90133 Palermo. ℃ **091-7720857.** www.allavucciria.com. 3 units. 70€–80€ double. Rates include breakfast. Free street parking. Bus: 101, 102, 103, 104, 107, or Linea Rossa. **Amenities:** Reading room. In room: TV, Wi-Fi (free).

Hotel Ambasciatori ★★★ 🏨 When looking for quality on a budget, this is the best place to stay in town. Over the din of Via Roma rises this gem of a hotel that offers respite from the noisy streets. The midsize, soundproofed rooms evoke the colors of the Mediterranean and have parquet floors, and the minimal bathrooms have either a tub or a shower. The quarters might seem cramped, but if you happen to land one of the rooms with a balcony, you'll forget about the limited space. The glorious rooftop terrace overlooking the city where breakfast is served in nice weather is reason enough to stay here.

Via Roma 111, 90133 Palermo. ℃ **091-6166881.** Fax 091 6100105. www.hotelambasciatori.it. 20 units. 60€–90€ double; 120€–175€ quadruple. Rates include continental breakfast. AE, DC, MC, V. Bus: 101, 102, 107, or Linea Rossa. **Amenities:** Exercise room; smoke-free rooms. In room: TV, minibar, Wi-Fi (free).

Hotel Moderno ★ 🍴 One of the city's best cost-conscious options lies on the third and fourth floors of a stately looking building that's among the grandest in its busy and highly congested neighborhood. Don't expect the same kind of grandeur inside that you see on the building's neoclassical exterior: You take a cramped elevator to the third-floor reception area, and then proceed to a clean but very simple guest room. Each unit comes with a tiled bathroom, lots of artwork, and not a great deal of direct sunlight. In view of the oppressive heat outside, and in light of the reasonable prices, few of this hotel's repeat visitors seem to mind.

Via Roma 276 (at Via Napoli), 90133 Palermo. ℃ **091-588683.** Fax 091-588260. www.hotelmodernopa. com. 38 units. 65€–75€ double. AE, DC, MC, V. Bus: 101, 102, 103, or 107. **Amenities:** Bar. In room: TV.

Hotel Orientale ★ 🍴 The former royal residence of Prince Alessandro Filangieri II, this 18th-century palace has been converted into a boutique hotel. Many of the original features were left intact, including a grand marble staircase, original hand-painted frescoes, and a courtyard. The location is in the historic center of the old city, near many famous landmarks, including the Teatro Massimo (p. 120). You can walk here from the central train station. I prefer room no. 7, because it's large and grandly comfortable, more like a ballroom than a bedroom. It was constructed over an archway through which traffic can reach the market streets behind the hotel. Antiques are mixed with 1950s-era furnishings. Not all rooms have bathrooms.

Via Maqueda 26, 90134 Palermo. ✆ **091-6165727.** Fax 091-6161193. www.albergoorientale.191.it. 24 units. 45€–70€ double. AE, MC, V. Bus: 101, 102, 103, 104, 107, 122, or 225. **Amenities:** Cafeteria next door for breakfast; smoke-free rooms; Internet (3€/hr). *In room:* A/C, TV.

Letizia ★ 👜 A once-dreary *pensione* has been reincarnated as a boutique hotel of charm, grace, and elegance. Surrounded by a decaying 18th-century palazzo from the golden age of Palermo, the hotel rises only two floors on the edge of Kalsa district, a half-block from the main drag, Corso Vittorio Emanuele. The public rooms are gracefully decorated with antiques and Persian carpets. The small-to-midsize bedrooms contain much of the same type of furnishings and are immaculately kept.

Via Bottai 30, 90133 Palermo. ✆/fax **091-589110.** www.hotelletizia.com. 13 units. 60€–130€ double; 120€–150€ suite; 150€–180€ family room. Rates include buffet breakfast. AE, MC, V. Parking 12€. Bus: 107. **Amenities:** Bar; room service; babysitting. *In room:* A/C, TV, minibar, hair dryer, Wi-Fi.

WHERE TO EAT

Palermo certainly offers no shortage of eateries for every price range and taste—ingredients are fresh and plentiful from land and sea. Start your morning off with one of the piping-hot croissants fresh out of the oven or the ubiquitous gelato with a brioche. Choices at lunchtime run the gamut, from the street food found at just about every corner served up piping hot to sit-down banquets. Dinner is a ritual, where friends and family gather around a table for a pizza or a multicourse meal that will put you on the treadmill first thing in the morning. Sweets alone are often a meal, and don't be surprised to see ice-cream parlors packed at lunchtime. Given Palermo's multiethnic heritage, there's no shortage of other cuisines around town and sushi bars are popping up like mushrooms. I only list restaurants that serve traditional cuisine, because that's what you're in Sicily for.

Expensive

Bellotero ★ SICILIAN Lying in Palermo's new town, this is one of the most traditional of all Sicilian restaurants. The 10-table restaurant draws mainly Palermo foodies, who feast on such dishes as fresh fish and shellfish, beginning with a seafood appetizer of calamari, mussels, and shrimp. Many diners begin their meal with a lobster-studded pasta, and you can order such fare as spaghetti with sea bass, sea urchins with lemon zest, or perhaps lamb with oven-roasted pistachios. The menu also features Sicilian rabbit and even serves filet of horse, which sounds revolting to many diners, although it is a traditional Sicilian dish with a long-standing reputation among gourmets. For dessert, I recommend the pistachio ice cream.

Via Giorgio Castriota 31. ✆ **091-582158.** Reservations required. Main courses 10€–20€. AE, MC, V. Tues–Sun 1–3pm and 8–10:30pm. Closed Aug 1–20. Bus: 101, 102, 107, or 806.

Il Ristorantino ★ SICILIAN This restaurant is justifiably celebrated for its finely honed cuisine. Francesco Inzerillo, hailed as the city's top chef by gourmet Italian guides, presides over an establishment that's not only elegant but also one of the most stunningly modern in the city. The menu is creative, although old-time favorites are also included. He won my heart with mackerel with caper sauce and a winning soup of fresh seafood. Try the lobster tortellini with cherry tomatoes or the well-crafted swordfish au gratin. Desserts are luscious, so save some room. The restaurant lies in the suburbs north of the center and is best reached by taxi.

Piazzale Alcide De Gasperi 19. © **091-512861.** Reservations required. Main courses 12€–20€. AE, DC, MC, V. Tues-Sat 12:30-3:30pm and 8:30pm-midnight. Closed 2 weeks in Aug and Jan 1-7.

Moderate

Cin-Cin ★★ 🏨 SICILIAN   One of the culinary treasures of Palermo, this is a favorite spot with locals. Behind an unpretentious facade, it's reached by going down a flight of steps off Via Libertà, near Piazza Croci. Start off with an improbable yet delectable mix: Bufala mozzarella topped with wild strawberry jam. Some of the best main courses feature *spaccatelle* (pasta) with pesto Ericino (a pesto made with basil, almonds, pistachio, pine nuts, and cherry tomatoes); risotto with red pumpkin and mascarpone cheese; swordfish rolls stuffed with basil, almonds, honey, and orange rind; and beef filet with mushrooms and mozzarella. The parfaits that come in three different flavors—chocolate, cinnamon, and Marsala—close the meal superbly.

Via Manin 22, off Via Libertà. © **091-6124095.** www.ristorantecincin.com. Reservations recommended. Main courses 7€–16€. AE, DC, MC, V. Sept-June Mon-Fri noon-3pm and 8pm-midnight, Sat 8pm-midnight; July-Aug Mon-Fri noon-3:30pm. Bus: 101, 102, 107, 806, or Linea Rossa.

Cucina Papoff ★ 🏨 SICILIAN   With a name like "Papoff's Kitchen," you'll think you've landed in Bulgaria. The restaurant is named for its Bulgarian founder, but this friendly little trattoria actually serves some of the most traditional of all Sicilian dishes. The setting is an atmospheric 18th-century building with stone vaulting in the heart of Palermo, just a few steps from the newly restored Teatro Massimo.

The basic recipes remain pretty much the same as they were 200 years ago. I recommend the batter-fried cardoon florets, which have the nutty taste of artichoke bottoms (only better). The stuffed radicchio is Palermo's best, as is the exquisite rabbit in red-wine sauce. You'll also see all those soul-food specialties that warm a Sicilian's heart, including *arancini di riso* (stuffed rice balls) and potato croquettes. Opt for one of the rare Sicilian vintage wines that are almost never found beyond the island's shores.

Via Isidoro La Lumia 32. © **091-586460.** www.cucinapapoff.com. Reservations recommended. Main courses 8€–12€. AE, MC, V. Mon-Fri 1-3:30pm and 8pm-midnight; Sat 8pm-midnight. Closed Aug. Bus: 101, 102, 104, or 106.

Il Maestro del Brodo ★ SICILIAN   What, 25 years ago, used to be just a mess hall serving up potfuls of boiled veal to the hungry working multitudes has come a long, long way. Never budging from the original location at the Vucciria, which was formerly an 1800s ice-cream parlor complete with wrought-iron columns, the broth masters still offer the veal, but fish figures prominently on the menu, as it should in Palermo. The best of the first courses is the fresh tortellini, cooked in the saffron and vegetable broth in which the veal is boiled.

Viale Panninieri 7 © **091-329523.** Main courses 7€–10€. AE, DC, MC, V. Lunch only except weekends. Closed Mon.

Lo Scudiero ★★ SICILIAN   Set directly across the busy street from the Teatro Politeama Garibaldi, this cozy restaurant and brasserie (its name translates as "The Shield Bearer") is not to be confused with the grander and more expensive restaurant with a roughly similar name out in the suburbs near the soccer stadium.

Honest, straightforward, and unpretentious, it's favored by locals, many of whom work or live in the nearby Via Libertà neighborhood. Fine raw materials and skilled hands in the kitchen produce such tempting dishes as grilled swordfish flavored with garlic and a touch of mint. The fish served here is really fresh, as the owner buys it every day at the market. This place gets my vote for some of Palermo's best roulades, grilled veal rolls with a stuffing of ground salami and herbs. Vegetarians can opt for the medley of grilled vegetables with balsamic vinegar and olive oil.

Via Turati 7. ✆ **091-581628.** Reservations recommended. Main courses 8€–18€. AE, DC, MC, V. Mon–Sat 12:30–3pm and 7:30–11:30pm. Closed Aug 10–20. Bus: 101 or 107.

Mi Manda Picone ★ 🏛 SICILIAN   Come here for three reasons: To sample the excellent and well-chosen Sicilian wines, to enjoy the tasty food at affordable prices, and to admire the facade of that Romanesque gem, Chiesa di San Francesco, rising a few steps from the restaurant's entrance.

The specialty here is wine (450 kinds), mostly from Sicily, accompanied by platters of hearty, robust food. Sit on the terrace in front of the church or retreat to the woodsy, medieval-style interior, which once functioned as a stable. Light snacks include stuffed and deep-fried vegetables; a marvelous flan of fava beans and Pecorino cheese; fresh salads; and antipasti platters. More substantial fare includes grilled tuna or swordfish steaks with capers and black pepper.

Via Alessandro Paternostro 59 (Piazza San Francesco d'Assisi). ✆ **091-6160660.** www.mimanda picone.it. Main courses 10€–14€. AE, MC, V. Wine 3.50€–7.50€ per glass. Mon–Sat 7–11pm. Bus: 103, 105, 108, or 164.

Osteria dei Vespri ★★ SICILIAN/ITALIAN   A few steps from Via Roma, this restaurant lies in what were once the stables of Palazzo Ganci, where the ballroom scene from *The Leopard* was filmed. A wine tavern and restaurant, it is filled with handcrafted wooden furniture resting on parquet floors. The wine list, with hundreds of vintages, is the best in town.

The chefs, using a razor-sharp technique, impress with such starters as a soup of mussels, lentils, potatoes, saffron, and wild fennel. I am also impressed with their imaginative and finely crafted dishes, especially the roulade of fish and dried prunes, pine nuts, tuna roe, and cauliflower mousse. The pasta dish that merits the most raves is ravioli with ricotta and fresh basil, homemade tomato sauce, and crispy onion. I want to go back to have my favorite dessert here, a mousse of black-and-white chocolate with glazed orange peel.

Piazza Croce dei Vespri 6. ✆ **091-6171631.** www.osteriadeivespri.it. Reservations recommended. Main courses 15€–25eu]; fixed-price menu 55€. AE, DC, MC, V. Mon–Sat 1–3pm and 8:30pm–midnight. Bus: 101, 102, 107, 122, or Linea Rossa. Closed 2 weeks in Aug.

Trattoria Biondo ★ SICILIAN   Where else can you find a pizzeria where the pizzas are so good the waiters actually talk you out of having a starter? This long-time establishment in town keeps the clientele coming with more than 50 types of pizzas—the bacon and bufala mozzarella one is out of this world. But it's not just the pizzas that'll make your mouth water; the pastas and the mixed grilled meats are just as tasty.

Via Carducci. ✆ **091-583662.** Main courses 10€–15€. AE, DC, MC, V. Mon–Tues and Thurs, Sun 10am–3pm and 7:30–11pm. Closed Wed & July 1–Sept 15. Bus: 101, 102, 106, or 806.

Inexpensive

Antica Focacceria San Francesco 🖐 SICILIAN   I have to give them credit for being around longer than the unified Italian nation, and for having taken on the Mafia (as a consequence they have police parked outside 24/7). Yes, the high ceilings and marble floors evoke the era in which the eatery was born, and the food has changed little since. You can still get the classic staple *panino con la milza* (spleen sandwich), some *panelle* (deep-fried chickpea fritters), and *arancini di riso* (rice balls stuffed with tomatoes and peas or mozzarella), but the anti-Mafia protest seems to be more of the selling point than the food.

Via A. Paternostro 58. ⓒ **091-320264.** www.afsf.it. Sandwiches 5€–8€; pastas 7€–10€. AE, DC, MC, V. Daily 10am–midnight. Bus: 103, 105, or 225.

Antico Caffè Spiannato ★★ CAFE/PASTRIES   Established in 1860, this is the most opulent cafe in its neighborhood. Set on a quiet, pedestrian-only street, it's the focal point for residents of the surrounding Via Libertà district, thanks to its lavish displays of sandwiches, pastries, and ice creams. Buy coffee at the bar and be tempted by the elaborate cannoli and almond cakes. If you're hungry, sit at a tiny table—indoors or out—for one of the succulent *piatti del giorno.* (These include fresh salads, grills, and succulent pastas such as spaghetti with sea urchins.) In the evenings, the focus shifts from coffee to cocktails and from pastries to platters. Live music entertains the nighttime crowd.

Via Principe di Belmonte 115. ⓒ **091-583231.** Pastries 1€–3€; platters 3€–12€. AE, DC, MC, V. Daily 7am–1am. Bus: 101,102, 104, 107, or 806.

Il Mirto e la Rosa ★ VEGETARIAN   "The Myrtle and the Rose" is no longer a strict vegetarian restaurant. True, it still serves some of the most flavorful vegetarian dishes in Palermo, made with only the freshest harvests from the fields; but these days, its customers are also treated to an array of well-prepared meat and fish dishes. It's set in a Liberty-style building from the turn-of-the-20th-century Belle Epoque days; a dining terrace is open in summer. The North African-inspired vegetable couscous is the best in town, as are any number of rice and pasta dishes with tantalizing sauces, such as ravioli stuffed with tomato mousse and basil jelly. If you want generous portions and good flavor, order the delectable grilled steak Florentine. Seasonal produce is always emphasized on the menu.

Via Principe di Granatelli 30, off Piazza Florio. ⓒ **091-324353.** www.ilmirtoelarosa.com. Reservations recommended. Main courses 8€–15€; fixed-price menus 13€–21€. AE, DC, MC, V. Mon–Sat noon–3pm and 7–11pm. Closed Aug 25–31. Bus: 101, 102, 103, 104, 107, or Linea Rossa.

Le Pergamène 🍴 ITALIAN/SICILIAN   This is one of two alfresco restaurants that sit adjacent to one another at the edge of Piazza Marina. The plastic armchairs of this restaurant are green, as opposed to the yellow chairs of the restaurant next door, with which there's a friendly rivalry. The menu lists two dozen pizzas; pastas that include the ubiquitous *pasta alla Norma (with eggplant/aubergine)*, as well as a version with either smoked salmon or smoked swordfish; and main courses that focus on grilled steaks (beef, pork, and veal), roulades, and fresh fish.

Piazza Marina 48-49. ⓒ **091-6166142.** Pizzas 6€–10€; main courses 7€–18€. MC, V. Daily 5pm–2am. Bus: 103, 105, or 225.

di Camillo Benso ★ ☺ 🔥 ITALIAN   In the tiny side street nes-
~~~Feltrinelli and the Banca D'Italia, this new eatery is by far the best
~~~taurant in town, and gives a whole new meaning to fast food. Housed in
~~~old movie theater where the Art Deco has been preserved, it serves up a plethora
of hot-and-cold pastas, meats, and vegetables, with nods to Sicilian cuisine like
caponatina and breaded vegetables.

Via Lucifora 11. ℂ **091-7573452.** All you can eat 10€. MC, V. Mon–Sun 11am–3pm. Thurs–Sat 7–9pm.
Bus: 101, 102, 103, 107, or Linea Rossa.

Pasticceria Alba ★ SICILIAN/PASTRIES   This bar has been a Palermo institution since 1955. This is the home of the famous regional dessert of candied fruit,
marzipan, and sponge cake—it's a delight if you're not afraid of a diabetic coma. The
homemade ice creams deserve an award, especially the creations made with pistachio, and the *frutta martorana* (fruits made of almond paste) will dazzle you. You can
also go the whole hog on savory dishes—their *arancine* (rice ball with ham and
cheese), a typical Sicilian specialty, is the best in town. The location is at the top of
Via della Libertà, near the entrance to La Favorita Park.

Piazza Don Bosco 7C. ℂ **091-309016.** www.pasticceriaalba.it. Pastries 1.50€–2€; main courses 4€–7€.
AE, DC, MC, V. Tues–Sun 7:30am–11pm. Bus: 603 or 833.

Strascinu ★★ 🎒 SICILIAN   It's a bit inconvenient to reach, as it's on the outskirts of town, but serious foodies head here knowing that it's worth the effort. This
eatery has been a local favorite since it was opened in 1974 by Don Peppino, an
expert on Sicilian gastronomy and a great devotee of island tradition. He wanted his
restaurant to be typically Sicilian, not just in its cuisine but in its atmosphere. Inside,
the decor is adorned with Sicilian handicrafts. Made only with market-fresh ingredients, dishes are based on time-tested recipes—nothing experimental here. The
fish is on display for clients to choose, as is the huge array of all-you-can-eat starters.
An appetizing selection of meat dishes is highlighted by *arrosto misto di carne*
(stuffed meat rolls, lamb cutlets, various slices of roasts, and sausages). You might
also opt for fresh prawns with chicory-flavored rice.

JUICE bars, GELATERIE, & STREET FOOD

Juice bars were once the place where *palermitani* would quench their thirst after a long stroll on a hot summer day. Today most are long gone, but a few are still found here and there: In Piazza Kalsa, in Piazza Beati Paoli, and at the Cala near Piazza Marina, where during the summer locals throng the place to eat fresh fruit, or have a *sciopettino,* a small bottle of water, spiked with *zammú* (anise). Gelaterie are ubiquitous around town, but if you can try only one, head straight to the Cremolada in Piazza Alberico Gentili, at the cross-section between Via Libertà and Via Notarbartolo. What Cremolada offers is neither ice nor ice cream; it's a smooth concoction, which the owner is trying to patent, offered in all flavors imaginable. For serious street food, head to Francu u' Vastiddraru, the dingy, rickety place at the end of Corso Vittorio Emanuele, near Piazza Marina. It has lines going around the corner at lunchtime.

Viale Regione Siciliana 2286. (✆ **091-401292.** Main courses 8€–18€ MC, V. Daily noon–4pm and 7:30pm–midnight. Closed Aug 14–30. There's no bus, so hop in a taxi to reach the place.

Zia Pina ★★★ 🍴 SICILIAN   You might risk passing this place up, or avoid it altogether, as the derelict, unsavory surroundings are very off-putting. But what looks like someone's outdoor kitchen is actually one of the busiest eateries in Palermo, with well-dressed businessmen packing the plastic tables that line the streets. The service is brusque, the locale very Spartan, and the impromptu entertainment consisting of the local drunk who sings songs in dialect add to the charm—the food is the freshest you can have, cooked right in front of you, and you get to choose your own fish, which the menacing-looking owner prepares for you. Open for lunch only.

Via Argenteria 67. No phone. Main courses 5€. Cash only. Daily 12:30–3pm. Bus: 101, 102, 103, 104, 139, Linea Rossa.

THE TOP FIVE ATTRACTIONS

You should give Palermo at least 3 days, and even then you will have grasped only some of its highlights. If you have only a day for the artistic monuments of Sicily's capital, here's how the top-five sights rank on a very short A-list:

1. **Palazzo dei Normanni/Cappella Palatina**
2. **San Giovanni degli Eremiti**
3. **Museo Archeologico Regionale**
4. **Catacombe dei Cappuccini**
5. **Galleria Regionale della Sicilia**

Palazzo dei Normanni (Palace of the Normans) ★★   This is Palermo's greatest attraction and the pinnacle of the cultural crossroads of Sicily. Allow 1½ hours and visit just this site if your time is really limited. It was here that Frederick II had his court of minstrels and literati that founded the Schola Poetica Siciliana, which marked the birth of Italian literature; what remains is an incomparable testimony to Palermo's cultural heyday. The foundations of the palace date back to Punic times in the 8th century B.C., when they set up an outpost in the highest part of the city. In the 9th century A.D. the Arabs built the palace for their emirs, and under Norman domination it was brought to its full splendor, hence the name Norman Palace. Of the four towers that once stood, only two remain. Under the decaying neoclassical facade that was added in the 18th century, you can still see the original medieval architecture. At the top of the Torre Pisana is the **Astronomical Observatory and Museum** ★ (✆ **091-233247**), from which Fra Giuseppe Piazza discovered Ceres, the first asteroid known to mankind. The museum also includes his famous Ramsden Circle.

Entering from Piazza Indipendenza, you'll go up a sweeping staircase to the splendid **Cappella Palatina (Palatine Chapel)** ★★★, representing the pinnacle of the Arabo-Norman collective genius and built by Roger II from 1132 to 1140. Once visible from the outside, it has since been hidden behind the palace walls. Before entering the chapel, you might want to pay attention to a seemingly unimportant slab of rock placed near the left of the entrance, enclosed in a glass casing: Inscribed in three languages, Latin, Greek, and Arabic, it celebrates the commissioning of the Hydraulic Clock by Roger II in 1132. Intended as his private house of worship, the

Palermo Attractions

ZISA

Airport

Piazza
Indipendenza

Via Phave

Viale delle Scienze

Corso Pisani

Corso Calatafimi

Colonna Rotta

Via Gaetano Mosca

Corso Re Ruggero

Via del Bene gettini

Corso Alberto

Amedeo

4   **3**

Corso Tukory

Via Alberghena

Via Antonio Mongitore

Via Porta di Castro

*VILLA
BONANNO*

Via Matteo Bonello

**Mercato
delle
Pulci**

**Palazzo di
Giustizia**

Corso

*Piazza
di Giustizia*

5

Piazza della
Vittoria

Duomo

6

IL CAPO

Via della
Zagara

Via Mura de San Vito

Via Volturno

**IL
BALLARÓ**

Piazza Ballaró

**Ballaró
Market**

7

Via del Celso

V. Francesco Raimondo

Sant' Agostino

28

Via Gaetano
Donizetti

**Teatro
Massimo**

*Piazza
Verdi*

Via Carlo Pisacane

Via Cesare Battisti

Via del Bosco

Via Vittorio

8

MEDIEVAL QUARTER

9

Via Maqueda

11

10

*Piazza
Pretoria*

**LA
VUCCIRIA**

Via Bandiera

Via S. Basilio

Via Giacalone

Rosolino Pilo

**Stazione
Centrale**

*Piazza
G. Cesare*

Via Torino

Emanuele

Via Roma

27

ALBERGHERIA

Via Garibaldi

13

Via Divisi

Via Sant'Anna

Via Calascibetta

12

**Vucciria
Market**

*Piazza
San Domenico*

Via Camillo Benso Conti di Cavour

14

Via Carlo Rao

22

23

Via Merlo

Via Bottai

Via Cassari

24

25

Via Giovanni Meli

Via Squarcialupo

26

Via Francesco Guardione

Via Onorato

21

*Piazza
Magione*

Via Alloro

15

Via Lincoln

LA KALSA

*Piazza
Marina*

17

20

*La
Cala*

Via Francesco Crispi

*ORTO
BOTANICO*

18

16

Via Niccolo
Cervello

Via Torre-
muzza

Via Buttera

19

Via Sammuzzo

Foro Italico

0		1/10 mi
0	100 m	

TERRAZZA A MARE

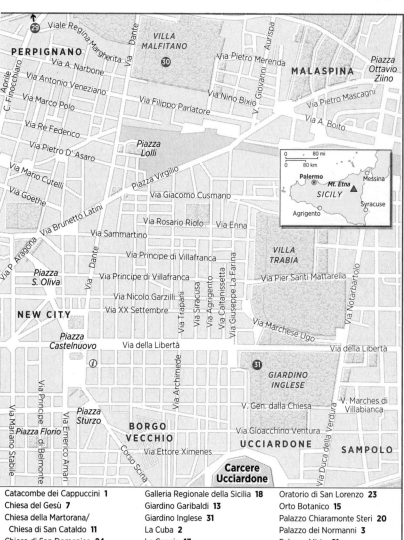

church is dedicated to St. Peter and was the first in Palermo to be adorned with some of the most spectacular Byzantine **mosaics** in the western world. If you can't make it all the way out to Monreale, think of this chapel as a miniature Monreale, though just as evocative. The wooden stalactite ceiling, or the **muquarnas ★★**, seems straight out of the Alhambra, with each nook and cranny decorated with scenes of everyday Arab life. You'll need a good pair of binoculars to see the decorations up-close, though.

The chapel features a nave and two aisles divided by oval arches. The central area is surmounted by a hemispheric dome set on corner niches over a mosaic floor with walls of marble wainscoting. Note the towering **Paschal candelabrum ★** carved with figures, wild animals, acanthus leaves, and, some believe, even the face of Roger II himself.

The whole mosaic cycle reads like a story from beginning to end. Biblical scenes decorate the walls, while the image of **Christ Pantocrator,** surrounded by angels and archangels dressed in Norman warrior garb, is on the cupola. Another Christ Pantocrator occupies the bowl of the central apse; below are the Madonna and some saints. If you look closely at these, you'll notice that these mosaics below the Christ Pantocrator of the apse differ slightly in refraction—some are from the 18th-century and are tri-dimensional, as opposed to the original two-dimensional ones. (This is due to restorations after an earthquake.) You'll also find similar period mosaics in the vestibule of the entrance depicting King Ferdinand and Queen Caroline, and the Genius of Palermo. The colors of the mosaics are vibrant and create exquisite detailing. This mixed inlay makes the surfaces gleam in the soft light. Note how the water is designed when depicting the scenes from the Universal Flood and the Baptism of Christ—it looks as if it's actually shimmering.

Visits to the **Royal Apartments ★★**, one flight up, are escorted, as this is a seat of government. (When parliament is in session, visitors may not enter.) Tours are almost always conducted in Italian; ask if there is an usher on duty who can lead the tour in English. You'll first enter **Salone d'Ercole,** from 1560, the chamber of the Sicilian parliament. The room is named for the mammoth frescoes, created by Giuseppe Velasco in the 19th century, depicting the *Twelve Labours of Hercules.* Two years are engraved on either side of the wooden paneling of the public seating area: 1131, the year the first-known parliament in Europe convened under Roger II, and 1947, when the first Sicilian Parliament convened. From here, you'll be taken to the **Room of the Viceroys,** which shows the paintings of all the viceroys that governed in Palermo on behalf of the Spanish kings. Note the painting of Giuseppe Caracciolo—he is the enlightened Neapolitan viceroy who put an end to the inquisition in Palermo. The **Sala dei Presidenti,** which may seem nothing out of the ordinary, was given a new importance in 2002, when the earthquake that damaged the palace knocked down a wall of the room that had been covered for centuries, unveiling the original medieval structure.

From there, you are led to the **Torre Gioaria** (tower of the wind), one of the two existing towers of the Palace. This is probably the most impressive part of the building, as it was a harbinger of the modern air-conditioning system. A fountain placed in the middle of the tower (since removed) spouted water that, when met with the breezes coming from the four hallways, cooled off the building. In the Torre Gioaria is the **Sala di Ruggero II ★★**, where King Roger himself slumbered. It's decorated with mosaics, but as opposed to the biblical figures of the Palatine Chapel, this room

FREDERICK II: THE EMPEROR HAD street CRED

When you're the grandson of two of the most powerful rulers of the middle ages, Roger II (on your mother's side) and Frederick Barbarossa (on your father's), saying that you have it made is an understatement. Yet that wasn't the case with Frederick II. He was born on December 24, 1194 in Jesi, on the Adriatic coast—his mother, Constance of Hauteville, the daughter of Roger II, was on her way down to Palermo from Germany for the coronation of her husband, Henry VI of the Hohenstaufen lineage, as King of Sicily. Constance had been yanked out of a convent at age 32 by her nephew, Norman king William II, and married off to the Swabian heir to continue the Hauteville dynasty. She ultimately gave birth at 40 to her only child, going into labor in a public square to quell any doubts about her pregnancy. Left fatherless at the age of 3, Frederick's mother also died a year after her husband. He was entrusted to tutors who were to give him an education fit for a king, but he was often neglected and abandoned. Left to his own devices, he got his education by roaming the streets of the poorest areas of Palermo, coming into contact with all of Palermo's diverse cultures and religions—Arab, Jewish, Byzantine, and the merchants who came from all over the Mediterranean. This unconventional education would prove to be integral in the formation of the young king. He ruled with respect for other traditions, in the same vein as his grandfather, Roger II.

is laden with nature and hunting scenes—the one in the center of the ceiling is most symbolic; an eagle, representing temporal power, grabs on to a hare, representing secular power. It's a depiction of the conflicts of the times between church and state. Notice the table at the center of the room: It is not marble, but petrified wood. You'll wind up the tour traversing the **Red Room,** or the Throne Hall, and the once grand ballroom known as the **Yellow Room.** If it's open to the public, make your way down to the **Segrete ★★** to get the real feeling of what palace life must have been like—at least for prisoners. Etchings of Norman warriors sailing on their warships adorn the dungeon walls, in which, it's said, a woman was buried alive. **The Punic Foundations ★**, one floor below, are the oldest part of the building, dating back to the 8th century.

Piazza del Parlamento. ℂ **091-6262833.** Admission 8.50€, Palatine Chapel 7€; free admission children 17 and under and EU citizens 65 and over. Mon–Sat 8:15am–5:45pm; Sun 8:15am–1pm. Bus: 104, 105, 108, 109, 110, 118, 304, 309, or Linea Verde. Metro: Palazzo Reale/Orleans.

San Giovanni degli Eremiti (St. John of the Hermits) ★★★ A short walk from the Norman Palace, this now-deconsecrated church is the epitome of Arabo-Norman architecture in the city. In fact, were it not for the Norman bell tower that flanks it, it would seem like a mosque when seen from afar, capped as it is by five red domes. This is probably as close as you'll get to understanding what the city was like at the time of Roger II. Commissioned by the king himself as a Benedictine monastery, it is set amid a splendid garden of palm and fragrant citrus trees. Stripped of any interior decoration, the oldest part of the church was, with all probability, a mosque, where the cross vaulting of the rectangular hall was once divided by a row of columns. A single nave divides the simple interior into two bays, surmounted by a dome. A small cupola tops the presbytery. The right-hand apse is covered by one of the red domes. Surrounding the left-hand apse is a bell tower with pointed windows; it, too, is crowned by one of the church's red domes. To the right of the entrance is a portico of five arches and an open courtyard. The small, late-Norman **cloister ★**, added a century later, with an Arab cistern in the center, was part of the original Benedictine monastery that once stood here. It has little round arches supported by fine, paired columns.

Via dei Benedettini 18. No phone. Admission 6€ adults, 3€ children 11 and under. Tues–Sun 9am–7pm. Bus: 104, 105, 108, 109, 110, 118, 304, 309, or Linea Verde. Metro: Palazzo Reale/Orleans.

Museo Archeologico Regionale "Antonino Salinas" (Regional Archaeological Museum) ★★★ This is one of the most impressive archaeological museums in Italy, filled as it is with artifacts from prehistoric times to the Arab era. Spread over several wings of this former monastery, the museum's collection includes major Sicilian finds from the Phoenician, Punic, Greek, Roman, and Saracen periods, with several noteworthy treasures from Egypt. The museum is currently undergoing an extensive renovation, meaning that it's only partially open until 2012.

You'll pass through small **cloisters ★** on the ground floor, centered on a beautiful hexagonal 16th-century fountain bearing a statue of Triton. In room 3 is some rare Phoenician art, including a pair of **sarcophagi** that date from the 5th century B.C.

In room 4 is the **Pietra di Palermo (Palermo Stone),** a black diorite slab known as the Rosetta stone of Sicily. Dating from 2700 B.C., and discovered in Egypt in the 19th century, it was intended for the British Museum. Somehow, because of red tape, it got left behind in Palermo. It contains carved hieroglyphics detailing information about the pharaohs, including the delivery of 40 shiploads of cedarwood to Snefru.

The most important treasures of the museum, in room 13, are the **metopes of Selinunte ★★** (closed for renovation until 2012). These finds were unearthed at the temples of Selinunte, once one of the major cities of Magna Graecia (Greek colonies along the coast of southern Italy). The Selinunte sculptures are extraordinary for their beauty, casting a light on the brilliance of Siceliot (Greek Sicilian) sculpture in general. Displayed are three magnificent metopes from Temple C, a quartet of splendid metopes from Temple E, and, in the center, a 5th-century bronze statue, **Ephebe of Selinunte ★**. These decorative friezes cover the period from the 6th century B.C. to the 5th century B.C., depicting such scenes as Perseus slaying Medusa, the Rape of Europa by Zeus, and Actaeon being transformed into a stag.

Etruscan antiquities grace rooms 14 to 17. Discoveries at the Tuscan town of Chiusi, such as the unearthing of funereal *cippi* (stones), shed more light on these mysterious people. The **Oinochoe Vase,** from the 6th century B.C., is one of the most detailed artifacts of Etruscan blackened earthenware (called *bucchero*).

Other exhibit halls on the ground floor display underwater archaeology, with the most complete collection of **ancient anchors,** mostly Punic and Roman, in the world.

Finds from Greek and Roman sites in western Sicily are to be seen on the second floor in rooms 2 and 12. Here are more artifacts from Selinunte and other ancient Sicilian sites such as Marsala, Segesta, Imera, and Randazzo near Catania. These include **funereal aedicules** (openings framed by two columns, an entablature, and usually a pediment), **oil lamps,** and **votive terra cottas.**

In room 7 is a remarkable and rare series of large Roman bronzes, including the most remarkable, a tremendously realistic **bronze Ram ★★**, a Hellenistic work from Syracuse. It's certainly worth the climb up the steps. Another notable work here is ***Eracle e il Cervo*** (H ***ercules Killing the Stag*) ★**, discovered at Pompeii, a Roman copy of a Greek original from the 3rd century B.C. In room 8, the most remarkable sculpture is ***Satiro versante in Marmo* (*Satyr Filling a Drinking Cup*) ★**, a Roman copy of a Praxitelean original.

On the third floor is a prehistoric collection along with Greek ceramics, plus Roman mosaics and frescoes. The highlight of the collection is panels illustrating ***Mosaico con Orfeo* (*Orpheus with Wild Animals*) ★**, from the 3rd century A.D.

Piazza Olivella 24. (☎) **091-6116805.** Only partially open due to until 2012. Admission 4€ adults, 2€ children 18 and under. Tues-Fri 8:30am-1:30pm and 2:30-6:30pm; Sat-Sun and holidays 8:30am-1:30pm. Bus: 101, 102, 103, 104, 107, or Linea Rossa.

Catacombe dei Cappuccini (Catacombs of the Capuchins) ★★

If you've got a secret penchant for mummified cadavers, and your tastes lean to borderline grotesque, you should spend at least an hour at the catacombs at the Capuchin Monastery.

Some 500 years ago, it was discovered that the catacombs' walls contained a mysterious preservative that helped mummify the dead. Placed in what was called a *colatoio*, or dripping room, the bodies were sealed in this chamber for 1 year, after which they were perfectly preserved. When word got out, at least 8,000 Sicilians (from nobles to maids) demanded to be buried here. The oldest corpses date from the late 16th century, with the first one being Fra Silvestro da Gubbio, one of the monks, who died in 1599. The last corpse to be placed here was that of 2-year-old Rosalia Lombaro, who died in 1920. (The man who had embalmed her, Giuseppe Salafia, had also traveled to the U.S. to preserve the corpses of Civil War heroes; he died without ever revealing what the secret embalming formula was.) Rosalia still appears so lifelike that locals have dubbed her "Sleeping Beauty." Giuseppe Tomasi, prince of Lampedusa and author of one of the best-known works of Sicilian literature, *The Leopard,* is buried in the outdoor cemetery next door.

Visitors wander through the catacombs' clammy corridors among the mummified bodies propped up on the walls. Some faces are contorted, as if posing for Edvard Munch's *The Scream,* while others seem straight out of *Planet of the Apes.* Although many corpses are still remarkably preserved (some were dipped in arsenic), time and decomposure have been cruel to others. Some are downright creepy, with body parts such as jaws or hands missing. ***Note:*** think twice about taking your kids here—while it all may seem very exciting for them, these are, in fact, dead bodies, and I've seen many a child run out of the place crying from fright.

Capuchins Monastery, Piazza Cappuccini 1. (☎) **091-212117.** Admission 2€ adults & children. Daily 9am-noon and 3-5pm (until 6pm in summer). Closed holidays. Bus 105, 309, or 389.

Galleria Regionale della Sicilia (Regional Gallery) ★★★

This is the greatest gallery of regional art in Sicily and one the finest art galleries in all of Italy. It's housed in the **Palazzo Abatellis ★**, itself an architectural treasure, a Catalan-Gothic structure with a Renaissance overlay designed by Matteo Carnelivari in 1490. Carnelivari constructed the building for Francesco Abatellis, the harbormaster of Palermo. After World War II bombings, the architect Carlo Scarpa restored the palazzo in 1954.

CHEAP eats

With all the wandering around that you'll be doing trying to take it all in, you'll probably work up an appetite, and Palermo certainly has no shortage of eateries. Do as the locals do—grab a slice of *sfincione* or a *panino* with *panelle* from any street vendor who sells them. Or if you're really brave, try the de rigueur Palermo street food—*pane 'ca meusa*—spleen sandwich—plain or topped with cheese, usually ricotta or caciocavallo. If the thought of the gory, greasy sandwich isn't your thing, grab a quick, sit-down meal in any of the charming little eateries in and around the Champagneria, the area enclosed between the Massimo Theater and the Archaeological Museum. The streets and alleyways are crammed with tiny trattorie serving up local favorites at reasonable prices.

The outstanding collection shows the array of the arts in Sicily from the 13th to the 18th centuries. Sculpture predominates on the main floor. Beyond room 2, the former palazzo chapel contains the gallery's most celebrated work, the **Trionfo della Morte (Triumph of Death)** ★★★, dating from 1449 and of uncertain attribution (though it's sometimes credited to Pisanello) and originally housed in the Palazzo Sclafani. In all its gruesome brilliance, it portrays a horseback-riding skeleton (representing Death) treading on his victims. The painter is believed to have depicted himself in the fresco, seen with an apprentice praying in vain for release from the horrors of Death. The precision of this astonishing work, including the details of the nose of the horse and the men and women in the full flush of their youth, is truly remarkable, especially for its time.

The second masterpiece of the gallery lies at the end of the corridor exhibiting Arab ceramics in room 4: the white-marble, slanted-eyed bust of **Eleonora di Aragona** ★★, by Francesco Laurana, who created it in the 15th century. This is Laurana's masterpiece.

The second-floor galleries are filled mainly with paintings from the Sicilian school, including the impressive **Annunciation** ★★, the creation of Antonello da Messina, in room 11. It is one of the two Annunciations he painted; the other is at the Bellomo museum in Syracuse.

In the salon of Flemish paintings rests the renowned, intriguing **Triptych of Malvagna** ★★, the work of Mabuse, whose real name was Jean Gossaert. His 1510 work depicts a Madonna and *bambino* surrounded by singing angels with musical instruments.

Via Alloro 4, Palazzo Abatellis. 𝒞 **091-6230011.** Admission 8€ adults, 3€ children 9 and under. Tues–Sat 9am–1:30pm. Bus: 103, 105, 139, Linea Gialla, or Linea Verde.

CATHEDRAL & CHURCHES

The listings below are all worth seeing if you have some additional time in Palermo.

Chiesa del Gesù Constructed in 1564, but extended and modified by several later architects, this was the first church in Sicily built by the Jesuits. Regrettably, it was another victim of the 1943 bombings. Don't judge this church by its plain facade, however. Its **interior** ★★ is a triumph of baroque extravagance. Everywhere you look is an outstanding example of exuberant Sicilian Baroque, with marble adornments, stucco reliefs, polychrome intarsias, and a collection of paintings and sculpted works. All this overlay took centuries to complete. The magnificent porticoed courtyard gives access to the **Biblioteca Comunale,** the public library known as "Casa Professa." Filled with ancient manuscripts and incunabula, it also displays 300 portraits of illustrious men.

Piazza Casa Professa 21. ⓒ **091-581880.** Free admission. Daily 7am–noon and 5–6:30pm. Bus: 101, 102, 107, or Linea Rossa.

Chiesa della Martorana ★★   Founded in 1141 as Santa Maria dell'Ammiraglio by George of Antioch, Roger II's faithful admiral, the church was subsequently bestowed to Eloisa Martorana who founded a nearby Benedictine convent. History was made here as well: It was in this church that Sicily's noblemen convened to offer the crown to Peter of Aragon.

The baroque facade you see today conceals the original Norman front, usurping the original splendor. You enter through an exquisite combined portico and bell tower with a trio of ancient columns and double arch openings. Once you go inside, you'll know why your time spent seeking out this church was worthwhile. The stunning **mosaics** ★ were ordered by the admiral himself, a man of Greek descent who loved mosaics, reminiscent of the Byzantine iconography of his homeland. It's believed that the craftsmen who designed these mosaics also did the same for the Cappella Palatina. The mosaics are laid out on and around the columns that hold up the principal cupola. They're at their most beautiful in the morning light when the church opens. The one at the right of the entrance is particularly impressive: It is the only known portrait of King Roger II.

Dominating the dome is a rendition of Christ, surrounded by a multitude of angels with the Madonna and the apostles pictured off to the sides. Even with the passage of centuries the colors remain vibrantly golden, and the flooring looks more like a wild garden, with peacocks and frogs inlaid in the marble and porphyry floor. Unfortunately, it succumbed to baroque devastation: The subsequent Latin plan altered the original Byzantine one, and the frescoes have no business being here, but you still get a feeling of how splendid this church once was. The church has been part of the archdioceses of Piana degli Albanesi since 1935 and still celebrates the Orthodox rite.

Piazza Bellini. No phone. Free admission (donation appreciated). Mon–Sat 9:30am–1pm and 3:30–5:30pm; Sun 8:30am–1pm. Bus: 101, 102, 103, 104, 105, 107, Linea Gialla, Linea Rossa, or Linea Verde.

Chiesa di San Cataldo ★★   The Chiesa di San Cataldo is of Norman origin and, like the Martorana, built atop the remains of Roman walls around 1154 by Maio of Bari, chancellor to William I. But because he died in 1160, the interior was never completed, yet it presents a fine example of Arab artistry in Norman times. Over the course of the centuries it has served many purposes: Burial ground, hospital, and post office. The church has a parallelepiped outer structure of layered rectangular stones, while the interior presents a perfect rectangular plan, divided into a nave and two aisles. The altar is the original, and has the inscription of the four evangelists on the front. The church is topped with three red domes; it was spared any alterations and left in its original Arabo-Norman splendor. It now belongs to the Order of the Knights of the Holy Sepulcher. Gregorian chants are always playing in the background, complementing the medieval atmosphere.

Piazza Bellini. ✆ **091 348728.** Admission 2€ adults & children. Mon–Sat 9:30am–1pm and 3:30–6:30pm; Sun 9:30am–1pm. Bus: 101, 102, 103, 104, 105, 107, Linea Gialla, Linea Rossa, or Linea Verde.

Chiesa di San Domenico   Although its oratory (p. 103) is a more intriguing artistic expression because of the delightful *putti* by Giacomo Serpotta, the Church of St. Dominic is one of the city's most remarkable baroque structures, its elegant baroque facade often depicted on postcards. It was constructed in 1640 to the design of the architect Andrea Cirrincione. The facade, however, wasn't added until 1726. Many antique buildings on the square were demolished to give this church more breathing room.

The facade rises in a trio of carefully ordered tiers, graced with both Corinthian and Doric pillars along with square pilasters that form a sort of picture frame for a statue of St. Dominic. Unlike the lavishly decorated oratory, the church has a severe interior that only emphasizes the beauty of the architecture. Its chapels, on the other hand, are richly decorated, forming a pantheon of tombs and cenotaphs of some of the more noble Sicilians, including Francesco Crispi, the former prime minister of Italy. The tomb of the painter Pietro Novelli (1608–47) is in the north aisle.

Adjacent is the headquarters of the Sicilian Historical Society, with its own tiny **Museo del Risorgimento (Resurgence Museum),** containing mementos of Garibaldi. The fragmented 14th-century cloister was part of the first church erected on this site.

Piazza San Domenico. ✆ **091-584872.** Free admission to church, 2€ to cloisters adults; free for children 9 and under. Mon–Fri 9–11:30am; Sat–Sun 5–7pm. Bus: 101, 102, 103, 104, 107, 122, or Linea Rossa.

Chiesa di San Francesco d'Assisi   In Kalsa district, north of Via Alloro, this church remains a gem despite earthquakes, raisings, and the devastating bombardment by Allied planes in 1943. It was built between 1255 and 1277 as a shrine to St. Francis of Assisi. The church is known for its facade with a shallow porch and zigzag ornamentation. Its Chiaromontano **rose window** ★ is one of the finest in Sicily, and its flamboyant **Gothic portal** ★ is from the original 13th-century structure.

After the 1943 bombardments, restorers set about to return the interior to its original medieval appearance, removing the overlay added by decorators who found the neoclassical style more alluring. The interior today is rather austere, with a trio of cylindrical piers and wide Gothic arches. But it still has the light, airy sense of space evocative of Franciscan churches erected in medieval times.

A few notable works of art survive. In the north aisle, fourth chapel on the left, note the magnificent **arch** ★★, superbly sculpted by Pietro de Bonitate and Francesco Laurana in 1468. This arch was the earliest major Renaissance work in Sicily. The sanctuary has beautiful **choir stalls** carved by Paolo and Giovanni Gili in 1520.

Piazza di San Francesco d'Assisi, off Via Paternostro. ✆ **091-6162819.** Free admission. Mon–Fri 7am–noon and 4:30–6pm; Sat 9am–noon. Bus: 103, 105, Linea Gialla, or Linea Verde.

Chiesa di Santa Cita/Oratorio del Rosario di Santa Cita ★★★   The Oratory of the Rosary of St. Cita is a far greater artistic treasure than the church of St. Cita, on which Allied bombs rained in 1943. Only a shadow of its former self, the church still contains a lovely **marble chancel arch** ★ by Antonello Gagini. Look for it in the presbytery. From 1517 to 1527, Gagini created other sculptures in the church, but they were damaged in the bombing. In the second chapel left of the choir is a **sarcophagus of Antonio Scirotta,** also the creation of Gagini. To the right of the presbytery is the lovely **Capella del Rosario ★**, with its polychrome marquetry and intricate lace-like stuccowork. The sculpted reliefs here are by Gioacchino Vitaliano.

On the left side of the church, and entered through the church, is the **oratory,** the real reason to visit. This was the crowning achievement of the leading baroque decorator of his day, Giacomo Serpotta, who worked on it between 1686 and 1718. His cherubs and angels romp with abandon, delightfully climbing onto the window frames or spreading garlands of flowers in their path. They can also be seen sleeping, eating, and simply hugging their knees deep in thought.

The oratory is a virtual art gallery containing everything from scenes of the flagellation to Jesus in the Garden at Gethsemane. The *Battle of Lepanto* bas-relief is meant to symbolize the horrors of war, while other panels depict such scenes as *The Mystery of the Rosary.* At the high altar is Carlo Maratta's *Virgin of the Rosary* (1690). Allegorical figures protect eight windows along the side walls.

Via Valverde 3. (℃) **091-332779.** Free admission (donation appreciated). Entrance to oratory 2€ adults & children. Mon–Sat 9am–1pm. Bus: 101, 102, 103, 104, 107, 122, or Linea Rossa.

Chiesa di Sant'Agostino   Its **facade ★** is the most beautiful part of this church, which was financed in the 13th century by two prominent Palermo dynasties, the Chiaromonte and Sclafani families. Both the lava-mosaic-enclosed main portal and the distinctive rose window are in the Norman architectural style.

In contrast to the classic medieval front is the interior, which was reconstructed with baroque adornment centuries later. Here you'll see the last stuccoes of followers of the Serpotta School, completed between 1711 and 1729. You can still see Serpotta's mark, a *serpe* (Sicilian for snake). The medieval cloister was originally built in the Catalan-Gothic style, surrounding a central fountain. Lying at a corner of the cloister, the chapter house preserves many of its original 13th-century architectural features. Embedded in the wall of the stairs leading from the church's side entrance is an ancient Roman tomb. Sant'Agostino lies adjacent to **Mercato di Capo,** the city's largest outdoor market.

Via Sant'Agostino. (℃) **091-584632.** Free admission. Mon–Sat 7am–noon and 4–5:30pm; Sun 7am–noon. Bus: 225.

Duomo ★★   All those who came, saw, and conquered in Palermo needed to leave their mark, and when this mark-making conglomerated on the cathedral, it created an architectural pastiche that is somewhere between exquisite and eyesore. It is still a striking building, however, and well worth an hour or more of your time. Regrettably, the various styles—Byzantine, Arabic, Norman—were not blended successfully with the overriding baroque overlay, and many of the original lines were destroyed to make way for the new elements.

In 1184, during the Norman reign, the archbishop of Palermo, the Englishman Walter of the Mill, launched the cathedral on the site of a Muslim mosque, which had been built over an early Christian basilica. As the Palermo Duomo took shape, it became an architectural battleground (known as "The Battle of the Two Cathedrals") between the one launched by the bishop and the one launched by William II in Monreale.

Today, the facade is closed between two soaring towers with double lancet windows. The middle portal, dating from the 15th century, is enhanced by a double lancet with the Aragonese coat of arms. The four impressive campaniles (bell towers) date from the 14th century, the south and north porticos from the 15th and 16th centuries. Take note of the column on the left of the south portico as you go in: Incredibly, you'll see a Koranic inscription on the column. It is believed that the column was recycled from the mosque that once stood there.

But if anyone could be considered the offender for the cathedral's clashing styles, it is the Neapolitan architect Ferdinando Fuga, who went with the mood of his day and, in 1771 and 1809, gave both the exterior and the interior of the Duomo an all-encompassing neoclassical style, adding a cupola to the building, which sticks out like a sore thumb on the original Norman design. In retrospect, he should have left well enough alone. The only sections that the restorers didn't touch were the **apses ★**, which still retain their impressive geometric intarsia decoration. As overwhelming as the exterior may seem, the interior is a stark disappointment and, in some patches, it's in dire need of restoration.

The Duomo is also the pantheon of Norman–Swabian royalty. Entering from the south portico, the second chapel on the left holds the remains of Roger II, the first king of Sicily, who died in 1154; his daughter Constance, who died in 1198; her husband Henry VI of Hohenstaufen, who died the year before; and Constance and Henry's son, Frederick II, known to the world as Stupor Mundi and who died in 1250. The Norman and Hohenstaufen tombs are all in porphyry, a color of royalty. Constance of Aragón, the first wife of Frederick II who died in 1222, is buried in a sarcophagus to the right, while Peter of Aragón, who died in 1342, is inexplicably lumped together with Frederick II. What's more, when the tomb was opened some years ago, the body of a woman, perhaps a girl, was also found in the tomb.

Accessed from the south transept, the **Tesoro,** or treasury, is a repository of rich vestments, silverware, chalices, holy vessels, altar cloths, and ivory engravings of Sicilian art of the 17th century. The true rarity here, however, is the bejeweled, cap-like **crown of Constance of Aragón ★**, designed by local craftsmen in the 13th century, and removed from her head when the tomb was opened in the 18th century. Other precious objects removed from the royal tombs are also on display here. *Tip:* If you're really pressed for time and your visit is not centered on religious motives, buy a combined ticket to see the royal tombs, the crypt, and the treasury—the room that leads down to the crypt allows you to see what remains of the original interior of the church, while the crypt itself shows the original Byzantine plan.

Piazza di Cattedrale, Corso Vittorio Emanuele. (ℭ **091-334373.** www.cattedrale.palermo.it. Duomo: free admission (donation appreciated); crypt, royal tombs, and treasury 3€ (combined ticket); free for children 9 and under. Mon–Sun 8am–7pm. Bus: 104, 105, or Linea Verde.

 THE mystery **OF THE STOLEN PAINTING**

In 1969, a shocked art world learned that Caravaggio's last large painting, *The Nativity,* had been stolen from the Oratory of San Lorenzo, where it once hung over the altar. Caravaggio created the work in 1609, a year before his death. No one for sure knows who stole it, or for what motives, but what might have become of it has sparked off dozens of urban legends, including the one that it was shredded and fed to pigs. More than 40 years have passed, yet its whereabouts still remain a mystery.

THE church THAT NEVER WAS

One of the most evocative moments you can experience in Palermo is to stand in the church ruins of Santa Maria dello Spasimo on a dying summer day, watching the remains of this late Gothic building catch fire with the rays of the setting sun. This sight evokes the spirit of Raphael, who came here to paint his famous portrait of the anguish of the Madonna before the cross. You'll have to go to the Prado in Madrid to see the actual masterpiece, but the inspiration for it is right here in La Kalsa.

La Gancia   Constructed in 1485 and dedicated to Santa Maria degli Angeli, this church stands next door to the Regional Gallery and can be easily visited at the same time. In the late Middle Ages, this was an enclave of the Franciscans. Much changed and altered over the centuries, the exterior of La Gancia contains a Gothic portal with a bas-relief on the arch. Inside, the nave is without aisles but contains a total of 16 side chapels and a marble floor in different hues.

The sculptor Giacomo Serpotta added baroque stucco decorations. The patterned **wooden ceiling ★** is romantically painted with stars on a blue background. The chief treasure of La Gancia is a splendid **organ ★★** by Raffaele della Valle that dates from the late 1500s, making it the oldest in Palermo. At the marble pulpit, look for the **relief tondi of the _Annunciation,_** the work of Antonello Gagini in the 16th century. As a curiosity, note the **novice monk ★** peering over the top of a cornice in the chapel to the left of the main altar.

Via Alloro 27. ℂ **091-6165221.** Free admission. Mon-Sat 9:30am-noon and 3-6pm; Sun 10am-12:30pm. Bus: 103, 105, or Linea Gialla.

Oratorio del Rosario di San Domenico ★★★   Located in the area of the colorful Vucciria, the Oratory of the Rosary of St. Dominic was founded in the closing years of the 16th century by the Society of the Holy Rosary. Two of its most outstanding members were the sculptor Giacomo Serpotta and the painter Pietro Novelli, both of whom left a legacy of their artistic genius in this oratory.

In allure, this oratory is the equal of the Oratorio di San Lorenzo, which also displays Serpotta's artistic flavor. The sculptor excelled in the use of marble and polychrome, but it was in stucco that he earned his greatest fame. From 1714 to 1717, he decorated this second oratory with his delightfully expressive _putti_ (cherubs), who are locked forever in a playground of happy antics.

Themes throughout the oratory are wide ranging, depicting everything from Allegories of the Virtues to the Apocalypse of St. John. Particularly graphic is a depiction of a writhing "Devil Falling from Heaven." At the high altar is a masterpiece by Anthony Van Dyck, the _Madonna of the Rosary_ (1628). Pietro Novelli frescoed the ceiling with the _Coronation of the Virgin._

Via dei Bambinai.ℂ **091-332779.** Free admission (donation appreciated). Mon 3-6pm; Tues-Fri 9am-1pm and 3-5:30pm; Sat 9am-1pm. Bus: 101, 102, 103, 104, 107, 122, or Linea Rossa.

Oratorio di San Lorenzo ★★★   No longer as rich in treasures as it once was, the Oratory of San Lorenzo lies to the left of, and faces, the church of San Francesco d'Assisi. A local Franciscan order, Compagnia di San Francesco, commanded this

FROM TREE decorations TO SICILY'S FAVORITE SWEET

In the Middle Ages, every convent in Sicily specialized in creating a different kind of confectionery. Many of those old recipes are gone forever, but one of the most enduring is still sold at *pasticcerie* all over the city: *frutta martorana,* named after the old Benedictine convent of La Martorana. Incredibly, this marzipan was molded into various fruit and vegetable shapes to decorate the barren trees in the winter months. Today, these almond-paste goodies resemble anything from frogs to cars. The *frutta martorana* are most abundant in the bakeries and pastry shops before the feast day of All Saints, in early November, when the marzipan is freshest.

oratory constructed back in 1569. Its stunning mahogany pews, laced with mother-of-pearl, were created during the 18th century and rest on carved supports.

Of extraordinary elegance, the interior's **stucco decoration ★★** is the masterpiece of Giacomo Serpotta, who worked on it between 1698 and 1710. It features a series of 10 symbolic statues, plus panels relating the details of the lives of St. Francis and St. Lawrence. Art historians have written of these wall paintings as "a cave of white coral." Some of the most expressive of the stuccoes depict the martyrdom of St. Lawrence. Paintings alternate with statues of the Virtues. In total contrast to the serene Virtues and the solemn nudes is the cavalcade of *putti,* who romp gaily, making soap bubbles or kissing one another.

Via dell'Immacolatella. (*C*) **091-582370.** Free admission. Mon–Sat 9am–1pm. Bus: 103, 105, or Linea Gialla.

THE BEST OF THE PALACES

La Cuba ★ "Cuba" is a Sicilian derivation of the Arabic *Ka'aba,* meaning "cube" or "square-shaped structure," which is the shape of this building. Built in 1180 by King William II, it was a kind of summer palace, or *sollazzo,* with vast royal gardens where the court came to escape the heat. A tall building with a rectangular plan, it is a magnificent piece of Fatimid architecture. The interior of the original structure had a hall that rose the full height of the building and was covered by a dome.

Giovanni Boccaccio made La Cuba a setting in his tales of *The Decameron.* After it fell from royal use, it was privately owned, becoming a leper colony. While you're there, make sure to pop into the **Punic Necropolis ★** next door.

Corso Calatafimi 100 (in the Tukory Barracks opposite Via Quarto dei Mille). (*C*) **091-590299.** Admission 2€ adults; free for children 17 and under and EU citizens 65 and over. Mon–Sat 9am–7pm; Sun 9am–1pm. Bus: 105, 304, 309, 339, or 389.

La Zisa ★ Only the shell of the former Moorish palace remains, yet an aura of *Arabian Nights* still lingers about the place. With a little imagination you can conjure up dancers who entertained the various sultans centuries ago.

Moorish craftsmen started the palace in 1166 under William I; it was finished in 1175 for his son, William II. La Zisa (from the Arabic "*al-aziz,*" meaning "the splendid") was the major building in a royal park that also embraced La Cuba. This beautifully landscaped park was called "Genoard," meaning "terrestrial paradise," and was celebrated throughout Europe in the Middle Ages. The park was fenced in so that wild animals could roam about. Unfortunately, by the 16th century, the palace's heyday was all but a memory, and it was used as a depository for objects contaminated by the plague. When the north wing of the building collapsed in 1971, the local government finally decided to intervene. It was fully restored in 1992.

The structure you see today is high and compact. Two square towers flank the short sides of the castle. With its richness long stripped away, the interior is no longer remarkable, but you can still get some impression of the former sultan's palace. On the ground floor as you enter is the **Fountain Hall** ★, built on a cross plan and still embellished with a strip of mosaics. On the second floor is the **Museum of Islamic Art,** which houses a good collection of Arabic art and artifacts.

Piazza Gugliemo il Buono (near Piazza Camporeale at the end of Via Dante). ℂ **091-6520269.** Admission 6€ adults; free for children 17 and under and EU citizens 65 and over. Mon–Sat 9am–noon and 3–7pm; Sun 9am–1pm. Bus: 106, 124, or 134.

Palazzo Chiaramonte Steri ★★★   Overlooked by many visitors to Palermo, the palace that dominates Piazza Marina deserves at least 2 hours of your time, because for centuries the city's vicissitudes revolved around this building. Built in 1307 as a home and fortress by the powerful Chiaromonte family, the descendants added the second floor some 40 years later. But it was Manfredi Chiaromonte, the last of the descendants, who commissioned the masterpiece **Hall of the Barons** and its **wooden ceiling** ★★★, with more than 200 sq m (2,153 sq ft.) of richly decorated beams depicting Biblical episodes, stories of mythology, and moments of the chivalric cycle. It is considered a veritable medieval encyclopedia. The Aragonese made this their palace when they killed off the dynasty, and in 1601 the Spanish Inquisition officially set up shop here for 180 years. On the ground floor are the **Philippine Prisons,** where those even merely suspected of dubious crimes against the church were packed into miniscule cells to await their fate—torture or death. The spectacular **graffiti** ★★★ recovered from the walls of the old cells screams of their despair. Another wing of the building, with even more detailed, rich graffiti, is set to open in 2012. For many years, this palazzo was also the courthouse of Palermo; today it is the administrative headquarters of the University of Palermo. Renato Guttuso's most famous work, *La Vucciria,* is on display here.

Piazza Marina 61. ℂ **091-6075306.** Admission 6€, 3€ children 11 and under and EU citizens 65 and over. Tues–Sat 9am–6:30pm; Sun 9am–2pm. Bus: 103, 105, 139, Linea Gialla, or Linea Verde.

Palazzo Mirto ★★   A visit to the nobleman's residence of the princes of Lanza Filangieri is like a journey through the past decades. Though many of the other palazzi constructed at the same time and in the same area are all but abandoned, this one is still relatively intact. Its history as a lavish abode dates back to the early 17th century; in 1982, the last surviving family member donated the palazzo to the Sicilian government to preserve as a memorial to a vanished era.

Pause to take in the grace of the principal facade, with its double row of balconies, open to view on Via Lungarini. No other residence in Palermo can give you a better idea of a princely residence from the 18th and 19th centuries. As you enter the palazzo, look to the left, where magnificent **19th-century stables** ★ feature stalls and ornamental bronze horse heads. Take the fabulous red marble staircase up to the first floor, which is still decorated as it was when the last of the princes departed.

The first of the elegant drawing rooms is the **Sala degli Arazzi,** or tapestry hall, with mythological scenes that were painted by Giuseppe Velasco in 1804. Some of the salons open onto a patio garden with a flamboyant rococo fountain flanked by a pair of aviaries. My favorite spot is the exquisite **Chinese sitting room ★**, with its *trompe l'oeil* ceiling, leather floor, and painted silk walls showing scenes from daily life. After dinner, the princes gathered here to smoke, talk, and play cards. As a note of curiosity, the next room has a series of remarkable Neapolitan plates from the 19th century, decorated with party costumes. At masked balls, each guest was assigned a plate that featured his or her costume. From the vestibule, you can visit another **smoking room ★**, this one painted and paneled with embossed leather. For a final bit of frippery, seek out the **Pompadour sitting room ★**, with a mosaic floor and silk walls embroidered with flowers, elegance so divine as to be decadent.

Via Merlo 2, off Piazza Marina. ⓒ **091-6167541.** Admission 4€ adults; free for children 17 and under, and EU citizens 65 and over. Mon–Sat 9am–7pm; Sun 9am–1pm. Bus: 103, 105, or 139.

Villa Malfitano ★★   One of Palermo's great villa palaces, built in the Liberty style, sits within a spectacular **garden ★★**. The villa was constructed in 1886 by Joseph Whitaker—grandson of the famous English gentleman and wine merchant, Ingham, who moved to Sicily in 1806 and made a fortune producing Marsala wine. Whitaker had trees shipped to Palermo from all over the world to plant around his villa. These included such rare species as Dragon's Blood, an enormous banyan tree that happens to be the only one found in Europe. Local high society flocked here for lavish parties, and even George V and Queen Mary of England visited. In World War II, Gen. George Patton temporarily stayed here as he planned the invasion of southern Italy. The villa today is sumptuously furnished with antiques and artifacts from all over the world. The **Sala d'Estate (Summer Room)** is particularly stunning, with *trompe l'oeil* frescoes covering the walls and ceiling. A few years ago this aristocratic villa became the subject of controversy: It was discovered that Mafiosi were hiding weapons in and around the villa gardens.

Via Dante 167. ⓒ **091-6816133.** Admission 6€ adults, 3€ children 11 and under. Mon–Sat 9am–1pm. Bus: 106, 122, 134, 164, or 824.

OTHER RECOMMENDED MUSEUMS

Galleria d'Arte Moderna Sant'Anna ★★★   Finally finding its permanent home in the ex-convent of the church of the same name, the Galleria d'Arte Moderna Sant'Anna houses a prestigious collection of 214 works from national and international artists spanning the last 150 years, many of which have been pieces shown at various Biennale exhibitions in Venice. The installations all revolve around a historical theme, from mythology to the Italian Risorgimento.

Piazza Sant'Anna 21. ⓒ **091-8431605.** Admission 6€ adults; 3 € children 11 and under. Tues–Sat 10am–6pm. Bus 101, 102, 107, 122, or Linea Rossa.

Museo Internazionale delle Marionette (International Puppet Museum) ★★ ☺   For those who are into puppets (or *pupi,* as the Sicilians say), this is the greatest museum of its kind in the world. In their shiny armor and with their stern expressions, these marionettes remain as an evocation of Norman Sicily, an era of legendary chivalry and troubadours. In the world of the puppet, the exploits of William the Bad (1120–66) and others live on, as do the legends of Charlemagne and the swashbuckling Saracen pirates. All the puppets on display are handmade antiques, some of them centuries old, from Sicily as well as from other parts of Italy. Most were used at one time in the *opera de pupi,* a local tradition fast dying out. The collection also includes puppets crafted in other parts of the world, notably Indonesia, India, and other countries from the Far East, as well as the English "Punch and Judy." The most outstanding artisan represented here is Gaspare Canino, who achieved fame with his theater puppets in the 1800s.

Piazzetta Niscemi 1. ℭ **091-328060.** Admission 5€ adults; 3€ children 11 and under. Daily 9am–1pm; Wed–Fri 3:30–6:30pm. Bus: 103, 105, 139, 225, or Linea Verde.

Riso: Museo d'Arte Contemporanea della Sicilia ★★★ In the recently restored **Palazzo Riso,** across from Piazza Bologni, Palermo finally gets its permanent headquarters for contemporary art. This eclectic space houses the works of some of the most avant-garde artists in Italy, and it's also a "happening" center, abuzz with activities and vernissages. The restoration was thought out purposely to use the entire grounds of the building, so that works can be displayed indoors and out. The cafe (equipped with Wi-Fi) is a hangout of art-lovers and profanes alike.

Corso Vittorio Emanuele 365 ℭ **091-320532.** Admission 6€ adults; 3 € children 11 and under. Tues–Sat 10am––8pm; Sun 9am–1pm. Bus: 104, 105, or Linea Verde.

CITY LANDMARKS & TREASURES

Fontana Pretoria ★★ In the heart of Palermo's loveliest square, **Piazza Pretoria ★★,** stands this magnificent fountain, the work of the Florentine sculptor Francesco Camilliani in 1554 and 1555. It overlooks the facades of the two churches on the square, Santa Caterina and San Giuseppe dei Teatini. This fountain is hardly subtle: It's adorned with depictions of allegories, animal heads, nymphs, monsters, ornamental staircases and balustrades, and, of course, gods and goddesses who make up an encyclopedia of Mount Olympus. One of the statuettes guarding the ramps is Ceres, the classical patroness of Sicily, depicted with a horn of plenty. The fountain is floodlit at night, making it a 24-hour sight.

 SHOCKING, outrageous, DISGRACEFUL!

When the **Fontana Pretoria** was first unveiled in 1575 at Piazza Pretoria, the outcry was so loud it could practically be heard across the city. Originally intended for a private Florentine villa and not a public square, it was uprooted from a garden and transplanted to Palermo as a showcase of its waterworks system, which rivaled Messina's. The fountain is adorned with nude figures galore. In time, Palermitans learned to live with this "outrage," although they forever afterward referred to it as *Fontana della Vergogna,* or "Fountain of Shame."

GETTING AIR IN confined QUARTERS

In the 1800s, it wasn't proper for a woman, especially if she was widowed, to go for a breath of fresh air along the Foro Umberto, as people might "talk." The solution? Right below Palazzo Butera, a promenade in confined quarters, the *Mura Delle Cattive* (the Wall of the Captives), was the area designated for these "outcasts," where they could stroll in peace and not attract accusing looks.

Quattro Canti ★ The actual name of the square is Piazza Vigliena, after the viceroy who commissioned it, although locals refer to it as Quattro Canti. Via Maqueda dates from the 1580s, when it converged with the ancient Via Càssaro, now called Vittorio Emanuele. The square is also known as Theater of the Sun, because at any given time of day, the sun will shine on one of the four corners. Here was the starting point of each of the historical neighborhoods of Old Palermo.

Each of the corners is decorated with a niche in three tiers. The first tier of each niche contains a fountain and a statue representing one of the four seasons. The second tier of each niche displays a statue of one of the Spanish Habsburg kings, while the third tier of each niche is a statue of the patron saint of each *mandamento*: Starting from the southeast *mandamento* of the Albergheria and in clockwise order, they are Cristina, Ninfa, Oliva, and Agata.

Unfortunately, Quattro Canti is no longer the meeting place of Palermitani as it was in the old days. Instead of creamy white facades, think soot-blackened gray—even if they are cleaned off from time to time. And be careful when admiring the former beauty of the place, or you might be run down by a king of the road on a speeding Vespa.

ESPECIALLY FOR KIDS

Palermo is not the world's most child-friendly city. Because of roaring, dangerous traffic, it is difficult to walk the city's streets, especially the narrow ones, without constantly keeping an eye out for your *bambini*. There is one attraction that kids adore in Palermo, however, and that's the **Museo Internazionale delle Marionette (International Puppet Museum,** p. 106). Sicilians call their famous puppets *pupi,* and they are truly works of folkloric art. To see how puppets are actually made, head to the workshop owned by **Vincenzo Argento,** in Corso Vittorio Emanuele 445 (© **091-6113680;** www.argentopupi.it). He also puts on daily shows at the Palazzo Asmundo in front of the Cathedral (daily at 5:30pm).

Away from the traffic, noise, and pollution of Palermo, the city's public parks offer refreshing interludes for families. Especially inviting is the landscaped oasis of the **Orto Botanico,** or botanical gardens (p. 114).

Another delight for families is a trip up to **Monte Pellegrino** (p. 124), a mountain that looms over north Palermo. With its greenery and parkland, the 600m (1,969-ft.) mountain evokes Yosemite. Keep in mind that the park is likely to be crowded on Sundays with Sicilian families in search of a respite from Palermo's smog.

5

Especially for Kids

PALERMO

Finally, if you're in Palermo on a summer day, you might want to escape the city altogether and head for **Mondello Lido,** with its long, sandy beaches. Even on a summer night, this is the place to be; many families can be seen walking along the water and ducking into one of the eateries when the kids get hungry. For more on Mondello Lido, see p. 124.

WALKING TOUR: OLD PALERMO

START:	**San Giovanni degli Eremiti.**
FINISH:	**Piazza Marina.**
TIME:	**3 to 3½ hours. (Interior visits, of course, will consume far more time.)**
BEST TIME:	**Early morning or at opening time in the afternoon.**
WORST TIME:	**Mid-morning, when all the tour buses converge.**

Begin your tour by the iron gates that protect the palm-shaded garden surrounding:

1 San Giovanni degli Eremiti

The best known of all the Arabo-Norman monuments of Palermo, San Giovanni degli Eremiti is at Via dei Benedettini. Five typically Arab domes reveal the origins of the Moorish craftsmen who constructed this monastery for Benedictine monks in 1132. It honors St. John of the Hermits. The church's tranquil, beautiful gardens are devoted to such species as the pomegranate and the jasmine. The gardens lead to the ruins of the original church that once stood here, a structure built in 581 for Pope Gregory the Great.

After a visit, walk north toward the sound of roaring traffic coming from the nearby Piazza del Pinta. En route to the piazza, you'll pass a wall niche dedicated to Maria Addolorata, which is usually embellished with plants and fresh flowers.

Cross to the opposite side of Piazza del Pinta. From here, you'll see the severely dignified stone archway pierced with formidable doors, leading to:

2 Palazzo dei Normanni

The chief attraction of Palermo, this mammoth palace and artistic treasure was constructed by the Arabs in the 11th century over the ruins of a Punic fort, in the highest part of the city. Over time it was expanded and turned into the royal residence of Roger II, the first Norman king. Much of the look of the present palace is from alterations it received from the 16th to the 17th century. The chief attraction inside is **Cappella Palatina (Palatine Chapel),** a magnificent example of the Arabo-Norman artistic genius.

Exit from the compound's stately entrance gate (the same one through which you entered), walk about 50 paces downhill, and then turn left onto Via del Bastione. You'll have trouble seeing the street sign at first.

The M Word

"The Mafia is not invincible; it is a human fact, and like all human facts, it has a beginning and will also have an end"

—Giovanni Falcone

From here, you'll skirt the Norman Palace's massive and sharply angled foundations. After two narrow and claustrophobic blocks, climb the first set of granite steps rising from Via del Bastione's left side. This will lead you into a verdant garden called:

3 Villa Bonanno

Imbued with the scent of jasmine and citrus trees, this public park separates the rear entrance of the Palazzo dei Normanni from the Duomo compound you'll be visiting soon. Dotting the garden are monuments and effigies erected in honor of Sicilian patriots. If it's a hot day, this is an idyllic place to cool off. Pop into the remains of the Roman villa to get an idea of daily life in Roman patrician times.

Walk through the garden, exiting at its opposite end, which will lead you to:

4 Palazzo Arcivescovile

Lying across the busy Via Bonello, a street of uncontrolled traffic, a portal is all that survives from the palace constructed here in 1460. The present structure is from the 18th century. It is also the **Museo Diocesano (Diocese Museum)**, housing artifacts from the cathedral and other works of art from churches about to be demolished.

On the other side of Palazzo Arcivescovile on Via Bonello is the 16th-century **Loggia dell'Incoronazione (Coronation Corridor),** with ancient columns and capitals that were incorporated into the present structure. The kings of Sicily used to "display" themselves to their subjects here following a coronation. As a slight detour from this walking tour, head two blocks north after the Loggia to Via Gioeni to visit the Norman church of **Santa Cristina La Vetere,** one of the churches of the ancient Via Francigena, and which once housed the remains of the saint.

After viewing the palace, head east along the major artery, Corso Vittorio Emanuele. The sidewalk at this point becomes very narrow, barely passable, as cars roar by. The pavement will open within a short time onto a sweeping view of the:

5 Duomo

At Piazza di Cattedrale, right off Corso Vittorio Emanuele, the duomo (cathedral) of Palermo, dedicated to Our Lady of the Assumption, was built on the site of an early Christian basilica, which was later turned into a mosque by Arab rulers. Although launched in the 12th century, the cathedral has seen many architects and much rebuilding over the centuries. The cathedral today is a hodgepodge of styles, its baroque cupola added in the late 18th century.

After a look or a visit, continue east along Corso Vittorio Emanuele on narrow sidewalks until you come to:

6 Biblioteca Centrale della Regione Siciliana

Once a Jesuit college called Collegio Massimo dei Gesuiti, this building is today the home of Palermo's main public library, providing shelter for more than half a million volumes and many ancient manuscripts, including several from the 15th and 16th centuries. A double arcaded courtyard is its architectural centerpiece. It is entered by the portal of the adjacent Chiesa di S. Maria della Grotta.

Walking Tour: Old Palermo

1 San Giovanni degli Eremiti
2 Palazzo dei Normanni
3 Villa Bonanno
4 Palazzo Arcivescovile
5 Duomo
6 Biblioteca Centrale della Regione Siciliana
7 Museo d'Arte Contemporanea
8 Galleria Coffee Shop
9 Chiesa San Giuseppe dei Teatini

10 Quattro Canti (Four Corners)
11 Piazza Pretoria
12 Chiesa San Cataldo
13 Chiesa della Martorana
14 Pizzeria Bellini
15 Chiesa San Francesco d'Assisi
16 Palazzo Mirto
17 Piazza Marina

Continue to head east along Corso Vittorio Emanuele until you come to the intersection of Piazza Bologni, from here visit the:

7 Museo d'Arte Contemporanea

The spanking new contemporary art gallery is housed in the restored noble palace of Palazzo Riso and exhibits one of the finest art collections on the island, if not in all of Italy.

8 Galleria Coffee Shop ☕

While in the museum, stop at this Palazzo Riso coffee shop, which offers lots of local goodies and opens onto the magnificent Piazza Bologni. There's Wi-Fi here, in case you need to connect.

After a refueling stop, continue east for a short distance until you come to:

9 Chiesa San Giuseppe dei Teatini

Forming one of the Quattro Canti (see below), this lavishly decorated church was built by the Theatine congregation. The interior has a dancing baroque spirit, although the facade, not completed until 1844, is along more severe neoclassical lines. The cupola of the church is adorned with majolica tiles. If you go inside (hours are Mon–Sat 8:45–11:15am and 5–7pm; Sun 8:30am–1pm), you'll find a two-aisle nave. Flanking it are towering columns resting under a frescoed ceiling, holding up walls covered with a marble polychrome decoration. The main altar is constructed of semiprecious gems, and the chapels are lavishly frescoed with stucco decoration. The church was designed by Giacomo Besio of Genoa (1612–45).

At this point of the walking tour, you are in the very heart of Old Palermo at the famous:

10 Quattro Canti (Four Corners)

Corso Vittorio Emanuele intersects with Via Maqueda, the latter street a famous piece of Palermitano civic planning, carved out of the surrounding neighborhood in the 16th century by the Spanish viceroy Maqueda. On each corner you'll find, on the lower tier, one of the allegories of the season; in the middle, one of the four Spanish Habsburg kings; and on top, the patron saint of each *mandamento*.

Directly east of this "crossroads" of Palermo lies:

11 Piazza Pretoria

This lovely square is Palermo's most famous. It's beautiful but controversial fountain, originally intended for a Tuscan villa, is adorned with nude statues and mythological monsters—thus, it was called **Fontana della Vergogna,** or "Fountain of Shame," by outraged churchgoers. **San Giuseppe dei Teatini** is the church directly to the west; the eastern end of the square is flanked by **Chiesa Santa Caterina (St. Catherine's Church).** Climb the stairs of Santa Caterina to get a bird's eye view of the square. On the south axis stands **Palazzo Pretorio,** the City Hall. Note the plaque on the front of the building commemorating Garibaldi's 1860 triumph, ending the Bourbon reign in Sicily.

SEE PALERMO THE dolce VITA WAY

All the walking around town can be very tiring, and some of the tiny side streets can seem off-putting. To get into those tiny little alleyways 1950s-style, entrust your tour to one of the men who drive specially outfitted, three-wheeler *ape* that get you around town with little hassle. To reach a serious, reputable driver, call ✆ **328-1543377.**

Now walk to the southern edge of the Piazza Pretoria and go through the narrow gap between the City Hall and the Chiesa Santa Caterina. A vista over the Piazza Bellini will open up before you. At its far end rise two of the most distinctive churches in Palermo, the first called:

12 Chiesa San Cataldo

Standing side by side with Chiesa della Martorana (see below), this is one of two Norman churches built on the remains of a Roman wall. The church, with its rose-colored cupolas, was founded in 1154 by Maio da Bari, the emir of William I. After serving various purposes—the church was turned into a post office in the 19th century—San Cataldo today is the seat of the Knights of the Holy Sepulcher.

Next door to San Cataldo is:

13 Chiesa della Martorana

With its handsome Norman bell tower, this is the more intriguing of the two churches, thanks to its splendid mosaics. It is the loveliest Greek church remaining in Sicily. It was founded in 1143 by George of Antioch, called Roger II's "Emir of Emirs." Regrettably, the linear symmetry of the original Norman church is today covered by a baroque facade.

14 Pizzeria Bellini 🍽

Set directly at the base of the Church of San Cataldo, with a pleasant terrace that's shielded from the dust and congestion of the surrounding neighborhood by an evergreen hedge and latticework barrier, this is the kind of cafe where you almost fall into the chairs, then slug back a half liter of liquid refreshment. It doubles as a restaurant, in case you want a full meal, but most participants on this walking tour opt for gelato, a coffee, or a drink. Piazza Bellini 6; ✆ 091-6165691. Closed Mondays.

Retrace your steps along Via Maqueda north to Quattro Canti (Four Corners). Once there continue east along Corso Vittorio Emanuele on the street's right-hand side. Here the neighborhood grows increasingly battered, commercial, and decrepit. In about 4 minutes, turn right onto Via Alessandro Paternostro, a narrow street one short block after Vicolo Madonna del Cassaro. Walk uphill along Via Alessandro Paternostro through a commercial section of shops. After a brief walk, note the intricately carved Romanesque facade of the:

15 Chiesa San Francesco d'Assisi

This is one of the most outstanding churches in Palermo, thanks to its dignified simplicity and unusual combination of Romanesque and baroque detailing; you get the sense that it's still very much involved in the day-to-day life of this

RESPITE IN THE city

The Arabs, who knew the joy of a green oasis, were the ones who introduced gardens to Palermo. The Normans extended the idea by creating extensive parklands and summer retreats to escape the heat. Today, you can wander among gardens and greenery and encounter incredible, centuries-old banyan trees and other exotic plantings. An hour or two in one of Palermo's parks allows you to take a breather from the noise and pollution, while admiring the stunning Mediterranean landscape.

Villa Bonanno, behind the Palazzo dei Normanni, is among the most beautiful public gardens of Palermo. Enter from Piazza della Vittoria. The city added palm trees in 1905, making the park look like an oasis in North Africa. Note the roof covering the ruins of a Roman villa, the only such artifacts of their kind left in Palermo. Entrance is free, so take advantage—some of the mosaics are well preserved.

The **Giardino Garibaldi (Garibaldi Garden),** in Piazza Marina, has stunning **banyan trees,** with their exposed, trunklike "aerial" roots, along with fig trees and towering palms.

The **Orto Botanico (Botanical Garden),** at Via Abramo Lincoln 2B (℡ **091-6238241;** www.ortobotanico. palermo.it), was laid out in 1795.The garden is known to botanists the world over thanks to the richness and variety of its plant species. Among the curiosities are the *Bombacaceae* and *Chorisias* plants shipped here in the late 19th century from South America. These have swollen, prickly trunks and, in spring, bloom with beautiful pink flowers that turn into a strange fruit. Upon ripening, the fruit bursts open and drops its seed on the ground along with what is called "fake cotton." Admission to Orto Botanico is 4€. It is open April to October daily 9am to 7pm; November to March, Monday to Saturday 9am to 5pm, Sunday 9am to 2pm. Take bus no. 139, 211, 221, 224, 226, or 227.

Villa Giulia, next door to the Orto Botanico and also opening onto Via Abramo Lincoln, is an Italianate oasis created in 1778 and enlarged in 1866. This was the city's first public park, named for its patron, Giulia Avalos Guevara, the wife of the ruling viceroy. Goethe came this way in 1787 and had much praise for the garden, which is also called "La Flora." Its beautiful trees and flowers are in better shape than the monuments, which include neoclassical band shells. The best-known statue is called *Genius of Palermo,* by Marabitti.

The **Parco Della Favorita** is reached by going 2.8km (1¾ miles) north of Palermo along Viale Diana. This was part of an estate acquired in 1799 by Ferdinand of Bourbon, who came here after he was driven out of Naples by Napoleonic troops. He ordered that the land be laid out according to his rather Victorian taste. In time, it became the ruler's private hunting estate. The fantastic **Casina Cinese (Chinese House)** built for Ferdinand is still standing. It was in this exotically decorated palace that the king, along with his wife, Maria Carolina, entertained Horatio Nelson and Lady Hamilton.

In the heart of the city center, just after Piazza Croci and ending at Via Duca della Verdura, is the **Giardino Inglese (English Garden),** the "green lung" of the city. Laden with sky-high palm trees and busts of Sicilian notables, it's where workers come to get air during their lunch break.

ancient parish. First constructed in the 13th century, it was destroyed by Frederick II after he was excommunicated by the pope. A new church was constructed and completed in 1277, although it's seen much alteration over the years. A 1943 Allied bombing didn't help matters, either.

From the square directly in front of the church (Piazza di San Francesco d'Assisi), head east on the narrow, unmarked street on the right-hand side of the church as you face it. Walk 1½ short blocks until you reach:

16 Palazzo Mirto

This is your greatest opportunity to visit a palace from yesteryear and to see how a Sicilian noble family lived. Of the many other palaces in the neighborhood, most are closed to the public and still not restored. Palazzo Mirto miraculously remains as it was, with its original furnishings. It dates from the 18th century, having been built over earlier structures that went back to the 15th century.

After a visit, walk a few steps to the west into the broad 19th-century vistas of:

17 Piazza Marina

This is the largest square in Palermo. Its most significant architectural monument is **Palazzo Chiaromonte Steri,** constructed in 1307 by one of Sicily's most influential noble families. The palace was built in a Gothic style with Arabo-Norman influences. In the middle of Piazza Marina is the **Giardino Garibaldi,** a beautiful park around which there's no shortage of nightlife; it comes alive on the weekend with a flea market.

CITY MARKETS & SHOPPING

Palermo is like a grand shopping bazaar. You'll find a little bit of everything here, including boutiques of high fashion. Many shoppers seek out the expert artisans known for their skill in producing any number of goods, especially beautiful coral jewelry. Along the streets and alleyways of La Kalsa you'll still find ironworkers and other craftsmen who continue centuries-old traditions. Embroidered fabrics are another specialty item. Some visitors come to Palermo just to purchase ceramics and antiques.

Palermo markets (see below) are the most colorful in southern Italy. At these markets, all the bounty of Sicily—fruits, vegetables, fish—is elegantly displayed. Since it is unlikely you will be staying in accommodations with kitchen facilities, the markets are mainly for sightseeing, although they do offer an array of clothing and crafts as well.

For the best shopping, head for **Via Ruggero Settimo** and **Via della Libertà,** north of the city's medieval core, within a 19th-century residential neighborhood of town houses and mid-20th-century apartment buildings that evoke some of the more upscale residential sections of Barcelona. Within this same neighborhood, **Via Principe di Belmonte** is an all-pedestrian thoroughfare with many hip and elegant shops, as well as fashionable cafes. The two other principal shopping streets in the Old Town are **Via Roma** and **Via Maqueda.**

ONE PERSON'S junk IS ANOTHER PERSON'S TREASURE

Steps away from the cathedral on a tree-lined street that looks like a row of abandoned bodegas, the **Mercato delle Pulci (Flea Market)** is a treasure-trove for everything from tacky trinkets to fine pieces of period furniture; even entire ceramic floorings have been uplifted from abandoned palaces and are sold in some makeshift storefronts. Of course, I can't guarantee the authenticity of what you're buying, and you'll need a trained eye to distinguish genuine antiques from fakes. But know this: Some years ago, a university student was seeking some cheap furniture. He purchased a coffee table, paying literally peanuts for it. When he re-sold it, much to his delightful shock, he found out that the table was an Art Nouveau original, meaning he got the equivalent of 2,000€ for it!

Monday morning is the worst time to shop, as nearly all stores are closed. Otherwise, general shopping hours are Tuesday to Friday 9am to 1pm and 4 to 7 or 7:30pm, Saturday 4 to 8pm. Some department stores are open on Mondays, and some shops in the city center are open at lunchtime and generally on the first Sunday of the month. Outdoor markets such as the Capo are closed on Wednesday afternoon.

Books

Feltrinelli   See "Bookstores," under "Fast Facts: Palermo," p. 76.

Ceramics

De Simone   For majolica-style stoneware, this old favorite, a family-run business, has been producing quality ware since the 1920s. It also offers some of the most tasteful ceramics and finest tiles in Palermo. Most tiles are painted with scenes of Sicilian country life, including seascapes and bird-filled landscapes. Also for sale are porcelain dinner and tea services, along with ceramic chandeliers. While visiting the shop, you can inquire about visits to the factory at Via Lanza di Scalea 960 (🕐 **091-6711005**), open Monday through Friday from 8am to 5pm. Via Gaetano Daita 13B. 🕐 **091-584876.** www.lafabbricadellaceramica.it. Bus: 103, 106, 108, or 122.

Tre Erre ★   Near the port, Tre Erre sells ceramics based on 19th-century Sicilian models, but always with a sophisticated, modern twist. The result is a shop that's frequented by visitors on shore excursions from cruise ships who stock up on jardinières, planters, anthropomorphic vases, lace-edged bowls and platters, and holders for votive candles. Prices are lower than you'd expect. Via Emerico Amari 49. 🕐 **091-323827.** www.treerreceramiche.com. Bus: 108.

Department Stores

La Rinascente   Recently opened up here at its new location on Via Roma. Rinascente occupies five floors selling high-end designer accessories; women's, men's, and children's designer lines; and homewares. The top floor has a selection of eateries offering everything from sushi to classic Sicilian staples, not to mention spectacular views over Palermo. Via Roma 255. ℰ **091-601781.** www.larinascente.it. Bus 101, 102, 103, 104, 107, 122, or Linea Rossa.

Eyewear

Spektor   This place is for glasses, the latest sunglasses, contacts, and just about everything else for your vision-related needs. The owner speaks fluent English. Via Villareale 68. ℰ **091-3815696.** Bus 101, 102, 103, 104, or Linea Rossa.

Fabrics

Giuseppe Gramuglia   Traditional Sicilian decor—at least that inspired by the late 19th century—usually involves lots of fabric, in the form of rich-looking upholsteries and heavy curtains that block out the intense sunlight. If you want to duplicate this look in your own home, consider a visit to this store. Set at the corner of Palermo's most fashionable shopping street (Via Principe di Belmonte), it contains hundreds of bolts of fabric in every conceivable pattern. It also sells decorative ropes, fringes, and tassels. Via Roma 412–414 (at Via Principe di Belmonte). ℰ **091-583262.** Bus: 101,102,103, 104, 107, or Linea Rossa.

Fashions for Men

Carieri & Carieri   This is a store for serious menswear shoppers—and if you express the slightest interest, a member of its staff is likely to "adopt" you, leading you to selections in your size and along a wide spectrum of fashion-related statements. The only thing wrong with this store is its intimidatingly large size, which might confuse you (or delight you) when you first walk in. The staff is about as upscale and attentive as any you're likely to find in Palermo, and if there aren't a lot of other customers, they're likely to descend upon you, en masse, to attend to your needs. The selection of suits and office wear is very extensive—the best and classiest displays in town. Via Enrico Parisi 4 (corner of Via Libertà). ℰ **091-321846.** www.carieri.it. Bus: 101, 102, 104, 106, or 806.

Pustorino   Walk into this shop at the Quattro Canti and feel as if you've just taken a step back 100 years—the decor of the place has not changed, nor has the merchandise, which is the finest menswear that doesn't scream trendy but classic. You'll find good-quality, tried-and-true labels. Via Maqueda 174. ℰ **091-580984.** www.pustorino.it. Bus 101, 102, 103, 104, or Linea Rossa.

Fashions for Women

Giglio   This where all the socialites and wannabes in town flock to when they need to buy a new evening dress. Given the vast assortment of designer labels available, it's hard to narrow it down to just one choice—budget, of course, permitting. Piazza Antonio Mordini 9. ℰ **091-625 7727.** www.giglio.com. Bus 101, 102, 106, or 806.

Mazzara   More accessible price-wise than Giglio, it nonetheless offers good-quality clothes, and even has a range of choices for plus sizes. Via Notarbartolo 3H. ℰ **091-6259855.** www.mazzaragroup.com. Bus: 101, 102, 106, 704, or 806.

SEVEN layers **OF HEAVEN**

I might not ever find out the original ingredients—it's a secret kept under lock and key—but the **Sette Veli** cake, the seven heavenly layers of chocolate, has been delighting palates and threatening waistbands since time immemorial. Layers of fudge, praline, devil's food, and mousse are mysteriously commingled to form this attack on the waistline. There's been a heated debate throughout the nation as to who can really lay claim to ownership, but food historians seem to concur that the inventor of this sinfully rich cake came out of the workshop of **Pasticceria Cappello,** Via Colonna Rotta 68 (near the Norman Palace). ✆ **091-489601; www.pasticceriacappello.it.**

Food

Cibus   A gastronome's paradise, Cibus offers all the abundance of Sicily, from gold-colored olive oils to ruby-red wines to pastas in intricate and peculiar shapes. The on-premises catering allows you to try some of their delectable goods. Via Emerico Amari 64. ✆ 091-6122651. Bus 108.

I Peccatucci di Mamma Andrea ★   This small-scale boutique contains one of the most diverse collections of gastronomic abundance in Palermo, each item artfully wrapped into the kind of gift that will delight recipients back home. Elegant bottles contain liqueurs distilled from herbs or fruits you might never have thought suitable, such as almonds, basil, myrtle, fennel, figs, and rose petals. Jams and honeys showcase the agrarian bounty and aromas of Sicily. There is also an array of *peccatucci* ("small sins")—utterly delightful candies made from almond paste, sugar, and liqueur—that resemble fruit or sleeping cherubs. Via Principe di Scordia 67. ✆ 091-334835. www.mammaandrea.it. Bus: 101, 102, 103, 104, 107, 122, 124, 224, or 225.

Jewelry

Fiorentino   A Palermo tradition since 1890, this jeweler is still going strong, offering both traditional and contemporary designs. The pieces are exquisite; there's also a vast array of gift items, silverware, and watches. Via Libertà 33. ✆ 091-7495318. www.fiorentinogioielli.it. Bus: 101, 102, 104, 107, or 806.

Matranga   In the heart of the shopping district, this is one of Palermo's best jewelry stores. Top names in watches are featured along with tastefully styled rings, necklaces, and bracelets. Via Ruggero Settimo 56. ✆ 091-581863. www.matranga.it. Bus 101, 102, 103, 104, or Linea Rossa.

Markets

The Muslims were active traders, and Palermo's markets, which spill over into narrow alleys shaded by colorful awnings, still have an Arab feel. Nothing else connects you with local life more than a visit to a bustling Palermo market.

The most fabled market in Palermo is **La Vucciria ★★**. In Sicilian dialect, *vucciria* means the "place of loud voices," and that's what you'll hear here; some maintain that the word is a corruption of the French *"boucherie,"* (butcher). The market spills onto the narrow side streets of Piazza San Domenico, off Via Roma between Corso Vittorio

Emanuele and the Cala. This is one of Europe's great Kasbah-like markets, with mountains of food ranging from fresh swordfish steaks to all sorts of meat and recently harvested produce, reflecting the bounty of the Sicilian countryside. Sadly, it's no longer as vibrant and bustling as it once was, as supermarkets have come to fill the needs of shoppers. This market trades Monday through Saturday until 2pm. Try to go before 10am, when it's at its most frenetic and colorful. The markets described below keep roughly the same hours.

If you're seized with market fever, you can also visit **Mercato di Capo,** the largest of the street markets that captures some of the spirit of the city's Saracen past. This market sprawls around the area of Chiesa di Sant'Agostino. Clothing stalls flank the streets of Via S. Agostino and Via Bandiera; the items here tend to be cheap and poorly made. More interesting is the food section off Via Volturno, which spreads along Via Beati Paoli and Via Porta Carini. The most colorful part of this market converges around Piazza Beati Paoli. The stalls wind toward the old gate, Porta Carini, which used to be a part of the city wall surrounding Palermo. At the Capo, make sure to visit the spiceman, the polyglot Antonello, at his well-stocked bodega at Via Porta Carini 45.

The third great market of Palermo is **Ballarò,** in the Albergheria district, roughly between Piazza Carmine leading to Piazza Casa Professa and Piazza S. Chiara. This is mainly a food market, with mountains of fruits and vegetables along with fishmongers and hawkers of discount clothing.

Perfumes & Cosmetics

Arena Barranco   Come here for the experience: This is the last of the historical *perfumeries* in Palermo, where you are doted on as the *venduses* open up old drawers and cabinets to get you what you need. Things don't come cheap here, but they're still the only ones in town who have exclusive labels. Via Notarbartolo 47. © **091-344085.** Bus: 103, 118, 702, or 704. Metro: Notarbartolo.

Shoes

Saccone   For the more budget-oriented, Saccone offers a range of shoes for the whole family, as well as accessories. Via Roma 300. © **091-321659.** Bus: 101, 102, 103, 104, 107, 122, or Linea Rossa.

Schillaci   Shoe shops seem to be everywhere in town, and for every price range, but for top-quality designer shoes—no bargains to be had here—make your way to this boutique to buy the very latest in national and international labels, both for men and women. Via Libertà 37. © **091-585452.** Bus: 101, 102, 106, or 806.

JUST relax!

Experience what it must have been like when the Moors had these baths all over the city. At **Hammam,** Via Torrearsa 17/d (© **091-320783;** www.hammam.pa.it), there is an oasis of vigorous scrubs, sensuous steam baths, and soothing massages. Sybaritic doesn't even begin to cover it.

PALERMO AFTER DARK

Considering its size, Palermo has a scarcity of nightlife and is considerably out-classed by Catania. Although they are improving somewhat, many areas of Palermo with bars and taverns (such as La Kalsa (p. 72) or Albergheria) are still not safe for walking around at night. And some of the bars and taverns in the medieval core of Palermo last the blink of an eye.

The liveliest squares at night—and the relatively safest because lots of people are here—are **Piazza Castelnuovo** and **Piazza Verdi.** Another "safe zone" is a pedestrian strip flanked by bars and cafes, many with sidewalk tables, along **Via Principe di Belmonte,** between Via Roma and Via Ruggero Settimo. Some of these bars have live pianists in summer. If you're into the student/rock scene, head to **Via Candelai** near the Quattro Canti for lively evenings.

If you're interested in the arts and cultural venues, stop by the tourist office (p. 71) and pick up a copy of *Lapis* (www.lapis.it), which documents cafes and other venues offering live music in summer.

THE ARTS Palermo is not the thriving cultural capital it was in the late 1800s, but it still does have an impressive opera and ballet season running from November to July, with programs attracting audiences from around the world. These take place at the **Teatro Massimo ★★** in Piazza Verdi (© 800-907080; www.teatro massimo.it). It boasts the largest indoor stage in Europe after the ones at the opera houses of Paris and Vienna, and according to some experts it has the best acoustics in Europe. Francis Ford Coppola shot the climactic opera scene here for *The Godfather: Part III.* The two lions flanking the staircase rival those at the central branch of the New York Public Library. The theater was built between 1875 and 1897 by the architect G.B. Filippo Basile in a neoclassical style, and reopened after a restoration in 1997 to celebrate its 100th birthday. The box office is open Tuesday to Sunday 10am to 3pm. **Tours** of the theater take place from Tuesday to Sunday 10am to 3pm, except for rehearsal days. Visits cost 5€, with discounts for seniors and children. Bus: 101, 102, 103, 104, 107, or Linea Rossa.

If you have only 1 night for theater in Palermo, make it the Teatro Massimo. However, **Politeama Garibaldi,** Piazza Ruggero Settimo (© 091-6053315), is also extravagant (though the acoustics are terrible), and it too presents a wide season of operatic and orchestral performances. Built around the same time as the Massimo Theater, it came to be known as the "poor man's opera house:" Patrons couldn't afford—nor could they mingle with—the upper classes at the Massimo. It is lavishly decorated on the outside in the neoclassical style of the time, topped with a stunning bronze quadriga. Bus: 101, 102, 103, 104, 106, 107, 124, 806, or Linea Rossa.

BARS/CAFES Start off an evening by heading to one of the many cafes in town that offer *aperitivo rinforzato,* a happy hour that is literally a full-fledged meal. The area in front of the Massimo Theater, known as the Champagneria, is crammed with these places that offer all-you-can-eat with drinks, and is without a doubt the liveliest place in town. If you have to choose one, then let it be the original **Champagneria,** Via Spinuzza 59 (© 091-335730), and enjoy a glass from its well-stocked wine cellar.

LIVE MUSIC Palermo lacks live music venues, which is surprising considering its concentration of young people. The city's main venue is **I Candelai,** Via Candelai

WHERE THE go-getters GO

The *movida* of Palermo, where the see-and-be-seen converge and move like a pack of wolves, is pinpointed in two locations: The **Kursaal Kalhesa,** Foro Umberto I 21 (© **091-6167630;** www.kursaalkahlesa.it), is a bar, lounge, restaurant, bookshop, travel agency, and music venue rolled into one palace overlooking the sea. In the Palazzo Forcella de Seta, it has evocative interiors—the bare, tufaceous stone walls are enhanced by lighting that brings out the best of this grand space. And its lush interior gardens are a hideaway from the din of the traffic flow nearby. Some locals literally "live" here. The other go-to place is **La Cuba,** (p. 104). Young ones in the know, yuppies, and fashionistas congregate in this structure that resembles a small palace from the *Thousand and One Nights.* Aperitifs lead to DJ sets of thumping beats and free-flowing dances. The restaurant is just as good, serving international cuisine.

65 (© **091-327151;** www.candelai.it), which has been going strong for 10-plus years. It features mainstream rock throughout the night in a crowded complex of teens and university students. The club hosts cover bands, up-and-coming acts, the occasional international artist, and, on weekdays, anything goes from DJ sets to tango lessons. There is no cover, but it is necessary to buy a membership card for 15€. Another place that's been going strong for many years, and is always packed with locals, is **I Grilli,** Largo Cavalieri di Malta (© **091-584747**). It's really alive and kicking on weekends. For something more subdued, see the listing below for Mikalsa.

PUBS   For great jazz and over 70 types of beer, head to the **Mikalsa,** Via Torremuzza (© **339-3146466;** www.mikalsa.it), in the heart of La Kalsa. It's where aficionados flock for live, smoky sets. You can also order meats or cheese platters here along with your drinks. Bus: 103,105, Linea Gialla, or Linea Verde.

GAY & LESBIAN   Gay and lesbian bars in Palermo are picking up, though most are more politically-oriented associations than hangouts. Many gay encounters occur on the streets, in cafes, and around squares. That said, gays and lesbians from 18 to 70 converge at **Exit,** Piazza San Francesco di Paola 39–40 (© **348-7814698;** www.exitdrinks.com), daily 10pm to 3am. Live rock or pop is often presented. In summer, tables are placed outside, fronting the beautiful square. Bus: 108, 118, 122, or 124.

FARTHER AFIELD

Palermo is blessed with attractions in its environs that can be explored easily as side trips. **Monreale** (p. 127), with its cathedral, is such an important sight that it is considered among greater Palermo's major attractions.

If you don't have time to range far in your explorations, however, you have the choice between land and sea: You can take an excursion to 600m (1,969-ft.) **Monte Pellegrino** (p. 124), towering over the city, or head to **Mondello** (p. 122), the beach of Palermo.

6

SIDE TRIPS FROM PALERMO

I f you want to escape the stifling chaos of Palermo, fortunately, there is no shortage of attractions in the environs: From the top of its headland, **Monte Pellegrino,** you can admire some of the most beautiful **panoramas ★★★** in the area, while for some seaside respite, head to **Mondello,** Palermo's beach of choice.

Monreale would be just another anonymous village if it weren't for its splendid Duomo (cathedral) that is a world treasure, and in the fishing village of **Cefalù,** a town grew up around the massive Duomo, the first of its kind in the area. From its high perch on top of a rocky crag, **Cáccamo** dominates the inland with its medieval castle, while aristocrats once made **Bagheria** home with their baronial manors and villas. For a true removal from civilization, the volcanic island of **Ustica** offers some of the best diving underwater activities in the Mediterranean.

MONDELLO

12km (7½ miles) W of Palermo.

When the summer sun burns hot, when the old men on the square seek a place in the shade, and when *bambini* tire of their toys, it's beach weather. For Palermo residents that means Mondello Lido. In the Belle Epoque heyday it was the place European aristocrats flocked to, and the still-standing Art Nouveau villas are a testament of the carefree era. A good sandy beach stretches for about 2km (1¼ miles), even though it is commandeered by endless rows of cabanas from June to August, leaving little or no elbow room.

GETTING THERE   To reach all the locations below by bus, take no. 806 to Mondello, leaving from Piazza Sturzo behind the Teatro Politeama. By car, take Viale Regina Margherita from the northern end of Parco della Favorita, going through the western slope of Monte Pellegrino. On your way back, you can drive from Valdesi, at the southern tip of Mondello, along the Lungomare Cristoforo Colombo toward the heart of

Side Trips from Palermo

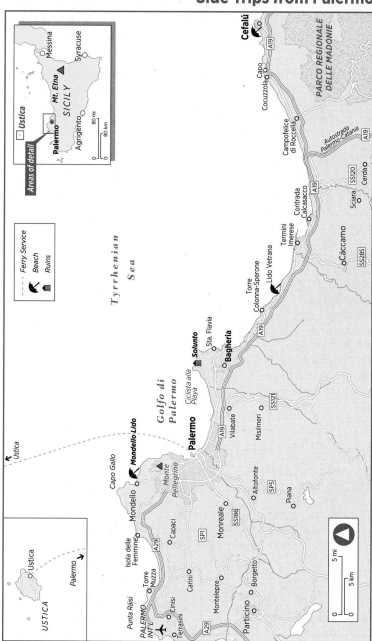

Palermo, going via the rock-strewn coastline at the foot of Monte Pellegrino, known as the Addaura.

HITTING THE BEACH   If you find yourself in Palermo in July or August, **Mondello Lido** ★★ is the place to be. The wide, sandy beach extends for 2km (1¼ miles) from Monte Pellegrino to Monte Gallo, where the latter has the cleanest waters and least crowds. It is the place for showing off your most daring swimwear and for living the good life, including lots of late-night staggering along with the young Palermitani from bar to bar (largely in the center, around **Piazza Mondello** in **Piazza Valdesi**). In the center of the beach, rising from concrete piers above the surface of the water, and connected to the Sicilian "mainland" with a bridge, you can still see the *kursaal*, a whimsical bathhouse (now a restaurant, **Charleston Le Terrazze**) designed in the Art Nouveau style and adorned with sea dragons and other mythological creatures.

MONTE PELLEGRINO ★

15km (9 miles) N of Palermo.

The parkland and nature reserve of the crown-shaped mountain of Monte Pellegrino looms over north Palermo. It was known to the Arabs as "Gebel Grin," and during his visit, Goethe called it "the most beautiful headland on earth." The mountain has an almost symbiotic connection with the people of Palermo: Not only is it where the first traces of civilization of the city were located, for many years it held the remains of a young girl, Rosalia (see box below), who became the city's patron saint, and where a shrine in her honor now stands.

Along its caves are the earliest traces of civilization: In the **Grotte dell'Addaura** are hunting scenes dating back to the Paleolithic times.

GETTING THERE   The mountain rises sharply on all sides except to the south. You can reach the mountain by **driving** from Piazza Generale Casino in Palermo, close to Fiera del Mediterraneo, the fair and exhibition grounds. From here, take Via Pietro Bonanno, following the signs toward the Santuario di Santa Rosalia (see below). If you're not driving, you can take **bus** no. 812 from Piazza Sturzo (Politeama) in Palermo (trip time: 30 min.), the cost is 1.30€.

What to See & Do

After a 15km (9-mile) drive to the north of Palermo, you will reach the peak of Monte Pellegrino. Along the way to the top, you'll be rewarded with some of Sicily's most **panoramic views** ★★★, taking in the old city of Palermo and a sweeping vista of Conca d'Oro, the valley. The paved road you see today dates from the 1600s, when it was a footpath for people climbing the mountain. On your way up your attention will be drawn to a peculiar-looking pink edifice: The **Castello Utveggio,** despite its name, was never a castle; it was intended to be a hotel, which never materialized, and today it is a meeting and research center.

The chief attraction of Monte Pellegrino is **Santuario di Santa Rosalia** (© 091-540326), a cave where the patron saint of Palermo lived. Santa Rosalia holds a special place in the hearts of the Palermitani, who have affectionately nicknamed her *La Santuzza*, or Little Saint. You enter the sanctuary through a little chapel constructed over a cave in the hillside, where the bones (read: Alleged bones)

THE legend OF SANTA ROSALIA

No one knows for sure who Santa Rosalia was. She's more legend than real woman. She was born in 1130, supposedly to a patrician Norman family said to be descended from Charlemagne. Never a swinger, she was a very pious young lady. In order to escape an arranged marriage, she fled to a cave in Monte Pellegrino in 1159 and died there in 1166.

When the Black Death swept over Palermo in 1624, the story goes, the figure of Rosalia appeared to a hunter. She directed him to her remains in the cave and ordered him to bring her bones to Palermo. She was then carried in a procession through the streets and properly buried.

After that, the plague disappeared. Ever since, Rosalia—now Santa Rosalia—has been revered as the patron saint of the city.

A festival held in her honor, every year on July 14, is a major social and religious event in Palermo. You can join the faithful on September 4, when the true believers walk barefoot from Palermo to the saint's sanctuary.

of Rosalia were found in 1624. Supposedly a descendant of William II, Santa Rosalia lived and died as a hermit on this mountain, retreating here in 1159.

As a curiosity, note the thin spikes of flattened "steel cobweb" hanging from the ceiling. This isn't contemporary art; it's done to direct the water seeping from the mountain surface into a container.

Admission is free, and the sanctuary (in theory, at least) is open daily from 7am to 8pm (closes at 6:30pm in winter). Frequent masses may disrupt your visit.

Note the little pathway leading to the left of the chapel. If you take it, after about 30 minutes you'll be at a cliff-top promontory with a view and a statue of the saint. The pathway to the right of the sanctuary leads to the top of Pellegrino, a leisurely hike of about 40 minutes. Families use the grounds and trails on Pellegrino as a picnic site.

You can take the bus back or else descend from the mountain along the **Scala Vecchia (Old Steps),** a stepped path that winds down the mountain by the sanctuary going all the way to the Fiera del Mediterraneo fairgrounds. (This is where the devoted march up—some on their knees—from the base of the hill to the sanctuary to give thanks to Santa Rosalia.) As you wind northward down the mountain, you'll come to the intersection with Viale Regina Margherita—the beginning of Mondello (p. 122).

Where to Stay

Albergo Conchiglia d'Oro 🏷 Situated a 6-minute walk inland from the Lido (beach) in a residential neighborhood loaded with bougainvillea and private homes, this well-maintained hotel has a setting that's calmer and more sedate than those of other hotels close to the oceanfront frenzy. It's sometimes favored by Palermo-based business travelers who appreciate the easy parking after a day in the big sweaty city. Guest rooms are contemporary and somewhat generic-looking, though very comfortable. The hotel's garden—in the midst of which is a swimming pool—is one of the most appealing in Mondello. The beach is private. The in-house restaurant is large, airy, and welcoming, serving a good regional cuisine.

Via Cloe 9, 90151 Mondello, Palermo. ℰ **091-450032.** Fax 091-450359. www.hotelconchigliadoro.com. 50 units. 75€–100€ double. AE, DC, MC, V. Free parking. **Amenities:** Restaurant; bar; outdoor pool; Wi-Fi (free). *In room:* A/C, TV.

Mondello Palace Hotel ★★   This is the most prestigious hotel in Mondello, set on its own private beach. It's favored by resort-goers and business travelers who prefer the relative peace of Mondello to the crush of Palermo. Modern and minimalist, it has an appealing kind of simplicity—a hint of the 1950s-derived glamour of *la dolce vita*. Originally built in 1953, it sits on prime real estate that's separated from the sands of the Lido only by a garden, an iron fence, and a busy oceanfront boulevard. The mix of privacy and seclusion on one side of the hedge, and the crush of holiday-making flesh on the Lido, is very appealing. Guest rooms are conservative, contemporary, and comfortable. Most contain private balconies; the luxurious bathrooms have tub/shower combinations.

Viale Principe di Scalea, 90151 Mondello, Palermo. ℰ **091-450001.** Fax 091-450657. www.mondello palacehotel.it. 93 units. 195€–225€ double. Extra bed 70€. AE, DC, MC, V. **Amenities:** Restaurant; bar; outdoor pool; gym; watersports equipment/rentals; room service. *In room:* A/C, TV, minibar, hair dryer.

Splendid Hotel La Torre ★ 🍴   Tucked away at the distant edge of Mondello's fishing port, this postmodern building rises in stark contrast to the low cement structures that line the harbor. Inside the hotel, you'll find clean lines, oak floors, skylights, sweeping views of the sea, and mobs of European tourists, many of them on group tours. Originally built in 1959, the hotel has a hip but busy staff and mid-size guest rooms filled with comfortable, bland-looking furnishings and tub/shower combinations. One highlight is this hotel's location, on a rocky peninsula jutting into the sea at the edge of the harbor. Terraces descend several steps to sweeping views over the water and the sands of the Lido, about 1km (½ mile) away. Also on-site are a park, a garden, and a solarium.

Via Piano Gallo 11, 90151 Mondello, Palermo. ℰ **091-450222.** Fax 091-450033. www.latorre.com. 169 units. 136€–172€ double; 161€–217€ triple. AE, DC, MC, V. **Amenities:** Restaurant; piano bar; saltwater outdoor pool; tennis court; solarium; room service; babysitting; Wi-Fi (free). *In room:* A/C, TV, minibar.

Villa Esperia ★ 📇   Set on a busy commercial boulevard in the center of Mondello, this charming hotel occupies a majestic villa built around 1890. Touches of stateliness remain, thanks to high ceilings, a walled-in garden, and a Liberty-era decor that's more or less authentic to the late 19th century. Rooms are small to medium in size, with vague references to the 19th century, plus lots of cozy comfort. Those facing the street can be noisy, although air-conditioning and double layers of glass help somewhat. Four of the rooms are in a comfortable annex that was originally conceived as a stable. The pleasant on-site restaurant has a glassed-in terrace.

Viale Margherita di Savoia 53, 90146 Mondello, Palermo. ℰ **091-6840717.** Fax 091-6841508. www.hotel villaesperia.it. 22 units. 100€–150€ double. Rates include continental breakfast. AE, DC, MC, V. **Amenities:** Restaurant; bar; outdoor pool; tennis court; Wi-Fi (free). *In room:* A/C, TV, hair dryer, Internet.

Where to Eat

Bye Bye Blues ★★ 📇 SICILIAN   Savvy locals all know of this place, an innocuous-looking private house that's set alarmingly close to a busy street in the neighborhood of Valdesi. The cuisine is among the finest in the greater Palermo area, though it falls just short of the viands concocted at Charleston. The casual, relaxing dining room is run by Antonio, who used to work on American cruise ships, and his wife, Patrizia, who inherited time-tested Sicilian recipes from her mother and grand-mother. The kitchen shapes raw materials from the surrounding countryside into dishes filled with flavor and passion. You'll be won over by the mussel soup with potatoes and pumpkin flowers; the extraordinary pasta with prawns; or the grilled calamari, a fragrant delight. If the watermelon gelatin tart is too experimental for you, finish with hot chocolate cake.

Via del Garofalo 23. © **091-6841415.** Reservations required. Main courses 8€–20€. AE, DC, MC, V. Wed–Mon 8pm–midnight. Closed Nov 1–15.

Da Calogera ★★★ A stones' throw away from the shoreline, this little place adjacent to the medieval Mondello tower is one of the area's best—and that includes Palermo. The colorful, ceramic-tiled exterior of the eatery is a clam bar, where the owners, who call themselves "the poets of the liturgy of throat and palate," will cut open and serve up shellfish on the spot. Indoors, enjoy an array of fish pasta dishes—no meat/fish main courses here—or the restaurant's original dish: Boiled octopus, which the owner used to sell from a wooden stall not too far from the current location. If you're not a lover of seafood, no worries: A pizza will satisfy your appetite.

Via Torre 22. © **091-6841333.** Reservations preferred. Main courses 8€–15€. AE, DC, MC, V. Daily lunch/dinner. Closed lunchtimes and Tues in winter.

MONREALE ★★★

10km (6 miles) SW of Palermo.

On the Mons Regalis overlooking the Conca d'Oro (the Golden Valley), this hilltop village would be just another of the many that dot this fertile area south of Palermo—that is, if it weren't for its majestic Duomo (cathedral, see below) that is one of the greatest medieval treasures. The interior with over 6,400 sq m (53,820 sq ft.) of mosaics has no rivals in the world. Those who dismiss Monreale as "just another church with mosaics" are subjected to the old local saying: "To come to Palermo without having seen Monreale is like coming in like a donkey and leaving like an ass."

GETTING THERE From Palermo, take **AMAT bus** no. 389, which runs every half-hour from Piazza Indipendenza (© **848-800817** or from a mobile line © **199-240800;** www.amat.pa.it); tickets cost: 1.30€. The **AST bus** (© **840-000323;** www.aziendasicilianatrasporti.it) from Palermo's Piazza Giulio Cesare (Central Train station) and Piazza Indipendenza costs 2.10€ one way, 3.30€ round-trip. If you are **driving,** leave your vehicle at the municipal car park at Via Ignazio Florio. From there you can either walk up the 99 (!) steps that lead to the cathedral, or take a cab, at the cost of 2€ per person.

What to See & Do

Duomo ★★★ Legend has it that William II had the idea of this cathedral in a dream when, during a hunting expedition, he fell asleep under a carob tree. While slumbering, the Virgin Mary appeared to him, indicating where a treasure chest was located—and with this loot he was to build a church in her honor. Legends aside, the real motives that led William to build a new church were dictated by supremacy: The struggle between temporal and secular power was ever-present. It is the last—and the greatest—of the series of Arabo-Norman cathedrals with Byzantine interiors.

THE battle OF THE TWO CATHEDRALS

In Palermo, Walter of the Mill, the very powerful bishop and William II's former tutor, tried, unsuccessfully, to convince the young king to grant him and other nobles more power. He had already commissioned the cathedral of Palermo as proof of papal supremacy while the young William was still a minor. When he was crowned, young William's first act was to confirm his sovereignty, proving to the bishop and the Sicilian nobles who was really in charge. By establishing a bishopric in Monreale, William very cleverly curtailed the omnipotence of the bishop of Palermo. By also building and annexing an abbey to the cathedral, and assigning it to the Benedictine monks from Cluny, William enabled the abbot to automatically become an archbishop without the need of papal approval, thus exacerbating the fierce antagonism between the French monks and the papacy (the latter included Walter). Justifying the cathedral dedicated to Santa Maria La Nova (Saint Mary The New) with the story of the dream, William endeavored to outdo his old tutor. What resulted was a mammoth complex that took less than 20 years to build—a miracle for its time. Unlike the cathedral of Palermo, which has most of its artistic splendor on the exterior, Monreale's cathedral features all its beauty on the inside. Luckily, as an independent archbishopric, it never underwent any of the horrendous "improvements" that were applied to the cathedral of Palermo, and therefore its original beauty was preserved—it's a true miracle that it was left intact.

For the most part, the exterior of the building is nothing remarkable: The facade, facing west in Piazza Guglielmo, is flanked by two towers, one of which was never completed. The addition of a portico in the 18th century covered the fine bronze doors created by Bonanno of Pisa in 1186, who also created the Bell Tower atop the Leaning Tower of Pisa. The northern portico, which is the main entrance to the cathedral, has a doorway created by Barisano da Trani (1179). The portico also has two bronze statues from the 1970s; on the left is the Virgin Mary, while on the right is William II offering a model of his cathedral to her. The real highlight of the exterior are the exquisite apses ★★, seen from Via dell'Arcivescovado (go under the small archway just after the north portico) with their interlacing of limestone and lava to create intricate geometric shapes.

The interior of this rather unadorned rough-looking church, measures 102m x 40m (335 ft. x 131 ft.) and presents a floor plan that combines elements of both a Latin and Byzantine basilica, which was typical of Norman architecture. It has a wide central nave and two smaller aisles, each flanked by nine columns on either side topped with different capitals with religious symbols and figures. Of all the eighteen columns, only one is not made of granite: The first on the right side is made of cipollino marble, frailer than granite, representing the archbishop. The roof made of wood and showing a stark Saracen influence, is an 1811 replica of the original, which was destroyed in a fire.

Needless to say, the **mosaics** ★★★ are the principal attraction of the cathedral, covering some 6,400 sq m (68,889 sq ft.) of the interior and utilizing some 2,200 kg

(4,850 lb.) of gold. The mosaics cover the entire surface of the cathedral except for the ground level, which is decked out in marble. There are in total about 130 individual mosaics, depicting biblical and religious events. Episodes from the Old Testament are depicted in the central nave (the ones representing the life and times of Noah are particularly noteworthy), while the side aisles illustrate scenes from the New Testament. The dominating mosaic is the **Christ Pantocrator** ★ on the central apse of the main altar, similar to the ones in the Palatine chapel and in the cathedral in Cefalù. Right below it is the mosaic of the **Teokotos** (Mother of God) with the Christ child on her lap. The small window above the main entrance always casts a light on this mosaic. Teokotos is flanked by angels and saints, the most remarkable being the one of Thomas à Becket, the Archbishop of Canterbury who was murdered on the orders of William's father-in-law, Henry II. It is one of the earliest portraits of the saint. (He is the second from the right.)

Two other mosaics worth mentioning are on other side of the presbytery, over the royal and episcopal thrones: The one over the former shows William II being crowned by Christ, while the latter depicts William offering a model of the cathedral to the Virgin Mary. The **north transept** leads to the heart of St. Louis, who was buried here after a funeral cortege stopped in Monreale on the way back from Tunisia; it also houses the **Treasury.** In the south transept lies the pantheon of the cathedral—William I, William II, and Margaret of Navarre. William I's tomb is preserved intact in its royal porphyry casing, while his son's, presumably destroyed in a fire, was made from scratch in typical 16th-century funeral style, with his life and accomplishments etched on the sarcophagus. From the **rooftop** ★ entrance to the right of the main door, after a very steep—and sometimes perilous—climb, you're offered the most wonderful panorama over the golden valley, eastern Sicily and, on a clear day, the Aeolian Islands.

The fine **cloisters** ★★ is the only remaining original part of the abbey. It is perfectly square and lined with groups of twin columns on each side, four at every corner, for a total of 228 columns; each group supports a capital (no two are alike) adorned with scenes from Sicily's Norman history. The knights depicted resemble those in the *Bayeux Tapestry,* which chronicles the Battle of Hastings and strongly reflects the style of 12th-century Provence. Also among the designs are animals, monsters, Christian symbolism, and even the sacrifice of a bull. In the cloisters the

HOW THE mosaics ARE MADE

The millennia-old art of creating mosaics takes a precision and skill that few possess today. Around the Duomo in Monreale there are, however, a couple of workshops that still invest time and passion into the craft. If you make your way under the archway just beyond the north portico to view the apse of the cathedral, you'll find one of the few mosaic makers in town. The shop, Mosaico Arte e Artigianato, at Via Arcivescovado 13 (✆ **091-6406036**) creates everything from very simple landscapes (costing just a few euros) to elaborate replicas of famous paintings (costing thousands of euros), and they even offer basic starter kits for the kids to keep them busy.

monks grew the trees of paradise—palms, olives, figs, and pomegranates. In the southwest corner is an exquisite enclosure that outlines a splendid **fountain** ★ in the shape of a palm tree.

Piazza Guglielmo il Buono. ℂ **091-6404413.** Free admission to the cathedral; 2€ north transept and treasury; 2€ roof; 8€ cloisters, 4€ 18-25, free for children 17 and under and EU citizens 65 and over. Mon-Sat 8am-1pm and 2:30-6:30pm, Sunday 8am-1pm; Cloisters: daily 9am-7pm.

Where to Stay

Baglio Conca d'Oro ★ 🍴🛏 This 18th-century paper mill at Borgo Molara was completely restored and turned into a retreat of old-fashioned charm with 21st-century comforts. Guest rooms are modernized and come with small bathrooms with shower stalls. Most units open onto panoramas of the beautiful bay of Conca d'Oro, Monreale itself, or the Gulf of Palermo. In the antique redbrick building, the use of dark wood and Oriental rugs adds to the allure. You'll find this a convenient base for exploring both Palermo and Monreale.

Via Aquino 19, Borgo Molara 90126. ℂ **091-6406286.** Fax 091-6408742. www.hotelbaglioconcadoro. com. 27 units. 170€-195€ double. AE, DC, MC, V. Located 3km (1¾ miles) from Monreale. From Palermo, take Viale Regione Siciliana and follow signs to Sciacca and N624. **Amenities:** Restaurant; bar; room service; Wi-Fi (free). *In room:* A/C, TV, minibar, hair dryer.

ON THE OUTSKIRTS

Casale del Principe ★★ 🍴🛏 This is an *agriturismo* (farm estate) lying 23km (14 miles) south of Palermo in the Jato Valley. The historic residence, turned into a delightful country hotel, grew from a 16th-century watchtower and was converted into a Jesuit monastery in the 18th century. Most guests arrive to enjoy the regional cuisine at its 150-seat restaurant, but you can also spend the night in a setting of vineyards, fruit orchards, and olive groves. The interior is rustic but elegant with a fireplace, paintings, and country furniture. No two rooms are alike, and most of the guest rooms open onto a private terrace with a panoramic view.

Contrada Dammusi, 90046 Monreale. ℂ **091-8579910.** Fax 091-8579168. www.casaledelprincipe.it. 7 units. 50€ double; 75€ suite. Rates include buffet breakfast. AE, DC, MC, V. Follow the SS624 Palermo-Sciacca truck road to the San Giuseppe Jato exit (signposted from this point). **Amenities:** Restaurant; bar. *In room:* A/C, TV.

Where to Eat

Drop in at **Bar Italia,** Piazza Vittorio Emanuele (ℂ **091-6402421**), near the Duomo. The plain cookies are wonderfully flavorful; in the morning, order a croissant and a cappuccino, Monreale's best. Open Wednesday to Monday 5am to 1am.

Dietro l'Angolo SICILIAN   For a modest meal, consider this simple *trattoria* that's positioned within a maze of narrow streets, about 4 blocks uphill (and west) from the cathedral. During clement weather, the preferred seating is on the cobble-covered terrace. Inside, you'll find a pizza oven and a TV that's likely to be blaring the latest soccer match. The straightforward cuisine is typical of what you might find in the home of a local family: Roulades (thin slices of veal that are stuffed, rolled, and fried), lamb or veal cutlets, and *Spaghetti alla Norma* (somehow eggplant always tastes better in Sicilian pastas). Your best bet might be the catch of the day, which is usually grilled along with roasted vegetables. Two specialties include *caserecce* (homemade pasta) with fresh sardines and fennel or roasted Sicilian sausages.

Via B. Civiletti 12. © **091-6407770.** Main courses 7€–10€. AE, DC, MC, V. Fri–Wed 12:30-2pm and 7:30pm-midnight.

Taverna del Pavone ★ SICILIAN/ITALIAN   The most highly recommended restaurant in Monreale faces a small cobblestone square, about a block uphill from the cathedral. Inside, you're likely to find a friendly greeting, an artfully rustic environment that's akin to an upscale tavern, and tasty Sicilian food. You might take delight in the zucchini flowers braised in a sweet-and-sour sauce; a delightful *pennette* with fava-bean sauce; or the house-made *maccheroni*, which is loaded with country cheese and absolutely delicious. For dessert, the most soothing choice is *semifreddo*—whipped cream folded into ice cream, given extra flavor with baked almonds.

Vicolo Pensato 18. © **091-6406209.** Reservations recommended. Main courses 9€–16€. AE, DC, MC, V. Tues–Sun noon-3:30pm and 7:30–11:30pm.

BAGHERIA

14km (8¾ miles) E of Palermo.

In the 18th and 19th centuries, Bagheria became the summer retreat of the Sicilian aristocracy, who built magnificent villas here to escape the scorching heat of Palermo; some even went so far as to abandon their stately homes in Palermo to tend to their vast farmlands. Today it is just a shadow of its former, fabulous self, as the villas were abandoned and left in a state of neglect and decay. Some have been recovered and put to good use, but the grandeur and countrified gaiety have been replaced by hideous eyesores of modernity, often the fruits of Mafia money laundering.

   When the Phoenician settlers landed here in the 8th century B.C., they called it *Bayharia,* meaning "the area toward the sea," yet for centuries Bagheria was mostly an anonymous farming area. That's not to say, however, that this city of former stately manors is not without any luster. It was the birthplace of the contemporary painter Renato Guttuso; another local son, Oscar-winner Giuseppe Tornatore, directed the 2009 film *Baaria,* which was about his hometown. The novelist Dacia Maraini, whose mother was of Palermitan nobility, spent her childhood summers here at her ancestral home of Villa Valguarnera; she recounts the atmosphere in her memoir, the aptly titled *Bagheria.*

GETTING THERE   Several **trains** on the Palermo–Messina line from Palermo Stazione Centrale arrive at Bagheria (© **892021;** www.trenitalia.it). The train runs approximately every 20 minutes and costs 2.10€ single for the 15-minute journey. The hourly **bus no. 4** operated by **AST** (© **840-000323;** www.aziendasiciliana trasporti.it) runs here from Palermo, leaving from the Stazione Centrale, and takes an hour. If you're coming by **car** from Palermo, taking the coastal route (SS113) via Ficarazzi is easier than going to the trouble of getting on the autostrada (A19).

What to See & Do

Villa Butera   This is the oldest of the villas, built by prince Giuseppe Branciforti in 1658, who decided to live here in self-imposed exile after suffering political disappointment in the capital. It was his palatial estate that set off the rush for other nobility to come here, a sort of "keeping up with the landed Joneses." Built like a medieval fortress, Villa Butera was protected by surrounding walls and two crenellated towers, one of which was knocked down in the 19th century because of its precarious state. Its rectangular plan has two sweeping stairways, as was the style of the times. A clock was installed on the facade of the new wing; also added was an eerie chapterhouse, with life-size wax figures of monks. Regrettably, the villa has been ransacked over the years, most recently in 2009, when a collection of majolicas from the 1700s were stolen. It's only viewable from the outside.

Corso Butera 1. No admission.

Villa Cattolica ★   The Modern and Contemporary Art Gallery, now known as the **Museo Guttuso (Guttuso Museum),** was established here in 1973. Most of the works in the gallery were donated by Renato Guttuso, a neorealist painter who is Sicily's, if not Italy's, best-known modern artist. Born in 1912, Guttuso was also a staunch anti-fascist and politician. Many of his works reflect his involvement in the social upheavals of his time (he was a member of the Italian Communist Party). Although the influence of Van Gogh and Picasso is felt in some of his early works, he abandoned realism for expressionism, opting for the strong colors and boldly decisive lines that would characterize his art. His works from the late 1960s and 1970s are dense with sensuality (some critics have even come to dub them as borderline pornographic, as they depict his long-time lover in, well, every shape and form).

His portrait of French Impressionist Paul Cézanne is a particularly astounding tribute to the artist. Guttuso died in 1987 and, though he is not buried in Bagheria, his sculptor-friend Giacomo Manzù designed a bizarre "blue capsule" tomb for him. Placed in the midst of succulent cacti and fragrant citrus trees near the villa, the tomb evokes the blue of the Sicilian sky. In the gardens of the villa there is also a *Camera dello Scirocco,* an artificial cave built under the mansion that provided relief on days when the scorching winds from Africa swept across the land.

Via Ramacca. ✆ **091-933315.** www.museoguttuso.it. Admission 5€ adults, 4€ students and children 17 and under. Tues-Sun 9am-6pm.

Villa Cutò   In the proximity of the train station, it has seen more than its fair share of change of aristocratic ownership over the centuries; its most notable owners—besides the princes of Aragona, who commissioned it as their summer residence in the early 1700s, and the Filangeri Cutò family who subsequently acquired it—was Giuseppe Tomasi di Lampedusa, author of *Il Gattopardo (The Leopard).* Unlike other villas in the area that emulate a bucolic feel, this one resembles a fabulous city *palazzo,* complete with a loggia on the second floor, yet it lost its grandeur once the surrounding gardens were sacrificed to make room for the railway. The building was purchased by the city of Bagheria in 1991 and now houses, among other cultural initiatives, the **Museo del Giocattolo (Toy Museum)** ★, with a rich collection of rare children's pastimes and an annexed restoration workshop. The wax figures that were once a part of the Chapterhouse of Villa Cattolica are also kept here.

Via Consolare 105. ✆ **091-943801.** www.museodelgiocattolo.org. Admission 4€ adults, 2 € children 5 and under. Tues-Fri 9am-1pm and 3-6:30pm; Sat-Sun 9am-1pm.

Villa Palagonia ★★   If Villa Valguarnera (see below) is the most spectacular manor home in town, this is certainly the creepiest. It's known around the world as the "Villa of Monsters;" when Goethe came here on his grand tour, he was extremely put off by its "bad taste and folly." It was built in 1715 by Tommaso Maria Napoli for Francesco Gravina, prince of Palagonia, yet it was eccentrically decorated by the prince's oddball grandson, the hunchbacked Ferdinando Gravina Alliata. He commissioned a series of grotesque statues to be inserted along the top of the wall in front of the facade. Goethe described this pageant of hideous figures as "beggars of both sexes, men and women of Spain, Moors, Turks, hunchbacks, deformed persons of every kind, dwarfs, musicians, Pulcinellas;" he described the animals as "deformed monkeys, many dragons and snakes, every kind of paw attached to every kind of body, double heads and exchanged heads." So repulsive were the statues that pregnant women steered clear of the area, fearing that they would bear similar creatures. Less than 60 of the original 200 remain today.

The reason for such bizarre decor was dictated by revenge: Knowing that his wife had a bevy of lovers, Ferdinando ordered artisans to make monstrous caricatures of these men to mortify his wife and her paramours. He also created an eccentric interior not unlike a haunted house, with spikes hidden under elegant velvet seats and sets of rare Chinese porcelains purposely broken and glued together. A **Hall of Mirrors ★** was built into the walls to distort the figures of visitors—thus, the hunchback got his revenge on those who stood tall and straight, often making them seem as if their legs had been cut off. When he died, in a final act of self-pity, he ordered that the villa be painted over in black. Spanish surrealist painter Salvador Dalí fell in love with the place when he visited and wanted to buy it and turn it into his atelier, but that never happened.

After years of decay and neglect the villa was restored by the Castronovo family, opening to the public once again in 2007.

Piazza Garibaldi (at the end of Corso Umberto I). ✆ **091-932088.** www.villapalagonia.it. Admission 4€ adults, 2€ students and children 17 and under. Apr–Oct daily 9am–1pm and 4–7pm; Nov–Mar daily 9am–1pm and 3:30–5:30pm.

Villa Valguarnera Without doubt, this is the most sumptuous villa in Bagheria. Built in 1714, it is situated in an enormous park enclosed within gates and balustrades—a rarity nowadays for villas. Its splendid rococo decor and sweeping views over the gulf were famed the world over; the villa hosted many notables, including Marie Caroline of Austria, wife of king Ferdinand III, and Stendahl, who wrote that the panorama "drew sounds of the soul, like an arc from a violin." It was here that the world-famous Corvo wine started production. The novelist Dacia Maraini, a descendant of the Alliata di Salaparuta nobility that are now the proprietors, sings the praises (and the mysteries) of this, her childhood ancestral dwelling, in her novels *Bagheria* and *Lunga Vita a Marianna Ucria* (*Long Life of Marianna Ucria*). The latter is a biography of princess Marianna Gravina Valguarnera del Bosco, the founder of the villa. After a costly and painstaking restoration, the villa has been returned to some of its former splendor.

Piazza Sturzo. No admission.

Where to Eat

Ristorante Don Ciccio ★★ Owned by the same family for three generations, Don Ciccio is always a favorite with the locals: The patrons have been dining in the same quarters since the 1940s, which is steeped with old farmer's tools along the walls. The menu hasn't changed much either: The typical starter is a boiled egg(!) downed with a glass of *zibibbo*, while a delectable pasta dish is a ragout made with tuna.

Via Cavaliere 87. ✆ **091-932442.** Main courses 7€–15€. MC, V. Tues–Sat noon–3pm and 7:30pm–10pm.

CÁCCAMO

45km (28 miles) SE of Palermo.

The Middle Ages live on at **Castello Cáccamo ★**, a huge 12th-century fortress overlooking the San Leonardo River Valley—the greatest fortress in Sicily and one of the most majestic in all of southern Italy. Dominating the tranquil village of Cáccamo, the feudal castle was built by the Normans on the site of an older Saracen fortress.

Essentials

GETTING THERE   Buses run by **Randazzo** (✆ **091-8148235;** www.randazzo. altervista.org) bound for Cáccamo leave throughout the day from Palermo's Central Station and get there in 1 hr 20 mins. Cost: 2.50€. If you're **driving,** take the Palermo–Catania autostrada, the exit for Cáccamo is signposted, 10km (6 miles) to the south.

VISITOR INFORMATION   For information, contact the **Ufficio Turismo del Commune di Cáccamo,** Piazza Duomo (✆ **091-8122032**). It's open in July and August, Monday and Friday 7:30am to 2pm, Tuesday to Thursday 7:30am to 2pm and 3 to 6pm; and September to June, Wednesday and Friday 8am to 2pm, Tuesday and Thursday 9am to 1pm.

What to See & Do

Castello Cáccamo ★   With its massive towers and battlements, the gray stone castle looks like something created by Disney, but it's the real thing. It has 130 rooms, its most impressive being the armory-filled **Sala della Congiura (Conspiracy Hall).** You can visit the theater hall, the court chapel, the 17th-century residence of various lords, the gatehouse, the knight's house, the keep, and the guard tower as well as the ramp wall. The castle is rather bare-bones inside, but worth seeing is the **panoramic view ★** from the tower, **Torre Mastra.** The entrance is from Via Termitana on a rocky spur.

✆ **091 8103248** to book visits. Admission 2€ for adults, free for children 17 and under. Daily 9am–1pm and 3–7pm.

After visiting the castle, take an hour to walk around the medieval village. The highlight is the main square, **Piazza Duomo ★**, built on two different levels. The higher part contains a spectacular complex of structures, including the 17th-century **Palazzo del Monte di Pietà,** flanked on the right by **Chiesa delle Anime Sante del Purgatorio** and on the left by **Oratorio del Santissimo Sacramento.** The whole square looks like a stage set. On the western side of the square is the town's most interesting church, **Chiesa Madre,** open Monday to Saturday 8am to 1pm. Dating from 1090, it was largely rebuilt in the 1400s and given a heavily baroque overlay centuries later. The church contains some treasures, including a painting from 1641 by Mattia Stomer, called the *Miracle of Sant'Isidoro Agricola.*

Where to Eat

Don't get your hopes up if you're hungry: Restaurants at Cáccamo are very limited.

A Castellana SICILIAN   In business for over 25 years, the finest dining choice in town is located in the stables of the castle and serves hearty, affordable Sicilian fare. The pastas are the best, with more than a dozen varieties prepared fresh every day. The chefs also make 55 different pizzas. Gluten-free cuisine available.

Piazza Caduti 4. (🕐 **091-8148667.** www.castellana.it. Main course 10€–15€. AE, DC, MC, V. Open noon–3pm and 7–11pm. Closed Mondays.

CEFALÙ ★★

81km (50 miles) E of Palermo, 38km (24 miles) NE of Termini Imerese, 170km (106 miles) W of Messina.

The major destination along the Tyrrhenian coast, the former fishing village of Cefalù has grown into one of northern Sicily's premier stopovers. It hardly rivals Taormina in appeal, but it's trying. The town is most noted as being captured in the Oscar-winning film *Cinema Paradiso.* You can tour Cefalù in half a day and spend the rest of your time enjoying its beach. The town is not only in possession of a great patch of sand; it's also blessed with a Romanesque cathedral and a museum that houses Antonello da Messina's masterpiece *Portrait of an Unknown Man.*

Anchored between the sea and a craggy limestone promontory, Cefalù is a town of narrow medieval streets, small squares, and historic sites. Towering 278m (912 ft.) above the town is La Rocca, a massive and much-photographed crag. The Greeks thought it evoked a head, so they named the village *Kephalos,* which in time became Cefalù.

Essentials

GETTING THERE   From Palermo, some three dozen **trains** (🕐 892021; www. trenitalia.com) head east to Cefalù (trip time: 1 hr.). The cost is 4.70€ one-way. From Messina, about a dozen trains run daily, costing 8.50€ and taking about 3 hours. Trains pull into the Stazione Termini, Piazza Stazione (🕐 892021). **SAIS buses** (🕐 091-6171141) run between Palermo and Cefalù, charging 6€ one-way for the 1½-hour trip. By car, follow Route 113 east from Palermo to Cefalù; count on at least 1½ hours of driving time (longer if traffic is bad). Once in Cefalù, park along either side of Via Roma for free, or pay 1€ per hour for a spot within one of the two lots signposted from the main street; both are within an easy walk of the town's medieval core.

VISITOR INFORMATION   The **Cefalù Tourist Office,** Corso Ruggero 77 (🕐 0921-421050), is open Monday to Saturday 8am to 7:30pm, Sunday 9am to 1pm. Closed on Sunday in winter.

GETTING AROUND   Taxis are the easiest way to get about and take advantage of the city's history-rich environs. **Cefalù Taxi** (🕐 0921-422554) operates the taxis, most of which can be found clustered at Piazza Stazione or Piazza Colombo.

[FastFACTS] CEFALÙ

Currency Exchange
Go to **Banca Credito Siciliano,** at Via Roma and Via Giglio (🕐 0921-423922), near the rail depot. Open Monday to

Friday 8:30am to 1:30pm and 2:45 to 3:45pm. The **Banco di Sicilia,** Piazza Garibaldi (🕐 0921-421103), has 24-hour ATM access.

Emergencies   For the police, call 🕐 0921-420104; for first aid, 🕐 0921-424544; and for Guardia Medica, 🕐 0921-423623. The latter is open daily 8pm to 8am and located at Via Roma 15.

Hospital The **Cefalù Hospital—San Raffaele** is at Contrada Pietrapollastra (✆ **0921-920111**).

Internet Access The most central option is **Kef-aonline,** Piazza San Francesco 1 (✆ **0921-923091**), at Via Mazzini and Via Umberto; it is open Monday to Saturday 9:30am to

1:30pm and 3:30 to 7:30pm and charges 6€ per hour.

Pharmacies The two most central drugstores are **Cirincione,** Corso Ruggero 144 (✆ **0921-421209**), open Monday to Friday 9am to 1pm and 4:30 to 8:30pm, Saturday and Sunday 4:30 to 11pm; and **Dr. Battaglia,** Via Roma 13 (✆ **0921-421789**), open

Monday to Saturday 9am to 1pm and 4 to 8pm.

Police The municipal police headquarters are along Via Roma (✆ **0921-420104**).

Post Office The post office is at Via Vazzana 2 (✆ **0921-923930**). Open Monday to Friday 8am to 6:30pm, Saturday 8am to 12:30pm.

What to See & Do

Getting around Cefalù on foot is easy—no cars are allowed in the historic core. The city's main street is **Corso Ruggero ★**, which starts at Piazza Garibaldi, site of one of a quartet of "gateways" to Cefalù. This is a pedestrian street that you can stroll at leisure, checking out the shops and viewing the facades of its palazzi, even though these are hardly comparable to those found in Palermo's medieval core.

The Romans designed a main street to bisect the village on a north–south axis. Basically that same plan is carried out today. The medieval sector is found to the west, where the poor folks once lived. Noblemen and their families and the rich clergy settled in the more posh eastern sector.

Across from the tourist office lies **Osteria Magno,** at the corner of Via Amendola and Corso Ruggero. Constructed in the 1300s but massively altered over the years, this was the legendary residence of Roger II. The palace remains closed but serves occasionally as a venue for temporary art exhibitions. For information on what's happening here, call the tourist office at ✆ **0921-421050.**

Duomo ★★★   Set along Corso Ruggero, this magnificent Norman cathedral opens onto a wide square that is the center of the town. Legend has it that Roger II ordered this mighty church to be constructed after his life was spared following a violent storm off the coast. Construction stretched on until 1240.

Your first impression may be that you've arrived at a fortress rather than a duomo. Anchored at the foot of towering La Rocca, the twin-towered facade of the duomo forms a landmark visible for miles around. Splitting the facade is a two-story portico that had to be rebuilt in the 1400s. I enjoy viewing this splendid facade in the late afternoon, when the building is bathed in golden light.

To the right of the facade on the south side, you'll find an entrance that may disappoint, if you've already been dazzled by the mosaics of Palermo's Cappella Palatina or Monreale's Duomo. But press on to the apse and vault, where you'll find a stunning array of **mosaics ★★★** in all their shimmering glory. Completed in 1148, they are the oldest Byzantine–Norman mosaics in Sicily and among the world's most brilliant. The tour de force of the cycle is the Byzantine figure of the Pantocrator in the apse. Since this was a Norman church, Christ is depicted as a blond, not a brunette; but his nose and mouth look Greek, his brows and beard black like a Saracen's.

Regrettably, there's little else to see here. The duomo seems to be in a perpetual state of restoration, hampered by lack of funds.

Piazza del Duomo. ✆ **0921-922021.** Free admission. Summer daily 8am-noon and 3:30-7pm; off season daily 8am-noon and 3:30-5pm.

La Rocca ★★ During the dog days of August, it's a long, hot, sweaty climb up to this rocky crag, but once you're here, the view is panoramic, one of the grandest in Sicily. If you're stout-hearted, count on 20 minutes to approach the ruins of the so-called Temple of Diana and another 45 huffing-and-puffing minutes to scale the pinnacle.

From Piazza Garibaldi, along Corso Ruggero, a sign—ACCESSO ALLA ROCCA—will launch you on your way. In summer, I recommend taking this jaunt either in the early morning or when evening breezes are blowing.

In Cefalù's heyday, this was the site of the acropolis of Cephaloedium, with a temple dedicated to Hercules on the top. Over the centuries, residents from below used this zone as a stone quarry.

You'll come first to the ruins of the **Tempio di Diana,** which popular tradition has attributed as a temple to the goddess Diana. Now consisting of mammoth trapezoidal blocks, the temple was constructed or reconstructed in various stages from the 9th century to the 4th century B.C.

As you continue to the top, you'll see the restored **ancient Arab** and **medieval fortifications.** From here, you can see all the way to the skyline of Palermo in the west or to Capo d'Orlando in the east. The lookout tower here, now in ruins, was called Torre Caldura and guarded an unfriendly coastline. On a clear day you can't see forever, but you will get a stunning view of the Aeolian Islands.

Museo Mandralisca 🖐 I come here just to gaze at the wonder of *Ritratto di un Uomo Ignoto (Portrait of an Unknown Man)* ★★, the 1465 work of Antonello da Messina. Unfortunately, the painting is badly framed and a velvet rope requires you to keep your distance. Still, this is clearly a masterpiece by the great Renaissance artist from Messina.

After being dazzled by Antonello, you may find the rest of the exhibitions disappointing. Baron Enrico Piraino di Mandralisca (1809–64) seemed to have randomly purchased anything that caught his fancy, including coins and medals, artifacts unearthed at digs at Lipari, and even such esoteric items as a Chinese puzzle in ivory. After searching for something intriguing, I did come upon a **4th-century-**B.C. **vase** ★, depicting a fish vendor and a customer in heated argument. After that, you must face a barrage of 20,000 shells.

Via Mandralisca 13. ✆ **0921-421547.** Admission 5€. Daily 9am-1pm and 3-7pm.

HITTING THE BEACH

Cefalù's crescent-shaped beach is one of the best along the northern coast. Regrettably, it's always packed in summer. In town, I prefer **Lido Poseidon.** At the best bar here, **Poseidon,** Via Lungomare Giuseppe Giardino (✆ **0921-424646**), you can rent an umbrella or a deck chair for 10€. It's open daily May to September. Another good beach is **Spiaggia Attrezzata,** where you'll find free showers. Other recommended beaches are found west of town at **Spiaggia Settefrati** and **Spiaggia Mazzaforno.**

Where to Stay

If you want to spend the night in Cefalù, and you have wheels, you'll find the hotels outside of town more comfortably satisfying.

Astro Hotel   Originally built in 1969 and intelligently renovated several times since, this is the first hotel many visitors see when they approach Cefalù from its western outskirts. Small-scale and unpretentious, with a hardworking and sensitive staff, it offers well-equipped albeit simple rooms, each with terrazzo or tile floors and a shower-only bathroom. (*Note:* Hot water here means tepid.) About a third of the rooms have balconies. Parking is usually difficult in the traffic-clogged neighborhoods adjacent to the city's car-free inner core, but here it's free and readily available within a walled-in lot directly across the street. The hotel lies just uphill from the private beach, about a 12-minute walk from the medieval core.

Via Roma 105, 90015 Cefalù. ℭ **0921-421639.** Fax 0921-423103. www.astrohotel.it. 30 units. 80€–180€ double; 110€–220€ triple. Rates include buffet breakfast. AE, DC, MC, V. Free parking. **Amenities:** Restaurant; bar; babysitting; laundry service. *In room:* A/C, TV.

Hotel Tourist 🏆   Despite its lackluster name, this is a desirable hotel dating from 1970 but renovated many times since. It enjoys a tranquil position on the beach, about a 10-minute walk from the center, and is situated to offer scenic views of not only the water but also Cefalù itself. Bedrooms are midsize and simply adorned, each equipped with a shower-only bathroom. The most desirable units have balconies with views of the sea. A private beach lies across the highway from the hotel. The staff is one of the most helpful in the area, serving an excellent breakfast to fortify you for the day ahead.

Lungomare Giardina, 90015 Cefalù. ℭ **0921-421750.** Fax 0921-923916. www.touristhotel.it. 46 units. 90€–230€. Rates include continental breakfast. AE, MC, V. Free parking. **Amenities:** Restaurant; bar; outdoor pool; laundry service. *In room:* A/C, TV, minibar, hair dryer.

Kalura ★ ☺   Set amid palm trees, Kalura has something of a North African feel to it. This snug retreat is 3km (2 miles) east along the coast on a little promontory, a 20-minute walk from the center of Cefalù (follow the street signs from town to reach it). Run by the same family for nearly 3 decades, it's a friendly, inviting oasis. Guest rooms are well furnished; most open onto a sea view. Nothing is too elaborate here, including the simple shower-only bathrooms. A special park is reserved for children, one reason this is a very family-friendly place. The private beach offers good swimming in unpolluted waters. The hotel is also the most sports-conscious in the area, and can arrange excursions to nearby attractions as well.

Via Cavallaro 13, 90015 Contrada Caldura. ℭ **0921-421354.** Fax 0921-423122. www.hotel-kalura.com. 73 units. 190€ double. Rates include continental breakfast. AE, DC, MC, V. Closed Nov 1–Mar 7. **Amenities:** Restaurant; 2 bars; outdoor pool; mountain bikes; watersports equipment/rentals; children's park; room service; babysitting; laundry service. *In room:* A/C, TV, hair dryer.

Riva del Sole ★   The town's finest accommodations are in a three-story building rising along the seafront. Completely refurbished, it has its own discreet charm and harmonious styling in both its public and private rooms. Run by the Cimino family since it opened in 1966, it offers both attentive service and a welcoming atmosphere. Special features include a graceful garden, a solarium, a panoramic terrace, and an intimate bar. Bedrooms are midsize, tastefully furnished, and well equipped,

SIDE TRIPS FROM PALERMO | Cefalù

each with a private balcony or veranda opening onto the water. The chefs do best with their take on Sicilian cuisine, but also turn out well-crafted Italian dishes and international specialties.

Lungomare G. Giardina, 90015 Cefalù. ⓒ **0921-421230.** Fax 0921-421984. www.rivadelsole.com. 28 units. 140€–150€ double; 190€–200€ triple. Rates include buffet breakfast. AE, MC, V. Free parking. Closed Oct to mid-Dec. **Amenities:** Restaurant; bar; room service; babysitting; laundry service; smoke-free rooms. *In room:* A/C, TV, minibar.

Where to Eat

If you're thinking of a picnic, you can pick up some delights at **Gatta Gaetano Alimentari e Salumeria,** Corso Ruggero 152 (ⓒ 0921-423156). This well-stocked deli offers the best of Sicilian cheeses and sausages, along with cured meats, to-die-for olives, and luscious fruits—everything except bread, which you'll find sold in many places all over town.

For the best cakes and cookies, stop by **Pasticceria Serio Pietro,** V. G. Giglio 29 (ⓒ 0921-422293), which also sells more than a dozen flavors of the most delicious gelato in town.

MODERATE

Al Porticciolo ★ SICILIAN   At the seafront end of the old town, nearly adjacent to the old port, this restaurant is set within a cave-like stone-sided room that used to be a storage point for fish (long before the days of refrigeration). During the day, dine indoors in air-conditioned comfort to avoid the heat, but at night (when all traffic is stopped along this street), opt for an outdoor table. The traditional pasta with sardines is well prepared here, but I'm also fond of the tagliatelle of octopus, the addictive grilled radicchio, and the country-style kettle of mussel soup—just right for a seafaring town. The *cassata Siciliana* (layered sponge cake filled with ricotta, chocolate, and candied fruits) here is among the best I've ever tasted.

Via Carlo Ortolani di Bordonaro 66. ⓒ **0921-921981.** Main courses 8€–19€; fixed-price menus 20€–35€. AE, DC, MC, V. Thurs–Tues noon–3pm and 7pm–midnight. Closed Nov to mid-Dec.

Kentia ★★ ITALIAN   This restaurant manages to evoke a bit more glamour, and a lot more style, than some of its nearby competitors. It's a cool hideaway from the oppressive sun, thanks in part to tiled floors, high masonry vaulting, and an understated elegance. A dozen homemade pasta dishes are prepared daily, and you'd have to walk to Messina to find swordfish as good as it's grilled here. I generally stick to the *pesce del giorno* (catch of the day), which can be grilled to your specifications. The chefs also prepare a daily vegetarian fixed-price menu as well as one devoted entirely to fish.

Via N. Botta 15. ⓒ **0921-423801.** Reservations recommended. Main courses 7€–15€; fixed-price vegetarian menu 18€; fixed-price fish menu 30€. AE, DC, MC, V. June–Sept daily noon–3pm and 7:30–11pm; Oct–May Wed–Mon noon–3pm and 7:30–11pm.

La Brace SICILIAN/INTERNATIONAL   This has been a landmark restaurant in Cefalù since 1977. It's near the Duomo, on an impossibly narrow cobblestone street about a block downhill from the center of town. The Sicilian cuisine here has a number of imaginative Asian and other international touches—a surprise in this part of the world. I recommend the tagliatelle with porcini mushrooms and the mouth-watering *spiedini di pesce spada* (marinated swordfish roasted with sweet peppers and served in a lemony mustard sauce). As a bow to Tex-Mex cuisine, chili con carne appears on the menu, but serious foodies prefer the gratin of octopus. Other recommended main dishes include turkey filet with cherry sauce, swordfish kabob with a mustard lemon sauce, and spaghetti with prawns and swordfish. The house dessert, justifiably celebrated locally, is a banana doused with orange liqueur, baked, and then topped with whipped cream.

Via XXV Novembre 10 (off Corso Ruggero). ✆ **0921-423570.** Reservations recommended. Main courses 7€–15€; fixed-price lunch 19€–35€; fixed-price dinner 29€–40€. AE, DC, MC, V. Tues–Sun 1–2:30pm and 7–11:30pm. Closed Dec 15–Jan 15.

Osteria del Duomo ★★ SICILIAN/INTERNATIONAL The hippest, most sophisticated restaurant in Cefalù is right in front of the town's famous cathedral, at the bottom of steps that have been trod upon by Norman knights and *La Dolce Vita* movie stars alike. Many tables sit in the open air on cobblestones, others under the vaulted ceiling of the air-conditioned interior. I think the chefs here top those at La Brace (Michelin's Cefalù favorite; see above): They will enthrall you with their smoked fish, their seafood salads are the town's best (and the ideal food on a hot summer day), and their truly excellent carpaccio of beef will appeal to serious carnivores. Count on freshly made salads and desserts as well.

Via Seminario 3. ✆ **0921-421838.** Reservations recommended Sat–Sun. Main courses 8€–16€. AE, DC, MC, V. Tues–Sun noon–midnight. Closed mid-Nov to mid-Dec.

INEXPENSIVE

Al Gabbiano SICILIAN/SEAFOOD Unlike most of the other restaurants in Cefalù, which are tucked into hideaway alleys within the medieval core, this one sits directly across from the town's most popular beach, allowing sun-kissed diners access throughout the day and evening. The atmosphere evokes a woodsy-looking tavern with breezy access to the outdoors and touches of heavy timbers and exposed stone. Fresh fish, a menu constant, tastes best grilled and served with spinach or fava beans. The mainstay of the north coast, swordfish, is served here with a tasty onion sauce. You can also order couscous with fresh fish. No pasta in town compares to this place's linguine with shrimp, clams, and mussels. And one of my favorite items is zucchini flowers, which the chefs are skilled at deep-frying or grilling.

Via Lungomare Giardina 17. ✆ **0921-421495.** Main courses 7€–12€. AE, DC, MC, V. Thurs–Tues noon–3pm and 7:30–11pm.

L'Antica Corte SICILIAN The authentic Sicilian cuisine served here is market fresh and satisfying, despite the restaurant's slight touristic bent (the waiters, for example, appear with red bandannas and sashes like those worn by the Saracen pirates of yore). In good weather, try to get a table set under grapevines in the old courtyard. Otherwise, you'll find the air-conditioned seats inside a welcome relief from the heat. The pizzas are among the best in town—try the "Drago," with spicy sausage. Tempting pastas include one with hot peppers (*all'arrabbiata*) and another with shrimp, mushrooms, and a dousing of limoncello. The best bet is the catch of the day, which the chefs flavor with herbs and grill to your specifications.

Cortile Pepe 7, off Corso Ruggero. ✆ **0921-423228.** Reservations recommended. Main courses 9€–13€; pizza 5€–9€; menu turístico 15€. AE, MC, V. Fri–Wed noon–3pm and 7–11:30pm; Sat–Sun only in Feb and Nov.

Lo Scoglio Ubriaco (The Drunken Rock) SICILIAN   This restaurant is set high atop a rocky cliff at the edge of the old town. Walk in boldly and bypass the less desirable tables in the narrow dining room. Near the back, you'll find a staircase that meanders down onto a terrace perched atop jagged rocks, just above sea level and overlooking the fortifications on either side of the old port. If a table is available, this is where you should sit. Menu items are well prepared, albeit relatively predictable in light of the roughly equivalent food served in the town's other restaurants. A tangy mussel soup might tempt you before you proceed to the mixed grill of either fish or meat. The house-style tagliatelle is understandably a local favorite, served with a well-flavored mussel and cream sauce. You can also order another pasta dish, farfalle with tuna roe.

Via Carlo Ortolani di Bordonaro 2-4. ℂ **0921-423370.** Reservations recommended. Main courses 8€–18€. AE, MC, V. July-Aug daily noon-2:30pm and 7pm-midnight; Sept-June Wed-Mon noon-2:30pm and 7pm-midnight.

Cefalù after Dark

Many townspeople like to go home, eat their catch of the day, and retire early after watching some TV. The liveliest spot in Cefalù is **Bip Bop Pub, Bar & Bistro,** Via Nicolà Botta 4 (ℂ **0921-923972**). The rock-'n'-roll music and youthful (or at least young-at-heart) crowd in this English-style pub pull you very far away from the medieval setting of old Cefalù. Opt for a cocktail or beer on tap, crepes, sandwiches, salads, or a plate of pasta. Open daily from 11am to 4am; closed Mondays from October to March.

USTICA ★★★

57km (35 miles) NW of Palermo.

The lone volcanic island of Ustica is known as "The Black Pearl," dramatically surging as it does out of the cobalt sea surrounding it.

Initially inhabited by the Phoenicians, the Greeks followed, naming the island Osteodes ("ossuary"), in memory of the skeletons of 6,000 Carthaginians who were brought here and abandoned without food or water.

Attempts to colonize it in the Middle Ages failed because of raids by Barbary pirates. The Bourbons repopulated it in 1762 with people from the Aeolian Islands and Naples. They constructed a trio of towers to defend the island against pirates.

As late as the 1950s, Ustica was a penal colony, a sort of Alcatraz of Sicily. Antonio Gramsci, the theorist of the Italian Communist Party, was once imprisoned here. And, in one of the most secret meetings of World War II, British and Italian officers met here in September 1943 to discuss a switch in sides from Mussolini to the Allies.

Ustica is tiny, only 8.6 sq km (3⅓ sq miles), with a population of roughly 1,370, yet it is the oldest island in the Sicilian outer archipelago—even older than the Aeolian Islands. Because its jagged coastline is riddled with creeks, bays, and caves, Ustica is best explored by a rented boat (see below) circling the island.

In 1987, Sicily designated part of the island a national marine park, and today its clear waters, filled with aquatic flora and fauna and archaeological trails, attract sea lovers from around the world.

Essentials

GETTING THERE Hydrofoils and ferries operate daily from Palermo's Stazione Maríttima to Ustica. The ferry is the cheapest and slowest transport, costing 14€ each way and taking 2½ hours. The hydrofoil, at a cost of 21€ does it in half the time. For tickets for either transport, go to **Siremar** (✆ **892123;** www.siremar.it), at Via Francesco Crispi 118 in Palermo (✆ **091-336632**), and on Piazza Bartolo in Ustica (✆ **091-8449002**). Hydrofoil service runs from April to December; ferries run year-round, but not on Sundays in winter.

GETTING AROUND Arrival from Palermo is at Ustica village, the only port and home to 90% of the islanders. The heart of the village is reached by climbing a flight of steps from the harbor. You'll emerge onto the main square of town—actually a trio of interlocking squares that include the piazzas of Bartolo, Umberto I, and Vito Longo. I recommend that you take care of any shopping needs before you leave Palermo; otherwise, you'll have to buy it here, as whatever Ustica has to offer is found in this area.

Once you arrive, you can always do as the locals do and rely on your trusty feet. Otherwise, take one of the orange minibuses that circumnavigate the island, hugging the coastline. These leave from the center of Ustica village daily on the hour. Figure on 2½ hours for the entire bus ride around the island; a ticket between any two points along the route costs 1€.

Summer boat excursions are run by local fishermen who not only know the most scenic beauty spots, but also will allow you time out for swimming during an island trip. **Hotel Ariston,** Via della Vittoria 5 (✆ **091-8449042**), organizes sightseeing boat trips, rents boats to scuba divers, and hires out motorcycles. Its three-seater boats cost 50€ a day, gasoline not included. A boat trip around the island, which lets you see the caves and stop at secluded spots for swimming, lasts 2½ hours and costs 20€. If you'd like to tour on your own—expect rough roads—it costs 29€ to 40€ a day to hire a motorcycle, with gas and two helmets included.

Scuba divers can go to **Ailara Rosalia,** Banchina Barresi (✆ **091-8449605**), which rents boats for 70€ a day. You should bring your own diving gear, however.

VISITOR INFORMATION The tourist office has closed because of financial reasons. However, you can visit the headquarters of **Parco Marino Regionale,** on the main square of town (✆ **091-8449456**). The staff here can provide information about the marine park. Hours are daily 8am to 8pm.

Attractions near the Port

It's fun just to stroll around the village, taking in views of the bay, Baia Santa Maria. The little town is made more festive by a series of murals that decorate the facades of the buildings.

Directly south of the village stands **Torre Santa Maria,** housing the **Museo Archeologico (Archaeological Museum)** (no phone). It's open daily from 9am to noon and 5 to 7pm; admission is 3€. Its most fascinating exhibits are fragments and artifacts recovered from the ancient city of Osteodes, now submerged beneath the sea. Many of the artifacts, such as crusty anchors, were recovered from ships wrecked off the coast. You'll see amphorae, Bronze Age objects from the prehistoric village of Faraglioni, and contents of tombs from the Hellenistic and Roman eras.

EXPLORING A watery WONDERLAND

J. Y. Cousteau claimed that the waters off the coast of Ustica were among the most beautiful he'd ever seen, ideal for diving and underwater photography—and I agree. The best spot for diving is the **Grotta del Gamberi,** near Punta Gavazzi, at the southern tip of the island beyond Grotta del Tuono. Nearby is the famous **Sub-Aqua Archaeological Trail;** lying off the headland is Punta Gavazzi with its lighthouse. Many anchors and even Roman amphorae can still be seen in these waters.

The best dive spot on the north coast is **Secca di Colombara,** to the west of Grotta dell'Oro. Here you can see a vast array of gorgonians and Ustica's most beautiful sponges. **Scoglio del Medico ★★,** or "doctor's rock," lies off the west coast of the island directly north of the bay called Baia Sidoti. This outcropping of basalt, riddled with grottoes and gorges, plunges to murky depths in the Atlantic, and offers a panoramic seascape unequaled anywhere else in Sicily.

To the east of the tower are the ruins of a Bronze Age settlement, **Villaggio Preistorico,** at Faraglioni. Excavations began in 1989 on what was a large prehistoric village dating from the 14th century to the 13th century B.C. The foundations of some 300 stone-built houses were discovered, and the defensive walls of the settlement are among the strongest fortifications of any period known in Italy. It is believed that these early settlers came over from the Aeolian Islands. Admission is free; the site is always open.

If you walk north of Ustica village, you'll come to the remains of the **Rocca della Falconiera,** at 157m (515 ft.). Figure on a 20-minute walk. (Along the way you'll see many cisterns, as water remains a precious commodity on Ustica, even though a desalination plant has been installed.) The defensive tower was constructed by the Bourbons to protect the island from raids by pirates. This site was first settled back in the 3rd century B.C. by the Romans. If you look toward the sea you'll see the lighthouse, **Punta dell'Uomo Morto (Dead Man's Point)** on a cliff, where a cave contains vestiges of centuries-old tombs.

From the fort you can take in a view of **Guardia dei Turchi,** at 244m (801 ft.). This is the highest point on the island. That object you see in the distance, evoking a mammoth golf ball, is in fact a meteorological radar system installed by the Italian government.

The **view ★** from the fortress ruins stretches from the harbor to the core of the island, with the mountains of **Monte Costa del Fallo** and **Monte Guardia dei Turchi** clearly outlined.

Exploring the Island

Since it is the top of an extinct volcano, Ustica doesn't have sandy beaches. But as you traverse the island, you'll find jumping-off points for swimming. The biggest attraction is the grotto-lined coastline and, because distances are short, hiking is a viable option.

Wildflowers cover the island except in late July and August, when the blistering sun burns them away. You'll also see island-grown produce, such as lentils, figs, capers, grapes, prickly pears, wheat, and almonds.

Of all the caves or grottoes on the island, the most celebrated and fascinating is the **Grotta Azzurra ★★**, the first cave south of Ustica village as you head down the coast by boat. It's named for the more fabled cave in Capri, but both grottoes share an incredible iridescent glow from light reflections from the sea.

Almost as stunning is the next sea cave directly to the south, **Grotta Pastizza ★**. This is a stalactite cave behind a great pyramidal rock. Directly down the coast, another grotto, **Grotta della Barche,** is also intriguing. *Barche* means "boats," and Ustica fishermen anchor in this safe haven during storms.

Parco Marino Regionale ★★

The Marine National Park was created in 1986, the first marine reserve ever established in Italy. Since Ustica lies at the center of an inward current surging through the Straits of Gibraltar directly from the Atlantic Ocean, its waters are always clean and free of pollution.

Underwater photographers flock to the park to film the stunning **aquatic flora and fauna ★★★**. A rare seaweed, *Poseidonia oceanica,* is called "the lungs of the sea" because it oxygenates the water. You may also see an array of magnificent red gorgonians, stunning black coral, plentiful turtles (now that they are protected), swordfish, lobster, and *cernia* (a kind of sea perch). Some divers claim to have had close encounters with grouper as big as a Fiat 500.

The park comprises three zones. **A area** extends along the western part of the isle from Cala Sidoti to Caletta and as far as 935m (3,068 ft.) offshore. Swimming is allowed here, but boats and fishing are prohibited. **B area** extends from Punta Cavazzi to Punta Omo Morto, taking in the entire southwest-to-northeast coastline, and extending out into the sea a distance of 3 nautical miles. Swimming is permitted here. Finally, **C area** is a partial reserve made up of the rest of the coast. Swimming is allowed here, as is fishing.

Hiking around Ustica

You can circumnavigate the island in 3 to 4 hours, depending on your pace. The best hike is along the coastal path heading north of town, where you'll see the Municipio, or island headquarters. Head left here, taking the trail along the north coast that leads past an old cemetery. This hike hugs the steep cliffs on the northern side of the island, part of the marine reserve, and the views are stunning.

Eventually you'll come to **Punta di Megna,** on the western coast, on the exact opposite side of the island from Ustica village. The offshore rock so appreciated by scuba divers, **Scoglio del Medico,** can be seen from here.

The road continues along the southwestern coast as far as the battered ruins of the old tower, **Punta Spalmatore,** where you can go swimming. (There is no beach here, however.)

Below this point, at **Punta Cavazzi,** along the southern rim of the island, is **Piscina Naturale ★**, a sheltered seawater pool and the best place on Ustica for swimming. If there are a lot of tourists on the island at the time of your visit, this "hole" is likely to be crowded with bathers in the briefest of swimwear.

At this point, the route no longer follows the coast and cuts inland all the way northeast to Ustica village once again.

Where to Stay

Accommodations are scarce and fill up quickly from April to September. Many islanders rent rooms when the hotels are fully booked, but if you count on that, you're taking a chance. It's far preferable to arrive with a reservation. If you don't have one, go to the Piazza Umberto and start asking around for a *camera*, or room. In winter, many places close down.

Hotel Clelia ⚜ This is the most typical of Ustica's little island inns, situated off Piazza Umberto I, the main square of Ustica village. It was the first little boarding-house on the island to receive visitors, who began arriving in 1950 during the lean postwar years. It is also one of the island's best bargains. For most of its life, it was a *pensione*, or boardinghouse. But after so many improvements, it has been upgraded by the government to three-star status. Nonetheless, its prices have remained reasonable in spite of the installation of soundproof windows and modern furnishings. Guest rooms are small but comfortable, each with a little shower-only bathroom. Hotel extras include a lovely patio with scenic views, a shuttle bus that makes trips around the island, and scooter and boat rentals. This is one of the few places that remain open year-round.

Via Sindaco I 29, Ustica 90010. ℂ **091-8449039.** Fax 091-8449459. www.hotelclelia.it. 26 units. 65€–150€ double; 84€–195€ triple. Rates include continental breakfast. AE, DC, MC, V. **Amenities:** Restaurant; bar; babysitting. *In room:* A/C, TV, minibar, hair dryer.

Hotel Diana ★ 🏨 Located on the beach at Contrada San Paolo, this is one of the island's oldest hotels, but it's still in good shape following renovations. Opened in 1973 at the dawn of tourism on the island, the Diana's most attractive feature is its landscaping, which features fruit trees and wild island plants. The hotel's panoramic position allows some good views from the terraces of its guest rooms. Accommodations are a bit bare-bones but comfortable, with good beds, marble floors, and small bathrooms. The helpful owner/manager can offer advice on setting up island tours.

Contrada San Paolo, 90010 Ustica. ℂ/fax **091-8449109.** www.hoteldiana-ustica.com. 30 units. 55€–80€ per person double. Rates include half board. AE, DC, MC, V. Closed Sept 25–Mar 31. **Amenities:** Restaurant; bar; outdoor pool. *In room:* A/C, TV.

Hotel Grotta Azzurra ★★ This is Ustica's best hotel bet, lying a 5-minute walk from the center. Modern and comfortable, the Grotta Azzurra stands on a wide plateau above the ocean, with a steep drop to a spot for swimming. A natural grotto carved out of a cliff face below gives the hotel its name and its most alluring feature. All of the well-appointed guest rooms open onto sea views; each comes with a small but neat private bathroom with shower. Set among lush gardens, this hotel feels like a Mediterranean retreat, with such resort-style amenities as beach towels and umbrellas. Sports-oriented people can rent scooters and boats for island tours, sailing, and windsurfing. The hotel also attracts a lot of divers. Even if you're not a guest, consider a meal at **La Cala dei Fenici,** known on the island for its refined Sicilian cuisine.

Contrada San Ferlicchio, Ustica 90010. ℂ **091-8449807.** Fax 091-8449396. 51 units. 160€–285€ double. Rates include breakfast. AE, DC, MC, V. Closed Oct–May. **Amenities:** Restaurant; bar; outdoor pool; hydromassage; babysitting. *In room:* A/C, TV, minibar.

Villaggio Lirial Punta Spalmatore ★ Sicily's coastal towns are riddled with self-contained tourist villages, and this is the island's best such choice. Set 4km (2½ miles) from Ustica village on the western coast, it's entirely surrounded by native trees and plants. Most visitors spend their days in the terraced pool area with a panoramic view of the ocean; some guests from Palermo never even leave the grounds. The buildings rise only two floors, and small but comfortable guest rooms are in bungalows that have shower-only bathrooms. The cuisine is typical resort fare, but much use is made of fresh produce when available. Otherwise, foodstuffs have to be shipped over from Palermo. The wide range in rates depends on when you're here—the highest prices are charged in July and August.

Località Punta Spalmatore, Ustica 90010. ✆ **091-8449388.** Fax 091-8449472. 110€–230€ double. Rates include continental breakfast, lunch, and dinner. AE, MC, V. Closed Sept 20–May 31. **Amenities:** Restaurant; bar; outdoor pool; gym; Jacuzzi; sauna; wellness center/massage. *In room:* A/C, fridge.

Where to Eat

La Luna sul Porto SICILIAN One of the handful of restaurants that's open even after the tourists have gone, this charming little restaurant facing the port is run by a welcoming woman who goes out of her way to make sure you get the best in local cuisine. As you've guessed, fish is king here; even timeless Italian classics such as *spaghetti all' amatriciana* is made with tuna (in place of bacon). If you're lucky enough to be on the island on August 15th or 24th, you'll be treated to fish lasagna—a rarity, since it's only made on these particular days.

Via Vittorio Emanuele 11 90010-Ustica (PA) ✆ **091-8449799.** AE, MC, V. Fish menu 40€–45€ per person. Daily noon–3pm and 8pm–1am. Closed Fridays.

WESTERN SICILY

Blessed with crystalline waters, golden sunshine, fertile land, and unspoiled nature, western Sicily is an extraordinary place known for its prized wines, olive oil, and rock salt. The influence of Phoenician and Arab culture can still be felt in its cuisine and architecture, giving the area a North African feel.

The capital of the area, **Trapani,** has a peculiar sickle shape stretching out to sea and its shoreline is dotted with centuries-old tuna processing plants that are a testament to its vibrant fishing industry. Connoisseurs from around the world (even from as far as Japan) flock here to buy the prized tuna.

Marsala, further down the coast and where Garibaldi landed in 1860 in the name of Italian Unification, is known for the dessert wine of the same moniker. This is also Elymian country, where the refugees from the war of Troy settled and which they turned into their legendary kingdoms. The greatest legacy left by the Elymians is **Erice ★★★**; the historic town perched on top of a rocky crag not far from Trapani has sweeping views that, on a clear day, stretch as far as Tunisia.

Western Sicily wasn't immune to Greek influence. The mighty **Selinunte,** founded by settlers of Megara in this unexpected part of Sicily (Greeks predominantly populated the east) in fact has the largest extension of Greek ruins in Europe, including Greece itself. **Segesta ★★★**, also an Elymian city, equally felt the influence—this is the best-preserved Doric temple in the world with a stunning Greek theater (still used for summer plays).

The tiny, privately owned island of **Mozia ★★★** with its archaeological site is in the Stagnone lagoon off the coast of Marsala and is as close as you'll get to Punic (Carthaginian) civilization in Sicily without crossing over to Carthage. This is also the place for some serious swimming—the area offers a plethora of choices, from the Caribbean-like sands of **San Vito Lo Capo** to the protected area of **Lo Zingaro.**

The lone island of **Pantelleria** in the Sicilian channel, with its exotic surroundings and dotted with converted *dammusi* (lava-stone former peasant homes), is a jetsetters' paradise and is as close as you'll get to Tunisia without leaving the country.

SEGESTA ★★★

30km (19 miles) NE of Trapani, 75km (47 miles) SW of Palermo.

The main reason to visit Segesta is to see a single amazing temple in a lonely field, the **Tempio di Segesta.** For some visitors, that's reason enough because it's one of the best-preserved ancient Doric temples in all of Italy, but the temple's rural setting also means that it's a pretty spot, and its grayish stone changes hue with the light. The temple is part of the ruined ancient city of Segesta, and close by lies an ancient Greek amphitheater on top of Monte Barbaro (431m/1,414 ft.). The theater was hewn out of the rock and has a view stretching toward the surrounding hills and sea at the Gulf of Castellamare. The trip to Segesta takes about an hour from Palermo; it's a good place to stop for half a day en route to Trapani (p. 157).

Essentials

GETTING THERE   Three **trains** (✆ 892021; www.trenitalia.it) per day arrive from Trapani (p. 157) to the stop at Segesta Tempio, taking 25 minutes and costing 3.25€ per person. From Palermo (p. 69), three trains a day make the 1¾- to 2-hour journey at a cost of 6.10€ one way. The station is about a 1km (½-mile) walk to the park entrance. Segesta is also reached **by bus** with a couple of companies: **AST** (✆ 840-000323; www.aziendasicilianatrasporti.it), which leaves from Piazza Montalto in Trapani and **Tarantola** (✆ 0924-31020; www.tarantolabus.it) who operate three buses a day from Piazza Ciaccio in Trapani (journey time: 1 hour), and three to four buses from Piazza Giulio Cesare (Central Train Station) in Palermo (journey time: 1¾-hour).

By **car,** take the autostrada (A29) running between Palermo and Trapani. The exit at Segesta is clearly marked. The journey takes a little under an hour from Palermo.

Parco Archaeologico (The Archaeological Park)

The **Tempio di Segesta (Temple of Segesta) ★★★** is perhaps the best-preserved Doric temple in the world, and the only freestanding limestone temple in Sicily (all the others are made of sandstone). It stands on a 304m (997-ft.) hill, on the edge of a deep ravine carved by the Pispisa River. Built in the 5th century B.C., the temple is shrouded in mystery. It has all the specifications of a typical Doric temple, but the columns were surprisingly never fluted. The inner architectural components are also missing—a roof was never added, the tabs used to transport the stones were never removed which has led historians to suggest that the temple was hastily built to impress the Athenian ambassadors, to whom Segesta had turned in search of an ally against Selinunte.

When observing the temple from afar, the best **views ★★★** are from the hillside as you reach the theater on Monte Barbaro; the columns all look deceptively alike, but upon close inspection, the entases (the diametrical differences at the top, bottom, and middle of a column) along each of them, create an optical illusion that balances out any irregularities. The Temple of Segesta was one of the favorite subjects of the 18th-century artists traveling in Sicily. Their paintings often included herds of sheep and cattle in or surrounding the temple—this was, after all, an open farmland, since Segesta ceased to exist as a city after the Norman times. Recently, and most sensibly, the theater has been fenced off and can only be admired from the

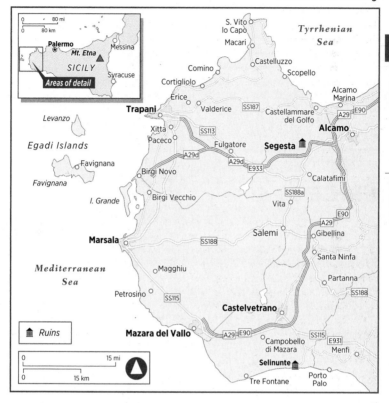

outside. **Note:** There is a bit of a steep, precarious climb to reach the temple from the entrance, and no facilities for wheelchair accessibility.

After visiting the temple, you can either hike up the nearly 4km (2½ miles) or take a bus to the **Teatro (Theater)** ★★, at the top of Mount Barbaro (431m/1,414 ft.). The hike to reach the theater allows you to view little-known areas of the old city, with some foundations dating back to medieval times. The fastest way up, however, is the bus, which departs every half-hour. Once you're off the bus, take a few moments to visit the **excavations** ★ currently underway. What is believed to have been the *agorà,* or public square, is currently being unearthed, allowing greater insight into Segesta's past. The theater, which dates from the 3rd century B.C. or maybe earlier, has been perfectly restored. A semicircle with a diameter of 63m (207 ft.), it was hewn right out of the side of the mountain and allows for some spectacular views, stretching out to Castellamare del Golfo and all over the surrounding farmland. In ancient days, the theater could hold nearly 4,000 spectators along its *cavea* of 20 semicircular rows—there are still etchings on some of them to distinguish the "rich-folk" sections from the cheap seats. The site is still used for the staging of operas, concerts and plays every summer, so if you have the time you can watch a work by one of the ancient Greek playwrights performed in Italian against a spectacular backdrop on a balmy summer evening, just as audiences would have done thousands of years ago. Beneath the theater lies a grotto dating back to the Bronze Age.

The site, which is still the subject of study by archaeologists from around the world, is open daily 9am to 5pm in winter and 9am to 7pm in summer; admission is 9€ for adults, 4.50€ for ages 18 to 25, and free for children 17 and under and adults 65 and over who reside in the EU, Canada, or Australia. The ticket is valid for 3 days and includes admission to the Parco Archeologico in Selinunte (p. 170). The ticket office closes an hour before the park's closing time. On-site bus transportation between the temple and the theater is not included in the ticket; it costs 1.50€. The park also has a small, canopied eating area opposite the only cafe, where visitors can unwind or rest during their visit.

ERICE ★★★

96km (60 miles) SW of Palermo, 14km (8⅔ miles) NE of Trapani, 45km (28 miles) NW of Marsala, 330km (205 miles) W of Messina.

The enchanting medieval city of Erice is a lovely place to spend a day drinking in the incomparable views. From its panoramic setting on top of Mount Erice (743m/2,438 ft.)—reached by cablecar (see below)—two sheer cliffs drop to vistas across the plains of Trapani (p. 157) and down the west coast of Sicily. On a clear summer's day, you can see west to the Egadi Islands, east to Mount Etna and south to Africa, glimpsing Tunisia's Cape Bon. But the Sicilian aerie of Erice is often shrouded in a mist that only adds to its mystique. The cool fog that descends on the city is known as "the veil of Venus" because Erice's highest point, the **Castello di Venere (Castle of Venus)**, is where a temple to the Roman goddess of love once stood, and seeing the city's towers and craggy rocks shrouded in a hazy blanket of gray is quite magical.

Erice is an atmospheric place, where you'll stop to perhaps admire an arch, a door, or a bell tower, as you wander its steep cobblestone streets flanked by churches and stone houses with elaborate baroque balconies packed with cascading geraniums, peeking in on tiny courtyards crammed with potted plants. There's plenty to buy too; in addition to local wines and tuna-based products, Erice is known for its colorful handmade ceramics and rugs. The city is famous throughout Sicily for its pastries, so you can justifiably pause from sightseeing and shopping to sample delights such as the tangy *dolci di Badia* cakes, which are made from almond paste and citron juice according to a traditional recipe that originated from the former convent of San Carlo (St. Charles).

Essentials

GETTING THERE   From Palermo, there are four **trains** (© 892021; www.trenitalia. com) a day to Trapani, taking about 2¼ hours and costing 7.40€ one way. After you pull into the station at Trapani (p. 157), head to Piazza Giovanni Paolo II and board bus no. 21, run by **ATM Trapani** (© 0923-559575; www.atmtrapani.it), which leaves Trapani every 30 minutes and costs 1.20€ if you pay your fare on the bus. This will bring you to the Casa Santa section of Erice, where the cablecar station is on Via Capua.

From here you then board the **funivia (cableway)** (© 0923-560023; www.funiviaerice.it) that will whisk you up to the top in about 10 minutes at a cost of 6€ round-trip (wheelchair accessibility is available). *Note:* The cableway is usually closed on Monday mornings for general maintenance and does not operate in inclement weather; check first before going. **AST buses** (© 840-000323; www.azienda sicilianatrasporti.it) to Erice depart from Trapani's Piazza Montalto and service is year-round, daily 6:40am to 7:30pm. The trip—along winding, uphill turns—lasts 50 minutes. If you are prone to carsickness, you might want to opt for the cableway.

By **car** from Palermo, follow the A29 all the way to Trapani, then turn right on Via Fardella. Near the end of the street, you'll see signs pointing the way to Erice and the cableway, should you decide to park your car.

Discovering Erice

No matter how you reach Erice, you will arrive at Porta Trapani, one of three entrance gates of the city (the other two are Porta Spada and Porta Spagnola, farther north). Porta Trapani is incorporated in the **Elymian-Punic walls,** the extensive defensive barrier laid out by the Eymians around 1200 B.C. and fortified subsequently by the Carthaginians that guarded the city from attacks coming from the west, as it was the most vulnerable part of the town. The gate itself was built in Norman times.

Once you're through the door, turn left at the first street, leading to the **Chiesa Matrice** (© 0923-869123), the Royal Duomo of Erice. It was constructed in 1312 using stones from the ancient Temple of Venus that once stood in Erice—quite the contradiction, considering that when the Normans re-Christianized Erice, they purposely dismantled any and all pagan symbols in town. Its Gothic, crenellated walls speak of the church's regal foundations. The fine rose window on the church facade is as beautiful as the one adorning the Basilica of San Francesco di Assisi in Palermo. Its splendid porch, dubbed the Gibbena (from the Latin *agi bene,* meaning "act well"), was added in 1426 with the purpose of accommodating penitents who were not allowed to partake in the mass. The staircase was added in the 18th century. The interior of the church, which is not particularly large, contains three naves with two transepts, one just before the presbytery and one at the entrance. Some of Sicily's finest neo-Gothic architecture is found here, especially along the vaulted, arabesque **ceiling ★★**, which was rebuilt in 1853 after the original had collapsed from neglect and decay. In the sanctuary is an enormous altarpiece in Carrara marble, depicting the life and times of Jesus Christ; to the left, in a circular niche in the wall, is the medieval fresco of the *Angelo Musico* ★, one of the few examples of the original artwork in the church. A lovely marble *Madonna Assunta,* patroness of the church, with an exceptional bas-relief by Domenico Gagini, is in a chapel on the right nave, while on the left nave is the chapel dedicated to the Madonna of Custonaci, patroness of Erice. The **treasury,** just beyond this chapel, houses ecclesiastical regalia such as vestments, altar cloths, and gold- and silversmithery. *Note:* An admission fee of 2€ is required for entrance to the cathedral, free for children 12 and under. The church is open Monday to Friday 9:30am to 12:30pm and 3:30 to 5:30pm, Saturday and Sunday 9:30am to 1pm and 3:30 to 6pm. Tours are prohibited during mass.

If you climb the steep, often perilous, 108 steps of the church's **campanile** (bell tower) right next door, you'll be rewarded with a spectacular **view ★** across the Gulf of Trapani to the Egadi Islands. Ordered by Frederick of Aragon at the end of the 1200s, who long sojourned in Erice when French troops blocked him here, it is built on top of a preexisting Punic watchtower. Decorated with splendid monofora (single-arch) and bifora (double-arch) windows, it rises 28m (92 ft.) high.

As you make your way back to Via Vittorio Emanuele and up its arduous cobblestone street you'll bypass some churches and monasteries that have only been recently opened to the public (thanks to local efforts promoting the past Christian history of the city), as well as shops selling local crafts and souvenirs. Before reaching the main square at Piazza Umberto, reward yourself at Maria Grammatico's world-renowned pastry shop, Pasticceria Grammatico (p. 157).

In the historic core of Erice, and also at the highest point, stands the **Museo Civico Antonio Cordici,** Piazza Umberto I, at Corso Vittorio Emanuele (*©* **0923-869172**), open Monday and Thursday 9am to 1pm and 3 to 5pm; Tuesday, Wednesday, and Friday 9am to 1pm; admission is free. Named for a local historian, the building was originally a library dating from 1867. In its entrance hall is a magnificent 1525 relief of the *La Annunciazione (Annunciation)* ★ by Antonello Gagini, one of his most impressive pieces of art. Upstairs are displays of the more intriguing artifacts from archaeological digs in the area, including a small Attic head of Venus dating from the 5th century B.C., and tombstones with Greek, Latin, and Hebrew inscriptions.

Heading east, down Via Guarnotti and past Piazza San Giuliano, you'll arrive at the public gardens of the **Giardino del Balio ★**, initially constructed by the Normans as a forward defense for their castle (see below). From the gardens, make your way to the spectacular ancestral home of the Pepoli family, the **Castello Pepoli;** it's now a hotel, though the family still occupies a tower of the castle. The family, having descended from the Saxon King Alfred, were the benefactors of the town, investing much into the restoration of monuments. Situated on the summit of a hill, the castle promenade has one of the most **spectacular views ★★★** in western Sicily, embracing the peaks of Monte Cofano (known also as Shark Tooth mountain for its odd shape) with distant views of the Egadi Islands. On a clear day you can see all the way to Tunisia, a distance of 170km (106 miles). The gardens are always open.

A ramp will lead you down from the Castello Pepoli to a promenade overlooking the southern vista from Erice—make a left, and you'll come to **Castello di Venere,** or Castle of Venus, built at the extremity of Mount San Giuliano (as Erice was called for many years, before reclaiming its original name in 1927) on the same spot where in ancient times a temple to the goddess, known as Venus Ericina to the Romans and Astarte to the Carthaginians, once stood. Dating from the 12th century, the present *castello* was constructed as a defensive fortification by the Normans. Massive and majestic, it became the seat of Norman authority in the west. It's still encircled by mammoth medieval towers. Inside it also has all the traces of a previous Roman dwelling, including a small spa. The well, according to the legend, was where Venus threw men when she was fed up with them. Above the entrance to the castle, note the coat of arms of the Holy Roman Emperor, Charles V (1500–58) and an original Gothic window. Through the defensive openings in the walls you can see the plains of Trapani and the Egadi Islands to the southwest. In fair weather, you can even spot the offshore island of Ustica (p. 141).

THE WORLD'S oldest PROFESSION, SANCTIFIED

Besides conquering the world, the Romans were also known for all sorts of debaucheries, and Erice was not immune to this. As they venerated the goddess Venus from the temple built in honor of king Eryx's mother, Romans and foreigners alike flocked to the temple to offer young girls as *hierodules,* or holy salves, to the temple in gratitude of fulfilled vows. Barely pubescent, these girls, once "sacrificed" to the temple, underwent boot camp in the art of all things physically pleasurable. When men came to "pay their respects" legend has it that the girls turned into Venus herself. When their stances as holy slaves ended, usually at the ripe old age of 21, their careers—and reputations—were far from tarnished: Not only did they retire with a princely sum of money, they were the most desired bachelorettes in town, and, like Venus, were not stick thin: A diet of milk and honey added to their voluptuous allure.

The castle is open from November to March, visits can be made via booking during weekdays, (📞 **366-6712832**); weekends and holidays open 10am to 4 pm; April to October daily 10am to sunset. Admission is 3€ for adults and 1.50€ for children aged 8 to 14 and seniors aged 65 and over, and when buying a combined ticket for cableway passage. Entrance is free for those with limited mobility and for children 7 and under.

Where to Stay

EXPENSIVE

Hotel Baglio Santa Croce ★   On the way up to Erice in the town of Valderice, this converted farmhouse dates from 1637 and lies on the slope of Mount Erice, opening onto the Gulf of Cornino. The newer wing, built in 2006, has doubled the hotel's capacity, though you'll want a room in the old quarters to get a real feel for country living. This is a most delightful choice and, for many, the most relaxing way to enjoy the pleasures of historic Erice without staying in the center. The original architectural elements, including wooden beams, have been retained. The delightful terraced gardens have panoramic vistas, and the atmosphere is one of country charm and elegance. Guest rooms are simply but comfortably furnished, with terra-cotta floors and wooden beams, along with rustic, country-style furnishings. The on-site restaurant serves excellent local dishes.

SS187, Km 300 (Contrada Ragosia), 91019 Erice. 📞 **0923-891111.** Fax 0923-891192. www.bagliosanta croce.it. 67 units. 120€–140€ double; 180€–220€ suite. Rates include breakfast. AE, DC, MC. Free parking. Located 2km (1¼ miles) east of Valderice on N187. **Amenities:** Restaurant; bar; outdoor pool. *In room:* A/C, TV.

Hotel Elimo ★   Set in the heart of Erice's historic core and uphill from Porta Trapani, a few steps from the Hotel Moderno (see below), this art hotel was built 400 years ago as a private *palazzo* and transformed into a hotel in 1986. Its public areas feature an appealing combination of old frescoed ceiling beams, antique masonry, oriental rugs, and contemporary leather sofas, all nestled around a library-style TV den that adds considerable Sicilian coziness to the space. A roaring fireplace is a warm welcome in winter on those cold, foggy Erice days. Spectacular views, seen through the enormous windows of the restaurant, sweep over the golden plains of western Sicily. The outdoor terrace offers even more astounding views. Choose one of this hotel's conventional guest rooms, which tend to be of average size, comfortable, and very tidy. Avoid the claustrophobic duplex suites.

Via Vittorio Emanuele 75, 91016 Erice. © **0923-869377.** Fax 0923-869252. www.hotelelimo.it. 22 units. 110€ double; 185€ suite. AE, DC, MC, V. **Amenities:** Restaurant; bar. *In room:* A/C, TV, minibar.

MODERATE

Hotel La Pineta As the name implies, this hotel is nestled in a pine wood, away from the din of the town center, yet it's close enough to be within walking distance. It calls itself a resort, though it's really a conglomeration of small cottages; all have private terraces (a rarity in these parts), and most have sea views—make sure to ask for one. The rustic stone exterior and natural light of each roomy cottage are reminiscent of turn-of-the-20th-century country dwellings, and this is best exemplified in the period furniture in each room. Bathrooms (shower-only) are proportional to the room size. For sports enthusiasts, a tennis court and a soccer (football) field are nearby.

Viale Nunzio Nasi, 91016 Erice. © **0923-860127.** Fax 0923-860143. www.lapinetadierice.com. 20 units. 60€–90€ double. Rates include breakfast. AE, DC, MC, V. Free parking. **Amenities:** Restaurant; bar; babysitting. *In room:* A/C, TV, minibar, Wi-Fi (free).

Hotel Moderno ★ Another hotel on the main thoroughfare, the snug and warm Moderno has plenty of charm. The family that runs this hotel makes visitors feel welcome. The name "moderno" dates to just after World War II, when a 19th-century stone house and, later, the 14-room annex across the street, were converted into one of central Erice's most appealing hotels. Rooms in the annex are bigger than those in the hotel's main building. All units have elements of 19th-century decor, some antiques, and bentwood, brass, and wicker furniture. The colors are subdued and relaxing. About a dozen of the rooms open onto private balconies or terraces. The view from the terrace, where breakfast can be taken in warm weather, is stunning. If you arrive on a cold day, you're likely to be welcomed by a glowing fire. The on-site restaurant is a favorite with locals and visitors alike.

Via Vittorio Emanuele 67, 91016 Erice. © **0923-869300.** Fax 0923-869139. www.hotelmodernoerice.it. 40 units. 80€–110€ double; 110€–130€ quadruple. Rates include breakfast. AE, DC, MC, V. Free parking nearby. Pets welcome. **Amenities:** Restaurant; bar; babysitting. *In room:* A/C, TV, minibar.

Hotel San Domenico ★★★ 💼 Compared to the Elimo and the Moderno, this well-located hotel offers the exclusivity of only seven rooms. It was carefully re-created from a 14th-century palazzo, and it's run by a gracious family that has owned the building for centuries. The reception and restaurant areas still show the original tuff stones used in the masonry and are laden with period furniture and decor. The guest rooms, reached via a few flights of stairs, are average sized yet welcoming; they feature period furniture and terra-cotta flooring; the shower-only bathrooms are spanking new. Room no. 501 has its own private terrace with the most superb view; if you aren't lucky enough to land it, no worries—the hotel terrace has vistas all the way to Monte Cofano.

Via Tommaso Guarrasi 26 91016 Erice. ℰ **0923-860128.** Fax 0923-309978. www.hotel-sandomenico. it. 7 units. 95€–115€ double; 115€–145€ double with terrace; 145€–170€ triple. Rates include continental breakfast. AE, DC, MC, V. Free street parking or private optional garage upon request. **Amenities:** Bar. *In room:* A/C, TV, minibar, hair dryer, Wi-Fi (free).

Santa Teresa ★★ If it's a self-catering option you are looking for, this is the ideal choice. Located in the town's medieval center and converted from an old blacksmith and cutlery shop, it has been meticulously restored to bring forth the original feel and masonry of the place. Outfitted to accommodate up to five people per apartment, the rooms evoke the medieval epoch of Erice yet are well-appointed, with a full working kitchen in which to prepare meals. The thick stone walls don't allow much external light to come in, and the bathrooms (shower only), while new, can be rather small. The owner is always present to tend to your needs without being overbearing.

Via Vito Carvini 86–88, 91016 Erice. ℰ **0923-892242.** Fax 0923-833285. www.vacanzeagroericino.it. 2 units. 33€–40€ for 2 people, minimum 2-night stay; 550€–850€ for 5 people, 1-week stay. Free parking nearby. **Amenities:** *In room:* TV, kitchen.

INEXPENSIVE

Hotel Belvedere San Nicola ★ ☺ A sister lodging of the Hotel Moderno (see above), this country home stands in a secluded setting with sweeping views over the shoreline of Trapani and the city itself. A family-friendly country inn with lots of on-premises activities for the little ones, it's less expensive than hotels in Erice's historic core, and an excellent choice if you need to get your bearings with kids in tow. Built in 2000 adjacent to a complex of summer homes, it gives you the impression of a postmodern version of a thick-walled, big-windowed farmhouse. None of the tiny, tile-floored guest rooms have air-conditioning, but thanks to Erice's high altitude and cooler temperature, you won't need it. Some rooms have high, sloping ceilings, and all have an efficient, no-frills styling. The social center is the large outdoor pool.

Contrada San Nicola, 91016 Erice. ℰ **0923-860124.** Fax 0923-869139. www.hotelmodernoerice.it. 10 units. 80€ double. Rates include continental breakfast. AE, DC, MC, V. Free parking. **Amenities:** Restaurant; bar; outdoor pool; children's playground; room service. *In room:* TV.

Il Carmine ★★ 🎒 For the price, this is a true gem. Located near Porta Carmine, one of the three historical entrances to Erice, Il Carmine is a refurbished 15th-century convent that still shows traces of monastic living (the chapel still exists; services are held). The no-frills rooms are simple, with shower-only bathrooms, yet they're spacious enough for families. Erice's high altitude makes air-conditioning unnecessary, and Il Carmine's guest rooms don't have any. Some have views out to the verdant gardens that are a part of the complex. There's no curfew, as an independent entrance allows you to come and go at your leisure. An attentive, friendly staff makes your stay here an enjoyable one.

Piazza del Carmine 23, 91016 Erice. ℰ **0923-1941532,** or 0923-869089 (evenings and weekends). www.ilcarmine.com. 6 units. 55€–80€ double; 85€–120€ quadruple. Rates include buffet breakfast. AE, MC, V. Free parking (except in summer). Pets welcome. **Amenities:** Restaurant; Internet. *In room:* TV.

Where to Eat

Il Tulipano ☺ 🍴 CAFE This cafe/self-service joint right next door to Maria Grammatico's pastry shop (p. 157) is a sound choice for those who don't have time for a full sit-down meal. Fresh Sicilian and national dishes are prepared daily with a wide variety of choices from pastas, rice salads, frittatas, couscous, meats, and fish. Sandwiches and sliced pizza are also available, as well as the ubiquitous rice balls. Options for vegetarians are plentiful. Dining is either outside (on the street in quaint wooden booths) or indoors (upstairs).

Via Vittorio Emanuele 10. ⓒ **0923-69672.** Main courses 4€–6€. AE, MC, V. Daily 8am–10pm.

La Pentolaccia ★ SICILIAN   You'll be greeted by a colorful Sicilian cart at the entrance to La Pentolaccia, which is in an old convent that dates back to the early 1600s. The setting is laid back yet elegant, attracting a crowd from the nearby international research center who love to savor the local offerings: Starters include *antipasto paolina,* a mixed platter of *caponatina,* and bruschetta and roulades. Be sure to leave some room for a delectable pasta dish, *ravioli all'ericina,* stuffed with ricotta, prosciutto, pecorino, spinach, and tomatoes. The main courses feature either the catch of the day or a wide assortment of meats.

Via G.F. Guarnotti, 17. ⓒ/fax **0923-869099.** www.ristorantelapentolaccia.it. Main courses 8€–16€. AE, DC, MC, V. Sept–May Fri–Wed noon–3pm and 8pm–midnight; June–Aug daily noon–3pm and 8pm–midnight.

Monte San Giuliano ★★★ 🍴 SICILIAN   To reach this garden hideaway, make your way through a labyrinth of narrow stone alleys that begins a few steps downhill from Erice's Piazza Umberto I. Then pass through an iron gate and wander beyond stone walls and shrubbery to the restaurant's terraces and dining rooms. The setting is very rustic, typical of Erice. The freshest and finest seafood is served here. That the Arabs once ruled the land is evidenced in the seafood couscous. My favorite pasta is something to savor: *Busiate* (a homemade pasta) made with *pesto alla Trapanese,* which in this case means garlic, basil, fresh tomatoes, and almonds. Other worthy pasta dishes include *caserecce* (a homemade pasta) with fresh shrimp and artichokes, or else fettuccine with sea urchins.

Vicolo San Rocco 7. ⓒ **0923-869595.** www.montesangiuliano.it. Reservations recommended. Main courses 8€–15€. AE, DC, MC, V. Tues–Sun 12:15–2:45pm and 7:30–10pm. Closed Jan 7–21.

Ulisse SICILIAN   Enter this airy indoor/outdoor dining room by walking up a series of ramps and stairs that seem to go on forever, past hidden pockets of greenery loaded with hibiscus and palmettos. At the top of your climb is a family-managed restaurant lined with paintings by local artists. Pizzas are available here, but only at dinnertime, and they're less popular than the well-prepared fresh fish, meat, and pasta platters for which the place is best known. The house specialty is spaghetti with lobster. Another pasta favorite with locals is *pappardelle* (wide noodles) with fresh mushrooms.

Via Chiaramonte 45. ⓒ **0923-869333.** www.ristorantiitaliani.it/ulisse. Main courses 8€–16€. AE, DC, MC, V. Sept–May Fri–Wed noon–3pm and 8pm–midnight; June–Aug daily noon–3pm and 8pm–midnight.

PASTRIES

Erice is renowned throughout Sicily for its pastries. These delectable goodies were carefully refined by cloistered nuns in Erice from the 14th to the 18th century. Even if you're dining in one of the restaurants in the central core, skip dessert and head to one of the best pastry shops in town.

Pasticceria Grammatico Maria Grammatico, who was raised in the nearby San Carlo convent, became famous in Italy when she wrote her autobiography, *Bitter Almonds*. The book tells of her melancholic recollections and recipes from a Sicilian girlhood spent in forced spiritual confinement. Her almond creations have made her celebrated all over Italy, especially her crunchy almond cookies, rum- or orange-filled marzipan balls, and confections fashioned from chocolate-covered almond paste. The almond-paste creations are works of art, shaped into a variety of forms such as whimsical animals, one of which was even on display at a crafts fair in New York. Do not miss the delectable, attack-on-the-waistline *cassatella*, a fried dumpling stuffed with ricotta and powdered with sugar and cinnamon. The pastry shop, which retains its original 1960s interior, also sells Marsala and local wines.

Via Vittorio Emanuele 14. ℂ **0923-869390.** Pastries from 1.50€. AE, MC, V. Daily 7am–10pm.

Pasticceria San Carlo ★ Taking its name from the now-defunct convent that made the famous almond treats, San Carlo is on the same par with Maria Grammatico—it might not have the same history, but the delights are just as good. Grab one of the mixed assortments on the counter and nibble as you make your way around town, or have the salespeople prepare one for you.

Via S. Domenico 18. ℂ **0923-869235.** Pastries from 1.50€. AE, MC, V. Daily 7:30am–9pm (until 2am July–Aug).

Shopping

Altieri 1882 This small, charming shop lies a few steps uphill from the heart of Erice, Piazza Umberto I. It sells coral jewelry, silver frames, and Sicilian pottery, some of it produced locally. Via Cordici 14. ℂ **0923-869431.**

Bazar del Miele ★★★ This is one of the most impressive food shops in Sicily, with some items that are esoteric even by local standards. You'll see 15 different honeys; several preparations of anchovies; Marsala wines, arranged by vineyard, year, and degree of sweetness; and liqueurs, including a pale-green one made from fermented pistachios. The array of cheeses and almond-based candies is the most comprehensive in town. Via Cordici 16. ℂ **0923-869181.**

Ceramica Ericina ★ Erice craftspeople are as famous for their rugs as they are for their ceramics. This is basically a ceramics store, but I also found the best selection of Erice carpets here. These highly valued rugs are hand-woven, the most traditional colors being red, yellow, and blue. Sometimes the colors are broken up by even brighter hues, with both floral and geometric designs in zigzags and diamonds. There is also a good selection of Sicilian lace here. Via Vittorio Emanuele 7. ℂ **0923-869140.**

TRAPANI

100km (62 miles) SW of Palermo, 14km (8⅔ miles) SW of Erice, 150km (93 miles) NW of Agrigento.

The most westerly of Sicilian provinces, here the coast from Trapani to Marsala (p. 164) is lined with dazzling white salt pans—the salt flats are a nature reserve populated by migratory birds, and the sight of the vast white stretches of rock salt against a blue skyline broken by red-and-white stone windmills is spectacular. The province covers a land of great natural beauty, while the provincial capital, Trapani, lies below Mount Erice on a promontory stretching into the sea. A fishing and ferry port, Trapani is known for its fine seafood—particularly tuna—and wine from the region's vineyards. The local cuisine is influenced by the region's proximity to North Africa and Trapani is famed for its couscous.

The old town extends westwards out to sea, and a stroll through its narrow streets takes in old palazzi; ornate churches like the Cattedrale di San Lorenzo; the Torre della Colombaia offshore fortress; and at the tip of the headland, a former defensive outpost, the Torre del Ligny. Modern Trapani is marred by some ugly modern buildings, but merits a visit to see the Santuario dell'Annunziata and the Museo Regionale Pepoli. When you're shopping, look out for the salt and the exquisite coral jewelry made locally. The best time to visit is at Easter for Good Friday's **Processione dei Misteri** (Procession of the Mysteries), when 20 groups of wooden statues are carried through the streets in keeping with a centuries-old tradition.

Getting There

BY PLANE   The **Vincenzo Florio Airport** at Birgi, 15km (9 miles) from the center of Trapani (✆ **0923-842502;** www.airgest.it), has rapidly become the third major airport on the island and the main Ryanair hub for Sicily from the U.K. An excellent alternative to landing at Palermo, it is served by daily flights from the mainland, from the island of Pantelleria, and from abroad. From here, take any one of the **buses** that connect you to the city or to Palermo. **AST** (✆ **840-000323;** www.aziendasicilianatrasporti.it) has an hourly service from the airport to Trapani at a cost of 4.50€; **Salemi** (✆ **0923-981120;** www.autoservizisalemi.it) runs a service to Marsala for 4€ and to Palermo for 9€. **Lumia** (✆ **0922-20414;** www.autolineelumia.it) runs to Agrigento at a cost of 11€, while **Terravision** (✆ **0923-981120;** www.terravision.eu) operates to Trapani for 8€ and to Palermo for 12€. Alternatively, you can book a **taxi** (✆ **329-9128821;** www.trapanitaxidriver.it) for 25€ to 30€.

BY TRAIN   Frequent trains from Palermo make the 2½-hour run to Trapani; there are also about a dozen per day from Marsala, taking 30 minutes. Trains pull in at the **Piazza Stazione,** where luggage storage is available. For general information and ticket prices, call ✆ **892021,** or see www.trenitalia.it.

BY BUS   **AST** (✆ **840-000323;** www.aziendasicilianatrasporti.it) runs seven buses per day to Erice, departing from Piazza Montalto in Trapani. The one-way ride takes 50 minutes. From Palermo, **Salemi** (✆ **0923-981120;** www.autoservizi salemi.it) and **Segesta** (✆ **091-6167919;** www.etnatrasporti.it) make several daily runs to Trapani. **Note**: Both lines require reservations for passage; tickets are non-refundable.

BY FERRY   Trapani is a major embarkation point for ferries and hydrofoils. Most departures are for the Egadi Islands of Marettimo, Levanzo, and Favignana. Service is also available to Ustica, Pantelleria, Civitavecchia near Rome, and even Tunisia in North Africa. Ferries depart from the docks near Piazza Garibaldi. Service is offered by **Ustica** (✆ **0923-22200;** www.usticalines.it) or **Grimaldi** (✆ **0923-593673;** www.grimaldi-lines.com).

BY CAR   From Palermo, follow the A29 autostrada all the way southwest into Trapani. From Marsala, head north along Route 115 to Trapani.

Getting Around

BY BUS   The limited municipal bus service **ATM** (✆ **0923-559575**; www.atm trapani.it) gets you to where you need to go at the cost of 1€; tickets are valid for 90 minutes. If bought on board, expect to pay an extra 20 cents.

BY TAXI   Taxi ranks are found at the train station and at the port; to call one, dial ✆ **0923-22808** or ✆ 0923-23233.

Visitor Information

The **tourist office,** at Via San Francesco d'Assisi (✆ **0923-545511**), is open Monday to Saturday 8am to 8pm, Sunday 9am to noon.

[FastFACTS] TRAPANI

Pharmacies   There are two in the city center at Piazza Ciaccio Montalto 15 and Viale Regina Margherita 9. Pharmacies operate on a rotational system for night hours and weekends, with at least one open every night of the week and weekends and holidays.

Hospital   Serious medical needs are attended to at **Ospedale Sant'Antonio Abate,** Via Cosenza, in the northeast of the city (✆ **0923-809111**).

Internet   For Internet access, head to **Phone Center GGE,** Stazione Marittima (✆ **0923-549840**), where the rate is 4€ per hour.

Post Office   The post office, Piazza Vittorio Veneto (✆ **0923-28914**), is open Monday to Friday from 8:30am to 6:30pm and on Saturday from 8:30am to 12:30pm.

Exploring Trapani

Start off from the *centro storico* ★, the medieval core lying on the "sickle" into the sea. The oldest part of Trapani has a typical North African style and feel, creating a tightly wound labyrinth of narrow streets. As was typical of Saracen fortification, these streets lay behind defensive walls that guarded against unexpected invaders.

The most intriguing street is **Via Garibaldi** (also known as Rua Nova, or "New Road"), which is flanked with churches and palaces. The Aragonese laid out this street in the 18th century. The best shops in the old town line **Via Torrearsa,** which leads down to a bustling *pescheria* **(fish market)** where tuna—caught in nearby waters—is king. The spacious central square, **Piazza Vittorio Emanuele,** laid out in 1869 and planted with palm trees, is a relaxing oasis.

The pedestrianized main street of Trapani is **Corso Vittorio Emanuele,** sometimes called Rua Grande by the locals. Many elegant baroque buildings are found along this street, which makes for a grand promenade. At the eastern end of the street rises the **Palazzo Senatorio,** the 17th-century town hall, done up in pinkish marble.

Along the way, you can visit the **Cattedrale** (✆ **0923-432111**), open daily from 8am to 4pm. Built on the site of an earlier structure from the 14th century, the cathedral is dedicated to San Lorenzo (St. Lawrence) and has a 1743 facade.

GETTING TO the ISLANDS

A time-tested travel agency is **Panfalone,** Via Ammiraglio Staiti 91 (*℃* **0923-542470**), across the street from Trapani's harbor. The agency knows all the boat schedules and can sell tickets from Trapani to any of Sicily's offshore islands. A selling agency for most fleets, it also sells tickets for departures from other ports, for example from Palermo or Genoa.

Artworks inside include a *Crucifixion,* by Giacomo Lo Verde, a local artist, on the building's south side, fourth altar.

Another major church is **Chiesa Santa Maria del Gesù,** on Via San Pietro, with a facade that incorporates both Gothic and Renaissance features, dating from the first half of the 16th century. Its major work of art is a beautiful *Madonna degli Angeli* (Madonna with Angels), a glazed terra-cotta statue by Andrea della Robbia. Regrettably, the church is often closed.

Also worthy but perpetually closed is **Chiesa di Sant'Agostino,** Piazzetta Saturno, adjacent to the tourist office. This church is known for its exquisite rose window from the 14th century, and even more so for occasional concerts staged here. Ask at the tourist office for details.

Another church in the heart of the old town, **Chiesa del Purgatorio,** is in the 17th-century baroque style. In theory, it's open daily 8:30am to 12:30pm and from 4 to 8pm. It's across from Stazione Marittima, one block up from Piazza Garibaldi. The entire atmosphere of this church remains medieval, with intoxicating incense and otherworldly music. It houses the single greatest treasure in Trapani, however: The *Misteri* ★, 20 life-size wooden figures from the 18th century depicting Christ's Passion, and carried out every year during the Good Friday procession.

At the edge of town that extends out to the sea is the **Torre di Ligny,** built in 1671 as a defensive fortress on the northern tip of Trapani's "hook." It is the supposed home of the Museo Preistorico, but it is regrettably closed to the public. From this outpost you can see the **Isola Colombaia** and the decaying **Castello della Colombaia,** built during the Punic times as a fortification and enhanced by the Aragonese.

Villa Margherita lies between old and new Trapani. These public gardens offer a welcome respite from a day of tramping the cobblestone streets. Fountains, banyan trees, and palms rustling in the wind make for an inviting oasis. **Luglio Musicale Trapanese** (p. 37) a festival of opera, ballet, and cabaret, is staged here in July.

Modern Trapani has two sights worth a visit. **Santuario dell'Annunziata** ★ is a 14th-century convent whose cloisters enclose the major museum of Trapani (see below). The 14th-century church was forever altered in the 18th century by new decorators, although its Gothic portal remains, surmounted by a beautiful rose window. The **chapels** ★★ are a treasure and include two dedicated to the fishermen of Trapani who risk their lives daily to harvest the sea. The major chapel to seek out is the **Cappella della Madonna,** with its sacred Virgin and *Bambino,* attributed to Nino Pisano in the 14th century. The bronze gates to the chapel are from 1591. On its left flank is **Cappella dei Marinai,** a tufa-made chapel crowned by a dome and built in the Renaissance style.

Adjacent to the church is Trapani's major museum: **Museo Regionale Pepoli ★**, Via Conte Agostino Pepoli 200 (© **0923-553269**), open Monday to Saturday 9am to 1pm and Sunday 9am to 12:30pm. Admission is 4€, 2€ for children 12 and under. The former Carmelite convent has been converted into a showcase of regional art that emphasizes archaeological artifacts but also has a worthy collection of statues and coral carvings. The artistic Gagini family is better represented here than any other artist. Especially striking is *San Giacomo il Grande* by Antonello Gagini. The folk-art figurines are noteworthy, including a brutal depiction of the biblical legend of Herod's search for the Christ Child. Other works of art include a moving 14th-century *Pietà* ★, by Roberto di Oderisio, and some impressive triptychs by anonymous artists.

Where to Stay

Crystal Hotel ★   This is the most architecturally dramatic and urban-style hotel in Trapani. Attracting a predominantly business crowd, it's the most distinctive ultramodern building in an otherwise old town, characterized by an all-glass facade that curves above a piazza directly in front of the town's not-particularly-busy rail station. Guest rooms are comfortable and efficiently organized, as would be expected of the chain it belongs to.

Piazza Umberto I, 91100 Trapani. © **0923-20000.** Fax 0923-25555. www.crystalhoteltrapani.it. 70 units. 120€–190€ double; 260€–290€ suite. Rates include buffet breakfast. AE, DC, MC, V. Free parking. **Amenities:** Restaurant; bar; room service; babysitting; smoke-free rooms. *In room:* A/C, TV, minibar, Wi-Fi (free).

Duca di Castelmonte ★   Visitors seeking country atmosphere and good food can drive outside of town to this *agriturismo* in the countryside. Here you are housed in rustic comfort in little flats that can accommodate from two to six people. The dukes of Castelmonte still live at this castle. The original barns, stalls, and warehouses have been restored and turned into guest lodgings.

The setting is one of olive groves, citrus trees, and century-old pines. The owners grow their own vegetables, olives, and various fruits. The cooks prepare traditional recipes using time-tested family recipes that have been handed down from generation to generation.

Via Salvatore Motisi 3, 91020 Xitta (Trapani). ©/fax **0923-526139.** www.ducadicastelmonte.it. 9 units. 40€–50€ per person. Rates include breakfast. AE, MC, V. 5km (3 miles) west of Trapani along Via Florio. **Amenities:** Restaurant; outdoor pool; tennis court; babysitting. *In room:* No phone.

Hotel Russo   The oldest hotel in Trapani has been welcoming visitors for over 50 years. Newer, hipper places have since sprung up like mushrooms, but once you walk into its art-filled lobby, you feel that you're about to stay at one of the most deeply entrenched hotels in western Sicily. There are marble and tile floors throughout, an amusing set of frescoes in the breakfast room, and a sense of old-fashioned Trapani everywhere. Rooms are well maintained, comfortable, and without any particular sense of drama or theatricality.

Via Tintori 4, 91100 Trapani. © **0923-22163.** Fax 0923-26623. www.sicily-hotels.net. 35 units. 76€–85€ double. Rates include continental breakfast. AE, DC, MC, V. **Amenities:** Bar; room service; babysitting; Wi-Fi. *In room:* A/C, TV, minibar.

Hotel Vittoria ★★   On the shorefront with easy access to beaches, Hotel Vittoria combines both the convenience of being in the center of town and lido services for its guests. But that's not the only plus of this place—the staff are courteous, attentive, and make you feel at home immediately. Rooms are large with many facing the sea, and though the decor might seem a bit somber, it's the hotel efficiency and comfort that trumps the furnishings in this case. The generous buffet breakfast is the perfect way to start a day around town or at the beach.

Via Francesco Crispi 4, 91100 Trapani. ✆ **0923-873044.** Fax 0923-29870. www.hotelvittoriatrapani.it. 65 units. 80€–100€ double. Rates include breakfast. AE, DC, MC, V. Free street parking. **Amenities:** Breakfast lounge; bar; room service; Wi-Fi (free). *In room:* A/C, TV, minibar. Wi-Fi (free).

Ligny ★★ 🎁 Simply put, location, location, location: Ligny is on the tip of the "sickle," a stone's throw from the Ligny Tower and within walking distance of a beach and the port. The B&B is up two flights of stairs in an old palazzo, and it has comfortable, cozy rooms that combine northern African decor with the original elements of the building. Bathrooms are shower-only, but not all are en suite. The panoramic balconies in each guest room encompass the entire gulf and Erice. The neighborhood, made up of the city's fishermen for the most part, gives you a feel of authenticity; it's surrounded by a plethora of eateries.

Via Torre Ligny 114 91100 Trapani. ✆ **0923-1941515** (Mon–Fri 9:30am–5:30pm), or 328-9253805 (mobile). www.ligny.it. 5 units. 45€–80€ double. Rates include breakfast. No credit cards. Free street parking. **Amenities:** Wi-Fi (free). *In room:* A/C, TV.

Where to Eat

Ai Lumi Tavernetta ★ SICILIAN   Many locals cite this artfully rustic tavern, established in 1993 on the ground floor of what used to be an important family-owned palazzo, as one of Trapani's best restaurants. It's located two blocks from the cathedral and features a long, narrow dining room capped with a series of medieval-looking brick arches. During the 17th century it functioned as a stable, but today the venue is filled with wines from virtually everywhere, dark furniture, and a clientele that includes actors, politicians, and journalists. And, thanks to thick masonry walls and air-conditioning, it's a cool retreat from the blazing heat outside. Flavorful dishes include roast lamb in a citrus sauce, local rabbit that's larded and then roasted, and seafood pasta with shrimp and calamari that taste so fresh they could have just leapt from the boat.

Corso Vittorio Emanuele 75. ✆ **0923-872418.** www.ailumi.it. Reservations recommended Fri–Sat night. Main courses 8€–18€. AE, DC, MC, V. Sept–July Mon–Sat 7:30–11pm; Aug daily 7:30–11pm.

P & G ★★ 🍴 SICILIAN/SEAFOOD   This restaurant, one of the best in town, is located near the train station across from the public gardens of Villa Margherita (see above). It's also near the historic center, Via Fardella, and the shopping district. The decor is simple but classic, and service is impeccable. A highly recommended house specialty is *busiate,* the homemade pasta of the region, served with tomatoes, lots of garlic, anchovies, and almonds. Since North Africa is just across the sea, expect a wickedly delicious couscous prepared with fresh fish. Desserts are luscious, so save room.

Via Spalti 1. ✆ **0923-547701.** Reservations recommended. Main courses 7€–18€. AE, DC, MC, V. Mon–Sat 10am–3:30pm and 7pm–midnight.

Ristorante da Peppe SICILIAN   Convivial meals are served in this one-room restaurant, where large murals and a blue-green color scheme brighten up the varnished wood and white plaster. Menu items feature a well-rehearsed, oft-repeated

THE salt MARSHES ★★★

Stretching from Trapani to Marsala along route SP21, the salt pans along the coast have been in use since antiquity, and the windmills used to harvest it are centuries old. Used as a preservative for perishable food and as monetary compensation for mercenaries during the Roman times (the word "salary" derives from the Latin *salaries* meaning "soldier's allowance for the purchase of salt") it reached its pinnacle in the 19th century, when this salt was exported as far as Scandinavia. Today, it is still sought after by many gourmet chefs. When the Carthaginians first landed in the area they immediately understood the favorable natural and meteorological conditions offered, and set about to create basins from which to harvest salt. Exploiting the high level of salinity in the seawater and the wind and sun that contribute to the evaporation process, water is pumped in mid to late winter into the pans through a canal driven by an Archimedes screw. Over the next few months the water is left to evaporate, when it assumes a reddish color dense with mineral pigment. Around July, just as it reaches a sluggish consistency, the salt is raked and harvested, and brought on to terra firma to complete the exsiccation process. What look like little salt huts line the road, covered in terra-cotta tiles to protect them from the elements. Once completely dry, the salt is cleansed of debris and ready for packaging. The salt today is still being extracted, albeit not with the same urgency as in the past; nonetheless its history and technique has been preserved, and a fascinating insight into how the process is still carried out, is visible at Paceco, 5km (3 miles) south of Trapani. The area has now been designated a World Wildlife Fund reserve, the **Riserva Naturale Orientata "Saline di Trapani e Paceco"** (✆ **0923-867700;** www.wwfsalineditrapani.it), covering 1,000 hectares (2,471 acres). At **the Museo del Sale (Salt Museum),** at Nubia (✆ **0923-867442;** www.trattoriadelsale.com) guided tours are offered in what used to be an old salt worker's house dating back to the 1700s, where tools and artifacts used during the course of history to harvest salt are on display. Doubling as a restaurant, you'll also have the chance to sample local cuisine, which consists of home-style cooking and the catch of the day. If possible, visit in the afternoon, when you'll witness sunsets against a terse evening sky that changes color as the sun goes down and as the migrating birds perform their spectacular in-flight choreographies.

medley of mostly Sicilian dishes, such as spaghetti with squid and squid ink; three kinds of couscous; risotto paella (a Sicilian adaptation of the famous dish of Valencia); and a time-honored favorite, *spaghetti rustica,* with swordfish, tuna, salmon, dried tomatoes, Abruzzi herbs, and breadcrumbs.

Via Spalti 50. ✆ **0923-28246.** Reservations recommended Fri–Sat night. Main courses 8€–15€; fixed-price menus 14€–22€. AE, DC, MC, V. Daily 1–11pm.

Taverna Paradiso ★ SICILIAN   This tavern, established in 1996 in an old warehouse on the seafront, is the town's most prestigious restaurant. The warren of medieval-looking stone rooms is stylishly decorated with rustic artifacts that show off the antique masonry to its best advantage. The food is excellent, and prices aren't nearly as high as you might expect from a place of this quality. Care and precision go into every dish, especially the house specialties: A maritime version of couscous; spaghetti with tangy sea urchins; and a marvelous pasta dish with lobster, shrimp, and fresh artichokes. In winter, well-flavored meat and poultry dishes are likely to be featured when fish catches are slim due to rough waters.

Lungomare Dante Alighieri 22. © **0923-22303.** Reservations recommended. Main courses 10€–18€. AE, DC, MC, V. Mon–Sat 1–3:30pm and 8–11:30pm.

Shopping

Cinzia Gucciardo This is one of the few stores in Trapani that specializes in jewelry made from coral gathered in nearby waters. Inventories include necklaces, bracelets, and coral-crafted votive portraits of saints that are larger and more elaborate than anything else in Trapani. There's also a collection of 19th-century engravings and art objects, most of them focusing on 18th-century selections, usually in music rooms or salons. Corso Vittorio Emanuele 23–25. © **0923-25542.**

Gioielleria Enzo Catania This might be the most elegant shop in town, the kind of place where a security system "buzzes" you inside after you've been checked out by the staff through a plate-glass window. Inside, you'll find clocks; silver picture frames and chalices; religious icons; and impressive gold, silver, and platinum jewelry. Corso Vittorio Emanuele 39–41. © **0923-21148.**

Libreria del Corso One of the town's best bookstores sells Italian-language (and to a lesser degree, English-language) books, many of them about Sicily and its art treasures. Corso Vittorio Emanuele 61. © **0923-26260.**

MARSALA

134km (83 miles) NW of Agrigento, 301km (187 miles) W of Catania, 124km (77 miles) SW of Palermo, 31km (19 miles) S of Trapani.

A thriving little port on Cape Boeo, the westernmost tip of Sicily overlooking the Egadi Islands and Tunisia, Marsala is where the world-famous Marsala sweet wine is produced thanks to the area's fertile red earth, sunshine, and sea breezes. This is an elegant town with baroque buildings, Roman ruins, a lively fish market, and a long sandy coastline stretching to the north and south.

Like the town itself, Marsala wine has antique origins, but it was first popularized in 1770 when an English trader, John Woodhouse, was forced to anchor here during a violent storm. Woodhouse headed for a tavern, downed some local wine, and realized it had commercial potential: The rest is history. You can drink some of the amber yellow Marsala in one of the town's quaint wine shops, or head through the hills along roads lined with prickly-pear cacti to one of the vineyards nearby. Townspeople drink the dark, vintage Marsala, which is best sipped as a dessert wine with hard piquant cheese, fruit or pastries, and it's also used to flavor the local *cassatelle* cakes made from fried ricotta and cinnamon.

Wine isn't the only gastronomic delight in Marsala; it's a good place to try what's considered to be the oldest handmade pasta in the world, *busiati*. The curly pasta has a firm texture and mealy taste, and is good eaten with pesto sauce made Trapanese style with cherry tomatoes.

Marsala

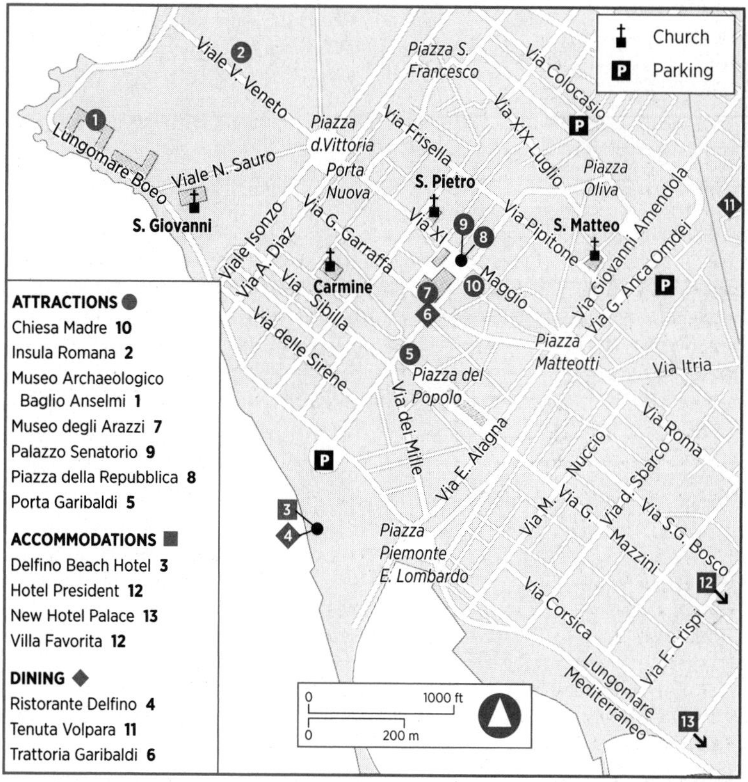
Church
Parking
Viale V. Veneto
Piazza S. Francesco
Via Colocasio
Lungomare Boeo
Viale N. Sauro
Piazza d.Vittoria
Porta Nuova
Via Frisella
Via XIX Luglio
Piazza Oliva
S. Pietro
S. Giovanni
Viale Isonzo
Via A. Diaz
Via G. Garraffa
Via XI
Via Pipitone
S. Matteo
Via Giovanni Amendola
Via G. Anca Omdei
Via Sibilla
Carmine
Maggio
Via delle Sirene
Piazza Matteotti
Via Itria
Piazza del Popolo
Via dei Mille
Via E. Alagna
Via Roma
Via M. Nuccio
Via G. Mazzini
Via d. Sbarco
Via S.G. Bosco
Piazza Piemonte E. Lombardo
Via Corsica
Via F. Crispi
Lungomare Mediterraneo
0 1000 ft
0 200 m
ATTRACTIONS
Chiesa Madre 10
Insula Romana 2
Museo Archaeologico Baglio Anselmi 1
Museo degli Arazzi 7
Palazzo Senatorio 9
Piazza della Repubblica 8
Porta Garibaldi 5
ACCOMMODATIONS
Delfino Beach Hotel 3
Hotel President 12
New Hotel Palace 13
Villa Favorita 12
DINING
Ristorante Delfino 4
Tenuta Volpara 11
Trattoria Garibaldi 6

The best time to visit the town is in early May when its inhabitants don red shirts to re-enact one of the most important events in Italian history: The landing of Garibaldi and his brigade of Red Shirts at Marsala on May 11, 1860, which was the start of the freedom-fighter's campaign to unify Italy.

GETTING THERE Multiple **trains** run daily south from Trapani and Palermo. The journey takes 30 minutes from Trapani, up to 3 hours from Palermo. For schedules and fares call ✆ **892021,** or see www.trenitalia.it.

AST Buses for Marsala leave from Piazza Montalto in Trapani at the rate of three per day. The one-way trip lasts 35 minutes. For schedules, call ✆ **0923-21021** or see www.aziendasicilianatrasporti.it. From Palermo, **Salemi** (✆ **0923 981120;** www.autoservizisalemi.it) runs several buses to the town center. The journey takes 1 hour 45 minutes.By **car,** head south from Trapani along Route 115.

VISITOR INFORMATION The **tourist office,** at Via 11 Maggio 100 (✆ **0923-714097**), is open Monday to Saturday 8am to 1:45pm and 2:10 to 8:10pm, Sunday 9am to noon.

FLORIO, WOODHOUSE, nelson, & WHITAKER

Even a brief history of Marsala would not be complete without mentioning John Woodhouse and Vincenzo Florio. Woodhouse landed at Marsala in 1773, and 'discovered' that the local wine produced in the area, and aged in wooden barrels, tasted similar to the Portuguese "Porto." Eventually, this fortified wine found such success in England that he returned to Sicily in 1796, and became a pioneer in the mass production and commercialization of **Marsala wine.**

The legendary Admiral Horatio Nelson, who defeated Napoleon Bonaparte in the Battle of the Nile, spent a great deal of time in the northwest region of Sicily, between Palermo and Marsala. It was he who introduced Marsala wine to the British Navy as an alternative to Port, and even suggested a regimen of one glass per day.

Joseph Whitaker, a young English entrepreneur and archaeologist, inherited a vast vineyard in Marsala, upon which he founded a "*baglio*," or typical Sicilian wine estate. From this *baglio*, Whitaker made a fortune exporting wine to the U.S. and England around the turn of the 19th century. In his later years, Whitaker is known to have bought the island of Mozia (p. 175), where he founded an archaeological museum and published important studies of Tunisian birds. However, his influence on Marsala's development and economy, even today, cannot be overstated.

At the beginning of the 19th century, Vincenzo Florio, an entrepreneur from Palermo, purchased the Woodhouse wine industry and set out to create his very own vintage, with a more exclusive breed of grapes. During that time, often referred to as *la belle epoque*, the Florio family were considered one the richest of Italy. They also owned one of the first tuna canneries, from the *tonnare* (fisheries) of the Egadi Islands, as well as a large fishing vessel that was one of the first to take tuna from Marsala across the Atlantic to New York. Although the family retired from industry after World War I, their name remains one of the largest and most recognizable in Marsala wine production.

GETTING AROUND   For a **taxi,** call ✆ **339-5497849.**

FAST FACTS   In an **emergency,** call the *Carabinieri* (army police corps) at ✆ **112.** The most convenient drugstore is the **Farmacia Calcagno,** Via 11 Maggio 126 (✆ **0923-953254**). When it's closed, a notice is posted listing what other pharmacies are open. For medical care, go to the **Hospital San Biagio,** Via Colocasio 10 (✆ **0923-782111**).

What to See & Do

Enter the city from the **Porta Garibaldi** (formerly Porta di Mare), a glorious gateway from the 1600s crowned by an eagle. Garibaldi is honored because it was at Marsala that he and his red-shirted volunteers overthrew the Bourbon reign. The road from the gate leads on to **Via Garibaldi,** where it ends at the busy **Piazza della Repubblica,** the heart of the city. The **Palazzo Senatorio,** now the Town Hall, dating from the 18th century and nicknamed "Loggia," is located here, as is the cathedral.

The largest church in Marsala is the **Chiesa Madre** (℃ **0923-716295**), open daily 7:30am to 7pm. Originally constructed during the Norman occupation, the church was dedicated to St. Thomas à Becket, which in hindsight seems rather fitting, considering Marsala's English connections. Legend has it that a ship carrying materials to build a church dedicated to the saint was on its way to England when a storm forced it to seek shelter in the harbor of Marsala. It was with all probability the first church dedicated to the martyred English saint, and it was in Sicily that Becket's family took refuge when he was exiled from England. The church was completely overhauled in baroque fashion in the 1700s. The cupola collapsed in 1893 and was partially reconstructed in the 20th century. The sandstone facade is decorated with statues of saints and flanked by two small campaniles (bell towers) that are incorporated into the facade, which itself was ultimately completed in the 1950s. The three-nave interior is graced with slender marble columns and houses noteworthy works of art, including 15th- and 16th-century sculptures by the Gagini brothers. Seek out, in particular, the lovely *Madonna del Popolo* in the right transept, a 1490 creation of Domenico Gagini.

Behind the Chiesa Madre is the entrance to **Museo degli Arazzi (Tapestry Museum)**, Via Garraffa 57 (℃ **0923-711327**). It houses a formidable collection of eight **Flemish tapestries** ★, made in Brussels between 1530 and 1550. All are from the Royal Palace of Phillip II in Madrid. These exquisite tapestries depict such scenes as the capture of Jerusalem and the war fought by Titus against the Jews in A.D. 66 to A.D. 67. After undergoing meticulous restoration, the tapestries are kept in darkened rooms to avoid damage. The museum is open Monday to Saturday 9am to 1pm and 4 to 6pm, Sunday 9am to 1pm; admission is 2.50€.

North from Piazza Repubblica is the main thoroughfare, **Via 11 Maggio,** extending from west to east from Piazza della Vittoria to Piazza Matteotti, flanked by the town's most splendid baroque palazzo. From here make your way northwest toward the sea, where you'll find the archaeological museum—the **Museo Archaeologico Baglio Anselmi** ★, at Lungomare Boéo (℃ **0923-952535**). The museum occupies a former warehouse (*baglio*) for Marsala wine. The installation occupies two sections of the warehouse and displays among other things prehistoric gold jewelry, remnants coming from the Tophet, (the sacrificial burial area of Mozia), and amphorae from shipwrecks. Labeled according to date, origin, and contents, it sheds light on the fascinating ancient Mediterranean trade route. The museum's main attraction is the relic of a well-preserved **Punic ship** ★★ discovered in 1971 off Isola Longa in the Stagnone lagoon. The ship is thought to have been originally constructed for the Battle of the Egadi Islands in 241 B.C. yet sunk on its maiden voyage; it's amazing to think that any vessel dating back to the First Punic War has been discovered. Measuring 35m (115 ft.) long and carefully reconstructed in 1980, the ship has nails that have eluded corrosion (how, exactly, is a mystery). Manned by 68 oarsmen, it was the type of warship that made the Romans green with envy. Objects that were on board—including cannabis leaves and stalks—are also on display. The museum is open Wednesday to Saturday 9am to 7pm, and Sunday to Tuesday 9am to 1pm. Admission is 4€ for adults and 2€ for children 17 and under and adults 65 and over.

After your visit to the museum, head north along the **Lungomare Boéo,** dotted with many old *bagli,* or Marsala wine warehouses, some still in use while others have been converted into restaurants. As you make your way along the bend, stop in either of the two wine shops next door to one another, **Enoteca La Ruota** (at number 36/A, ✆ **0923-715241**) and **Enoteca Luminario** 34/A, ✆ **0923-713150**), where the friendly owners will welcome you in and where you can sip the local wines while admiring the Stagnone lagoon lying in front of you. At the intersection with Via Piave are the excavations of the ancient Lilybaeum or the **Insula Romana,** an archaeological area open to the public 24 hours a day. It contains the remains of a Roman villa, true to Marsala's imperial past, (which had a steam room, among its other trappings), and well-preserved mosaics ★.

Where to Stay

Baglio Fontanasalsa ★★ ☺ Consider this olive farm your retreat from the outside world. Belonging to the same family for centuries, the last of the heirs gave up her medical practice to tend to her ancestral home, creating award-winning olive oils in the process. As a guest, you can have a first-hand look at how the olive oil is made, while you stay in one of the rustic rooms of the farmhouse. Rooms are simple, light-drenched, and decorated with country flair; the public areas have warm, cozy niches that make you feel at home. The home-cooked meals on the premises are some of the best in the area.

Via Cusenza, 78, 91020 Fontanasalsa ✆ **0923-591120;** www.fontanasalsa.it. 9 units. 100€–150€ double; 120€–170€ suite. Rates include breakfast. AE, DC, MC, V. Free parking. **Amenities:** Restaurant; outdoor pool; Internet (5€/hr). *In room:* A/C, TV.

Delfino Beach Hotel This is the closest thing to a large-scale resort in Marsala. Set 5km (3 miles) south of town, behind a neo-baroque facade across a busy highway from the beach, it was designed as a compound of cement-sided buildings within a walled garden, centered on a splashy-looking core that evokes a theatrical stage setting.

Most of the double bedrooms are midsize, with modern furnishings, often with a sitting area. Each is well supplied with modern gadgets, including individual controls for the air-conditioning. The 16 well-furnished apartments are far more generous in size, with sitting and living areas separate from the bedrooms. Many of these are suites suitable for families of about four persons. The hotel restaurant and its beachfront lie a dusty 10-minute walk across the busy highway from the hotel's core. I prefer the Hotel President (see below), closer to the center of town.

Lungomare Mediterraneo 672, 91025 Marsala. ✆ **0923-751076.** Fax 0923-751647. www.delfinobeach. com. 50 units. 92€–180€ double. Rates include half board. AE, DC, MC, V. Free parking. **Amenities:** Restaurant; bar; outdoor pool; tennis court; exercise room; room service; babysitting. *In room:* A/C, TV, minibar, Jacuzzi (in some), hair dryer, Internet.

Hotel President ★ Modern and pleasingly designed, this is a welcoming, efficient hotel with a whiff of jazzy insouciance that might have been inspired by Las Vegas. You may be surprised to learn that this favorite stopover of business travelers is rated only three stars by the local tourist authorities, since it looks very much as if it deserves four. The entrance is prefaced with a row of palms; inside, a sheathing of travertine marble adds a touch of sober dignity. Guest rooms are located in two five-story towers, connected at the bases by a granite-floored lobby strewn with leather sofas and chairs. Guest rooms are comfortable, sunny, and relatively large, each with a bathroom that—with three separate kinds of marble sheathing and tub/ shower combinations—looks like a testimonial to the stonemason's art.

Via Nino Bixio 1, 91025 Marsala. ℂ **0923-999333.** Fax 0923-999115. www.hotelpresidentmarsala.com. 128 units. 95€–105€ double. AE, DC, MC, V. Free parking. **Amenities:** Restaurant; 2 bars; outdoor pool; gym; room service. *In room:* A/C, TV, minibar, hair dryer.

New Hotel Palace ★ ☺ This 19th-century estate was built by an English wine importer, but it has been completely redone as a modern hotel, enough to warrant a five-star government rating. Amazingly, the original architectural and historical appearance has been maintained as much as possible, despite the addition of another 48 guest rooms. Newer units duplicate the style of the original eight units in the main house. Bedrooms are spacious and furnished in the style of a grand hotel. Some of the units are adorned with frescoes by local artists. The bar is the spot for an elegant rendezvous, and the first-class restaurant serves market-fresh ingredients in delightful concoctions. A tree-lined park lies in front of the hotel, and stately old trees are a backdrop for the swimming pool. Children enjoy the playground.

Lungomare Mediterraneo 57, 91025 Marsala. ℂ **0923-719492.** Fax 0923-719496. www.newhotelpalace. com. 56 units. 95€–130€ standard double; 140€–220€ superior with sea view; from 300€ family room/ suite. Rates include buffet breakfast. AE, DC, MC, V. Free parking. Pets welcome. **Amenities:** Restaurant; bar; outdoor pool; room service; babysitting; all smoke-free rooms. *In room:* A/C, TV, minibar, hair dryer, Internet (free).

Villa Favorita ★★ 🏠 This elegant and offbeat choice was established in the early 19th century, when it became a rendezvous for Sicilian intellectuals and aristocrats. Today the retreat is part of the cultural heritage of Marsala and has been given a new lease of life. Much of the original architecture of the main building has been preserved, with its wide oak floors and arched loggias opening onto a courtyard. You have a choice of a more traditional room in the main building or, for greater privacy, a whitewashed igloo-shaped bungalow in the garden. Bedrooms are spacious. First-rate Sicilian and Italian dishes are a feature of the on-site restaurant that's a popular choice for weddings and parties.

Via Favorita 23, 91025 Marsala. ℂ **0923-989100.** Fax 0923-980264. www.villafavorita.com. 29 bungalows, 13 units (in the main building). 85€–105€ double in bungalow; 100€–125€ double (in the main building). Rates include buffet breakfast. AE, DC, MC, V. Free parking. From the center of Marsala, take the SS115 toward Trapani. The hotel is signposted. **Amenities:** Restaurant; bar; outdoor pool; tennis court; babysitting; Internet. *In room:* A/C, TV, minibar.

Where to Eat

Ristorante Delfino ★ SEAFOOD/SICILIAN This restaurant lies adjacent to the beachfront and across the highway from the hotel that bears the same name. It was established in the 1960s and has done rip-roaring business ever since. The setting is a very large, always-bustling series of terrazzo-floored, slightly battered dining rooms, with a row of large windows and a terrace overlooking the sea. A huge array of antipasti, plus a steamy hardworking kitchen that's open to view, greets visitors as they enter. The fish soup is the best in town, but the homemade *bucatini* pasta in a tuna and mint sauce may be your starter of choice. Several kinds of carpaccio, often flavored with balsamic vinegar, are presented nightly. The chef is justifiably proudest of his wide variety of fresh fish, much of which is exhibited in a display case near the entrance.

Delfino Beach Hotel (see above). ℂ **0923-998188.** Main courses 8€–17€; pizzas 5€–8€; fixed-price menu 20€. AE, MC, V. Daily 8:30am–11pm. Closed Tues Oct–Mar.

Tenuta Volpara ★ 🎒 SICILIAN   Follow a labyrinth of winding country roads, then pass between a stately pair of masonry columns, to reach Marsala's quintessential country inn—a jumble of light, noise, and energy in an otherwise isolated rural setting, 6km (3½ miles) south of the city center. Vast and echoing, with one of the largest dining rooms in western Sicily, it was rebuilt in 1993 on the site of a ruined tavern that had been here for centuries. Many diners come as part of a wedding reception or baptism, which adds to this place's sense of fun. Beneath soaring stone arches, you'll dine on such items as steak braised in a Barolo wine sauce, homemade sausages roasted with a herb-flavored liqueur, fettuccine with fresh mushrooms, and the dessert specialty, *zabina*, a pastry with ricotta cheese.

In an annex somewhat removed from the bustle of the restaurant are 18 motel-style guest rooms, each with a shower-only bathroom, air-conditioning, minibar, TV, and phone. With breakfast included, a double costs 80€.

Contrada Volpara. 📞 **0923-984588.** Fax 0923-984667. Reservations recommended Fri-Sat night. Main courses 7€–15€; fixed-price menu 15€. AE, DC, MC, V. Daily 1:30–3pm and 8:30pm–midnight. Closed Mon Oct-Mar.

Trattoria Garibaldi ★ 🦐 SICILIAN/SEAFOOD   Located in the historic center near the cathedral, this unpretentious restaurant has been feeding locals well since 1963. Patrons come here, some once or twice a week, to enjoy the dishes, which despite their low prices are made with fresh, quality ingredients. The chef is justly proud of his array of antipasti, including succulent mussels and sea urchins (the latter dish an acquired taste for many). I especially like his *busiate* (the local home-made pasta) served with fresh fish. He also does a Moroccan-inspired couscous with fish. The signature dessert is *cappidruzzi,* fried ravioli filled with ricotta.

Piazza dell'Addolorata 35. 📞 **0923-953006.** www.trattoriagaribaldi.com. Reservations recommended. Main courses 7€–13€. MC, V. Mon-Fri noon–3pm and 7:30–10pm; Sat 7:30–10pm; Sun noon–3pm.

SELINUNTE ★★★

122km (76 miles) SW of Palermo, 113km (70 miles) W of Agrigento, 89km (55 miles) SE of Trapani.

A day spent wandering around Selinunte's archaeological park (Parco Archelogico Selinunte) is a must on any trip to Sicily. Vast and, at 270 hectares (670 acres), Europe's largest archaeological park, it's not just that you can walk around ancient Greek temples, crane your neck looking up at stout columns, peek in on what were once sacred shrines, and clamber across heaps of awe-inspiring rubble, it's also a fabulous place to relax and enjoy a picnic. The ruins look out to sea and the park is so large it's easy to find a peaceful spot where you're unlikely to be disturbed. You can gaze out at the deep blue waters of the Mediterranean Sea, and realize that the ancient Greeks had an eye for a great view, while perhaps witnessing a shepherd taking a flock of sheep past where his distant ancestors lived and worked.

Strolling around the various ruins it's easy to gain an impression of just how large and important a city Selinunte was at its height before Hannibal virtually destroyed it in 409 B.C., and it still has an air of noble, albeit faded, beauty. In the summer, the heat bears down on this exposed spot as if from a furnace, bleaching the long grasses almost white; but on a spring day, you'll admire the colors of the numerous wild flowers, vegetables, and herbs that pepper the bright green grass. The shrub and vegetation add an air of wildness to the site, which takes its name from the Greek

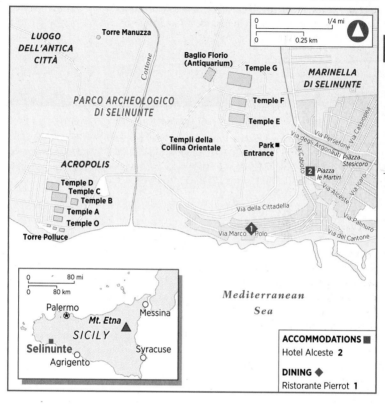

word *selinon,* meaning parsley, and it's possible that the ancient inhabitants foraged here just as the food-loving Sicilians do today.

Essentials

GETTING THERE   Selinunte is on the southern coast of Sicily and is easily reached by **car.** From Agrigento, take the scenic Route 115 northwest into Castelvetrano; then follow the signposted secondary road marked SELINUNTE, which leads south to the sea. From Palermo or Trapani, take the A29 autostrada and get off at Castelvetrano, following the signs thereafter. Allow an hour from Trapani and at least 2 hours from either Palermo or Agrigento.

If you prefer to take the **train** (© **892021;** www.trenitalia.it) from Palermo, Trapani, or Marsala, you can get off at Castelvetrano, 23km (14 miles) from the ruins. The trip from Palermo to Castelvetrano takes a little over 2 hours (you need to change trains; cost is 7.40€); from Trapani five trains make the 1¼-hour journey and cost 5.50€; from Marsala, it's only 40 minutes, with trains leaving five times a day and costing 3.80€.

GETTING around THE ARCHAEOLOGICAL PARK

At 270 hectares (667 acres), the ruins of Selinunte cover the most extensive area of Classical artifacts in Europe, including Greece. To make your visit swifter and more relaxing, **Ecotour**

Selinunte runs a hop-on-hop-off service to all the sites within the park on a train of golf carts. For more info, call ℂ **347-1645862** or visit www.selinunte service.com.

Once at Castelvetrano, board a **bus** for the final lap of the journey to Selinunte. **Autoservizi Salemi** (ℂ **0923-981120;** www.autoservizisalemi.it), which also operates a service from Palermo to Castelvetrano, will take you to the archaeological park in 20 minutes. **Lumia buses** (ℂ **0922-20414;** www.autolineelumia.it) run to Castelvetrano station from Agrigento.

VISITOR INFORMATION   The **tourist office,** Via Giovanni Caboto (ℂ **0924-46251**), near the archaeological garden, is open Monday to Saturday 8am to 2pm and 3 to 8pm, Sunday 9am to noon and 3 to 6pm.

Exploring the Archaeological Garden ★★

The archaeological grounds are designated into three distinct zones: The **East Hill and temples,** the **Acropolis and ancient city,** and the **Sanctuary of Demeter Malophorus.** The Doric temples, faithfully rebuilt as best they could be and still the subject of study as to which deity they were dedicated to, are simply denoted by letters of the alphabet. You'll occasionally see fragments of the stucco finish on them, which was painted on to make the columns look like marble, just like the originals in the motherland. The stones used to build Selinunte came from the nearby quarry of **Cave Di Cusa.** You will most likely start your visit from the East Hill, adjacent to the main entrance.

   East Hill: This was the sacred district of the city, surrounded by an enclosure. Here you will find three temples, beginning with impressive **Temple E,** which was with all probability dedicated to Hera (Juno), according to a votive *stele,* or upright stone bearing a monumental inscription, found in the temple. Built between 490 and 480 B.C and measuring 67.7m by 25.3m (212.5 ft. x 83 ft.), it has a staggering 68 columns (consider that the temple in Segesta, in comparison, has half as many) and still contains remains of the inner temple. Reconstructed in 1958 after being toppled by an earthquake, the precious Metopes, the reliefs between two triglyphs of the entablatures, are now housed at the archaeological museum in Palermo. Next is **Temple F.** Not much is known about this temple except that it was the oldest of the three (560–540 B.C.); it's believed to be dedicated to Aphrodite, Athena, or Dionysius. In its original state it had a double row of 6 columns at the eastern entrance and 14 columns on either side, with the lower part of the peristyle enclosed by a wall. The last temple, **Temple G,** a heap of rubble except for a lone standing column restored in 1832, was destined to be of colossal proportions had it been completed in 480 B.C., as the size of its base attests: 110.36m (362 ft.) by 50.1m (164 ft.), it had 8 columns on either entrance and 17 on either side, matching the Parthenon. Dedicated to Zeus, it is second largest temple in Sicily.

After viewing Temples E, F, and G, all near the parking lot at the entrance, you can get in your car and drive along the Strada dei Templi west to the **Acropolis** or walk there (20 min). **This site that included the western temples,** was enclosed within defensive walls and built from the 6th century to the 5th century B.C. The streets of the Acropolis were laid out along classical lines, with a trio of principal arteries bisected at right angles by a grid of less important streets. The Acropolis was the site of the most important public and religious buildings, and it was also the residence of the town's aristocrats.

At the highest point of the hill is **Temple C.** In 1925, 14 of the 17 columns of Temple C were re-erected. This is the earliest surviving temple of ancient Selinus, built in the 6th century B.C. and probably dedicated to Hercules or Apollo. In order to accommodate the huge sacrificial altar within, the *temenos,* or sacred enclosure, was modified and steps were added to the original internal structure. Temple C towers over the other ruins and gives you a better impression of what all the temples might have looked like at one time. Artifacts such as a cross were found around the area, a testament to the Orthodox settlement in Selinunte. Nearby once stood the small **Temple B. Temple D,** also built in the mid-6th century, is the second oldest temple and once supported 34 columns. Just beyond the temple is the so-called **Temple of Small Metopes,** which are now housed at the archaeological museum in Palermo.

At the tip of the cliff overlooking the sea, near the custodian's house, lie the twin temples, **Temple A** and **Temple O,** built in the 5th century B.C. and which, like the others, remain in scattered ruins.

Sanctuary of Demeter Malophorous: As you follow the road leading west of the Acropolis, you cross the Modione River, arriving at the most ancient part of the area, believed to predate the actual Megaran settlement. Within a large enclosure are the ruins of several shrines where worshipers placed stone figurines to honor or appease the gods; 5,000 such figurines have been unearthed in the surrounding area. Many *stele* carved with male and female heads have also been recovered, and a few are displayed in Palermo. Next to this is the Sanctuary of Zeus. Excavations of the nearby Manicalunga necropolis, extending down to the shore, have resulted in heaps of bones amassed for all to see.

The park is open from 9am to one hour before sunset daily. Admission is 9€ for adults, 4€ for adults 18 to 25, and free for children 17 and under and adults 65 and over from the EU, Australia, and Canada. The ticket is valid for 3 days and is also good for entrance to Segesta (p. 148). Given the enormity of the area, allow yourself at least 3 hours to visit, preferably in the early morning. Bring or buy drinks before starting your visit, as you can get rather thirsty under the sun.

Where to Stay Nearby

The site of the ruins has no lodgings and restaurants, but you can find many of them in the adjacent seaside villages of Marinella and Triscina, which are both the seaside resort towns of Castelvetrano (p. 171). East of Marinella lies a wildlife reserve at the mouth of the Belice River and along what used to be the old Castelvetrano–Sciacca railway.

Hotel Alceste   This concrete structure is about a 15-minute walk from the ruins. Guest rooms have small tiled bathrooms with tub/shower combos. Most visitors, however, stop only for a visit to the plant-filled courtyard, where in summer there's musical entertainment, dancing, cabaret, and theater. The somewhat shy and very kind owner, Orazio Torrente, is charming, as is his family. The airy, bustling restaurant is open daily for lunch and dinner (main courses 7€–14€); it's sometimes filled with busloads of visitors from as far away as Hungary. Note that in July and August a large number of academics stay at the hotel.

Via Alceste 21, 91022 Marinella di Selinunte. © **0924-46184.** Fax 0924-46143. www.hotelalceste.it. 30 units. 50€–87€ double; 115€ triple. Rates include continental breakfast. AE, DC, MC, V. All smoke-free rooms. **Amenities:** Restaurant; room service; Internet (5€/hr). *In room:* A/C, TV.

Where to Eat

Hotel Alceste, recommended above, is also a good choice for dining.

Ristorante Pierrot ★ 🍴 SICILIAN   With a terrace opening onto the Mediterranean, this is the best place in the area for regional food. With a seafront table and a rustic decor, you can enjoy fresh produce from the market and fish caught that same day. Travelers tired from visiting the ruins are quickly refreshed here with the invigorating cuisine prepared by skilled cooks. Since you're so close to North Africa, fish couscous regularly appears on the menu. *Orecchiette* (their homemade pasta) is served with succulent scampi. Another homemade pasta, and one I like even better, is *spaccatelle con melenzane e pesca spada* (pasta sautéed with swordfish, eggplant, and tomato sauce). Nearly everyone orders one of the seafood pasta dishes, such as one with sea urchins, mussels, and shrimp. But you can also order your catch of the day grilled or sautéed to your specifications.

Via Marco Polo 108, Marinella. © **0924-46205.** Reservations recommended. Main courses 8€–15€; fixed-price menus 15€–30€. AE, DC, MC, V. Daily 10am–3pm and 7pm–midnight.

Farther Afield: Mazara del Vallo

WHERE TO STAY

Kempinski Hotel Giardino di Costanza ★★★   Set in a landscaped park of olive groves and vineyards, this German chain hotel is the only Kempinski property in Italy. You wander among Vegas-y fountains and gazebos before entering a refined world of understated elegance and sublime comfort. The spacious, beautifully furnished guest rooms are a harmonious blend of typical Sicilian decor and warm colors that open onto a private balcony or terrace.

The children's programs here are the best along the coast while, for the adults, the on-site spa is named for the noted Austrian aesthetician Daniela Steiner, whose clinics in St. Moritz and Monte Carlo are always packed. Steiner suggests preserving skin beauty by using natural methods, in this case Sicilian products such as sea salt. Patrons are also smeared with volcanic clay. The sublime Sicilian cuisine highlights regional produce. An hour's drive from Palermo, the location is ideal for exploring such ancient sights as Segesta, Selinunte, Erice, and Marsala.

Via Salemi, Km. 7,1000, 91026 Mazara del Vallo. © **0923-675000.** Fax 0923-675876. www.kempinski sicily.com. 91 units. 200€–387€ double; 640€ junior suite; 4,900€ penthouse suite. AE, DC, MC, V. **Amenities:** Restaurant; 2 bars; 2 pools (indoor and outdoor); spa; room service. *In room:* A/C, TV, minibar, Wi-Fi (free).

WHERE TO DINE

Trattoria delle Cozze-Basiricó ★ 👜 SEAFOOD/SICILIAN   Set on the southern outskirts of the town of Mazara del Vallo, about 5km (3 miles) from the center, this restaurant might remind you of an oversize railway car that just happens to serve vast amounts of seafood to hundreds of diners every night throughout the summer. Don't expect grandeur; this is a gutsy, two-fisted place whose walls are open to the sea breezes. There are no printed menus here: A fast-talking waiter will tell you that the only options are selections from the buffet-style antipasti table, several different preparations of mussels, and steamed octopus in either lemon or tomato sauce. Drinks of choice include wine or beer, a suitable accompaniment for the restaurant's widely acknowledged specialty, mussels.

Litoranea Mazara-Granitola. (✆ **0923-942323.** www.trattoriadellecozze.it. Reservations not accepted. Main courses 7€–10€. AE, DC, MC, V. Mazara del Vallo is reached by heading southeast of Marsala along Rte. 115 for 22km (14 miles). May–Sept daily 8pm–midnight. Closed Oct–Apr.

MOZIA ★★★

2km (1.2 miles) W of Marsala, 15 km (9.3 miles) SW of Trapani.

For lovers of ancient art, Mozia is a delight. Located on the tiny island of San Pantaleo—one of the small islands in the Stagnone, a lagoon and nature reserve among the salt flats between Marsala and Trapani—this archaeological site is home to the ruins of the Carthaginian city of Motya. The island is also a wonderful place to observe the many birds that visit the lagoon, including pink flamingoes, curlews, and egrets. It's a pretty spot for a picnic, particularly in the summer when plants such as the exotic white sea daffodil and the delicate sea lavender are in bloom.

Mozia was a Phoenician stronghold (the name means "mills"), and by the 6th century B.C. it was surrounded by nearly 2.5km (1½ miles) of defensive walls. In 397 B.C., Dionysius the Elder of Syracuse mounted a massive attack on the Carthaginians, who retreated to Lilybaeum (now Marsala).

The island is owned by the Whitaker family, who came to prominence as traders and vintners of Marsala wine, and many of the splendid artifacts excavated on the island are at the **Villa Malfitano** (www.fondazionewhitaker.it/villa.html) museum. Among the most impressive is a sensual marble statue of a young man in a wet tunic, the **Giovane di Mozia (Young Man of Mozia),** which dates to around 440 B.C. and is a marvellous example of ancient Greek art. Among the most interesting ruins on Mozia are the **Casa dei Mosaici (House of Mosaics),** with scenes from animal life dating to the 4th to 3rd century B.C., and the Tophet, a Phoenician burial ground for victims of child sacrifice with various carved *stele.*

There is a vineyard on the island, too, owned by the Tasca D'Almerita winery. On the edge of the lagoon an old salt mill has been converted into an interesting museum and hotel, **Saline Ettore and Infersa** (✆ **0923-733003**; www.saline ettoreinfersa.com), and explains how salt is extracted using a technique dating back to the Punic times.

GETTING THERE   **Arini and Pugliese ferries** (✆ **347-7790218;** www.arini pugliese.com) runs a daily, year-round service to Mozia from Marsala and costs 5€ return, 2.50€ for schoolchildren and adults 65 and over.

CASTELLAMMARE DEL GOLFO & SCOPELLO

Occupying a dramatic point on the bay with sweeping views to Monte Cofano to the west and Terrasini to the east, Castellammare del Golfo is an active fishing town that draws tourists from all around as they make it their base to visit the natural reserve of Lo Zingaro (see below). Founded by the Elymians, it was the port for Segesta for centuries. Owing its name to the splendid **castle** on the tip of its shores, it was first built by the Arabs as a means of defense, subsequently re-fortified by the Normans and then again by the Swabians. It now houses the **Museo Civico (Civic Museum),** which displays such wares as antique clothes, tools, pots and pans, and equipment for making wine and olive oil. As a testament to its fishing traditions, tunneries line the seafront, though many of these buildings are now being converted into summer homes and restaurants. The writer Gavin Maxwell actually lived within the castle walls while writing his sociological tome about this area, *The Ten Pains of Death* (1959). For those with a sweet tooth, Castellammare is famous for its *cassatelle,* a pocket of fried dough filled with ricotta and dusted with powdered sugar and cinnamon, and all self-respecting bakeries and cafes will be happy to serve you one.

Lying 10km (6 miles) northwest of Castellammare is **Scopello,** or **Scopello di Sopra,** the town that marks the beginning of some of the best **beaches** and coastlines in Sicily, with hidden coves and alternating sand and pebble shores. Inhabited by little more than a few shops and a few roads, and governed by building restrictions to preserve the beauty of the town, it can get quite claustrophobic in summer, as well as pricey—this is one of the most desired vacation spots in Italy. From here you access the southern entrance of the Riserva Naturale dello Zingaro (see below). The bulk of seaside activity culminates around the **Tonnara di Scopello,** just beyond Scopello proper. Known also as Marafaggio, this 13th-century tuna-processing plant retains an almost picturesque melancholy about it: Seemingly abandoned, it is surrounded by wind-shaped rocks and lined with hundreds of old anchors in front of the buildings, almost as a testament to the vibrant life that once revolved around the place. The tunnery has now been lovingly restored, even rented, and day-trippers are allowed to swim off its sparkling cove— provided, however, that they don't turn up with chairs, radios, or anything else that would disrupt the idyll.

RISERVA NATURALE DELLO ZINGARO & SAN VITO LO CAPO

In this stretch of land (12km/7½ miles) extending from north Scopello all the way to San Vito Lo Capo, the **Riserva Naturale dello Zingaro (© 092-435108;** www.riservazingaro.it) was the first designated wildlife area in Sicily, covering nearly 1,600 hectares (3,954 acres) and 7km (4 miles) of coastline. The facilities here are threadbare and the beaches impossibly crowded in summer, but it nonetheless makes for a paradisiacal delight—fishing and motorized vehicles are prohibited (the only transport is by mule). Dense with Mediterranean maquis comprising indigenous flora, wheat is still harvested here the old-fashioned way, by hand and sickle. Within the reserve is also the precious **Grotta dell'Uzzo,** a cave that served as a dwelling place in Paleolithic times, and now is a refuge for six different types of bats.

EGADI ISLANDS

10km (16 miles) SW of Trapani.

The charming Egadi Islands are really a place to get away from it all. An archipelago of three islands (Favignana, Levanzo, and Marettimo), this is the westernmost point of Sicily. The islands are popular in the summer when people are drawn to their crystalline azure waters that are good for swimming and scuba-diving, but the rest of the year their 4,600 inhabitants are left to live from the fruits of the sea much as they have done for centuries.

Each of the islands has a distinct character, and it's possible to take in Roman ruins, Paleolithic and Neolithic cave paintings, grottoes, and natural springs. None of the islands is large, two are free of cars, and their deserted mountain paths make them attractive spots to go walking. All of the islands are great places to eat fish, but be prepared to find that—as with many in Sicilian fishing villages—not all seaside restaurants will have a menu; rather, each morning a restaurant owner will go down to see what the fishermen have caught and that's what gets cooked. The great thing is that you'll get to eat fresh fish just as the locals like it, and concoctions like couscous with poached fish, or tuna simmered in a pot with tomatoes, capers, anchovies, and herbs.

The islands are home to the largest tuna fishery in Sicily, and famous for the annual *mattanza,* an age-old method of culling tuna (p. 178).

Getting There

BY BOAT   Ustica Lines (© 0923-873813; www.usticalines.it) runs a daily ferry and hydrofoil service almost every hour from Trapani and Marsala to Favignana, Levanzo, and Marettimo. Cost: 9.80€, free for children 3 and under, half price for children 11 and under.

What to See & Do: Favignana

The island sought out by most vacationers, Favignana presents two distinct landscapes: Flat pastures to the east, with many disused tufa quarries, and desolate crags to the west. In the middle of it all is Favignana proper, built in 1637, when it supplanted the original medieval layout. The grandeur of the Florio wine dynasty is still present on the island, as you will see (albeit only from the outside) at the **Villino Florio** (now the police headquarters) and the numerous tuna-canning facilities that were once a thriving business on the island. Also worth seeing are the so-called **Bagno Delle Donne**, a Roman bath house for women. Many of the shops here sell the local specialty, *bottarga,* or dried tuna roe. The best swimming is at the rocky bay at **Cala Rossa**, while other overcrowded beaches are between **Grotta Pergiata** and **Punta Longa**. Despite its relatively small size, Favignana isn't immune to building speculation; sadly, many new edifices are built over prehistoric ruins.

What to See & Do: Levanzo

The smallest of the archipelago is also one of the historically richest, as the first traces of human settlements in Sicily dating back to the Paleolithic times are along the caves of the **Grotta del Genovese.** The cave is reached by an exhausting 2-hour hike or by boat, though you won't be able to see much: It is now closed to

LA mattanza

It is hardly a spectacle for those against animal cruelty, and the sight can be gruesome even for those not faint of heart, but *La Mattanza*—the centuries-old method of catching tuna—still draws crowds from all over the world wanting to witness this gory event. Taking place from May to June, the local fishermen, led by a head fisherman called the *Rais*, head out to the waters to catch the tuna that have come to breed in the deep waters between the islands of Favignana and Levanzo. Nets are placed in the water to form a corridor, through which the fish are forced and end up in the last, toughest net, called the *camera della morte*, or chamber of death. At this stage the tuna, which are packed together, have wounded and stunned each other in an attempt to make an escape. When the *Rais* deems that enough fish have been caught, he orders the hauling of the nets—an arduous task done in synchronized movements kept in time by the chanting of ancient fishermen songs. Once pulled to the surface, the tuna are harpooned and pulled on board and the sea becomes ruby red. It is a show that has changed very little since the Bronze Age, and there are several animal protection organizations that are asking for this sort of fishing to be banned.

the public after vandals damaged some of the graffiti. To arrange a visit, contact **Natale Castiglione** (✆ **0923-92403**).

Known to Pliny the Elder as *Bucinna,* the island has no natural water reserves, but also no cars, and with its patches of maquis of fragrant plants and cobalt blue seas it makes for a paradise. Among other precious artifacts that have been found around the island's waters is a cargo of *garum*—a sauce (much used in Roman times) made of fish intestines, salt, sea water, and herbs and spices.

What to See & Do: Marettimo ★

The remotest of the islands is also a Crusoe's paradise—this was where Samuel Butler suggested that the island of Ithaca might have been in the *Odyssey,* as the islets of Le Formiche were the rocks hurled at Ulysses by Polyphemus. Known as the ancient Hieromesus, it has no cars and no hotels, and is without a doubt the most beautiful of the Egadi Islands. Filled with natural springs and grottoes, and limestone pinnacles leading up to **Monte Falcone** (686m/2,250 ft), it is home to many rare species of plants and the occasional wild boar and *mouflon* (wild sheep). In the tiny village of **Marettimo** proper there are some Roman ruins and a Paleochristian church. Amazingly, what few inhabitants there were on the island at the beginning of the 1900s—it had long been a stronghold for pirates—emigrated to Monterey, California, and took the art of tuna canning to the U.S. This craft was immortalized in John Steinbeck's novel *Cannery Row.*

Where to Stay

Bouganville ☺ Bouganville has its devoted clientele—and it's not difficult to see why: This family-run place right in the center of town is close enough to the sea for you to enjoy the best of both worlds. The basic, no-frills rooms have high ceilings and are spacious. The on-site restaurant serves some of the most delectable food on the island, with outdoor dining in warmer months.

Via Cimabue 10, 91023 Favignana ✆ **0923-22033.** www.albergobouganville.it. 13 units. 180€–280€ double. Rates include breakfast. AE, MC, V. Free parking. **Amenities:** Restaurant; bar; Internet (5€/hr). *In room:* A/C, TV, minibar.

Paradiso Within walking distance of the beach, this no-frills *pensione* offers Spartan comfort without much brouhaha. All rooms are spacious and with shower-only bathrooms, yet each room, with its own private terrace facing the sea, clearly makes up for the frugalness of the decor. The gracious hosts go out of their way to make you feel at home without being smarmy, and when the restaurant starts calling patrons like the song of the sirens, you'll be glad you have first pick as a guest.

Via Lungomare Levanzo ✆ **0923-924083.** www.isoladilevanzo.it. 15 units. 160€–200€ double. Rates include breakfast. AE, MC, V. **Amenities:** Restaurant; bar; Internet (5€/hr). *In room:* A/C, TV. Closed mid Dec–Mar.

Where to Eat

La Bettola Favignana One of the most popular places to eat in town. By the size of the clientele it attracts it would seem to serve the best home-style island food, but you may have to put up with the somewhat rude staff. Order the pasta with an original rustic pesto of tuna, tomatoes, basil, and anchovies and follow up with the catch of the day grilled on lava rocks. For a complete meal, nothing beats the fish couscous. If you really have your heart set on eating here, book an early meal to avoid disappointment.

Via Nicotra 47 91023 Favignana ✆ **0923-921988.** Reservations recommended. AE, MC, V. Main course 13€–22€. 12:30pm–3pm and 7:30pm–12:30am. Closed Thurs and Dec.

PANTELLERIA

110km (62 miles) S of Trapani.

The exotic island of Pantelleria is the hideaway of choice for jetsetters. Some 110km (62 miles) from Sicily and 70km (44 miles) from Tunisia, and covering 83 sq km (32 sq miles) it is the largest of the outer lying islands, with a population of approximately 8,000. Of volcanic origin, the island's central cone is now dormant, and its hot springs are a great place to relax. The sea surrounding the island is a haven for lovers of water sports, and dolphins are commonly sighted. Because of the island's isolated location, it is home to some endemic species such as the slender Pantescan donkey, as well as species no longer found on the Sicilian mainland, like the green tortoise.

Inhabited since the Neolithic times, Pantelleria was known as *Cossyra* (meaning "small one") to the Greeks. The island has always been known for its strong winds and little rain, and when the Arabs overtook Pantelleria, they renamed it *Bent-al-Riah,* or daughter of the wind. The winds have been a crucial influence on the landscape, flora, agriculture, and even architecture. From the 10th to 17th centuries, the islanders built thick-walled stone houses with domed roofs to collect water, and enclosed gardens to shelter crops. Known as *dammusi,* many of these former peasant dwellings are now summer getaways for the rich. Much of the island is covered with thick maquis, as well as pines, rosemary, and heather. Despite a lack of rain and natural water Pantelleria's capers and grapes are highly renowned—the former are thought to be the best in the world, while the *zibibbo* grapes are used to make the sweet dessert wines, Moscato and Passito.

Getting There

From Trapani, **Siremar** ferries (☏ **892123,** or ☏ **02-26302803** from outside Italy; www.siremar.it) runs a **ferry** service twice a day Monday to Saturday, once on Sunday. The journey takes roughly 4 hours; there is also night service. Tickets from Pantelleria to Trapani can be purchased at the **Agenzia Rizzo,** Via Borgo Italia (☏ **0923-911104;** www.agenziarizzo.com). For tickets from Trapani, see "Getting There," under "Trapani" (p. 158). The cost for passage starts at 30.10€.

Meridiana (☏ **0789-52682;** ☏ **892-928** from abroad; www.meridiana.it) has daily flights from Palermo and Trapani to the airport located at the hamlet of San Vito (☏ **0923-911398**). From here, a bus connects you to the town of Pantelleria, dropping you off in Via De Amicis next to the town hall after a 15-minute ride.

Exploring Pantelleria

The **Tourist Information** office, Via San Nicola (☏ **0923-911838**), provides information and timetables on the local bus lines that reach all the villages of the islands, where to rent out bicycles, scooters, diving equipment, and boats; it even lists places to stay if you've not booked anything. Starting from the town of Pantelleria, where the port lies, a 45km (28-mile) coastal road allows easy circumnavigation and a scenic tour of the island—though be forewarned that it can be rough, especially if using a bicycle or scooter. The town itself does not offer much in terms of monuments, as it was leveled during the Allied bombings of 1943; the one remaining edifice, however, is the impressive Spanish fortification of the **Barbacane castle** (open daily 9am–6pm). Heading southwest, the road leads to the **Cuddie Rosse,** the volcanic red rocks marking the site of a prehistoric settlement. Bypassing the village of **Cossyra,** head to the archaeological area of **Mursia,** where the enclosure of prehistoric, domed lava tombs, known as *sesi* in the local dialect, are located. Only 27 tombs still exist, with human remains still inside, laid to rest in fetal positions. The highest is the **Sese Grande,** over 6m (20 ft.) high, which creates a spooky setting to an otherwise lunar landscape. At **Punta Fram,** where some resorts are located, signposts mark where you can walk down to the sea. **Sataria** is a quaint little getaway (expect crowds, however, during the high season) where the basalt rocks have created a natural pool next to warm springs. Bring a sandwich and a towel, as this is the only place for miles that has an actual shaded area. **Scauri** is one of the bigger villages, and from here you can see Cape Mustafá in Tunisia on a clear day. The town is perched above its harbor, the two separated by a 20-minute steep climb. Scauri has a few eateries where you can stop for refreshments or have a meal. Farther south, the smaller village of **Nicà** is another hot-spring source, while inland, the village of **Rehkale** is a picturesque hamlet that best exemplifies the essence of Pantelleria—*dammusi,* the low, lava-stone homes with surrounding walls to protect from the wind, and luxuriant gardens. Following the bend of the island, you'll come to the aptly named **Dietro l'Isola** (meaning "behind the island"), a stretch of prohibitive barren wilderness carved with dirt roads that lead you to the east. The long road leads you to **Cava Elefante** and to the lava outcropping of **Arco dell'Elefante ★★**, whose name comes from the volcanic outcropping that resembles an elephant's snout dipping in the water. From here, you can either make your way inland, climbing the steep path to the two hamlets of **Tracino** and **Kamma,** where you'll encounter holiday homes and lavish grounds, or continue along the coast. The twin villages are also an excellent base from which to start hiking around the inner island, particularly if you want to reach its main attraction, the green lake known as the **Specchio di Venere (Venus's mirror),** a sulfuric spring said to have been Venus's mirror into which she peered when comparing her beauty to Psyche, her rival. From the *specchio* you can easily make your way along the coastal road again, turning right eastbound and winding up your exploration at another lake, the **Lago delle Ondine,** where waves are collected into the hallow lava to form brilliant pools. From here, descend into the waters at the **Cala Cinque Denti,** one of the most breathtaking coves on the island.

Where to Stay

Cossyra ☺ Located in the village of Mursia, the hotel has all the trappings you would expect of a seaside resort, including three pools. The rooms are basic, with wood and wicker furniture, and all have a terrace. The resort spreads out like a military base and clashes with the natural landscape, but if you just want to lounge around without venturing beyond the hotel property, this makes an excellent choice for families.

Localita Rosso, Mursia, 91017 Pantelleria Ⓒ **0923-911154.** Fax 911026. www.mursiahotel.it. 74 units. 40€–80€ double. Rates include breakfast. AE, DC, MC, V. **Amenities:** Restaurant; saltwater pool; freshwater pool; children's pool; tennis court; Internet. *In Room:* A/C, TV, minibar (in some).

Lago di Venere ★ On the banks of the lake of the same name—known for its therapeutic mud and waters—a former military barracks has been craftily converted into a little-known yet sought-after hotel. Located inland, it's far removed from the touristy chaos. There are two buildings; the older one still preserves the lava masonry in its walls, while the rooms are a nod to northern Africa both in feel and design. For the sports lover, numerous activities can be arranged by the friendly staff, from diving to horseback riding.

Contrada Lago, Corso Vittorio Emanuele, 91017 Pantelleria Ⓒ**0923-914130.** www.hotellagodivenere.it. 14 units. 55€–110€ double. Rates include breakfast. MC, V. **Amenities:** Bar/lounge; Internet. *In room:* A/C, TV, minibar, hair dryer.

Le Stele di Rekale ★★ One of the few hotels open year-round, this complex made up of four individual *dammusi* is an alternative to hotel living, with apartments overlooking the sea. Each unit is furnished with country-style furniture and basic appliances, while the bedrooms have a distinctively Arab feel. Expect to pay through the nose, but the exclusivity can't be beaten.

Via dei Limoni 18, 91017 Pantelleria Ⓒ/fax **0923-916871.** www.lesteledirekale.com. 4 units. 700€–2,000€ per week for up to four people. AE, DC, MC, V. **Amenities:** full kitchen.

Papuscia In a centuries-old *dammuso* near the sea, each room is furnished with simple decor that evokes the island ambience, and each has its own canopied terrace, though don't expect too much of a dramatic view from most rooms—it's the comfort you want here. If you want a sybaritic retreat however, the Jacuzzi for the guests is filled with the therapeutic waters of the Lago di Venere. The in-house restaurant, **Malacucina,** is one of the island's favorites, so make sure you reserve.

Contrada Sopra Portella. Ⓒ **0923-915463.** www.papuscia.it. 11 units. 40€–60€ per person. Rates include breakfast. MC, V. **Amenities:** *In room:* A/C, TV.

Where to Eat

La Nicchia ★ SICILIAN   What started on a whim in an old *dammuso* has grown to be one of the chicest places to eat on the island. The tiny dining room circles an orange tree that gives an exotic feel to the ambience. Produce might be limited on an island, but it's always fresh and local: From starters like tuna carpaccio or a crunchy *caponatina* (vegetarian stew) with almonds, to main courses such as shrimp in grape gelatin. The creativity of the chef is accompanied—and washed down— with some of the finest wines produced locally.

Contrada Scauri © **0923-916342.** www.lanicchia.it. Reservations recommended. AE, DC, MC, V. Main course 15€–25€. Daily lunch & dinner.

La Risacca ★★ SICILIAN   La Risacca offers good down-to-earth, home-style cooking. The dining area overlooks the port in an unpretentious, convivial environment, where the gracious owners will satisfy your palate with traditional recipes. Try the mint-infused ravioli, a Pantelleria staple. If that sounds too much, you can always play safe and order pizza.

Via Milano 65 © **0923-912975.** Reservations recommended. MC, V. Main courses 7€–15€. Tues–Sun dinner only. Closed Mon; closed Oct.

Le Lampare ★★ SICILIAN   The in-house restaurant of the Mursia Hotel is a favorite with devoted visitors to the island, and the renowned chef keeps the faithful with original twists on local staples. The couscous *pantesco* (fish sauce with capers), made with all the surrounding bounty on offer, goes quickly; as does the curiously named *sciaki-sciuka,* a Pantelleria-style ratatouille laden with the island's most famous produce, capers.

Localita Rosso Mursia, © **0923-911217.** Reservations recommended. AE, DC, MC, V. Main courses 12€–20€. Daily dinner only.

CENTRAL SICILY

No visit to Sicily is complete without venturing to the sleepy heart of the island and its hilltop towns, which offer spectacular views of the surrounding fertile hills and valleys. The area is also home to one of the island's most impressive archaeological treasures, the **Villa Romana del Casale** at **Piazza Armerina**—the largest and best-preserved collection of Roman mosaics in the world.

Often overlooked by most visitors to Sicily, the rest of the area, comprising four provinces, has a wealth of lesser-known (read: Less crowded) yet fascinating archaeological sites, such as the one discovered at **Morgantina.** You can explore breathtaking castles and the highest provincial capital in Italy at **Enna,** and unspoiled bucolic landscapes and fecund fields in the **Parco Regionale delle Madonie** mountains and Sikanian hills.

It is an area steeped in mythological tales, and is the closest you'll ever get to experiencing island life the way it was 100 years ago, when the main source of income was farming, and when industry thrived on sulfur mining in the area around **Caltanissetta.** The mines are now closed and the wheat fields on the hills are no longer as vast (during Roman domination the area served as the breadbasket of the Empire, and today they still supply durum wheat to most of Italy). But the centuries-old farmhouses that pop up now and then on hilltops, and the grazing sheep and cattle on them, are testament to how this area has not really changed much—if it weren't, however, for the wind farms that have unequivocally disfigured the landscape.

The Sikanian hills—an explosion of colors and rolling hillsides that emulate the Irish countryside on a blustery spring day, yet look like no-man's land during the scorching summer—are the repository of the oldest traces of civilization on the island, owing to the fact that the Sikanians, the most ancient of the indigenous peoples of Sicily, dwelled among these mountains. Through its mounds, the dairy capital of the west has been carved with the *Via dei Formaggi,* "the road of the cheeses," where dairy products are still churned according to age-old methods.

ENNA

135km (84 miles) SE of Palermo

The most engaging aspect of this town is to wander its winding streets that snake up the side of the hill, popping in on churches to admire the frescoes, and pausing in a cafe to sit back and watch people about their daily life. Thanks to its high elevation, it's also a place to escape the fierce summer heat of the lowlands and coastal areas, and in the winter it often snows, adding to its sense of secluded charm.

At 931m (3,054 ft.) Enna is not only the highest provincial capital in Italy but also the capital of the only land-locked Sicilian province. Dubbed the "navel of Sicily" by the Greeks, it is divided into two sections: *Enna Alta,* or the historical center, and *Enna Bassa,* along the plains. Often considered off the beaten path, Enna deserves a visit, not only to admire the spectacular landscape from atop the center of the island, with views of smoking Mount Etna to the east, but also to savor some of the local products like saffron-imbued Piacentino cheese. The vertiginous climb to reach Enna will reward you with an aspect of Sicily that's rarely seen in the travel brochures.

GETTING THERE **SAIS bus** lines (✆ **800-211020,** from mobiles ✆ **199-244141;** www.saisautolinee.it) runs an early morning service from Palermo for 9.40€ one way taking 1¾ hours; from Catania there are 10 buses a day costing 7.30€ one way and taking 1 hour 20 minutes. Check the website for other locations. **Trains** (✆ **802021;** www.trenitalia.it) stop quite a way down the hill at Enna Bassa, where a bus then whisks you to the historical center, however there are no direct trains from Palermo, so the bus is a much better option. From Catania, the train takes 1 hour 20 minutes and costs 6.10€ one way. If you're **driving,** take the A19 (Catania–Palermo) autostrada, exiting at Enna.

What to See & Do

Starting your visit from the heart of the city at **Piazza Vittorio Emanuele;** on the north side you'll encounter the church of **San Francesco d'Assisi,** where the only original part is the bell tower from the 1500s. In the Piazza is a bronze replica (the original is in Rome, at the Galleria Borghese) of Bernini's *Rape of Persephone*; Persephone was the daughter of Demeter, goddess of agriculture and fertility, whose cult was rooted here in Sicily. From the square make your way east along Via Roma, Enna's main thoroughfare lined with impressive buildings where most of the tourist attractions are located. As you climb your way up the street you'll traverse a succession of small squares: At Piazza Umberto, you'll see on the right hand side the elegant facade of the **Municipio** (town hall), a neoclassical structure which has expanded over the years to incorporate the adjacent opera house. On the left, at Piazza Colajanni, is the 17th-century church of **Santa Chiara**—a war memorial and burial ground, it oddly enough pays homage to a non-religious event: Part of the decor of the majolica tiled floor depicts the beginning of steam navigation. Just beyond the square are the remains of the 15th-century **Palazzo Pollicarini,** which still retains some Catalan Gothic elements. It has now been converted into a private apartment complex. This is the last of the small squares before you reach the **Duomo,** the city's main church. Launched by Queen Eleanor, wife of Frederick III of Aragon, in 1307 on the site of a temple dedicated to Persephone, and nearly wiped out by a devastating fire in 1446, restoration was only begun one hundred years later. As a consequence, its architectural styles span

three eras, from medieval Gothic to late Renaissance to baroque. The graceful Gothic apse and transept were part of the original structure, while the rest of the church boasts many fine works of art from the baroque period including paintings by Flemish artist Willem Borremans. Behind the Duomo lying east is the **Museo Alessi (Alessi Museum),** which houses a collection of area artifacts, among which are the missiles, or *glandes,* used during the Servile War. Also of note are the 7th- to 6th-century B.C. Egyptian ushabti figurines said to have been found here. The **Duomo Treasury** (*Tesoro*) on the first floor showcases exquisite examples of Renaissance jewelry, with the crowning glory, so to speak, the splendid gold and jewel encrusted "Crown of the Virgin," from 1653. The Duomo is open from 8am to 7pm daily, and the Treasury is open Tuesday through Sunday from 9am to 1pm and 4 to 7pm.

Across from Piazza Mazzini is the recently reopened **Museo Archeologico Varisano (Varisano Archaeological Museum)** housed in the palace of the same name. It houses finds from the environs, from prehistoric artifacts to medieval pieces. The museum is open daily 9am to 1pm and 3 to 6pm and costs 2€ for adults, 1€ for children 11 and under and seniors over 65.

As you make your way toward the end of Via Roma you'll arrive at Enna's main attraction, the **Castello Lombardo (Lombard Castle)** ★★ built by Frederick II in the early part of the 13th century over a pre-existing Arab fortification. It is thought that its name had to do with the fact that Frederick II called in troops from Lombardy in northern Italy to defend the castle. In the 14th century the Aragonese Frederick III was crowned here as King of Sicily and enhanced the castle's defenses. Originally having 20 towers, only 6 have survived to the present day: The Pisan Tower is the highest, offering spectacular **views** ★ of Sicily's countryside. Built on three levels of courtyards, one level is also an open-air theatre. Archaeological excavations are underway in the other two and you can see the remains of a church and a few tombs. From the ramparts to the north, you can view the **Rocca di Cerere,** where the old temple to the goddess of agriculture once stood, and beyond in the distance, Mount Etna.

Heading towards Enna Bassa, Enna's other defensive fortification from the Middle Ages is **Torre Federiciana (Frederick's Tower),** known also as Castello Vecchio, standing 24m (79 ft.) high on top of a hill in the public gardens on the opposite side of town. Local legend has it that Frederick II, wanting to mark the exact center of Sicily, built this tower and labeled it "the tower of the winds." Originally having three floors, the top floor collapsed in time. The tower was built on an octagonal foundation instead of the more common round or square floor plan.

Where to Stay

B&B Del Centro ★★★ 📖   In the heart of town, this hidden B&B is a true gem—an old *palazzo* refurbished back to its original splendor. The staff is very welcoming and helpful. Small but cozy rooms have wrought-iron beds and wooden flooring; the bathrooms, though proportionate to room size, are spanking new and outfitted with massage showers—a rarity in hotels, let alone in a B&B.

Via Sant'Agata 108, 94100 Enna, ✆ **327-7460800** (mobile). www.bedandbreakfastenna.com. 6 units. 50€–70€ double; 65€–90€ triple. Rates include breakfast. AE, MC, V. Pets accepted. All smoke-free rooms. **Amenities:** Bar; bicycle rental. *In room:* A/C, TV, minibar, Wi-Fi (free).

Grande Albergo Sicilia   This renovated three-star hotel has long been the only viable choice in the area, yet the friendly, family-run staff and excellent service are what keeps it going. Rooms have a touch of country flavor in the furnishings that are a nod to Enna's surroundings; brightly colored and comfortable. All rooms have a spacious bathroom and tub. The superb views from the rooms are memorable; some even have balconies from which to admire the picturesque countryside (ask for a room facing the back).

Piazza Napoleone Colajanni 7, 94100 Enna. ⓒ **0935-500850.** Fax 0935-500488. www.hotel siciliaenna.it. 60 units. 75€–140€ double. Rates include breakfast. AE, DC, MC, V. **Amenities:** Bar. *In room:* A/C, TV, minibar, Wi-Fi (free).

Where to Eat

Antica Hostaria ★★ 🎒   Look no further than this place for authentic Ennese cuisine, hidden in a back street as if it were exclusive to cognoscenti. The starter itself is a banquet, and the chef prepares dishes according to seasonal offerings, so expect hearty, mouth-watering ragout pastas in winter, while in summer you can choose from delectable twists on classics, such as carbonara with wild asparagus, fresh-picked from the nearby fields. The homemade desserts will find their way to delight your palate, even if you're about to explode.

Via Castagna 9. ⓒ **0935-22521.** Reservations recommended. Main courses 7€–12€. AE, MC, V. Wed-Mon noon–3pm and 7pm–11pm. Closed Tues.

Farther Afield: Morgantina & Aidone

The environs of Enna have been dealt the most striking landscapes man and mother nature could conjure, and almost every village affords a view. This fertile area was the breadbasket of Rome, and wheat-growing predominates still. Consequently any drive through the hills is a pleasure as you negotiate the numerous twists and bends to be met with yet another striking panorama, and marvel at how every tiny patch of land is cultivated. After harvest time in late summer, the mustard, pale yellow, burnt apricot, and sage green colors of the fields striated with dark brown lines make this a painter and photographer's dream. Such is the area's beauty, it's sometimes hard to concentrate at the wheel, and there's a constant temptation to stop on a perilous curve to take snaps.

The countryside is steeped in mythological, agricultural, and regal connotations, and what are now sleepy villages were once the homes of the ancient gods and hideaways of kings. While all the surrounding towns are enticing and merit a visit, if you are pressed for time and can only make one side trip from Enna then make it the adjacent cities of **Morgantina** and **Aidone.**

Morgantina's archaeological site was a once-powerful Siceliot (Sicilian Greek) city state that occupied a vast area (more than 20 hectares/51 acres) and is a testament of the power of this ally of Syracuse. Your first stop should be at Morgantina, and then return to the modern town of Aidone, where many of the artifacts found at the site are displayed in the archaeological museum.

GETTING THERE   Although the **SAIS bus** (ⓒ **800-211020;** www.saisauto linee.it) runs buses twice daily at 2pm and 6pm from Enna at a cost of 3.90€ one way, or 6.10€ return, there is no return bus until the next day. If you're **driving** from Enna, proceed southbound along state road SS117-bis and follow the directions to Contrada Ciappino; from here, make a left on provincial road 228 and follow the signpostings to Aidone. To Morgantina, continue along the 228 from Aidone.

THE myth OF THE SEASONS AND LAKE PERGUSA

One day, the goddess Persephone was picking flowers along the shores of what is Lake Pergusa when she plucked a beautiful narcissus from the earth. When uprooted, the earth caved in and from the abyss came Hades on his mighty chariot and carried her off. Upon her kidnapping, her mother, Demeter (or Ceres) the goddess of agriculture, went in search for her daughter, and as such abandoned the crops she governed over, leaving them to become barren and unfruitful. Zeus, the father of Persephone, put a stop to the famine by ordering the release of his daughter; Hades obliged (by now he and Persephone had a son, Pluto) but not without her first consuming a pomegranate seed as a sign of fidelity to him, and her promising to return to him for 4 months every year. Every time, Demeter would again plunge into sorrow, and the fields once again were ungerminated. This myth of the cycle of abandonment and reunion mirrors the winter which fails to produce bounty, while the springtime leads to joy and plenty.

WHAT TO SEE & DO

Morgantina Archaeological Site ★★   Abandoned for centuries, the site of one of the most boisterous cities of Magna Graecia was first excavated in the 1950s by a group of archaeologists from Princeton University, who have since unearthed a full city, complete with shops, markets, the meeting hall for the city council (*bouleuterion*), as well as the mainstays of all Greek cities—a theater and an agora, and even a mint.

As the excavations proceeded unscrupulous looters made their way on to the grounds, ransacking what they could dig up and selling it off on the black market. Among these pieces were the statue of the Venere di Morgantina, which somehow made its way to the Getty Museum in Malibu, and some silver coins, housed at the Metropolitan Museum of New York. After much bickering between U.S. and Italian authorities, the pieces have finally returned home and are on display at the Museo Archeologico in Aidone (see below).

Morgantina. ℂ **0935-87955.** Admission 4€ adults, 2€ children 11 and under and seniors 65 and over. Daily 8am–1 hr before sunset.

Museo Archeologico Regionale di Aidone ★★   Located in the former Capuchin convent on Piazza Torres Trupia, the museum houses artifacts coming from the excavations at nearby Morgantina. Besides the statue of the **Venere di Morgantina** and coins from the mint, the museum also houses pieces dating back to the Bronze Age, utensils found in Morgeti dwellings, and a fine bust of Persephone (around 3rd century B.C.), coming from the sanctuaries dedicated to her and her mother Demeter in Morgantina.

Piazza Torres Trupia. ℂ **0935-87037.** Admission 4€ adults, 2€ children 11 and under and seniors 65 and over. Tues–Sun 8am–6:30pm. Closed Mon.

CALTANISSETTA

23km (14 miles) W of Enna, 91km (56 miles) W of Catania, 44km (27 miles) NE of Agrigento, 93km (60 miles) SE of Palermo.

Caltanissetta's best feature is its views of the surrounding rolling hills with their tiny stone houses, lone olive trees, ploughed fields, and rocky crags. Once an important royal city thanks to its strategic location 588m (1,929 ft.) above sea level and between three mountains—Sant'Anna, Monte San Giuliano, and Poggio Sant'Elia— Caltanissetta afforded its knights an extensive view of the surrounding countryside of the Salso Valley.

Perhaps the least-visited provincial capital of Sicily, Caltanissetta suffered from the heavy damage incurred during fighting in World War II, the demise of its sulfur industry in the 1960s, and its reputation as one of the island's poorest cities. Yet what remains of Caltanissetta's heyday, when its wealthy inhabitants constructed numerous churches and mansions, is interesting to see, particularly the **Palazzo Moncada** and the **Palazzo Vescovile.** The best time to visit the city is at Easter during Settimana Santa because the *nisseni,* as the inhabitants are called, re-enact the **Passione di Cristo** (Passion of Christ).

If you decide to finish a meal with a native liqueur, this is the place to do so— Caltanissetta is famous throughout Italy for being where the **Amaro Averna** liqueur originated. Drunk as a digestive, the bitter-tasting drink was invented by Capuchin monks belonging to the local order, who passed their recipe on to benefactor Salvatore Averna in the 1800s. Initially, Averna made the drink for family and friends, but such was the demand he decided to set up a business. Today the herbs, roots, and citrus rinds, which form the base of the brown-colored drink, are still mixed in Caltanissetta, although the rest of the manufacturing process takes place elsewhere.

GETTING THERE By **car,** the autostrada A19 has direct links from both Palermo and Catania; taking an average of 1 hour and 20 minutes from either way. There are frequent, direct **trains** (✆ **892021;** www.trenitalia.it) from Palermo, Enna, and Catania: Five trains from Palermo take 2½ hours and cost 7.95€; from Enna there are four trains that make the 40-minute journey for 3.25€; and from Catania the journey takes 2 hours, and you should expect to pay 7.70€ on one of the four trains a day. **SAIS** (✆ **800-102021;** www.saisautolinee.it) runs a **bus** from Enna costing 3.90€ one way for a 50-minute trip.

What to See & Do

The city's foundation as a fortified settlement dates from the Saracens' rule of Sicily. Like many Arab towns, Caltanissetta's name shares the Arabic prefix *kal* indicating that it was indeed a fortified, or castled, city. In this case, it derived its name from *Kalat Nisa* or "the castle of women," as it is said that the Emir of Palermo kept his women here. Considerably broadened in Norman times, this fortress, the **Castello Pietrarossa,** is visible on the edge of the city, although only part of a tower and some walls remain. The castle was sacked during the War of the Vespers but the looters were subsequently pardoned by the new sovereign, Peter of Aragon.

Caltanissetta has a large 17th-century **Duomo** built on the site of a previous medieval church, and a handful of late-medieval churches in the old part of town, though most of the latter, having been extensively modified in successive centuries, reflect little of their origins. There are also some exquisite baroque palaces, particularly **Palazzo Moncada** on Corso Vittorio Emanuele and the **Palazzo Vescovile** in Viale Regina Margherita.

The exquisite **Abbazia dello Spirito Santo ★★**, lying roughly 4kms/2.4 miles from the center of town, is a Norman abbey built upon Saracen fortifications, the purpose of which was to create a house of worship for the landworkers, as the Normans continued their quest to re-Christianize Sicily.

Where to Stay

Hotel San Michele   This modern hotel is popular as a base for venturing around the environs. Rooms are quite large compared to island standards, and are soundproofed. Almost all have private balconies. It is also a business hotel, so you may find that it is occasionally full for conferences. If you decide to stay in, the hotel also has a good restaurant that will satisfy your appetite.

Via Fasci Siciliani, Caltanissetta ℰ **0934-553 750.** Fax 0934-598 791. www.hotelsanmichelesicilia.it. 136 units. 110€–130€ double. Rates include breakfast. AE, DC, MC, V. **Amenities:** Restaurant; bar; outdoor pool; fitness center; smoke-free rooms. *In room:* A/C, TV, minibar, Wi-Fi (free).

Where to Eat

Vicolo Duomo ★   Renowned in the area for its fine home cooking, this charming little restaurant serves traditional-style farmers' dishes. This is best exemplified by the *farsumagru*, a Sicilian-style meatloaf. The dish is hearty, and served with one of the main wines in the cellar.

Vicolo Neviera, 1, ℰ 0934 582331. Reservations recommended. AE, DC, MC. V. Main courses 8€–15€. Tues–Sat 12:30–3pm and Mon–Sat 7:30–11:30pm. Closed Sun.

PIAZZA ARMERINA

84km (52 miles) SW of Catania, 181km (112 miles) SW of Messina, 164km (102 miles) SE of Palermo, 103km (64 miles) NW of Ragusa, 134km (83 miles) NW of Syracuse.

Piazza Armerina is where you can see the most magnificent mosaics in all of western Europe. Art lovers journey from all over the world to visit the ruins of an extraordinary Roman villa, the **Villa Romana del Casale ★★★,** which houses mosaics that are admired for their preservation and masterful craftsmanship. A visit to the villa makes a trip to Piazza Armerina worthwhile, but the town itself merits a visit for at least an hour, although most tour buses rush through here delivering their passengers directly to the villa at Casale on the outskirts of Piazza Armerina.

A stroll through the historic center takes in pretty squares, streets graced with imposing but decaying palazzi with ornate facades and billowing baroque balconies, and numerous churches in a range of architectural styles. The grandest church is the **Duomo,** and its shiny blue cupola dominates the skyline. The town is actually two-in-one: The original "Piazza," a village that dates from the heyday of the Saracens in the 10th century; and a 15th-century medieval "overflow" town that extends to the southeast.

The best time to visit Piazza Armerina is during the **Palio dei Normanni** (Norman Palio). Held every year from August 12 to 14, the Palio celebrates the arrival of

Norman Count Roger in the town in 1061 during his campaign to liberate Sicily from the Saracens, and locals dress up in costume as nobles and soldiers to join in the event that culminates in the Saracen Joust, which involves four teams of modern-day "knights" on horseback.

Essentials

GETTING THERE   Piazza Armerina can be reached by **SAIS bus** (© 800-211020; www.saisautolinee.it): Five buses a day (3 at weekends) from Palermo take 2 hours and cost 12€; four buses a day make the 40-minute journey from Enna and cost 5.20€. If you're **driving** from Enna, it will take about an hour. Drive south along the S561, which then merges with the S117-bis.

VISITOR INFORMATION   The **tourist office,** at Via S. Rosalia 5 (© 0935-683049), is open Monday to Friday 8am to 2pm, and on Wednesday 3 to 6:30pm.

GETTING AROUND   If you've arrived in Piazza Armerina by bus, you can take yet another bus to reach the Roman villa at Casale. The **Piccola Società Cooperativa** (© 0935-85605) runs buses (no. B) to the site daily from 9 to noon and 3 to 6pm (trip time: 15 min.), costing 1€ one way.

What to See & Do

The city was founded during the Norman era, and today is filled with mansions showing both baroque and Renaissance architectural influences. Its historic **medieval quarter** ★ is graced with many beautiful churches, the most impressive of which is the **Duomo,** crowning the highest point in town at 720m (2,364 ft.) on the Via Cavour (© 0935-680214).

The old town's maze of narrow streets sprouted around this cathedral. The bell tower is from 1490, a surviving architectural feature of an even earlier church. The present building was inaugurated in 1627, the facade dating from 1719 and the dome from 1768. The facade is adorned with pilasters and columns, and the grand central door is surmounted by a large, square window topped by an eagle. The interior is spacious and filled with light. Among the best-known works of art here is the **Vergine delle Vittorie** ★, above the main altar at the far end of the nave in a 17th-century tabernacle. It is believed that it was given by Pope Nicholas II to Count Roger, ruler of Sicily, and is the traditional standard used during the Palio dei Normanni. An impressive **wooden cross** ★ dating from 1455 is on view in the small chapel to the left of the chancel. Its back depicts a scene of the Resurrection that has been much reproduced in art books on Sicily. The Duomo is open daily from 8:30am to noon and 3:30 to 7pm.

Villa Romana del Casale ★★★   Located 6km (3½ miles) from Piazza Armerina, this magnificent villa is one of the largest dwellings of its kind to have survived from the days of the Romans. Its 40 rooms are carpeted with 11,340 sq m (122,063 sq ft.) of some of the greatest, most magnificent mosaics in western Europe. *Note*: be forewarned that opening times can change without notice due to ongoing restoration; call or check the website first before making the trek out (see below).

It is obvious that a wealthy patrician built this mansion, and some scholars have even suggested that it was the hunting lodge of Maximanus, the co-emperor of Diocletian. The exact date of the villa's construction is hard to ascertain, however—perhaps the end of the 3rd century A.D. or the beginning of the 4th century. The complex was destroyed by fire in the 12th century and over the years was buried in mudslides. Parts of the villa were unearthed in 1881.

Many of the mansion's walls are still standing, but most visitors come to take in the mosaics on the floors and the surviving wall paintings. Many of the mosaic scenes are mythological. Since this was a hunting lodge, most of the tableaux involve the pursuit of wild animals.

Rooms branch out from a central courtyard, or peristyle. Among the discernible rooms still left are the **Terme,** or steam baths, which supplied water and also heated the villa with steam circulating through cavities in the floors and walls. In the **Sala delle Unizioni (Room of Unguents),** slaves are depicted massaging the bodies of their masters.

The Peristylium, directly east of the peristyle, contains the splendid **Peristylium mosaic** ★★, which you can see on every side of the portico. It's a romp of birds, plants, wild animals, and domesticated creatures such as horses. Adjoining it is the **Salone del Circo (Room of the Circus)** ★★, the narthex (portico) of the Terme. Its name comes from the scenes of the Roman circus depicted in its mosaics. The chariot race at Rome's Circus Maximus can clearly be seen.

Directly south of the peristyle is the **Sala della Piccola Caccia (Room of the Small Hunt)** ★★★, with mosaics depicting everything from a sacrifice to the goddess of the hunt, Diana, to the netting of a wild boar.

To the immediate west of the peristyle is the **Ambulacro della Grande Caccia (Corridor of the Great Hunt)** ★★★, measuring 60m (197 ft.). The mosaics discovered here are among the most splendid from the ancient world. One of the most dramatic scenes depicts wild animals, ranging from rhino to elephant, being loaded onto a ship.

In a salon at the northwest corner of the peristyle is the most amusing room of all: **Sala delle Dieci Ragazze (Room of the 10 Girls).** Wearing strapless two-piece bikinis, the young women are dressed for gymnastic exercises; one even has a stitched knee. Their outfits would be appropriate for a beach in the 21st century.

Directly north of the peristyle is the **Triclinium** ★★★, a large central space that spills into a trio of wide apses. This was probably the dining area, and it's known for its magnificent rendition of the Labors of Hercules. In the central apse, the mosaics depict "The Battle of the Giants," five mammoth creatures in their death throes after being attacked by the poisoned arrows of Hercules.

Among the final salons is the **Vestibolo del Piccolo Circo (Vestibule of the Small Circus)** ★★, depicting circus scenes such as chariot racing; and the **Atrio degli Amorini Pescatori** ★★, with mosaics illustrating fishing scenes.

Cubicolo della Scene Erotica ★ features a polygonal medallion depicting a panting young man locked in a tight embrace with a scantily clad seductress. Yes, there is a gratuitous bottom shot.

Contrada Casale. ℰ **0935-680036.** www.villadelcasale.it. Daily 10am to 30 minutes before sunset. Admission 10€; free for children 17 and under and EU citizens 65 and over.

Where to Stay

Hotel Ostello del Borgo   This small hotel in the historic center occupies a wing of the ancient monastery of San Giovanni, once filled with Benedictine nuns and dating from the 14th century. It is the most atmospheric place to stay in the area. The small to midsize guest rooms are well maintained and equipped with small shower-only bathrooms. All the sights, including several restaurants, lie within reach of the front door. Five rooms operate as eight-bed dormitories.

Largo San Giovanni 6, 94015 Piazza Armerina. © **0935-687019.** Fax 0935-686943. www.ostellodei borgo.it. 21 units. 60€ double; 80€ triple. Rates include continental breakfast. MC, V. **Amenities:** Breakfast room; Internet. *In room:* TV, no phone.

Park Hotel Paradiso This modern hostelry has the best location for those who want to be near to Villa Romana del Casale (see above). Located outside of town and surrounded by a forest, this is a well-kept building with comfortably furnished guest rooms. Each bathroom has either a shower or a hydromassage tub. The hotel has good on-site dining and drinking facilities, so you don't have to wander into Piazza Armerina at night.

Contrada da Ramaldo, 94015 Piazza Armerina. © **0935-680841.** Fax 0935-683391. www.parkhotel paradiso.it. 95 units. 95€–110€ double; 150€–180€ suite. Rates include buffet breakfast. AE, DC, MC, V. Free parking. Located 1km (½ mile) beyond Chiesa di Sant'Andrea. **Amenities:** Restaurant; 2 bars; outdoor pool; gym; fitness center; sauna; solarium; smoke-free rooms. *In room:* A/C, TV, minibar, Jacuzzi (in superior rooms), hair dryer.

Where to Eat

Al Fogher ★★★ 📖 SICILIAN/ITALIAN This rustic restaurant, 3km (1¾ miles) north of Piazza Armerina, is one of the best in Italy, attracting epicureans from all over the nation. If you like to eat well but shun flashiness, you will instinctively warm to the cuisine here—the chef travels the world in search of ingredients to interpret back home. His uniqueness is expressed in such dishes as risotto with pumpkin, ricotta, and gooseliver seasoned with fresh rosemary, and pork in a pepper sauce under a pistachio crust. The real specialty of the house is duck breast with a champagne vinegar sauce, dried tomatoes, and a green apple mousse. Equally good is the crispy red mullet filet with cream of yellow pepper, served with black rice studded with pistachio. The wine cellar is one of the best in the area, with 400 different local and international choices.

Contrada Bellia, Strada Statale 117. © **0935-684123.** www.alfogher.net. Reservations recommended. Main courses 10€–35€. AE, DC, MC, V. Tues–Sat 12:30–2:30pm and 8–11pm; Sun 12:30–2:30pm. Closed July 20–Aug 5.

Mosaici da Battiato SICILIAN This classic countryside restaurant lies 3km (1¾ miles) west of Piazza Armerina, en route to the famous mosaics. Unless a tour group has stopped off here (a frequent occurrence), this is a good place to order some of the best homemade Sicilian dishes in the area. Begin with delectable pennette pasta with rich cream, fresh tomatoes, and mushrooms. Most plates are reasonably priced, except the copious meat platter of grilled specialties—for trenchermen only.

Contrada Casale Ovest. © **0935-685453.** www.hotelmosaici.com. Reservations recommended. Main courses 9€–15€; fixed-price menu 20€. No credit cards. Daily 1–3pm and 7–11pm.

Trattoria La Ruota SICILIAN Opt for a table on the terrace of this atmospheric restaurant, which was created from a defunct water mill. You'll be served a typical Sicilian lunch (the only meal offered) evocative of the plains of central Sicily. The good, homemade country cooking may include *tagliatelle alla Boscaiola* (with minced beef in a zesty tomato sauce laced with cream, fresh peas, and mushrooms); stewed rabbit with olives, capers, and tomatoes; and homemade pork sausages.

Contrada Casale Ovest. © **0935-680542.** Reservations recommended. Main courses 6€–8€. AE, MC, V. Daily noon–3pm.

REGIONALE DELLE
NIE ★★★

of Catania, 181km (112 miles) SW of Messina, 164km (102 miles) SE of Palermo, of Ragusa, 134km (83 miles) NW of Syracuse.

One of Sicily's most attractive areas of natural beauty, the Parco Regionale delle Madonie is home to mountains, hills, forests, and glades punctuated by medieval hill-top villages, making it an ideal place to go hiking, mountaineering, and—in the winter—skiing. Just 6km (3¾ miles) south of Cefalù (p. 135), you can explore its 39,679 hectares (98,049 acres) on your own if you have plenty of time.

The park has been called a botanic paradise, and is considered to be the meeting point of three continents because it contains species endemic to central Europe, Asia, and north Africa, including olive, basilisk, fir, oak, and holly trees, and in springtime the hillsides are covered with a colorful carpet of wild flowers. Some of the most ancient rocks and mountains on the island are found here, and many buildings made from the local stone contain fossils. The highest peak is **Pizzo Carbonara,** at 1,979m (6,493 ft.), but wherever you are in the park you're likely to have a spectacular view.

But the park is far from a wilderness: You can also explore the picturesque charms of villages such as **Petralia Soprana** and **Petralia Sottana,** with their stone fountains of spring waters, steep cobbled streets, tiny alleys, and ceramic-tiled church spires. The area surrounding **Castelbuono** is also the only place in the world where manna, the sap from manna ash trees, is harvested. Locals eat manna both raw and flavored with cheese or chocolate, as well as using it as a natural sweetener.

GETTING THERE   **AST bus** (© 840-000323; www.aziendasicilianatrasporti.it) runs the best network of buses from Palermo and Cefalú to Castelbuono and Collesano and is the best way to reach the area if you're not driving. From Palermo, five buses daily make the 2¼-hour journey. **Trains** from Palermo and Messina (© 892021; www.trenitalia.it) pull into the station at Cefalú (see p. 135) and from here you can take one of the AST buses inland.   If you're **driving** from Palermo or Catania take the A19 autostrada and exit at Scillato. From Messina, take the A20, exit at Scillato.

What to See & Do

Follow the road directions to the **Santuario di Gibilmanna.** From the belvedere at this town, in front of the little 17th-century church, you can take in a **panoramic view ★★** of the Madonie, including the peak of Pizzo Carbonara. The Santuario di Gibilmanna is a shrine to the Virgin Mary. The Madonna is said to have shown signs of life in the 18th century when she was restoring sight to blind pilgrims and speech to a mute. Since the Vatican confirmed this claim, Gibilmanna has been one of the most important shrines in Sicily.

After taking in the view, continue southeast, following the signs to **Castelbuono,** an idyllic town that grew around a *castello* (castle) constructed in the 1300s that dominates the town. The church here, **Matrice Vecchia,** dates from the 14th century, when it was built on the ruins of a pagan temple. You can stop over to visit its historic core, **Piazza Margherita.** By this time, you will no doubt have worked up an appetite, and no visit to Castelbuono is complete without a stop at **Fiasconaro,** Piazza Margherita 10 (© 0921-677132) for some of the most delectable pastries in western Sicily.

Hollywood, POLIZZI GENEROSA

Vincent Schiavelli was a gifted character actor who appeared in films such as *One Flew Over the Cuckoo's Nest* and *Amadeus*. As a child he grew up steeped in his grandfather's tales about his time as a nobleman's in-house cook in Sicily. So enamored was he with the stories of his homeland that Schiavelli sought to come back to his roots, electing to leave the dehumanized cinematic world and move to Polizzi Generosa, his ancestral village. Granted honorary citizenship to the town, Schiavelli died in 2005 after a long illness and requested burial in the town of his roots.

The road continues south to **Petralia Soprana ★★**, at 1,147m (3,763 ft.) the loftiest town in Madonie and one of the best-preserved medieval villages of Sicily, with narrow streets and houses of local stone. A grand belvedere is found at Piazza del Popolo, with a **stunning vista ★★** toward Enna in the east.

At the end of Via Loreto, you can visit the church of **Santa Maria di Loreto,** built on the site of a Saracen fortress and framed by a set of campaniles. At the back of the church is Madonie's greatest **panorama ★★★** of Mount Etna.

The next stop is **Petralia Sottana,** overlooking the River Imera Valley. This little village, perched 1,000m (3,281 ft.) above sea level, is the headquarters of the national park service, **Ente Parco,** Corso Paolo Agliata 16 (© **0921-684011**), open Monday to Friday 9:30am to 1:30pm and 3:30 to 6:30pm.

At this point, head west along the S120, stopping at **Polizzi Generosa,** another hilltop magnificently situated on a limestone spur. The **view ★★★** at Piazza XXVII Maggio is one of the most spectacular in Madonie, taking in its loftiest peaks and the scenic valley of the River Himera.

Here you can begin your journey north back to Cefalù (p. 135), passing through **Scillato** until you reach **Collesano,** where the aura of the Middle Ages still lingers. The **Chiesa Madre,** reached by going up a flight of stairs, is filled with art treasures. This church contains masterpieces by the 16th-century painter Gaspare Vazzano, who signed his name "Zoppo di Gangi;" his cycle of **frescoes ★** illustrates scenes from the lives of Jesus Christ, St. Paul, and St. Peter. He also painted another magnificent canvas, *Santa Maria degli Angeli ★*, found in the north aisle. Collesano is the home of the **Targa Florio** in September every year, where, since 1906, cars have been racing along the death-defying hairpin turns of the mountains. It still runs today, but only vintage cars can participate.

Where to Stay

Hotel Pomieri ★★ ☺ 👜   You'll feel as if you're in the Swiss mountains thousands of miles away—this chalet is surrounded by the highest peaks in the Madonie, and is ideal for those who seek a base within the park. The rustic wooden interior immediately gives you a sense of coziness, as do the rooms, which are spacious, rustic, and most importantly, heated when necessary. All have spectacular views overlooking the landscape. The hotel also has a good restaurant on the premises, which serves up hearty meals after a day spent trekking.

Contrada Pomieri, Petralia Sottana. ☏ **0921-649998.** Fax 0921-649855. www.hotelpomieri.it. 40 units. 134€ double. Rates include breakfast. No credit cards. Special discounts for children under 10. Free on-premises parking. **Amenities:** Restaurant; Internet (4€/hr). *In room:* A/C, TV.

Masseria Susafa ★★★   Country living at its finest—you can watch the sheep being milked and the ricotta being made at this centuries-old farm that preserves the tradition and the history of the territory. The welcoming owners have converted the old buildings, maintaining their original outer stone structure, while inside you'll be welcomed into a restored manor that maintains the original charm of the property, including the soaring, wooden-beamed ceilings. The rooms were once the farmers' apartments but now have some of the plushest beds in Sicily, while the furniture and flooring date back to the last century. The delectable, generous breakfasts are lovingly prepared. Given the plethora of activities in and around the Masseria, such as their cookery courses, or just the quiet hideaways where you can relax with a book, you might want to stay for good.

Contrada Susafa, Polizzi Generosa. ☏ **338-9608713.** www.susafa.it. 14 units. 70€—150€ double. Rates include breakfast. AE, DC, MC, V. Free on-premises parking. **Amenities:** Restaurant; bar; outdoor swimming pool; Internet (3€/hr). *In room:* A/C, TV.

Paradiso delle Madonie   This is one of the few modern structures found in these parts, albeit totally reconverted from an old building. In the historic center of Castelbuono, rooms are spacious with basic yet well-kept furnishings; the second-floor rooms have balconies facing the main road. Bathrooms are shower-only. Its only drawback is that it's rated as a four-star hotel, when it should really be three, but the courtesy makes up for the "missing" star.

Via Dante Alighieri 82, Castelbuono ☏ **0921-676197.** Fax 0921-673958. www.paradisodellemadonie.it. 16 units. 82€—116€ double. Rates include breakfast. AE, DC, MC, V. Free street parking. **Amenities:** Bar; babysitting. *In room:* A/C, TV, minibar, Wi-Fi (free).

Where to Eat

Nangalarruni ★★★ SICILIAN   In the heartland of the Madonie, chef Giuseppe Carollo has made it his mission to use only the ingredients provided by his environs, creating dishes that honor his childhood and his people. From the bread flan stuffed with fresh ricotta and topped with tomato sauce, or lamb cooked in a crust of pistachios, you feel as if you are at home among old friends, and the convivial setting brings the faithful back time and again. If you really want to take the memories home with you, Nangalarruni also offers cooking classes.

Via delle Confraternite, 5, Castelbuono ☏ **0921-671428.** Fax 0921-677449. www.hostariananalarruni. it. Reservations strongly recommended. AE, DC, MC, V. Main Courses 10€—20€. Thurs-Tues 12:30-3pm and 7:30-11pm. Closed Wed.

Romittaggio ★ SICILIAN   Specializing in simple yet delicious mountain food, the restaurant is within a monastery from the Middle Ages, where you dine within the centuries-old tufa walls. In summer, tables are set up outside in the arcades of the cloister. This is a place where local mushrooms are king, and are served with pastas, meat dishes, and as side dishes. Pizza is also available.

Località San Guglielmo Sud, Castelbuono. ☏ **0921-671323.** www.romittaggio.it. Reservations recommended. AE, MC, V. Main Courses 8€—20€. Thurs-Tues 12:30-3pm and 7:30-11pm. Closed Wed and June 15–July 15.

TAORMINA & MOUNT ETNA

S icily attracts visitors from around the world, but perhaps there are two places that instantly come to mind when referring to the island: The chic resort town of **Taormina ★★★**, and the menacing **Mount Etna ★★**, the highest volcano in Europe.

Although lying near to one another (30km/18.6 miles), they could not be further apart in ambience and mentality: Taormina draws in the jetsetters, the nouveau riche, and everything in between to its romantic alleyways and dazzling hotels, while the rugged mountain offers an alpine scenery more in tune with nature-lovers and those seeking seclusion. Where Taormina offers a breathtaking landscape dense with man-made archaeology, Etna offers perhaps the most stunning vistas ever created by nature.

Yet despite these stark contrasts, both are steeped in tales of mythology: It was in Taormina that the Oxen of the Sun roamed the plains in Odysseyean tales, and Etna was the home to Hephaistos, the god of fire. Chance has placed these two wonders in relative proximity, and you won't have difficulty choosing between them: Both can be seen in one day should you be pressed for time, and either one makes a perfect base from which to visit the other.

If you still have time on your hands and your curiosity runs rampant, the choices for side trips are endless: **Giardini-Naxos,** the actual shoreline of Taormina, was the first Greek settlement of the island; the **Gole dell'Alcantara (Alcantara Gorges) ★**, created by lava and carved by rushing waters, offers a refreshing getaway from the stifling summer heat, and the many towns at the foothills of Etna, such as **Linguaglossa** and **Randazzo,** are all excellent bases from which to explore Etna, each with unique histories of their own, and with gastronomical traditions far removed from anything seaside.

TAORMINA ★★★

53km (33 miles) N of Catania, 53km (33 miles) S of Messina, 250km (155 miles) E of Palermo.

The spectacular views of the smoldering **Mount Etna ★★** and across two bays out to the Ionian Sea have helped make Taormina Sicily's most famous—and fabled—resort town. Cascading down the slopes of Mount Tauro at some 200m (656 ft.) above sea level, Taormina first became a

Taormina

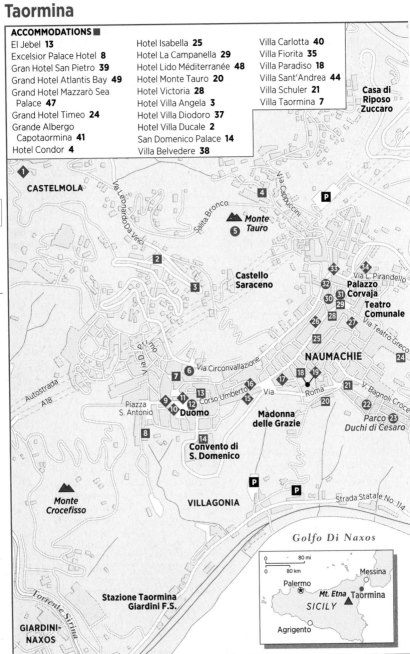

Casa di
Riposo
Zuccaro

CASTELMOLA

Via Leonardo Da Vinci

Salita Bronco

Via Cappuccini

Monte
Tauro

Castello
Saraceno

Via L. Pirandello

Palazzo
Corvaja

Teatro
Comunale

Via Teatro Greco

NAUMACHIE

Via P. Rizzo

Via Circonvallazione

Autostrada A18

Corso Umberto

Via Roma

V. Bagnoli Croce

Piazza
S. Antonio

Duomo

Madonna
delle Grazie

Parco
Duchi di Cesaro

Convento di
S. Domenico

Monte
Crocefisso

VILLAGONIA

Strada Statale No. 114

Golfo Di Naxos

Torrente Sirina

Stazione Taormina
Giardini F.S.

GIARDINI-
NAXOS

0   80 mi
0   80 km

Palermo

Messina

Mt. Etna Taormina

SICILY

Agrigento

9

TAORMINA & MOUNT ETNA | Taormina

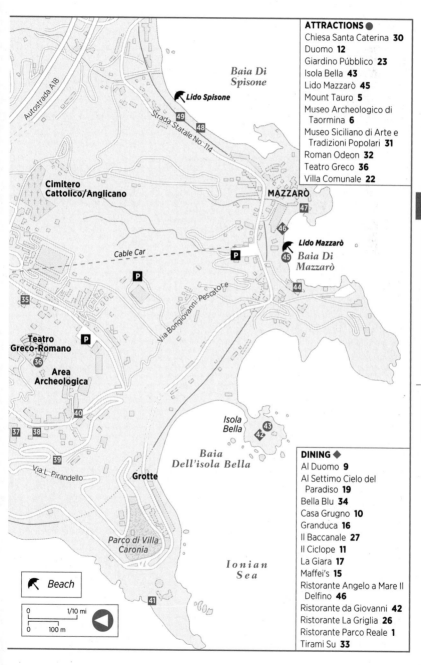

ATTRACTIONS ●
Chiesa Santa Caterina **30**
Duomo **12**
Giardino Púbblico **23**
Isola Bella **43**
Lido Mazzarò **45**
Mount Tauro **5**
Museo Archeologico di
Taormina **6**
Museo Siciliano di Arte e
Tradizioni Popolari **31**
Roman Odeon **32**
Teatro Greco **36**
Villa Comunale **22**

DINING ◆
Al Duomo **9**
Al Settimo Cielo del
Paradiso **19**
Bella Blu **34**
Casa Grugno **10**
Granduca **16**
Il Baccanale **27**
Il Ciclope **11**
La Giara **17**
Maffei's **15**
Ristorante Angelo a Mare Il
Delfino **46**
Ristorante da Giovanni **42**
Ristorante La Griglia **26**
Ristorante Parco Reale **1**
Tirami Su **33**

Baia Di
Spisone

Lido Spisone

Strada Statale No. 114

Cimitero
Cattolico/Anglicano

MAZZARÒ

Cable Car

Via Bongiovanni Pescatore

Lido Mazzarò

Baia Di
Mazzarò

Teatro
Greco-Romano

Area
Archeologica

Isola
Bella

Baia
Dell'isola Bella

Grotte

Via L. Pirandello

Parco di Villa
Caronia

Ionian
Sea

Beach

0   1/10 mi
0   100 m

port of call in the 18th century when it formed part of The Grand Tour, and travelers flocked to see the well-preserved **Teatro Greco ★★★** amphitheater, where you can still see plays and concerts against the backdrop of distant Etna.

Soon Taormina evolved into the destination of choice for aristocracy, bohemians, artists, and jetsetters alike, and among the famous names who hung out in the town is D.H. Lawrence, who was inspired to write *Lady Chatterley's Lover* when he was there. Over the years, the town became Sicily's answer to Monte Carlo, today Taormina still has an air of chic, which is evident in the prices, but as the island's prime tourist destination it can also get incredibly crowded during the summer months. Its winding medieval streets are packed with Arab, Norman, and baroque monuments, as well as numerous restaurants, cafes, and shops. The town is a shopper's paradise with a plethora of souvenir shops, plus a host of jewelers, smart designer boutiques, and funky stores selling everything from hats to chandeliers.

In summer, you can hang out at the beaches below the town at **Giardini-Naxos** by day but, if you want to escape the tourist hordes, seek out adventures: Perhaps climbing Mount Etna, walking to the **Castelmola,** or making a trip to **Syracuse** (see p. 285).

Essentials
GETTING THERE
BY TRAIN   Trains (✆ **892021;** www.trenitalia.it) to Taormina/Giardini-Naxos arrive from both Sicily and the mainland. The train station for Taormina/Giardini-Naxos is not in Taormina proper but in Naxos, below the town (about 1.6km/1 mile away). Along the east coast, service to Taormina is frequent and direct. From Messina, the train runs approximately every hour, the journey takes an hour, from Catania, it's 40 minutes; both trains cost 3.80€. From Syracuse, it takes approximately 2 hours; there are about five direct trains a day and it costs 7.95€. From Palermo, the journey can take up to 5 hours; you need to change, and the costs varies from 12€ to 30€ depending on what type of train you take.

From the station, **Interbus** (✆ **0942-625301;** www.interbus.it) run a service daily from 9am to midnight, every 15 to 45 minutes past the hour. Tickets cost 1.30€, which you can buy from the driver. Buses stop in Taormina. You can also take a taxi for about 15€; book one by calling ✆ **335-5398799;** www.naxosonline.it/taxi-taormina.

BY BUS   Buses pull directly into town at the **bus station** in Via Luigi Pirandello, arriving from Catania (journey time 1½ hr and stopping at Giardini-Naxos), Catania Airport (hourly costing 5€), and Messina station. For details, contact **Interbus** (✆ **0942-625301;** www.interbus.it).

BY CAR   From Messina, head south on the A18. From Catania, continue north on the A18. Most of the city is off-limits to traffic, so leave your car at one of the car parks in town. **Lumbi Parking,** Contrada Lumbi, is signposted off the Taormina Nord autostrada junction; there's another garage at **Mazzarò Parking,** on Via Nazionale in Mazzarò, in the vicinity of the cablecar station off the coastal road. For 24-hour parking, count on paying 20€ to 25€.

VISITOR INFORMATION
The **tourist office** is in the Palazzo Corvaja, Piazza Santa Caterina (✆ **0942-23243**); it's open Monday to Saturday 8:30am to 2pm and 4 to 7pm. Here you can get a free

map, hotel listings, bus and rail timetables, and a schedule of summer cultural events staged at the Greek Amphitheater and during the Taormina Film Festival.

SPECIAL EVENTS

The **Taormina Film Festival** (www.taorminafilmfest.it) takes place every year in June, when industry giants and cinema buffs from around the globe convene here to view national and international works. The **Teatro Greco** (p. 202) has a rich summer program with local and well-known international artists performing here, usually their only stop in Italy.

GETTING AROUND

Everything is within walking distance in Taormina, though you might encounter a steep climb now and then—this is a hilltop town. If you're venturing off on day excursions, a network of buses goes to such places as Giardini-Naxos (p. 217) and Mount Etna (p. 220). The tourist office has a complete list of brochures and timetables.

The more distant parts of Taormina are linked by minibus, which leaves from the terminal at Via Luigi Pirandello in town and costs 1€ for a one-way ticket. Most visitors use the minibus that goes from the terminal to Madonna della Rocca, since it passes most of the major hotels.

Taxi ranks are found at Piazza Vittorio Emanuele and at Piazza San Pancrazio. These are used primarily if you're leaving the heart of Taormina and venturing into its hinterlands. A typical fare—say, from the center of Taormina to Madonna della Rocca—is 15€.

If you prefer to get around by moped, **Jet Car,** Via Nazionale 8 (✆ **0942-56190**), rents scooters for 45€ per day. It's open year-round daily 8am to noon and 4 to 8pm.

[FastFACTS] TAORMINA

American Express The travel agency **La Duca Viaggi,** Via Don Bosco 39 (✆ **0942-625250**), handles AmEx clients Monday to Friday 9am to 1pm and 4 to 7:30pm. However, the most comprehensive travel agency in Taormina is **Dr. Silvestri Travel Bureau,** Corso Umberto I, 143–145 (✆ **0942-23052**). Established in 1905, it offers services ranging from car rentals and airline tickets to currency exchange and bus excursions. It's open Friday to Wednesday 9am to 1pm and 4 to 8pm.

Currency Exchange There are dozens of possibilities, especially at the banks along Corso Umberto I and Via Pirandello. **Cambio Valute,** Corso Umberto I, 224, near Piazza Sant'Antonio (✆ **0942-24806**), has ATMs and is the most convenient; it's open Monday to Saturday 9am to 1pm and 4 to 8pm. You can also get money exchanged at the post office at Piazza Sant'Antonio (✆ **0942-213011**), open Monday to Saturday 8am to 6:30pm.

Emergency Dial the *Carabinieri* at ✆ **113** or the police at ✆ **112.**

Hospital/Medical Needs Serving the entire Taormina area is **Ospedale San Vincenzo,** Piazza S. Francesco Di Paola (✆ **0942-628040**). In an emergency, call **Guardia Medica** (✆ **0942-625419**), open Monday to Friday 8am to 8pm, Saturday and Sunday 24 hours.

Internet Access The best place to go is the **Internet Café,** Calle Umberto I, 214 (✆ **0942-628839**), which charges 4€ per hour.

Left Luggage A kiosk inside the Taormina/Giardini-Naxos train station is open daily from 8am to 9pm; it charges 4€ for an hour per piece and up to 11€ over a 24-hour period.

Pharmacy The most central drugstore is **Farmacia Ragusa,** Piazza Duomo 9 (℡ **0942-23231**), open Thursday to Tuesday 8:30am to 1pm and 5 to 8:30pm. It posts a schedule of other pharmacies open at night and on weekends; this list changes weekly on a rotating basis.

Post Office The post office is at Piazza Sant'Antonio (℡ **0942-213011**). Hours are Monday to Friday 8am to 6:30pm and Saturday from 8am to 12:30pm.

Exploring the Area

The center of Taormina is incredibly easy to visit, and you can view all the main attractions in under two hours. The **Teatro Greco** (theater) ★★★, Via del Teatro Greco (℡ **0942-23220**), is Taormina's most visited monument, offering a view of rare beauty of the seacoast and Mount Etna. The ruins lie on the upper reaches of Taormina, near the Grand Hotel Timeo. In the Hellenistic period, the Greeks hewed the theater out of the rocky slope of Mount Tauro; the Romans remodeled and modified it greatly. What remains today dates from the 2nd century A.D. Reserved seating existed even in Greek times; a seat bears the inscribed name of Philistide, wife of Hieron II of Syracuse. The famous view of Mount Etna and the sea beyond the theater is breathtaking. The conquering Arabs, who seemed intent on devastating the town, slashed away at the theater in the 10th century, which is why it's a rather sparse and dusty ruin. On the premises is a display of artifacts from the classical and early Christian periods. Today, this Greek Theater (though some consider it a Greco-Roman theater) is the site of the annual Taormina film festival, and in the summer is the home of a robust entertainment program, attracting artists from around the world, making Taormina their only stop in Italy. The theater is open from April to September, daily from 9am to 7pm; and from October to March, daily from 9am to 4pm. Admission is 8€ for adults, 4€ for those ages 18 to 25, and free for adults 65 and older and children 17 and younger, coming from the EU, Canada, and Australia.

Behind the tourist office, on the other side of Piazza Vittorio Emanuele, is the **Roman Odeon,** a small theater partly covered by the church of Santa Caterina next door. The Romans constructed this theater around A.D. 21. Much smaller than the Greek theater and with similar architecture, it was discovered in 1892 by a blacksmith digging in the area. A peristyle (colonnade) was also discovered here, perhaps all that was left of a Greek temple dedicated to Aphrodite.

Chiesa Santa Caterina, Piazza Santa Caterina, off Corso Umberto I (℡ **0942-23123**), was consecrated to St. Catherine of Alexandria (exact consecration date unknown); it may have been built in the mid-17th century. It sits on a piazza that abuts the highest point of the town's main street, Corso Umberto I. Within its severely dignified exterior are baroque detailing and a trussed wood-beamed ceiling. Chiesa Santa Caterina is the temporary replacement for Taormina's cathedral (which, at the time of writing, is due to open in the spring of 2011). It's open daily 9am to noon and 4 to 7pm.

Farther along the main drag, **Corso Umberto I** ★, you'll arrive at Piazza del Duomo and the **Duomo,** or cathedral, of Taormina. Built around 1400 on the ruins of a church from the Middle Ages, this fortress cathedral has a Latin-cross plan and a trio of aisles. The nave is held up by half a dozen monolithic columns in pink marble; a fish-scale decoration graces their capitals, in honor of the island's maritime tradition. For information, call ✆ **0942-23123.** The cathedral's role has been temporarily assumed by Chiesa Santa Caterina (see above).

Museo Archeologico di Taormina, in the Palazzo Badia Vecchia, on Via Circonvallazione (✆ **0942-620112**), is set on the site of the ancient Roman baths. It is a repository for the hundreds of archaeological remnants discovered during excavations in and around the city. Expect to find pottery shards and lingering artifacts of the ancient Roman world. Admission is free; it's open Tuesday to Sunday 9am to 1pm, also on Tuesday and Thursday 4 to 8pm.

The Palazzo Corvaja, one of the most famous palaces in Taormina, contains the tourist office as well as the **Museo Siciliano di Arte e Tradizioni Popolari (Museum of Art and Popular Traditions),** Piazza Santa Caterina at Corso Umberto I (✆ **0942-23243**). It's filled with 18th-century oil portraits, painted glass and donkey carts, and embroidery. The most charming pieces in the collection are secular portraits of the mid-19th-century Sicilian bourgeoisie. Entrance to the ground floor of the palace (also the town's tourist office) is free. Admission to the museum is 3€. It's open Tuesday to Sunday 9am to 1pm and 4 to 8pm.

A local sightseeing oddity here is **Villa Comunale,** sometimes called **Parco Duca di Cesarò ★★,** Via Bagnoli Croce, off Corso Umberto I. It's one of the most beautiful little parks in all of Sicily, with gardens created by Lady Florence Trevelyan in the late 19th century. This Scottish lady was "invited" to leave Britain after a well-publicized romance with the future king, Edward VII, son of Victoria. She built various amusements in the gardens, including a fanciful stone-and-brick pavilion that might have been conceived as a teahouse. The gardens are open daily 8:30am to 7pm (6pm in winter); admission is free.

Another flower-filled garden in Taormina is the **Giardino Púbblico (Public Garden),** Via Bagnoli Croce. Bequeathed to the city by an English aristocrat who fell in love with Taormina, it overlooks the sea, making it a choice spot for views. You can order drinks at a bar in the park. The garden is open from dawn until dusk.

It's worth a trip to the nearby village of **Castelmola ★,** 3km (2 miles) northwest of Taormina. This is one of the most beautiful places in eastern Sicily, with a panoramic view of Mount Etna on clear days. You might also visit the ruined *castello* (castle) on the summit of **Mount Tauro** (390m/1,280 ft.), about 3km (2 miles) northwest of Taormina along the Castelmola road. Hikers can follow a footpath here. Ruins of a former acropolis are visible, but most people come simply for the panoramas.

Many visitors to Taormina come for the beach, although the sands aren't exactly at the resort. To reach the best and most popular beach, **Lido Mazzarò ★★,** you have to go south of town via a cablecar (✆ **0942-23605**) that leaves from Via Pirandello every 15 minutes. A one-way ticket costs 2€. This beach is one of the best equipped in Sicily, with bars, restaurants, and hotels. You can rent beach chairs, umbrellas, and water-sports equipment at various kiosks from April to October. To the right of Lido Mazzarò, past the Capo Sant'Andrea headland, is the region's prettiest cove, where twin crescents of beach sweep from a sand spit out to the minuscule **Isola Bella** islet. You can walk here from the cablecar in a minute, but it's more fun to paddle a boat from Mazzarò around Capo Sant'Andrea, which hides a few grottoes with excellent light effects on the seaward side.

North of Mazzarò are the long, wide beaches of **Spisone** and **Letojanni,** more developed but less crowded than **Giardini,** the large, built-up resort beach south of

Isola Bella. A local bus leaves Taormina for Mazzarò, Spisone, and Letojanni, and another heads down the coast to Giardini.

Where to Stay

Lodging options in Taormina range from army cots to sumptuous suites. Be prepared, however, to pay a king's ransom, and don't be too surprised if what's deemed four-star here passes for a nondescript three-star anywhere else.

If you're coming primarily to hit the beach, at least in July and August, you may want to stay at **Mazzarò,** 5km (3 miles) from the center, and trek up the hill for shopping, nightlife, and dining. Mazzarò is the major beach and has some fine hotels (see the Grand Hotel Mazzarò Sea Palace, below). Buses and cablecars connecting Mazzarò and Taormina leave every 30 minutes daily from 8am to 9pm; the fare is 1.50€. Otherwise, I recommend that you stay in Taormina—it has far more charm than anything down by the sea.

In summer, the curse of Taormina hotels is the noise, from traffic as well as from visitors who turn the town into an all-night party. If you're a light sleeper and you've chosen a hotel along Corso Umberto, ask for a room in the rear—you'll be trading a view for a good night's sleep.

If you're driving to a hotel at the top of Taormina, call ahead to see what arrangements can be made for your car. Ask for exact driving directions as well as instructions on where to park—the narrow, winding, one-way streets can be bewildering once you get here.

VERY EXPENSIVE

El Jebel ★★ 💼   The new kid on the block, opening in 2009, is a boutique hotel right in the heart of town. It's a beautifully restored compound from the 1300s, which masterfully combines Arab decor with plush modern elements. Although it's a bit of climb to get here (you can't drive to the hotel), you'll nonetheless be rewarded with 5-star service unparalleled at other places. Rooms are spacious and comfortable, creatively combining modern and arabesque pieces; some have hardwood floors, and all have tub-only bathrooms. Although it's still ironing out a few kinks and lacking other amenities most luxury hotels provide (no on-premises pool, no reading room), El Jebel stands out for personalized attention.

Salita Ciampoli, 9, 98039 Taormina. 🕜 **0942-635494.** Fax 0942-625677. www.hoteljebel.com. 12 units. 400€ double; 700€–1500€ suite. Rates include breakfast. AE, DC, MC, V. **Amenities:** Bar; restaurant; spa: *In room:* A/C, TV, minibar, free laptop use.

Gran Hotel San Pietro ★★★   This is one of the most elegant hotels in town. A Relais & Châteaux member, it's a 15-minute walk to Taormina's center, with daily shuttle service available. The interiors are elegant and welcoming, with added touches like a wood-paneled library. Guest rooms are elegantly furnished, each with a private balcony overlooking either Mount Etna or Naxos Bay. They are rated classic and superior, or else junior and executive suites. The location of this Mediterranean-style building, rising six floors, is set on a hillside overlooking the sea, with dramatic views on Isola Bella.

Via Pirandello 50, 98039 Taormina. 🕜 **0942-620711.** Fax 0942-620770. www.grandhotelsanpietro.net. 63 units. 260€–540€ double; 560€–1,210€ suite. Rates include buffet breakfast. AE, DC, MC, V. Free parking. **Amenities:** 2 restaurants; bar; outdoor pool; fitness center; room service; babysitting; smoke-free rooms; private beach. *In room:* A/C, TV, minibar, Wi-Fi.

FOR THAT rainy DAY

Taormina has one of the most charming public libraries in Italy, **Biblioteca di Comune di Taormina,** Piazza XXV Aprile 3 (ℂ **0942-610260**). It's lacking in its range of books, but the setting is the severely dignified **Chiesa di**

Sant'Agostino, originally built in 1448 and majestically transformed into a library around 1900. It's open Monday to Friday 8:30am to 1:30pm, Tuesday and Thursday 3:30 to 6pm.

Grande Albergo Capotaormina ★★   A short driving distance from the center, this cape was transformed in the 1960s with the addition of the most avant-garde architectural statement in or around Taormina—an oasis of posh comfort within a spectacularly inhospitable natural setting. Surrounded by the Ionian Sea on three sides, and with a layout that resembles an irregular pentagon, the hotel contains five floors with wide sun terraces. Elevators take you through 46m (151 ft.) of solid rock to the beach and to a large, free-form pool far below the level of the hotel, directly adjacent to the sea. Guest rooms are generous with dated but well-maintained furnishings, each with a private terrace and a spacious bathroom.

Via Nazionale 105, 98039 Taormina. ℂ **0942-572111.** Fax 0942-625467. www.atahotels.it/ en/ capotaormina. 202 units. 222€–500€ double; 460€–1,100€ suite. Rates include breakfast. AE, DC, MC, V. Parking 15€. **Amenities:** 3 restaurants; 3 bars; outdoor seawater pool; golf; tennis; gym; seawater Jacuzzi; sauna; massage; room service; watersports program (supplemental charge) including deep-sea fishing and scuba; smoke-free rooms. *In room:* A/C, TV, minibar, hair dryer, Wi-Fi.

Grand Hotel Atlantis Bay ★   This government-rated five-star hotel has its own private beach along the Taormina coast. Associated with the excellent Mazzarò Sea Palace, it blends artfully into a landscape of pebbly beachfronts and cliffs. Great care was taken for an ecologically sensitive approach to the natural surroundings. The result is a jagged and earthy-looking combination of rough-hewed stones, terra-cotta tiles, and primal colors that don't stand out when viewed from afar. There's something stylish and postmodern about this youthful, sports-oriented hotel, with its bubbling aquariums and neo-Roman accessories in the lobby. Rooms are spacious and comfortable, with dining by the shoreline in summer months.

Via Nazionale 161, 98030 Taormina Mare. ℂ **0942-618011.** Fax 0942-23194. www.atlantisbay.it. 86 units. 300€–500€ double; from 570€ suite. Breakfast not included. AE, DC, MC, V. Parking 45€. **Amenities:** 2 restaurants; 2 bars; outdoor pool; fitness center; wellness center; smoke-free rooms. *In room:* A/C, TV, minibar, hair dryer, Wi-Fi.

Grand Hotel Mazzarò Sea Palace ★★★   The leading hotel in Mazzarò opens onto the most beautiful bay in Sicily and has its own private beach. Completed in 1962, this government-rated five-star deluxe hotel has been renovated frequently since. From the coastal highway, you won't be able to see very much of this spectacular lodging—only a rooftop and masses of bougainvillea. You'll register on the top floor, and then ride an elevator down to sea level for access to a stylish, airy set of marble-sheathed public rooms. The hotel is very elegant, genuinely charming, and well staffed. Big windows let in cascades of light and offer views of the coast. Guest rooms are well furnished, filled with wicker and veneer pieces along with original art and wood or tile floors; most have panoramic views.

9

TAORMINA & MOUNT ETNA   Taormina

Via Nazionale 147, 98030 Mazzarò. ✆ **0942-612111.** Fax 0942-626237. www.mazzaroseapalace.it. 88 units. 350€–600€ double; 600€–1,000€ suite. Rates include breakfast. AE, DC, MC, V. Parking (nearby) 25€. **Amenities:** Restaurant; bar; outdoor pool; fitness center; room service; babysitting; smoke-free rooms. *In room:* A/C, TV, minibar, hair dryer, Wi-Fi.

Grand Hotel Timeo ★★   Hidden in a tranquil private park just below the Teatro Greco, the Timeo opened in 1873 and has hosted everyone from King Umberto II to Liz Taylor. It's perched at the eastern edge of Taormina, on a precarious but panoramic terrace that's flooded with light and views upward to the amphitheater and down across town to the sea. It evokes a 19th-century neoclassical villa that manages to be lighthearted and baronial at the same time. You get the feeling that the Timeo was built purely for pleasure, and it carries the aura of a sophisticated and very secular private villa. Guests are treated to a winning combination of old-world elegance and contemporary conveniences. From the tiniest room to the most sumptuous suite, the Art Nouveau decor in each one is a clear nod to the grandeur of this property.

Via Teatro Greco 59, 98039 Taormina. ✆ **0942-23801.** Fax 0942-628501. www.grandhoteltimeo.com. 87 units. 400€–600€ double; 550€–1,900€ suite. Rates include buffet breakfast. AE, DC, MC, V. Free parking. **Amenities:** Restaurant; piano bar; outdoor heated pool; fitness center; Turkish bath; room service; massage; babysitting; smoke-free rooms; shuttle service to the beach. *In room:* A/C, TV, minibar, Wi-Fi.

San Domenico Palace ★★★   This is one of Italy's greatest hotels, so impressive that it evokes a national monument. Set in the town's oldest neighborhood, it originated in the 14th century as a Dominican monastery. Today it's surrounded by walled-in terraced gardens that are lit at night by flickering torches.

Inside you'll find massive and dignified areas (reception rooms, hideaway chapels, paneled salons) outfitted with museum-quality antiques that have been in place for at least 75 years, a genuinely impressive patina, and a physical setting that no one would dare modernize. The result is old-fashioned in the most appealing sense of the word. Guest rooms are located in either the old monastery part of the hotel, where furnishings are severely dignified and very comfortable, or in the more opulent "newer" wings, which evoke the Gilded Age. Views extend over the bougainvillea, palms, and citrus trees in the garden to the sea.

Piazza San Domenico 5, 98039 Taormina. ✆ **0942-613111.** Fax 0942-625506. sandomenicopalace.hotels insicily.it. 108 units. 400€–650€ double; from 850€ suite. Rates include buffet breakfast. AE, DC, MC, V. Free parking outside; 3 spaces inside (summer only) 20€. **Amenities:** 4 restaurants; piano bar; outdoor heated pool; gym; room service; babysitting; smoke-free rooms. *In room:* A/C, TV, minibar, hair dryer.

EXPENSIVE

Excelsior Palace Hotel ★★   This four-star hotel in Taormina is used more by tour groups than virtually any other hotel in town. It's set on a rocky ridge in the lower reaches of Taormina, midway between a busy piazza and an isolated, somewhat dusty garden. Part of the allure of this place derives from its outrageous facade (ca. 1903), which artfully mimics the grand Moorish architecture you might expect in Marrakech. Most of the rather formal-looking guest rooms were recently upgraded and inspired by late-19th-century models. Older, not-yet-renovated rooms are a bit blander but equally comfortable.

Via Toselli 8, 98039 Taormina. ✆ **0942-23975.** Fax 0942-23978. www.excelsiorpalacetaormina.it. 88 units. 350€ double. Rates include breakfast AE, DC, MC, V. **Amenities:** Restaurant; bar; outdoor pool; babysitting. *In room:* A/C, TV, minibar, Wi-Fi (free).

Hotel Isabella   Only one other hotel, the Victoria, enjoys a location directly on the main street of Taormina; the Isabella is the better rated of the two. Small-scale and chic in a way that only a boutique hotel can be, it welcomes visitors with a lobby that might remind you of a living room with a peaches-and-cream color scheme. Its pleasing decor was inspired by a sun-flooded English country house. Guest rooms are not particularly large, though they are cozy and plush. Some have views over the all-pedestrian hubbub of the town's main street. On the rooftop is a solarium.

Corso Umberto I 58, 98039 Taormina. ℂ **0942-23153.** Fax 0942-23155. www.hotel-isabella.it. 32 units. 112€–194€ double. Rates include buffet breakfast. AE, DC, MC, V. **Amenities:** Restaurant; bar; free access to beach club w/watersports equipment/rentals; babysitting; smoke-free rooms. *In room:* A/C, TV, minibar, hair dryer.

Hotel Monte Tauro   This hotel was built into the side of a hill rising high above the sea. Each room has a balcony with a sea view. Rooms are furnished to a high standard, with tiled bathrooms. Junior suites have Jacuzzis. The social center is the outdoor pool, whose cantilevered platform is ringed with dozens of plants.

Via Madonna delle Grazie 3, 98039 Taormina. ℂ **0942-24402.** Fax 0942-24403. www.hotelmonte tauro.it. 100 units. 250€–370€ double; 350€–450€ junior suite. Rates include continental breakfast. AE, DC, MC, V. Closed Jan 15–Mar. **Amenities:** Restaurant; 2 bars; outdoor pool; room service; babysitting. *In room:* A/C, TV, minibar, hair dryer, Internet.

Hotel Villa Diodoro ★   This is one of Taormina's better hotels, with tasteful design through and through. There are sunny spots where you can swim, sunbathe, and enjoy the view of mountains, trees, and flowers. The vistas of Mount Etna, the Ionian Sea, and the eastern coastline of Sicily are reason enough to stay here. Guest rooms are elegant and comfortable, with wrought-iron headboards, terra-cotta floors, balconies, and compact bathrooms. From June to October, a shuttle bus runs to the beach at nearby Lido Caparena.

Via Bagnoli Croce 75, 98039 Taormina. ℂ **0942-23312.** Fax 0942-23391. www.hotelvilladiodoro.com. 99 units. 178€–326€ double. Rates include buffet breakfast. AE, DC, MC, V. Free parking. **Amenities:** Restaurant; outdoor pool; room service; babysitting. *In room:* A/C, TV, minibar, hair dryer.

Hotel Villa Ducale ★★   This restored old villa is a charming and romantic choice. Villa Ducale sits on a hillside, a 10-minute walk up from the center, in the quiet hamlet of Madonna della Rocca (midway between the heart of the resort and high-altitude Castelmola). It boasts magnificent views of the Mediterranean, the town, and Mount Etna. Each guest room has a veranda, terra-cotta floors, wrought-iron beds, and a compact bathroom. The service is warm and helpful. Breakfast is usually served on an outdoor terrace with a gorgeous view.

Via Leonardo da Vinci 60, 98039 Taormina. ℂ **0942-28153.** Fax 0942-28710. www.hotelvilladucale.it. 15 units. 100€–280€ double; 200€–480€ suite. Rates include buffet breakfast. AE, MC, V. Parking 10€. **Amenities:** Lounge; Jacuzzi; room service; shuttle service to the beach. *In room:* A/C, TV, minibar, hair dryer.

Villa Carlotta ★★   Only Villa Ducale and Grand Hotel Timeo enjoy the same tranquility and romantic position as this house, situated in a mock castle with an alluring roof garden—it's a charmer in every way. The staff, the service, the guest rooms, and the price combine to make this a little gem. Furnishings are well chosen for comfort, tradition, and style, and each guest room is beautifully furnished and inviting. The cuisine at the restaurant is first-rate.

Via Pirandello 81, 98039 Taormina. ⓒ **0942-626058.** Fax 0954-23732. www.hotelvillacarlotta taormina.com. 23 units. 250€–320€ double; 320€–480€ suite. Rates include buffet breakfast. AE, DC, MC, V. Parking 15€. **Amenities:** Restaurant; outdoor pool; Jacuzzi; room service; babysitting; smoke-free rooms. *In room:* A/C, TV, minibar, hair dryer, Wi-Fi (free).

Villa Sant'Andrea ★   Staying here is like going to a house party at a pretty home. The atmosphere draws return visits by artists, painters, and other discerning guests. The Sant'Andrea lies at the base of the mountain, directly on the sea, and opens onto a private beach. Guest rooms are well maintained and comfortable, though size and decor vary. Many have balconies or terraces; the tiled shower-only bathrooms are small. A cablecar, just outside the front gates, runs into the heart of Taormina.

Via Nazionale 137, 98030 Taormina Mare. ⓒ **0942-23125.** Fax 0942-24838. www.framon-hotels.com. 80 units. 256€–388€ double; from 420€ suite. Rates include buffet breakfast. AE, DC, MC, V. Parking 20€. Closed Nov 3–Apr 2. **Amenities:** 2 restaurants; 3 bars; fitness center; boat rental; room service; massage; babysitting; smoke-free rooms. *In room:* A/C, TV, minibar, hair dryer.

Villa Taormina ★★   In the heart of Taormina, this antique residence is imbued with more Sicilian character than any other similar establishment in town, and its terrace opens onto one of the resort's most panoramic views. The residence stands above the Piazza del Duomo, with the cathedral clearly visible from the balconies of the hotel. Villa Taormina combines elegance, charm, and comfort; it's filled with antiques and objets d'art. Each spacious bedroom is individually decorated with hand-chosen fabrics, warm colors, Oriental rugs, and traditional Sicilian furniture. Baroque, neoclassical, and imperial styles are blended harmoniously. The superb bathrooms contain a hydromassage bathtub or shower, and the bedrooms use hypoallergenic materials. Breakfast is served on a sun-filled terrace, opening onto views of the Mediterranean and Mount Etna. The location is just two flights up from the main street, Corso Umberto.

Via T. Fazzello 39, 98039 Taormina. ⓒ **0942-620072.** Fax 0942-623003. www.hotelvillataormina.com. 8 units. 180€–280€ double; 260€–350€ suite. Rates include buffet breakfast. AE, DC, MC, V. Parking (nearby) 20€. Closed Jan–Feb. **Amenities:** Bar; Jacuzzi; room service; babysitting; smoke-free rooms. *In room:* A/C, TV, minibar, Wi-Fi (free).

MODERATE

Baia Taormina ★★   On a rocky hillside overlooking the sea, Baia Taormina is distinctly Mediterranean, with its local stone and Sicilian terra cotta. The resort lies a 30-minute (13km/8-mile) drive north of Taormina. Guests find more sports facilities here than at resorts in the center. Here there are two swimming pools (one saltwater, one freshwater), and you can take part in such activities as hang gliding, tennis, rock climbing, water-skiing, and surfing. The health and beauty center offers a Turkish bath, a hydromassage, and a regular massage. Il Picciolo Golf Club, on the slopes of Mount Etna, is a 30-minute drive from this luxury hotel. Admittedly, some of the bedrooms are small, but most are midsize, and each is furnished handsomely, comfortably, and attractively. All the rooms overlook the sea, and there is a sunbathing terrace. The Sicilian and international cuisine served here offers a mouthwatering roster of carefully prepared dishes.

Statale dello Ionio 39, 98030 Forza D'Agrò. ⓒ **0942-756293.** Fax 0942-756603. www.baiataormina.com. 60 units. 88€–186€ per person double; 150€–202€ per person suite. Rates include buffet breakfast. AE, DC, MC, V. Free parking. **Amenities:** Restaurant; bar; 2 outdoor pools; golf (30-min drive); health club; spa; room service; babysitting; smoke-free rooms. *In room:* A/C, TV, minibar, hair dryer, Wi-Fi (free).

Hotel Lido Méditerranée ★ Less stylish and a bit more dowdy than some of the five-star palace hotels that lie within a 3-minute drive along the coast, this solidly reliable choice offers less-expensive rates than those around it. Originally built in 1968 next to a gravel beach, and renovated a few times since, it resembles a private bougainvillea-draped villa. Guest rooms are unpretentious, reminiscent of a simple beachfront hotel in the Caribbean.

Via Nazionale, 98030 Taormina Mare (Spisone). ℂ **0942-24422.** Fax 0942-24774. www.taormina hotels.com. 72 units. 180€–280€ double. Rates include continental breakfast. AE, DC, MC, V. Closed Nov–Easter. **Amenities:** Restaurant; piano bar; massage; room service; babysitting; smoke-free rooms. *In room:* A/C, TV, minibar, hair dryer, Wi-Fi (free).

Villa Belvedere With a friendly reception, professional maintenance, and old-fashioned style, this hotel offers the same view enjoyed by guests at more expensive hotels nearby. Head to the cliff-side terrace at the rear to enjoy the vista of the Ionian Sea, the cypress-studded hillside, and smoldering Mount Etna. The small to midsize guest rooms feature functional furniture with a touch of class. Most units have slivers of balconies from which to enjoy views over the neighboring public garden to the sea; top-floor rooms have small terraces. The hotel is located near the cablecar and the steps down to the beach.

Via Bagnoli Croce 79, 98039 Taormina. ℂ **0942-23791.** Fax 0942-625830. www.villabelvedere.it. 47 units. 120€–228€ double; 190€–380€ suite. Rates include breakfast. MC, V. Parking 10€. Closed late Nov to mid-Dec and mid-Jan to mid-Feb. **Amenities:** 2 bars; outdoor pool; room service; smoke-free rooms. *In room:* A/C, TV, hair dryer.

Villa Paradiso ★★ This charming boutique hotel is set within a warren of narrow streets adjacent to the town's most beautiful public gardens. The Paradiso contains tastefully furnished public rooms outfitted with antiques and fine art. Each of the cozy, individually decorated guest rooms has a balcony, conservative furnishings, and a tiled bathroom. Between June and October, the hotel offers free shuttle service and free entrance to the also-recommended **Paradise Beach Club,** about 6km (4 miles) to the east, in the seaside resort of Letojanni. The hotel's restaurant, **Al Settimo Cielo del Paradiso** (p. 212), serves excellent cuisine on the panoramic rooftop.

Via Roma 2, 98039 Taormina. ℂ **0942-23921.** Fax 0942-625800. www.hotelvillaparadisotaormina. com. 35 units. 155€–222€ double; 195€–245€ junior suite. Rates include breakfast. AE, DC, MC, V. Parking 15€. **Amenities:** Restaurant; bar; massage; room service; shuttlebus and free access to beach club (6km/4 miles). *In room:* A/C, TV, hair dryer.

AN evening PROMENADE

I like to stroll at twilight along Corso Umberto I until I reach the resort's most charming small square. **Piazza IX Aprile** ★★ overlooks the sea with the grandest panorama of Mount Etna looming in the background. One side of the square is open; its other three sides are enclosed by the 17th-century church of San Giuseppe, San Agostino (converted into a library), and Torre dell'Orologio, from the late 1600s. Choose any of the bars with outdoor seating and sit back to enjoy the show—Piazza IX Aprile is the favored rendezvous point for the young men of Taormina to meet ladies.

INEXPENSIVE

Hotel Condor ★★★ 🛡 When it comes to value for money in a town where you pay for the air you breathe, nothing tops this place. This charming family-run hotel in a Spanish-style villa is a stone's throw from the city center and commands some of the most impressive views around. The staff, who speak English, will make you feel at home immediately. The rooms, though spacious, have furniture that is rather uninspiring, but with the views you'll enjoy from most of the rooms, you won't even notice. Bathrooms are basic and shower-only. The breakfasts taken on the terrace will set you up for the day.

Via Dietro Cappuccini 25, 98039 Taormina. ⓒ 0942-23124. Fax 0942 675226. www.condorhotel.com. 12 units. 80€–100€ double. Rates include breakfast. AE, DC, MC, V. Parking nearby 10€ daily. Pets accepted. All smoke-free rooms. **Amenities**: Bar. *In room:* A/C, TV, Wi-Fi (free).

Hotel La Campanella This hotel is rich in plants, paintings, and hospitality. It sits at the top of a seemingly endless flight of stairs, which begin at a sharp curve of the main road leading into town. You'll climb past terra-cotta pots and the dangling tendrils of a terraced garden, eventually arriving at the house. The owners maintain clean, simple, homey guest rooms.

Via Circonvallazione 3, 98039 Taormina. ⓒ **0942-23381.** Fax 0942-625248. lacampanella@tao.it. 12 units. 90€ double. Rates include continental breakfast. No credit cards. **Amenities:** Lounge, Internet (5€/hr). *In room:* A/C, TV.

Hotel Victoria It's unusual to find a good, government-rated, two-star hotel in Taormina, and this one is conveniently positioned smack in the middle of the night-time action, on the town's all-pedestrian main street. It was established in 1885 within a 300-year-old, four-story building that has been frequently upgraded over the years. Rooms are accessible via a flight of stone steps; they're high-ceilinged, well maintained, and comfortable, with hints of manorial style. All but a few have air-conditioning; eight have minibars; and all contain shower-only bathrooms. Rooms overlooking the Corso Umberto I get more light but also more noise.

Corso Umberto I 81, 98039 Taormina. ⓒ **0942-23372.** Fax 0942-623567. www.albergovictoria.it. 22 units. 93€–125€ double. Rates include buffet breakfast. AE, MC, V. Closed Jan–Feb. *In room:* A/C (most), TV.

Villa Fiorita ★ 🛡 This small inn stretches toward the Teatro Greco from its position beside the road leading to the top of this cliff-hugging town. Its imaginative decor includes a handful of ceramic stoves, which the owner delights in collecting. A well-maintained garden lies alongside an ancient but empty Greek tomb whose stone walls have been classified a national treasure. The guest rooms are arranged in a step-like labyrinth of corridors and stairwells, some of which bend to correspond to the rocky slope on which the hotel was built. Each unit contains antique furniture and a shower-only bathroom; most have private terraces.

Via Luigi Pirandello 39, 98039 Taormina. ⓒ **0942-24122.** Fax 0942-625967. www.villafioritahotel.com. 26 units. 125€ double; 165€ suite. Rates include breakfast. AE, MC, V. Parking 12€. **Amenities:** Outdoor pool; room service; smoke-free rooms. *In room:* A/C, TV.

Villa Schuler ★ 🛡 Filled with the fragrance of bougainvillea and jasmine, this hotel offers style and comfort at a good price. Family owned and run, it sits high above the Ionian Sea, with views of Mount Etna and the Bay of Naxos. It's only a 2-minute stroll from Corso Umberto I and about a 15-minute walk from the cablecar to the beach below. Guest rooms are comfortably furnished; many have a small balcony or terrace. Rooms are mostly shower-only. Breakfast can be served in your room or taken on a lovely terrace with a panoramic sea view. Service is impeccable.

The most luxurious way to stay here is to book the garden villa suite with its own private access. It's spacious and beautifully furnished, with two bathrooms (one with a Jacuzzi). The villa comes with a kitchenette, patio, private garden, and veranda, and costs from 240€ per day for two, including breakfast.

Piazzetta Bastione, Via Roma, 98039 Taormina. *C* **0942-23481.** Fax 0942-23522. www.villaschuler. com. 27 units. 128€–182€ double; 182€–196€ junior suite. Rates include continental breakfast. Booking for at least 2 nights is required in peak season. AE, DC, MC, V. Parking 15€ in garage; free outside. Closed Nov 23–Mar 6. **Amenities:** Bar; room service; free bicycles. *In room:* A/C, TV, hair dryer, Wi-Fi(free).

IN CASTELMOLA

Hotel Villa Angela ★ Rocker Jim Kerr, who has made Taormina his second home, converted this old villa, a stylish brick-and-stone retreat that is a short walk downhill from Castelmola's town square, into one of the hippest places to stay. Built on a ridge beside the winding road that accesses the village, it has spectacular views from both the front and back sides. Guest rooms feature modern lines and manorial Sicilian touches such as wrought-iron headboards. The ebullient staff arranges excursions all over the area, while the tasty Scottish brunches are unlike anything to be found in Sicily.

Via Leonardo da Vinci, 98030 Castelmola. *C* **0942-28513.** www.hotelvillaangela.com. 36 units. 180€–230€ double; 340€ suite. Rates include buffet breakfast. AE, DC, MC, V. Free parking. **Amenities:** Restaurant; bar; outdoor pool; Internet (free). *In room:* A/C, TV, minibar.

Where to Eat
VERY EXPENSIVE

Casa Grugno ★★★ SICILIAN/INTERNATIONAL The most exciting restaurant in Taormina is making a bold statement about modern Sicilian cuisine. Austrian-born chef Andreas Zangerl presides over this increasingly famous place, where the snows of the Austrian Tyrol seem to mingle with the torrid Sicilian scrublands. The setting is a stone-sided house that contains a bar, an ocher dining room outfitted like a *trompe l'oeil* rendition of Carnevale in Venice, and a walled-in terrace ringed with plants. The hip and alert young staff gets excellent supervision from the town's most successful *maître d'hôtel,* Stephano Lo Guidice.

The sublime food here is reinvented Sicilian cuisine at its finest, a haute cuisine that draws from a pan-European sensibility. The fixed-price menus might include tuna steak with sweet-and-sour onion and mint sauce; *pasta alla Trapanese* (with almonds, tomatoes, and chili peppers); roasted pigeon with lentils from the island of Pantelleria; and an impeccable version of Parmesan eggplant that might be the most deliciously fragrant dish in this part of town.

Via Santa Maria de Greci. *C* **0942-21208.** www.casagrugno.it. Reservations recommended. Main courses 15€–25€. AE, DC, MC, V. June–Sept daily 7:30pm–midnight; off season Thurs–Tues 7:30pm–midnight. Closed Nov 4–Dec 26 and Jan 4–Mar 4 (dates may vary).

EXPENSIVE

La Giara ★★ SICILIAN/ITALIAN Glossy, airy, and reminiscent of Rome during the heyday of Gina Lollobrigida, La Giara evokes a warmed-over *la dolce vita.* The restaurant is almost excessively formal, and it has remained predictably stable since its founding in 1953. Views sweep from the veranda's outdoor tables over the bay of

Taormina. The Art Deco ambience is also inviting, with marble floors and columns shaped from stone quarried in the fields outside Syracuse. The pastas are meals in themselves; I'm especially fond of the ricotta-stuffed cannelloni. The fresh fish of the day is grilled to perfection, and meats are cooked equally well. Other enticing menu items include filet of pork cooked with dried fruit and dressed with Marsala wine, or rolled sea bass stuffed with aromatic breadcrumbs with cherry tomatoes and capers.

Vico la Floresta 1. ℂ **0942-23360.** www.lagiara-taormina.com. Reservations required. Main courses 19€–25€. AE, DC, MC, V. Apr–July and Sept–Oct Tues–Sun 8:15–11pm; Nov–Mar Fri–Sat 8:15–11pm; Aug daily 8:15–11pm.

Maffei's ★ 🎁 SICILIAN/SEAFOOD   Maffei's is very small, with only 10 tables, but it serves the best fish in Taormina. Every day the chef selects the freshest fish at the market, and you simply tell him how you'd like it prepared. I often choose the house specialty, swordfish *alla Messinese,* braised with tomato sauce, black olives, and capers. The *fritto misto* (a mixed fry with calamari, shrimp, swordfish, and sea bream) is made superbly light by good-quality olive oil.

Via San Domenico de Guzman 1. ℂ **0942-24055.** Reservations required. Main courses 10€–16€. AE, DC, MC, V. Daily noon–3pm and 7pm–midnight. Closed early Jan to mid–Feb.

MODERATE

Al Duomo ★ SICILIAN/MESSINESE   Known for its romantic terrace dining (with a view of the square and cathedral), this restaurant prepares its dishes using the freshest local produce and regional ingredients. It's an attractive place, with brickwork tiles and inlaid marble tables. Try the stewed lamb with potatoes and red Sicilian wine; fried calamari sautéed in extra-virgin olive oil; or *rissolé* of fresh anchovies.

Via degli Ebrei 11. ℂ **0942-625656.** www.ristorantealduomo.it. Reservations required. Main courses 9€–18€. AE, DC, MC, V. Nov–Mar Mon–Sat noon–2:30pm and 7–11pm; Apr–Oct Thurs–Mon noon–2:30pm and 7–11pm.

Il Ciclope 🍴 SICILIAN/ITALIAN   This is one of the best of Taormina's low-priced *trattorie.* Set back from the main street, it opens onto the pint-size Piazzetta Salvatore Leone. In summer, try to snag an outside table. The food is fairly simple, but the ingredients are fresh and the dishes well prepared. Try the fish soup, Sicilian squid, or grilled shrimp.

Corso Umberto I, 203. ℂ **0942-23263.** Main courses 7€–18€. AE, DC, MC, V. Thurs–Tues noon–3pm and 6:30–10:30pm. Closed Jan 10–Feb 15 and Wed Oct–May.

Ristorante La Griglia ★★ SICILIAN   This restaurant seems much older than it is, thanks to its country-elegant location within the thick stone walls of what was a private *palazzo* in the 1600s. My favorite seats are those against the most distant back wall, where windows overlook one of Taormina's oldest streets, a ravine-like alley known as Via Naumachia, whose walled edges were built by the ancient Romans. Start with one of the best selections of antipasti in town or with a classic island pasta dish. The chef will be happy to prepare grilled fresh vegetables for vegetarians. The wine list is wonderful.

Corso Umberto I, 54. ℂ **0942-23980.** www.ristorantelagrigliataormina.com. Reservations recommended for dinner during midsummer. Main courses 9€–18€. AE, DC, MC, V. Wed–Mon noon–3:30pm and 7–11pm.

INEXPENSIVE

Al Settimo Cielo del Paradiso ★ 🍴 SICILIAN   It's far from being the most popular restaurant in Taormina, but in some ways it's my undisputed budget favorite, thanks to its superb view, sense of chic, and high-altitude view that seems to sweep over half of Sicily. To reach it, take an elevator from the lobby of the also-recommended Villa Paradiso hotel (see above), and then dine on a rooftop where Orson Welles and John D. Rockefeller IV once ate. Dishes are likely to include well-crafted versions of pennette or risotto with salmon; succulent salads of grilled prawns with a limoncello sauce; and roulades of grilled swordfish layered with vegetables and herbs. *Note:* Arrive early as it has the shortest opening times of any place along the coast.

In the Villa Paradiso hotel (p. 209), Via Roma 2. ⓒ **0942-23922.** www.hotelvillaparadisotaormina.com. Reservations recommended. Main courses 9€–20€. AE, DC, MC, V. Daily 12pm–3pm and 7:30–9pm.

Bella Blu ★ SICILIAN   This chic international spot is a restaurant and pizzeria, as well as a piano bar and disco. In addition to offering fine cuisine, Bella Blu is one of the most entertaining places in Taormina after dark. Located a 150m (492-ft.) walk from the center, it has a rich, luxurious aura. Its menus and fine food are based on the freshest local ingredients. The chef specializes in barbecued and grilled meats flavored with fresh herbs, as well as fresh fish. Sicilian favorites include homemade pasta with fresh sardines in a savory tomato sauce with wild fennel and pine nuts.

Via Luigi Pirandello 28. ⓒ **0942-24239.** www.bellablutaormina.com. Reservations required June–Aug. Main courses 7€–13€; fixed-price menu 18€. AE, DC, MC, V. Daily 10am–3pm and 6–11pm.

Granduca ★ ITALIAN/SICILIAN   This is the most atmospheric choice in town, entered through an antiques store; it also serves an excellent, carefully executed cuisine. In fair weather, request a table in the beautiful gardens. My favorite pasta here is *spaghetti alla Norma* (with tomato sauce and ricotta). If you want something truly Sicilian, ask for pasta with sardines. The best meat dish is the grilled roulades. At night, various pizzas are baked to perfection in a wood-fired oven.

Corso Umberto I, 172. ⓒ **0942-24983.** www.granduca-taormina.com. Reservations recommended. Main courses 8€–18€. AE, DC, MC, V. Daily 12:30–3pm and 7:30pm–midnight.

Il Baccanale SICILIAN   This trattoria/grill serves what islanders call *cucina tipica Siciliana*. A slightly better dining venue than its many competitors that flank it, this eatery lies at the end of a pedestrian-only street. It's the Taormina equivalent of a French bistro, with checkered tablecloths and a bustling kitchen visible on an upper balcony. The 30 or so tables spill onto the piazza in front.

Piazzetta Filea 1 (Via Di Giovanni). ⓒ **0942-625390.** Reservations recommended. Main courses 9€–17€. MC, V. Daily noon–3pm and 6–10pm. Closed Thurs Oct–Mar.

Tirami Su ★ SICILIAN   This is one of the most frequently praised inexpensive restaurants in Taormina, drawing appreciative comments from both residents and visitors. It's small and basic-looking, set beside a busy, narrow commercial street. You'll enjoy dishes that may include beef with mushrooms and cream sauce; swordfish roulades; and spaghetti with seafood.

Via Costantino Patricio. ⓒ **0942-24803.** www.ristorantetiramisutaormina.it. Reservations recommended. Main courses 8€–14€; pizzas 5€–9€. AE, DC, MC, V. Wed–Mon 12:30–3pm and 7:30pm–midnight.

IN MAZZARÒ

Ristorante Angelo a Mare-Il Delfino MEDITERRANEAN/ITALIAN   This late-19th-century building is about 5km (3 miles) from Taormina and a 2-minute walk from the cablecar station. From the flower-filled terrace, you can enjoy views over the bay.

THE CASE OF THE bouncing CHECK

The writer Truman Capote visited Taormina to finish his novel *Answered Prayers*. One drunken night at the San Domenico, he closed a deal to purchase the island Isola Bella. It's actually a gloriously conical peninsula—small, ringed with sand, and absolutely beautiful. The asking price from a local landowner was $10,000. Everyone was happy with this amazing deal until the check was returned from New York, marked "insufficient funds."

Both decor and menu items were inspired by the sea. Specialties include mussels *Delfino* (with garlic, parsley, olive oil, and lemons), house-style steak (with fresh tomatoes, onions, garlic, capers, and parsley), and risotto *pescatoro* (fisherman's rice).

Via Nazionale. ✆ **0942-23004.** Reservations recommended. Main courses 7.50€–18€. AE, DC, MC, V. Daily noon–3pm and 6pm–midnight. Closed Nov–Mar.

IN ISOLA BELLA

Ristorante da Giovanni   Perched precariously between the coastal road and the cliff that drops vertiginously down to the sea, this restaurant enjoys a view that sweeps over the peninsula of Isola Bella. The glassed-in dining room is simple and airy, accented with blue tile floors and very few adornments other than the view. The flavorful menu items include a fish soup that might win the approval of Neptune, as well as a mixed grill of fish caught that morning in the Ionian Sea. For my pasta fix, I gravitate to pennette with succulent crabmeat. Meat aficionados should find the veal scaloppine with white-wine sauce heartwarming.

Via Nazionale, Isola Bella. ✆ **0942-23531.** Reservations recommended. Main courses 8€–18€. AE, DC, MC, V. Tues–Sun 12:15–3pm and 8–11pm.

IN CASTELMOLA

Ristorante Parco Reale ★ 📷   Artful and romantic, the best restaurant in Castelmola offers lots of international pizzazz. Some members of the staff are Australian, with an offbeat sense of humor that might contribute to your understanding of this very Sicilian venue. The airy and rambling dining room is awash with displays of wine and rolling food carts. The menu is constantly changing, but the grilled catch of the day is always done to perfection. I also recommend the risotto with fresh mushrooms; the macaroni with garlic, tomatoes, and ham; and the veal escalope cooked in almond wine.

In the Hotel Villa Sonia, Via Porta Mola 9, Castelmola. ✆ **0942-28082.** www.hotelvillasonia.com. Reservations recommended for dinner in midsummer. Main courses 8€–19€. AE, DC, MC, V. Daily 12:30–2:30pm and 7–9:30pm.

Shopping

Shopping is easy in Taormina—just find **Corso Umberto I,** the main street. The trendy shops here sell everything from lacy linens to fashionable clothing to antique furniture. More adventurous types can veer off the Corso and search out little shops on the side streets.

Bar Pasticceria A Chemi ★   Everything in this store comes from Sicily. The array of candies is amazing: Expect to find at least four kinds of *torrone* (nougat); local honey fortified with slices of dried fruit; and every conceivable kind of marzipan. Bottled

Sicilian liqueurs are also available, including a worthy collection of Marsalas and an almond-flavored dessert wine. Corso Umberto I, 102. ℰ **0942-24260.**

Carlo Panarello This shop offers a good selection of Sicilian ceramics, plus deluxe umbrellas, tablecloths, and an eclectic mixture of antique furnishings, paintings, and engravings. Corso Umberto I, 122. ℰ **0942-23910.**

Gioielleria Giuseppe Stroscio ★ This is the best outlet for antique gold jewelry from 1500 to the early 1900s. It also sells a good selection of modern jewelry. I've seen more helpful staff, however. Corso Umberto I, 169. ℰ **0942-24865.**

Giovanni di Blasi ★ Ceramics stores are found all over Sicily, but this is one of the best for quality and design. It specializes in the highly valued "white pottery" of Caltagirone. Corso Umberto I, 103. ℰ **0942-24671.**

Il Quadrifoglio Here you'll find a rich collection of amber jewelry from the Dominican Republic and the Baltic, antique jewelry from estate sales throughout Sicily, antique porcelain from Dresden, and papier-mâché masks that might be suitable for Carnevale in Venice. The venue is artsy, antiquey, and charming. Corso Umberto I, 153. ℰ **0942-23545.**

La Torinese Loaded to the rafters with the agrarian bounty of Sicily, this delicatessen was established in 1936 by—you guessed it—a one-time resident of Torino. Pick up cheeses, sliced meats, pâtés, bread, and pastries for a picnic on any of the city's panoramic outcroppings. There's also an impressive collection of wines, liqueurs, and grappas. Corso Umberto I, 59. ℰ **0942-23321.**

Taormina after Dark

Sicilian cities aren't known for their nightlife. The best—and certainly the most sophisticated—after-dark amusements can be found in Taormina, though be prepared to shell out an arm and a leg even for bottled water. The resort is also the best spot in Sicily for gay and lesbian visitors.

Many visitors are content to relax at cafe tables on outdoor terraces. The most popular form of evening entertainment is the *passeggiata,* or promenade, along the Corso Umberto I. Join in—it's fun.

You might also catch a bus to Giardini-Naxos (see below) for a waterfront stroll in the evening. Most bars and clubs there stay open way past midnight, at least in the summer.

Bar at the Palazzo San Domenico ★ For a (relatively) inexpensive way to see one of Italy's most legendary hotels, drop by here for a drink. Within a sprawling labyrinth of public areas—some of which evoke the Gilded Age, others the inner sanctums of medieval monasteries—you can order drinks and listen to live piano music. Bar service is technically available daily from 4 to 11:30pm, but the place is most romantic after 9pm, when flickering torches illuminate the gardens. Piazza San Domenico 5. ℰ **0942-613111.**

Bar San Giorgio Perched on the main square of Castelmola, adjacent to a rocky drop-off guaranteed to induce vertigo, this might be the only building in the town's historic core that was able to beat the local building codes and alter its otherwise medieval-looking architecture. The result is a boxy, glass-sided upper story that looks like something from the German Bauhaus. Many visitors opt for coffee or gelato in the ground-floor cafe, but if you prefer to contemplate the Sicilian views that sweep over the surrounding hills, simply negotiate the steep steps that cling to the building's exterior to reach the upper story. The place serves only coffee, sandwiches, light snacks, and drinks. Open year-round, daily 7:30am to midnight. Piazza S. Antonio, Castelmola. ✆ **0942-28228.**

Bella Blu   On a crazy summer day, you can bet that the most fun is being generated by the high-energy 20- and 30-somethings who flock to this previously recommended restaurant/pizzeria (p. 213). It's also one of the most elegant and popular piano bars and dance clubs in town. The disco is open only on Saturday 11pm to 2:30am; the piano bar is also open only on Saturday, 9pm to 2am. Via Luigi Pirandello 28. ✆ **0942-24239.** www.bellablutaormina.com.

Caffè Wunderbar   I always begin my evening here, as Tennessee Williams did on his yearly visits to Taormina. This bar/cafe is on Taormina's main street, opening onto a panoramic view of the bay and Mount Etna beyond. Ice cream and *granite* (crushed-ice drinks) are served at outdoor tables or inside an elegant salon where you might hear the soft notes of a cafe concert. Open daily from 9am to 2:30am; closed Tuesdays from November to February. Piazza IX Aprile 7 (Corso Umberto I). ✆ **0942-625302.** www.wunderbar.it.

La Cisterna del Moro   The focal point of this restaurant/pub is a stone-sided cistern, built during the Middle Ages by the Arabs, that's set deep within a basement used for wine storage. A staff member will show it to you upon request, but you're more likely to be drinking and eating on the upper floors. Located in a narrow alley a few steps downhill from Corso Umberto I, the club is most fun after 8pm. An attached restaurant, set on a terrace draped in bougainvillea, serves 25 kinds of pizza (including a version with grilled radicchio, smoked cheese, and bacon). Beer is the preferred drink. Open Tuesday to Sunday, noon to 3pm and 6pm to midnight. Via Bonifacio 1. ✆ **0942-23001.**

Mocambo Bar ★   My favorite outdoor bar in Taormina occupies an enviable location on the main square, smack in the center of the evening hubbub. It was established in 1952, during the peak of *la dolce vita,* when Truman Capote and Tennessee Williams held court at the sidewalk tables. You can opt for a seat on the piazza throughout the year, weather permitting, but during colder months many visitors migrate inside, where there's a satirical mural showing a busy night at the Mocambo. There's live piano music every evening between 9pm and midnight. Open in summer daily 8pm to at least 2am; in winter, Saturday and Sunday 9pm to 12:30am. Piazza IX Aprile 8. ✆ **0942-23350.** www.mocambobar.com.

Morgana Bar   This ultrahip bar is tucked into one of the narrow alleys that run downhill from Corso Umberto I. Centered on a semicircular bar, it spills onto a candlelit terrace with lighting guaranteed to make anyone look fabulous. Don't expect this place to even begin hopping until around midnight. The clientele is international and attractive, and mating games between regulars and incoming holiday-makers sometimes get serious. Open nightly 9pm to 5am. Scesa Morgana 4. ✆ **0942-620056.**

O-Seven Irish Pub   One of my favorite bars in Taormina is a woodsy, high-ceilinged affair, staffed with attractive Europeans. It welcomes 20- and 30-somethings from around the world, many flirting and philosophizing with one another over foaming mugs of beer. Open from June to September, daily 4pm to 6am; October to May, Thursday to Tuesday 5pm to 2am. Largo La Farina 6 (at Corso Umberto I). ✆ **0942-24980.**

Re di Bastoni   Favored by locals as a convivial and almost claustrophobically crowded hideaway, this bar gets impossibly loud after 10pm with its live or recorded music reverberating off sienna-colored walls, a beamed ceiling, and oversize paintings.

Patrons usually come here late at night, sometimes with their pets, and always with their fetishes, to slurp down the house specialty of strawberry caipirinhas. Open Tuesday to Sunday 11am to 3am. Sandwiches are the only food served. Corso Umberto I 120. © **0942-23037.** www.redibastoni.it.

GIARDINI-NAXOS

5km (3 miles) S of Taormina, 47km (29 miles) N of Catania, 54km (34 miles) S of Messina.

If you're seeking a holiday by the beach and prefer to enjoy Taormina only on day trips, then **Giardini-Naxos** is your best choice, and here you can walk straight from your hotel room to the sands, lying off the long main street, **Lungomare,** running parallel to the sea.

The beach here opens onto the bay, lying between Capo (Cape) Taormina in the northwest and Capo Schisò in the south. Its point formed by an ancient lava flow from Mount Etna, Capo Schisò was the natural landfall for mariners rounding the toe of Italy on their way from eastern Mediterranean ports.

Over the years, beach development at Giardini-Naxos has been so great that the resort now competes with Taormina for visitors, although it lacks the older resort's medieval charm. (As a local said, "Taormina has the class, we have the sands.") Indeed, all the trappings of tourism are evident in this once-tranquil fishing village, with its many sports facilities and amusement parks, discotheques, souvenir shops, hotels, trattorie, and beachside bars, making it a lively place. Giardini-Naxos caters mainly to package-tour operators from the north of Europe, and much of the resort continues to function during the winter, although the wind can be cold.

Even if you're staying in Taormina, you should set aside some time to visit the archaeological park, the site of the first Greek colony in Sicily dating back to 735 B.C. (see below).

Essentials

BY BUS Interbus (© **0942-625301**) runs buses from the terminal in Taormina at Via Luigi Pirandello; a one-way ticket costs 1.50€. Service is daily, every half-hour from 8am to midnight and takes 30 minutes.

BY TRAIN Giardini-Naxos shares the same rail depot as Taormina (see "Getting There," earlier in this chapter). If you're driving from Taormina, take the SS114 south. From Messina, follow autostrada A18 south, exiting at the turnoff for Giardini-Naxos.

VISITOR INFORMATION The **tourist office,** Via Lungomare 20 (© **0942-51010**), is open Monday to Friday 8:30am to 2pm and 4 to 7pm, Saturday 8:30am to 2pm.

Exploring Ancient Ruins

In a setting of citrus trees and prickly pears, on the headland of Capo Schisò, lie the ruins of the **Naxos excavations ★**, the site of the first Greek colony in Sicily. This site has been inhabited since 735 B.C., and has gone through the various tribulations of all such colonies, thriving and prospering until conquered and devastated—only to rise again out of the ashes.

If you're driving, head out on Via Naxos, which becomes Via Stracina. The ancient site lies in the dusty, barren scrubland above Giardini-Naxos. The actual excavations are behind a rusted iron fence facing the uphill (landward) side of the main road leading into Giardini-Naxos. Inside, you'll find the repository of artifacts that remained after Dionysius of Syracuse razed the city in 403 B.C.

This is not Pompeii, so don't be disappointed. What the tyrant didn't raze to the ground, centuries of builders carted off for other structures. Little remains today, with the exception of some structural foundations and the pavement stones of ancient streets.

The best of what was dug up is displayed in the **Archaeological Museum,** on two floors of an old Bourbon-built fort. The most evocative artifact is a statuette of Aphrodite Hippias from the 5th century B.C. As a curiosity, one exhibit displays objects removed from a surgeon's grave, including a strigil, a speculum used to examine injuries, and tiny ointment jars.

The site is open daily from 9am to 4:30pm. Admission is 2€ for adults, free for children 17 and under. For information, call ✆ **0942-51001.**

Where to Stay

Arathena Rocks Hotel ★ ✦ This government-rated three-star hotel contains one of the most appealing collections of decorative objects along the Taormina coastline. This includes bas-reliefs, sculptures, wrought-iron balustrades, gilded baroque door frames, and hand-painted tilework tastefully assembled into a complete whole. The overall effect is that of a whimsical private villa that happens to rent out rooms. Built in the 1970s atop a jagged strip of eroded lava rocks, it has compensated for its lack of sandy beach with a terraced pool and masses of potted flowers. Its rock-studded beach is private. Guest rooms are cozy and clean; many contain balconies or loggias. Half of the units have air-conditioning.

Via Calcide Eubea 55, 98035 Giardini-Naxos. ✆ **0942-51349.** Fax 0942-51690. www.hotelarathena.it. 50 units. 116€–130€ double. Rates include continental breakfast. AE, DC, MC, V. Free parking. Closed Nov–Easter. **Amenities:** Restaurant; bar; outdoor pool; free shuttle transfers to Taormina. In room: TV.

Hellenia Yachting Club Set in the heart of Giardini-Naxos, closer to the town's bars than some of its competitors, this is a gracefully modern hotel whose public areas have some of the most lavish marble decoration anywhere, often with classical Greek touches. Built in 1978 and radically upgraded in 2004, it features a sun terrace (with a pleasant but not overly large pool) and black-lava steps that descend to a private gravel beach. The place has the aura of a private club—perhaps one in Greece that welcomes a nautically minded British clientele. Be warned that guest rooms are not as opulent as the lobby would imply. They have a sparsely furnished, somewhat cold decor, with hints of 18th-century French styling.

Via Jannuzzo 41, 98035 Giardini-Naxos. ✆ **0942-51737.** Fax 0942-54310. www.hotel-hellenia.it. 112 units. 147€–230€ double; 360€ suite. Rates include buffet breakfast. AE, DC, MC, V. Free parking. **Amenities:** Restaurant; 2 bars; babysitting; outdoor pool; fitness room; room service; smoke-free rooms; tennis nearby. In room: A/C, TV, minibar, hair dryer, Wi-Fi (7€/hr).

Hotel Sabbie d'Oro The on-site restaurant (see below) is genuinely charming and more alluring than the hotel that administers it. Nonetheless, this simple lodging is acceptable in every way, though hardly grand. Built in 1990, and named after the public beach (Sabbie d'Oro/Golden Sands) that's just across the street, this government-rated three-star hotel is clean, only a bit battered, and completely unpretentious.

Via Schisò 12, 98035 Giardini-Naxos. ✆ **0942-51227.** Fax 0942-56913. www.hotelsabbiedoro.it. 39 units. 90€–120€ double. Rates include buffet breakfast. AE, DC, MC, V. Parking 15€. **Amenities:** Restaurant; bar; Internet. In room: A/C, TV, minibar, hair dryer.

Sant Alphio Garden Hotel ★   This is the biggest and most opulent hotel in Giardini-Naxos. Its rich style evokes the scope and imagination of Las Vegas, and its centerpiece is a free-form outdoor pool with lavish landscaping and a swim-up bar, set adjacent to the best-looking cluster of swimming pools along the Taormina coastline. The hotel is outfitted in contemporary tones of navy and white, with touches of chrome and a jazzy combination of Sicilian and European styling. Bedrooms range from midsize to spacious, each with a well-maintained bathroom with shower or tub. Most visitors opt to spend at least a week here, decompressing from overburdened schedules in other parts of (usually northern) Europe. Come here for a retreat, with the understanding that the medieval attractions of Taormina are just an easy taxi ride away. A private beach lies within a 3-minute walk; tennis, horseback riding, and golf are available through outside concessions.

Marina di Recanati, 98030 Giardini-Naxos. ℂ **0942-51383.** Fax 0942-53934. www.santalphiohotel. com. 124 units. 130€–214€ double; 230€–290€ suite. Rates include buffet breakfast. AE, DC, MC, V. Free parking. **Amenities:** 2 restaurants; 2 bars; indoor pool, outdoor pool w/sunken bar; health club; spa; room service; babysitting. *In room:* A/C, TV, minibar, hair dryer, Wi-Fi (7€/hr).

Where to Eat

Ristorante Sabbie d'Oro SICILIAN   Amicable and laid-back, this restaurant sits in a covered open-air pavilion adjacent to both the beach and the hotel that manages it (see above). You'll dine in a setting that evokes a woodsy tavern, with tables loaded with grappa and a ceiling draped with fishnets and nautical bric-a-brac. The cooks, though not world-class, are attentive. You'll enjoy such dishes as a curious marriage of beef and clams; pennette with swordfish and almonds; and macaroni with fresh tomatoes.

Via Schisò 12. ℂ **0942-52380.** www.hotelsabbiedoro.it. Reservations recommended Sat-Sun. Main courses 10€–20€. AE, DC, MC, V. Daily noon–3pm and 7–11pm.

Ristorante Sea Sound ★★ SICILIAN/SEAFOOD   From a position beside a commercial street in the center of town, adjacent to the Hellenia Yacht Club Hotel, you'll walk for a few minutes along a private footpath flanked by flowering vines. Just when you suspect you've made a wrong turn, you'll see a low-rise concrete bungalow adjacent to the sea. Its focal point is the terrace, surrounded by walls adorned with cheerful pottery. The antipasti selection, ranging from smoked tuna to swordfish, is the best in the area. More than a dozen pastas are made daily, including *spaghetti alla bottarga* (with tuna roe) and risotto with fresh seafood. Meat choices are limited, but dishes such as veal scaloppine in Marsala sauce are competently made. The chef specializes in freshly caught fish and grilled shrimp.

Via Jannuzzo 37A. ℂ **0942-54330.** Reservations recommended. Main courses 9€–22€. AE, DC, MC, V. Daily 12:30–2:30pm and 7–11:30pm. Closed Nov–Easter.

Farther Afield: Alcantara Gorges

To see some beautiful rapids and waterfalls, head outside of town to the **Gole dell'Alcantara** ★ (ℂ **0942-985010**), which is a series of gorges. The waters are extremely cold—uncharacteristic for Sicily, but quite refreshing in August. It's usually possible to walk up the river from May to September (when the water level is low), though you must inquire about current conditions before you do so. From the parking lot, take an elevator partway into the scenic abyss and then continue on foot.

You're likely to get wet, so bring your bathing suit. If you don't have appropriate shoes, you can rent rubber boots at the entrance. Allow at least an hour for this trip. From October to April, only the entrance is accessible, but the view is always panoramic. It costs 4€ to enter the gorge, which is open daily 7am to 7:30pm. By car, head up the SS185 some 17km (11 miles) from Taormina; the gorges are signposted. Or take **Interbus** (© 0942-625301) for the 1-hour trip departing from Taormina at 9:15 and 11:45am and 1:15, and 4:45pm. Buses from Gole dell'Alcantara return to Taormina at 9:25am, 12:35, 2:35, and 3:45pm. The round-trip fare is 5€. You can also take a taxi from Taormina, but you'll have to negotiate the fare with your driver.

MOUNT ETNA ★★

23km (14 miles) SW of Taormina, 31km (19 miles) N of Catania, 60km (37 miles) S of Messina.

Looming menacingly over the coast of eastern Sicily, Mount Etna is the highest and largest active volcano in Europe, and there's always a layer of smoke drifting from its summit. The peak has changed in size over the years, and continues to do so thanks to constant eruptions, but at the time of writing was 3,329m (10,922 ft.). Etna has been very active in modern times, wiping out entire villages and wreaking havoc along its way.

Nevertheless, Etna is a continually changing entity: The experience you have will depend on the day you find yourself there, and the time of year. You may witness an explosion from the side of the crater, as a new crater forms and, along with a fright, see a column of rock, ash, and smoke burst into the sky. Whenever you visit there's likely to be some volcanic dust swirling around, which can make life awkward for asthma sufferers and wearers of contact lenses. On a clear summer's day you can see some great views, but equally on a cloudy day visibility is poor and you may find the trip disappointing. It's best to try and go in the morning when generally it's clearer. At any time of year bear in mind that temperatures at the summit will be cooler than those below, so take layers of clothing including a hat and gloves because even in May it can be bitterly cold and windy.

There is no shortage of activities along the mountain: Besides volcano buffs, it attracts skiers, hikers, cyclers, and all who want to be at one with nature in this place so seemingly removed from the Mediterranean. From its domineering position over the island, the **views ★★★** go on forever on a clear day.

Getting There

BY BUS AST buses (© 840-000323; www.aziendasicilianatrasporti.it) runs a daily service from the central railway station in Catania (leaving at 8:15am, and departing Etna at 4:30pm) at a cost of 5.90€ return, making the climb up from the south side in 2 hours.

BY CAR By **car,** the ascent to the summit can be approached from the northern side, leading up to the ski area at Piana Provenzana (see below), or southern side, arriving at the base camp at **Rifugio Sapienza** (© 095-915321; www.rifugio sapienza.it) at 1,900m (6,233 ft.).

BY CABLECAR From Rifugio Sapienza, you will be whisked up to 2,504m (8,215 ft.) in a cablecar run by the **Funivia dell'Etna** (© 095-914141; www. funiviaetna.com, open 9am–5:30pm and on Monday evenings from 5:30pm for sunset hiking) up to Montagnola (2,500m/8,200 ft.) and from there you can board

Mount Etna & Environs

an all-terrain vehicle with a mountain guide to take you to the highest point possible at 3,323m (10,902 ft.). The combined cost for cablecar and bus excursion is 51€, or 27€ for cablecar passage only. The 2-hour guided excursions run from March to November, with the buses operating as ski transport in the winter months. **Note:** Climbs to the summit can be suspended without warning due to inclement weather.

What to See & Do

Visitors will have to decide whether to ascend Mount Etna from the northern or southern approach. I prefer the north-facing side, more forested, and much richer in wildflowers that thrive in the volcanic soil. The south side is mostly covered with barren black rock from the lava flows, which gives it an eerie, otherworldly appearance. Its access routes are more crowded, and its views less appealing. Nonetheless, many visitors to Catania come up Etna's south side (for details, see Chapter 11).

If you decide to come up the north side, simply take the highway to its end, **Piano Provenzana,** which stops at a complex of Alpine-inspired chalets selling souvenirs. During the heat of a Sicilian summer, they appear visibly out of place, but in winter, because of the high altitude (2,700m/8,858 ft.), they function as the centerpiece of a small-scale but thriving ski colony. The ski facilities include five downhill ski lifts and a network of cross-country ski trails.

It is from this artificial-looking alpine hamlet of Piano Provenzana that you buy tickets for bus excursions (see above) to the top of Mount Etna. Many hikers walk from Piano Provenzana to the cone of Etna in about 3 hours, following the track used by the buses.

The buses are specially equipped for the harsh terrain, and resemble an armored car. They wind their way laboriously uphill, through gravel beds and rocky gullies, past barren, lichen-covered, gray-green landscapes. At the top, the bus parks near a seismic exploration station, which is mostly abandoned, and visitors walk a bit farther to a point near the top, across gravel-covered ground, but the main crater is often out of bounds when it's too dangerous to get that close. If the crater is active, bus trips are stopped immediately, so you won't see molten lava spouting out unless it's from a great distance.

The Foothills of Mount Etna

The village of Linguaglossa, 18km (11 miles) west of Taormina, is the best base for excursions to Mount Etna. From here, you can access Piano Provenzana (see above), the main ski resort on Etna. The road around the foot of the volcano takes you through magnificent countryside where the rich soil has spawned many orchards and vineyards. If you're driving in the morning you can usually see the summit, although on hazy summer days it's often hidden by the afternoon.

LINGUAGLOSSA

Before climbing the mountain, you may want to linger in the village of Linguaglossa. Built from black lava, it is traversed by a main street called Via Roma. At the most distant end of this street is the 17th-century church **Chiesa Madre Madonna della Grazie,** capped with an iron cross and opening onto Piazza Matrice.

Via Roma is covered with large and very heavy black-lava cobblestones. It begins at the **Chiesa di San Francesco de Paola,** known for its lavish baroque frescoes and plasterwork. Via Roma continues to the 17th-century Duomo, which is also known as **Chiesa della SS. Annunziata.** The stately pink-stucco **Il Municipio (Town Hall)** opens on Piazza Municipio, overlooking a Liberty-style monument dedicated to the Italian dead of World War I.

The tourist office, **Associazione Turistica Proloco Linguaglossa,** Piazza Annunziata 7 (© **095-643094**), is open Monday to Saturday 9am to 1pm and 4 to 8pm (3–7pm in winter), Sunday 9:30am to noon. Pick up brochures for area attractions and check out the mini display that showcases the local geology, including insights on the abundant lava flows.

A bus from Giardini-Naxos (p. 217) leaves for Linguaglossa daily at 2:55pm. If you're driving from Taormina to Linguaglossa, take the A18 south. After 12km (7½ miles), take the exit marked FIUMEFREDDO. After 815m (2,674 ft.), turn left and follow the SS120 into Linguaglossa.

Where to Dine

Chalet delle Ginestre SICILIAN   As you navigate your way uphill through the scrubby pine forests and occasional snows of the north slope of Mount Etna, you'll find this isolated, cement-sided chalet a welcome sight. Set 9km (5½ miles) from the uppermost terminus of the highway, it was built in 2000 and offers a cozy, weatherproof venue for a fortifying meal or drink. Menu items include a mixed grill of meat; asparagus with risotto, butter, and sage; and roasted veal. The food is satisfying and filling—nothing more.

Strada Mareneve, Km 10.8. ☎ **0347-7629436.** Main courses 7€-15€; fixed-price menu 25€. No credit cards. Oct-Feb Fri-Wed 12:30-4pm; Mar-Sept Fri-Wed 12:30-4pm and 8-10pm. Closed 2 weeks in Nov.

RANDAZZO

After you explore Linguaglossa and Mount Etna, you may want to continue west to the intriguing "black town" of Randazzo, 20km (12 miles) away on Route 120. Amazingly, this town, built of lava and with a history going back to antiquity, has never been destroyed by the volcano. Most of its destruction came in 1943, when the Germans made Randazzo their last stand of resistance, and the Allies bombed the town.

Chiesa di Santa Maria ★, Piazza della Basilica 5 (☎ **095-921003**), is a study in contrasts, its building materials of black lava contrasting with its white trim. Its black-and-white tower is a prime example of brilliant Sicilian masonry. The church dates from the 13th century and contains a 15th-century south portal built in the Catalan Gothic style. The interior opens onto impressive black-lava columns. It's open daily from 10am to noon and 4 to 6pm.

The other notable church in town, **Chiesa di San Martino,** Corso Umberto I (☎ **095-921003**), is open daily 10am to noon and 4 to 6pm. Its impressive **campanile ★**, or bell tower, is from the 13th century, although the church was reconstructed in the 17th century. The black-and-white stone tower stands in dramatic contrast to the church, whose facade is adorned with reliefs of martyrs and saints.

The **tourist office** is at Corso Umberto I, 197 (☎ **095-7991611**). It's open daily 9am to 1pm and 2 to 8pm.

Where to Stay

L'Antica Vigna ★★ ☺ Take the SS120 out of Randazzo to get to this stunningly situated little hotel, located 4km (2½ miles) southeast of town at the foot of the volcano. L'Antica Vigna is actually a converted farm surrounded by 3 hectares (7½ acres) of olive trees. The farmyard menagerie includes horses and Sicilian goats. The place is ideal for families with children; there's even a small park set aside for them. Guests are housed in small, comfortable villas, furnished with everything from kitchens to fireplaces.

Località Montelaguardia, 95036 Randazzo. ☎ **095-924003.** Fax 095-923324. www.anticavigna.it. 14 units. 50€ per person (includes breakfast and dinner). No credit cards. **Amenities:** Restaurant; tennis court. *In room:* No phone.

Where to Dine

Trattoria di Veneziano SICILIAN   Randazzo's most elegant restaurant is separated from the town's medieval zone by a deep valley, along the bottom of which runs a busy boulevard. It's set on the ground floor of an airy, modern building decorated in tones of Chinese red. Among the well-prepared menu items are grilled tenderloin steaks, grilled and smoke-cured ham, salted codfish, grilled sausages, and rigatoni or pappardelle with fresh mushrooms.

Via del Romano 8. ☎ **095-921418.** www.ristoranteveneziano.it. Main courses 7€-13€. AE, DC, MC, V. Tues-Sat noon-3:30pm and 7-11:30pm; Sun noon-3:30pm.

MESSINA &
THE AEOLIAN
ISLANDS

The Aeolian Islands' volcanic archipelago is the most exotic location in the Mediterranean, and seeing the night sky lit up by the natural firework display provided by Stromboli's volcano makes any visit to northeast Sicily memorable. Starting from the ancient port of **Messina** you can hop from one island to another taking in turquoise waters, hissing fumaroles, and mud baths.

10

Just off the northern coast of Sicily, the many charms of this volcanic archipelago of seven islands and five small islets are such that it has been declared a Unesco World Heritage Site. And they are truly fabulous: Whether you want to go hiking, fishing, canoeing, snorkeling, diving, swimming, sailing, or just relax, the islands have it all. There are beaches and coves with black sand, pumice stone, and tiny pebbles, steaming craters, bubbling mud baths, sulfur springs, strange-shaped grottoes, crystal-clear turquoise waters, craggy cliffs, and archaeological sites.

Each island has a distinct character: Lively **Lipari** is where most visitors stay, choosing to island-hop to the upmarket **Panarea,** peaceful **Salina,** wild **Filicudi,** unspoiled **Alicudi,** smelly **Vulcano,** and highly active **Stromboli.** On Vulcano you can take a dip in natural sulfur bubbling mud baths and then head off to relax in the warm thermal waters nearby. If you're feeling energetic you can climb to Stromboli's fiery crater with a guide. To cap it all, the islands offer amazing views as you can look from one to another, seeing their conical forms stretch out across the sea, and on some evenings, if Stromboli spouts lava, there's even a natural fireworks show.

MESSINA

233km (145 miles) E of Palermo, 683km (424 miles) SE of Rome, 469km (291 miles) S of Naples.

Overlooking the Straits of Messina to the wooded Calabrian hills, the city of Messina is the gateway to Sicily by virtue of the fact that only 5km (3 miles) separate it from the Italian mainland. Located on Sicily's

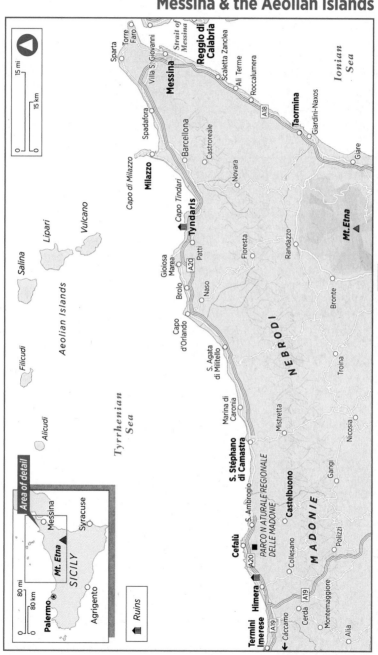

Ruins

BRIDGING THE gap

The long-delayed development in Messina—the Straits of Messina bridge project, which will link the city with Reggio Calabria on the mainland— was announced in 2002. Construction began in late 2005 but was discontinued for 3 years. It was slated for completion in 2012 but as of yet the project has barely seen any building. The project has been a mess since its inception and fiercely opposed by nature conservationists. Check out www.strettodimessina.it for updates, drawings, and even computer simulations of the new bridge.

easternmost tip, the provincial capital is a thriving industrial port, particularly in the summer when boats make their way back and forth along the Straits. Most visitors pass on seeing the city itself in their haste to reach their final destination, but that's a shame, because the city does offer some treasures, such as the **Chiesa SS. Annunziata dei Catalani** and the **Duomo** (cathedral).

It's also a good base to take trips to **Santo Stefano Di Camastra,** which is famed for its ceramics, and to **Tindari** to visit the ancient ruins of **Tyndaris ★** and the **Santuario Maria SS. Madonna del Tindari** (Sanctuary of Mary the Holy Madonna of Tindari), with its breathtaking views down to the turquoise blue lagoons and white sands of Marinello beach.

If you can face the crowds, the best time to visit is mid-August, to see the **Passegiata dei Giganti** (Ride of the Giants) on August 14, when two large statues of the city's mythical founders are paraded through the streets on horseback. A day later, citizens celebrate the Assumption holy day with the "Vara," when they haul a huge litter festooned with papier-mâché figures through the city.

Essentials

GETTING THERE

BY BOAT   Messina is linked to the Italian mainland by **ferries** and **hydrofoils** crossing the Straits of Messina from either Villa San Giovanni or Reggio di Calabria. Ferries leave from **Villa San Giovanni,** which is 12km (7½ miles) north of Reggio and closer to Messina. Ferry services are called *traghetti;* **FS** (✆ 892021 in Villa San Giovanni) is state run, while **Caronte** (✆ 090-37183214; www.carontetourist.it) is independent. Offices for both companies can be found at the harbor where the ferries depart. Both ferries charge a fare of 28€ to Messina. If you're leaving from **Reggio di Calabria,** you can take the **Meridiano** ferry (✆ 0965-810414; www.meridianolines.it), which charges 2€ for foot passengers on the 40-minute crossing to Messina. Cars cost 12€. Crossings take about 20 minutes.

BY PLANE   The nearest airport to Messina is on the Italian mainland at Reggio di Calabria. **Aeroporto dello Stretto** (✆ 0965-640517) is 5km (3 miles) south of Reggio. From here take the **Metromare** (✆ 0923-873813; www.metromare dellostretto.it) service—a combination of bus and hydrofoil transportation. Journey time 1 hour; cost 9€. The nearest airport in Sicily, Aeroporto Vincenzo Bellini in Catania (p. 253), is 110km/68.3 miles south of Messina. **SAIS buses** (✆ 800-211020; www.saisautolinee.it) run hourly at a cost of 8.50€ one way to Messina. Journey time: 2 hours.

BY TRAIN   Several trains a day come from the mainland, including Rome, and take up to 9 hours (cost 41.50€). There are also frequent rail links to Palermo, with 15 trains going between Messina and the island's capital, taking approximately 3½ hours and costing 11.55€ one way. There are also hourly trains between Messina and Taormina, Sicily's major resort to the south (see p. 197), taking 1 hour and costing 3.80€ each way. For rail information, call ✆ **892021** or see www.trenitalia.it.

BY BUS   SAIS buses (✆ **800-211020;** www.saisautolinee.it) operate from Catania daily with at least one an hour, taking 1½ hours and costing 7.70€ one-way. There are eight buses a day from Palermo, a 2¾-hour trip that costs 15.10€ one way.

BY CAR   From the mainland of Italy, follow the A3 south to Reggio di Calabria, getting off at Villa San Giovanni and taking a car ferry across the Straits of Messina to Messina itself. Along the northern coast, travel the A20/SS113 east from Palermo and Cefalù. The A18 from Taormina runs north to Messina.

VISITOR INFORMATION

For information and a map, head to the **Azienda Autonoma per L'Incremento Turistico,** Via Calabria 301 (✆ **090-674236**), near Piazza della Repubblica and Stazione Centrale. It's open Monday to Saturday 9am to 1:30pm.

ORIENTATION

If you come by hydrofoil or ferry from Reggio di Calabria, you'll arrive 1km (½ mile) north of Stazione Centrale on Via Vittorio Emanuele II. Those taking a ferry from Villa San Giovanni reach land 3km (1¾ miles) farther on or about 500m (1,640 ft.) north of Fiera, the site of Messina's trade fairs.

Messina grew around its sickle-shaped harbor. The tip of the sickle is marked by a towering statue, **Madonna della Lettera,** atop one of the tall towers of **Forte San Salvatore,** built in 1546 by the Spanish viceroys. **Via Garibaldi,** running parallel to the sea, is the main street. It goes through **Piazza del Duomo,** the town's major square. South of this square is the second-most important square in Messina, **Piazza Carducci,** site of the university, founded in 1548 and reconstructed in 1927.

To the east, the port is protected by the lighthouse known as the **Lanterna di Raineri,** on the peninsula of the same name. **Via 1 Settembre** leads from the sea to the heart of town. The transportation hub of Messina is **Piazza della Repubblica,** in front of Stazione Centrale. Most of the major bus lines converge on this square. To reach the heart of Messina from Piazza della Repubblica, head across the busy square and walk directly north along Via 1 Settembre to **Piazza del Duomo,** a square crowned by Messina's cathedral.

GETTING AROUND

Most hotels and attractions lie in the center and are best reached on foot. If you need to go farther afield, **ATM buses** (✆ **090-22851;** www.atmmessina.it) depart from the transportation hub, Piazza della Repubblica. Bus tickets can be purchased at *tabacchi* (tobacco shops) or news kiosks throughout the city; they cost 1€ for a ticket valid for 1½ hours or 2.60€ for an all-day ticket. The most useful route is **no. 79,** which stops at the Museo Regionale and the Duomo. **Taxis** are found mainly at the Stazione Centrale, at Piazza Cairoli, and along Via Calabria. For a 24-hour radio taxi, call ✆ **090-2934880.**

[FastFACTS] MESSINA

Currency Exchange
The most convenient currency exchange is **Cambio/ Ufficio Informazioni** (℃ **090-675234**), inside the Stazione Centrale. Open daily 7am to 9pm. There are also ATMs in the station.

Emergencies Call ℃ **113** for the police, ℃ **118** for first aid.

Hospitals Try **Ospedale Policlinico Universitario,** Via Valeria (℃ **090-2211**), or **Ospedale Piemonte,** Viale Europa (℃ **090-2221**).

Internet Access Internet Caffè, Via Garibaldi 72 (℃ **090-662758**), is open Monday to Saturday 9am to 8pm and charges 4€ per hour.

Luggage Storage A kiosk at the Stazione Centrale will store your bags for 4€ for one hour and up to 11€ for 24 hours; open daily from 6am to 10pm. Photocopied ID is required when leaving luggage.

Post Office The main post office is on Corso Cavour 138 (℃ **090-6015752**); it's open Monday to Friday 8:20am to 6:30pm and Saturday 8:20am to 12:30pm.

What to See & Do

As you wander around Messina, you'll come to the ruins of the church of **Santa Maria Alemanna,** built in 1220 by the crusading Teutonic Knights. The church—or what's left of it—stands at the corner of Via dei Mille, off Corso Garibaldi, directly north of Via del Vespiro and to the immediate west of Piazza Cavallotti. It's one of the few Gothic churches on the island, as the Gothic style of architecture never swept Sicily the way it did other parts of Europe. The Messinese seemed to dislike the style, and the unfinished church was left abandoned in the 15th century.

Chiesa SS. Annunziata dei Catalani   When the Messinese saw their beloved church on this square after the 1908 earthquake, they called it a miracle. The earthquake stripped away much of the latter-day alterations and additions to the church, leaving its original 12th- and 13th-century architectural style intact. But because the quake leveled the earth on which the church sits, the structure seems to be sinking into the street today. Try to view the church from its western facade, where you'll see a trio of 13th-century doors.

The interior, now used as the chapel for the university, is in red, yellow, and white stone with tall Corinthian columns. The most outstanding feature is the **apse ★**, a stellar example of the Norman composite style. A nave and two aisles run to the apse, resting under a severe, brick-built cupola. This church is a kind of Arabic-Byzantine hodgepodge: Romanesque architecture blended with such Moorish features as geometrical motifs, with suggestions of the Byzantine.

In the back of the church is a famous statue of **Don Juan of Austria,** the "natural" son of Emperor Charles V and a hero in the 1571 Battle of Lepanto. Amusingly, he's depicted with his foot resting proudly on the head of the Ottoman commander, Ali Bassa. The sculptor Andrea Calamech carved this monument in 1572. Incidentally, an even more famous sailor sailed from Messina to take part in that battle: Miguel de Cervantes, author of *Don Quixote*. Wounded, he was brought back to recover in a local hospital.

Piazza dei Catalani, Via Garibaldi. ℃ **090-6684111.** Free admission. Mon–Sat 9:30–11:30am; Sun 9–11:30am.

Duomo ★   This Romanesque and Norman cathedral has had a rough time of it since Roger II ordered it built in 1160. Henry VI, the Holy Roman Emperor, attended its consecration in 1197. The 1908 quake and a 1943 Allied firebombing didn't help. The cathedral has more or less been reconstructed from scratch, although some original architectural features remain.

Its **central doorway** ★ was reconstructed using fragments originally from the 15th century. The lower part of the facade is decorated with 15th-century carvings depicting Sicilian agrarian life. The gray-and-pink interior has a trio of aisles divided by ogival arches and columns, resting under a trussed and painted ceiling. Many of the duomo's treasures were re-created, using fragments pulled from the ruins after the Allied bombings.

The statue of **John the Baptist** in the south aisle is attributed to Antonello Gagini in 1525. Dominating the main altar is a copy of the Byzantine **Madonna della Lettera,** the original having been destroyed by the 1943 firebombing. A pupil of Michelangelo, Jacopo del Duca, designed the **Cappella del Sacramento** in the north apse. It holds the cathedral's only original mosaic, a 14th-century work that depicts the Virgin seated with saints, queens, and archangels.

The church's treasure-trove is found in its **Tesoro,** which contains valuable candlesticks, chalices, and gold reliquaries. Much of the silverwork was created by artisans from Messina in the 17th and 18th centuries. Displayed for the first time in 3 centuries is the **Manta d'Oro** (golden mantle), a special cover for the Virgin and Bambino on the Duomo's altar.

Piazza del Duomo. ℂ **090-675175.** Free admission. Guided tours in English 5€ adults, 3.50€ for children 17 and under and seniors 65 and over. Oct 15–Apr 15 Mon–Sat 9am–1pm, Sun 10am–1pm and 4–6:30pm; Apr 16–Oct 14 daily 9am–1pm and 3:30–6:30pm.

Fontana di Nettuno (Neptune's Fountain)   This landmark fountain stands on the seafront, at the intersection of Via della Libertà and Via Garibaldi. It's a reconstruction of the heavily damaged fountain created by Montorsoli in 1557. The original of the muscular marble god has been in the Museo Regionale (see below) ever since the statue was "castrated" by some roaming youths from Palermo. The sculpture of Neptune is depicted pacifying the sea, guarding the Straits of Messina from those wicked terrors, Scylla and Charybdis. *Take note:* Enjoy this fountain during the day, as the port area here isn't safe at night.

Fontana di Orione (Orion's Fountain) ★   Standing in the center of the cathedral square, Piazza del Duomo, this elegant fountain was the prebaroque creation of Giovanni Angelo Montorsoli in 1547. It honors Orion, the city's mythical founder, who is seen surmounting a bevy of giants, nymphs, and crocodile-wrestling *putti* (cherubs). The fountain was built to honor the construction of the city's first aqueduct. The major figures represent the rivers Nile, Ebro, Camaro, and Tiber.

Museo Regionale ★★   Situated in a former silk mill from 1914, the Museo Regionale, north of the Duomo, is one of Sicily's finest provincial museums and contains the island's greatest collection of art from the 15th to the 17th centuries. Its main collection consists of works rescued from the 1908 earthquake.

Its most precious relic to the devout is found in the atrium: A dozen **18th-century gilded bronze panels** that relate the tale of the Holy Letter. As legend has it, during a famine the Madonna sent the Messinese a boat filled with food but devoid of crew. The Virgin is also said to have sent along a letter containing a lock of her hair.

The museum displays many medieval and baroque treasures, including a mosaic of the Virgin and Child, known as *La Ciambretta* and dating from the 13th century. A marble low relief of **St. George** is attributed to Domenico Gagini. There is nothing finer than Antonello da Messina's beautiful but damaged **polyptych ★★** of the Madonna with St. Gregory, St. Benedict, and the Annunciation, from 1473. Also on exhibit are two large **Caravaggio masterpieces ★★**, the work of "the divine" artist during his sojourn in Messina from 1608 to 1609. They represent the raising of Lazarus and the Nativity.

Greek and Roman antiquities are on view in the newly created garden pavilion. Look for the magnificent 1742 **Senator's Coach ★**, with its flamboyantly painted panels. The statues of **Neptune, Scylla,** and **Charybdis,** removed from the Fontana di Nettuno (see above), are also on display.

Viale della Libertà. ℭ **090-361292.** Admission 6€. June–Sept Tues–Sat 9am–1:30pm and 4–6:30pm, Sun 9am–12:30pm; Oct–May Tues–Sat 9am–1:30pm, Tues, Thurs, and Sat 3–5:30pm, Sun 9am–12:30pm.

Orologio Astronomico ★   The Duomo is upstaged by its 60m (197-ft.) campanile, or bell tower, with its astronomical clock standing to the left of the cathedral facade. Created in 1933 in Strasbourg, France, the clock puts on "the show of shows" at noon every day. With Schubert's *Ave Maria* scraping away on a loudspeaker in a note of high camp, the bronze automata goes into action. A lion waves his banner and roars, while a cock flaps its wing and crows. Dina and Clarenza, the heroines of Messina at the time of the Sicilian Vespers, take turns ringing the bell, and Jesus pops out of the tomb for instant resurrection. Be sure to gather in the square to check out this show.

Piazza del Duomo. No admission. Free show at noon.

Where to Stay

Jolly dello Stretto Palace Hotel   It isn't as architecturally dramatic, plush, or well located as its rival, NH Liberty, but this boxy-looking *moderno* (ca. 1953) hotel draws loyal travelers, many of them in town on business. It was the first large-scale modern hotel in Messina, and was once the reigning choice in town. All rooms have double windows for insulation from the roar of traffic, and about half open onto views of the harbor. Units are well maintained, modern, and a bit banal looking but very comfortable, each with a tiled bathroom. The in-house restaurant is reviewed under "Where to Eat," p. 231.

Via Garibaldi 126, 98100 Messina. ℭ **090-363860.** Fax 090-5902526. www.medeahotels.com. 96 units. 90€–110€ double. AE, DC, MC, V. Free parking. **Amenities:** Restaurant; bar; room service; babysitting; smoke-free rooms. *In room:* A/C, TV, minibar.

NH Liberty ★★★   This is the most elegant, appealing hotel in Messina, and one of the finest hotels in Sicily. It originated as a battered rooming house, but it's been beautifully transformed. Throughout, you'll find rich paneling, marble-inlaid floors, ornate plasterwork, and lavish stained-glass windows. Guest rooms are as plush as anything you'll find in Sicily, with marble-trimmed bathrooms, fine hardwoods, high ceilings, and color schemes of champagne and gold. Thanks to this and to the welcome that's extended with genuine concern to single women traveling alone, the hotel enjoys one of the highest occupancy rates in town.

Via I Settembre 15, 98123 Messina. ✆ **090-6409436.** Fax 090-6409340. www.nh-hotels.it. 51 units. 105€–147€ double; 202€–225€ suite. Rates include buffet breakfast. AE, MC, V. Parking 11€ daily. **Amenities:** 2 bars; room service; babysitting; smoke-free rooms. Wi-Fi (5€/hr). *In room:* A/C, TV.

Royal Palace Hotel Built in the 1970s and recognized as a reputable hotel for business travelers, this large, boxy-looking hotel lacks the high-blown style and elegance of the NH Liberty, but both are operated by the same chain. It's a suitable choice, thanks in part to its comfortable guest rooms, its streamlined styling, and a genuinely charming lobby bar.

Via T. Cannizzaro 224, 98123 Messina. ✆ **090-6503.** Fax 090-2921075. nhroyalpalace.hotelsinsicily.it. 107 units. 90€–110€ double; 165€–240€ suite. Rates include buffet breakfast. AE, MC, V. Parking on premises (fee). **Amenities:** Restaurant; bar; room service; babysitting; smoke-free rooms; Wi-Fi (5€/hr). *In room:* A/C, TV, minibar.

Where to Eat

EXPENSIVE

Jolly Restaurant dello Stretto ★ ITALIAN/SICILIAN   This contemporary hotel restaurant has the town's most panoramic view (in this case, of the wharves that service the ships coming in from Reggio Calabria), along with a floor crafted from mollusc-encrusted russet marble and a sense of *la dolce vita* pizzazz. To start, select an array of smoked local fish; there's nothing better on the menu. The staff also does very well with even a simple dish such as cream of tomato soup with basil.

In the Jolly dello Stretto Palace Hotel, Via Garibaldi 126. ✆ **090-363860.** www.medeahotels.com. Reservations recommended Fri–Sat. Main courses 14€–18€; fixed-price menus 30€–35€. AE, DC, MC, V. Daily 1–3pm and 8–10pm.

MODERATE

Piero 🔪 SICILIAN   Dating from 1959, this is one of the town's most recommended restaurants. It has an attractive interior that's outfitted with exposed paneling, terracotta floors, and a sense of bustling good cheer and workaday efficiency. Menu items may remind many Sicilians of their childhoods: Spaghetti with mussels and crabmeat (my favorite); pennette sautéed with swordfish, clams, shrimp, tomatoes, and capers; and, finally, scampi prepared any way you ask for it. Don't overlook the luscious temptations of the antipasti table—a serve-yourself buffet that shouldn't be missed.

Via Ghibellina 119. ✆ **090-6409354.** Reservations recommended Fri–Sat nights. Main courses 12€–20€. AE, DC, MC, V. Mon–Sat 12:30–3:15pm and 8–11:30pm. Closed Aug.

INEXPENSIVE

Al Padrino MESSINESE/SICILIAN   Part of the charm of this place is its rough-edged, unpretentious nature. Virtually no effort has been spent on the glaringly white decor, and tables are hot and cramped, yet Al Padrino has flourished for a quarter of a century in a dreary neighborhood of heavy industry. The impossibly small kitchen churns out Messinese-style food that includes a creamy homemade *maccheroni;* swordfish meatballs with a fresh tomato and olive sauce; and many different preparations of beef. Flavors are robust and hearty, portions large. Get ready for loud voices, an in-your-face welcome, and an insight into working-class Messina at its most vivid.

Via Santa Cecilia 54–56. ✆ **090-2921000.** Main courses 10€–20€. MC, V. Mon–Fri noon–3pm and 7–11pm; Sat noon–3pm. Closed Aug.

Le Due Sorelle 🍴 SICILIAN Set beside the square that flanks the front entrance to Messina's town hall, this restaurant occupies a long, narrow room that contains fewer than 10 tables, walls covered with wine bottles, and a carved screen that rises high above the terra-cotta floor. At lunchtime, the place is loaded with municipal office workers, one of whom often happens to be the town's mayor. The unpretentious fare includes two different versions of couscous; veal with roasted vegetables; a *padellata di pesce* (panful of fish) with vegetables; and a full roster of house-made desserts.

Piazza Municipio 4. 📞 **090-44720.** Reservations recommended on Fri–Sat nights. Main courses 12€–20€. MC, V. Mon–Fri 1–3pm and 8pm–midnight; Sat–Sun 8pm–midnight. Closed Aug.

Pasticceria Irrera PASTRIES Set directly beside Messina's largest and most verdant square, this well-known cafe was established in 1910. The marble bar serves coffee and drinks; the *granita* tastes especially wonderful on warm days; and the pastry shop is widely renowned for its almond-based *Fiori di Mandorlo,* its succulent *Torta Letizia* (made with almonds and vanilla), and a chocolate-covered version of almond paste known as *Le Amarilde.*

Piazza Cairoli 12. 📞 **090-673823.** Pastries 2€–6€. AE, DC, MC, V. Tues–Sat 8am–1:30pm and 4–8pm; Sun 4–8pm.

Messina after Dark

If you're here in July or August, head for Piazza del Duomo, the central cathedral square where free concerts devoted to rock, jazz, or classical music are presented. Posters advertise cultural events, and the tourist office (see "Visitor Information," p. 227) will have details.

Easy Excursions to the Beach

If the streets look a little deserted in July or August, it's because the Messinese are hanging out at **Mortelle,** the beach resort 12km (7½ miles) north of Messina, at the northeastern tip of the island. The beachfront is a narrow strip of pebble-strewn sand known as the **Lido del Tirreno** (📞 090-321001). Thanks to large numbers of parasols and chaises longues, as well as easy access to beachfront restaurants, it's the best-accessorized beach in and around Messina. Entrance costs 4€ per person; parking is free. A day's rental of a *cabine* goes for 20€ to 25€, while a chaise longue and parasol cost 10€.

From Messina, Mortelle is an easy ride on bus no. 79 or 81; cost 1.20€ one way, 1.70€ return. Even when the sun goes down, Mortelle continues to stay busy until late at night; be careful not to get run down by cycles and scooters. The area is filled with pizzerias and bars, and in July and August, **open-air films** are screened at Arena Green Sky, opposite Duc Palme pizzeria.

If you find Mortelle too crowded, continue to the west, where you'll encounter more sandy beaches and little seaside resorts, the best of which is **Acqualadrone.**

WHERE TO STAY

Grand Hotel Lido di Mortelle ☺ Set at the Messina end of the best beachfront in Mortelle, this simple hotel was built in the late 1970s as the best lodging in town. The simple, airy guest rooms attract holiday-makers from the region, including families with young children. Nothing is particularly plush, but in this unpretentious beach resort, no one really seems to mind. Access to the nearby beach is free.

SS113, Mortelle, 98164 Messina. ☎ **090-321017.** Fax 090-321666. www.giardinodellepalme.com. 24 units. 80€–120€ double. DC, MC, V. Free parking. **Amenities:** Restaurant; bar; outdoor pool; babysitting; smoke-free rooms; Internet (4€/hr). *In room:* A/C, TV, minibar.

Farther Afield: Heading West from Messina

TYNDARIS ★

At **Capo Tindari,** approximately 62km (38.5 miles) from Messina, stand the ruins of Tyndaris, on a lonely, rocky promontory overlooking Golfo di Patti. It was known to the ancients since it was founded by Dionysius the Elder in 396 B.C. after a victory over the Carthaginians. For a long time it formed a protective union with its ally, Syracuse, until that eastern Sicilian city fell to the Romans in 256 B.C. Tyndaris has had a rough time of it: It was partially destroyed by a landslide in the 1st century A.D., and then suffered an earthquake in A.D. 365. The Arabs in the 10th century were particularly vicious in destroying its buildings.

The **view ★★** alone is almost reason enough to go; it stretches from Milazzo in the east to Capo Calavà in the west. On a clear day, there are stunning vistas of the Aeolian Islands, with Vulcano the nearest.

The most serious excavations of the site began after World War II, although digs were launched much less successfully in the 19th century. Most of the ruins you see today date from the Roman Empire, including the **basilica,** the exact function of which remains unknown. Just beyond the basilica is a **Roman villa,** which is in rather good condition (you can still see the original mosaics on the floor). Cut into a hill at the end of town is a wide **theater,** built by the Greeks in the late 4th century B.C. The **Insula Romana** contains the ruins of baths, patrician villas with fragments of mosaics, and what may have been taverns or drinking halls. Beyond the entrance to the site on the left is a small display of dug-up artifacts. You can also see the ruins of defensive walls constructed during the dreadful reign of Dionysius.

The ruins are open daily from 9am until 1 hour before sunset. Admission, including the theatre, is 4€ for adults, 2€ for adults aged 18 to 25, and free for children 17 and under, and adults 65 and over, coming from the EU, Canada, and Australia. For information on the archaeological area, call ☎ **0941-675184.**

The site is also a place of pilgrimage for the devout who flock to the **Santuario di Tindari** (☎ **0941-369167**), which contains a Byzantine Black Virgin, or the *Madonna Nera.* Legend has it that this Madonna washed up on the shores of Tyndaris centuries ago. The sanctuary is open Monday to Friday 6:45am to 12:30pm and 2:30 to 7pm, Saturday and Sunday 6:45am to 12:30pm and 2:30 to 8pm. Admission is free.

GETTING THERE   Four **trains** (☎ **892021**; www.trenitalia.it) daily on the Messina–Palermo line stop at the station at Oliveri-Tindari costing 4.95€ one way. Journey time: 1 hour. If you're **driving** from Messina, head west along the main coastal routes (A20/SS113) for 62km (38.5 miles), exiting at Falcone. A small **tourist office** (☎ **0941-369184**), at the site at Via Teatro Greco, is open Monday to Friday 9am to 1pm and 3 to 7pm, Saturday 9am to 1pm.

SANTO STEFANO DI CAMASTRA

Lying at 128km/79.5 miles west of Messina, Santo Stefano di Camastra is one of the cities in Sicily well-known for its ceramic art, an industry that grew here because the area in the hinterlands is said to have some of the best clay in Sicily. The town also commands some outstanding views of the Aeolian Islands.

Once you enter the town, you'll see dozens of vendors hawking ceramics and pottery. If the many choices overwhelm you, head for the shop I've found the most reliable over the years: **Ceramiche Franco,** Via Nazionale 8 (𝄆 **0921-337222**). Craftsmanship and skill go into the Franco family's ceramics, which are inspired by various artistic movements in Italy, especially the Renaissance and the baroque. Hours are Monday to Saturday 9am to 7:30pm.

Before buying anything, familiarize yourself with the area's artisanal creations by visiting the **Museo della Ceramica ★**, Via Palazzo (𝄆 **0921-331110**), in the heart of town in the Palazzo Trabia. The restored palace itself is a thing of beauty, especially its **tiled floors ★**, **antique furnishings** (mainly from the 1700s), and beautifully **frescoed ceilings.** You'll learn how varied ceramics can be and the technique and skills that go into making them. It's open from May to September, Tuesday to Sunday 9am to 1pm and 4 to 8pm; and from October to April, Tuesday to Sunday 9am to 1pm and 3:30 to 7:30pm. Admission is free.

GETTING THERE   Hourly **trains** (𝄆 **892021;** www.trenitalia.it) depart daily from Messina, at a cost of 7.95€, taking roughly 1 hour. From Messina by **car**, take the A20 autostrada which becomes the SS113 on its approach to Santo Stefano. Journey time: 45 minutes.

THE AEOLIAN ISLANDS ★★★

The Aeolian Islands are as exotic and Mediterranean as you can get, recognized as a Unesco World Heritage site and a protected nature area. Up to the early 1980s some islands didn't even have electricity. Nowadays, the islands are one of the most sought-after vacation spots in Europe thanks to sparkling waters and lava-created landscapes.

Lipari (36 sq km/14 sq miles) is the largest of the islands and the most inhabited, **Stromboli** (13 sq km/5 sq miles) is the most distant and volcanically active, and **Vulcano** (21 sq km/8 sq miles), with its puffing, potentially unpredictable summit and sulfur-rich malodorant mud baths that bubble from beneath the surface, is the first island you reach when arriving from Sicily. **Panarea** (3.5 sq km/1½ sq miles) is the tiniest and most exclusive island, while **Salina** (27 sq km/10½ sq miles), the second largest of the islands, is famous for its Malvasia dessert wine and tranquility. The wild island of **Filicudi** (9.5 sq km/3¾ sq miles) has traces of the Bronze Age, and **Alicudi** (5 sq km/2 sq miles) the westernmost and furthest from Lipari, is a step back in time (no cars, no hotels).

 ## WHEN TO visit THE ISLANDS

In summer, the islands are most populated and can be somewhat claustrophobic (and expensive). Your best bets are May, early June to mid July, and September, when the northern Italians still haven't flocked down from their foggy cities. Off-season visits are relaxing and probably best if you want to appreciate the islands for their beauty. Bear in mind, however, that many businesses and lodgings close for the season at the end of September, and the wind can be bitterly cold in winter.

The Aeolian Islands have been inhabited since Paleolithic times; in fact, they are probably Sicily's oldest human settlements, as well as an area of volcanic activity. According to mythology, this is where Aeolus (hence the name), god of the winds, dwelled and when the winds kick up in the afternoon, it's easy to imagine why.

GETTING THERE Ferries and **hydrofoils** alike service all the Aeolian Islands, principally from the port of **Milazzo,** 40km (25 miles) west of Messina. Hydrofoils are faster than ferries, getting you to Vulcano in an hour (ferries take twice as long), yet ferries are roomier, and allow you to stay out on the deck on your way there. **Ustica Lines,** Via Rizzo (℃ **090-9287821;** www.usticalines.it), operates numerous daily ferry and hydrofoil routes to all islands, as well as seasonal routes from the mainland at Reggio Calabria. Trips can cost from 15€ per adult to 22€ (prices vary according to which island). **N.G.I.,** Via dei Mille 26 (℃ **800-250000** toll free from Italy or 090-9284091; www.ngi-spa.it), offers ferry services to certain islands. From Naples, **SNAV** (℃ **081-4285555;** www.snav.it) offers a seasonal service (late May to early Sept) to all the islands except Filicudi and Alicudi. Note that all ferry services charge a 1€ fee per person for entry to the islands. In the event of a storm or inclement weather, service can be halted for days.

Of course, you'll need to get to Milazzo first before embarking by sea. By **train** (℃ **892021;** www.trenitalia.it) from Messina, the cost is 3.25€ and takes 30 minutes; from Palermo, the cost is from 10€ and takes 2½ hours; the stop is at Milazzo. From there, take the shuttle bus that drops you off at the port (1€), or take a taxi, which will cost you around 10€. **Giuntabus** (℃ **090-673782;** www.giuntabus. com) runs buses approximately every hour from Messina on weekdays with some going all the way to the port. If you're **driving** from Messina or Palermo, take the A20 autostrada until you come to the turnoff for the port at Milazzo, and follow the directions for *"garage/imbarchi,"* where you can also park your car safely.

Lipari ★★

37km (23 miles) N of Milazzo, 41km (25 miles) W of Messina.

Known to Greeks as *Meligunis,* Lipari is the largest of the islands and it's the best base for exploring the entire archipelago. Lipari town sits on a plateau of red volcanic rock on the southeastern shore, framed by two ports: **Marina Lunga,** where the larger vessels dock, and **Marina Corta,** the smaller fishermen's harbor.

Nearly all activity is centered on the area between these two harbors, where locals convene, and which includes the largest concentration of tourist facilities in all of the Aeolian Islands. There are four other villages on the island, including **Canneto,** which is only 2km (1¼ miles) north of Lipari town. **Acquacalda** is found on the northern tip of the island. Inland and to its southwest is **Quattropani.** If you're heading southeast from Quattropani back to Lipari town, you'll pass through the small town of **Pianoconte.**

Marina Lunga and Marina Corta flank, at the base, the acropolis of Lipari, which includes the castle and its 15th-century walls. Inside these walls are the imposing Duomo, two decaying baroque churches, and the Museo Archeologico (archaeological museum), one of the most important in Sicily.

Corso Vittorio Emanuele is the main thoroughfare in Lipari and where most of the daily hubbub unfolds; it is where you'll find the bulk of local businesses, including

Lipari & Vulcano

LIPARI
Acquacalda **3**
Canneto **6**
Cave di Pomice **2**
Lipari **8**
Mount Pilato **5**
Pianoconte **7**
Porticello **1**
Quattropani **4**

VULCANO
Gelso **11**
Gran Cratere **9**
Piano **10**

bars, banks, souvenir shops, grocery stores, and eateries. The local **Tourist Office** is located at no. 202 (✆ **090-9880095**).

ESSENTIALS

GETTING AROUND Large **boats** dock at the deepwater port of **Marina Lunga,** while the smaller vessels call in at **Marina Corta.** Most of the city life lies between these two ports and its side streets, so if you need anything once you disembark, it's all nearby. **Taxis** are found at the port ready to whisk you to wherever you need to go; to pre-book service, call one of the local drivers at ✆ **338-525603**. *Note:* most hotels and B&Bs offer courtesy shuttle-services to and from the port; check to see if the one you're staying at provides a transfer service.

Lipari is serviced by a **bus** network, run by **Guglielmo Urso** (✆ **090-9811026**; www.ursobus.it), which also offers sightseeing trips. Buses leave from Marina Lunga about every hour (more frequently in summer), stopping at various points around the island. No point on the island is less than a half-hour ride away. A bus schedule is provided by the tourist office and at the website. Tickets can be bought at the ticket kiosk at the port or purchased on board from the driver, at no extra charge, for 2€.

To get around on your own (cars are not allowed on the island during the summer), a cheap, efficient option is to **rent a bike** (average rates 10€ per day) or motor scooter (20€ daily, not including fuel, but including the safety helmet). A security deposit (cash or credit card) is required, together with identification. Two rental outlets are **Da Marcello,** Via Sottomonastero, Marina Lunga (℮ **090-9811234**); and **Da Tullio,** Via Amendola 22, Marina Lunga (℮ **090-9880540**). To rent a small car, try **Aveden** (℮ **090-9811026;** www.aveden.it), Via dei Cappuccini, which provides small vehicles at a reasonable fee.

VISITOR INFORMATION The **tourist office** in Lipari is at Via Vittorio Emanuele 202 (℮ **090-9880095**). In July and August, it is open Monday to Friday 8:30am to 2pm and 4:30 to 7:30pm, Saturday 8am to 2pm. From September to June, hours are Monday to Friday 8:30am to 2pm and 4:30 to 7:30pm.

[FastFACTS] LIPARI

Banks The major bank is **Monte dei Paschi di Siena,** Via Vittorio Emanuele 209 (℮ **090-9880432**), which has an on-site ATM available 24 hours. There is also a branch of **Banco di Sicilia** at Via Castelfidardo 4 (℮ **090-9819424**), also with 24-hour ATM service.

Emergencies Call ℮ **113** for the police, ℮ **118** for first aid. For **medical services,** head to the **Guardia Medica** in Via Porto Levante (℮ **090-9852220**) or in Via Garibaldi (℮ **090-9885426**).

Hospitals Head to the **Ospedale Civile,** Via Sant'Anna (℮ **090-983040**); the **hyperbaric chamber** for divers (℮ **090-9885457**) is also located here.

Internet Access Go to **Net Cafe,** Via Garibaldi 61 (℮ **090-9813527;** www.netcafelipari.com/bar.html), which charges 4€ per half-hour.

Pharmacy Pharmacies in town are the **Farmacia Morsillo,** Via Marina Garibaldi 72 (℮ **090-9811428**),

and the **Farmacia Internazionale,** Via Vittorio Emanuele 128 (℮ **090-9431011**).

Police For the local *Carabinieri* (army police corps), call ℮ **090-9811333.**

Post Office The main post office is at Corso Vittorio Emanuele 207 (℮ **090-9810051**); open Monday to Friday 8:20am to 6:30pm and Saturday 8am to 12:30pm. It also has an ATM for cash withdrawal.

WHAT TO SEE & DO
Citadel/Upper Town

Lipari is the only island of the archipelago with a distinct urban plan. The city is dominated by the **castle,** situated on top of a volcanic-rock crag, which also served as a natural fortress throughout the centuries. It was the acropolis of the Greek *Lipara* and the starting point at which the Romans refounded the town. Since Lipari was so vulnerable to attacks, its inhabitants were forced to live for months on end enclosed within the castle walls, which were refortified in the 1500s and again in the 1700s. Excavations around the castle area, which began in 1946, have provided extraordinary insight into Lipari's past; many of these findings are housed at the archaeological museum (see below). To access the castle, your best bet is to start your trek uphill (ideally in the early morning) from the ancient entrance at Piano della Civita (Piazza Mazzini), where you can still find traces of the Greek settlement in the remains of the **walls** on the south side of the square; from the Marina Corta, it can be reached via the Salita Meligunis.

As you make your way from Piazza Mazzini, you will bypass the imposing **Spanish fortifications** built to defend the city from pirate attacks; on the right, among the interesting remains of several churches, is a vast archaeological area. As you reach the summit, you'll see a few decaying churches, the former bishop's palace (now a part of the museum), and a few old homes, also incorporated into the museum. On the highest point is the **Duomo (cathedral),** dedicated to the patron saint Bartholomew, and dating back to the 15th century. The building contains both baroque and Norman elements; the facade and bell tower from 1761 evoke the architecture of the times, while the only remaining Norman part of the cathedral lies on the south side, in the **abbey ★** built with materials salvaged from Lipari's classical era. The cathedral's three baroque naves have frescoed vaults with scenes from the New Testament. A short distance away is the church of the Madonna delle Grazie with its fine 17th century facade. Go behind the church toward the ramparts for the most amazing **views ★★★** over Lipari and Marina Corta.

Museo Archeologico Luigi Bernabo' Brea ★★★ This is one of southern Italy's most impressive archaeological museums, housing one of the world's finest Neolithic collections. It is spread out over six pavilions, occupying among other edifices the former 17th-century **Palazzo Vescovile,** or bishop's palace, which contains the Neolithic and Bronze Age exhibits; the **Sezione Classica,** on the south side of the cathedral, focuses on the classical and Hellenic periods.

The collection is laid out chronologically and with English explanations, beginning with the Neolithic to Bronze Age discoveries unearthed nearby as well as those from Milazzo and southern Italy. Among the artifacts on display are: Glossy red ceramics, known as the "Diana style," from 3000 to 2500 B.C., getting its name from the nearby area of Contrada Diana; a display of obsidian, the glass-like black volcanic rock that was crafted into blades used throughout the ancient world before it was eventually replaced by metal; and the only Late Bronze Age (8th century B.C.) necropolis found in Sicily.

Over in the Sezione Classica section is a formidable collection of classical artifacts, many coming from in the nearby necropolis. Particularly noteworthy are **burial urns** from Milazzo; archaeologists discovered that in the 11th century B.C., Lipari islanders buried bodies in fetal positions in large jars. The upper level holds a spectacular array of **decorated vases ★★**, many from the ancient Roman site of Paestum, that depict gods and goddesses, satyrs and courtiers, and scenes of daily life in ancient times. The museum also contains the world's greatest collection of **theatrical masks ★★★**, unearthed in tombs from the 4th century to the 3rd century B.C. Those gruesome grins on the masks of Hercules and Hades will haunt your dreams.

The final and least interesting section of the museum is the **Sezione Epigrafica,** in a smaller adjoining building (it's not always open). It displays engraved stones and the remains of several Greek and Roman burial tombs.

Via del Castello. ℂ **090-9880174.** Admission 6€ adults, 3€ for ages 18–25, free for children 17 and under and adults over 65 residing in the EU, Australia, and Canada. Daily 9am–1:30pm and 3–6pm (4–7pm May–Sep), Sun/holidays 9am–1:30pm.

Lower Town

After visiting the citadel, another site of archaeological interest in the Lower Town is the **Parco Archeologico Contrada Diana,** west of Corso Vittorio Emanuele, the main street. Sadly lying in a state of neglect, you can see the remains of Greek walls dating from the 5th and 4th centuries B.C., the old city gate through which the Romans came and expunged the island, and the altar dedicated to the cult of Demeter. Ancient tombstones and other funerary relics were retrieved from the necropolis that held up to 2,500 bodies. The burial grounds are visible off Via Marconi. The park is usually locked, so you can only stroll by and look in. Any major finds discovered here are housed in the archaeological museum in the Upper Town.

Around the Island

Twenty-nine kilometers (18 miles) of road circle the island, connecting all of its villages and attractions. Buses run by **Guglielmo Urso** (p. 236), make the rounds of the island. The trip to the little towns of **Quattropani** and **Acquacalda** (aptly named because of the hot springs in the sea) on the north coast costs 2€. Buses leave Lipari town from Marina Lunga, opposite the service station.

Besides the town of Lipari proper, the major destination is the village of **Canneto,** 2km (1¼ miles) north on the east coast. It's where some of the best, accessible beaches are found (no sand, though, just rocks and deep waters). You can see daily life unfold on the island far from the tourist traps. Canneto can be reached by bus or a 30-minute walk from Marina Lunga. Just north of Canneto is **Spiaggia Bianca,** named for the (supposed) white sand, though it's really in hues of gray. White sand, in fact, is a rarity here—the rest of the island's beaches are predominantly black volcanic sand or rock. To reach the beach from Canneto, take the waterfront road, climbing the stairs along Via Marina Garibaldi, and then veer right down a narrow cobbled path for 297m (974 ft.).

Buses run north of Canneto, passing the **Cave di Pomice** at Campobianco, located between Spiaggia Bianca and Porticello. To get here, rent a scooter. Other than tourism, pumice is the principal industry of Lipari. Pumice is used for everything from a building material to an ingredient in toothpaste. Some daring visitors slide down a pumice chute directly into the waters along the north coast.

From Cave di Pomice, you can see **Mount Pilato,** at 476m (1,562 ft.). This is the ancient crater of a volcano that last erupted in A.D. 700. Fields around this crater are the source of the pumice. You can walk to the crater, passing through barren fields locals call *Rocce Rosse,* or the "red rocks," because of the hue of the stone. A path leading to the crater from the northern tip of Campobianco stretches for 1.2km (¾ mile).

The bus stops in the village of **Porticello,** which has a beach. I suggest you avoid it, however, as it's rocky and not very noteworthy. If you do stop here, the most rewarding feature is the **panoramic view ★★** of the other Aeolian Islands such as Alicudi, Filicudi, and Salina.

The island's northernmost little town is **Acquacalda,** or "hot water," a settlement known for its obsidian and pumice quarries. But few people go to the black-sand beaches here because they're rocky and there's also no shade. Acquacalda itself is virtually a one-street town with some snack bars and waterfront dives.

The bus moves along the northern tier of Lipari and then heads southwest to the little town of **Quattropani,** which is to the west of Mount Chirica at 602m (1,975 ft.). In the town, you can make a steep climb to **Duomo de Chiesa Baraca,** where the point of interest is most definitely not the cathedral but the **panoramic view ★** from the grounds of the church. The distance between Quattropani and Acquacalda is 5km (3 miles); some hikers prefer to traverse this route on foot, enjoying scenic vistas at every turn.

There is yet another grand view to be enjoyed before leaving Lipari. West of Lipari town (4km/2½ miles), and reached by buses departing from Marina Lunga, is a lookout point at **Quattrocchi** ("four eyes"). Once at Quattrocchi, you can make the steep climb to **Quattrocchi Belvedere,** which will reward you with one of the most **panoramic vistas ★★** in the Aeolian Islands.

WHERE TO STAY
Expensive

Gattopardo Park Hotel ★★   Set in an 18th-century villa and enveloped by white bungalows, this is the island's most architecturally interesting hotel. In comfort, it also ranks among the top choices on the island. Spacious terraces opening onto scenic views are yet another allure. The hotel provides a free minibus service to some of the best beaches on the island, although there's also free swimming from the rocks in a bay nearby. For Aeolian style, this place is unbeatable, with beautifully planted grounds, tiled floors, and wood-beamed ceilings. The furnishings are a blend of antique and modern, the rooms come with small shower-only bathrooms, and the best units are some of the most comfortable in Lipari. For a resort hotel, the dining and drinking facilities are among the island's best.

Vico Diana, 98055 Lipari. ℂ **090-9811035.** Fax 090-9880207. www.gattopardoparkhotel.it. 60 units. 130€–260€ double. Rates include half board (breakfast and dinner). AE, DC, MC, V. Closed Nov–Feb. **Amenities:** Restaurant; bar; outdoor pool; room service; babysitting; Internet (6€/hr). *In room:* A/C, TV.

Giardino sul Mare ★   This first-class option is only minutes from Marina Corta, opening onto the sea. It's a real Mediterranean resort hotel, with covered terraces for dining and a smallish pool surrounded by chaises longues and umbrellas. Guest rooms are well tended and comfortably furnished, with small shower-only bathrooms. Many guests spend all their vacation time here except for an occasional island trip. The drinking and dining facilities equal those found at Villa Meligunis.

Via Maddalena 65, 98055 Lipari. ℂ **090-9811004.** Fax 090-9880150. www.giardinosulmare.it. 41 units. 180€–270€ double. Rates include half board. AE, DC, MC, V. Closed Oct 30–Mar 21. **Amenities:** Restaurant; bar; outdoor pool; room service; babysitting; Wi-Fi (free). *In room:* A/C, TV.

Villa Meligunis ★   This hotel literally puts you right in the heart of it all. Less than 45m (148 ft.) from Marina Corta, this charming Mediterranean-style building derives from a compound of 17th-century fishermen's cottages. It's dense with stylish allure, from its lovely fountain to its dramatic rooftop terrace to its wrought-iron bedsteads used by fashion photographers as backdrops. The rooftop pool for both adults and children is a rarity in Lipari, and in the summer breakfast is served poolside. Guest rooms are comfortably furnished with summery pieces and spacious, though not exactly modern, bathrooms with either tubs or showers. Some have a sea view, which naturally costs more. The restaurant serves excellent regional specialties.

Via Marte 7, 98055 Lipari. ℂ **090-9812426.** Fax 090-9880149. www.villameligunis.it. 32 units. 170€–320€ double; 225€–380€ suite. Rates include continental breakfast. AE, DC, MC, V. Free parking. **Amenities:** Restaurant; 2 bars; outdoor pool; room service; babysitting; smoke-free rooms; Wi-Fi (free). *In room:* A/C, TV, minibar.

Moderate

Hotel Oriente ★   Located in the historic center of Lipari town, this hotel is only steps from the archaeological park and 300m (984 ft.) from the port. On a hot day, its shady terrace is one of the best places to be on the island. The interior is like a museum, stuffed with knickknacks and artifacts made from wrought iron. The rooms are light and airy, with small tiled bathrooms that have hydromassage showers. A generous breakfast is served in the garden amid bougainvillea and citrus blossoms.

Via Marconi 35, 98055 Lipari. ✆ **090-9811493.** Fax 090-9880198. www.hotelorientelipari.com. 32 units. 80€–150€ double; 100€–180€ triple; 140€–250€ quad. AE, DC, MC, V. Closed Oct 30–Mar 30. **Amenities:** Bar; room service; babysitting; Wi-Fi (free). *In room:* A/C, TV, minibar.

Hotel Poseidon   A favorite with scuba divers and discerning travelers in general, this well-run hotel lies off the main street, just 100m (328 ft.) from the sea, with guest rooms opening onto an inviting courtyard. Diving instruction can be arranged, as can equipment rentals, cylinder refills, and guided underwater trips. There is a fresh, breezy Mediterranean feel to this place. The guest rooms are well maintained, with wicker decorations and small tiled bathrooms.

Vico Ausonia 7, 98055 Lipari. ✆ **090-9812876.** Fax 090-9880252. www.hotelposeidonlipari.com. 18 units. 75€–150€ double; 90€–180€ triple. Rates include continental breakfast. AE, DC, MC, V. Closed Nov 15–Feb 28. **Amenities:** Bar; room service; babysitting; smoke-free rooms. *In room:* A/C, TV, minibar, hair dryer.

Villa Augustus ★ 🏨   Set in the historic center, close to the port, this hotel is surrounded by luxuriant gardens and has a dramatic roof terrace overlooking the sea. It's just 100m (328 ft.) above the main harbor and 2km (1¼ miles) from the whitish beaches north near the pumice quarries. The hotel is reached along a narrow island road and relatively hidden from the street. Rooms are attractively furnished; those with balconies or terraces are preferred. Attractive amenities include a reading room, a piano bar, and a solarium.

Vico Ausonia 16, 98055 Lipari. ✆ **090-9811232.** Fax 090-9812233. www.villaaugustus.it. 35 units. 110€–200€ double. Rates include buffet breakfast. AE, MC, V. Closed Nov 1–Feb 28. **Amenities:** Restaurant; 2 bars; fitness room; sauna; room service; massage; babysitting; roof garden. *In room:* A/C, TV, hair dryer.

At Canneto

Casajanca ★ 🏨   It looks like a private home, and for good reason: Before it was converted into this little inn, Casajanca was the home of Ruccio Carbone, a native son who was celebrated as "the poet" of the Aeolian Islands. Rooms are little more than basic, motel-like accommodations, with small, shower-only bathrooms, but there is reasonable comfort here. Furnishings mix contemporary pieces with the occasional antique. The little garden is studded with tropical plantings and tables and chairs. The friendly owners provide a grand welcome to what they call "the inn of everlasting love."

Marina Garibaldi 115, Canneto (Lipari). ✆ **090-9880222.** Fax 090-9813003. www.casajanca.it. 10 units. 80€–200€ double; 110€–243€ triple. Rates include continental breakfast. AE, DC, MC, V. **Amenities:** Bar; room service. *In room:* A/C, TV, minibar.

WHERE TO DINE

E Pulera ★★ SICILIAN/AEOLIAN   Owned by the same family who run the Filippino (see below), this restaurant emphasizes its Aeolian origins. Artifacts and maps of the islands fashioned from ceramic tiles are scattered about. Some tables occupy a terrace with a view of a flowering lawn. Specialties include a delightful version of fishermen's soup, swordfish ragout, and risotto with squid in its own ink. A delightful pasta dish is fettuccine with yellow pumpkin, shrimp, and wild fennel.

Via Diana. ✆ **090-9811158.** www.pulera.it. Reservations recommended. Main courses 10€–13€. DC, MC, V. Daily 8pm–midnight. Closed Oct–May 15.

Filippino ★★ SICILIAN/AEOLIAN   It's a pleasant surprise to find such a fine restaurant in such a remote location. Filippino has thrived in the heart of town, near the town hall, since 1910. You'll dine in one of two large rooms or on a terrace ringed with flowering shrubs and potted plants. Menu items are based on old-fashioned Sicilian recipes and prepared with flair. The chef's signature pasta dish is "Aeolian orchids," a curly pasta topped with tomatoes, pine nuts, capers, garlic, basil, mint, and pecorino cheese.

Piazza Mazzini. ℂ **090-9811002.** www.filippino.it. Reservations required July–Aug. Main courses 8€–15€. AE, DC, MC, V. Daily noon–2:30pm and 7:30–10:30pm. Closed Nov 10–Dec 26.

La Nassa ★ 🍴 SICILIAN/AEOLIAN   At this enchanting restaurant, the delectable cuisine of Donna Teresa matches the friendly enthusiasm of her son Bartolo, who has thousands of interesting stories to tell. The food is the most genuine on the island, prepared with respect for old traditions and modern tastes. After the *sette perle* (seven pearl) appetizer—a combination of fresh fish, sweet shrimp, and spices—you can try your choice of fish, cooked to your specifications. Local favorites include *sarago, cernia,* and *dentice,* as delicate in texture as their names are untranslatable. For dessert, try cookies with Malvasia wine.

Via G. Franza 41. ℂ **090-9811319.** Reservations recommended. Main courses 8€–18€. AE, MC, V. Apr–June Fri–Wed 8:30am–3pm and 6pm–midnight; July–Oct daily 8:30am–3pm and 6pm–midnight. Closed Nov–Easter.

Ristorante Pizzeria Pescecane 🍴 SICILIAN/AEOLIAN   The oldest restaurant on the island is a warm, rustic place located right on the main street of town. It offers tables both inside and out on a terrace. The pastas are savory, especially those made with freshly caught seafood. *Lipparata* is the most regional pasta dish, prepared with capers, olives, anchovies, and tomatoes. Pizzas are also good, especially the Desirée, made with mozzarella, fresh tomato, and ham.

Via Vittorio Emanuele 249. ℂ **090-9812706.** www.pescecanelipari.com. Reservations recommended. Main courses 5€–10€; fixed-price menu 15€. AE, DC, MC, V. Daily 10:30am–3pm and 6pm–midnight. Closed Nov–Dec.

LIPARI AFTER DARK

On a summer night, most of the scantily clad visitors congregate around one of the bars with outdoor tables at Marina Corta. The early evening begins at the **Net Cafe,** Via Garibaldi 61 (ℂ **090-9813527;** www.netcafelipari.com/bar.html) where people come not only to surf the Web but also to enjoy drinks and burgers, the big-screen TV, and a beautiful garden. **Turmalin** (ℂ **338-6418362**) is a summer dance club off Piazza Municipio near the castle. May through August, it's open nightly from 11pm to 6am, charging a cover of 15€.

Otherwise, nightlife consists of bars and more bars. Both live and recorded music are featured at **Chitarra Bar,** Salita San Giuseppe 5 (ℂ **090-9811554**), drawing a young to middle-aged crowd. In summer, it's open daily from 7pm to 4am (until midnight in winter). It shuts down in January and February. A hard-drinking place, **Bar Caffè La Vela,** Piazza San Onofrio 2 (ℂ **090-9880064**), is open 24 hours a day in summer, daily from 7am to midnight off season.

Vulcano ★★★

55km (34 miles) NW of Milazzo, 18km (11 miles) NW of Lipari.

Vulcano, the ancient Thermessa, figured heavily in the mythologies of the region. The island was thought to be not only the home of Vulcan, the god of fire, but also the gateway to Hades; Ulysses even stopped here in Homer's *Odyssey,* delaying his return home to Ithaca. Ancient historians Thucydides, Siculus, and Aristotle each recorded eruptions. Other dormant volcanoes (including Vulcano Piano and Vulcanello) exist on the island, but a climb to the rim of the active **Gran Cratere (Big Crater),** or Vulcano della Fosse, draws the most attention. It hasn't erupted since 1890, but one look inside the sulfur-belching hole makes you understand how it inspired the hellish legends surrounding it. The 418m (1,371-ft.) peak is an easier climb than the one on Stromboli, taking just about an hour—though it's just as hot, and the same precautions prevail.

For centuries, the island was uninhabited because of fear of the volcano. Today, however, Vulcano is a stamping ground of the party crowd. Rich Italians from the mainland have erected fancy villas here as second homes. Vulcano's thermal baths, known for their curative powers and said to be especially helpful in relieving rheumatic suffering, also draw visitors.

Vulcano is the island closest to the Sicilian mainland. Ferries and hydrofoils stop here before going on to the other islands. If the wind is blowing in the right direction, you can smell the island's prevalent sulfurous fumes. Vulcano also has the best beaches in the Aeolians, if you don't find black volcanic sands off-putting.

ESSENTIALS

VISITOR INFORMATION   The tourist office no longer operates here. Information on Vulcano is available by calling the tourist office in Lipari (✆ 090-9880095).

GETTING AROUND   Most people walk, but a private company, **Scaffidi** (✆ 090-9853017), runs **buses** from the port area to Piano, a village in the southwestern interior of the island, and to Gelso at the southern tip. Seven buses operate Monday through Saturday; two on Sunday. If you'd rather rent a bike or scooter, go to **Da Paolo,** Via Porto Levante (✆ 090-9852112), open May through November daily from 8am to 8:30pm. Mountain bikes cost from 6€ to 10€ per day; scooters range from 15€ to 40€.

[FastFACTS] VULCANO

Banks   The **Banco di Sicilia,** Via Marina Garibaldi 152 (✆ 090-9811140), has an ATM and keeps regular banking hours Monday through Friday.

Currency Exchange   Money can also be exchanged at the **Thermessa Agency,** Via Porto Levante

(✆ 090-9852230), open daily from 6:30am to 8:30pm.

Emergencies   Call ✆ 113 for the police, ✆ 118 for first aid. For **medical services** from June to September, a doctor is on call at ✆ 090-9852220.

Pharmacy   The island **pharmacy,** Bonarrigo, Via

Favaloro 1 (✆ 090-9852244), is open daily 9am to 1pm and 7 to 9pm.

Police   The *Carabinieri* (army police corps) can be called at ✆ 090-9852110.

Post Office   The post office is on Via Piano, off Porto di Levante (✆ 090-9853143).

WHAT TO SEE & DO

It might be, as the ancients believed, the entrance to hell, nonetheless, Vulcano is the most visited of the Aeolian Islands, no doubt because of its proximity to the Sicilian mainland. Only the late, great film director Federico Fellini could have done justice to a movie about visitors flocking here to bathe in the mud.

To reach these fabled mud baths, **Laghetti di Fanghi,** go to the docks and enter along Via Provinciale. Walk over to a 56m-high (184-ft.) *faraglione,* or "stack:" It's one massive pit of thick, sulfurous gunk that is said to greatly relieve certain skin diseases and rheumatic suffering. ***Take note:*** The mud discolors everything from clothing to jewelry—one reason for the prevalent nudity. Also, because the mud baths are radioactive, don't stay in them for more than 10 to 15 minutes. In summer, expect to encounter muddy pools brimming with (naked) tourists. The water from the sea bubbles up like a giant Jacuzzi nearby, and it's here that mud bathers wash off the gunk. Take care that you don't scald yourself while cleaning yourself off. The beach nearby isn't bad, but the aroma from the mud baths may have you holding your nose if you attempt to sunbathe here. The baths are open from Easter to October, daily from 6:30am to 8pm; admission is 1€.

You can, of course, skip this muddy cauldron altogether and head directly to the dramatic **Spiaggia Sabbie Nere (Black Sands Beach) ★**, the finest in the archipelago. Regrettably, its black sand gets so hot by midday that flip-flops are a virtual necessity if you plan to while away your day here. This beach is on the distant side of the peninsula from Porto di Levante to Porto di Ponente; get here by going along Via Ponente. Porto di Ponente is a 20-minute walk north from the mud baths.

If you tire of the black sands, leave the beach and take the only road north to **Vulcanello** at the northern tip. Locals call this a "volcanic pimple." It erupted from the sea in 183 B.C., spiking its way up through the earth to become a permanent fixture on the island's landscape. As late as 1888, this toy-like volcano erupted a final time, creating what the islanders call a *Valle dei Mostri* (Valley of Monsters) of bizarrely shaped lava fountains.

The Gran Cratere ★★★

To the south of Porto di Levante lies one of the greatest attractions in the Aeolians, the Gran Cratere. From Porto di Levante, follow Via Piano away from the sea for about 182m (597 ft.) until you see the first of the AL CRATERE signs. Once you do, follow the marked trail; allow 3 hours to make it there and back. ***Tip:*** This walk is unshaded, so go early in the morning or late in the day; load up on sunscreen and water; and wear sturdy hiking shoes.

For your trouble in making this steep, hot climb, you'll be rewarded with **dramatic views ★★** of some of the other Aeolian Islands. As you near the mouth of the crater, you see rivulets caused by previous eruptions. At the rim, peer down into the mammoth crater itself. Vapor emissions still spew from the crater, whose lips measure 450m (1,476 ft.) in diameter. The steam is tainted with numerous toxins, so you may not want to hang out here for long.

South to Gelso

Most of the tourist activity is concentrated in northern Vulcano, but an offbeat excursion can be made by taking a bus that cuts inland to the remote, almost forgotten villages of **Piano** and **Gelso.** For details on the island buses, see "Getting Around," above.

Islanders who live inland are likely to reside in the remote village of Piano, 7km (4⅓ miles) from the port. Piano lies between two peaks, **Mount Saraceno,** (48m/ 157 ft.) and **La Sommata** (387m/1,270 ft.). There's not much here, and many of the homes are abandoned in the off season. If you continue on the bus to the southern-most village of Gelso, you can view the inland scenery of Vulcano along the way. At Gelso, the end of the line, you'll find some summer-only places to eat and good sea bath-ing. *Gelso* is Italian for "mulberry," one of the crops cultivated here along with capers.

The best beach is immediately east of Gelso. **Spiaggia dell'Asino** is a big cove reached by a steep path from the village of Gelso. Hydrocycles, deck chairs, and umbrellas can be rented from kiosks on the beach in summer.

Another little road goes to **Capo Grillo,** which has some of the best **panoramic views** ★★ on the island, with a sweeping vista of the Aeolians.

BOAT EXCURSIONS ON VULCANO

You can rent your own boat at **Centro Nautico Baia Levante,** Porto di Levante (✆ 339-3372795; www.baialevante.it). With a boat, you can visit the hamlet of Gelso and explore the caves and bays that riddle Vulcano's western shores. Rentals prices range from 170€ to 700€ per day, fuel not included.

EXCURSIONS TO OTHER ISLANDS

From Vulcano, excursions to other Aeolian Islands can be arranged through **Centro Nautico Baia Levante,** Porto di Levante (✆ 339-3372795; www.baialevante.it), open April through October daily from 8:30am to 8pm. Day excursions, which head for the islands of Lipari, Filicudi, Alicudi, and Salina, begin at 10am and last until 6pm. The cost can range from 40€ to 100€ per person. Night excursions begin at 6pm and end at midnight, with similar costs.

WHERE TO STAY

Hotel Conti ★   This is the second-best hotel on the island, surpassed only by Les Sables Noirs (see below). Just a few minutes' walk from the port where the hydro-foils and ferries pull in, the hotel opens onto the black sands of Ponente Bay. Its architecture is distinctively Aeolian, and luxuriant vegetation surrounds the main building and bungalows. Inside, you'll find cool tiled floors and dark-wood furnish-ings. Guest rooms are simply though comfortably furnished, each with a private entrance opening onto the gardens and a small tiled bathroom. The terraces, solar-ium, and restaurant (serving excellent local specialties) all boast sea views.

Via Porto Ponente, 98050 Vulcano. ✆ **090-9852012.** Fax 090-9852064. www.contivulcano.it. 67 units. 54€–97€ per person double. Rates include half board. AE, DC, MC, V. Closed Oct 21–Apr 30. **Amenities:** Restaurant; bar. *In room:* TV, hair dryer.

Hotel Eolian ★ 🍴   This hotel opens onto Ponente Bay. In typical Aeolian style, the main building is surrounded by stucco bungalows and set in a lush garden stud-ded with palms. None of the bungalows have a view of the water—that's reserved for the restaurant and bar—but most guests spend their days beside the sea anyway. Guest rooms are midsize and furnished in a minimalist style. Walk down from the terrace of the bar to reach the beach, where you can indulge in various water sports, or rent a small boat to explore the more remote parts of the coastline. The thermal sulfurous pool is said to aid poor circulation.

Via Porto Levante, 98050 Vulcano. ✆ **090-9852151.** Fax 090-9852153. www.eolianhotel.com. 88 units. 124€–176€ double; 148€–214€ per person with half board. Rates include continental breakfast. AE, DC, MC, V. Closed Oct to mid-May. **Amenities:** Restaurant; bar; 2 outdoor saltwater pools; tennis courts; babysitting; smoke-free rooms. *In room:* A/C, TV, minibar, hair dryer.

Les Sables Noirs ★★ Les Sables Noirs is the most elegant place to stay on Vulcano, offering a surprising level of luxury and excellent service in this remote outpost. Its rooms overlook a black-sand beach and front a panoramic sweep of the Bay of Ponente. The stucco and bamboo touches evoke a Caribbean resort. Guest rooms are spacious, comfortably furnished, and decorated in typical Mediterranean style; many units open onto a wide balcony. There's a solarium as well. The restaurant, which serves impressive regional specialties, opens onto a broad terrace in front of the beach.

Via Porto di Ponente, 98050 Vulcano. ✆ **090-9850.** Fax 090-9852454. www.framonhotels.com. 48 units. 230€–290€ double; 270€–350€ suite. AE, DC, MC, V. Closed Oct–Mar. **Amenities:** Restaurant; 2 bars; outdoor pool; babysitting; smoke-free rooms. *In room:* A/C, TV, minibar, hair dryer.

WHERE TO DINE

Il Palmento AEOLIAN/SEAFOOD The terrace opening onto the beach is a potent lure, but so is the cuisine. Although the food never rises to the sublime, it's still good, hearty fare. There is an accurate and thorough understanding of flavor here, especially in the house specialty: Spaghetti with chunks of lobster in a zesty tomato sauce. The fish soup with homemade croutons was the best I've sampled in Vulcano, and that Sicilian classic, pasta with fresh sardines, was prepared admirably here, with tomato sauce, olive oil, pine nuts, and wild fennel.

Via Porto Levante. ✆ **090-9852552.** Main courses 6€–16€ fixed-price menu 22€. MC, V. Daily noon–4pm and 6pm–12:30am. Closed Nov 1–Mar 30.

L'Approdo ★ AEOLIAN/SICILIAN Known for its shady oasis of a garden and its good food, this local eatery is decorated in a typical Aeolian style, with white walls, tile floors, and dark wooden tables. Most of the ingredients are shipped over from mainland Sicily, although the fish is caught locally and some of the foodstuffs are grown on the island. Chefs are expert at grilling the fresh fish. They also reveal their skilled technique in their combinations of flavors, including octopus salad with olive oil and lemon flavoring, as well as swordfish carpaccio. Linguini is paired with clams, thyme, and parsley. Another pasta dish, pennette, comes with fresh tuna and wild fennel.

Via Porto di Levante. ✆ **090-9852426.** www.lapprodovulcano.it. Reservations recommended. Main courses 8€–16€ AE, DC, MC, V. Daily noon–3pm and 7:30–11:30pm. Closed Nov 1 to the week before Easter.

Ristorante Belvedere AEOLIAN/SICILIAN I like to come here for the food, but I also enjoy sitting out on the beautiful terrace with a view of other Aeolian Islands. The seafood dishes are typically superb; I favor the catch of the day grilled with fresh herbs and lemon. Grilled Sicilian lamb is another savory treat. My all-time favorite pasta here is the homemade ravioli stuffed with ricotta and spinach.

Via Reale 42. ✆ **090-9853047.** Reservations recommended. Main courses 7€–13€. AE, DC, MC, V. Daily 1–3pm and 8pm–midnight. Closed Oct 1–Mar 30.

Vincenzino 🍴 AEOLIAN/SICILIAN This is the most appealing of the *trattorie* near the ferry port. Known for its hefty portions and affordable prices, it serves clients in a rustic setting. You might begin your meal with spaghetti with crayfish, capers, and a tomato sauce. I'm fond of the *risotto alla pescatora,* with crayfish, mussels, and other seafood. Another good choice is the house-style macaroni. From October to March, the menu is limited to a simple array of platters from the bar.

Via Porto di Levante. ℰ **090-9852016.** www.ristorantevincenzino.com. Reservations recommended. Main courses 8€–10€; fixed-price menu 20€. AE, DC, MC, V. Daily noon–3pm and 7–10pm.

VULCANO AFTER DARK

One of your best bets for a drink is **Ritrovo Remigio,** Porto di Levante, open daily from 6am to 2am. It offers terrace seating overlooking Porto di Levante, where the ferries and hydrofoils from the mainland come in. In addition to its soothing cocktails, it serves excellent pastries and gelato.

The best nightlife—virtually the only nightlife—is found at **Cantine Stevenson ★**, Via Porto di Levante (ℰ **090-9853247**), the former wine cellars of James Stevenson, a virtual Renaissance man who did much to change the face of the island. Born in Wales, Stevenson's many interests led him to Vulcano, where he exported sulfur and pumice. In 1870, he purchased most of the island and planted the first vineyards. Here, in his former wine cellars, live music is featured nightly—folk, Sicilian, pop, rock, jazz, or blues—and more than 600 types of wine are sold. The old-style cantina, with seats outside in summer, is open April through September, daily from noon to 3am.

Stromboli ★★★

63km (40 miles) N of Milazzo, 40km (25 miles) N of Lipari.

This is the easternmost of the islands, and its volcano, whose single cone measures 926m (3,038 ft.), has caused the island to be evacuated several times. Today Stromboli maintains a small population and attracts summer visitors.

The island has two settlements. **Ginostra,** on the southwestern shore, is little more than a cluster of summer homes with only 15 year-round residents. **Stromboli,** on the northeastern shore, is a conglomeration of the villages of Ficogrande, San Vincenzo, and Piscita, where the only in-town attraction is the black-sand beach. You won't see volcanic eruptions from any of these villages, as they occur on the northwest side of the volcano.

The entire surface of Stromboli is the cone of its sluggish but still-active volcano; puffs of smoke can be seen during the day. At night along the **Sciara del Fuoco (Slope of Fire),** lava glows red-hot on its way down to meet the sea with a loud hiss. The main attraction is a steep, difficult climb to the lip of the 92m (302-ft.) **Gran Cratere.** The view of bubbling pools of ooze is accompanied by rising clouds of steam and a sulfuric stench.

The most far-flung island in the archipelago, Stromboli achieved notoriety and became a household word in the United States in 1950 with the release of the Roberto Rossellini *cinéma vérité* film *Stromboli,* starring Ingrid Bergman. The American public was far more interested in the love affair between Bergman and Rossellini than in the film. Although tame by today's standards, the affair temporarily ended Bergman's American film career, and she was even denounced on the Senate floor. Movie fans today are more likely to remember Stromboli from the film version of the Jules Verne novel *Journey to the Center of the Earth,* starring James Mason.

ESSENTIALS

GETTING AROUND To book **hydrofoil** or **ferry** rides, head for the office of **Siremar** (℃ **090-986016;** www.siremar.it) along the harbor road at the port and easy to spot. Siremar offers year-round boat trips from Stromboli to Naples at 38€ to 48€ per person. Boats arrive from Milazzo from April to September only. From July to September, it's possible to book hydrofoil tickets on **Ustica Lines** (℃ **090-9287821;** www. usticalines.it) from Stromboli direct to Naples for 57€ to 62€ per person one-way.

Although several agencies at the port hawk deals ranging from cruises to boat trips, Sabbia Nera, Via Marina (℃ **090-986390;** www.sabbianerastromboli.com), is the most reliable. From Easter to September, it's open daily 9am to 1pm and 3 to 7pm. Boat rentals for tours around Stromboli begin at 140€ a day (fuel extra). You can also rent a scooter here for 20€ a day (fuel extra). The staff can arrange guided boat excursions to Vulcano; the cost is 30€ per person. Guided excursions to Panarea cost 45€ per person. The excursion to Filicudi and Alicudi costs 85€ per person. The agency can also book boat trips around Stromboli, calling at Ginostra and Strombolicchio. Trips last 3 hours and cost 20€ per person. Trips at night to see Sciara del Fuoco (see below) last 2 hours and cost 25€ per person. Most of these excursions leave from the beach at Ficogrande.

[FastFACTS] STROMBOLI

Pharmacy The local **pharmacy** is **Farmacia Bonarrigo Pietro,** Via Favaloro 1 (℃ **090-9852244**), open daily from 8:30am to 1pm and 4:30 to 9pm (8am–midnight August).

Post Office The **post office** is at Via Roma (℃ **090-986261**). Open Monday to Friday 8:20 am to 1:30pm and Saturday 8:20am to 12:30pm.

EXPLORING THE ISLAND

By law, the cone of the volcano, **Gran Cratere ★★★**, can be visited only with a guide. **Guide Alpine Autorizzate** (℃ 090-986211) charges 20€ per person and leads groups on the 3-hour one-way trip up the mountain, leaving at 5pm and returning at 11pm. (I don't recommend taking the trip during the day—it's far less dramatic then.) The trip down takes only 2 hours, but you're allowed an hour at the rim. About halfway up is a view of the **Sciara del Fuoco ★**, which at night glows a fiery red.

Climbing the volcano is the big deal here; otherwise, there isn't much to see in town. Film buffs can follow Via Vittorio Emanuele to the **Chiesa di San Vincenzo,** a church so unremarkable it barely merits a visit. However, just two doors down on the right, near the Locanda del Barbablu, is the **little pink house** where Ingrid Bergman and Roberto Rossellini "lived in sin" during the filming of the 1950 flick *Stromboli.* The house can be viewed only from the outside.

On the northeast coast is a striking rock, **Strombolicchio,** a steep basalt block measuring 43m (141 ft.). It is reached by climbing steps hewn out of rock. Once at the top, you'll be rewarded with a **panoramic view of the Aeolians ★★**, and on a clear day you can see as far as Calabria on the Italian mainland.

WHERE TO STAY

B&B Ginostra ★ 🌶 For the money, this guesthouse is the best deal on this volcanic island. It lies on a hill, a 5-minute walk from the sea, with its windows opening onto views of the port. The typical whitewashed Aeolian building has a certain charm and grace, and offers much comfort in its simply furnished rooms with terra-cotta floors. The bedrooms are midsize and beautifully maintained, and each has a terrace overlooking the sea. The breakfast is homemade and generous.

Via S. Vincenzo (Ginostra), 98050 Stromboli. ℂ **090-9811787.** www.ginostrabb.com 4 units. 45€–55€ per person double. Rates include buffet breakfast. No credit cards. *In room:* Electric fan.

La Locanda del Barbablu ★ 🏨 This quirky choice is a charming, isolated little Aeolian inn with only a few rooms, standing against turn-of-the-20th-century breakfronts. This *locanda,* or inn, has enjoyed a certain renown since the early 1900s, when sailors used to stop here for some R&R en route to Naples. Today, the place is rather chic and has a lovely garden. Guest rooms are small but comfortably furnished, often with four-poster beds encrusted with cherubs and mother-of-pearl inlay. A wide terrace opens onto dramatic views of the volcano and the sea. The restaurant, La Locanda del Barbablu (see below) is worth a visit even if you're not a guest.

Via Vittorio Emanuele 17–19, 98050 Stromboli. ℂ **090-986118.** Fax 090-986323. www.barbablu.it. 6 units. 130€–210€ double. AE, DC, MC, V. Closed Nov–Feb.

La Sirenetta Park Hotel ★★ This has the island's finest guest rooms. It's the best-equipped hotel, with a scenic terrace, a nightclub, and a restaurant serving the best cuisine of any hotel here. It also has an idyllic location on the Ficogrande Beach in front of Strombolicchio, the towering rock that rises out of the waters at San Vincenzo. Guest rooms are attractively furnished, with tiled floors and an airy feel. The hotel is justly proud of having the island's finest pool as well, complete with hydromassage. Facilities include a dive center that also offers water-skiing, sailing, and windsurfing.

Via Marina 33, 98050 Ficogrande (Stromboli). ℂ **090-986025.** Fax 090-986124. www.lasirenetta.it. 60 units. 120€–300€ double; 160€–370€ double with half board. Rates include breakfast. AE, DC, MC, V. Closed Nov 1 to mid-Mar. **Amenities:** Restaurant; 2 bars; saltwater outdoor pool; tennis court; fitness center; room service; massage; water sports; smoke-free rooms. *In room:* A/C, TV, minibar, hair dryer.

WHERE TO DINE

Il Canneto This typical island restaurant was constructed in the old style, with white walls and dark tables. Among the local trattorie, it's nothing fancy, but it's one of the more reliable joints in town. The specialty is always the fish caught in local waters. A delectable pasta dish is the macaroni with minced swordfish or whitefish cooked in a light tomato sauce with fresh herbs. Swordfish roulades are also prepared with a certain flair here.

Via Roma 64. ℂ **090-986014.** Reservations recommended. Main courses 10€–18€. AE, MC, V. Daily 7–11pm. Closed Oct–Mar.

La Locanda del Barbablu ★ The food at this quaint locanda is classically Italian, with no experimentation whatsoever. Excellent dishes include *ravioli di melanzane,* fried ravioli with a tomato sauce; *matarocco,* pasta flavored with tomato sauce, garlic, pine nuts, and fresh basil and parsley; and that old Sicilian reliable, pasta with fresh sardines.

Via Vittorio Emanuele 17-19. ✆ **090-986118.** www.barbablu.it. Reservations recommended in summer. Main courses 8€-15€. AE, DC, MC, V. Daily 7:30-11:30pm. Closed Nov 1-Feb 1.

Punta Lena ★★ The island's best cuisine is served at this old Aeolian house tastefully converted into a 17-seat restaurant, with a terrace opening onto the sea. The restaurant lies on the beach, a 10-minute walk from the center of town. There is a genuine effort here to cook with fresh products whenever possible. Stick to whatever the fishermen have brought in that day. The *gnocchi alla Saracena*, with whitefish, capers, olives, and tomatoes, is also excellent. The restaurant stocks the island's widest selection of wines.

Via Marina 8 (Località Ficogrande). ✆ **090-986204.** Reservations recommended. Main courses 8€-16€. AE, DC, MC, V. Daily noon-2:30pm and 7-11pm. Closed Nov-Mar.

STROMBOLI AFTER DARK

As the sun sets and the volcano lights up the sky, it seems that everyone heads for **Bar Ingrid,** Via Michele Bianchi 1 (✆ 090-986385). Naturally, it's named for Ingrid Bergman. Drinks, beer, and sandwiches are the casual offerings, but mainly people come here to see and be seen. It's open 6 days a week from 6pm to 2am. It closes Monday one week, Sunday the next.

Also popular is **Il Malandrino,** Via Marina (✆ 090-986376), where you can hang out, drink, and even order a pizza. It's open 6 days a week from 5:30pm to 3am. It closes Monday one week, Sunday the next, a rotation it jointly maintains with Bar Ingrid.

For live music, head to **La Tartana,** Via Marina 33, Ficogrande (✆ 090-986025), opening onto the beach. It's open June through September, daily from 9pm to 2am. Patrons come here to dance to disco or enjoy live pop. La Tartana is part of La Sirenetta Park Hotel, right near the port.

Panarea

The smallest of the Aeolian archipelago is also the chicest—its Greek-like setting, dense with white-washed houses wrapped in brilliantly colored bougainvilleas, attracts jetsetters from Italy and abroad. Presenting a jagged landscape surrounded by cobalt waters, much of daily life takes place around the port area of San Pietro. Inhabited since Neolithic times, traces of prehistoric civilization have been uncovered at **Punta Milazzese,** and date back to the 14th century B.C. Artifacts from the digs are on display at the Museo Archeologico at Lipari (p. 238). A walking tour around the island will take you 30 minutes—perhaps to peer into the villas of the idle rich—but also to find quaint little corners from which to dive into the sea, such as at Zimmari beach.

[FastFACTS] PANAREA

Banks You'll find an **ATM** machine located near the port.

Pharmacy **Farmacia Sparacino,** Via Iditella ✆ **090-983148**

Post Office The **post office** is on Via S. Pietro. ✆ **090-983028.** Open Monday to Friday 8:20am to 1:30pm and Saturday 8:20am to 12:30pm.

WHERE TO STAY & DINE

Hotel Quartara   Here you'll find island living at its finest, with a white-washed exterior and terrace dominating the sea. With a balance of friendliness yet exclusivity, you are close enough to the center of town, yet secluded in a heavenly hideaway. The luminous rooms are elegantly furnished with four-poster beds and luscious amenities, and each have their own terrace (only four have sea view). The in-house restaurant is one of the best on the island, serving up scrumptious Aeolian dishes, with outdoor dining on the terrace.

Via S. Pietro 15, Panarea. ✆ **090-983027.** Fax 090-983621. www.quartarahotel.com. 13 units. 200€–350€ double, 300€–450€ double superior. Rates include breakfast. AE, MC, V. Closed Nov–Mar. **Amenities:** Restaurant; bar; outdoor pool; Jacuzzi. *In room:* A/C, TV, minibar, Internet (free).

Salina

The second largest—and some say the most beautiful—of the Aeolian islands was known to the ancients as Didyme, meaning twin, due to the identical now-dormant volcanoes at the center of the island, the Monte dei Porri and Monte Fosse delle Felci. The name Salina (meaning salt) comes from the salt lake near the village of Marina di Salina. The other two main villages on the island are Malfa and Leni.

You'll find one of the best beaches of the Aeolians on this island at **Pollara ★**, and Salina shot to notoriety when scenes from the movie *Il Postino* (*The Postman*; 1994) were filmed here.

Salina is also famous for its grapes that create **Malvasia,** the sweet dessert wine. The capers produced on the island rival those of Pantelleria, and each year they are celebrated at the Caper Festival (*Sagra del Cappero*) in the first week of June.

[FastFACTS] SALINA

Banks   The **Banca Antonveneta** is located at Santa Marina di Salina in Via Lungomare, while the **Banca Nuova** is at Malfa in Via Provinciale 2.

Pharmacy   **Farmacia Meccio** (✆ **090-9844188**) is in Malfa on Via Umberto I , 3, while the **Farmacia Cucinotta** is in Leni on Via Libertá 48 ✆ **090-9809053**

Post Office   A **post office** is at Santa Marina Salina at Via Risorgimento 130 ✆ **090-9843402.** Open Monday to Friday 8am to 1:30pm and Saturday 8am to 12:30pm.

WHERE TO STAY & DINE

Capofaro ★★★   Brainchild of the Tasca d'Alemerita wine family, Capofaro occupies several homes in a vineyard near the island lighthouse that have been artfully turned into an enticing boutique resort with some of the most impressive views over the surrounding islands. The subdued minimalist interiors creatively blend island traditions and ethnic findings, as do the rooms, which are spacious, each with a private balcony and/or terrace. Many are touting this place of understated elegance as one of *the* places to stay in Sicily. The in-house restaurant stays true to Aeolian traditions, and if you fancy learning, you can sign up to one of the in-house cookery classes.

Via Faro 3, Salina ✆ **090-9844330.** www.capofaro.it. 20 units. 150€–440€ double; 240€–580€ suite. Rates include breakfast. AE, DC, MC, V. **Amenities:** Restaurant; bar; outdoor pool; room service. *In room:* A/C, TV.

Filicudi & Alicudi

The quaint island of **Filicudi** attracts vacationers looking to forgo the crowds on the eastern islands and seek out threadbare, authentic, and unspoilt surroundings. The island has three villages that collect all the 250 souls living here: Porto, Pecorini, and Val di Chiesa. Inhabited since the Bronze Age (artifacts are housed at the Museo Archeologico in Lipari) the basalt coastlines plunge dramatically into the sea below. The best way to enjoy the spectacular natural setting is by boat—negotiate a trip around the island with one of the cooperative fishermen at the port.

The most westerly of the islands, **Alicudi,** is also the furthest removed from civilization—there are no paved roads, and the only means of transport are donkeys and the three-wheel Piaggio Ape vehicle. With a population of little more than 100, the locals take great pride in their island, with spectacularly designed terraces, and a firm "no" to urban expansion. Time hasn't changed things here, where electricity was only introduced in the early 1990s. Only a handful of shops sell the basics, but Alicudi's slow pace is probably the true essence of island living.

CATANIA

One of the liveliest cities in southern Italy, Catania is a bustling town with much *joie de vivre*. Many visitors to Sicily bypass this baroque gem on the way to Taormina, but Catania merits at least 2 full days for its art treasures, church museums, and Roman ruins, if not for its liveliness as well as its to-die-for fresh food-stuffs such as those you'll find at the lively fish market (*la pescheria*).

The city has suffered natural disasters throughout the centuries. Much of the history of Catania is linked to its volcanic neighbor, **Mount Etna.** In 1669, the worst eruption in Catania's history occurred when Etna buried much of the city under lava that literally ran through the streets.

The architects **Giovan Battista Vaccarini** (1702–68) and **Francesco Battaglia** (1701–1788) helped turn the city into one of the baroque capitals of Europe. Builders used solidified black lava in the masonry, which also fortified the buildings. The result was so unique that word spread, and in the 18th and 19th centuries, Catania was a compulsory stopover on the "Grand Tour" of Europe.

Catania's industry has earned it the appellation of "the Milano of the South." The city's airport has always been the island's largest, and many department store chains open up in Catania long before heading westward. It is also a cultural capital of sorts, having provided to the Arts its favorite sons—Bellini, Verga, and Greco. Catanians are deeply proud of their heritage and have gone to great lengths to restore antique *palazzi* to their original splendor. They are also crafty at putting abandoned buildings to good use: An exhibition complex occupies a former sulfur refinery at Il Ciminiere, a contemporary art foundation has taken over an old licorice factory, and the old tobacco processing plant is slated to become the home of the long-overdue Archaeological Museum.

ESSENTIALS

Getting There

BY PLANE Flights from mainland Italy and from the U.K. arrive at Italy's third largest airport, **Aeroporto Vincenzo Bellini** at Fontanarossa (© **095-7239111;** www.aeroporto.catania.it), 7km (4 miles) from the city center. For information about which carriers fly into Catania, see p. 39.

From the airport, **AMT** city bus **no. 457** (also known as **Alibus; ☎ 800-018696;** www.amt.ct.it) runs into town every 20 minutes from 5:00am to midnight, with stops at Piazza Stesicoro and the Central Station. Another line, **no. 524,** makes stops along Via Dusmet and at Piazza Borsellino. Tickets cost 1€ and must be bought before boarding at the Money Exchange Office/Bus Ticket Office in the Arrivals area.

You can catch a **taxi** outside the arrivals hall, or book one at **Radio Taxi Catania** (☎ **095-330966;** www.radiotaxi.org). Expect to pay a flat rate between 25€ and 40€, depending on where you're headed in the city. *Tip:* Always negotiate the fare before getting in.

BY TRAIN   Arrivals are at the **Stazione Centrale,** Piazza Papa Giovanni XXIII (☎ **892021;** www.trenitalia.it). Trains arrive daily from Turin, Venice, Milan, Bologna, Florence, Rome, and Naples, though not all are direct. From Milan, the journey cost starts at 86.60€, while from Rome it starts at 45.50€. Catania also has good, direct rail links to cities all over the east coast of Sicily (Messina, Taormina, Syracuse) and has good connections to other cities such as Ragusa and Noto. Train rides to cities like Palermo or Agrigento, to the west, can take 3 to 4 hours long and involve some transfers.

BY BUS   There is a direct bus service to Catania from Rome and other northern cities, but unless you really want to be sitting for 12 hours in crammed quarters with limited leg room, I highly discourage it. **SAIS Trasporti** (☎ **091-6166028;** www. saistrasporti.it) runs a daily service from Rome's Tiburtina station; the 12-hour trip costs 35€. **Etna Trasporti** (☎ **095-530396;** www.etnatrasporti.it) runs a service from Milan, Pisa, and Rome's Tiburtina station to Catania, with the journey from Milan taking nearly 18 hours.

BY BOAT   Ferry service to Catania from Naples is run by **TTT lines** (☎ **800-915365;** www.tttlines.it), and from Civitavecchia the service is handled by **Grimaldi Lines** (☎ **081-496444;** www.grimaldi-lines.com). Both are excellent alternatives to driving all the way to Catania from the mainland, as you can board the car onto the ferry and relax the rest of the way.

BY CAR   There are two national autostrade that link Catania to the rest of the island: from Messina, which will probably be your gateway into Sicily, take the A18 south, passing Taormina and continuing on to Catania. From Palermo, you can take the A19. From Syracuse, take the national highway SS114 northbound.

Visitor Information

Tourist offices are found at the Stazione Centrale, Piazza Giovanni XXIII (☎ **095-7306255;** www.apt.catania.it), and at Via Cimarosa Domenico 10 (☎ **095-7306211**), both open daily 8am to 8pm. There is also a branch at the airport (☎ **095-7306266**), open daily 8am to 8pm. Stop by one of the three to ask for a map highlighting the monuments and places of interest around town.

City Layout

Catania was rebuilt using antiseismic measures. Its major boulevards were made straight and wide, virtually eliminating anything that had existed from medieval Catania. Broad piazzas punctuate many streets. The aim was to make streets wide enough to allow Catanians to escape in case lava flows through the streets again.

In recent years, unchecked growth has sent Catania crawling up the southern slopes of the ferocious Etna and sprawling across the fertile lands of the Simeto River.

The old center of the city is the **Piazza Duomo,** with the fountain of the ancient elephant. Splitting Catania in two parts is its main street, **Via Vittorio Emanuele II,** which begins east at **Piazza del Martini** running west past Piazza Duomo.

Running on a north–south axis, **Via Etnea** ★ is the grand boulevard of Catania that runs north from Piazza Duomo for 3km (2 miles). Along this avenue are the best restaurants and boutiques. Eventually Via Etnea reaches **Villa Bellini,** the beautiful public gardens.

In western Catania, **Via Crociferi** ★ is the city's gracious street of the baroque, flanked by churches and palazzi.

GETTING AROUND

BY BUS   AMT (Azienda Municipale Trasporti), Via Plebiscito 747 (✆ **095-7519111;** www.amt.ct.it), operates a good network of buses, branching out across the city. Tickets cost 1€ and are valid for 90 minutes. A ticket valid for a day goes for 2.50€. You can purchase tickets at *tabacchi* (tobacco shops), news agents, and AMT kiosks. *Tip:* If you take circular bus no. 410, you'll be treated to a round-trip of all the major sightseeing attractions for the cost of a one-way fare. The service is run only by appointment; call ✆ **095-7517111.**

BY METRO   The very limited subway system—with only six stations it is the shortest metro system in the world—has trains running every 15 to 30 minutes daily from 7am to 8:45pm, costing 1€ for a ticket valid for 90 minutes. Metro tickets, like bus tickets, are available from newsagents and tobacco shops. The metro runs from Stazione Centrale at Platform 11 south to Catania Porto and north and northwest all the way to Catania Borgo, the terminus for the Stazione Circumetnea via Caronda 490. *Tip*: Don't count on buying tickets at the station from automatic vendors, which are often out of service.

BY TAXI   Radio Taxi Catania (✆ 095-330966) operates 24-hour taxi service. Taxi ranks are found at the Stazione Centrale and Piazza Duomo.

[Fast FACTS] CATANIA

American Express   AmEx is represented by **La Duca Viaggi,** Viale Africa 14 (✆ **095-7222295**). Open Monday to Friday 9am to 1pm and 4 to 7:30pm, Saturday 9am to noon.

Books   **La Feltrinelli,** Via Sant'Euplio 38, carries English-language bestsellers and classics.

Consulates   There is an honorary U.K. consulate in Via N. Coviello 27 (✆ **095-7167336**), which operates Tuesdays and Thursdays from 10:00am to 12:30pm and by appointment. The nearest U.S. Consular Agency is in Palermo (see p. 76).

Currency Exchange   Most banks lie in the center along Corso Sicilia; these include **Deutsche Bank,** Piazza Buonarroti 14 (✆ **095-722931**), and

Banco di Sicilia, Corso Sicilia 8 (✆ **095-368215**), both open Monday to Friday 8:30am to 1:30pm and 2:30 to 4pm. You can also exchange currency at the airport, at the train station, and at the AmEx office (see above).

Emergencies   For the police, dial ✆ **112;** the *Carabinieri* (army police corps) can be reached at ✆ **113.** For an ambulance, dial ℭ **118**; to report a fire, ℭ **115.** For road assistance, call ACI (Italian Automobile Club) at ℭ **803116** or toll-free ℭ **800-116800.**

Hospitals The major hospital is **Garibaldi,** Piazza Santa Maria del Gesù (ℭ **095-7591111**), while the **Ospedale Cannizzaro** is at Via Messina 829 (ℭ **095-7261111**). The **Children's Hospital** is

within the Policlinico, Via Santa Sofia 78 (ℭ **095-743 1111**).

Internet Access
Your best bet is **WebCam,** Via Etnea 678 (ℭ **095-434999**), open Monday to Saturday 10am to 9pm. It charges 2.50€ per hour.

Pharmacies **Farmacia Consoli** is on Via Etnea 400, the **Farmacia Centrale** at Via Etnea 238, and the

Farmacia Crocerossa on Via Etnea 274. One night pharmacy is **Croceverde,** on Via Ruggero Settimo 43 (ℭ **095-441868**), open daily 4pm to 1am.

Post Office The main post office is at Via Etnea 215 (ℭ **095-7155071**), next to the Villa Bellini Gardens. It is open Monday to Friday 8am to 6:30pm, and Saturday 8am to 12:30pm.

WHERE TO STAY

Expensive

Excelsior Grand Hotel ★★   No other hotel in Sicily so gracefully manifests the flowing sense of *la dolce vita* modernism as Catania's leading establishment. It brought postwar tourism to Catania with a stately and monumental facade, built in 1954, that's almost a mirror image of the Palazzo di Giustizia (Courthouse), which lies immediately across Piazza Verga, the most impressive square in Catania.

Expect a *moderno*-style lobby in perfect taste, with a resident pianist, deep and comfortable settees, and a posh bar. Half of the bedrooms overlook Piazza Verga and faraway Mount Etna, and all units are soundproof. These standard double rooms are called deluxe rooms, and each comes with a loggia-style balcony. The remainder ("superior rooms") are just as large, plush, and comfortable, but they face the back of the hotel and in most cases lack balconies. The in-house restaurant, **Le Zagare,** is reviewed on p. 261.

Piazza Verga, 95129 Catania. ℭ **095-7476111.** Fax 095-537015. www.thi.it. 176 units. 215€–265€ double; 275€–568€ suite. Rates include breakfast. AE, DC, MC, V. Free street parking. Bus: 443, 457, 721, or 722. **Amenities:** Restaurant; piano bar; fitness center; steam room; room service; babysitting; smoke-free rooms. *In room:* A/C, TV, minibar, hair dryer, Wi-Fi (5€/hr).

Una Hotel Palace ★★   Giving the Excelsior a serious run for its money, this splendid hotel occupying a former grand palazzo is fast becoming the place to stay in town. A part of the prestigious Una chain, you are welcomed into a plush yet minimalist lobby; rooms are a creative mix of ethnic/arabesque pieces against pristine white walls, the beddings are of the highest quality to guarantee guests a pampered sleep. The generous bathrooms have either tubs or showers, and are vividly decorated in Mediterranean hues. The roof-garden bar is one of the liveliest places in town for happy hour, while the in-house restaurant has been getting rave reviews from guests and locals alike.

Via Etnea 218, 95131 Catania. ℭ **095-2505111.** Fax: 095-2505112. www.unahotels.it. 94 units. 150€–260€ double; 200€–350€ suite. Rates include buffet breakfast. AE, DC, MC, V. Parking on premises 20€. **Amenities:** 2 Restaurants; bar; outdoor pool; health club; spa with hammam; room service; babysitting; smoke-free rooms. *In room:* A/C, TV, minibar, Wi-Fi (18€/24hr).

Villa del Bosco ★★★   Guests at Villa del Bosco will enjoy a true taste of the aristocratic life of a landowning Sicilian family during the early 19th century. The stately looking Bosco is set behind a high wall that separates it from a suburban neighborhood, 5km (3 miles) south of Catania's historic core. It was originally built in 1826 as a private home and converted into a dignified boutique hotel, rich with antiques and a sense of another time. The hotel's social center is an elaborately detailed salon with a bar at one end. Guest rooms are elegant, with four-poster beds, plus tiled or stone-sheathed bathrooms. Suites come with either a Jacuzzi or hydro-massage showers. The artfully frescoed breakfast room is the most beautiful in Catania. The in-house restaurant, **Il Canile,** is reviewed on p. 261.

Via del Bosco 62, 95125 Catania. ℰ **095-7335100.** Fax 095-7335103. www.hotelvilladelbosco.it. 33 units. 260€ double; 320€–450€ suite. AE, DC, MC, V. Bus: 129, 314, or 421. **Amenities:** Restaurant; bar; outdoor pool; smoke-free rooms. *In room:* A/C, TV, minibar, Wi-Fi (.75€/hr).

Moderate

Albergo Savona   A definite cut above the Hotel Centrale Europa (see below), which sits across the street, this solid, well-located hotel lies a 2-minute walk from the Duomo. Converted into a hotel about a century ago, it has three floors of quiet, soundproof bedrooms with high ceilings, severely dignified yet comfortable furniture, and shower-only bathrooms. Guest rooms are accessed via a grandiose flight of marble-capped stairs flanked with elaborate wrought-iron railings. Although some have views of the cathedral, room nos. 102 and 104 are the best, with views over a medieval-looking courtyard. One of the best aspects of this place is the plush, paneled bar, complete with soaring ceiling vaults, deep armchairs, and plenty of dignified style. It doubles as a breakfast room. Some members of the staff could use a refresher in manners.

Via Vittorio Emanuele 210, 95124 Catania. ℰ/fax **095-326982.** www.hotelsavona.it. 30 units. 100€–160€ double. AE, DC, MC, V. Bus: 401, 429, 432, or 457. **Amenities:** Bar; smoke-free rooms. *In room:* A/C, TV, minibar.

Hotel Mediterraneo ★   Well designed and unpretentious, with three stars from the local tourist authorities, this is one of Catania's most modern hotels, and is a member of the Best Western hotel chain. The blue-floored lobby's best features include a tactful, hardworking staff and dramatic murals inspired by the great masterpieces of the Italian Renaissance. Guest rooms are angular, simple, and uncomplicated, with big windows and bathrooms with tub/shower combinations.

Via Dottor Consoli 27, 95124 Catania. ℰ **095-325330** or 800/528-1234 in the U.S. Fax 095-7151818. www.hotelmediterraneoct.com. 64 units. 170€ double. Rates include buffet breakfast. AE, DC, MC, V. Parking 10€–18€ per day, depending on vehicle size. Bus: 431. **Amenities:** Lobby cafe and bar; smoke-free rooms. *In room:* A/C, TV, minibar, Wi-Fi (free).

Jolly Hotel Bellini   This older (around 1959), more central, of Catania's two Jolly Hotels has only three government stars, a low ranking for a chain more noted for its four- and five-star properties. Detractors find it a wee bit dated; I find it comfortable, well maintained, and, despite a few remaining touches of retro-dowdiness, an acceptable choice.

Piazza Trento 13, 95129 Catania. ℰ **095-316933.** Fax 095-316832. www.jollyhotels.it. 130 units. 155€–230€ double. Rates include buffet breakfast. AE, DC, MC, V. Bus: 443, 721, or 722. **Amenities:** Restaurant; bar; room service; smoke-free rooms. *In room:* A/C, TV, minibar.

Where to Stay & Eat in Catania

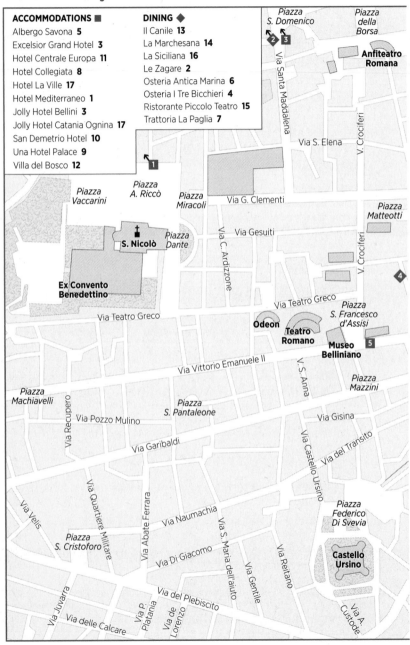

ACCOMMODATIONS ■

Albergo Savona **5**
Excelsior Grand Hotel **3**
Hotel Centrale Europa **11**
Hotel Collegiata **8**
Hotel La Ville **17**
Hotel Mediterraneo **1**
Jolly Hotel Bellini **3**
Jolly Hotel Catania Ognina **17**
San Demetrio Hotel **10**
Una Hotel Palace **9**
Villa del Bosco **12**

DINING ◆

Il Canile **13**
La Marchesana **14**
La Siciliana **16**
Le Zagare **2**
Osteria Antica Marina **6**
Osteria I Tre Bicchieri **4**
Ristorante Piccolo Teatro **15**
Trattoria La Paglia **7**

Piazza S. Domenico

Piazza della Borsa

Anfiteatro Romana

Via Santa Maddalena

V. Crociferi

Via S. Elena

Piazza Matteotti

Piazza Vaccarini

Piazza A. Riccò

Piazza Miracoli

Via G. Clementi

Via Gesuiti

Via C. Ardizzone

V. Crociferi

S. Nicolò

Piazza Dante

Ex Convento Benedettino

Via Teatro Greco

Via Teatro Greco

Piazza S. Francesco d'Assisi

Odeon

Teatro Romano

Museo Belliniano

Via Vittorio Emanuele II

V. S. Anna

Piazza Mazzini

Piazza Machiavelli

Via Recupero

Via Pozzo Mulino

Piazza S. Pantaleone

Via Gisina

Via Castello Ursino

Via del Transito

Via Garibaldi

Via Quartiere Militare

Via Vells

Via Abate Ferrara

Via Naumachia

Via S. Maria dell'aiuto

Piazza Federico Di Svevia

Piazza S. Cristoforo

Via Di Giacomo

Via Gentile

Via Reitano

Castello Ursino

Via Juvarra

Via delle Calcare

Via P. Platania

Via de Lorenzo

Via del Plebiscito

Via A. Custode

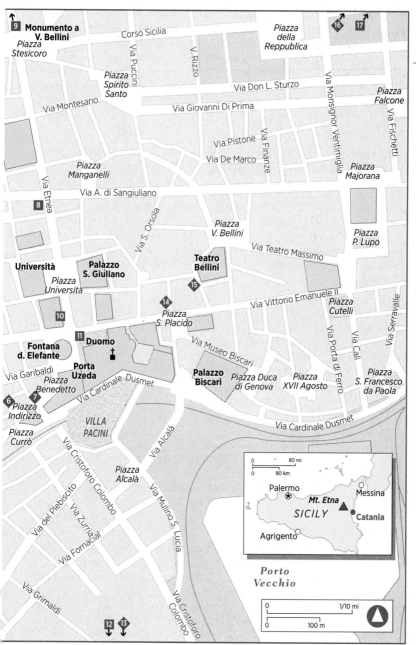

9 Monumento a
V. Bellini

Piazza
Stesicoro

Corso Sicilia

Piazza
della
Reppublica

16 **17**

Via Puccini

V. Rizzo

Piazza
Spirito
Santo

Via Don L. Sturzo

Via Monsignor Ventimiglia

Piazza
Falcone

Via Montesano

Via Giovanni Di Prima

Via Fischetti

Via Pistone

Via Finanze

Via De Marco

Piazza
Majorana

Piazza
Manganelli

Via A. di Sangiuliano

Via Etnea

8

Via S. Orsola

Piazza
V. Bellini

Piazza
P. Lupo

Via Teatro Massimo

Università

Palazzo
S. Giuliano

Teatro
Bellini

Piazza
Università

15

Via Vittorio Emanuele II

Piazza
Cutelli

10

14

Piazza
S. Placido

Via Porta di Ferro

Via Cali

Via Serravalle

Fontana
d. Elefante

11 Duomo
✝

Via Museo Biscari

Piazza
S. Francesco
da Paola

Via Garibaldi

Porta
Uzeda

Palazzo
Biscari

Piazza Duca
di Genova

Piazza
XVII Agosto

6
Piazza
Indirizzo

7
Piazza
Benedetto

Via Cardinale Dusmet

VILLA
PACINI

Via Alcalà

Via Cardinale Dusmet

Piazza
Currò

Via Cristoforo Colombo

Piazza
Alcalà

Via Mulino S. Lucia

Via del Plebiscito

Via Zurria

Via Fornaci

Via Cristoforo Colombo

Via Grimaldi

12 **13**

Porto
Vecchio

0 — 80 mi
0 — 80 km

Palermo

Messina

Mt. Etna

SICILY

Catania

Agrigento

0 — 1/10 mi
0 — 100 m

Jolly Hotel Catania Ognina ★ Set at the point in Catania where the city devolves into a seaside strip of beach resorts that eventually lead to such towns as Acireale, this boxy-looking, government-rated three-star hotel is favored by business travelers. A somewhat blasé staff will check you into a contemporary-looking guest room, outfitted with bland but comfortable furniture. About half of the units have harbor views. There's no on-site restaurant, but a respectable choice of dining options lies within a few minutes' drive or walk.

Via Messina 626–628, 95126 Località Ognina Catania. (✆) **095-7528111.** Fax 095-7121856. www.jollyhotels. it. 56 units. 190€ double. Rate includes breakfast. AE, DC, MC, V. Free parking. Bus: 334 or 448. **Amenities:** Bar. *In room:* A/C, TV, minibar.

Inexpensive

Hotel Centrale Europa This age-old government-rated two-star hotel occupies a site that's closer to the cathedral than any other lodging in town. It's been here since 1900, still evoking a battered but genteel *pensione* whose staff has seen thousands of art lovers and business travelers come and go. The small lobby is filled with sepia-toned photos of old Catania. Rooms are very simple and bland-looking, with few frills but acceptably comfortable furniture. More than half overlook the Duomo and the historic buildings around it. No meals are served, but the Caffè del Duomo (p. 272) lies a few steps away.

Via Vittorio Emanuele 167 (Piazza Duomo), 95124 Catania. (✆) **095-311309.** Fax 095-317531. www. hotelcentraleuropa.it. 17 units. 85€ double. AE, MC, V. Bus: 401, 429, 432, or 457. *In room:* A/C, TV.

Hotel Collegiata ★ 👔 All the floors in this 17th-century building are devoted to private apartments except for two, which contain a series of high-ceilinged guest rooms that, however spartan-looking, are airy, comfortable, and bigger than you'd expect. The setting is close to one of Catania's most beautiful churches, La Collegiata, a short walk from the Duomo. The staff is hip and friendly.

Via Vasta 10 (at Via Etnea), 95100 Catania. (✆) **095-315256.** Fax 095-322848. www.lacollegiata.com. 14 units. 65€–85€ double. Rates include continental breakfast. AE, DC, MC, V. Bus: 448, 449, or 457. *In room:* A/C, TV.

Hotel La Ville ★★★ 👔 This is considered by many to be the friendliest hotel in Catania, and in a city where you are a stranger, it's a relief. This three-star property near the main railway station is a splendid mix of old-world charm and modern furnishings, with very spacious, soundproofed rooms elegantly decorated with wooden pieces and terra-cotta floorings; the marble bathrooms are shower/bath combos. For its location and quality of service, the accolades are well-deserved.

Via Claudio Monteverdi 15, 95131 Catania. (✆) **095-322709.** Fax: 095-7465189. www.hotellavillecatania. com. 14 units. 90€–100€ double. Rates include breakfast. AE, DC, MC, V. Street parking. **Amenities:** Breakfast lounge; smoke-free rooms; Wi-Fi (free). *In room:* A/C, TV, Internet.

San Demetrio Hotel ★ 👔 Small-scale, personal, and deeply idiosyncratic, this hotel occupies one of the upper floors of a grandiose building near the cathedral; it shares the floor with the branch of the local bureaucracy that fines motorists for parking and traffic violations. (To reach the entrance to the hotel, you pass somewhat scary-looking government offices, traverse a courtyard, and take a claustrophobic elevator to an upper floor.) The hotel was converted from a private apartment in 2000, and it still evokes a private home. It is graced with some of the most beautiful ceiling frescoes of any hotel in Catania. The appealing paintings on the walls are done in a "post-Renaissance kind of modernism." Room no. 22 is particularly charming, but the others compete worthily with early-19th-century grace notes. In contrast, furnishings are spartan.

Via Etnea 55, 95124 Catania. ℂ 095-2500237. Fax 095-311845. www.hotelsandemetrio.com. 6 units. 90€ double; 120€ triple; 140€ quad. Rates include continental breakfast. MC, V. Free parking. Bus: 448, 449, 457, 722, or 733. **Amenities:** Babysitting. In room: A/C, TV, hair dryer.

WHERE TO EAT

Expensive

Le Zagare ★★ CONTINENTAL/SICILIAN   When designers renovated the dining room of the Excelsior Grand Hotel in 2001, they took pains to retain the original lines of its *dolce vita* decor (around 1954). The result is a genuinely elegant dining experience complemented by superb food and access to a terrace lined with flickering candles and flowering shrubbery. Menu items are a cut above the standard fare served in other hotel dining rooms. Delectable starters include Sicilian king prawn in a corn-and-cheese crust served on a bed of red onions and green tomatoes; or else purée of dried cod served on small pancakes of chickpeas, olives, and dried tomatoes. Natural flavors and the skill of the chefs combine to create such main dishes as grilled gilthead sea bream filets served with vegetables flavored with almond essence, or a casserole of Mediterranean fish and shellfish flavored with saffron. Desserts are especially yummy here, especially the crème brûlée flavored with pistachio or the crispy chocolate "pyramid" with iced nougat and orange sauce.

In the Excelsior Grand Hotel (p. 256), Piazza Verga. ℂ 095-7476111. Reservations recommended. Main courses 20€–30€. AE, DC, MC, V. Daily 12:30–2:30pm and 7:30–10:30pm. Bus: 443, 457, 721, or 722.

Osteria I Tre Bicchieri ★★★ CONTINENTAL   This is the finest and most appealing restaurant in Catania. Established in 2000 in partnership with one of the best-respected wine merchants (Benanti, Inc.) in Sicily, it welcomes visitors to a location on a narrow, quiet street two blocks northwest of the cathedral.

Note that this building contains two dining venues, the other a well-conceived wine tavern, called **Cantina,** in a woodsy-looking room near the front entrance. Food here includes the likes of fondue, steak tartare, carpaccio, pasta, and crepes, costing from 6€ to 15€. But the real culinary vision of the place is found in the three high-ceilinged, vaulted rooms outfitted in a graceful 18th-century style, reached by walking through the Cantina.

The best pasta I tasted in Catania was the tagliatelle with ragout of suckling pig here. Wonders are also done with fish, especially *triglia,* a local saltwater fish served with onion-stuffed artichokes and a sauce of smoked foie gras. The signature gnocchi comes with a cheese from Ragusa. The wine list includes at least 1,000 Italian vintages, many from Sicily.

Via San Giuseppe al Duomo 31. ℂ 095-7153540. www.osteriaitrebicchieri.it. Reservations required. Main courses 15€–25€. AE, DC, MC, V. Mon–Sat 8pm–12:30am. Bus: 443, 457, 721, or 722.

Moderate

Il Canile SICILIAN   Elegant and traditional, this restaurant in the Villa del Bosco hotel (p. 257) is very appealing. You can dine in a richly frescoed interior room or take a seat on a terrace without a hint of Sicilian traffic. Menu items include a *risottino* of porcini mushrooms from the slopes of Mount Etna. I sampled my finest seafood pasta in Catania here, and went on to devour a succulent sea bream under an oven-crisp potato crust. The restaurant's name, which translates as "The Kennel," is taken from the pair of 18th-century stone dogs that stand near its entrance.

In the Villa del Bosco, Via del Bosco 62. © **095-7335100.** Reservations recommended. Main courses 14€–21€. AE, DC, MC, V. Daily 1–2:30pm and 8–11pm. Bus: 129, 314, or 421.

La Siciliana SICILIAN   Decorated in a classic and rustic style, this restaurant was established in 1968 and is now managed by two sons of the original owner. Located in north Catania, it's set in a 19th-century villa that's furnished in provincial island style. In winter, diners sit in one of four cozy rooms; in summer, tables overflow onto a garden terrace. The cuisine is both innovative and respectful of tradition. I've enjoyed carpaccio of fresh swordfish, grilled stuffed calamari, and risotto with squid ink and fresh ricotta. For dessert, typical local favorites are always on the menu.

Viale Marco Polo 52A. © **095-376400.** www.lasiciliana.it. Reservations required. Main courses 6€–16€. AE, DC, MC, V. Tues–Sat 12:30–3pm and 8–11pm; Sun 12:30–3pm. Closed July 1–15.

Inexpensive

La Marchesana ★ SICILIAN 🍴   The charm of this place lies in its well-managed simplicity, the genuinely friendly welcome from the staff at the bar near the entrance, and the flavorful cuisine. Outdoor tables fill part of the quiet street during nice weather; otherwise, you can dine in a high-ceilinged, vaulted dining room that manages to stay cool even on hot days. The Di Dio family, well versed in welcoming diners from the English-speaking world, prepares dishes that include delectable risotto, salads, and succulent spaghetti with squid, cuttlefish, shrimp, and tomatoes.

Via Mazza 4–8 (at the Piazza San Placido). © **095-315171.** www.lamarchesana.com. Reservations recommended on weekends. Main courses 10€–15€. AE, DC, MC, V. Daily 11am–4pm and 7pm–1am. Bus: 1–4.

Osteria Antica Marina ★★ SICILIAN   Only a handful of other restaurants convey as effectively the earthy, grimy, teeming maze of humanity that hauls food in and out of central Catania. Established just after World War II, and sheathed with wooden panels, this *osteria* is set amid the densest concentration of open-air food stalls in town, two labyrinthine blocks south of the cathedral, on a piazza that by day teems with food merchants, but by night is calmer and quieter. You'll be separated from the outside by plate-glass windows and cooled with air-conditioning, but you'll still get a sense of the freshness and variety of raw material just a few steps away. Menu items include ultrafresh homemade pasta, garnished (you guessed it) with seafood and shellfish, including sea urchins and scampi; every imaginable kind of grilled gilled creature in the Mediterranean; and fresh cuts of beef, pork, veal, and lamb.

Alla Pescheria di Catania, Via Pardo 29. © **095-348197.** www.anticamarina.it. Reservations recommended. Main courses 15€–20€. AE, DC, MC, V. Thurs–Tues 1–3pm and 8pm–12:30am. Bus: 1–4, 2–5, or 3–6.

Ristorante Piccolo Teatro SICILIAN   Set a few steps from the Teatro Massimo is this cozy pub whose battered wood panels and prominent bar might remind you of an Italian beer hall. It attracts after-work businesspeople and a pre-theater crowd of young hipsters and hipster-wannabes. Expect dishes that include fresh fish (especially swordfish), risotto, and hot-weather favorites such as octopus salad and sorbets. "A dish for the gods," as one habitué described it, is spaghetti with sea urchins, eggs, and extra-virgin olive oil, given additional flavor by fresh parsley, garlic, and hot peppers. Pennette with swordfish is made enticing by the addition of fresh mint, pine nuts, and hot peppers.

Via Michele Rapisardi 6-8. 𝒞 **095-315369.** Reservations not needed. Main courses 12€-22€. AE, DC, MC, V. Wed-Mon 8pm-12:30am. Bus: 14.

Trattoria La Paglia ★ SICILIAN   If you like your food ethnic and your atmosphere hale and hearty, you can enjoy the most authentic Catanian dining experience at the site of the lively fish market. If you don't like the day's offerings, one of the staff might step out to the market and buy a fish you like, cooking it to your specifications. Start with *la triaca pasta*, an excellent pasta in fresh bean sauce, or *sarda al beccafico* (sardines fried in bread crumbs with pecorino cheese). I'm also fond of the spaghetti whipped with sea urchins in an extra-virgin olive oil with fresh garlic. One local dish that's highly favored is *tonno con cipollata* (broiled tuna with onions and a dash of vinegar). Most of the dishes are based on the sea, and the atmosphere is very rustic.

Via Pardo 23. 𝒞 **095-346838.** No reservations Fri-Sat. Main courses 10€-20eu]. MC, V. Mon-Sat 12:30-2:30pm and 8-11pm. Bus: 457.

WHAT TO SEE & DO

The **Duomo** ★ (𝒞 **095-320044**) at the very heart of Catania is dedicated to the memory of the martyred St. Agatha. The Duomo was originally ordered to be built by Roger I, the Norman king, but it was destroyed in the earthquake of 1693 and had to be reconstructed. Its **facade** ★ is its most enduring architectural feature, the work of Giovan Battista Vaccarini (1702–68), who redesigned the city after the earthquake. For the granite columns of the facade, the architect "removed" them from the city's Roman amphitheater. Only the lovingly crafted medieval apses, made from lava, survived the devastation of that earthquake.

Many opera fans come here to pay their respects at **Bellini's tomb,** guarded by a life-size angel in marble. It's to the right as you enter the Duomo through its right door. The words above the tomb are from *Sonnambula*, and in translation read, "Ah, I didn't think I'd see you wilt so soon, flower."

In the Norman **Cappella della Madonna (Chapel of the Madonna),** also on the right, precious metals envelop a magnificent Roman sarcophagus and a statue of the Virgin Mary, carved in the 1400s. To the right of the choir is the **Cappella di Sant'Agata.** In the sacristy is a fresco, said to have been created in 1774, that depicts the horrendous eruption of Mount Etna in 1669. Admission to the cathedral is free; it's open daily 7am–noon and 4:30–7pm.

Perhaps the most stunning part of the Duomo lies underground: The **Terme Achillane** ★★, an Imperial Roman thermal spa discovered after the devastating earthquake in 1693 that miraculously conserved some of its stuccoed decorations, including animals and grape bunches. The part of the complex open to the public is a rectangular hall with four pillars, surmounted by vaulted ceilings. At the center lies the original marble bath. Admission is 5€, half price for adults 60 and over, free for children 9 and under. To book a visit 𝒞 **095-281635;** www.museodiocesicatania.it.

The Duomo is not the only attraction on this landmark square. Lying in the very heart of Catania, the Piazza Duomo was also created by the city's planner, Vaccarini. The baroque elegance of Catania's heyday lingers on here.

Catania Attractions

Casa di Verga **4**
Castello Ursino & Museo Civico **5**
Chiesa di San Nicolò All'Arena **1**
Duomo **8**
Le Ciminiere **9**
Museo Civico Belliniano **3**
Museo Diocesano **7**
Museo Emilio Greco **2**
Piazza Duomo **6**

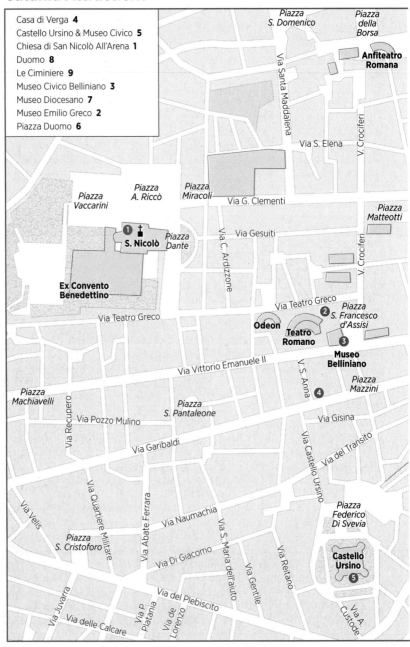

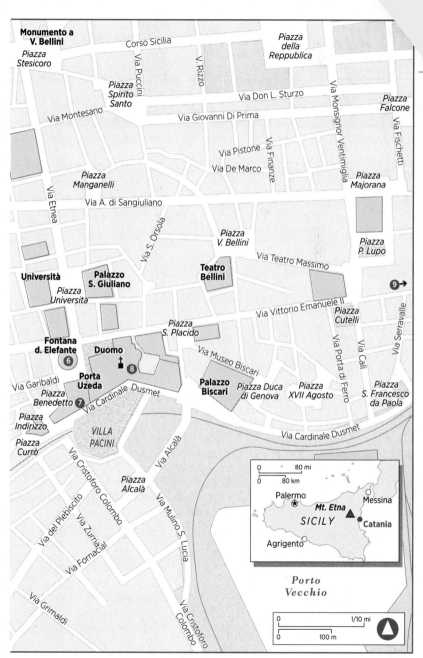

...een LUNG OF CATANIA

...y heat and conges-... ...ed **Villa Bellini ★**, ...Catania, reached ...rth along Via Etnea. Planted with such exotics as Brazilian araucarias, the park sprawls over several hills. This is one of the most attractive public parks in Sicily; the Catanians claim that the fig tree planted here is the world's largest. Unique in Italy is the floral clock and calendar on the hillside. Stand on a hill here and be rewarded with a panoramic view of Mount Etna.

The symbol of the city, the **Fontana dell'Elefante ★★**, was created in 1735. It was obviously inspired by Bellini's monument in Rome's Piazza Minerva. The elephant was hewn from black lava spewed forth by Mount Etna and stands on a Byzantine platform. The elephant is a beast of burden here, carrying on its back an Egyptian obelisk lettered with hieroglyphics celebrating the cult of Isis.

The less-imposing **Fontana dell'Amenano** lies on the south side of the piazza. Water cascades down from its top basin, evoking a sheer veil that caused the Catanians to dub it *acqua a lenzuolo,* or sheet water. On the north side of the square are the facades of **Palazzo degli Elefanti** (today the city hall) and **Palazzo Senatorio.** Palazzo degli Elefanti is usually open Monday through Friday from 8am to 7pm.

Standing beside the Duomo is the **Badia di Sant'Agata,** again dedicated to the patron saint of Catania. This is another stellar example of Vaccarini's mastery of baroque elegance. This church is one of seven in Catania dedicated to its patroness.

Lying east of Piazza Duomo is **Teatro Massimo** (or Bellini), one of the grandest and richest in Europe.

Directly uphill from Piazza Duomo lies the entrance to the **Teatro Greco Romano,** Via Vittorio Emanuele II 266, dating from 415 B.C. The Roman theater, where gladiators battled wild beasts shipped from nearby Africa, was constructed on the site of an even earlier Teatro Greco. At its apex, 7,000 spectators could view the grisly entertainment here. The marble was coated by Mount Etna's eruption in 1669. In the back of the theater is a similar but smaller **Odeon,** dating from the 2nd and 3rd centuries A.D. Concerts are sometimes staged here. The site is open daily from 9am to 1:30pm and 3 to 7pm; admission to the Odeon is 4€.

Casa di Verga (Verga's House) This is a memorial to Sicily's national poet, Giovanni Verga (1840–1922), who lived and wrote here for many years. Verga was a firebrand who wrote with poignancy about the plight of underpaid workers during the Industrial Revolution. Climb a flight of worn stairs for access to the battered, dusty, and not-particularly well-stocked museum that occupies the rooms where he completed some of his works. Despite the artist's powerful literature, you might leave with a sense of sadness that the local municipality has neglected this museum as obviously as it has. We recommend this place only for avid enthusiasts—the Bellini Museum (Museo Civico Belliniano), a few blocks away, is far more interesting.

Via Sant'Anna 8. ⓒ **095-7150598.** Admission 3€ adults, 2€ for ages 18-25, free for children 17 and younger. Tues and Thurs-Fri 9am-2pm and 3-7pm; Wed 9am-2pm and 3-5:30pm; Sat 9am-2pm. Apr-June also open Sun 9am-1pm. Bus: 1-4, 2-5, or 3-6.

Castello Ursino & Museo Civico ★ This castle, west of Piazza Duomo, was once the proud fortress of Frederick II in the 13th century. When it was originally built, the grim-looking fortress, surrounded by a moat, stood on a cliff overlooking the Ionian Sea. But Mount Etna's lava has shifted the land over the centuries. Now landlocked, Castello Ursino is reached by going through a rough neighborhood where caution is advised.

The castle was built on a square plan with a keep 30m high (98 ft.) on each corner and semicircular towers in the middle on each side. If you walk along the perimeter, you can still see the old moats and even some Renaissance windows embedded in the south side.

The castle's *pinacoteca* (portrait gallery) has an interesting (though unspectacular) series of paintings that date from the 1400s. Most of the work is from Sicily or southern Italy, including Antonello de Saliba's polyptych of the *Madonna ★*; de Saliba was a pupil of the legendary Antonello da Messina. One of the best-known Catanian artists was Michele Rapisardi, who is represented by two lovely studies: The Testa *di* Ofelia *Pazza (Head of the Crazed Ophelia)* and a **depiction of the Sicilian Vespers.** Surely the saddest *La Vedova (Grieving Widow)* in all of Catania was that depicted by another homegrown artist, Giuseppe Sciuti. The art of Lorenzo Loiacono is also worth noting for his vivid, even theatrical efforts.

Housed inside the Museo Civico are Prince Biscari's **archaeological collection**, along with objects from San Nicolò Monastery, and some of the best Sicilian painted carts on the island.

Piazza Federico di Svevia. (✆) **095-345830.** Free admission. Mon–Sat 9am–1pm and 3–7pm. Bus: 429.

Chiesa di San Nicolò All'Arena This is the largest and spookiest church in Sicily, stretching for 105m (344 ft.) with transepts measuring 42m (138 ft.). The cupola is 62m (203 ft.) high. Begun in 1687 by Giovanni Battista Contini, it was reconstructed in 1735 by Francesco Battaglia. Stefano Ittar designed the dome; the facade, with its mammoth columns, was left unfinished in 1796 but remains impressive. The interior is rather bare-bones. A beautiful 18th-century organ with 2,916 pipes is found behind the main altar. A meridian line was laid in the transept floor in 1841 to catch the sunlight precisely at noon. But because of the shifting volcanic land, today it catches the sun at 12:13pm. Sadly, the church will never be completed. Sporadic renovations try to keep it propped up, but the efforts seem doomed to failure.

The adjoining **Monastero di San Nicolò all'Arena** is the second-largest monastery in Europe, rivaled only by Mafra, outside Lisbon. This old Benedictine complex, dating from 1703, is now part of the University of Catania. Guided tours are available.

Piazza Cavour. (✆) **095-438077.** Free admission. Thurs 5–7:30pm; Sun 11am–1pm. Bus: 429 or 432.

Le Ciminiere What was once an old sulfur refinery, north of the central station, is now an eclectic Fairs and Convention (Centro Culturale e Fieristico) area exhibiting works and installations from artists from around the globe. It is the home of the **Museo Storico Sbarco in Sicilia (Museum of the Sicily Landing of 1943)**, and the **Museo del Cinema (Cinema Museum)**—and the Museo del Gioccatolo (Museum of Childhood), formerly housed at the Palazzo Bruca, will soon be finding a permanent location here as well.

Viale Africa. Museo Storico Sbarco: (✆) **095-4011929.** Admission 4€ adults, 1€ students, children 17 and under and senior citizens 60 and over. Tues–Sun 9am–12:30pm and Tues & Thurs 3–5pm. Museo del

WHERE GLADIATORS battled LIONS

Lovers of antiquity should head to the Piazza Stesicoro, Via Vittorio Emanuele 260 (© **095-7150405**), for a very evocative site, the ruins of a **Roman amphitheater** dating from the 2nd century A.D. Although the ruins lie below street level, the gladiator tunnels are still visible. This is one of the largest of all Roman amphitheaters; it is believed that some 17,000 spectators were once entertained here by blood games. Only a tiny part of the theater survives, so you'll have to use your imagination to conjure up the ancient gore. The reason? The Ostrogoths, not devotees of Roman glory, used the amphitheater as a quarry. In fact, the Goths found the Roman gladiator contests too vicious and outlawed them. They converted the stones into churches and public monuments. The site is open daily 9am to 1pm and 3 to 7pm. Admission is free.

Cinema: © **095-4011928.** Admission 4€ adults, 1€ students, children 17 and under and senior citizens 60 and over. Wed, Fri, Sat, & Sun 9am–1:30pm and Tues & Thurs 9am–5:30pm.

Museo Civico Belliniano ★★ One of the trio of nearly adjacent museums honoring local sons (Verga, Emilio Greco, and Bellini), this is the most compelling and the one that most easily evokes an emotional reaction from Catanians, many of whom view it as a national shrine. You enter a quiet courtyard off the Piazza San Francesco, and then climb to the drab, second-floor apartment where composer Vincenzo Bellini was born in 1801. Bellini is known for such titanic works as *La Straniera, Sonnambula, Norma, I Puritani,* and *I Cavalieri.*

Here you'll see original folios of his operas, his death mask, harpsichords and spinet pianos he rehearsed on as a child, and the coffin in which his body was transferred, in 1876, back to Catania from its original burial place near Paris. Signatures in the guest book read like a who's who of international musicians, ranging from Carlo Muti to Pavarotti. Many of the mementos of his life were donated by Rossini, a devoted latter-day fan of Bellini's brilliant *bel cantos.* If you're an opera fan, you will likely find this museum thrilling.

Piazza San Francesco 3. © **095-7150535.** Free admission. Tues–Thurs 9am–1pm and 3–6pm; Fri–Mon 9am–1pm. Bus: 1–4, 2–5, or 3–6.

Museo Diocesano This museum is dedicated for the most part to the cult of St. Agatha, patron saint of Catania. The museum is joined architecturally to the Duomo, its windows opening onto Piazza Duomo. Most of the artworks consist of vestments, altar furnishings, and relics from the bishops' palace. This minor museum need occupy no more than an hour of your time. The best of the treasure-trove is found in Hall II: Look for a relic arm of St. George as well as St. Cataldo's relic bust, attributable to Paolo Guarna, one of the most famous goldsmiths of Catania in the 16th century.

Via Etnea 8. © **095-281635.** www.museodiocesicatania.it. Admission 7€ adults, 3€ children 17 and under. Tues–Sun 9am–12:30pm and 4–7:30pm. Bus: 448, 449, 457, 722, or 733.

Museo Emilio Greco ★ Larger, plusher, and obviously better financed than either the Bellini or the Verga museums, this second-story museum showcases the oil paintings and engravings of Sicilian artist Emilio Greco (1913–95). Many locals are not that familiar with Greco and his abstract nude forms. He received more accolades in New York and Tokyo than in Sicily. Sure, I admire Emilio Greco, but I wonder why works by other Sicilian artists aren't also on display in this magnificent space.

Piazza San Francesco 3. ✆ **095-317654.** Free admission. Mon, Wed, and Fri–Sun 9am–1pm; Tues and Thurs 3–6pm. Bus: 31.

WALKING TOUR: HISTORIC CATANIA

START:	**Castello Ursino.**
FINISH:	**Piazza Università.**
TIME:	**4½ hours, including brief visits inside churches and monuments.**
BEST TIMES:	**Mornings before noon, when the food market is at its busiest.**
WORST TIMES:	**After dark, when the alleyways of the old town are unsafe.**

Begin your tour amid the palms and palmettos of the piazza in front of the massive and forbidding-looking:

1 Castello Ursino

Built on ancient Greek foundations, its towering, austere interior has some of the most impressive stone vaulting in Catania. The inside is devoted to a municipal museum that contains everything from archaeological remnants to 19th-century landscapes and portraits. When the *castello* (castle) was built in 1239, it directly fronted the sea although, since then, lava flows from Etna have raised the ground level to the point where it now lies some distance inland. Look for patterns of both menorahs and crosses set into the medieval masonry, a hallmark left by the masons.

After your visit, with your back to the *castello,* walk diagonally to the right, across Piazza Federico de Svevia, heading to a point immediately to the left of the iron fence that fronts the railway tracks. Pass through an alley that funnels into an unnamed triangular piazza, and from there continue onto Via Auteri. At Via Auteri 26, note the 18th-century facade of the privately owned **Palazzo Auteri.** Said to be haunted, and long ago divided into private apartments (none of which can be visited), it's just one example of the many grand buildings dotting this historic neighborhood.

From Via Auteri, turn right onto Via Zappala Gemelli, site of the beginning of Catania's:

2 Outdoor Fish, Meat, & Produce Market

I can't begin to describe the cornucopia of sights, sounds, and smells in this warren of narrow streets. Pay attention to your footing: Don't slip on the slime from fish guts or rotting vegetables.

Continue downhill, through the souk, to the bulk that rises on the right-hand side of Via Zappala Gemelli, the:

3 Chiesa Santa Maria dell'Indirizzo

Its elegant baroque facade—punctuated with a garish neon sign declaring VIVA MARIA—stands above a square (Piazza dell'Indirizzo) that rises above that part of the food market dedicated to meats. This is not a showcase church destined for the art books or tourist trade; it's the parish church of the meat- and fish-market district, with an evocatively battered interior, crumbling stucco, and scads of dusty baroque/rococo ornamentation. Opening hours are erratic, but are usually daily from 8am to noon and 3 to 6pm.

After your visit, walk to the church's southern side (the one on the left as you face it from the teeming meat market outside). Here, separated from the square by an iron fence, lies the ancient Roman ruins of the:

4 Terme dell'Indirizzo

Constructed by the ancient Romans out of black volcanic rock and terra-cotta brick, with only a few of its original vaults and arches still intact, these baths are best admired from outside the fence. Look also for a tiny domed Greek-cross building, constructed of black lava. It's virtually never open except to accommodate qualified archaeologists.

After your visit to the ruined baths, descend along basalt cobblestones in front of the Church of Santa Maria dell'Indirizzo. They lead downhill into the bowels of the rest of the food market. The largest open space in the market—a mass of parasols, blood, humanity, and grime—is the **Piazza Pardo** (also known as the Via Pardo), at the edge of which is the hard-to-see facade of a highly recommended restaurant, **Osteria Antica Marina** (p. 262).

With your back to the restaurant, turn left, noting the massive soaring archway, built of dark lava rock, on either side of which the food market teems wildly. It's the:

5 Porta Carlo V

Punctuating the entranceway to the indoor section of the city's food markets, this is one of the few structures of Catania that survived the earthquake of 1693. Pass beneath it and then turn left. After a few steps, you'll emerge into the open air again, into a neoclassical, traffic-free square filled with more food vendors selling, in this case, fish. Your map might identify it as the Piazza A. di Benedetto, but there is no sign. Most of the buildings date from the early 1600s. At the distant edge of this piazza, at the top of a short flight of stone steps, is a small stone obelisk marked FONTANA DELL'AMENANO. Built in 1867, it marks the location of a powerful underground river.

Visible at the bottom of a steep masonry-sided chasm from the obelisk's rear side is the:

6 Fontana dei 10 Canali
(Fountain of the 10 Rivers)

For years, this was the only water source in this neighborhood, and many local residents remember when a flood of water from this underground canal was diverted, thanks to conduits and channels, to an aboveground curtain of water used liberally by everyone in the food market. Today, because of urban renovations and difficulties with the plumbing, the waters remain mostly underground.

From here, walk to the top of the previously mentioned stone steps for a view over the:

7 Piazza Duomo

At the edges of this piazza sit several of the monuments that will be visited as part of this walking tour.

Walking Tour: Historic Catania

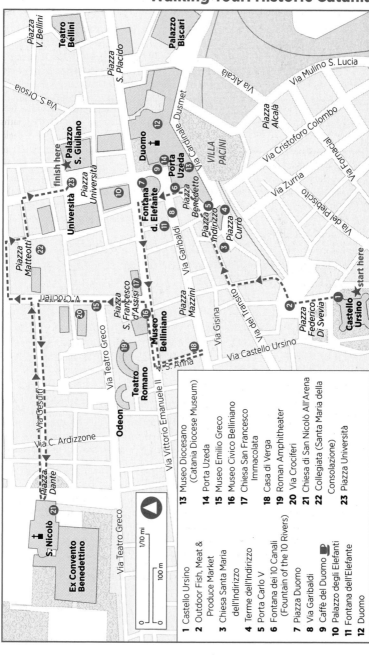

1 Castello Ursino
2 Outdoor Fish, Meat & Produce Market
3 Chiesa Santa Maria dell'Indirizzo
4 Terme dell'Indirizzo
5 Porta Carlo V
6 Fontana dei 10 Canali (Fountain of the 10 Rivers)
7 Piazza Duomo
8 Via Garibaldi
9 Caffè del Duomo 🍴
10 Palazzo degli Elefanti
11 Fontana dell'Elefante
12 Duomo

13 Museo Diocesano (Catania Diocese Museum)
14 Porta Uzeda
15 Museo Emilio Greco
16 Museo Civico Belliniano
17 Chiesa San Francesco Immacolata
18 Casa di Verga
19 Roman Amphitheater
20 Via Crociferi
21 Chiesa di San Nicolò All'Arena
22 Collegiata (Santa Maria della Consolazione)
23 Piazza Università

271

Before you start your visits of the monuments, look left (westward) along the wide, upward-sloping vista of the:

8 Via Garibaldi

At the most distant point on the street's faraway horizon, beyond the masses of people and cars, note the decorative triumphal arch that was built to celebrate the marriage, in 1768, of the Spanish king Ferdinand de Bourbon and Princess Carolina of Austria. About a century later, in 1862, it marked the processional route of Garibaldi for his triumphant entrance into Catania during the agonizing process of unifying Italy into a coherent political whole. The event marked Garibaldi's utterance, for the first time, of what eventually became a unifying political slogan, *"O Roma, o morte"* ("Give me Rome, or give me death").

9 Caffè del Duomo 🍵

Caffè del Duomo, Piazza Duomo 12 (📞 095-7150556), is the most charming of the cafes flanking the square. Built in the late 1800s, it has a marble counter, hints of the Belle Epoque, and a lavish tavola calda (buffet table of hot platters) adjacent to the bar. You can choose from at least 15 different snack items, most priced between 1.50€ and 3€. The cafe also sells some of the most artful almond candies in Catania, shaped like berries, pears, and apples. For a quick pick-me-up at the bar, do as the locals do and ask for seltzer water doctored with a tantalizing scoop of fruit-flavored *granita*. The cafe is open daily 5:30am to midnight.

After your refueling stop, walk across Piazza Duomo to the:

10 Palazzo degli Elefanti

This palace is now the Municipio, or town hall, of Catania. If it's open, walk into the building's central courtyard, where you'll see lava-rock foundations; bas-relief wall friezes dedicated to Catania's patron saint (St. Agatha); and a pair of 18th-century ceremonial coaches that are used every February to carry Catania's ecclesiastical and secular dignitaries (including the mayor) down the city thoroughfares for the Festival of St. Agatha. If the security guard allows it, proceed into the second courtyard. Here, note the wall-mounted 19th-century copy of an ancient Greek sundial. Proud Sicilians claim that the ancient Romans learned the art and science of sundials from the Greek colonists of Sicily. Regrettably, the rest of city hall is usually closed to casual visitors.

After your visit, cross the Piazza Duomo and take time to admire:

11 Fontana dell'Elefante

This fountain was created from black lava, and it is Catania's most famous monument. It stands on a Byzantine platform and carries on its back an ancient Egyptian obelisk covered with hieroglyphics. On top of that is an iron ornament that includes, among other symbols, a cross devoted to the patron saint, Agatha.

Piazza Duomo is dominated, naturally, by the:

12 Duomo

Begun by King Roger in 1070 and rebuilt by Caccarini after the earthquake, this cathedral used many ancient monuments of Catania in its construction, including stones from Roman theaters. Pause to admire its lugubrious baroque facade with its granite columns. Norman apses can be viewed from Via Vittorio Emanuele. The church was built over the ruins of a vaulted Roman bath, and inside, a Romanesque basilica lies under the Duomo's nave. The cathedral is a pantheon of some Aragonese royalty.

After you exit from the Duomo, with your back to the entrance, turn immediately left and walk a few steps to a building that functioned for many generations as a seminary for theologians and is now the:

13 Museo Diocesano (Catania Diocese Museum)

Located at Via Etnea 8, this museum gives insight into the lavish traditions associated with one of Sicily's most powerful undercurrents of religious ecstasy, the Cult of St. Agatha. Inside, you'll see photos of modern-day religious processions as well as the massive silver sledge that holds the iconic effigy of St. Agatha, which is hauled through the streets every February as part of the mystical rites associated with this powerful cult.

After your visit, with your back to the entrance of the Diocese Museum, turn left and walk a few paces to the south, passing beneath the massive ceremonial stone portal known as:

14 Porta Uzeda

Originally built by Sicily's Spanish overlords during the early 18th century, this archway contains some interesting shops selling folkloric pottery. On its opposite side is a pleasant and verdant park, **Villa Pacini,** where you can rest.

Now retrace your steps back into Piazza Duomo, walking diagonally across it toward Via Vittorio Emanuele, which flanks its northern edge. Continue westward. A point of minor interest en route is at Via Vittorio Emanuele 175, immediately adjacent to the Hotel de l'Europe. Here, note the **hidden doorway,** crafted from wood, whose panels were painstakingly designed to look like a continuation of the stone mullions of the building that contains it.

Continue west along the Via Vittorio Emanuele to Piazza San Francesco, site of three important attractions, each noted below. You'll recognize the square thanks to the contemporary-looking statue devoted to Cardinal Dusmet, a 19th-century benefactor of Catania's poor. The inscription on its base translates as "Because we have bread, we give it to the poor." The three attractions flanking the square include:

15 Museo Emilio Greco

Located at Piazza San Francesco 3, this archive-cum-museum displays the major artistic contributions of Catania citizen **Emilio Greco** (1913–95). He is most famous for his grand sculpture. For more information, see p. 268.

Accessible via the same entranceway on the western edge of the square is the more interesting:

16 Museo Civico Belliniano

The great **Vincenzo Bellini** (1801–35) was born in this house, which displays memorabilia and portraits. For details, see the review on p. 268.

Facing both of these museums at the eastern edge of Piazza San Francesco is:

17 Chiesa San Francesco Immacolata

The most interesting objects inside this church are the six massive, richly gilded candelabras (most at least 3.3m/11 ft. high and incredibly heavy), which are proudly displayed in the nave. Carved at the beginning of the 20th century, they're carried on the shoulders of the faithful during the Feast Day of St. Agatha. The largest and heaviest of them was carved in 1913, gilded in 1935, and donated to the church and to St. Agatha by the city's bakers' guild.

After your visit, continue westward along Via Vittorio Emanuele, turning left in 2 short blocks onto Via Santa Anna. On that street, you'll find the small-scale baroque facade of the tiny Chiesa Santa Anna (it's almost always closed to casual visitors) and a few buildings later, on the left, the former home of one of Sicily's most famous writers:

18 Casa di Verga

Known for his naturalistic fiction, **Giovanni Verga** (1840–1922) became one of Sicily's greatest writers. He was celebrated in his day, making friends with such greats as Emile Zola. Much of Catania turned out for his 80th birthday, where Luigi Pirandello appeared as orator. For details of the building at Via Sant'Anna 8, see the review on p. 266.

Retrace your steps to Via Vittorio Emanuele and turn right, back toward the Piazza San Francesco. En route, along that street's northern edge, see the deceptively modern-looking stone entrance to one of Catania's most cherished archaeological treasures, the:

19 Roman Amphitheater

Draped with ivy, and overlooked by a ring of 17th-century buildings and apartments, this charming theater at Via Vittorio Emanuele 260 is an ancient oasis concealed in the midst of an urban neighborhood. During classical times, it held as many as 17,000 spectators for plays and—to a lesser extent—water games, when boats would float on waters funneled in from nearby streams and aqueducts. It was also a site for gladiator contests. Ironically, part of the theater's graceful, crescent-shaped seating structure is blocked by a black-lava bridge added during the early 17th century as the base for the since-demolished Via Grotte, once a densely populated street within this residential neighborhood.

Via Grotte, most of its bridge-like foundations, and all of its buildings were demolished in the 1950s by Catania's historic buildings committee as a means of returning the ancient theater to some semblance of its original purity. Vestiges of the street remain within the circumference of the Roman theater, however, cutting surreally across one edge of the theater's sweeping, crescent-shaped bleachers.

Come with stamina, a good sense of balance, and sturdy walking shoes. Sandals are not recommended because of the steep, uneven steps, which lead visitors through ghostly tunnels that wind their way through and beneath the bleacher stands.

A smaller theater, the **Odeon,** is accessible near the back side of the Roman theater. To reach it, follow signs from the theater and walk uphill through some tunnels and steep vaulted stairs. Admission: 4€, free for children under 17 and EU, Canadian, and Australian citizens aged 65 and over.

After your visit, return to Piazza San Francesco, stand in front of its mammoth church, and turn uphill to face the lowest end of one of the most richly embellished baroque streets in Catania:

20 Via Crociferi

Above its downhill entrance is a soaring stone bridge, **L'Arco San Benedetto,** which allowed nuns, many of whom were in seclusion, to access the buildings on either side of this street during the convent's heyday (17th–19th centuries). Via Crociferi is so authentically baroque that it was filmed by Franco Zeffirelli for *Storia di una Capinera,* his cinematic tale of love during the baroque age.

In order of their appearance on this fabled but relatively short street, you'll see the following churches, convents, or monasteries: (1) **San Benedetto,** (2) **San Francesco Borgia,** (3) **San Giuliano,** and others whose facades aren't marked with name or number.

Three blocks from where you first entered Via Crociferi, turn left onto Via Gesuiti. Walk 4 blocks to reach Piazza Dante and the mammoth, never-completed:

21 Chiesa di San Nicolò All'Arena

The biggest church in Sicily was never completed, and it is almost ringed in scaffolding to keep it from falling down. Immediately adjacent is an abandoned monastery once intended as a library. Surrealistically large, this complex is Catania's symbol of the folly of large-scale projects gone awry. See p. 267.

Retrace your steps to Via Crucifero, turn left and walk about a block, and then turn right (downhill) onto Via San Giuliano. You'll be heading down the steep slope of a dormant volcanic crater associated with the geology of nearby Mount Etna. After 2 blocks, turn right onto Via Etnea and walk 2 blocks. On the right is a church with a baroque concave facade:

22 Collegiata (Santa Maria della Consolazione)

This royal chapel from 1768 is one of the masterpieces of the Catanese late baroque style, based on plans by Angelo Italia. The facade was completed by Stefano Ittar, and the vaults inside were frescoed by Giuseppe Sciuti. It's dearly beloved by many Catanians who attended religious celebrations here during their childhoods.

After your visit, continue another block south along Via Etnea to the:

23 Piazza Università

This elegant urban piazza is often the site of political demonstrations. One side is devoted to the back of the previously visited Municipio (town hall), the other side to the symbolic headquarters of the University of Catania. The university was founded in 1434, but the bulk of it lies in a modern educational complex 3km (2 miles) to the east, in the suburbs. The square was constructed at the request of the duke of Camastra. It's dominated by the **Palazzo Sangiuliano,** built in 1745, and by the main university building, **Palazzo dell'Università,** which was finished at the end of the 1700s. One of the richest libraries in Sicily is housed in the **Università degli Studi di Catania,** founded by Alphonese of Aragon in 1434.

SHOPPING

Dolci di Nonna Vincenza   Come here for marzipan and almond-based candies, made from recipes developed generations ago. You'll pay about 7€ per pound. The shop is on a quiet piazza, across from the main facade of the San Placido church. Piazza San Placido 7. ⓒ **095-7151844.** Bus: 3–6, 259, or 334.

L'Artigianato Siciliano   Chances are, during your stay in Catania you'll eventually wander beneath the Porta Uzeda, either on the above walking tour or as part of your exploration of the Piazza Duomo, which it fronts. Beneath it are vaulted spaces loaded with the fancifully hand-painted pottery skillfully made in Caltanissetta, a city in central Sicily that has churned out tons of the stuff during the past centuries. Look for gaily decorated serving dishes, candelabras painted like members of the 19th-century bourgeoisie, and all manner of art objects. Via Etnea 2 (beneath Porta Uzeda). © **095-345360.** Bus: 448, 449, 457, 722, or 733.

La Pescheria   Sicily's most colorful fish market fills the streets around the Duomo Monday to Saturday mornings, and if you have the stomach, it is worth popping along early to view the spectacle and watch the locals as they buy the wares. "If it swims we Catanians will eat it," is a phrase commonly used in the city. Vegetables and fruit stalls spill into the offshoot lanes. Behind Piazza del Duomo.

CATANIA AFTER DARK

Unlike Palermo, Catania has a really kicking nightlife, perhaps influenced by the fact that it lies closer to the mainland than the capital does, or that the university has more students. Pick up a free copy of *Lapis* (www.lapisnet.it), a bimonthly bulletin in Italian listing all that's buzzworthy in local entertainment and by night, published both in Catania and in Palermo. It is available at hotels, bars, cafes, and *tabacchi*.

Pubs and dance clubs rule the night, especially in the historical center of town. A fantastic way to start off the night and mingle with the locals is to head for an aperitivo. **Enoteca Sud Est,** at Via Di Sangiuliano 171 (© **095-7159096**), is a quaint, cozy little wine bar where hip Catanians flock to for a glass of red or white coming from the well-stocked cellar, accompanied by a platter of local delicacies. For something a bit more rambunctious, **The Stag's Head** in Via Michele Rapisardi 7–9 (no phone) is one of Catania's most jumping pubs with wall-to-wall go-getters, and no shortage of beers; even local brew (!) is on tap. If after all this hopping the night is still young, cut the rig over at **Discoteca Red Light** on Via Michele Gioia 16 (© **095-7237124**) where techno sounds and retro hits fill the dance floor quickly.

RAGUSA, SYRACUSE, & THE SOUTHEAST

The entire region of the Vale di Noto is a Unesco World Heritage site because of its monuments. The southeast is also an area known for its natural beauty: You can walk through the stunning coastal marshes of the **Vendicari** nature reserve, and laze on long sandy beaches at the **Marina di Ragusa.**

Inland, few visitors cut into the trails of central Sicily to discover the treasures this area holds, but even a short visit to the two cities of **Ragusa Superiore** and **Ragusa Ibla** and to **Noto ★★** will treat you to some of the most alluring baroque gems in all of Sicily, with Noto being arguably the most beautiful.

Southeastern Sicily is also a sightseeing mecca filled with glorious, evocative ruins. The baroque city of Noto is surrounded by Bronze Age sites, while the area's chief town is **Syracuse (Siracusa) ★★★**—one of the most important cities of the ancient world of Magna Graecia (Greater Greece). You'll find the best ruins at the **Parco Archeologico della Neapolis,** and the ruins of the Tempio di Apollo on **Ortygia Island (Isola Ortigia) ★★★** in the center of Syracuse, which should be one of the highlights of your trip to Sicily.

RAGUSA ★

267km (166 miles) SE of Palermo, 138km (86 miles) E of Agrigento, 104km (65 miles) SW of Catania, 79km (49 miles) SW of Syracuse.

Ragusa Ibla seems like a town from a fairytale, as its church domes and towers peek out among the cascade of terra-cotta roofs that spill down a hillside. One of the best-preserved old towns in Sicily, and a Unesco World Heritage Site, Ibla forms one part of the provincial capital Ragusa; the modern part, **Ragusa Superiore,** forms the other. The two are separated by a deep ravine, the Valle dei Ponti. The walk from Ragusa Superiore to a Maria delle Scale steps is a must for its vista of winding pathways ...liffs.

...orth a day of your valuable time because of its 18 Unesco-listed monu- ...g the glorious baroque church, the **Duomo di San Giorgio ★**. After ...ugh the town's steep alleys, pause at the pretty **Giardino Ibleo ★**, a small botanical garden with splendid views across the ravine, and home to three small churches.

From the twin towns, panoramas of the countryside unfold. The landscape around Ragusa is among the most memorable in Sicily, and is crisscrossed with low-lying, white, dry-stone walls, laboriously pieced together without mortar. If all this weren't enough, you can take a 25km (16-mile) drive to **Marina di Ragusa,** with its long, sandy beach. Many travelers prefer to anchor here, visiting Ragusa Ibla for the day. Marina di Ragusa is relatively modern, and its boardwalk is lined with shops, bars, and restaurants. In the summer, there's a party atmosphere when, at 10pm, the action is just getting started.

Essentials

GETTING THERE   From the east, Syracuse is often the rail gateway into Ragusa, with three **trains** (✆ **892021;** www.trenitalia.com) per day making the 2-hour journey. It's also possible to take one of three trains per day from Palermo; the 5- to 7-hour trip (with three changes) costs 14.30€ one-way—you have to change trains in Aragona, Calicat, and Gela. Ragusa also has a bus link with Syracuse. **AST buses** (✆ **0932-681818;** www.aziendasiciliatrasporti.it) runs seven times per day on the 3-hour run; the fare is 5.80€ one-way. The train and bus stations in Ragusa are at Piazza del Popolo and the adjoining Piazza Gramsci. At the time of writing, Ragusa's **airport** at Comiso was due to open in 2011.

Motorists touring southeastern Sicily who visited Noto (p. 304) can continue southwest along Route 115 to the town of Ispica, at which point the highway swings northwest toward Ragusa.

VISITOR INFORMATION   The **tourist office,** Via Capitano Bocchieri 33 (✆ **0932-221511**), is open Monday, Wednesday, and Friday 9am to 1:30pm and Tuesday and Thursday 9am to 1:30pm and 4 to 6pm.

GETTING AROUND   If you don't want to make the steep climb linking Ibla with Superiore, you can take city bus no. 3 departing from in front of the cathedral or from Piazza del Popolo. It's a hair-raising ride. The bus will let you off in Ibla at Piazza Pola or Giardini Iblei, which are most central for exploring the medieval and baroque town.

[FastFACTS] RAGUSA

Hospital   The local hospital is **Ospedale Civile,** Via da Vinci (✆ **0932-600111**).

Post Office   The main post office is at Piazza Matteotti (✆ **0932-232287**). It's open Monday to Saturday 8am to 6:30pm.

What to See & Do

If your time is limited, you can skip the upper town (Ragusa Superiore) and spend all your hours in Ragusa Ibla, as the older town holds far more intrigue. Those with more time can hike through the upper town.

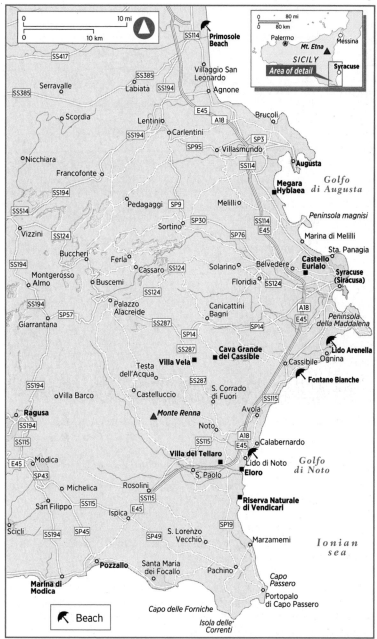

Ragusa

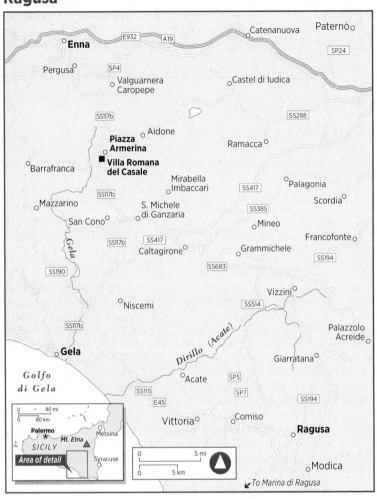

RAGUSA SUPERIORE

The long main street, **Corso Italia,** cuts through the upper town and makes for Ragusa's best promenade. The main attraction here is **Cattedrale di San Giovanni,** Via Roma 134 (✆ **0932-621658**), dating from the 18th century and dedicated to St. John the Baptist. Pause on the elegant square in front of the cathedral and look uphill to admire its decorative facade, which is made asymmetrical by a campanile on its western side. Its front elevation contains a wide terrace. The inside is ornate, especially the stucco decorations in the cupola. The Latin cross interior is notable for its two orders of pillars, each made of locally quarried asphaltite. Open daily 8:30am to noon and 4 to 7pm.

Museo Archeologico Regionale Ibleo, Palazzo Mediterraneo, Via Natalelli (📞 **0932-622963**), lies off Via Roma, within an easy walk of the Duomo, near the Ponte Nuovo bridge. The museum is rich in artifacts unearthed from ancient colonies in the province. The best of the collection is in the remnants of the civilization that flourished in Greek days at Rovine di Camarina, 16km (10 miles) northwest of Marina di Ragusa. Assaulted by the Carthaginians, the colony was finally leveled by the Romans as early as 598 b.c. Some of the artifacts at the museum in Ragusa are from a temple here once dedicated to Athena. Various necropolis reconstructions hold great interest. Hours are daily 9am to 1:30pm and 4 to 7:30pm; admission is 4€ for adults and 2€ for children aged 17 and under.

RAGUSA IBLA ★★

The most scenic way to reach the old town is by taking the long stairway, **Santa Maria delle Scale ★**, heading down from Ragusa Superiore to the historic core of Ibla. Take this walk for the **panoramic vistas ★★** alone, some of the finest in southeastern Sicily.

Head east until you come to the **Duomo di San Giorgio ★**, Piazza del Duomo (📞 **0932-220085**), which is open daily 9am to noon and 4 to 7pm. Characterized by an impressive neoclassical dome, this is one of the best examples of Sicilian Baroque in the south of Sicily, dating from the 18th century. The facade is a trio of tiers and looks like a glamorous wedding cake. In contrast, the interior may come as a disappointment, as it's quite plain.

Continuing east from the Duomo, you'll come to the **Chiesa di San Giuseppe ★**, Via Torre Nuova 19 (📞 **0932-621779**), open daily from 9am to noon and 4 to 6pm. It dates from 1590, and its oval-domed interior contains beautiful galleries and a striking pavement crafted of black asphalt interspersed with majolica tiles. Among the notable artworks is the painting *Gloria di San Giuseppe e San Benedetto (Glory of St. Benedict),* by Sebastiano Lo Monaco (1793).

If you continue walking all the way east through Ragusa Ibla, you'll reach beautiful public gardens, **Giardino Ibleo ★**, which are studded with religious buildings, notably **Chiesa di San Giacomo.** Dating from the 14th century, the church was hit by the 1693 earthquake, and much of the damage was never repaired. If it's open, you'll get to see a beautiful **triptych ★** by Pietro Novelli, depicting the Madonna flanked by St. Agatha and St. Lucy. At the edge of the gardens, enjoy the **panoramic view ★** sweeping across the Valley of Irminio. The gardens are the perfect place for a picnic and can be visited daily from 8am to 8pm; admission is free.

Where to Stay

RAGUSA SUPERIORE

Mediterraneo Palace ★ A healthy hike from the center of medieval Ragusa, this government-rated four-star hotel is a boxy concrete structure, but it's the finest lodging for miles around. It offers a high level of comfort, with attractively and comfortably furnished guest rooms. The decor is so modernized and minimalist that you could be anywhere from Nigeria to Alaska. Those who like to eat in will find decent on-site dining and drinking facilities.

Via Roma 189, 97100 Ragusa. 📞 **0932-621944.** Fax 0932-623799. www.mediterraneopalace.it. 92 units. 90 €–140€ double; 290€ suite. AE, DC, MC, V. Parking 12€. **Amenities:** Restaurant; bar; room service; smoke-free rooms. *In room:* A/C, TV, minibar, hair dryer, Wi-Fi (free).

Montreal Set in the modern part of Ragusa, a hellish climb from the medieval quarter, this completely renovated hotel is short on style but big on creature comforts. The location is 10 minutes by car from the baroque-style Ragusa Ibla, the historic center. Guest rooms are without frills but contain sturdy furniture and small tiled bathrooms. The Montreal is a favorite with businesspeople visiting Ragusa to hawk their wares.

Via San Giuseppe 8 (at Corso Italia), 97100 Ragusa. Ⓒ/fax **0932-621133.** www.montrealhotel.it. 50 units. 70€–90€ double. AE, DC, MC, V. Parking 8€. **Amenities:** Restaurant; bar; room service; smoke-free rooms. *In room:* A/C, TV, minibar, Wi-Fi.

MARINA DI RAGUSA

Eremo della Giubiliana ★★ 🏨 About .6km (¼ mile) inland from the barren highway, midway between Ragusa (7km/4 miles) and Marina di Ragusa, this stone estate is set in sun-blasted solitude against a landscape crisscrossed with low limestone walls. Maintained by local tenant farmers for at least a thousand years, the walls enclose grazing lands for cows and sheep. No other hotel I've seen in Sicily is as deceptive in the way it contrasts a baronial, severely dignified exterior with a walled-in compound of verdant greenery and lighthearted posh. Inside the compound, expect water fountains, lemon and almond trees, a kitchen garden burgeoning with life, and a truly unusual restaurant (p. 284). It's a warm, historically poignant hotel of discreet luxury and meticulous architectural detail. Guest rooms are cozy and as artfully authentic as rooms in a private home.

This is the only hotel in Sicily that maintains a private airstrip.

Contrada Giubiliana, 97100 Ragusa. Ⓒ **0932-669119.** Fax 0932-669129. www.eremodellagiubiliana.it. 11 units and 5 self-contained cottages. 149€–320€ double; 384€–920€ suite; 220€ cottage. Rates include buffet breakfast. AE, DC, MC, V. From Ragusa, take SP25 southwest toward Marina di Ragusa. Eremo is signposted at Km 7. **Amenities:** Restaurant; bar; outdoor pool, Wi-Fi (free). *In room:* A/C, TV.

Hotel Terraqua ★ This is the most appealing hotel in the seaside resort of Marina di Ragusa. Configured as a cement-and-glass cube dotted with balconies, it identifies itself mainly as a beachfront hotel with clean rooms. Don't expect any personalized service from the staff—they're familiar with hordes of vacationers coming and going. But as a base for exploration of the neighborhood, including Ragusa Ibla, the hotel is a worthwhile choice. Guest rooms have tile floors and a beachgoing simplicity. The hotel is inside its own walled garden, a 5-minute walk from the water and the beach. It also has the best and biggest pool in town.

Via delle Sirene 35, 97010 Marina di Ragusa. Ⓒ **0932-615600.** Fax 0932-615580. www.hotelterraqua. com. 77 units. 120€–160€ double; 160€–200€ junior suite. Rates include buffet breakfast. AE, DC, MC, V. Free parking. **Amenities:** Restaurant; bar; outdoor pool; tennis court; outdoor Jacuzzi; solarium; babysitting; Wi-Fi (free). *In room:* A/C, TV, minibar, hair dryer.

Where to Eat

RAGUSA SUPERIORE

Baglio La Pergola ★ SICILIAN This elegant restaurant offers the finest dining in the modern town of Ragusa. It's decorated in a style evocative of the late 19th century, with a Belle Epoque aura, marble floors, and comfortable chairs. Dishes are full of flavor and prepared with a certain flair, as exemplified by the swordfish in lemon sauce with capers and toasted pine nuts. If it's on the menu, the best tortellini in town is served here, with fresh shrimp and a saffron sauce. Other tasty dishes include *ricciola* (a local fish) cooked with a pistachio crust and fennel.

Contrada Selvaggio. ℂ **0932-686430.** www.baglio.it. Reservations recommended. Main courses 12€–18€; fixed-price menus 30€–35€. AE, MC, V. Wed–Mon noon–2:30pm and 8–11:30pm.

RAGUSA IBLA

Il Barocco SICILIAN   The name comes from the elaborate baroque-style doorway that dominates the restaurant's small, high-ceilinged dining room. In fact, you might get the impression that the restaurant is rather crammed into the anteroom of a very grand *palazzo*. Menu items are not as creative as those you will find at either of Ragusa's more prestigious eateries (Il Duomo and Locanda don Serafino), and the staff can be blasé, but food items are flavorful and filling. The best examples include lamb cutlets, crepes with ricotta and spinach, and a dessert specialty of orange mousse. The chef is also known for three of his pasta dishes—lasagna with pumpkin and ricotta; cavati with broccoli and anchovies; and tagliatelle with zucchini and sausage. *Note:* Don't confuse this restaurant with the gelateria, under the same name and management, about a block downhill.

Via Orfanotrofio 29. ℂ **0932-652397.** www.ilbarocco.it. Reservations recommended. Main courses 10€–18€. AE, DC, MC, V. Thurs–Tues 12:30–2:30pm and 7:30pm–midnight.

Il Duomo ★★★ SICILIAN   With its Michelin stars, this restaurant is one of the finest in Sicily—some say *the* best. It lies on an impossibly narrow street, uphill behind the cathedral. Inside, the small rooms are outfitted like private parlors in a 19th-century country-Victorian style, some with sweeping views over the hillsides. Come here for the intensely patriotic cuisine of Ciccio Sultano, a native *Ragusano* who commits himself to old-time traditions. Several varieties of bread are baked each day, using hard-to-find strains of wheat. At least 20 types of olive oil are on display, and staff will advise you on the best variety. Menus change with the seasons and make ample use of local products such as cherry tomatoes, pistachios, bitter almonds, wild fennel, and mint. One of the praised specialties is roasted baby pig with a chocolate sauce caramelized with Marsala wine.

Via Capitano Bocchieri 31. ℂ **0932-651265.** www.ristoranteduomo.it. Reservations recommended. Main courses 12€–25€; fixed-price menus 120€–130€. AE, DC, MC, V. Mon 7–11pm, Tues–Sat noon–2:30pm and 7–11pm. Closed Mon lunch & all day Sun.

La Bettola SICILIAN   A short walk through narrow winding streets from the town's cathedral, this restaurant shows few hints of any changes that might have been made since the days of Mussolini. That, coupled with the 1940s-era decor, provides much of its charm. Tables and chairs are arranged on a large piazza in front, amid potted flowers and ample doses of old-fashioned Italy. The chef often tells diners to leave matters in his own hands, and he'll compose a meal for you—perhaps fresh ricotta followed by a tender, herb-infused chicken breast with delectable roulades stuffed with ham and onions.

Largo Camerina 7. ℂ **0932-653377.** Reservations recommended. Main courses 10€–15€. MC, V. Mon–Sat 12:30–2:30pm and 7:30–11:30pm.

Locanda Don Serafino ★★ SICILIAN   This fine restaurant is set in a 17th-century palace in a labyrinth of intricately vaulted cellars, where the temperature remains cool in summer and comfortable even on the coldest days of winter. Any of the lavishly decorated tables presents a charming venue for lunch or dinner, but the most awe-inspiring are found in the deepest part of the labyrinth, a monastic-looking stone-sided room lined with wines selected personally by the owner. You'll enjoy dishes that may include *zuppa di pesce don Serafino* (fish soup); spaghetti with sea urchins, ricotta, and squid; fresh fish cooked to perfection, and herb-and-garlic-infused lamb cutlets. In July and August the restaurant does not serve lunch Monday to Wednesday.

Via Orfanotrofio 39. ℂ **0932-248778.** www.locandadonserafino.it. Reservations recommended. Main courses 25€–35€; fixed-price tasting menu 85 €. DC, MC, V. Wed–Mon 12:30–2:30pm and 5:30–11:30pm.

MARINA DI RAGUSA

Ristorante Don Eusebio SICILIAN   Even if an overnight stay at the Eremo della Giubiliana hotel (p. 282) isn't practical, we heartily recommend visiting for its fine cuisine and its eerily antique location. The setting, inside a walled compound that originated in the 1400s as a fortified monastery and later as a manorial home, has been meticulously restored to its full limestone glory. The restaurant serves well-prepared meals in a high-ceilinged room whose massive timbers are supported by soaring masonry arches. Lunches are relatively simple, consisting of a medley of omelets, salads, and focaccia (sandwiches stuffed with smoked fish, prosciutto, or local cheeses). Dinners are more elaborate, featuring *orecchiette* (one of their homemade pastas) with walnut sauce; roasted quail with spices; couscous; tuna carpaccio; and fresh salads usually culled from the hotel's walled-in garden. If you can, come and visit during daylight and make an effort to see the surrounding landscape.

Contrada Giubiliana. ℂ **0932-669119.** www.eremodellagiubiliana.it. Reservations recommended. Main courses 10€–20€; lunch platters 10€–15€; fixed-price tasting menu 95€. AE, DC, MC, V. Daily 1–3pm and 7:30–10pm.

Ristorante/Pizzeria La Falena 🔥 SICILIAN   Short on style but good in the kitchen, this rustic *trattoria* is known for its fresh fish, tasty pizzas, and welcoming reception. It attracts a beach-loving crowd for home-style dining, indoors or out. Quality ingredients go into the pasta with shrimp, the tortellini with ham and cream, and the savory rice dish with fresh shrimp, mussels, virgin olive oil, and garlic.

Via Porto Venere. ℂ **0932-239321.** Reservations required Sat–Sun. Main courses 10€–15€. AE, DC, MC, V. Wed–Mon 12:30–2:30pm and 7:30pm–12:30am. Closed Jan.

Ragusa after Dark

RAGUSA IBLA

Belle Epoque   Set in a tucked-away corner of the square directly in front of the cathedral, this place will welcome you for either daytime gelato or nighttime beer and cocktails. The homemade ice creams are likely to include *nocciola* (hazelnut), *pesca* (peach), and *arancia* (orange). From July to September, it's open daily 7am to 11pm or later. The rest of the year, it's closed on Monday. Via Convento, near Piazza Duomo. ℂ **0339-7528402.**

MARINA DI RAGUSA

Victoria Pub   Set directly across the street from the beach, this is the largest pub in Marina di Ragusa and one of the most whimsically decorated. The pseudo-Victorian decor includes pithy quotes from Shakespeare, expired New Jersey license plates, and banners advertising everything from Jack Daniel's to Newcastle Ale. The crowd tends to be young, on the make, and into rock 'n' roll. Open April to October, nightly 10pm to 4am; November to March, Saturday and Sunday 8pm to 4am. Lungomare Andrea Doria 20. ℂ **0339-2409247.**

SYRACUSE ★★★ & ORTYGIA ISLAND ★★★

182km (113 miles) S of Messina, 87km (54 miles) S of Catania, 330km (205 miles) SE of Palermo.

You'll be following in the illustrious footsteps of the scientist Archimedes, statesman Cicero, evangelist St. Paul, martyr St. Lucy, painter Caravaggio, and naval hero Admiral Lord Horatio Nelson, on a visit to Syracuse (Siracusa). Seeing its ruins will be one of the highlights of your trip to Sicily, because of all the Greek cities of antiquity that flourished in Sicily, Syracuse was the most important, a formidable competitor of Athens and, in its heyday, it dared take on Carthage and even Rome. What remains of the city's classical past, among some unattractive modern development, is impressive, and the still-functioning **Teatro Greco** amphitheater is where Aeschylus premiered his plays and Archimedes is said to be buried.

Much of what you'll want to see is on the miniscule island of **Ortygia** (Ortigia), accessible via the **Ponte Nuovo** ("New Bridge") built in 2004. The picturesque island is crammed with ancient monuments clustered around one of the most attractive squares in Italy, the **Piazza del Duomo,** and its beautiful **Duomo** (cathedral) is the oldest church in Europe. Where Archimedes ran through the streets shouting "Eureka!", Ortygia is a must on a trip to Sicily because of its temples, castle, palazzi, churches, and bustling market. Allow yourself at least 2 hours to explore, plus another hour to visit its labyrinthine alleys lined with crafts shops, boutiques, restaurants, bars, and cafes, which make it a lively spot during the summer. The local specialty is swordfish, freshly caught by local fishermen.

Syracuse is a cauldron in summer, when it's incredibly humid. Do as the locals do and head for the sea to the beaches at **Fontane Bianche,** about 19km (12 miles) away, and **Lido Arenella,** only 8km (5 miles) away.

Essentials

GETTING THERE　　From other major cities in Sicily, Syracuse can be reached by **train,** although many visitors find the bus (see below) faster. By train, Syracuse is 1½ hours from Catania, 2 hours from Taormina, and 5 hours from Palermo. Usually you must transfer in Catania. For information, call ✆ 892021; www.trenitalia.com. Trains arrive in Syracuse at the station on Via Francesco Crispi, centrally located between the Parco Archeologico (Archaeological Park) and Ortygia. The nearest airport is at Catania (p. 253).

From Catania, **Interbus buses** (www.etnatrasporti.it) make the 1¼-hour trip every hour to Syracuse. The one-way fare is 6€. Call ✆ 0931-66710 in Syracuse, or 095-7461333 in Catania, for schedules.

By **car** from Taormina, continue south along the A18 and then on the E45, past Catania. Allow at least 1½ hours.

VISITOR INFORMATION　　The **tourist office** is at Via San Sebastiano 43 (✆ 0931-481232), open Monday to Friday 8:30am to 1:30pm and 3:30 to 6pm, Saturday 9am to 1pm. There's another office in the historic center at Via della Maestranza 33 (✆ 0931-464255), open Monday to Thursday 8:30am to 1:45pm and 2:45 to 5:30pm, Friday 8:30am to 1:45pm.

SPECIAL EVENTS   Some of the most memorable cultural events in Sicily are staged in May and June, when actors from the Instituto Nazionale del Dramma Antico present a **cycle of classical plays** by Aeschylus, Euripides, and their contemporaries. The setting is the ancient **Teatro Greco** (Greek Theater) in the Parco Archeologico (Archaeological Park, p. 287). Tickets cost 30€ to 62€. For information, contact **INDA**, Corso Matteotti 29, 96100 Siracusa (© **0931-487200;** www.indafondazione.org).

CITY LAYOUT   The chief attraction, **Isola di Ortygia** (Ortigia island), is linked to mainland Syracuse by a bridge, **Ponte Umbertino.** The city's main street, **Corso Umberto,** runs from this bridge directly to the train station and crosses **Piazza Marconi,** a square from which most of the buses depart. Another main street is **Via Montedoro,** which runs parallel to, and to the immediate north of, Corso Umberto.

Other than Ortygia, Syracuse's grand attraction is the **Parco Archeologico della Neapolis.** To get to this garden of ruins from the heart of Syracuse, head north along **Corso Gelone.**

If you'd like to drive along the boulevard fronting the Ionian Sea, head up the **Dionisio Grande** for panoramic scenery. This route will also take you to the **Latomia dei Cappuccini,** one of the most ancient of the limestone quarries that supplied blocks of limestone for the construction of the major buildings and monuments of Syracuse.

Off Via Cavour is **Piazza del Duomo,** one of the city's most elegant squares. A 5th-century temple that the Greeks dedicated to Athena became in time a Christian cathedral, or *duomo.* From Piazza del Duomo, **Via Picherali** heads southwest to the sea and the **Fonte Aretusa (Fountain of Arethusa)** ★, a freshwater spring beloved by the ancient Greeks, who claimed that this was where the nymph Arethusa was turned into a fountain.

The oldest street in town, **Via della Maestranza,** is a sightseeing attraction in its own right. It passes the island's most aristocratic residences, mostly baroque in style. The two most interesting palaces, which can be admired from the outside, are **Palazzo Interlandi Pizzuti,** at no. 10, and **Palazzo Impellizzeri,** at no 17.

On the southernmost tip of Ortygia rises **Castello Maniace,** named in honor of George Maniakes, the Byzantine who, with aid from Norman soldiers, captured the city from the Muslims. Rebuilt by Frederick II in 1239, this castle is now a military barracks and is off-limits to the public. You can sail by the castle, however, if you take a boat tour (see "Syracuse from the Sea," below).

GETTING AROUND   Syracuse is served by a network of **buses** run by **AST** (© **840-000323;** www.aziendasicilianatrasporti.it). Buses leave from the center of Syracuse for Piazza della Posta, which lies across the bridge on Ortygia Island. The best

📷 Syracuse FROM THE SEA

I like to see this ancient city the way the Greeks first came upon it—from _____ launches operated by _____l **Selene** (© **0931-** _____ompagniadelselene.it) _____ **panoramic trip** ★★

around Porto Grande and Ortygia. It lasts an hour, and the scenes of the ancient ruins are evocative and inspiring. The most memorable boat trips occur around twilight, when the monuments are floodlit.

place to catch a bus in Syracuse proper is Piazza Marconi (also called Foro Siracusano). The most frequented routes are nos. 21 to 23, which also stop at the rail depot.

Sometimes it's better to call a **taxi** (✆ **0931-69722**). The fare from the train station to Ortygia is about 10€.

[Fast FACTS] SYRACUSE

Internet   Your best bet is **Internet Point,** Via Tunisi 36 (✆ **0931-411148**), lying on Ortygia Island. It offers 10 computers with fast connections, charging 3€ per hour. Open Monday to Saturday 10am to 9pm.

Luggage Storage   A kiosk in the train station along Via Francesco Crispi is open daily 7am to 10pm, charging 4€ per piece.

Medical   In case of medical emergency, **Guardia Medica,** Traversa Pizzuta 20 (✆ **0931-484629**), is open Monday to Friday 8pm to 8am, Saturday and Sunday 2pm to 8am. The regular hospital is the **Ospedale Umberto I,** Via Testaferrata (✆ **0931-724111**), near the end of Corso Gelone.

Pharmacy   The **Farmacia Zecchino,** Viale Zecchino 199

(✆ **0931-783384**), is open Monday to Saturday 8:30am to 1pm and 4:30 to 8pm. A list of pharmacies open at night is posted in the window.

Post Office   The post office is at Riva Posta 15 (✆ **0931-796011**), open Monday to Friday 8am to 6:30pm, Saturday 8am to 12:30pm. There is also a currency exchange here.

Seeing the Ancient Sites

Take bus no. 1 to reach these sites.

Parco Archeologico della Neapolis ★★★   Syracuse's Archaeological Park contains the town's most important Greek and Roman buildings, all on the mainland at the western edge of town to the immediate north of Stazione Centrale. The entrance to the park is down Via Augusto.

On Temenite Hill, the **Teatro Greco (Greek Theater)** ★★★, Viale Teocrito, was one of the great theaters of the classical period. Hewn from rock during the reign of Hieron I in the 5th century B.C., the ancient seats have been largely eaten away by time, but you can still stand on the remnants of the stone stage where plays by Euripedes were mounted. Today, the Italian Institute of Ancient Drama presents classical plays by Euripedes, Aeschylus, and Sophocles. In other words, the show hasn't changed much in 2,000 years.

Outside the entrance to the Greek Theater is the most famous of the ancient quarries, **Latomia del Paradiso (Paradise Quarry)** ★★, one of four or five from which stones were hauled to erect the great monuments of Syracuse in its glory days. Upon seeing the cave in the wall, Caravaggio is reputed to have dubbed it the "Ear of Dionysius" because of its unusual shape. But what an ear—it's nearly 60m (197 ft.) long. You can enter the inner chamber of the grotto, where the tearing of paper sounds like a gunshot. Although it's dismissed by some scholars as fanciful, the story goes that the despot Dionysius used to force prisoners into the "ear" at night, where he was able to hear every word they said. Nearby is the **Grotta dei Cordari (Ropemakers' cave),** where rope-makers plied their craft.

A rather evocative but gruesome site lies on the path down into the Roman amphitheater. The **Ara di Lerone,** or Altar of Heron, was once used by the Greeks for sacrifices involving hundreds of animals at once. A few pillars still stand, along with the mammoth stone base of this 3rd-century-B.C. monument. The longest altar ever built, it measured 198.4m (651 ft.).

The **Anfiteatro Romano (Roman Amphitheater)** ★ was created at the time of Augustus. It ranks among the top five amphitheaters left by the Romans in Italy. Like the Greek Theater, part of it was carved from rock. Unlike the Greek Theater with its classical plays, the Roman Amphitheater tended toward gutsier fare. Gladiators faced each other with tridents and daggers, and slaves were whipped into the center of a battle to the death between wild beasts. If a man's opponent, man or beast, didn't do him in, the crowd would often scream for the ringmaster to slit his throat. The amphitheater is near the entrance to the park, but you can also view it in its entirety from a belvedere on the road.

Via Del Teatro (off the intersection of Corso Gelone and Viale Teocrito). ℗ **0931-66206.** Admission 10€ adults; free for children 17 and under and EU, Australian, & Canadian citizens 65 and over. Apr–Oct daily 9am–5pm; Nov–Mar daily 9am–3pm.

Catacombe di San Giovanni (Catacombs of St. John) ★★ Evoking the more famous Christian burial grounds along Rome's Appian Way, the Catacombs of St. John contain some 20,000 ancient tombs, honeycombed tunnels of empty coffins that were long ago looted of their burial riches by plundering grave robbers.

In Roman times, Christians were not allowed to bury their dead within the city limits, so they went outside the boundaries of Syracuse to create burial chambers in what had been used by the Greeks as underground aqueducts. The early Christians recycled these into chapels. Some faded frescoes and symbols etched into stone slabs can still be seen. Syracuse has other subterranean burial grounds, but the Catacombs of St. John are the only ones open to the public.

You enter the "world of the dead" from the **Chiesa di San Giovanni,** now a ruin. St. Paul is said to have preached on this spot, so the early Christians venerated it as holy ground. Now overgrown, the interior of the church was abandoned in the 17th century. In its heyday, it was the cathedral of Syracuse.

The church's roots date from the 6th century, when a basilica stood here, but it was eventually destroyed by the Saracens. The Normans reconstructed it in the 12th century, but in 1693 an earthquake destroyed it. A baroque church was then built, but was left in ruins by the earthquake of 1908. All that remain are roofless Norman walls and about half of the former apse. A beautiful rose window is still visible on the facade of the Norman church.

Underneath the church is the **Cripta di San Marciano (Crypt of St. Marcian),** constructed on the spot where the martyr is alleged to have been beaten to death. His Greek-cross chamber is found 5m (16 ft.) below the ground.

Warning: Make sure that you exit well before closing. Two readers who entered the catacombs after 5pm were accidentally locked in.

Piazza San Giovanni, at end of Viale San Giovanni. No phone. Admission 6€ adults, 3€ children 15 and under. Tues–Sun 9:30am–12:30pm and 2:30–4pm. Closed Feb.

Museo Archeologico Regionale Paolo Orsi (Paolo Orsi Regional Archaeological Museum) ★★★ One of the major archaeological museums in southern Italy surveys the Greek, Roman, and early Christian epochs. Crafted from glass, steel, and Plexiglas, and designed as an ultramodern showcase for the objects

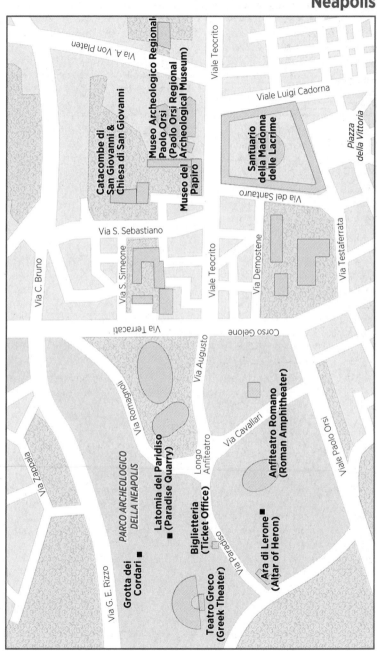

Syracuse Attractions

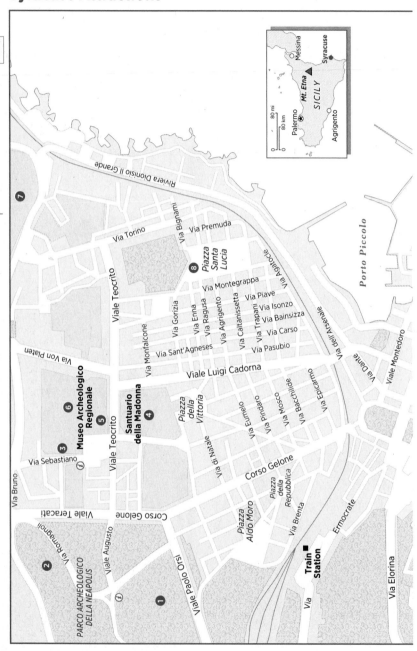

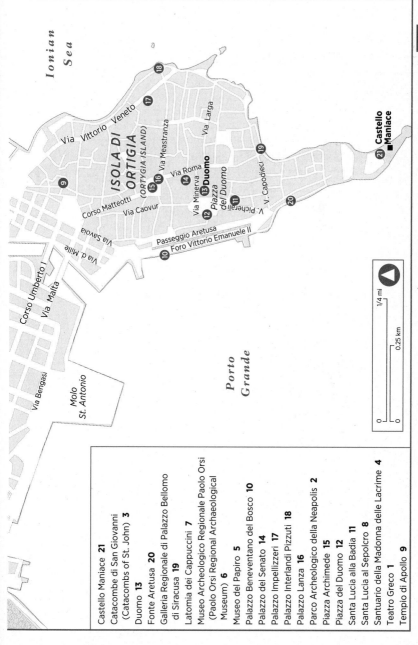

Castello Maniace **21**
Catacombe di San Giovanni
  (Catacombs of St. John) **3**
Duomo **13**
Fonte Aretusa **20**
Galleria Regionale di Palazzo Bellomo
  di Siracusa **19**
Latomia dei Cappuccini **7**
Museo Archeologico Regionale Paolo Orsi
  (Paolo Orsi Regional Archaeological
  Museum) **6**
Museo del Papiro **5**
Palazzo Beneventano del Bosco **10**
Palazzo del Senato **14**
Palazzo Impellizzeri **17**
Palazzo Interlandi Pizzuti **18**
Palazzo Lanza **16**
Parco Archeologico della Neapolis **2**
Piazza Archimede **15**
Piazza del Duomo **12**
Santa Lucia alla Badia **11**
Santa Lucia al Sepolcro **8**
Santuario della Madonna delle Lacrime **4**
Teatro Greco **1**
Tempio di Apollo **9**

unearthed from digs throughout Sicily, this is the kind of museum that reinvigorates an appreciation for archaeology. Its stunning modernity is in direct contrast to the sometimes startling portrait busts and vases unearthed from around the island. Laid out like a hexagon, the museum is set in a garden dotted with ancient sarcophagi.

Section A takes us back to before the dawn of recorded history. I'm always fascinated by the skeletons of prehistoric animals found here, including dwarf elephants. Many artifacts illustrate life in Paleolithic and Neolithic times. Look for the stunning red-burnished **Vase of Pantalica ★**.

Section B is devoted to Greek colonization. The celebrated **Landolina Venus ★★** is here, without a head but alluring nonetheless. After all these centuries, the anatomy of this timeless Venus is still in perfect shape. A Roman copy of an original by Praxiteles, the statue was found in Syracuse in 1804. When he visited the town in 1885, Guy de Maupassant fell in love with this Venus and left a vivid description of her. Although it's not the equal of the Landolina Venus, the singular limestone block of a **Mother-Goddess ★** suckling twins dates from the 6th century B.C. and was recovered from a necropolis.

Section C brings the subcolonies and Hellenistic centers of eastern Sicily alive once more. It's a hodgepodge of artifacts and fragments, including votive terra cottas, sarcophagi, and vases from Gela. Interspersed among some rather dull artifacts are stunning creations such as an enthroned male figure from the 6th century B.C., a horse and rider from the same era, a terra-cotta goddess from the late 6th century B.C., and a miniature 6th-century-B.C. altar with a relief depicting a lion attacking a bull. You can also seek out three rare wooden statues from the 7th century B.C. (found near Agrigento).

In the gardens of the Villa Landolina in Akradina, Viale Teocrito 66. (℗ **0931-464022.** Admission 8€ adults; free for children 17 and under and EU, Australian, & Canadian citizens 65 and over. Mon 3–5pm; Tues–Sat 9am–1pm and 3–5pm; Sun 9am–1pm.

Museo del Papiro (Papyrus Museum)   Located near the Paolo Orsi museum (see above), these galleries devoted to papyrus are unique in Italy. That's because Syracuse has the only climate outside the Nile Valley in which the papyrus plant can flourish. The word "paper," of course, comes from papyrus. But the plant has far more uses than making paper. Papyrus was used in the construction of lightweight boats, ropes, baskets, wigs, and fabric (papyrus sandals were all the rage in ancient Egypt). The most delicate part of the stalk might once have served as food. The most intriguing exhibit is of documents dating from the era of the pharaohs, featuring fragments from the Egyptian Book of the Dead.

Viale Teocrito 66. (℗ **0931-61616.** www.museodelpapiro.it. Free admission. Tues–Sun 9am–1:30pm.

Santa Lucia al Sepolcro   The original church here was constructed on the site where, in A.D. 304, St. Lucy (Santa Lucia) was said to have been martyred. Dating from the Byzantine period, the church was vastly altered in the 12th century and completely reconstructed in the 17th century. Beneath this sanctuary is a vast labyrinth of dank catacombs dating from the 3rd century, most of which, even today, have not been explored and are closed to the public. You can, however, visit the sanctuary. The famous Caravaggio painting depicting the burial of Santa Lucia once hung here, but is now in the Palazzo Bellomo museum (p. 294).

Indeed, there isn't much left to see of this church since all its former treasures have been hauled off. The doorway and apses are from Norman days, and a lovely rose window is from the 14th century. A granite column to the right of the presbytery marks the spot where Syracusans believe Santa Lucia suffered decapitation. Under the reign of Frederick III in the 16th century, the present ceiling was constructed with painted beams, reproducing a thick constellation of stars alternating with rose petals and small crosses.

Adjacent to the basilica and linked to it by a spooky 12th-century catacomb is a little baroque chapel containing the tomb of the martyred saint. She is long gone, however. In 1039, the Byzantine general Giorgio Maniace ordered that her corpse be sent to Constantinople. During the Crusades, the Venetians claimed the remains and shipped them back to Venice, where they remain today.

A marble statue placed under the sepulcher's altar is of particular, though morbid, fascination. From May 6 to May 8 1735, eyewitnesses reported that this statue miraculously "sweated" profusely.

The sanctuary lies at the northern end of one of the loveliest squares in Syracuse, Piazza Santa Lucia, lined on three sides by rows of trees.

Via Gignami 1. ℂ **0931-67946.** Free admission. Daily 9am–noon and 4–7pm.

Santuario della Madonna delle Lacrime The "Our Lady of Tears" sanctuary is one of the most bizarre monuments or churches in all of Sicily. Designed to evoke a gigantic teardrop, the structure was created by two Frenchmen, Michel Arnault and Pierre Parat, in 1994. It houses a statue of the Madonna that supposedly wept for 5 days in 1953. Alleged chemical tests showed that the liquid was similar to that of human tears. Pilgrims still flock here.

Although criticized by architectural purists, the contemporary conical structure dominates the skyline, rising 74m (243 ft.) with a diameter of 80m (262 ft.). The **interior ★** is amazing. You might get dizzy looking up at the vertical windows stretching skyward to the apex of the roof.

Lacrime is new, but just to the south of the sanctuary, on Piazza della Vittoria, you can stand and see the fenced-off excavations of an array of ancient Greek and Roman houses and streets.

Via Santuario 33. ℂ **0931-21446.** www.madonnadellelacrime.it. Free admission. Daily 8am–noon and 4–7pm.

ORTYGIA ISLAND ★★★

Ortygia, inhabited for many thousands of years, is also called the *Città Vecchia* (Old City). It contains the town's Duomo, many rows of houses spanning 500 years of building styles, most of the city's medieval and baroque monuments, and some of the most charming vistas in Sicily. In Greek mythology, it's said that it was ruled by Calypso, daughter of Atlas, the sea nymph who detained Ulysses (Odysseus) for 7 years. The island, reached by crossing the Ponte Nuovo, is about 1.5km (1 mile) long and half again as wide. Take bus no. 21 or 23 to get here.

Heading out on the Foro Italico, you'll come to the **Fonte Aretusa ★**, also famous in mythology. The river god Alpheius, son of Oceanus, is said to have fallen in love with the sea nymph Arethusa. The nymph turned into this spring or fountain, but Alpheius became a river and "mingled" with his love. According to legend, the spring ran red when bulls were sacrificed at Olympus.

At Piazza del Duomo, the **Duomo ★** of Syracuse, reached by heading down Via Minerva from Piazza Archimede, illustrates more than any other structure in town the changing colonizations and architectural styles that have dominated the city over the centuries. The present cathedral incorporates architectural fragments from a 5th-century-B.C. temple honoring Athena. In its heyday, this Greek temple was spoken of in revered tones by the people of the Mediterranean. From miles away, sailors could see the golden statue of Athena shining like a beacon. Twenty-six of the temple's **Doric columns** ★ are still in place. In 1693, an earthquake caused the cathedral's facade to collapse, and in the 18th century the structure was rebuilt in the baroque style.

Once inside, look in the first bay on the right for a beautiful **font** ★ fashioned from a Greek marble krater. It is held up by seven stunning 13th-century wrought-iron lions. The Duomo is also rich in statues adorning its chapels, including one honoring patron saint Lucia. Entry to the Duomo is free; it's open daily from 8am to noon and 4 to 7pm.

The irregular **Piazza del Duomo** ★ is especially majestic when the facade of the cathedral is dramatically caught by the setting sun or when floodlit at night. Acclaimed as one of the most beautiful squares in Italy, it's filled with fine baroque buildings. They include the striking **Palazzo Beneventano del Bosco,** with its lovely courtyard, and the **Palazzo del Senato,** with an inner courtyard displaying a senator's carriage from the 1700s. At the far end of the square stands another church, **Santa Lucia alla Badia.**

The other important landmark square is **Piazza Archimede,** with its baroque fountain festooned with dancing jets and sea nymphs. This square is directly northeast of Piazza del Duomo, forming the monumental heart of Ortygia. It, not the cathedral square, is the main piazza of the old city. Original Gothic windows grace the 15th-century **Palazzo Lanza** here. As you move about Ortygia, you'll find that Piazza Archimede is a fine place from which to orient yourself. Wander the narrow streets wherever your feet will take you, and when you get lost, ask for directions back to Piazza Archimede.

At Piazza Pancali on the island of Ortygia, the 6th-century B.C Greek **Tempio di Apollo** (Apollo temple) is the oldest peripteral (having a row of columns on each side) Doric temple in the world. The inscription says that the temple honors Apollo. However, after Cicero came to Syracuse, he wrote that the temple was dedicated to Artemis. Regardless, the temple faced a rocky future—it was first turned into a Byzantine church before the Saracens took over and converted it into a mosque. Later, under Norman rule, it was turned back into a church. You can see the fenced-off ruins anytime in the square across the bridge to Ortygia.

Galleria Regionale di Palazzo Bellomo di Siracusa ★★★ This elegant 13th-century palace is today home to one of the great art collections of Sicily, dating from the high Middle Ages through the 20th century. It's located next to San Benedetto (St. Benedict's) church close to Fonte Aretusa.

The palazzo is from the Swabian era and was enlarged in the 15th century by the powerful Bellomo family. The art is arranged chronologically on two floors. Much of it was rescued from deconsecrated monasteries and churches.

I like to gaze upon two exquisite masterpieces: *La Sepoltura di Santa Lucia* (*The Burial of St. Lucy* (1608) ★, by the "divine" Caravaggio, and Antonello da Messina's exquisite *Annunciazione* (*Annunciation*) (1474) ★. Caravaggio, the master of light, created a stunning canvas of grieving figures, graced with the serene expression of the martyr and the raw nudity of the gravediggers. The saint's death sleep was meant to signify her glorious rebirth in heaven. Although damaged, the *Annunciation* remains powerful in its imagery and majesty.

THE TEARS OF AN abandoned MISTRESS

One of the most evocative boat rides in and around Syracuse is along the **River Cyane,** 5km (3 miles) west of the city along Via Elorina. From May to September, a 2-hour boat trip can take you to the source of this river. Here you will see a pool that, according to legend, was formed by the tears shed by Cyane, a nymph attending her mistress, Persephone, who was abducted by Hades (Pluto in Roman mythology), leaving Cyane alone.

Along the way you'll see clusters of papyrus plants. The original plants were a gift from Ptolemy to Hieron II. The boat also goes by the meager ruins of **Olympeion,** a temple erected at the end of the 6th century.

Boat rentals cost between 8€ and 15€ per person, depending on the number of passengers. For tickets and information on departure times, call ✆ **0931-69076.** To reach the departure site, take bus no. 21, 22, or 23 from Piazza della Posta and get off at Ponte delle Fiane.

On the ground floor of the palazzo is an array of sculptures from the Middle Ages and the Renaissance, the most outstanding of which is from the Gagini school, including the tomb of Giovanni Cardinas, by Antonello Gagini, and a masterful *Madonna of the Bullfinch,* by Domenico Gagini. Look for the 17th- and 18th-century Sicilian carriages in the loggia.

The collection of Sicilian **decorative arts** ★ is full of charm and whimsy. It includes marble intarsia panels, ecclesiastical objects, 18th-century statuettes, church vestments, terra-cotta figurines, ceramics, and silver- and goldsmithery.

Note: At press time, this museum was closed for renovations. No reopening date has been announced. Before you visit, call to check on its current status.

Via Capodieci 16. ✆ **0931-69511.** Admission 8€, free for children 17 and under and EU, Australian, & Canadian citizens 65 and over. Mon–Sat 9am–6:30pm; Sun 9am–1:30pm.

Where to Stay

The best place to stay here is on Ortygia, at either the Grand Hotel or the Albergo Domus Mariae (p. 298). The island has far more character and charm than "mainland" Syracuse. On the downside, both of these hotels might be booked to capacity, especially in summer. In that case, we've included some backup choices.

EXPENSIVE

Algilà Ortygia Charme Hotel ★ 🏨   In a restored building in the historic heart of Ortygia, this stately old building opens onto panoramic views of the ancient Ortygia Sea. The last restoration saw the installation of the latest amenities, yet preserved its antique architecture. Each of the rooms is furnished differently with antiques, four-poster beds, and elegant decoration, and each contains a colorfully tiled bathroom. Rooms open onto a blissful inner courtyard. Both a Mediterranean and an international cuisine are served in the hotel restaurant, with a special menu offered to vegetarians.

Via Vittorio Veneto 93, 96100 Siracusa. ✆ **0931-465186.** Fax 0931-463889. www.algila.it. 30 units. 109€–280€ double; 230€–370€ junior suite. AE, MC, V. **Amenities:** Restaurant; room service, Wi-Fi (free). *In room:* A/C, TV.

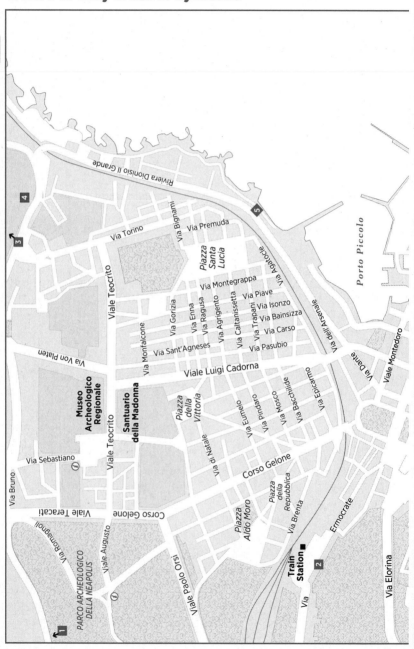

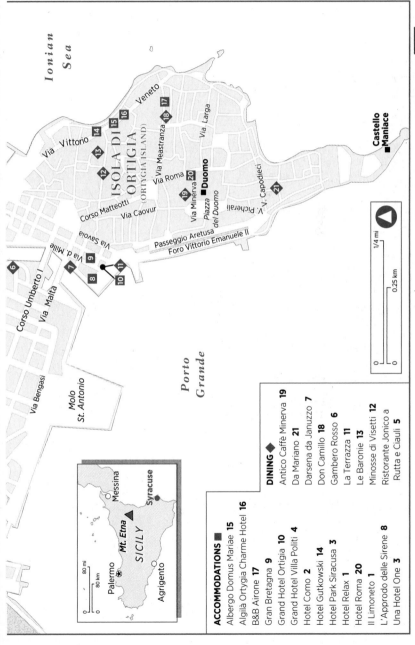

ACCOMMODATIONS ■

Albergo Domus Mariae **15**
Algilà Ortygia Charme Hotel **16**
B&B Airone **17**
Gran Bretagna **9**
Grand Hotel Ortigia **10**
Grand Hotel Villa Politi **4**
Hotel Como **2**
Hotel Gutkowski **14**
Hotel Park Siracusa **3**
Hotel Relax **1**
Hotel Roma **20**
Il Limoneto **1**
L'Approdo delle Sirene **8**
Una Hotel One **3**

DINING ◆

Antico Caffè Minerva **19**
Da Mariano **21**
Darsena da Januzzo **7**
Don Camillo **18**
Gambero Rosso **6**
La Terrazza **11**
Le Baronie **13**
Minosse di Visetti **12**
Ristorante Jonico a
Rutta e Ciauli **5**

297

Grand Hotel Ortigia ★★★   Originally built in 1905, this is the best hotel in Syracuse, with a very appealing mix of modernity and old-world charm. It's set directly on the waterfront, near Ortygia's main access bridge to the Italian "mainland," in a stately four-story building that contains lots of inlaid marble and polished Belle Epoque hardwoods. The vaulted cellar has a bar with comfortable sofas and a collection of remnants—some museum quality—unearthed from this site during long-ago excavations. Guest rooms are contemporary and comfortable, with color schemes of beige and champagne. In some of the suites, duplex setups include interior staircases of polished steel. The in-house restaurant, **La Terrazza,** is reviewed on p. 301.

Viale Mazzini 12, 96100 Siracusa. ✆ **0931-464600.** Fax 0931-464611. www.grandhotelsr.it. 58 units. 240€–250€ double; 300€–420€ suite. Rates include buffet breakfast. AE, DC, MC, V. Free parking. **Amenities:** Restaurant; 2 bars; babysitting. *In room:* A/C, TV, minibar, hair dryer, Wi-Fi.

Grand Hotel Villa Politi ★   For decades, this hotel (not to be confused with the Grand Hotel, described above) was one of the three most elegant and sought-after hotels in Sicily, rivaled only by Palermo's Villa Igiea (p. 77) and Taormina's Palazzo San Domenico (p. 206). Today, it's less prestigious, but if you know what you're getting beforehand, you'll probably be content to stay in its unusual premises. The hotel is awkwardly located in a residential neighborhood. It's situated above what was used thousands of years ago as a rock quarry, the historic Latomie dei Cappuccini. The result is bizarre, incorporating a dry, dusty garden with a deep chasm, all of it surrounded by the urban encroachments of the 21st century. Most rooms reflect the somewhat dowdy tastes of someone's Sicilian aunt: Lace curtains, high ceilings, comfy beds, and a definite sense of the south Italian bourgeoisie.

Via MP Laudien 2, 96100 Siracusa. ✆ **0931-412121.** Fax 0931-36061. www.villapoliti.com. 100 units. 210€–260€ double; 390€ suite. Rates include buffet breakfast. AE, DC, MC, V. Free parking. Bus: 1 or 4. **Amenities:** 2 restaurants; bar; outdoor pool; solarium; room service; smoke-free rooms. *In room:* A/C, TV, minibar, Wi-Fi.

Hotel Roma ★   A block from the city's magnificent cathedral, this government-rated four-star hotel opened in the much-renovated shell of a hotel that was originally built in the 1880s. The lobby's vaulted ceiling is crafted from chiseled stone blocks and ringed with Belle Epoque columns. Most of the very comfortable guest rooms have elaborate marquetry floors, original lithographs, and comfortable furniture vaguely inspired by Art Deco. About four of the rooms have computers. Overall, this is a fine hotel choice, with a location in the heart of monument-laden Ortygia Island.

Via Minerva 10, 96100 Siracusa. ✆ **0931-465626.** Fax 0931-465535. www.hotelromasiracusa.it. 45 units. 80€–210€ double; 270€ junior suite. AE, DC, MC, V. Parking 15 € per day. **Amenities:** Restaurant; bar; gym; sauna; room service. *In room:* A/C, TV, minibar, safe, Wi-Fi (in some rooms).

MODERATE

Albergo Domus Mariae ★ 🛍   This small-scale hotel originated in 1995 when a Catholic elementary school was transformed into a decent, well-managed lodging. It's owned by an order of Ursuline nuns, and although the desk staff and porters are likely to be laypersons, its manager is a hardworking, habit-clothed member of the order. This is the only hotel in Syracuse with its own chapel and a genuinely contemplative reading room. There's also a rooftop terrace for sunbathing. Rooms are fairly priced, with modern furniture and a no-nonsense approach to decor. There are no attempts to foist religious education on guests—for most purposes, this is a conventional hotel, without any evangelistic mission.

Via Vittorio Veneto 76, 96100 Siracusa. ☏ **0931-24854.** Fax 0931-24858. www.domusmariae1.it. 17 units. 140€-160€ double. Rates include buffet breakfast. AE, DC, MC, V. Free parking. **Amenities:** Restaurant; bar; solarium; room service; smoke-free rooms. *In room:* A/C, TV, minibar, hair dryer.

Gran Bretagna ★   No one knows the exact age of this three-story palazzo, but it has been restored with sensitivity with a location between two restaurant-flanked side streets lying at the north end of the old city in the heart of Ortygia. During a wholesale renovation, workers uncovered parts of the city's 16th-century fortifications in the lobby, which can be viewed through glass floor panels. In the courtyard you can also view some of the ancient wall. Bedrooms are well furnished and exceedingly spacious, with antique reproductions and in some cases 19th-century beautifully frescoed ceilings. Ask for rooms on the first floor. Some accommodations are suitable for three or four guests.

Via Savoia 21, 96100 Siracusa. ☏/fax **0931-68765.** www.hotelgranbretagna.it. 17 units. 90€-125€ double. Rates include breakfast. AE, DC, MC, V. Free parking. **Amenities:** Bar; room service, Wi-Fi. *In room:* A/C, TV, minibar, hair dryer.

Hotel Park Siracusa   The biggest hotel in Syracuse is architecturally uninspiring in its *moderno* statement, except for the private balconies, but it's still a solid, reliable choice. It offers airy, comfortably furnished guest rooms with tiled floors and mostly shower-only bathrooms. The service is good, though I found the restaurant rather mediocre. For the money, though, the place isn't a bad option.

Via Filisto 80, 96100 Siracusa. ☏ **0931-412233.** Fax 0931-38096. www.parkhotelsiracusa.it. 182 units. 120€-140€ double. AE, DC, MC, V. Free parking. **Amenities:** Restaurant; bar; outdoor pool; solarium; room service; babysitting; smoke-free rooms; Wi-Fi (2€/hr.). *In room:* A/C, TV, minibar, hair dryer, Internet.

INEXPENSIVE

B&B Airone   This converted old palazzo lies right in the historic center of Ortygia. It's the best B&B in the area, drawing young people, often backpackers, from all over the world. Furnishings are bare-bones yet comfortable, rooms are colorful, decor is vintage Sicilian, and the price is right. Only three of its units have private bathrooms, the others share a well-scrubbed hallway bathroom that's generally adequate for its purpose.

Via Maestranza 111, 96100 Siracusa. ☏/fax **0931-24781.** www.bedandbreakfastsicily.com. 6 units. 50€-70€ double with shared bathroom; 65€-80€ double with private bathroom. Rates include buffet breakfast. No credit cards. **Amenities:** Lounge. *In room:* No phone.

Hotel Como ★ 🗲 ☺   This small hotel, not far from the historic core, is one of the city's best bargains. It's located in the square at the train station and is convenient for those arriving on trains from Catania. It's little more than a utilitarian lodging, but many of the rooms are quite spacious and comfortably furnished. Since some of the units are triples, this is a favorite with families, often from other parts of Sicily. Plus, its low-slung design and sense of style set the place apart from a typically tacky train-station hotel.

Piazza Stazione 13, 96100 Siracusa. ☏ **0931-464055.** Fax 0931-464056. www.hotelcomosiracusa.com. 20 units. 70€-90€ double. Rates include buffet breakfast. AE, DC, MC, V. **Amenities:** Bar; smoke-free rooms. *In room:* A/C, TV, minibar, hair dryer, Wi-Fi (free).

Hotel Gutkowski This small hotel is a former fisherman's house on the waterfront in Ortygia and has been restored with a coastal feel and painted a fresh blue and white. Don't expect any particular luxury, as everything here is utilitarian and a bit less comfortable than rooms at the nearby Domus Mariae. Nonetheless it has a welcoming atmosphere. The only meal offered is breakfast, which is made up of organic local produce.

Lungomare Vittorini 26, 96100 Siracusa. © **0931-465861.** Fax 0931-480505. www.guthotel.it. 25 units. 90€–130€ double. Rates include buffet breakfast. AE, MC, V. Free parking. **Amenities:** Bar. *In room:* A/C, TV, Internet.

Hotel Relax ☺ This Mediterranean-style hotel lies 2km (1¼ miles) from the center in a rather tranquil residential area, so if you want to get around, you definitely need a car. On the grounds are a garden, a large pool, and solarium, making it a good choice for those who don't want to stay in the center of hot, dusty Syracuse. Guest rooms are light and airy, furnished in a minimalist yet comfortable fashion. Suites are a good buy, but there are only two and they must be reserved in advance. The restaurant serves typical but quite good Sicilian and international cuisine.

Viale Epipoli 159, 96100 Siracusa. © **0931-740122.** Fax 0931-740933. www.hotelrelax.it. 59 units. 108€ double; 145€ suite. Rates include buffet breakfast. AE, DC, MC, V. Free parking. **Amenities:** Restaurant; bar; outdoor pool; children's pool; solarium; room service; Wi-Fi (free). *In room:* A/C, TV, hair dryer.

Il Limoneto ★ ☺ This place brings you close to the heart of Sicily. The tranquil retreat of lemon groves and orchards lies 9km (5½ miles) from the center of Syracuse along SP14 Mare-Monti. You can stay at this estate and visit not only Syracuse but also Noto (p. 304) and Ragusa (p. 277) just over an hour away. Much of the food served has been grown on the grounds, and guests are invited to pick their own fruit. I enjoyed the hotel's house-party atmosphere, with guests gathering in the evening for wine and conversation. If you like the outdoors, this is the best choice in the area—you can take an aerobics class, or even archery instruction. Guest rooms are comfortably furnished in a farmhouse-rustic style. Families can opt for a room with a mezzanine, stashing the kids upstairs.

Via del Platano 3, 96100 Siracusa (Contrada Magrentino). © **0931-717352.** Fax 0931-717728. www. limoneto.it. 10 units. 95€–120€ double. Rates include continental breakfast. MC, V. Free parking. Closed Nov. Take the Palazzolo bus from Syracuse's central station. **Amenities:** Restaurant. *In room:* A/C (in some), no phone.

L'Approdo delle Sirene ✦ One of the town's best B&Bs is in an old palazzo by a canal; it's been restored and handsomely converted to receive guests. It offers excellent Sicilian hospitality with a panoramic terrace in a setting of jasmine and bougainvillea overlooking the sea. Despite the simple bright and fresh decor, there's an elegance to the comfortably furnished midsize bedrooms.

Riva Garibaldi 15, 96100 Siracusa. © **0931-24857.** Fax 0931-483765. www.apprododellesirene.com. 8 units. 100€ double; 110€–120€ triple. Rates include buffet breakfast. AE, DC, MC, V. Parking 20€. **Amenities:** Room service. *In room:* A/C, TV, minibar, hair dryer, Wi-Fi (free).

Una Hotel One ★ Previously the Bellavista, this modern design hotel lies in the commercial center, close to the archaeological zone. Guest rooms are bright white but can be small, while facilities are contemporary and design-led—some have round leather beds. The hotel has a Japanese sushi restaurant, but the treat here is the modern fitness center and spa with Turkish baths. If your room doesn't have the best view, head to the Sky roof terrace that's one of the coolest bars around.

Via Diodoro Siculo 4, 96100 Siracusa. ✆ **0931-411355.** Fax 0931-37927. www.onehotel.it. 44 units. 105€–209€ double; 341[eu–359€ suite. Rates include buffet breakfast. AE, DC, MC, V. Free parking. **Amenities:** Restaurant; bar; lounge; health club; spa with Turkish bath; room service. *In room:* A/C, TV/DVD, minibar, Wi-Fi (7€/24hr).

Where to Eat

For just a drink, snack, or coffee, nothing beats any one of the tiny little cafes along Piazza Duomo, in one of the most beautiful squares of Italy, where you can do a fair amount of people-watching. Within medieval tufa walls, the **Antico Caffè Minerva** on Via Minerva 15 (✆ **0931-22606**) a side street parallel to the Duomo, is a favorite of visitors and locals alike. It's open Thursday through Tuesday from 7am to 1am.

EXPENSIVE

La Terrazza ★ ITALIAN/SICILIAN   Set on the top floor of Ortygia's highest-rated hotel, this restaurant features a *dolce vita* ambience, formal service, and big-windowed views that sweep from the outdoor terrace way, way across Syracuse's bay. There's something festive about this place: The fine food includes starters like smoked salmon with mint sauce; jumbo shrimp with citrus sauce; and an antipasti platter containing smoked turkey. Equally alluring are the main courses, such as risotto with monkfish and saffron. The cuisine is admirably authentic and satisfying, prepared with the freshest of ingredients.

On the top floor of the Grand Hotel, Viale Mazzini 12. ✆ **0931-464600.** www.grandhotelsr.it. Reservations recommended. Main courses 10€–18€. AE, DC, MC, V. July–Aug and Jan–Feb Wed–Mon 7:30–10:30pm; Sept–Dec and Mar–June daily 12:30–2:30pm and 7:30–10:30pm.

MODERATE

Don Camillo ★★★ SEAFOOD/SICILIAN   This is one of the city's finest dining rooms, built near the historic center on the foundation of a 15th-century monastery that collapsed during an earthquake in 1693. The rather classy joint is full of atmosphere, with vaulted ceilings and potted plants. The cuisine is among the most creative in town, featuring lighter versions of time-tested Sicilian recipes. If you're a devotee of sea urchins (and not everyone is), the delectable morsels are particularly fresh-tasting here, especially when served with shrimp-studded spaghetti. All kinds of fish are served, and the catch of the day can be prepared almost any way you like. Another specialty is grilled tuna steak with pepper jam. More than 450 different wines are on offer.

Via Maestranza 96. ✆ **0931-67133.** www.ristorantedoncamillosiracusa.it Reservations recommended. Main courses 15€–20€. AE, DC, MC, V. Mon–Sat 12:30–2:30pm and 7:30–10:30pm. Closed Nov.

Gambero Rosso SICILIAN/SEAFOOD   This large restaurant is housed in an old tavern near the bridge to the Città Vecchia. The dining room extends onto a terrace facing the port. Two reliable choices are *zuppa di pesce* (fish soup) and *zuppa di cozze* (fresh mussels in a tasty marinade). The meat dishes feature a number of choices from the kitchens of Lazio, Tuscany, and Emilia-Romagna.

Via Eritrea 2. ✆ **0931-68546.** Reservations recommended. Main courses 8€–20€. AE, MC, V. Fri–Wed 11am–3pm and 7:30pm–midnight.

Minosse di Visetti ★ 🎁 This well-run restaurant is more formal and a lot more sedate than many of its competitors on Ortygia Island. It's set on an obscure alley in the heart of town, occupying a trio of paneled dining rooms. The restaurant entered the annals of local history in 1993, when it was selected as the dinner venue for the Pope on the occasion of his inauguration of the Our Lady of Tears sanctuary (p. 293). The chef wins praise for his fresh mussels with cherry tomatoes. The spaghetti with seafood is marked by intense, refined flavors, and the fish soup is one of the best in town. One final and most recommended specialty is baked swordfish and shrimp pie.

Via Vincenzo Mirabella 6. 📞 **0931-66366.** Main courses 9€–17€. MC, V. Tues–Sun noon–3pm and 7–11pm. Take any minibus leaving Piazza delle Poste and get off at Via Mirabella.

Ristorante Jonico-a Rutta e Ciauli ★★ SICILIAN This is one of the best restaurants in the area for typical Sicilian cuisine and wines. It's right on the sea, not far from Piazzale dei Cappuccini. The decor is pure Liberty (Art Nouveau) style. The antipasti array is dazzling, and the homemade pastas are superb—try *pasta rusticana,* with cheese, ham, and herbs. Swordfish appears here in roulades with raisins, pine nuts, and breadcrumbs. The dessert specialty is *cassatine Siciliane* (mocha-chocolate ice cream capped with sprinkles of coffee-flavored chocolate, all floating in a lake of English custard). A roof garden has a pizzeria serving typical Sicilian pizza.

Riviera Dionisio il Grande 194. 📞 **0931-65540.** Reservations recommended. Main courses 7€–12€; pizzas 5€–8€. AE, MC, V. Wed–Mon noon–3pm and 8–10:30pm. Closed Tues.

INEXPENSIVE

Da Mariano SICILIAN Set on a cobble-covered alley, much too narrow for a car, downhill from the Museo Bellomo, this hideaway has simple plastic tables and chairs, red-checkered tablecloths, and a good reputation. It is set in a cave-like warren of vaulted rooms that you'll find either charmingly intimate or impossibly claustrophobic. The chef's use of fresh ingredients is a compelling reason to dine here. We sampled a delightful homemade *cavatelli* (shell-like pasta) with wild boar sauce. Many dishes, such as baked rabbit, Sicilian tripe, and perfectly sautéed calves' liver, are full of good old country flavor. The grilled swordfish is immensely tasty, as is farfalle pasta with braised radicchio. Other menu items include spaghetti with pumpkin flowers, *cavatelli* with pork sauce, and grilled shrimp and calamari.

Vicolo Zuccolà 9. 📞 **0931-67444.** www.osteriadamariano.it. Reservations recommended. Main courses 11€–18€. MC, V. Wed–Mon 1–3pm and 8–11:30pm. Closed 3 weeks in July.

Darsena da Januzzo SICILIAN Well located, almost immediately adjacent to the older of the two bridges leading from the Sicilian "mainland" to Ortygia Island, this stylish enclave overlooks the artfully ratty harbor-front life that gives Ortygia such color. A veranda overlooks the Ionian Sea. I've enjoyed some good meals here, but be warned: This is not the friendliest oasis in town. Only time-tested local recipes are served: One specialty is a savory fish soup; another is spaghetti with a mass of little sea urchins. *Conchigliette al ragù di pesce* (minced fish in a rich tomato sauce) is another well-prepared dish.

Riva Garibaldi 8. 📞 **0931-66104.** www.ristorantedarsena.eu. Reservations recommended. Main courses 10€–20€. AE, DC, MC, V. Thurs–Tues noon–3pm and 7:15–11pm.

Le Baronie ★ 🎁 SICILIAN Longtime friends of mine living in Syr
me on to this delightful trattoria in an old Sicilian villa. Laid out like
set in a garden dotted with ancient sarcophagi and offers both patio
dining. The restaurant serves traditional island cuisine, but adds many crea
touches. The result is highly personal, inventive food. Try the homemade pasta with
a savory tomato sauce and shrimp. One of my other favorite pastas—and it's a
delight—is *pasta alla Siracusana* (with capers, anchovies, and olives). A standard
favorite is grilled swordfish or else grilled steak with a fresh salad. The chefs take
justifiable pride in their gnocchi sautéed with shrimp and cherry tomatoes.
Via Gargallo 24. ℭ **0931-68884.** Reservations recommended. Main courses 8€–15€. MC, V. Tues–Sun
noon–3pm and 7:30pm–midnight.

Shopping

Galleria Bellomo ★ Located across the narrow medieval street from the Museo
Bellomo, this is an art gallery with a twist: It sells colorful still lifes and landscapes
painted on papyrus that's manufactured on the premises. Part of the charm of this
place involves a free demonstration of how this waterlogged reed is soaked, pressed,
and layered between linen sheets to painstakingly produce the substance upon
which the day-to-day business of ancient Egypt was conducted. Via Capodieci 15.
ℭ **0931-61340.** www.bellomogallery.com. Bus: 21 or 22.

Syracuse after Dark

Much of the nightlife in summer takes place in satellite villages, particularly along
the coast. Unless specifically stated, hours can be irregular; check before heading to
one of the hotspots, especially those out of town.

In Syracuse itself, you can visit **La Nottola,** Via Gargallo 61 (ℭ **0931-60009;**
www.lanottolaricevimenti.it), on a small street near Via Maestranza. This stylish jazz
club/piano bar/disco attracts a well-dressed younger crowd.

Syracuse has a number of worthy bars and cafes, including **Bar Bonomo,** Corso
Gelone 48 (ℭ **0931-67845**), which is more of a bar/bakery. Its gelato is some of the
best in town. The spacious **Bar del Ponte,** Piazza Pancali (ℭ **0931-64312**), is near
Syracuse's most famous fountain and serves all kinds of drinks, snacks, and excellent
gelato. Tables overflow onto the square in fair weather. Also in the vicinity of the fountain
is the fashionable bar **Lungo la Notte,** Lungomare Alfeo 22 (ℭ **0931-64200**), open
only at night. The panoramic setting overlooking the harbor attracts a young clientele.

FARTHER AFIELD

Castello Eurialo ★ This boat-shaped structure is one of the most formidable
Greek fortresses to have survived from ancient times, set 9km (5½ miles) northwest of
Syracuse along Via Epipoli, in the Belvedere district. The castle was adapted and forti-
fied by Archimedes, the famous mathematician who was born in Syracuse in 287 B.C.

The castle was believed impregnable, but such was not the case. The Romans
conquered it without a struggle. The approach road crosses the **Mura Dionigiane
(Wall of Dionysius),** which once stretched for 27km (17 miles) across the Epipo-
lae high plateau, enclosing the northern tier of Syracuse. Two parallel walls were

ɔuilt of limestone blocks, the center filled with rubble. The walls, started by Diony-sius the Elder in 401 B.C. after the Athenian siege, were finished in 385 B.C.

As you survey the ruins, know that they are the most complete of any Greek military work extant. Three ditches precede the west front of the fortress. The main castle consisted of a keep, barracks, and cisterns. A warren of underground passages was cut through the fortress. From the castle precincts, you can enjoy a **panoramic view ★** back to Syracuse.

Take bus no. 11, 25, or 26 from the Archaeological Park to reach the site, which is open daily 9am to sunset. Admission is 4€ for adults and free for children 17 and under and over 65s. For information, call ℂ **0931-711773.**

Megara Hyblaea   If you don't suffocate passing through the industrial horror, *Zona industriale,* with its polluting oil refineries, you'll reach ancient Megara Hyblaea, near the major port of Prilo along the coast of southeastern Sicily, 16km (10 miles) to the north of Syracuse and reached along the SS114. The Greeks built the city to open onto the Gulf of Augusta, whose shoreline now contains the largest concentration of chemical plants in Europe. Pollution has killed nearly all marine life in the bay, and the air in this area is contaminated.

The Megarians, arriving in ships from Greece, founded Megara Hyblaea in the 8th century B.C., making it one of the oldest of all Greek settlements in Sicily. It was leveled by the tyrant Gelon in 483 B.C. By 340 B.C., Timoleon had founded a second city, but it, too, fell to conquerors, this time the Romans in 214 B.C. Serious excava-tions of the site began in 1949 and continue to this day.

Outside the old town walls are the remains of a necropolis. After a look, you can walk into the heart of the ruins, exploring foundations of buildings from both the Archaic period (indicated by red iron posts) and the Hellenistic era (green posts). Of particular interest is a Hellenistic house from the 4th century B.C. (the entry is marked by iron steps). Open Monday to Saturday 9am to 2pm and Sunday 9am to 1pm. Admission is free.

To the left of the old agora, or marketplace, are the ruins of Hellenistic baths, with a boiler still discernible in the rubble. Nearby is a small Doric temple in bad shape, which dates from the 4th century B.C. You can also view the Hellenistic west gate with its two square towers.

Although Megara Hyblaea is the finest and most complete model of an Archaic city still extant, all the valuable artifacts dug up here have been transferred to the Museo Archeologico Regionale Paolo Orsi (p. 288).

NOTO ★★

31km (19 miles) SW of Syracuse, 55km (34 miles) E of Ragusa.

The rich-looking, honey-colored buildings along Noto's **Corso Vittorio Emanuele** are some of the most captivating on the island, and the little town has been dubbed the 'Stone Garden' because of its sheer beauty. Justifiably the most popular day trip from Syracuse and a Unesco World Heritage site, Noto is a wonderful example of baroque town planning, since its palazzi, civic buildings, and churches were constructed after a devastating earthquake that hit the region in 1693. Its layout reflects the balance of power between the Roman Catholic Church, the state, and landowning nobles, and its curvilinear buildings sport wrought-iron balconies and breathtaking stone carvings. In the 17th century the town was wealthy, but its rich nobles only provided their eldest sons and daughters with inheritances and dowries, so they built numerous churches with accompanying convents and monasteries to house their remaining offspring. The result is a collection of architectural gems with windows shielded by billowing metal lattice work through which cloistered inhabitants could observe daily life while preserving their decorum. Chief among the fabulous churches is the **Duomo** (cathedral), which collapsed in 1996, but has been restored to its former glory.

Noto is set amid olive groves and almond trees on a plateau overlooking the Asinaro Valley, making for fabulous views. The town is even more magical at night, with all the buildings lit up—you may want to stay for dinner and then stroll around, or even stay overnight. The best times to visit are in May, during the Infiorata flower festival when the streets are transformed by carpets of floral designs, or in February when locals honor the town's patron saint, San Corrado, on the 19th with an exuberant procession.

Essentials

GETTING THERE

Noto is reached by **trains** (usually nine per day) heading southwest from Syracuse, which has good rail connections with the rest of Italy. The ride takes 30 minutes and costs 3.25€ one-way. The train station is on Via Principe di Piemonte, a 20-minute walk west of the historic core. For schedules, call ✆ **892021,** www.trenitalia.com. **Interbus** (✆ **0931-66710**) offers 13 buses per day from Syracuse; the trip takes 50 minutes and costs 4€ one-way. The bus station is on Piazzale Marconi, near Giardini Pubblici just east of the center, a 5-minute walk to Porta Reale and the main street, Corso Vittorio Emanuele. If you're **driving,** head southwest along Route 115.

VISITOR INFORMATION

To get your bearings, stop first at the **tourist office,** at Via Gioberti 13 (✆ **0931-836503**); it's open from May to September, daily 9am to 1pm and 3:30 to 6:30pm; October to March, Monday to Friday 8am to 2pm and 3:30 to 6:30pm.

What to See & Do

The main thoroughfare, **Corso Vittorio Emanuele,** cuts through a trio of squares, each with its own church. The main axis begins at **Porta Reale,** a giant gateway to Noto patterned on a Roman-style triumphal arch, except this one dates from the 19th century rather than ancient times. The three squares are Piazza Immacolata, Piazza Municipio, and Piazza XVI Maggio.

If it's a hot day, you can rest in the **Giardini Pubblici,** immediately to the right of Porta Reale opening onto Viale Marconi. These public gardens are filled with palm trees and flowering bougainvillea. Don't bother trying to figure out all those local figures honored by marble busts. Even most of the people of Noto today have forgotten these men of dubious achievement.

Heading west on Corso Vittorio Emanuele, you'll first approach **Piazza Immacolata.** The square is dominated by the handsome facade of **Chiesa di San Francesco all'Immacolata** (✆ **0931-573192**), which contains notable artworks rescued from a Franciscan church in the old town. The major work of art here is a painted wooden *Madonna and Child* from 1564, believed to be the work of Antonio Monachello. The most impressive aspect of this church is its grandiose flight of steps. Open daily from 8:30am to noon and 4 to 7:30pm.

Immediately to the right of the church as you face it is the **Monastereo del Santissimo Salvatore,** which can be admired from the outside. The building is characterized by windows adorned with "potbellied" wrought-iron balconies. The elegant tower is the hallmark of the fine 18th-century facade.

The next square is **Piazza Municipio ★**, the most majestic of the trio. It's dominated by the **Palazzo Ducezio,** a graceful town hall with curvilinear elements enclosed by a classical portico. The upper section of this palace was added as late as the 1950s. Its most beautiful room is the Louis XI–style **Salone di Rappresen- tanza (Hall of Representation),** decorated with gold and stucco. On the vault is a Mazza fresco representing the mythological figure of Ducezio founding Neas (the ancient name of Noto). The custodian will usually allow you a look around on the ground level during regular business hours; admission is free.

On one side of the square, a broad flight of steps leads to the **Duomo,** flanked by two lovely horseshoe-shaped hedges. The cathedral was inspired by models of Borromini's churches in Rome and was completed in 1776. In 1996, the dome collapsed, destroying a large section of the nave, and it's still under repair.

On the far side of the cathedral is the **Palazzo Villadorata,** graced with a classic facade. Its six extravagant **balconies ★★** are supported by sculpted buttresses of galloping horses, griffins, and grotesque bald and bearded figures with chubby-cheeked cherubs at their bellies. The palazzo is divided into 90 rooms, the most beautiful being the **Salone Giallo (Yellow Hall),** the **Salone Verde (Green Hall),** and the **Salone Rosso (Red Hall),** with their precious frescoed domes from the 18th century. The charming **Salone delle Feste (Feasts Hall)** is domi- nated by a fresco representing mythological scenes. In one of its aisles, the palazzo contains a *pinacoteca* **(picture gallery)** with antique manuscripts, rare books, and portraits of noble families. The building is under renovation and its status can change suddenly; check with the visitor center before heading here, or call ℂ **0931-573779** for up-to-date information.

The final main square is **Piazza XVI Maggio,** dominated by the convex facade of **Chiesa di San Domenico ★**, with two tiers of columns separated by a high cornice. The interior is filled with polychrome marble altars, but the church appears to have been shut indefinitely as it's in really bad shape. At least you can admire its facade. Directly in front of the church is a public garden, the **Villetta d'Ercole,** named for its 18th-century fountain honoring Hercules.

Right off Corso Vittorio Emanuele is one of Noto's most fascinating streets, **Via Nicolaci ★**, lined with magnificent baroque buildings.

In summer, Noto is also known for some fine **beaches** nearby; the best are 6km (3¾ miles) away at **Noto Marina.** You can catch a bus at the Giardini Pubblici in Noto; the one-way fare is 3€. Call ℂ **0931-836123** for schedules.

Where to Stay

Camere Belvedere   Set at the highest elevation of the historic district, this elegant stone structure opens onto the "balcony of the city," a short walk from the crumbling Duomo. From its terrace, you're treated to a panoramic view of the baroque city, and on a clear day, you can see all the way to the seashore at Noto Marina and up to Por- topalo, the extreme southeastern tip of the island. Constructed of ancient stones from other buildings, the belvedere is traditional all the way. Its guest rooms are sparsely furnished yet comfortable, resting for the most part under wood-beamed ceilings. Even though it's in the middle of a town, there is a rustic aura to this place.

Piazza Perelli Cippo 1, 96017 Noto. 🕾/fax **0931-573820.** 4 units. 55€–65€ double. Rates include continental breakfast. No credit cards. Free street parking. **Amenities:** Bar; breakfast room; solarium. *In room:* A/C, minibar.

La Sumalia Residence 🕮 This ancient mansion, a real discovery, lies in the hills less than 1km (½ mile) from the center of Noto. From its perch, a panoramic view of the Gulf of Noto and the town unfolds. The property, which dominates a valley planted with almond and olive trees, has been restored and renovated with a number of its original architectural features intact. The small guest rooms have wood-beamed ceilings; rustic, comfortable furnishings; and small, shower-only bathrooms. Guests can take breakfast on the terrace and use the communal kitchen.

Contrada San Giovanni, 96017 Noto. 🕾/fax **0931-894292.** www.lasumasumalia.com. 5 units. 60€–80€ double. Rates include continental breakfast. AE, DC, MC, V. Buses depart from Piazza Marconi in Noto for Contrada San Giovanni. Free parking. **Amenities:** Bar; Internet. *In room:* A/C, TV, no phone.

Villa Canisello ★ 🕮 Surrounded by lush vegetation, this offbeat discovery offers the chance to stay in a restored 19th-century farmhouse just a 10-minute walk from the historic core of Noto. You'll enter a world of peace and tranquility here. The property has been restored with sensitivity, and with tasteful decor throughout. The lounge in the garden can be used as a reading room, and the public rooms display local crafts. Guest rooms are small but beautifully kept, each with a private entrance and a small, shower-only bathroom.

Via Pavese 1, 96017 Noto. 🕾 **0931-835793.** Fax 0931-837700. www.villacanisello.it. 7 units. 75€–80€ double. Rates include buffet breakfast. No credit cards. Free parking. **Amenities:** Bar; breakfast room. *In room:* A/C in some, TV, fridge, no phone.

Villa Favorita/Villa Giulia ★★ 🕮 These two 18th-century residences have been beautifully restored and filled with modern comforts. Located between Noto and Noto Marina (the beach area), they provide the best-equipped lodgings in the area. Under the same management, and very similar in style, they actually lie 10km (6¼ miles) apart, but on the same road. Palm trees grace the grounds, and the look is one of elegance and serenity. Guest rooms are comfortably though somewhat austerely furnished. The dining rooms are handsomely appointed, and the cuisine of regional and international dishes is some of the best in the area.

Contrada Falconara, 96017 Noto. 🕾 **0931-820219.** Fax 0931-820220. www.villafavoritanoto.it. 73 units. 110€–180€ double. Rates include buffet breakfast. AE, DC, MC, V. Free parking. From May–Sept, a bus leaves Piazza Marconi in Noto and heads for Marina di Noto, stopping at both hotels. Free parking. **Amenities:** Restaurant; bar; outdoor pool; room service; Internet. *In room:* A/C, TV, fridge.

Villa Mediterranea ★ This is your best bet if you'd prefer to visit historic Noto on a day trip but stay on the best beach while in the area. This cozy hotel is set right along the seafront, in its own gardens with a small pool. The beach is accessible through a private gate. The public lounges are stylishly furnished. Guest rooms contain comfortable beds, tiled floors, and tidy shower-only bathrooms. In the tradition of beach hotels, there is no attempt to overdecorate here.

Viale Lido, 96017 Noto Marina. ©/fax **0931-812330.** www.villamediterranea.it. 15 units. 80€–150€ double. Rates include buffet breakfast. AE, DC, MC, V. Free parking. Closed Nov–Mar. **Amenities:** Bar; outdoor pool. *In room:* A/C, TV, minibar, hair dryer.

Where to Eat

Al Buco ★ SICILIAN   This restaurant is easy to reach, positioned only a few steps downhill from the town's main thoroughfare, Corso Vittorio Emanuele. Descend a flight of modern marble steps into a simply furnished interior that's kept cool by thick masonry walls and a location that's partially below the street's grade. The deep-fried zucchini blossoms here are the best I've ever had. Fresh grilled tuna is a delight in its simplicity. Japan meets Sicily in the raw swordfish marinated in citrus sauce. Meat-eaters don't get the same loving care fish devotees do, although steaks are good and served in pepper cream sauce.

Via Giuseppe Zanardelli 17. © **0931-838142.** Reservations recommended. Main courses 8€–14€. MC, V. Sun–Fri noon–3:30pm and 7pm–midnight.

Noto after Dark

Café Sicilia   Small-scale, cozy, and prefaced with outdoor chairs and tables, this is Noto's most enduring cafe/bar. Part of its allure comes from architectural adornments in place since 1892. Its clientele seems reluctant to take coffee or drinks anywhere else. The absolutely luscious pastries include a bomb-shaped *savarin al Marsala.* Jars of Sicilian honey and liqueurs are available for sale. Corso Vittorio Emanuele 125. © **0931-835013.**

La Fontana Vecchia   Set at the monumental end of Noto's main walkway, this popular and well-positioned bar has a huge terrace and a reputation for being mobbed most evenings after sunset. Established in 1996, but with a turn-of-the-20th-century design that might make you think it's much older, it has a helpful and good-looking staff, a wide selection of cocktails, and *granite* that taste fantastic when a scoop is dissolved in soda water. Open April to September, daily 7am to midnight, and October to March, daily 7am to 10pm. Corso Vittorio Emanuele 150. © **0931-839412.**

💬 THE SWEETEST tooth IN ALL OF SICILY

The denizens of Noto are said to love sugary concoctions and confections more so than people anywhere else in Sicily. To satisfy that need they are celebrated for their marzipan and often for their ice creams. The town's leading pastry shop is the named **Mandorio in Fiore ★★**, or "almond in bloom." It stands at Via Ducezio 2 (© **0931-836615**), close to the Church of Saint Carmine. Dozens of cakes are on sale, along with sweet cookies and a huge array of candied fruits. Locals flock here for the famous Sicilian *cassata,* among the best we've had on the island. Another delight is the **Pasticceria La Fontana Vecchia,** Corso Vittorio Emanuele 150 (© **0931-839412**), whose specialty is *panedi spagna* or sponge cake. It's filled with a sweet ricotta, and the ice cream here pleases the most demanding gelato aficionados.

Side Trip from Noto

RISERVA NATURALE DI VENDICARI ★★   Created as a government-protected nature reserve in 1984, this stretch of coast south of the Tellaro River is one of the most beautiful spots in southeastern Sicily. Open daily 9am to dusk, with free entry, it covers 574 hectares (1,418 acres) of lovely marshland that is an oasis for migratory birds and serious birders. Guides are available at the **office** (*©* **0931-67450;** www.oasivendicari.net) at the park entrance.

What you see depends on the season. In winter, all sorts of ducks can be spotted, ranging from the mallard to the red-crested pochard. In fall, you'll see the white egret, black stork, and even European flamingo. Most birds only check in and then fly away to other climes, with the exception of the black-winged stilt, the Kentish plover, and the reed warbler, which all breed here.

The reserve is always open, but it's best to go in the early morning or closer to twilight; don't forget binoculars. To get here from Noto, drive southeast to the coast. Then take the road south—signposted PACHINO—until you come to the marked entrance to the reserve.

If you first visited Eloro, continue driving south for 5km (3 miles), where you'll see the **Torre Vendicari,** an abandoned Norman tower. This artifact from Sicily's conquerors of yesterday overlooks a beautiful crescent of golden sand near old salt pans. It's a great place to log some time on the beach.

Motorists with the time can continue all the way to the extreme southeastern tip of Sicily. You'll pass first through the pleasant town of Pachino before reaching the cape, which lies 7km (4 miles) south of Pachino. A major tuna fishing ground, the **Capo Passero** rewards visitors with a **panoramic view** ★★ out to sea.

THE SOUTHERN COAST

13

The southern coast of Sicily has some fabulous sandy beaches, but its crowning glory is the spectacular ruins at the **Valley of the Temples ★★★** in Agrigento, where you'll find one of the most memorable sites of the ancient world made up of eight temples. Take half a day to visit this World Heritage Site.

After all that sightseeing, drive 7km (4½ miles south) and hop on the ferry to the remote Pelagie Islands, known for their unspoiled nature and exotic marine life. **Lampedusa ★★** is the main island, and although part of Sicily, it is actually part of the African continent and has the feel of a North African land. Here, you can relax and dive in some of the best waters of the Mediterranean.

AGRIGENTO/VALLEY OF THE TEMPLES ★★★

129km (80 miles) S of Palermo, 175km (109 miles) SE of Trapani, 217km (135 miles) W of Syracuse.

The reason to visit Agrigento is to see the magnificent **Valle dei Templi** (Valley of the Temples) and its ancient Greek ruins. Although much of the archaeological site consists of rubble, the **Tempio della Concordia** (Temple of Concord), is one of the best-preserved Greek temples in the world, and to see its impressive structure with its towering columns alone makes a trip to the city worthwhile. A visit to the **Museo Regionale Archeologico** (Regional Archaeological Museum) is a must, as it's one of the best museums in Sicily, and—unlike many museums on the island—there's information in English accompanying its numerous exhibits, the most notable being a fabulous stone **statue of Telemon,** or Atlas, measuring 7.65m (25 ft. high).

Visitors usually bypass the city itself, heading straight down to the temples. Yet Agrigento merits a stroll around the historic center to enjoy people-watching at a cafe along Via Atenea or take in the stunning views

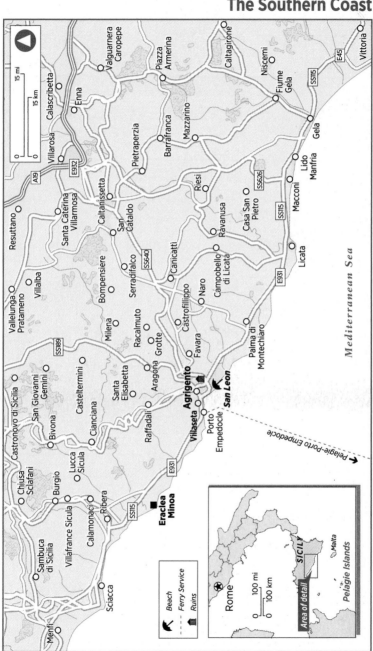

from Viale della Vittoria. Do pop in on the **Abbazia di Santo Spirito** church, which contains some amazing stucco work created by Giacomo Serpotta. What Michelangelo was to marble sculpture, so Serpotta was to stucco, and the white reliefs with their twisting figures are a joy to behold. The nearby village of **Caos** is home to **Casa di Pirandello** (Pirandello's House), where Agrigento's most famous inhabitant, the innovative writer and Nobel Prize winner, Luigi Pirandello, lived. Now a museum, it houses family photos, paintings, theatrical images, and manuscripts. In the summer months, locals flee the heat and take up residence at their summer homes at nearby **San Leone,** which has excellent, endless beaches.

Essentials

GETTING THERE   The main rail station, **Stazione Centrale,** Piazza Marconi (© **892021;** www.trenitalia.com), is downhill from Piazzale Aldo Moro and Piazza Vittorio Emanuele. The train trip from Palermo takes 1½ hours and costs 7.95€ one-way; there are 11 trains daily. From Syracuse, you must first take one of four daily trains to Catania; the 6-hour trip costs between 12€ and 30€ one-way. Three trains a day make the trip from Ragusa to Agrigento, at a cost of 10.10€ one-way. This is an extremely awkward connection, as you have to change trains at Gela and then at Canicattì. Depending on the train, the trip can last from 5 to 9 hours.

   Cuffaro (© **0922-403150;** www.cuffaro.info) runs four buses per day from Palermo; the trip takes 2 hours and costs 8.10€ one-way. By car from Syracuse, take the SS115 through Gela. From Palermo, cut southeast along the S121, which becomes the S188 and S189 before it finally reaches Agrigento. Allow about 2½ hours.

VISITOR INFORMATION   The **tourist office,** Piazzale Aldo Moro 7 (© **0922-20454**), is open Sunday to Friday 8am to 1pm and 3 to 8pm, Saturday 8am to 1pm. Another tourist office is at Via Empedocle 73 (© **0922-20391**), open Monday to Friday 8am to 2:30pm and Wednesday 3:30 to 7pm.

SPECIAL EVENTS   The **Settimana Pirandelliana** is a festival of plays, operas, and ballets staged in Piazza Kaos during 1 week in July or August. The tourist office can supply details and sells tickets.

GETTING AROUND   Agrigento is served by a network of orange **TUA buses** (© **0922-412024**). A ticket selling for 1€ is valid for 1½ hours. Bus no. 2 or 2/ runs to the beach at San Leone. Bus nos. 1 and 2 make frequent runs to the Valley of the Temples, and bus no. 11 goes to Casa di Pirandello. For a **taxi** service in Agrigento, call © **0922-21899** or 0922-26670.

[FastFACTS] AGRIGENTO

Hospital   **Ospedale Civile,** Via Rupe Atenea 1 (© **0922-492111**).

Pharmacy   **Farmacia Patti,** Via Atenea 129 (© **0922-20591**), open daily 9am to 1:30pm and 5 to 7:30pm.

Internet   **A.M. Servizi Telematici,** Cortile Contarini 7 (© **0922-402345**), open Monday to Saturday 9am to 1pm and 3:30 to 9pm. It charges 3€ per hour.

Post Office   Piazza Vittorio Emanuele (© **0922-551605**), is open Monday to Saturday 8am to 6:30pm. Currency can be exchanged here.

Wandering Among the Ruins

Many writers are fond of suggesting that the Greek ruins in the **Valley of the Temples (Valle dei Templi)** be viewed at dawn or sunset, when their mysterious aura is indeed heightened. The backdrop is idyllic, especially in spring, when the striking almond trees blossom.

Traveling down the Strada Panoramica, you'll first approach (on your left) the **Temple of Juno (Tempio di Giunone)** ★★, erected sometime in the mid-5th century B.C. Many of its Doric columns have been restored. As you climb the blocks, note the remains of a cistern as well as a sacrificial altar in front. The temple affords good views of the entire valley.

The **Temple of Concord (Tempio della Concordia)** ★★★, which you'll come to next, ranks with the Temple of Hephaestos in Athens as the best-preserved Greek temple in the world. With 13 columns on its side, 6 in front, and 6 in back, the temple was built in the peripheral hexastyle. You'll see the clearest example in Sicily of an inner temple. In the late 6th century A.D., the pagan structure was transformed into a Christian church, which might have saved it for posterity, although today it's been stripped down to its classical purity.

The **Temple of Hercules (Tempio di Ercole)** ★★ is the oldest, dating from the 6th century B.C. Badly ruined (only eight pillars are standing), it once ranked in size with the Temple of Zeus. At one time the temple sheltered a celebrated statue of Hercules. The infamous Gaius Verres, the Roman magistrate who became an especially bad governor of Sicily, attempted to steal the image as part of his temple-looting tear across the island. Astonishingly, you can still see black sears from fires set by long-ago Carthaginian invaders.

The **Temple of Jove/Zeus (Tempio di Giove)** ★ was the largest in the valley, similar in some respects to the Temple of Apollo at Selinunte, until it was ruined by an earthquake. It even impressed Goethe. In front of the structure was a large altar. The giant on the ground was one of several telamones (male caryatids) used to support the largest Greek temple in the world.

The so-called **Temple of Castor and Pollux (Tempio di Dioscuri** or **Tempio di Castore e Polluce),** with four Doric columns intact, is composed of fragments from different buildings. At various times it has been designated as a temple honoring Castor and Pollux, the twin sons of Leda and deities of seafarers; Demeter (Ceres), the goddess of marriage and of the fertile earth; or Persephone, the daughter of Zeus and the symbol of spring. The temples can usually be visited daily from 8:30am until 1 hour before sunset. City bus nos. 1, 2, and 3 run to the valley from the train station in Agrigento.

Ticket booths are found at the west and east entrances (✆ **0922-26191;** www. parcovalledeitempli.it); they're 10€ for adults and free for those 17 and under. Hours are daily 8:30am to 7pm. Nocturnal visits are from July 1 until September 5 Monday to Friday 7:30 to 9:30pm and weekends 7:30 to 11:30pm.

More Attractions

The **Museo Regionale Archeologico (Regional Archaeological Museum)** ★ is near San Nicola, on Contrada San Nicola on the outskirts of town on the way to the Valle dei Templi (✆ **0922-401565**). Its most important exhibit is a head of one of the telamones (male caryatids) from the Tempio di Giove. The collection of Greek vases is also impressive. Many of the artifacts on display were dug up when Agrigento was excavated. The museum is open Tuesday to Saturday 9am to 7:30pm, Sunday and Monday 9am to 1:30pm. Admission is 8€, and 4€ for children 17 and under. Take bus no. 1, 2, or 3. A combination ticket for admission to the Museo Regionale Archeologico and the Valley of the Temples costs 10€.

Casa di Pirandello (Pirandello's House), Contrada Caos, Frazione Caos (© **0922-511826**), is the former home of the 1934 Nobel Prize winner, known for his plays *Sei Personaggi in Cerca d'Autore* (*Six Characters in Search of an Author*) and *Enrico IV* (*Henry IV*). Although Agrigentans back then might not have liked his portrayal of Italy, all is forgiven now, and Pirandello is the local boy who made good. In fact, the Teatro Luigi Pirandello at Piazza Municipio bears his name. His *casa natale* is now a museum devoted to memorabilia pertaining to the playwright's life. His tomb lies under his favorite pine tree, a few hundred yards from the house and grounds, which are open daily 9am to 1pm and 2 to 7pm. Admission is 2€ for adults, and free to EU citizens aged 17 and under and 60 and over. The birthplace lies outside of town in the village of Caos (catch bus no. 1 from Piazza Marconi), just west of the temple zone.

The Churches of Agrigento

Abbazia di Santo Spirito (Abbey of the Holy Spirit) ★ There is one good reason to venture into the tacky modern city itself. Although this 13th-century church is rotting away, it is still a worthy goal, as you'll realize when you stand at its impressive Gothic entrance surmounted by a rose window. The single nave is adorned with a baroque interior of fantastic stucco work with **four high reliefs** ★ created by Giacomo Serpotta. The scenes depict *The Adoration of the Magi, The Nativity, The Presentation of Christ at the Temple,* and *The Flight into Egypt.* Take the exit to the right of the facade to look at the cloisters. Here you'll note a **lovely entrance** ★ into the chapter house, lined with Gothic arcades. A handsome doorway leads through a pointed arch. On each side are elaborate windows in the Arabo-Norman style. The nuns in the adjoining convent still sell a sweet confection called *kus-kus,* composed of chocolate and pistachio nuts.

Via Porcello at Via Santa Spirito. © **0922-20664.** Free admission. Tues–Sat 9am–1pm and 4–7pm; Sun 9am–1pm.

Duomo ★ Founded in the 12th century, the cathedral of Agrigento has faced rough times. There are still remnants from the early Norman days, particularly the windows, but most of the church was reconstructed in the 13th and 14th centuries. It was vastly restored in the 17th century, and later rejuvenated from the effects of a landslide in 1966. The bell tower, or campanile, is graced with a series of Catalán Gothic single lancet windows. The tower is from 1470, but because it was never completed, it gives the cathedral a strange, disturbing look, as if it were the victim of a windstorm. The **beautiful interior** ★ rests under an **impressive wooden ceiling** ★, the tie beams adorned with scenes from the lives of various saints. This work was carried out in the 16th century. The Duomo itself is dedicated to a Norman, San Gerlando, the town's first archbishop. His tomb is set in the right wing of the transept. Guides are fond of positioning you under the apse, where you can clearly hear even the whispers of people at the other end of the nave 80m (262 ft.)

Valley of the Temples

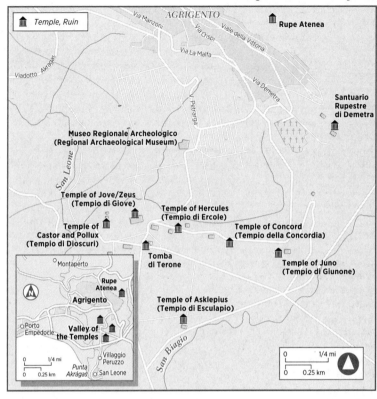

Temple, Ruin

AGRIGENTO

Via Manzoni · Via Crispi · Viale della Vittoria

Rupe Atenea

Via La Malfa

Viadotto Akragas

Via Demetra

V. Petrarca

Santuario
Rupestre
di Demetra

Museo Regionale Archeologico
(Regional Archaeological Museum)

San Leone

Temple of Jove/Zeus
(Tempio di Giove)

Temple of Hercules
(Tempio di Ercole)

Temple of
Castor and Pollux
(Tempio di Dioscuri)

Temple of Concord
(Tempio della Concordia)

Tomba
di Terone

Temple of Juno
(Tempio di Giunone)

Montaperto

Rupe
Atenea

Agrigento

Temple of Asklepius
(Tempio di Esculapio)

Porto
Empédocle

Valley of
the Temples

San Biagio

Villaggio
Peruzzo

Punta
Akràgas

San Leone

0   1/4 mi
0   0.25 km

0   1/4 mi
0   0.25 km

away. Standing in odd contrast to the rather somber chapels is the choir, a baroque romp of angelic angels and golden garlands.

Piazza Don Minzoni, off Via del Duomo. © **0922-490011.** Free admission. Tues–Sun 10am–1pm and 4–6pm.

Where to Stay
VERY EXPENSIVE

Foresteria Baglio della Luna ★★ 🎁 Restored by a local antiques dealer, this country inn has housed glamorous types who appreciate its stylish ways and its isolation from the crowds. Originating in the 1200s as a watchtower, then rebuilt in the 1500s by Emperor Charles V, it eventually evolved into an aristocratic manor house. You enter an immaculately maintained, cobble-covered courtyard, off which lie the stylishly decorated guest rooms. Each evokes a romantic lodging in an upscale home, and many have antique headboards, flowered upholsteries, and marble-clad bathrooms with showers and tubs. Some have faraway views of Agrigento's Greek temples. Hotel Villa Athena (see below) may have a closer view of the temples, but this place far surpasses it in charm and hospitality. To miss the experience of dining in the hotel's restaurant, Ristorante Il Dehor—the very best in this part of Sicily—would be unfortunate.

Contrada Maddalusa (SS640), Valle dei Templi, 92100 Agrigento. ☏ **0922-511061.** Fax 0922-598802. www.bagliodellaluna.com. 23 units. 200€–280€ double; 300€–501€ suite. AE, DC, MC, V. Bus: 1 or 3. On the SS640, about 4.8km (3 miles) west of Agrigento, and turn at the exit marked SPIAGGIA DI MADDALUSA. **Amenities:** 2 restaurants; Jacuzzi; room service; babysitting; smoke-free rooms. *In room:* A/C, TV, Jacuzzi (in suites), minibar, hair dryer, Wi-Fi (free).

EXPENSIVE

Hotel Villa Athena ★   This 18th-century villa rises from the landscape in the Valley of the Temples, less than 3km (1¾ miles) from town. It's worn and overpriced, but its location at the archaeological site is so dramatic that I like to stay here anyway, if only to see the ruins lit up at night from my room. Guest rooms are clean, with little style, and the tiled bathrooms have tub/shower combinations and aging though still-functioning plumbing. Ask for a room with a view of the temple, preferably one with a balcony. The perfect choice would be no. 205, which frames a panorama of the Temple of Concord. During the day, guests sit in the paved courtyard, enjoying drinks and fresh breezes. Even if you're not staying here, try to walk through the garden at night for an amazing view of the lit temple. You can also park here during the day and take a 10-minute walk along a trail to the temples.

Via Passeggiata Archeologica 33, 92100 Agrigento. ☏ **0922-596288.** Fax 0922-402180. www.hotelvilla athena.it. 40 units. 190€–330€ double; 290€–1,700€ suite. Rates include continental breakfast. AE, DC, MC, V. Free parking. Bus: 2. **Amenities:** Dining room; 2 bars; outdoor pool; room service. *In room:* A/C, TV, minibar, hair dryer, Wi-Fi (free).

MODERATE

Colleverde Park Hotel ★★   Sheathed in a layer of ocher-colored stucco, this is one of my favorite hotels in Agrigento, partly for its verdant garden, partly for its helpful staff, and partly for its location convenient to both the ancient and the medieval monuments of Agrigento. It has the finest hotel garden in town, a labyrinth of vine-covered arbors, terra-cotta terraces, and enormous sheets of white canvas stretched overhead as protection from the glaring sun. The hotel's eminently tasteful glass-sided restaurant is the site of many local wedding receptions. The decor throughout is discreetly elegant, providing refuge from the hysteria that sometimes permeates Agrigento, particularly its roaring traffic. Guest rooms have tiled bathrooms, lots of exposed wood, charming artwork, and big windows that in some cases reveal views of the temples of Concordia and Juno.

Via Panoramica dei Templi, 92100 Agrigento. ☏ **0922-29555.** Fax 0922-29012. www.colleverdehotel. it. 48 units. 135€–190€ double; 160€–210€ junior suite. Rates include continental breakfast. AE, DC, MC, V. Free parking. Bus: 1, 2, or 3. **Amenities:** Restaurant; bar; smoke-free rooms. *In room:* A/C, TV, minibar, hair dryer, Wi-Fi (6€/hr).

Grand Hotel dei Templi ★   Don't confuse this relatively conservative government-rated four-star hotel, which was originally built as a member of the upscale Jolly Hotel chain, with the more radical-looking three-star Grand Hotel Mosé next door. Originally built in an airy, high-ceilinged style in the mid-1970s, it's dignified and a lot more restrained, with less of a "let's party with *or* without the kids" motif, than what you'll find next door. It offers a pool surrounded by a wall, a tactful and

Agrigento

Stairs

1/4 mi

0.25 km

Via Imera

Via Gioeni

V. Degli Angeli

Via delle Mura

Via Plebis Rea

Via Girolamo

Via Gioeni

Via Giardinello

Via Fodera

V. Pirandello

Piazza Vittorio Emanuele

Piazzale A. Moro

S. Caolgero

Viale di Vittoria

Via Crispi

Statioze Centrale F.S.

Piazza Marconi

Via Callicratide

Via Manzoni

V. Matteotti

Chiesa del Purgatorio

Piazza Ravanusella

Via Atenea

Via Dante

Via Duomo

Museo Diocesano   Duomo

Seminario Vescovile

largo S. Giacomo

V. Recinto Oblati

V. Barone

Museo Civico

Piazza Pirandello

Piazza Sinatra

Viale Pietro Nenni

Via Garibaldi

Via Dante

SICILY

Messina

Syracuse

Mt. Etna

Palermo

Agrigento

80 mi

80 km

ACCOMMODATIONS ■
Colleverde Park Hotel **8**
Costazzura **1**
Foresteria Baglio della Luna **3**
Grand Hotel dei Templi **8**
Grand Hotel Mosé **8**
Hotel Kaos **1**
Hotel Tre Torri **8**
Hotel Villa Athena **8**
Hotel Villa Eos **1**

DINING ◆
Ambasciata di Sicilia **5**
Il Granaio di Ibla **7**
Ruga Reali **4**
Trattoria dei Templi **7**

ATTRACTIONS ●
Abbazia di Santo Spirito **6**
Duomo **2**

reserved staff, and guest rooms that are contemporary looking and comfortable—simple to the point of being a touch banal. Each unit comes with a small private bathroom. The high-ceilinged, extremely tasteful public areas reflect the best design standards of *la dolce vita* years.

Via Leonardo Sciascia, Villaggio Mosé, 92100 Agrigento. ℭ **0922-610175.** Fax 0922-606685. www. grandhoteldeitempli.eu. 148 units. 118€–155€ double. Rates include continental breakfast. AE, DC, MC, V. Free parking. Bus: 3. Pets welcome. **Amenities:** 2 restaurants; bar; outdoor pool; solarium; room service; babysitting; smoke-free rooms. *In room:* A/C, TV, minibar, Wi-Fi (6€/hr).

Hotel Kaos ☺   Set 2km (1¼ miles) southwest of the Valley of the Temples is this midsize hotel, which boasts a flowery garden, private beach, children's playground, and rooms opening onto the Mediterranean. The complex was formed by converting the residence of a former nobleman and two outbuildings once used to house servants. Many of the comfortable, well-furnished bedrooms have terraces; some units open onto the garden. Accommodations are well maintained and suitable for families, with tiled bathrooms. Unusually for a hotel of this size, Kaos contains three restaurants, each serving regional cuisine that features fresh produce.

Contrada Cumbo, Villaggio Pirandello, 92100 Agrigento. ℭ **0922-598622.** Fax 0922-598770. www. hotelkaos.it. 105 units. 74€–99€ double. AE, DC, MC, V. Free parking. Small pets welcome. **Amenities:** 3 restaurants; bar; outdoor pool; 2 tennis courts; solarium; babysitting; smoke-free rooms. *In room:* A/C, TV, minibar, Wi-Fi (free).

Hotel Tre Torri   Although it's near an unattractive commercial district 7km (4⅓ miles) south of Agrigento, this is among the area's busiest hotels. Behind a mock-medieval facade of white stucco, chiseled stone blocks, false crenellations, and crisscrossed iron balconies, Tre Torri is a favorite with Italian business travelers. The small guest rooms are comfortable, with modern furnishings and compact tiled bathrooms.

Viale Canatello 7, Villaggio Mosè, 92100 Agrigento. ℭ **0922-606733.** Fax 0922-607839. www.hotel tretorri.eu. 118 units. 60€–73€ double. Rates include continental breakfast. AE, DC, MC, V. Free parking. Bus: 3. **Amenities:** 4 restaurants; 3 bars; 2 pools (1 heated indoor); sauna; solarium; room service; smoke-free rooms. *In room:* A/C, TV, minibar (in some), hair dryer, Wi-Fi (7€/20 mins).

INEXPENSIVE

Costazzura   A government-rated three-star hotel, this is a sleek modern choice with enough comfort but little charm. It's located in San Leone, the seaside resort of Agrigento, 3km (1¾ miles) from the Valley of the Temples. Guests here can combine the beach with a tour of ancient monuments on the side. Bedrooms are comfortably furnished though a bit stark; each has a private balcony and a tiled bathroom. On-site is a good family-run restaurant specializing in Mediterranean dishes.

Via delle Viole 2, San Leone, 92100 Agrigento. ℭ **0922-411222.** Fax 0922-414040. www.hotelcostazzurra. it. 32 units. 50€–120€ double. AE, DC, MC, V. Free parking. **Amenities:** Restaurant; bar; Jacuzzi; room service; smoke-free rooms. *In room:* A/C, TV, minibar, hair dryer, Wi-Fi (free).

Grand Hotel Mosé ★★   This government-rated three-star hotel (not to be confused with the more formal four-star Grand Hotel immediately next door) is a well-designed architectural oddity that evokes a touch of Las Vegas. It sits beside the main traffic artery of Mosé Villaggio, a modern suburb stretching to the north of medieval Agrigento. Sheathed in stucco with the same honey tones as the sandstone used to build the Valley of the Temples, it's theme-ish and imaginative. Guest rooms are simple, colorful, and slightly spartan, like something you might expect in a Club Med. Most of the units have tiled floors, shower-only bathrooms, wrought-iron headboards, and touches of manorial Sicilian flair. The most dramatic are the units on the hotel's rooftop, which are designed on the outside like mud-walled huts in a North African kasbah, and which inside evoke a simple officer's barracks on the edge of the Sahara.

Viale Leonardo Sciascia, Villaggio Mosé, 92100 Agrigento. ✆ **0922-608388.** Fax 0922-608377. www. iashotels.com. 96 rooms. 100€–140€ double. Rates include continental breakfast. AE, DC, MC, V. Free parking. Bus: 3. **Amenities:** Restaurant; bar; outdoor pool; solarium; babysitting; smoke-free rooms. *In room:* A/C, TV, minibar, hair dryer.

Hotel Villa Eos ★ 🔥   Small and personalized, but isolated in a barren stretch of land between the SS640 and the sea about 4.8km (3 miles) southwest of Agrigento, this ramshackle hotel evokes a rambling, contemporary private home, thanks in part to its well-meaning staff and small scale. It sits in an oasis of greenery with views over the sea. Guests here generally opt to swim in the hotel pool rather than head for the beaches, which require a taxi or bus ride. Rooms are simple, modest, and comfortably furnished. Some, but not all, have minibars. Frankly, the hotel is best for those with cars—you may be guaranteed peace and quiet here, but the location is something of an inconvenience if you want to avail yourself of the area's many nearby attractions and dining options.

Contrada Cumbo, Villaggio Pirandello, 92100 Agrigento. ✆ **0922-597170.** Fax 0922-597188. www. hotelvillaeos.it. 23 units. 77€–150€ double. Rates include continental breakfast. MC, V. Free parking. Bus: 1. **Amenities:** Restaurant; bar; outdoor pool; tennis court; babysitting; smoke-free rooms. *In room:* A/C, TV, minibar.

SAN LEONE

Dioscuri Bay Palace ★★   The setting is more lavish than those of many nearby competitors, and this is a good choice if you want to be housed in comparative luxury close to Agrigento's beachfront. This modern hotel, renovated in 2009, rises three floors above a small bay at the northwestern tip of the boardwalks of Agrigento's waterfront resort of San Leone. Rooms are contemporary and comfortable, with tiled bathrooms.

Lungomare Falcone e Borsellino 1, 92100 San Leone (Agrigento). ✆ **0922-406111.** Fax 0922-411297. www.dioscurihotel.it. 102 units. 140€–220€ double; 230€–240€ junior suite. Rates include buffet breakfast. AE, DC, MC, V. Bus: 2. **Amenities:** Restaurant; 2 bars; outdoor pool; Jacuzzi; room service; babysitting; smoke-free rooms. *In room:* A/C, TV, minibar, hair dryer, Wi-Fi (3€/hr).

Hotel Akragas   This is one of the most appealing budget-priced hotels of San Leone, located on the busy main road leading from Agrigento. It isn't particularly near the water and, other than its restaurant, it has very few amenities—but in light of its reasonable prices, no one seems to care. The boxy 1950s structure is a pleasant place that's completely unpretentious, family friendly, and conducive to low-key holidays near the beach. Rooms are spartan, clean, and comfortable, with small shower-only bathrooms.

Viale Emporium 16–18, 92100 San Leone (Agrigento). ✆ **0922-414082.** Fax 0922-414262. 15 units. 80€ double. Rates include continental breakfast. AE, DC, MC, V. Free parking. Bus: 2. **Amenities:** Restaurant; Wi-Fi (free). *In room:* A/C, TV.

Where to Eat

Ambasciata di Sicilia ★ SICILIAN   This restaurant has been a city staple since the end of World War I, when a local family decided to celebrate the cuisine of their native Sicily in the form of this intensely vernacular *trattoria*. The cramped setting is accented with panels from antique donkey carts, frescoed ceiling beams, and marionettes salvaged from some long-ago street performance. In nice weather, the preferred seats are outside on four platforms built on the steeply sloping alley. (Some guests have commented that the flocks of birds that fly over the city rooftops far below are among the most soothing and mystical sights in Agrigento.) Menu items are based on 19th-century recipes. Stellar examples include beef roulades; an excellent *antipasti rustico* (sampling of antipasti); and *linguine al'Ambasciata* (prepared with meat sauce, bacon, calamari, and zucchini).

Via Gianbertoni 2, off Via Atenea. ⓒ **0922-20526.** Main courses 7€–12€. AE, MC, V. Sept–July Tues-Sun 12:30–3:30pm and 7–11:30pm; Aug daily 12:30–3:30pm and 7–11:30pm. Closed 2 weeks in Nov.

Il Granaio di Ibla ★ CONTINENTAL   The formally dressed staff here tends to be brusque, but the site can be so magical that a midsummer dinner on the terrace can be a memorable experience unaffected by food, staff, weather, or circumstances. If you opt for lunch, it will be served in a crescent-shaped stone-and-stucco building whose curtains are usually closed against the noon glare. But it's at dinner that the true magic emerges: Views sweep from the torch-lit terrace to the nearby Temple of Concordia (which literally looms before you) in ways unmatched by any other establishment in Agrigento. Begin, perhaps, with a duet of smoked salmon and swordfish or else a fresh shellfish salad. I'm fond of the sea bass flavored with saffron. The special risotto is made with pumpkin flowers, lobster, zucchini, and vodka. A "fantasy" of ice creams and sherbets is served to end the repast.

At the Hotel Villa Athena (see above), Via Passeggiata Archeologica 33. ⓒ **0922-596288.** Reservations required. Main courses 10€–20€. AE, DC, MC, V. Daily 12:30–2:30pm and 7:30–9:30pm (until 10pm June–Sept). Bus: 2.

La Trizzera ★ 🏛 SICILIAN   While visiting Pirandello's House (p. 314), you can also schedule a visit to this rustic trattoria. One reader called it "the best meal in Sicily." I'm not that enthusiastic but I found the food beautifully prepared, the ingredients fresh, and the dishes flavorsome. You may be turned off by the dusty stretch of road that runs in front, but wait until you sample the food. Each item is prepared fresh that day. You can delight in a dish, *bucaneve,* a savory crepe stuffed with ham and local cheese. The most regional dish is *sarde a beccafico* (sardines stuffed with breadcrumbs mixed with lemon juice and seasonings). A large variety of fish—either grilled or sauteed—is offered each day. The classic dessert, *cassata Siciliana* (made with ricotta cheese), is prepared with consummate skill here.

Via Fosse Ardeatine 57 (SS115), Contrada Caos, Villaseta. ⓒ **0922-512415.** www.latrizzera.it. Fixed-price menus 13€–27€. AE, DC, MC, V. Tues–Sun noon–3pm and 7–11pm. Closed 2 weeks in Aug.

Ruga Reali SICILIAN   Tables here spill onto one of Agrigento's most beautiful squares, high in the medieval center's upper zones. It's a short walk downhill from the cathedral, where there aren't a lot of other restaurants. I usually prefer the terrace, but if it's cold, rainy, or unbearably hot, descend into one of the nearby cellars, built in the 1400s as a stable, where other tables await. The chef shops at the nearby

fish market, later concocting such delights as a savory fish couscous or else lin̬
with a shrimp sauce. Regularly featured is the filleted fish of the day served w
fresh vegetables. The meat dishes are less inspired.

Piazza Pirandello (Piazza Municipio), Cortile Scribani 8. © **0922-20370.** Main courses 8€–17€. AE, DC, MC, V. Daily noon–3pm and 7:30pm–midnight. Closed mid-Oct to mid-Nov.

Trattoria dei Templi ★ SICILIAN   This charming, discreet, and extremely well-managed restaurant sits at the bottom of the hill between medieval Agrigento and the Valley of the Temples. Inside, you'll find brick-trimmed ceiling vaults, a polite crowd of diners from virtually everywhere in Europe, and excellent food that's served on hand-painted china. Menu items, served with efficiency by a staff of young, well-trained waiters, include *panzerotti della casa* (big ravioli stuffed with whitefish and served with a seafood sauce); and local fish with herbs, white wine, lemon juice, capers, olives, and orange zest.

Via Panoramica dei Templi 15. © **0922-403110.** www.trattoriadeitempli.com. Reservations recommended. Main courses 7€–20€. AE, DC, MC, V. Daily 12:30–3pm and 7:30–11pm. Closed Sun July–Aug and Fri Sept–June. Bus: 1, 2, or 3.

AT THE BEACH RESORT OF SAN LEONE

Il Pescatore ★ SICILIAN/SEAFOOD   Set right on the waterfront of Agrigento's beach resort of San Leone, this is the most famous of the 10 or so restaurants that flank it on either side. It's noted for its skillful preparations of fish, and also for a rough-and-tumble staff whose brusqueness is legendary—but which, almost perversely, has added to the restaurant's fame. The interior is more beautiful than you might expect, thanks to the four dining rooms' beamed ceilings and Romanesque-style columns and capitals salvaged from older buildings. Spaghetti with baby clams is always a smooth lead-in to a meal here, as is the *zuppa di cozze* (kettle of fresh mussels). Homemade bucatini comes with fresh sardines whipped into the pasta, and sole meunière is featured regularly.

Lungomare Falcone e Borsellino, San Leone. © **0922-414342.** Reservations recommended. Main courses 10€–15€. AE, DC, MC, V. Sept–June Tues–Sun 12:30–3:30pm and 7:30–11:30pm; July–Aug daily 12:30–3:30pm and 7:30–11:30pm. Bus: 2.

Leon d'Oro SICILIAN/SEAFOOD   Set in an undistinguished, cement-sided modern building that originated as a garage and car-repair shop, this restaurant is uncomfortably close to the busy boulevard that funnels most of the traffic from Agrigento into San Leone. Its festive interior, however, reveals one of the most respected restaurants in town. Expect savory dishes based on time-tested recipes. My favorite is *rotolini Emporium* (pasta with shrimp, tomatoes, fresh vegetables, and a pecorino cheese sauce).

Via Emporium 102, San Leone. © **0922-414400.** Reservations recommended. Main courses 8€–16€. AE, DC, MC, V. Tues–Sun 12:30–3:30pm and 7:45–11:30pm. Closed 2 weeks in Nov. Bus: 2.

Ristorante Il Dehor ★★★ SICILIAN/INTERNATIONAL   Set within the medieval walls of the Foresteria Baglio della Luna hotel (p. 315), this is one of the best restaurants in all of Sicily. The 50€ fixed menu is traditional Sicilian and a bit cliché-ridden, but the 53€ tasting menu truly shows off the chef's genius—Ferraro, an Agrigento-born, London-educated culinary whizz has reinve
tional Sicilian cuisine.

and shrimp with new potatoes in a bisque flavored with escargot ops with king prawns on cannellini beans with candied lemon in e. Wild salmon is served in a consommé of cherry tomatoes with lted fennel and chopped garlic. Desserts don't get much better fondant with a pistachio parfait and two sauces. Guests dine on a terrace or in one of two rooms that are ringed with important 19th-century paintings and tapestries.

In the Foresteria Baglio della Luna Hotel, Contrada Maddalusa (SS640), Valle dei Templi 92100. © 0922-511061. Reservations required. Main courses 10€-18€; fixed-price menus 50€-53€. AE, DC, MC, V. Tues-Sun 12:30-2pm and 7:30-10pm. Bus: 1 or 3.

LAMPEDUSA ★★

240km (49 miles) S of Agrigento.

For an offbeat adventure, unspoiled landscape and some fabulous beaches, take a ferry to the remote and rocky Pelagie Islands, where you can go swimming, snorkeling, and scuba diving. The main island is the arid **Lampedusa,** which is the name of both the largest island and its chief town.

To reach the islands from Agrigento, drive 7km (4½ miles) southwest to the Porto Empédocle to get the ferry. You'll stop first at **Linosa,** the northernmost of the islands and the tip of an ancient submerged volcano. The ferry continues to Lampedusa, its final stop. Lampedusa lies 50km (31 miles) south of Linosa and is shaped like a giant raft inclined to one side.

The best time to visit the islands is in July and August to go turtle watching at the miniscule **Isola dei Conigli** or Rabbit Island. A nature reserve, the island is one of the few places in the Mediterranean where the rare Caretta turtle lays its eggs. The sight of the turtles lumbering ashore en masse to make their nests, and their thousands of tiny hatchlings scurrying their way across the beach to the warm sea, is really special.

Essentials

GETTING THERE   The quickest way is to fly from Palermo to Lampedusa year-round on **Meridiana** (© 892928; www.meridiana.it); the trip takes only 1 hour. The small airport lies on the southeastern side of town. Always book your hotel in advance, and chances are a courtesy bus will be arranged for you at the airport.

Most arrivals are from Porto Empédocle on a **Siremar** (© 892123; www.siremar. it) ferry, operating year-round. Ferries from Porto Empédocle leave daily at midnight and arrive in Lampedusa at 8:15am, returning the following evening at 6pm. The trip costs 35€ to 65€ one-way depending on the season and where you stay on the boat; cars are transported for 63€ to 112€. The Siremar office in Porto Empédocle is at Via Molo 13 (© 0922-636683); in Lampedusa, the office is on Longomare L. Rizzo (© 0922-970003). Ferries arrive at the harbor, Porto Vecchio, in Lampedusa, a 10-minute walk into town. Taxis await arrivals, or else you can take a minibus into town in summer.

Visitor Information

The tourist office is on Via Vittorio Emanuele 80 (© 0922-970745). It is open ril to October but keeps such erratic hours you'll never know what hours it's open.

If you wish, you can rent a bike at **Autonoleggio d'Agostino,** Via Bix 1 (✆ **0922-970755**), and circle the island in a day. Bikes cost about 10€ a day, and motor scooters start at 25€.

What to See & Do

"We have the sun, we have the Mediterranean Sea," claims the island's director of tourism. "What more could you want?" That about says it.

The best beach on this 11km (6¾-mile) island is **Isola dei Conigli** or Rabbit Island, lying 7km (4⅓ miles) south of town. It's right off the shore, and you can swim over to it, except when the tide is out and then you can walk over. In addition to good sandy beaches, there is a small nature reserve here where the endangered Caretta turtle lays her eggs between July and August. A small bus in town runs to the departure point for Rabbit Island every hour during the day. There are no facilities on Rabbit Island, so take what provisions you need.

In summer you can go down to the wharf in Lampedusa and negotiate a boat tour around the island with one of the local fishermen. Count on paying 15€ per person for the half-day trip. Double the price for a full-day jaunt, with lunch included. There is little in the interior of interest.

Where to Stay

Cavalluccio Marino 🐟   This is one of the best bargains in town, although it's a simple place furnished very basically yet comfortably. Opened in 1980, it lies only 100m (328 ft.) from the sea and about 500m (1,640 ft.) from the center of town. Two of its units contain verandas and some of the others have balconies with a view. The food is good and hearty, with mainly fresh fish dishes.

Contrada Cala Croce 3, 92010 Lampedusa. ✆ **0922-970053.** Fax 0922-970672. www.hotelcavalluccio marino.com. 10 units. 170€–230€ double. Rates include half board. AE, DC, MC, V. Free parking. Closed Nov–Mar. **Amenities:** Restaurant; bar; room service. *In room:* A/C, TV, minibar.

Cupola Bianca ★   At 1km (½ mile) from the center of town, this modern hotel—decorated in a Mediterranean Arabesque style—is the best in the archipelago. On a headland studded with olive and palm trees, it rises from the earth like an oasis in Morocco. Its garden setting is the most attractive on the island. Bedrooms are spacious for the most part, ranging from standard to superior. The most expensive are in a North African-like structure called Dammusi, with its extensive verandas. Furnishings are in rattan, and the place has great style for this remote part of the world.

Contrada Madonna, 92010 Lampedusa. ✆ **0922-971274.** Fax 0922-973885. www.hotelcupolabianca. it. 23 units. 260€–440€ double; 250€–365€ suite. Rates include half board. AE, MC, V. Free parking. Closed Nov–May. **Amenities:** Restaurant; bar; outdoor pool; room service; massage; diving center; free airport transfer; smoke-free rooms. *In room:* A/C, TV, minibar, hair dryer.

Martello   This hotel could be placed in the center of Tangier and no one would know the difference. It lies on a spit of land dividing Cala Guitgia from Cala Salina, a small marina, at a point 80m (263 ft.) from the beach. Guests gather in the small garden to enjoy drinks and night breezes. Most of the rooms are spacious with a sea view from a private balcony. All are comfortably furnished in a standard motel style.

Contrada Guitgia, 92010 Lampedusa. ✆ **0922-970025.** Fax 0922-971696. www.hotelmartello.it. 25 units. 55€–110€ double. Rates include half board. AE, MC, V. Free parking. Closed Dec–Feb. **Amenities:** Restaurant; bar; solarium; diving center. *In room:* A/C, TV, hair dryer.

Where to Eat

In your search for a bar or restaurant, walk along **Via Roma** in the center of town at night. All the kitchens here serve fresh fish or else couscous from North Africa.

Gemelli MEDITERRANEAN/SICILIAN   This is the best restaurant in a town where the competition isn't very good. Nonetheless you get a cuisine that islanders have enjoyed for years. The local spaghetti appears with a fresh sardine sauce, and the chef even makes tasty Spanish paella. I am especially fond of the *seppie ripiene* or stuffed cuttlefish, and also couscous made with grouper. The Sicilian fish soup is also the best in town.

Via Cala Pisana 2. ✆ **0922-970699.** Reservations recommended July–Aug. Main courses 10€–30€. AE, DC, MC, V. Daily 7:30–11:30pm. Closed Nov–Mar.

FAST FACTS

FAST FACTS: SICILY

American Express Travel agencies representing AmEx are found in large cities, including **La Duca Viaggi,** Viale Africa 14, in Catania (✆ **095-7222295**); **La Duca Viaggi,** Via Don Bosco 39, in Taormina (✆ **0942-625255**); and **Giovanni Ruggieri e Figli,** Emerico Armari 40, in Palermo (✆ **091-587144**).

Area Code Dial ✆ **011,** then the country code for Italy (**39**), and then the city code (for example, **091** for Palermo or **095** for Catania). Then dial the specific phone number. To call abroad from Italy, dial the specific country code (**001** U.S. and Canada, **0044** U.K., **0061** Australia, **0064** New Zealand), then dial the area code and number.

ATM Networks See "Money & Costs," p. 45.

Business Hours Regular business hours are generally Monday to Saturday 8 or 9am to 1pm and 4 or 5 to 7 or 9pm. The *riposo* (mid-afternoon siesta) is observed in Sicily, though the shops on main thoroughfares in the big cities (Via Ruggero Settimo in Palermo and Via Etnea in Catania) stay open through lunchtime. Shops are also generally open the first Sunday of the month. If you're on the island in summer, when the heat is intense, you too may want to observe the custom of *riposo,* retreating back to your hotel for a long nap during the hottest part of the day. Banking hours vary from town to town, but in general are Monday to Friday 8:30am to 1:20pm and 3 to 4pm.

Cash Points See "Money & Costs," p. 45.

Currency See "Money & Costs," p. 45.

Drinking Laws In the last few years Italy has toughened up on the sale of alcohol to minors, as teenage drinking has become a nationwide problem. It is illegal to serve or sell alcoholic beverages to minors under the age of 16, though many establishments do not enforce this rule.

Driving Rules See "Getting There & Getting Around," p. 39.

Drugstores/Pharmacies Opening hours are usually from 8:30am to 1:30pm and from 4 or 5 to 8pm. Every *farmacia* (drugstore) posts a list of those that are on duty during afternoon closing hours, at night, and during the weekend and holidays. Over-the-counter medicines are also available at *parafarmacie,* which have a blue cross to distinguish them from pharmacies (green cross).

Electricity The electricity in Sicily varies considerably. It's usually alternating current (AC); the cycle is 50Hz 220V. Check the local current at the hotel where you're staying. I recommend obtaining a transformer if you're carrying any electrical appliances. Plugs have 2 or 3 prongs that are round, not flat; therefore, an adapter plug is also needed.

Embassies & Consulates   There's a **U.S. Consular Agency** at Via Vaccarini 1, in Palermo (📞 **091-305857**), while the U.S. Embassy is in Rome at Via Veneto 121 (📞 **06-46741**).

The **Canadian Embassy** is at Via Zara 30, in Rome (📞 **06-854441**).

There's a **U.K. Consulate** at Via Cavour 117, in Palermo (📞 **091-326412**), and a **U.K. Embassy** at Via XX Settembre 80A, in Rome (📞 **06-422-00001**).

The **Irish Embassy** is at Piazza di Campitelli 3, in Rome (📞 **06-697-9121**). For consular queries, call 📞 **06-697-9121.**

The **Australian Embassy** is at Via Antonio Bosio 15, in Rome (📞 **06-852-721**).

The **New Zealand Embassy** is at Via Zara 28, in Rome (📞 **06-441-7171**).

Emergencies   For a general crisis dial the police at 📞 **113** or the *Carabinieri* (army police corps) at 📞 **112**; for an ambulance, 📞 **118**; and to report a fire, 📞 **115.** To report a forest fire dial 📞 **1515**, and for distress at sea call 📞 **1530.** For road assistance, dial 📞 **803116.**

Emergency Money   If you need emergency cash over the weekend when all banks and American Express offices are closed, you can have money wired to you via **Western Union** (www.westernunion.com) or **Money Gram** (📞 **800-088-256** in Italy; (www.moneygram.com).

Gasoline (Petrol)   See "Planning Your Trip to Sicily," p. 44.

Holidays   Offices, banks, and shops in Sicily are closed on the following **national holidays:** January 1 (New Year's Day); January 6 (Epiphany); Easter and Easter Monday; April 25 (Liberation Day); May 1 (Labor Day); June 2 (Republic Day); August 15 (Assumption of the Virgin); November 1 (All Saints' Day); December 8 (Feast of the Immaculate Conception), December 25 (Christmas Day); and December 26 (Saint Stephen). Offices and shops are also generally closed on the day dedicated to a city or town's patron saint. Before a major holiday banks are often open only in the morning, closing before noon. Transportation is either on a reduced schedule or suspended altogether.

Insurance   Health Insurance   For travel overseas, most U.S. health plans (including Medicare and Medicaid) do not provide coverage, and the ones that do often require you to pay for services upfront and reimburse you only after you return home.

As a safety net, you may want to buy travel medical insurance, particularly if you're traveling to a remote or high-risk area where emergency evacuation might be necessary. If you require additional medical insurance, try **MEDEX Assistance** (📞 **410/453-6300;** www.medexassist.com) or **Travel Assistance International** (📞 **800/821-2828;** www.travelassistance.com; for general information on services, call the company's **Worldwide Assistance Services, Inc.** at 📞 **800/777-8710**).

Canadians should check with their provincial health plan offices or call **Health Canada** (📞 **866/225-0709;** www.hc-sc.gc.ca) to find out the extent of their coverage and what documentation and receipts they must take home in case they are treated overseas.

Travelers from the U.K. should carry their European Health Insurance Card (EHIC), which replaced the E111 form as proof of entitlement to free/reduced cost medical treatment abroad (📞 **0845/606-2030;** www.ehic.org.uk). Note, however, that the EHIC only covers "necessary medical treatment;" for repatriation costs, lost money, baggage, or cancellation, travel insurance from a reputable company should always be sought (www.travelinsuranceweb.com).

Travel Insurance   The cost of travel insurance varies widely, depending on the destination, the cost, and length of your trip, your age and health, and the type of trip you're taking, but expect to pay between 5% and 8% of the vacation itself. For U.S. visitors, you

FAST FACTS | Embassies & Consulates

can get estimates from various providers through **InsureMyTrip.com** (✆ **800/487-4722**). Enter your trip cost and dates, your age, and other information, for prices from more than a dozen companies.

U.K. citizens and their families who make more than one trip abroad per year may find an annual travel insurance policy works out cheaper. U.K. policies tend to cover both health and cancellation. Some bank accounts offer this as part of your package. Have a look at what you have, if not, check somewhere like **www.moneysupermarket.com** (✆ **0845/345-5708**), which compares prices across a wide range of providers for single- and multi-trip policies. Most big travel agents and airlines offer their own insurance and will probably try to sell you their package when you book a holiday. Think before you sign. Britain's Consumers' Association recommends that you insist on seeing the policy and reading the fine print before buying travel insurance. The **Association of British Insurers** (✆ **020/7600-3333**; www.abi.org.uk) gives advice by phone and publishes *Holiday Insurance*, a free guide to policy provisions and prices. You might also shop around for better deals: Try **Columbus Direct** (✆ **0870/033-9988**; www.columbusdirect.net).

Trip-Cancellation Insurance Trip-cancellation insurance will help retrieve your money if you have to back out of a trip or depart early, or if your travel supplier goes bankrupt. Trip cancellation traditionally covers such events as sickness, natural disasters, and State Department or Foreign Office advisories. The latest news in trip-cancellation insurance is the availability of **"any reason"** cancellation coverage—which costs more but covers cancellations made for any reason. You won't get back 100% of your prepaid trip cost, but you'll be refunded a substantial portion. **TravelSafe** (✆ **888/885-7233**; www.travelsafe.com) offers both types of coverage. For details, contact one of the following recommended insurers: **Access America** (✆ **866/807-3982**; www.accessamerica.com); **Travel Guard International** (✆ **800/826-4919**; www.travelguard.com); **Travel Insured International** (✆ **800/243-3174**; www.travelinsured.com); and **Travelex Insurance Services** (✆ **888/457-4602**; www.travelex-insurance.com).

Language Except in remote backwaters, Italian, of course, is the language of the land. (See p. 330 for a brief glossary of useful terms.) English is often understood at attractions such as museums and at most hotels and restaurants, especially in larger cities where there is a great influx of foreign visitors. Even if no one speaks English, with a good amount of pointing and gesticulating you'll make yourself understood. Most islanders also speak a Sicilian dialect, which is considered by some experts to be a distinct Romance language. It is an idiom composed of words and grammar structures left over from various conquerors, including Arabic, Greek, French, and Spanish, as well as elements absorbed into the vernacular after the American occupation.

Legal Aid The consulate of your country is the place to turn to for legal advice, although offices can't interfere in the Italian legal process. They can, however, inform you of your rights and provide a list of attorneys. You'll have to pay for the attorney out of your pocket—there's no free legal assistance. If you're arrested for a drug offense, about all the consulate will do is notify a lawyer about your case and perhaps inform your family. If the problem is serious enough, most nationals will be referred to their embassies or consulates in Rome.

Mail & Post Offices Mail delivery is infamously bad, and central post offices in big cities are a veritable competition of the survival of the fittest, especially at the beginning of the month, when customers start gathering outside at the crack of dawn just to secure a place in line for postal services. Although you most likely won't be paying bills or receiving your pension—the main reason why post offices are so crowded—even simple things like parcel-shipping or buying stamps may require a frustratingly long wait.

You are better off buying stamps at *tabacchi* (tobacco shops), even though they might not always be stocked. A stamp for a postcard within the E.U. costs .65€, for the U.S. & Canada .85€, for Australia and New Zealand 1€. To locate the nearest post office and other information call 𝄐 **803-160,** or visit www.posteitaliane.it.

Newspapers & Magazines   In major cities, most newsagents often carry English-language newspapers and magazines—your best bet is to head to newsagents at the main railway stations, as they are well-stocked with international reading matter. There are no English-language magazines or newspapers published in Sicily.

Police   See "Emergencies," above.

Safety   Despite what stereotyping and urban legends would lead you to believe, you won't be shaken down by any mafiosi, since the Mafia is virtually invisible to tourists. That's not to say however that there aren't shady types who like to improvise the part in the hopes of gouging naive tourists. Before agreeing to use a service always ask, "*Quanto costa?*" (How much does it cost?), and get a clear price—if the response is "*Non ti preoccupare!*" (Don't worry!), walk away; often that's the code word for "I'll take you to the cleaners." Pickpockets operate in crowded areas and on buses, while juvenile delinquents whizzing by on scooters won't think twice about knocking you down in an attempt to snatch your purse or valuables—regrettably Palermo, Messina, and Catania are full of them, and they often prey on tourists. Avoid walking alone at night, and even in the daytime be aware when walking in seedy areas. Never leave valuables in a car, even if they're well hidden, and never travel with your car unlocked. If your window is rolled down, keep valuables out of sight.

Smoking   In 2005 Italy launched one of Europe's toughest laws against smoking in public places, including bars and restaurants. All restaurants and bars come under the ruling except those with ventilated smoking rooms. Smokers face fines from 29€ to 290€ if caught lighting up. While outdoor bars and restaurants will allow smoking, it might bother your fellow diners; always ask if you can light up. Cigar smoking is usually frowned upon.

Taxes   As a member of the European Union (E.U.), Italy imposes a **value-added tax** (called **IVA** in Italy) on most goods and services. The tax that most affects visitors is the one imposed on hotel rates, which ranges from 9% in first- and second-class hotels to 19% in deluxe hotels.

Non-E.U. citizens are entitled to a **refund of the IVA** if they spend more than 155€ at any one store, before tax. For more information on the procedure, visit www.global refund.com. Many shops are now part of the **"Tax Free for Tourists"** network (look for the sticker in the window). After you have the invoice stamped at Customs, you can redeem the check for cash directly at the Tax Free booth in the airport at Palermo or Catania, or mail it back in the envelope provided within 60 days.

Telephones   See "Staying Connected," p. 54.

Theft   Be sure to inform all of your credit card companies the minute you discover your wallet has been lost or stolen; keep the emergency contact numbers found on the back of the card together with other emergency numbers. Your credit card company or insurer may also require you file a police report and provide a report number or record of the loss. Some credit card companies may be able to wire you a cash advance immediately; check if this option is available with your company before leaving. The emergency number for Visa in Italy is 𝄐 **800-819.** American Express cardholders should call collect 𝄐 **06/7220-348,** or contact an American Express office in Sicily (see above). MasterCard holders should call 𝄐 **800-870-866.** Before you begin your trip, inform your credit card company that you will be using your card overseas.

Before traveling abroad it's a good idea to make a color photocopy of your passport and keep it separate from other documents (it's also a good idea to leave a copy back home with a trusted person). The same goes for your driver's license, especially if you intend on renting a car. **Note:** By Italian law you are required to have ID with you at all times. You cannot use a photocopy of your driver's license when driving. If you're afraid of losing your documents, make a photocopy of your ID for non-official business (write the name and phone number of the place you are staying at on the photocopy, if stopped by a police officer or *Carabiniere* he/she might request to see the original).

Time Zone   Sicily is at GMT+1, that is 6 hours ahead of Eastern Standard Time in the United States. Daylight saving time goes into effect in Italy each year from the end of March to the end of October.

Tipping   In **hotels,** the service charge of 15% to 19% is already added to your bill. In addition, it's customary to tip the chambermaid .50€ per day, the doorman (for calling a cab) .50€, and the bellhop or porter 1.50€ to 2.50€ for carrying bags to your room. The concierge expects about 15% of his or her bill, as well as tips for extra services performed, which may include help with long-distance calls. In expensive hotels, these amounts are often doubled.

In **restaurants and cafes,** 10% to 15% is usually added to your bill as a service and cover charge. If you're not sure whether this has been done, ask, "*È incluso il servizio?*" (eh een-*cloo*-soh eel ser-*vee*-tsyoh?). An additional tip isn't expected, but it's nice to leave the equivalent of an extra couple of dollars if you're pleased with the service. If you feel you got bad service, do not feel compelled to leave a tip, even if the waiter starts to grumble. Restaurants are required by law to give customers official receipts (*ricevuta fiscale*), itemizing everything ordered. Checkroom attendants expect 1€; washroom attendants, .50€.

Taxi drivers expect 10% to 15% of the fare, but if you feel you've been overcharged or the driver was discourteous, you don't need to tip.

Toilets   All airport and rail stations have toilets, often with attendants who expect to be tipped. Many large rail stations apply a mandatory entrance fee (usually 1 €). Having hand sanitizers and pre-moistened tissues with you is a good idea. Public toilets are also found near many of the major sights. Usually they're designated *WC* (water closet), *bagno* (bath), *donne* (women), or *uomini* (men). The most confusing designation is *Signori* (gentlemen) and *Signore* (ladies), so watch that final *i* and *e!* Tip: if you happen to be around town and are desperate, head for the nearest department store—you're bound to find a restroom there.

Water   Most Sicilians have mineral water with their meals. Tap water is normally potable everywhere, including at public drinking fountains. Unsafe sources will be marked ACQUA NON POTABILE. Some cities along the southern coast get their water supply exclusively from a sea-water desalinator, making it non-potable. It's always good to ask first; if in doubt, stick to bottled water, even for cooking.

USEFUL TERMS & PHRASES

BASIC VOCABULARY

English	Italian	Pronunciation
Thank you	**Grazie**	*grah*-tzee-yeh
You're welcome	**Prego**	*preh*-goh
Please	**Per favore**	*pehr* fah-*vohr*-eh
Yes	**Si**	see
No	**No**	noh
Good morning or Good day	**Buongiorno**	bwohn-*djor*-noh
Good evening	**Buona sera**	*bwohn*-ah *seh*-rah
Good night	**Buona notte**	*bwohn*-ah *noht*-teh
How are you?	**Come sta?**	*koh*-meh *stah*
Very well	**Molto bene**	*mohl*-toh *behn*-neh
Goodbye	**Arrivederci**	ahr-ree-veh-*dehr*-chee
Excuse me (to get attention)	**Scusi**	*skoo*-zee
Excuse me (to get past someone)	**Permesso**	pehr-*mehs*-soh
Where is . . . ?	**Dovè . . . ?**	doh-*veh*
the station	**la stazione**	lah stat-tzee-*oh*-neh
a hotel	**un albergo**	oon ahl-*behr*-goh
a restaurant	**un ristorante**	oon ree-store-*ahn* -teh
the bathroom	**il bagno**	eel *bahn*-yoh
To the right	**A destra**	ah *deh*-stra
To the left	**A sinistra**	ah see-*nees*-tra
Straight ahead	**Avanti (*or* sempre diritto)**	ah-*vahn*-tee (*sehm*-preh dee-*reet*-toh)
How much is it?	**Quanto costa?**	*kwan*-toh *coh*-sta
The check, please	**Il conto, per favore**	eel kon-toh *pehr* fah-*vohr*-eh
What time is it?	**Che ore sono?**	keh *or*-eh *soh*-noh
When?	**Quando?**	*kwan*-doh
Yesterday	**Ieri**	ee-*yehr*-ree

English	Italian	Pronunciation
Today	**Oggi**	*oh*-jee
Tomorrow	**Domani**	doh-*mah*-nee
Breakfast	**Prima colazione**	*pree*-mah coh-laht-tzee-*ohn*-eh
Lunch	**Pranzo**	*prahn*-zoh
Dinner	**Cena**	*che*-nah
Monday	**Lunedì**	loo-neh-*dee*
Tuesday	**Martedì**	mar-teh-*dee*
Wednesday	**Mercoledì**	mehr-coh -leh-*dee*
Thursday	**Giovedì**	joh-veh-*dee*
Friday	**Venerdì**	ven-nehr-*dee*
Saturday	**Sabato**	*sah*-bah-toh
Sunday	**Domenica**	doh-*mehn*-nee-kah

NUMBERS

English	Italian	Pronunciation
1	**uno**	*oo*-noh
2	**due**	*doo*-eh
3	**tre**	treh
4	**quattro**	*kwah*-troh
5	**cinque**	*cheen*-kweh
6	**sei**	say
7	**sette**	*set*-teh
8	**otto**	*oh*-toh
9	**nove**	*noh*-veh
10	**dieci**	dee-*eh*-chee
11	**undici**	*oon*-dee-chee
20	**venti**	*vehn*-tee
21	**ventuno**	vehn-*toon*-oh
22	**ventidue**	*vehn*-tee doo-eh
30	**trenta**	*tren*-tah
40	**quaranta**	kwah-*rahn*-tah
50	**cinquanta**	cheen-*kwan*-tah
60	**sessanta**	ses-*sahn*-tah
70	**settanta**	set-*tahn*-tah
80	**ottanta**	ot-*tahn*-tah
90	**novanta**	no-*vahnt*-tah
100	**cento**	*chen*-toh

ARCHITECTURAL TERMS

Agorà   Marketplace in an archaeological site.

Apse   The half-rounded extension behind the main altar of a church; Christian tradition dictates that it be placed at the eastern end of an Italian church, the side closest to Jerusalem.

Atrium   A courtyard, open to the sky, in an ancient Roman house; the term also applies to the courtyard nearest the entrance of Byzantine churches.

Baldachin   A columned stone canopy, usually placed above the main altar of a church.

Baptistery   A separate building or a separate area in a church where the rite of baptism is held.

Basilica   A rectangular public building, usually divided into three aisles by rows of columns. In ancient Rome, this architectural form was frequently used for places of public assembly and law courts.

Capital   The top of a column, often carved and usually categorized into one of three orders: Doric, Ionic, or Corinthian.

Cavea   The curved row of seats in a classical theater; the most prevalent shape was that of a semicircle.

Chancel   Section of a church containing the altar.

Cornice   The decorative flange defining the uppermost part of a classical or neo-classical facade.

Cortile   Courtyard or cloisters ringed with a gallery of arches or lintels set atop columns.

Crypt   A church's main burial place, usually below the choir.

Entase   Convex curve in the shaft of a column.

Grotesques   Carved and painted faces, deliberately ugly, used by everyone from the Etruscans to the architects of the Renaissance; they're especially amusing when set into fountains.

Hypogeum   Subterranean burial chambers, usually of pre-Christian origins.

Loggia   Roofed balcony or gallery.

Narthex   The anteroom, or enclosed porch, of a Christian church.

Piano Nobile   The main floor of a *palazzo* (sometimes the second floor).

Pieve   A parish church.

Portico   A porch, usually crafted from wood or stone.

Pronaos   Vestibule at the front of a classical temple.

Pulvin   A four-sided stone that serves as a substitute for the capital of a column, often decoratively carved, sometimes into biblical scenes.

Putti   Plaster cherubs whose chubby forms often decorate the interiors of baroque chapels and churches.

Telamone   Structural column carved into a standing male form; female versions are called *caryatids*.

Transenna   Stone (usually marble) screen separating the altar area from the rest of an early Christian church.

Tympanum   The half-rounded space above the portal of a church, whose semicircular space usually showcases a sculpture.

MENU GLOSSARY

Agnolotti A crescent-shaped pasta shell stuffed with a mix of chopped meat, spices, vegetables, and cheese; when prepared in rectangular versions, the same combination of ingredients is identified as ravioli.

Anguilla alla veneziana Eel cooked in a sauce made from tuna and lemon.

Aragosta Lobster.

Arancini di riso Rice balls stuffed with peas, cheese, and meat, then coated with breadcrumbs and deep-fried.

Arrosto Roasted meat.

Baccalà Dried and salted codfish.

Bocconcini Veal layered with ham and cheese, then fried.

Bollito misto Assorted boiled meats served on a single platter.

Bottarga Dried and salted roe of gray mullet or tuna, which is pressed into loaves, cut into paper-thin slices, and dressed with lemon-laced virgin olive oil.

Bracciola Veal or pork chop.

Bresaola Air-dried spiced beef.

Bucatini Coarsely textured hollow spaghetti.

Cacciucco ali livornese Seafood stew.

Cannoli Crunchy fried tubular pastry filled with ricotta and studded with candied fruits, bits of chocolate, and pistachios.

Caponata Vegetable stew made with eggplants, capers, tomatoes, olives, onions, and celery in a sweet-and-sour sauce of vinegar and sugar. Served at room temperature.

Cappelletti Small ravioli ("little hats") stuffed with meat or cheese.

Carciofi Artichokes.

Carpaccio Thin slices of raw or cured beef, sometimes in a piquant sauce.

Cassata al galletto Cake made with vanilla-flavored frozen custard and, perhaps, candied fruits, bits of chocolate, hazelnuts, or pistachios.

Cassata Siciliana A richly caloric dessert that combines layers of sponge cake, ricotta cheese sweetened with Marsala or orange liqueur and candied fruit, bound together with a marzipan icing.

Cotoletta alla siciliana Thinly sliced breaded veal cutlet, fried, or grilled.

Cozze Mussels.

Fagioli Beans.

Fave Fava or broad beans.

Fontina Rich Alpine cow's-milk cheese.

Fritto misto A deep-fried medley of whatever small fish, shellfish, and squid are available in the marketplace that day.

Gnocchi Dumplings usually made from potatoes (*gnocchi alla patate*) or from semolina (*gnocchi alla romana*), often topped with combinations of cheese, spinach, vegetables; *alla romana* are strictly topped with parmigiano and butter.

Granita Flavored ice, with a smooth consistency.

Insalata di frutti di mare Seafood salad (usually octopus, shrimp and squid) garnished with lemon, olive oil, parsley, and spices.

Involtini Thinly sliced rolls of beef, veal, or pork, stuffed, and fried.

Mortadella Mild pork sausage, fashioned into large cylinders and served sliced; the original lunchmeat bologna (because its most famous center of production is Bologna).

Osso buco   Beef or veal shank slowly braised until the bone marrow is tender and then served with a topping of chopped fresh parsley, capers, garlic and lemon peel.

Pancetta   Herb-flavored pork belly, rolled into a cylinder and sliced.

Pancetta affumicata   Smoked pork belly, served in slices: The Italian bacon.

Panettone   A Christmas sweet consisting of a high dome-shaped loaf with a soft, spongy interior interspersed with candied fruit.

Panna   Heavy cream.

Peperoni   Green, yellow, or red sweet bell peppers.

Piccata al Marsala   Thin escalope of veal braised in a pungent sauce flavored with Marsala wine.

Piselli al prosciutto   Peas with diced ham.

Pizzaiola   A thick tomato and oregano sauce, usually used to top a thick slice of beef.

Polenta   Thick porridge or mush made from cornmeal flour, often served as a side dish.

Polenta e coniglio   Rabbit stew served with polenta.

Pollo alla cacciatore   Chicken with tomatoes, mushrooms, and carrots cooked in wine.

Salsa verde   Literally "Green sauce," it's made with capers, anchovies, lemon juice and/or vinegar, and parsley.

Saltimbocca   Veal scallop layered with prosciutto and sage; its name literally translates as "jump in your mouth," a reference to its tart and savory flavor.

Scaloppina alla Valdostana   Escalope of veal stuffed with cheese and ham.

Scaloppine   Thin slices of veal coated in flour and sautéed in butter.

Semifreddo   A frozen dessert; usually ice cream with sponge cake.

Sfincione   Sicilian square pizza with a sponge-like base topped with anchovies, onions, and tomatoes; sold in *focaccerias* and bakeries (but never in a pizzeria).

Sogliola   Sole.

Spiedini   Pieces of meat grilled on a skewer over an open flame.

Strozzapreti   Small twisted nuggets of pasta, usually served with sauce; the name is literally translated as "priest-choker."

Stufato   Beef braised in white wine with vegetables.

Trenette   Thin noodles served with pesto sauce, potatoes, and green beans.

Zabaglione/zabaione   Egg yolks whipped into the consistency of a custard, flavored with Marsala, and served warm as a dessert or as an ice-cream topping.

Zuccotto   A liqueur-soaked sponge cake, molded into a dome and layered with chocolate, nuts, and whipped cream.

Zuppa inglese   Sponge cake soaked in custard.

Index

See also Accommodations and Restaurant indexes, below.

General Index

A

AARP, 51
Abbazia dello Spirito Santo (near Caltanissetta), 190
Abbazia di Santo Spirito (Agrigento), 314
Academic Tours, 53
Accommodations, 56–57. *See also* Accommodations Index
best, 6–7
Acquacalda (Lipari), 239
Acropolis (Selinunte), 173
Aeolian Islands, 234–252
Agrigento, 310–322
  accommodations, 315–319
  getting around, 312
  restaurants, 320–322
  sights and attractions, 313–315
  traveling to, 312
  visitor information, 312
Aidone, 187
Air travel, 39–40
Albergheria (Palermo), 73
Alcantara Gorges, 219–220
Alessi Museum (Enna), 186
Alicudi, 252
Alitalia Vacations, 54
All Saints' Day (Tutti i Santi), 38
Almond Blossom Festival (Agrigento), 36
Altieri 1882 (Erice), 157
Amaro Averna, 189
American Express, 76, 201, 255, 325
Anfiteatro Romano. *See* Roman Amphitheater
Ara di Lerone (Syracuse), 287–288
Archaeological Museum
  Giardini-Naxos, 218
  Ustica, 142
Archaeological Park (Segesta), 148
Arco dell'Elefante (Pantelleria), 180–181
Area code, 325
Arena Barranco (Palermo), 119
Art, 21–25
Art Nouveau, 24–25
Assumption Day (Ferragosto), 37
Astronomical Observatory and Museum (Palermo), 91
ATMs, 46

B

Backroads, 52
Badia di Sant'Agata (Catania), 266

Bagheria, 131–133
Bagno Delle Donne (Favignana), 177
Ballarò (Palermo), 119
Barbacane castle (Pantelleria), 180
Bar Caffè La Vela (Lipari), 242
Bar del Ponte (Syracuse), 303
Bar Ingrid (Stromboli), 250
Baroque, 24
Bar Pasticerria A Chemi, 214–215
Bar San Giorgio (Taormina), 215–216
Battaglia, Francesco, 253
Bazar del Miele (Erice), 157
Beaches. *See also specific beaches*
  Cefalù, 137
  Messina area, 232
  Mondello, 124
  Noto, 306
  Scopello (Scopello di Sopra), 176
  Taormina, 203–204
Bella Blu (Taormina), 216
Belle Epoque (Ragusa), 284
Bellini, Vincenzo, 29, 268, 273
Biblioteca Comunale (Palermo), 99
Biblioteca di Comune di Taormina (Taormina), 205
Biking and mountain biking, 45
Bip Bop Pub, Bar & Bistro (Cefalù), 141
Birding, 52
Boat excursions, Ustica, 142
Boats and ferries, 41
Books, recommended, 26–28
Botanical Garden (Palermo), 114
Business hours, 325
Bus travel, 42, 43
Butterfield & Robinson, 52
Byzantine Empire, 16

C

Cáccamo, 134–135
Café Sicilia (Noto), 308
Caffè Wunderbar (Taormina), 216
Cala Rossa, 177
Calendar of events, 36–38
Caltanissetta, 189–190
Canneto (Lipari), 239
Cantine Stevenson (Vulcano), 247
Capella del Rosario (Palermo), 101
Capo Tindari, 233
Cappella dei Marinai (Trapani), 160
Cappella della Madonna
  Catania, 263
  Trapani, 160
Cappella del Sacramento (Messina), 229
Cappella di Sant'Agata (Catania), 263
Cappella Palatina (Palermo), 91, 94, 109

Car breakdowns and assistance, 44
Carieri & Carieri (Palermo), 117
Carlo Panarello (Taormina), 215
Carnevale, Acireale, 36
Car rentals, 43–44
Carthaginians, 13–15, 163
Car travel, 40, 43–45
Casa dei Mosaici (Mozia), 175
Casa di Pirandello (Agrigento), 314
Casa di Verga (Catania), 266, 274
Casina Cinese (Palermo), 114
Castelbuono, 194
Castellammare del Golfo, 176
Castellammare (Palermo), 73–74
Castello Cáccamo, 134
Castello di Venere (Erice), 150, 152
Castello Eurialo (near Syracuse), 303–304
Castello Lombardo (Enna), 186
Castello Pepoli (Erice), 152
Castello Pietrarossa (Caltanissetta), 189
Castello Ursino (Catania), 267, 269
Castello Utveggio (Monte Pellegrino), 124
Castelmola, 203
Castle of Venus (Castello di Venere), 150, 152
Catacombe dei Cappuccini (Palermo), 97
Catacombe di San Giovanni (Syracuse), 288
Catania, 60–61, 253–276
  accommodations, 256–261
  attractions, 263–275
  emergencies, 255–256
  getting around, 255
  layout of, 254–255
  nightlife, 276
  pharmacies, 256
  post office, 256
  restaurants, 261–263
  shopping, 275–276
  traveling to, 253–254
  visitor information, 254
  walking tour, 269–275
Cathedrals and churches. *See also* Duomo
  best, 4
Cava Elefante (Pantelleria), 180
Cave di Pomice (Lipari), 239
Cave paintings, 22
Cefalù, 135–141
Cellphones, 54–55
Central Sicily, 60, 183–196
Centro Nautico Baia Levante (Vulcano), 245
Ceramica Ericina (Erice), 157
Ceramiche Franco (Santo Stefano di Camastra), 234
Champagneria (Palermo), 120
Chiesa. *See under first significant word (e.g. San Cataldo)*

Restaurants